ROUTLEDGE HANDBOOK OF
SECURITY STUDIES

This revised and updated second edition features over twenty new chapters and offers a wide-ranging collection of cutting-edge essays from leading scholars in the field of Security Studies.

The field of Security Studies has undergone significant change during the past twenty years, and is now one of the most dynamic sub-disciplines within International Relations. This second edition has been significantly updated to address contemporary and emerging security threats with chapters on organised crime, migration, and security, cyber-security, energy security, the Syrian conflict, and resilience, amongst many others. Comprising articles by both established and up-and-coming scholars, the *Routledge Handbook of Security Studies* provides a comprehensive overview of the key contemporary topics of research and debate in the field of Security Studies. The volume is divided into four main parts:

- Part I: Theoretical Approaches to Security
- Part II: Security Challenges
- Part III: Regional (In)Security
- Part IV: Security Governance

This new edition of the Handbook is a benchmark publication with major importance for both current research and the future of the field. It will be essential reading for all scholars and students of Security Studies, War and Conflict Studies, and International Relations.

Myriam Dunn Cavelty is Senior Lecturer and Deputy Head of Research and Teaching at the Center for Security Studies (CSS), ETH Zurich, Switzerland. She is the author of *Cyber-Security and Threat Politics: US Efforts to Secure the Information Age* (Routledge, 2008).

Thierry Balzacq is Professor and Tocqueville Chair in International Relations at the University of Namur, Belgium, and Scientific Director at the Institute for Strategic Research at the French Ministry of Defence. His most recent books include *Contesting Security* (Routledge, 2014), and *Traité de Relations Internationales* (co-edited with F. Ramel, 2013).

ROUTLEDGE HANDBOOK OF SECURITY STUDIES

Second edition

*Edited by Myriam Dunn Cavelty
and Thierry Balzacq*

Routledge
Taylor & Francis Group

LONDON AND NEW YORK

Second edition published 2017
by Routledge
2 Park Square, Milton Park, Abingdon, Oxon OX14 4RN

and by Routledge
711 Third Avenue, New York, NY 10017

Routledge is an imprint of the Taylor & Francis Group, an informa business

First edition published 2010 by Routledge

British Library Cataloguing-in-Publication Data
A catalogue record for this book is available from the British Library

Library of Congress Cataloging-in-Publication Data
Names: Dunn Cavelty, Myriam, editor. | Balzacq, Thierry, editor.
Title: Routledge handbook of security studies / edited by
Myriam Dunn Cavelty and Thierry Balzacq.
Other titles: Handbook of security studies
Description: Second edition. | Abingdon, Oxon ; New York,
NY : Routledge, 2017. | Includes bibliographical references and index.
Identifiers: LCCN 2016002771| ISBN 9781138803930 (hardback) |
ISBN 9781315753393 (ebook)
Subjects: LCSH: National security. | Security, International. | Strategy.
Classification: LCC UA10.5 .R69 2017 | DDC 355/.033—dc22
LC record available at http://lccn.loc.gov/2016002771

ISBN: 978-1-138-80393-0 (hbk)
ISBN: 978-1-315-75339-3 (ebk)

Typeset in Bembo Std
by Swales & Willis Ltd, Exeter, Devon, UK

CONTENTS

Contents

Contents

Contents

CONTRIBUTORS

Delphine Alles is Professor of Political Science at Université Paris-Est, France, and an associate researcher at LIPHA and IRSEM (Paris). Her research focuses on religion in International Relations and peacebuilding, especially in archipelagic South East Asia.

Claudia Aradau is Reader in International Politics in the Department of War Studies, King's College London. Her research has developed a critical political analysis of security practices. Her current work pursues a critical exploration of security practices and the politics of (non-) knowledge, with a particular emphasis on how dangerous futures are made knowable and actionable.

Thierry Balzacq is Professor in the Department of Political Science and holder of the Tocqueville Chair in Security Policies at the University of Namur, Belgium. He is also the Scientific Director of the Institute for Strategic Research at the French Ministry of Defence in Paris.

Jiun Bang is a Ph.D. candidate at the Political Science and International Relations (POIR) programme at the University of Southern California (USC). She received her MA from the Security Studies Programme (SSP) at Georgetown University.

Thomas J. Biersteker is Curt Gasteyger Professor of International Security and Conflict Studies and Director of the Programme for the Study of International Governance at the Graduate Institute of International and Development Studies, Geneva.

Arjen Boin is Professor of Public Institutions and Governance at the Institute of Political Science, Leiden University. He is co-editor of *Public Administration* and a managing partner of Crisisplan BV.

Christian Bueger is Reader in International Relations at Cardiff University. His research is on maritime security, international organizations, security expertise, and international practice theory. Further information is available at http://bueger.info.

Oldrich Bures is Head of the Center for Security Studies at Metropolitan University, Prague. His research focuses on privatization of security and the fight against terrorism. He is the author of *EU Counterterrorism Policy: A Paper Tiger?* (2011).

Barry Buzan is Emeritus Professor of International Relations at the London School of Economics and Political Science (LSE) and an honorary professor at Copenhagen, Jilin, and China Foreign Affairs Universities.

David Chandler is Professor of International Relations and Director of the Centre for the Study of Democracy, Department of Politics and International Relations, University of Westminster. He founded the *Journal of Intervention and Statebuilding* and currently edits *Resilience: International Policies, Practices, and Discourses.*

Christopher Coker is Professor of International Relations at the London School of Economics and Political Science (LSE). He is the author of *Future War* (2015) and *Warrior Geeks* (2013) among other books.

Tobias Debiel is Professor for International Relations and Development Policy, University of Duisburg-Essen, and Director of the Institute for Development and Peace as well as of the Käte Hamburger Kolleg/Centre for Global Cooperation Research, Duisburg.

Ronald Deibert is Professor of Political Science and Director of the Citizen Lab at the Munk School of Global Affairs, University of Toronto.

Myriam Dunn Cavelty is Senior Lecturer and Deputy Head of Research and Teaching at the Center for Security Studies, ETH Zurich.

Adam Edwards is Reader in Politics and Criminology at Cardiff University, School of Social Sciences. His research interests include organized crime, urban security, and disruptive digital technologies. He is author of *Transnational Organised Crime* (with P. Gill, Routledge 2003).

Magnus Ekengren is Associate Professor of Political Science and Director of the European Security Research Programme at the Swedish Defence University.

Pierre Englebert is H. Russell Smith Professor of International Relations and Professor of African Politics at Pomona College. His recent publications include *Inside African Politics* (with Kevin Dunn) and *Africa: Unity, Sovereignty, and Sorrow.*

Sophie-Charlotte Fischer is currently a Mercator Fellow in International Affairs and Ph.D. Candidate at the Center for Security Studies (ETH Zurich) and holds an MA in International Security Studies from Sciences Po, Paris.

Sumit Ganguly is a Professor of Political Science, holds the Rabindranath Tagore Chair in Indian Cultures and Civilizations, and directs the Center on American and Global Security at Indiana University, Bloomington. His most recent book is *Deadly Impasse: India and Pakistan at the Dawn of a New Century* (2016).

Nada Ghandour-Demiri is a researcher, specializing on the Middle East. She is currently co-editor of Jadaliyya's 'Daily Acts of Resistance and Subversion' section. She holds a Ph.D. from the University of Bristol. Her doctoral research was on disciplining dissent in Israel and the Occupied Palestinian Territories.

Nils Petter Gleditsch is Research Professor at the Peace Research Institute Oslo (PRIO) and Professor Emeritus of Political Science at the Norwegian University of Science and Technology (NTNU) in Trondheim. He has served as president of the International Studies Association.

Aidan Hehir is a reader in International Relations at the University of Westminster. His research interests include the Responsibility to Protect (R2P) and the laws governing the use of force. He is co-convener of the BISA Working Group on R2P.

Kimberly Heinle is a research associate and editor for Justice in Mexico based in the Department of Political Science & International Relations at the University of San Diego. Recent publications include 'Building Resilient Communities in Mexico: Civic Responses to Crime and Violence' (2014) and 'Drug Violence in Mexico: Data and Analysis Through 2013' (2014).

Raymond Hinnebusch is Professor of International Relations and Middle East Politics at the University of St Andrews in Scotland and Director of the Centre for Syrian Studies.

Gunhild Hoogensen Gjørv is Professor of Political Science (specialization international relations) at the University of Tromsø – The Arctic University of Norway. She is also a member of the Norwegian Royal Commission on Afghanistan investigating the Norwegian efforts in Afghanistan from 2001 to 2014, and has recently been awarded a position as a Fulbright Arctic Initiative scholar.

Jef Huysmans is Professor of International Politics at Queen Mary University of London.

David C. Kang is Professor at the University of Southern California (USC), with appointments in both the School of International Relations and the Marshall School of Business. At USC, he is Director of both the Korean Studies Institute and the Center for International Studies.

Sonja Kittelsen holds a Ph.D. in International Politics from Aberystwyth University. Her Ph.D. thesis, on the process of securitizing pandemic influenza at the level of the EU, was awarded the UACES Best Ph.D. Thesis Prize in 2014.

Richard Ned Lebow is Professor of International Political Theory in the War Studies department of King's College London. He is also Bye-Fellow of Pembroke College, University of Cambridge and James O. Freedman Presidential Professor (Emeritus), Dartmouth College.

Jeffrey Mankoff is a senior fellow at the Center for Strategic and International Studies (CSIS) and Deputy Director of the CSIS Russia & Eurasia Programme.

Carlo Masala is Chair of International Relations at the University of the German Armed Forces in Munich and a member of the scientific advisory boards of the NATO Defence College, the Federal Academy for Security Policy, and the security research programme at the Federal Ministry of Education and Research.

Rens van Munster is Senior Researcher and Research Coordinator for Peace, Risk, and Violence at the Danish Institute for International Studies (DIIS), Copenhagen.

David Mutimer is Chair and Professor of Political Science at York University in Toronto, and the editor of *Critical Studies on Security*.

Sheila Nair is a Professor in Politics and International Affairs at Northern Arizona University and currently serving as Director of Women's and Gender Studies. She has published work on postcolonial International Relations (IR) and states of exception in IR. Her research interests include postcolonial feminism and international political economy, feminist theories, migration, and human rights, and memory and mass violence.

Robert W. Orttung is Associate Research Professor of International Affairs and Research Director of the Sustainability Collaborative at the George Washington University.

Rouzbeh Parsi is a senior lecturer at Lund University, Department of History and Human Rights, specializing on Iran (domestic and foreign policy) and the Middle East. He is also a co-founder and Director of the European Iran Research Group. Between 2009 and 2013, he worked as Senior Analyst at the EU Institute for Security Studies in Paris.

Heikki Patomäki is Professor of World Politics at the University of Helsinki, Finland. His most recent books in English are *The Great Eurozone Disaster: From Crisis to Global New Deal* (2013) and *The Political Economy of Global Security* (2008). His interests include methodology, peace research, economic theory, political economy and theory, and futures studies.

Karen Lund Petersen is Associate Professor at the Department of Political Science and Director of the Centre for Advanced Security Theory. Her primary research interests are security and risk governance, with a particular focus on corporate security and intelligence.

Mark Rhinard is Associate Professor of International Relations at Stockholm University and leads the Europe Programme at the Swedish Institute of International Affairs.

Patricia Rinck is a Ph.D. candidate at the University of Duisburg-Essen and Researcher at the Käte Hamburger Kolleg/Centre for Global Cooperation Research, Duisburg.

Octavio Rodríguez Ferreira is Programme Coordinator of Justice in Mexico, at the Department of Political Science & International Relations of the University of San Diego. He has written and co-authored several studies on Mexican policing and judicial reform.

David L. Rousseau is Founding Dean of the College of Emergency Preparedness, Homeland Security, and Cybersecurity at the University of Albany (State University at New York) and an associate professor in the Department of Political Science.

Simon Rushton is a faculty research fellow in the Department of Politics at the University of Sheffield and an associate fellow of the Centre on Global Health Security at the Royal Institute of International Affairs, Chatham House.

Amin Saikal is Distinguished Professor of Political Science, Public Policy Fellow, and Director of the Centre for Arab and Islamic Studies (the Middle East and Central Asia) at the Australian National University.

Alessandro Scheffler Corvaja is a research associate and academic coordinator of the MA International Security Studies programme at the University of the German Armed Forces in Munich and the George C. Marshall European Center for Security Studies.

Olivier Schmitt is an Associate Professor of Political Science at the University of Southern Denmark, where he is a member of the Center for War Studies. His research focuses on multi-national military operations, the transformation of European armed forces, and the work of the French sociologist Raymond Aron.

David A. Shirk is Director of Justice in Mexico and Associate Professor of Political Science & International Relations at the University of San Diego. His recent publications include: 'Contemporary Mexican Politics' (forthcoming) and 'Building Resilient Communities in Mexico' (2014).

Nancy Snow is the first titled professor of public diplomacy in Japan (Pax Mundi Professor of Public Diplomacy, Kyoto University of Foreign Studies). She served as Visiting Professor and Abe Fellow at Keio University in Tokyo, Japan. She is Emeritus Professor of Communications at California State University, Fullerton with visiting professor appointments in China (Tsinghua), Israel (IDC-Herzliya), Japan (Sophia/Keio), and Malaysia (UiTM), as well as at Syracuse University's Maxwell and Newhouse Schools and USC Annenberg.

Vicki Squire is Reader of International Security at the University of Warwick.

Gareth Stansfield is Professor of Middle East Politics at the Institute of Arab and Islamic Studies at the University of Exeter, and a senior associate fellow at the Royal United Services Institute (RUSI). He is also a global fellow at the Wilson Center in Washington DC.

Ole Magnus Theisen is Associate Professor in Political Science at the Norwegian University of Science and Technology (NTNU) in Trondheim and Associate Senior Researcher at the Peace Research Institute Oslo (PRIO).

Juha A. Vuori is Acting Professor of World Politics at the University of Helsinki in Finland. He is the author of *Critical Security and Chinese Politics* (Routledge 2014).

Thomas C. Walker teaches International Relations at Grand Valley State University. Before returning home to West Michigan, he taught at Dartmouth College, University at Albany–SUNY, and Rutgers, where he received his Ph.D. He has published in *International Studies Quarterly*, *Perspectives on Politics*, and *International Studies Review*.

Wilfred Wan is a JSPS-UNU postdoctoral fellow with the UNU Centre for Policy Research in Tokyo; his host institute is Hitotsubashi University. Among other topics, his current work examines multilateral cooperation in nuclear non-proliferation and security.

Annick T. R. Wibben is Professor of Politics at the University of San Francisco, where she chairs the interdisciplinary Peace & Justice Studies programme. She is the author of *Feminist Security Studies: A Narrative Approach* (Routledge 2011) and editor of *Researching War: Feminist Methods, Ethics & Politics* (Routledge 2016).

William C. Wohlforth is Daniel Webster Professor in the Department of Government at Dartmouth College and co-chairman of the editorial board of *Security Studies*.

ACKNOWLEDGEMENTS

Textbooks and other reference works on Security Studies, for both students and experts, are in high demand. This second edition of the *Routledge Handbook of Security Studies* offers a comprehensive collection of new and substantially updated cutting-edge essays on many aspects of the subject by a mix of established and up-and-coming international scholars. It identifies the key contemporary topics of research and debate in terms of theory, threats, areas of concern, and security solutions, and thus offers the most comprehensive overview that exists to date.

Compiling so many diverse chapters has been a great joy as well as a great challenge. Delays and setbacks are always inevitable, but having the final product in hand makes up for all the hurdles we encountered on the way. First and for all, we are indebted to our numerous authors: for agreeing to contribute to this ambitious project; for accepting the limits and constraints such a project inevitably brings about; for considering our suggestions and comments; for being patient about the editing process; and, finally, for delivering such rich content. We feel privileged to have worked with all of them, and this Handbook is a product of their devotion and commitment.

Also present at the creation was Andrew Humphrys, Senior Editor at Routledge, who, with the right mix of support, interest, and impatience, oversaw the project from beginning to end, showing a great deal of understanding for the extension of deadlines. As always, it has been a pleasure to work with him in preparing the book for publication. Special thanks also go to Routledge's Senior Editorial Assistant Hannah Ferguson, who was always there for us and dealt with our requests with great efficiency, the copy-editor Martin Thacker, as well as to Jonas Schmid and Darius Farman, research assistants at the Center for Security Studies, for their valuable assistance with the manuscript.

Myriam Dunn Cavelty and Thierry Balzacq
Zurich and Paris

INTRODUCTION

Thierry Balzacq and Myriam Dunn Cavelty

Handbooks such as this one are a bit like candy stores. Handbooks allow for a collection of appealing and varied articles, all of which are waiting to be sampled. If you try one, like it, and want more, the chapters in this research-oriented publication will give you indications for where you *can* get more, so that your cravings can easily be satisfied. Even better, the candies offered here in the second edition of the *Routledge Handbook of Security Studies* come with additional benefits: they are good for the brain, they do not make you gain weight, and you are not even constrained to brush your teeth afterwards.

What goodies can you find in this book? The name of our candy store is 'Security Studies'. Most often, this field of study is considered a sub-field of International Relations (IR) (Buzan and Hansen 2009: 1).[1] The story of how the sub-field formed, splintered, re-formed, shrunk, and grew has been told numerous times before (cf. Baldwin 1997; Buzan and Hansen 2009; Williams 2013) and will not be repeated here. We understand Security Studies broadly as the systematic, scholarly investigation of national and international security issues – and this is what this Handbook is about.

Not surprisingly, the concept of security itself has received a lot of scholarly attention. Security is variably seen as a condition, a value, a part of policy, a practice, a utopia, etc. Security is very old, but parts of security are new. You can add prefixes to the noun and thus turn it into things like national security, human security, food security, or cyber-security. Security touches everybody all the time, but sometimes, it benefits just a few. Security likes power, but power also creates insecurity. For some, security is always good, for others, security is never unproblematic. In sum, in the last few decades, security has been 'structured, systemised, broadened, deepened, gendered, criticalised, humanised, constructed and privatised' (Bourbeau et al. 2015: 111).

Security is a contested concept or even an 'essentially contested' one (Baldwin 1997), that is, its internal complexity and the contested values related to it produce rival versions of the concept, which in turn leads to perennial struggles over the 'true' meaning (Gallie 1956). As early as 1991, Barry Buzan identified 12 different definitions of security that important analysts have produced (Buzan 1991: 16), one of the more prominent examples being Arnold Wolfers' definition that 'security, in an objective sense, measures the absence of threats to acquired values, in a subjective sense, the absence of fear that such values will be attacked' (Wolfers 1952: 485). Since then, the definitions of security have multiplied considerably beyond the ones identified by Buzan. Security has fittingly been called 'a Tower of Babel' (Kolodziej 2005: 11), indicating both towering piles of texts and a great confusion as to the meaning of the conceptual foundations at the same time.

The point is: given these many takes on the concept, security can hardly be seen as just one thing – it is many things at the same time, often depending on who uses the term and for what purpose. This is the reason why this Handbook presents security and the way it is studied like a candy store would present its sweets: by offering the reader a large and diverse selection. In choosing our authors for this edition of the Handbook, neither meta-theoretical leaning nor methodological preferences were relevant categories. In other words, no school of thought was privileged. The only criterion we applied for the selection was a proven track record in excellent scholarly work, the greatest possible mix between men and women, diversity in seniority, and diversity in geographical location (within limits).[2]

If this book were a candy store and we editors owned it, going for 'maximum diversity' would still oblige us to limit the selection of candies we offer in our shop, given space constraints. Since this is not a newly opened candy store, we were fortunate to know that the basic stock (aka first edition) was very well received by our customers. But since we got the chance to renovate and even expand the shop for the second edition, we also had to choose new candies to be offered, and in the same process, exchange some of the old ones for others that we thought would bring even more pleasure to our customers. To select new candies, we looked at what the world had to offer – in other words, at what security issues were discussed at conferences, in academic journals, and in the media. Here, by choice and by expertise, we identified the key contemporary topics of research and debate today.

The second edition of this Handbook presents content that has considerably been updated, consolidated, and transformed. Of forty-two chapters, twenty-four are entirely new, either because new topics were added or because new authors were taken on board to write about first edition topics. Seventeen chapters were substantially updated by at least one of the original authors; some so much that they are basically new chapters. Only one chapter is a reprint. Of course, not everything was completely in our power. Some conditions had been predetermined, such as the maximum length of the volume. In addition, some of the exclusions are voluntary, while others are less deliberate. In more than one case, chapter delivery was simply not possible, even after we asked several potential contributors. Also, some authors ran into problems with production in the process of delivering to us, some very late in the process, and ultimately could not be included. Such things are never fully predictable. If they were, research would lack all surprise, all contingency, and – who knows? – all excitement. Still, the end result is what we aimed for: a Handbook that offers an appealing selection of highly different chapters on security issues and how they are studied.

The Handbook is organized into four parts:

- Part I looks at a wide variety of theoretical positions, from the historically dominant traditions to powerful critical voices.
- Part II addresses a number of contemporary security challenges, including terrorism, as well as health issues, and other topical transnational issues.
- Part III of the Handbook is dedicated to specific regional security challenges.
- Part IV focuses on some of the available tools and instruments to counter and manage security challenges on different levels.

Part I: theoretical approaches to security

Part I of the Handbook locates Security Studies within the broader landscape of IR. It brings together theoretical approaches to security and specific ways in which these approaches are currently extended. In this part, the central theses that underlie the different chapters may be condensed in two general propositions. First, because of its close connection with IR, Security Studies has been directly affected by all of the 'grand debates' in the field of IR. These exercises in defining the 'right way' to conduct scholarly inquiry are about questions of theory (and ultimately world views), involving 'idealist, realist, behavioralist, post-behavioralist, pluralist, neo-realist, rationalist, postpositivist, and constructivist' positions (Schmidt 2002: 3).

However, simplified and simplifying historical accounts give rise to specific and fairly powerful myths regarding the evolution of the field and especially the divisions in it (see also Bourbeau et al. 2015). Particularly the general image of a discipline divided between US scholars (following a rationalist tradition) and European security scholars (following a critical studies tradition) is overdrawn. Rather than taking different meta-theoretical positions and theories as invitations to create 'groups' and, ultimately, opposition between researchers, the current theoretical diversity should be seen as an asset (see also Jackson 2011). A much wider range of choices is now available when thinking about security issues, providing a very rich and fertile environment for the inquisitive analyst (Wæver and Buzan 2016).

Accounts of what Security Studies are or ought to be (Walt 1991) most often characterize the field via different sub-schools. In the formation of those, which happens either through the scholarly practice of assigning labels to one's own work or through assigning them to the work of others, theories, and the larger meta-theoretical families they are part of, have always served as the most important identity-element. In this light, the first part of this Handbook covers the two 'dominant' theoretical traditions in Security Studies, (neo)realism and (neo)liberalism. While describing the most influential thinkers in both research traditions and the differences between each other, both chapters also clearly establish how great the diversity within those theoretical traditions is. This discussion is followed by a new chapter on international political economy and security, which is looking at that particular intersection between security and political economy, thereby taking many of the topics in the neoliberalism chapter further. As in the first edition, the English school and its contributions to international security are represented as well.

The next five chapters cover different aspects of 'critical Security Studies', which have established themselves strongly as alternatives to the traditional theories over the last few years. An overview chapter over different strands of critical Security Studies is followed by a chapter on constructivism and securitization studies, and then rounded off by three chapters on important research traditions: poststructuralist approaches to security (one of the growth areas in Security Studies), feminist Security Studies, and postcolonialism.

Our second proposition can be phrased as follows: grand theories are increasingly losing ground in Security Studies to problem-focused investigations, which challenge and reconfigure how scholars approach the field itself. The new problems are seen as requiring a combination of conceptual lenses, and the application of methods that enable us to have a grip on how security is experienced. This tallies with what happens in the policy world. In fact, for policy-makers theoretical debates have never been a driver for the imperative to understand (and react to) security issues: it has been the issues *themselves*. Security issues or challenges are either treated as 'real', material threats by traditional approaches to security or are seen as constructed as security issues in a (security) political process by the critical approaches, with different consequences for how they are studied.

Accordingly, this Handbook includes chapters that are dedicated to different types of security or particular ways of understanding security: a chapter on human security and a chapter on the link between security and risk, covering some of the most recent theoretical innovations in Security Studies concerned with 'the unknowable, the new threat, the uncertain future, and the following difficulty of management and prevention'. Risk has become a very relevant category through which governments conceptualize public dangers in Western security practice. Particular to risk narratives is the understanding that national security is not (or no longer) defined by known and current dangers, but by potentials of unforeseeable catastrophic harm (Williams 2008). Narratives of inestimable upcoming harm are empowering an important range of specific government rationalities today, be it the permanent surveillance of populations, precautionary arrests of suspects, or pre-emptive invasions of foreign countries. This part concludes with a chapter on security as practice, covering an important shift in Security Studies (the 'practice turn'), with methodological consequences, such as the insistence on ethnographic approaches.

Part II: security challenges

If the first part of the Handbook was concerned with the referent point of security, the second focuses on what constitutes threats or what are the different sources of security problems. The theoretical discussions raised in the first section cross the thematic chapters vertically, which enables readers to assess the degree to which different perspectives affect our understanding of substantial security matters.

While war and the threat of the use of force are still part of the security equation, it is not exclusively so: Security Studies now encompass dangers that range from pandemics and environmental degradation to the more readily associated security concerns of direct violence, such as terrorism and inter-state armed conflict. The issues selected for inclusion in this part reflect this evolution. They range from classic security issues like war, ethnic and religious violence, and the link between resources, the environment, and conflict, to a range of 'new' security issues (terrorism, organized crime, migration, cyber-security, energy security, and pandemics). Among these issues, some are relatively new, while others have been long-standing focuses of attention for policy-makers and scholars.

Yet, whether traditional or not, old or new, threats morph. The nature they take usually command different kinds of actions. The contributions gathered in this part situate security issues in a decidedly multidisciplinary perspective. One of the noteworthy developments in the field of Security Studies in the last decades has been a consistent interest in insights gleaned from sociology, philosophy, anthropology, law, history, to name but a few disciplines that are woven into the fabric of Security Studies. For instance, chapters on terrorism and counterterrorism, organized crime, and migration draw on a diverse range of fields, which enables them to go beyond mono-disciplinary accounts of these phenomena. Be that as it may, chapters on cyber-security, pandemics and global health, and energy security address issues that are, indeed, regarded as emerging threats. But this is not entirely accurate. While cyber-security and global health are connected to, or derivative of, new modes of communication, energy security is not that new. The oil crises in 1973–4 and 1979 are there to remind us that, throughout history, states, or more generally polities, have often fought in order to secure access to natural resources. In other words, 'newness' in form is not 'newness' in content.

These issues arise from factors and actors that do not map on to the geographical remits or the military actions of sovereign states. Further, these moves result in policy (and scholarly) attention on issues previously not considered in the realm of 'Security Studies'. Importantly, this also breaks with the tradition of seeing security mainly as outwards-oriented and looks more closely at how security also works on the inside of political borders. Today, scholarship (and the policy world) accept more amorphous and ambiguous characteristics of national security, composed of a mixture of security problems – international, local, regional, domestic, and global security issues are intertwined.

The picture that emerges from this is that security is no longer primarily about threats and battles against an enemy, but is characterized by an inward-looking narrative about vulnerabilities. Its referent object is often not the population, or life more broadly, but technical and social systems that are designated vital to collective life. The sources of insecurity (classically, the 'enemy') are put to the background, as the stability of technical and societal systems becomes a primary target of security interventions. It is no longer, or not only, about widening or deepening security; rather, it is about rethinking its rationale.

Part III: regional (in)security

There is always a danger of overstating change – the vulnerability-focused Western debate in Security Studies is no exception to this. Amorphous and ambiguous types of security are not 'the' new paradigm. Put differently, security practices neither shift from one ideal type to another, nor are they universal or without alternatives. Traditional national security – state, government, and elite-centered – still prevails as a dominant rationality in many countries of the world. In addition, war and conflict remain the prime driver for many of the most deadly security issues for human life in the world. This is why this Handbook has a dedicated section on ongoing 'conflicts'. The third part of the Handbook is intended to provide us with a rich and nuanced picture of tensions whose ramifications often go beyond their immediate geographical context.

Conflict studies are a very well established field in Security Studies. One type of research is concerned more with mechanisms of conflict, with less interest in the particularities of particular cases (Sandole et al. 2010). Another type of research, often considered at the periphery of Security Studies if we look at the major journals for reference, is providing in-depth knowledge of particular regions and their conflicts. Scholarship in this tradition often does not aim to generalize from their particular case to broader mechanisms but lives from the intricate knowledge of local specificities. Part III of this Handbook follows the second tradition. Because of the fluid situation in many of these countries or regions, it may happen that some chapters are out-dated before this second edition is published. However, since all the authors focus their chapters not on the current situation only, but give a much broader overview over important factors and historical developments that shape the particular security situation, the chapters are able to deliver pointers for further research.

The selection of chapters for this part was probably the most difficult – sadly, there would have been so many additional conflicts to cover. This edition has chosen a particular focus on the Middle East (five chapters), a crisis-ridden region on the verge of a long struggle for a re-establishment, or reinvention, of regional and intra-state order. The effects of this struggle, and of competing concepts of the state and concepts of ruling within the Middle East, touch Europe and the rest of the Western world directly – not least through a new 'territorial terrorism' embodied by the Islamic State movement (Mahadevan 2015) but also through the large numbers of refugees fleeing their homes.

Iraq, Iran, and Syria are now part of a security complex, whose tremor is felt worldwide. Each chapter, however, pays particular attention to the peculiarities of these countries as some of them are also in conflict with countries that do not belong to the complex per se. Moreover, the internal dynamics and the organizational and ideological structures of these countries differ, so much so that authors have spent a great deal of effort in clarifying stakes, opportunities, and deadlocks. The added value in our understanding of these countries is significant. The same goes with the chapters on Afghanistan, on the one hand, and Israel-Palestine conflict on the other. In the former, peace remains fragile and the Taliban maintain an enormous pressure on the central government in Kabul. In the latter, negotiations, we know, are stalled. But in both cases, communities live in a state of permanent war, which varies in intensity, as a consequence of periodic outbursts of violence.

Furthermore, there are three chapters on big powers and world politics. The first, on China, shows that fears about China's rise are completely unfounded, whereas the chapter on Russia's revival paints a picture of a far more aggressive grand power that endangers the post-Cold War liberal international order. The chapter on Indian security policy also warns about the potential for further conflict in the region. Another chapter that was added turns the attention to a special type of conflict that is very bloody: the South American drug war. Finally, this version of the Handbook includes one chapter on an African conflict (the Democratic Republic of the Congo): attempts to commission papers for additional ones sadly failed.

Part IV: security governance

The last part of the Handbook seeks to present and discuss the various ways in which security challenges – like the ones elaborated in Part II – are dealt with. In the language of public policy, it is concerned with tools or instruments of security (Balzacq 2010). Here, too, the Handbook explores continuities and ruptures in the ways security issues are practically handled. We see continuities in approaches that accord a pre-eminent role to military power in dealing with threats. One of the new tools that extend military power in time and space are drones. Theoretically, we treat it through both the lenses of traditional and critical approaches to security. Some instruments are about pooling, and sometimes sharing, military power (e.g. alliances); others are concerned with containing military power (e.g. deterrence and nuclear non-proliferation); still others are about obtaining a desired strategic outcome without the use of military power (e.g. public diplomacy) or by relying upon individuals' resources (resilience). The basic assumption is that the (in-) security of a subject is not only dependent on the character and severity of the threat it is exposed to (its vulnerability), but also on the subject itself – namely its resilience to detrimental events. The concept thus aspires to describe mechanisms for maintaining stability, survival, and safety – mechanisms that seem equally applicable to the individual, society, nature, and technical systems.

As you read on, you will notice that the state holds no monopoly over most of the new instruments of security. The global governance of security, for instance, is a multi-layered arrangement that involves a wider range of actors, rules, and practices. It operates in a context wherein power is dispersed and sources of authority are hotly disputed. Further, humanitarian intervention, state building, and resilience cannot be carried out or supported exclusively by states. Much of the discussion in this part concerns the nature and uses, as well as the limits, of security instruments, including the normative challenge they raise. Thus, the Handbook offers one of the most compelling landscapes on the evolving character of security governance, one which accounts for the development of instruments, but also for the ways instruments shape interactions between different strategic agents.

Notes

1 At times, scholars have argued that IR was in fact a sub-field of Security Studies and not the other way around, as IR was depicted as dealing almost exclusively with deterrence and compellence (Jervis 1991: 80).
2 Owing to our own personal networks, this diversity does not extend to the inclusion of non-Western scholars.

References

Baldwin, D. A. (1997) 'The Concept of Security', *Review of International Studies* 23(1): 5–26.
Balzacq, T. (2010) 'A Theory of Securitization: Origins, Core Assumptions, Variants', in T. Balzacq (ed.) *Understanding Securitization Theory: How Security Problems Emerge and Dissolve*, London: Routledge, 1–30.
Bourbeau, P., Balzacq, T. and Dunn Cavelty, M. (2015) 'Celebrating Eclectic Dynamism: Security in International Relations', in P. Bourbeau (ed.) *Security: Dialogue across Disciplines*, Cambridge: Cambridge University Press, 111–36.

Buzan, B. (1991) *People, States and Fear: An Agenda for International Security Studies in the post-Cold War Era*, 2nd edn, Boulder, CO: Lynne Rienner.

Buzan, B. and Hansen, L. (2009) *The Evolution of International Security Studies*, Cambridge: Cambridge University Press.

Gallie, W. B. (1956) 'Essentially Contested Concepts', *Proceedings of the Aristotelian Society* 56(1): 167–98.

Jackson, P. T. (2011) *The Conduct of Inquiry in International Relations*, London: Routledge.

Jervis, R. (1991) 'Models and Cases in the Study of International Conflict', in Robert L. Rothstein (ed.) *The Evolution of Theory in International Relations*, Columbia: University of South Carolina Press, 61–81.

Kolodziej, E. A. (2005) *Security and International Relations*, Cambridge: Cambridge University Press.

Mahadevan, P. (2015) 'Resurgent Radicalism', in O. Thränert and M. Zapfe (eds.) *Strategic Trends 2015, Key Developments in Global Affairs*, Zurich: Center for Security Studies, 45–62.

Sandole, D. J. S., Byrne, S., Sandole-Staroste, I. and Senehi, J. (eds.) (2010) *Handbook of Conflict Analysis and Resolution*, London: Routledge.

Schmidt, B. C. (2002) 'On the History and Historiography of International Relations', in W. Carlsnaes, T. Risse, and B. A. Simmons (eds.) *Handbook of International Relations*, London: Sage, 1–22.

Wæver, O. and Buzan, B. (2016) 'After the Return to Theory: The Past, Present, and Future of Security Studies', in A. Collins (ed.) *Contemporary Security Studies*, 4th edn, Oxford: Oxford University Press, 417–35.

Walt, S. (1991) 'The Renaissance of Security Studies', *International Studies Quarterly* 35(2): 211–39.

Williams, M. J. (2008) '(In)Security Studies, Reflexive Modernization and the Risk Society', *Cooperation and Conflict* 43(1): 57–79.

Williams, P. (2013) *Security Studies: An Introduction*, 2nd edn, London: Routledge.

Wolfers, A. (1952) 'National Security as an Ambiguous Symbol', *Political Science Quarterly* 67(4): 481–502.

PART I

Theoretical approaches to security

1

REALISM AND SECURITY STUDIES

William C. Wohlforth*

It is impossible to understand contemporary Security Studies without a grounding in realism. After all, many of the most influential theories that have ever been advanced about violence and security among human groups fall within this intellectual tradition. And in many countries realism is a standard part of practitioner's lexicon, informing headline debates on foreign policy. To many analysts, moreover, realism's focus on power shifts and power politics seems as relevant as ever, as a rising China and a reassertive Russia upend complacency about the stability of the Western-dominated international system. Given the many scholarly criticisms of realism, ongoing debates about its place in Security Studies, and the proliferation in recent years of such realist 'brands' as defensive, offensive, and neoclassical realism, gaining this grounding might seem a formidable undertaking. In fact, the controversy and complexity have eased the task.

As this chapter shows, realist thinking is now far more robust and rigorous than ever, making it much more accessible and useful to security scholars. The chapter provides the four key elements that students of international security need to make use of realism: a simple definition of realism that distinguishes it from other approaches; an introduction to the various sub-schools of realist thought, such as neoclassical realism, which help bring order to the daunting diversity of realist scholarship; an outline of some of the most prominent realist theories, which do the actual work of explaining puzzling real-world phenomena, and a sketch of the contemporary realist contribution to Security Studies.

Defining realism

Realism is a school of thought based on three core assumptions about how the world works:[1]

1. *Groupism.* Politics takes place within and between groups. Group solidarity is essential to domestic politics and conflict and cooperation between polities is the essence of international politics. To survive at anything above a subsistence level, people need the cohesion provided by group solidarity, yet that very same in-group cohesion generates the potential for conflict with other groups. Today, the most important human groups are nation-states, and the most important source of in-group cohesion is nationalism. But it is important to stress that realism makes no assumption about the nature of the polity. It is as applicable to relations between ISIS and the Kurds as it is between the United States and China.

2. *Egoism*. When individuals and groups act politically, they are driven principally by narrow self-interest. Although certain conditions can facilitate altruistic behaviour, egoism is rooted in human nature. When push comes to shove and ultimate trade-offs between collective and self-interest must be confronted, egoism tends to trump altruism. As the classic realist adage has it, 'Inhumanity is just humanity under pressure.'

3. *Power-centrism*. Once past the hunter-gatherer stage, human affairs are always marked by great inequalities of power in both senses of that term: social influence or *control* (some groups and individuals always have an outsized influence on politics) and *resources* (some groups and individuals are always disproportionately endowed with the material wherewithal to get what they want). Key to politics in any area is the interaction between social and material power, an interaction that unfolds in the shadow of the potential use of material power to coerce.

Realism's most important single argument builds on these assumptions to illuminate a relationship between political order and security: if human affairs are indeed characterized by groupism, egoism, and power-centrism, then politics is likely to be conflictual unless there is some central authority to enforce order. When no authority exists that can enforce agreements – in a state of 'anarchy' – then any actor can resort to force to get what it wants. Even if an actor can be fairly sure that no other will take up arms today, there is no guarantee against the possibility that one might do so tomorrow. Therefore, all tend to arm themselves against this contingency. Disputes that would be easy to settle if actors could rely on some higher authority to enforce an agreement can escalate to war in the absence of such authority. The signature realist argument is therefore that anarchy renders security problematic and potentially conflictual, and is a key underlying cause of war.

This argument is not restricted to international politics. It identifies a fundamental and universal human problem that may apply to individuals as well as city-states, tribes, empires, or nation-states. The point simply is that insecurity is endemic to anarchy. To be secure, people need to overcome anarchy. One way to do this is to strengthen the bonds within a group to provide governance. This is what states do – or what they are supposed to do. If they fail, then life within a state can become just as threatened by insecurity as life among states. The dilemma is that solving the anarchy problem within one group only magnifies it between groups. Much realist thought is thus focused on how the security problem manifests itself in inter-group relations, but its insights are applicable to politics at all levels of analysis.

Realism's diversity: theoretical schools

Realism today is marked by the coexistence of numerous sub-schools, notably defensive, offensive, and neoclassical realism. These sub-schools are the outgrowth of sharp debates among scholars as well as unceasing efforts to check realist ideas against international political reality.

Classical realism

It all began with classical realism – a term scholars use to describe the whole realist tradition in all its diversity as it unfolded up to the 1970s. For the subsequent development of International Relations (IR) theory, however, one classical realist text stands far above all others: Hans J. Morgenthau's *Politics among Nations* (Morgenthau 1948). This book inaugurated the practice of seeking to translate the realist tradition of scholarship and statecraft into what Morgenthau, in the famous first chapter of his text, called 'a realist theory of international politics.'[2]

Morgenthau's major text did bring realist arguments to bear on a very large number of phenomena: war, peace, cooperation, international law, diplomacy, ethics, international organization, world public opinion, and more, but it simply failed to hold together as a unified theory, at least in the eyes of his critics. Even fellow realists found Morgenthau's theory beset by 'open contradictions, ambiguity, and vagueness' (Tucker 1952: 214). Key concepts such as the 'national interest' or 'the balance of power' were either undefined or defined in multiple and mutually contradictory ways. Not surprisingly, arguments deployed in different issue areas did not always cohere.

By the 1960s, many scholars of IR had come to see the natural sciences as models for social sciences. For them, a 'theory' had to be a coherent set of linked propositions, preferably falsifiable and empirically verified, that explains some phenomenon. In this context, Morgenthau's more modest and more humanistic understanding of what a theory of international politics can and should be seemed increasingly anachronistic (Williams 2007). And these scholarly criticisms mounted just as the world's security preoccupations were moving from the great-power contest between the US and the Soviet Union towards issues such as inequality between the wealthy North and the developing South, resource scarcity, and human rights. Morgenthau's version of realism seemed out of sync with the times. Out of this first post-war 'crisis' of realism came a revival of realist thinking that came to be called 'neorealism.'

Neorealism

As scholarly criticism of realism mounted in the 1960s and 1970s and the interest in the scientific approach to the study of politics grew (especially in the US), Kenneth Waltz sought to revivify realist thinking by translating some core realist ideas into a deductive, top-down theoretical framework first known as 'structural realism' but now most commonly called neorealism. Waltz (1959) held that classical realists' powerful insights into the workings of international politics were weakened by their failure to distinguish clearly between arguments about human nature, the internal attributes of states, and the overall system of states. His *Theory of International Politics* (1979) brought together and clarified many earlier realist ideas about how the features of the overall system of states affect security affairs. He presented the book as the transformation of classical realist 'thought' into a theory on the scientific model, in keeping with the contemporary expectations of the wider discipline of political science.

By restating, in the clearest form yet, realism's key argument about how the mere existence of groups in anarchy can lead to powerful competitive pressure and war – regardless of what the internal politics of those groups might be like – Waltz presented a theory that purported to answer a few important but highly general questions about international politics: why the modern states-system has persisted in the face of attempts by certain states at dominance; why war among great powers recurred over centuries; and why states often find cooperation hard. In addition, the book forwarded one more specific theory: that great-power war would tend to be more frequent in multipolarity (an international system shaped by the power of three or more major states) than bipolarity (an international system shaped by the power of two major states, or superpowers). Events in the real world seemed to underline the salience of Waltz's seemingly abstract ideas: right after the publication of the book, the Cold War heated up, reinforcing the sense that bipolarity was indeed a powerful structural force shaping international security.

Yet even in the 1980s, it was clear that neorealism left a great many questions about international security unanswered: why alliances form, why arms races begin and end, why states create international institutions, why the Cold War began, and why the superpower rivalry waxed and waned, and many more. The overwhelming majority of scholars seeking to address those questions found Waltz's general theory insufficient. Most responded by using Waltz's work as a foil for developing self-consciously non-realist explanations of specific puzzles or, more ambitiously, for developing alternative theoretical schools, most notably institutionalism (Keohane 1984) and constructivism (Wendt 1999). But some responded by developing their own realist theories based on Waltz's. For example, in seeking to explain alliance behaviour, Stephen M. Walt (1987) integrated insights from Waltz into a new, related but clearly distinct 'balance of threat' theory (discussed below), while Glen Snyder (1997) combined Waltz's theories with other complementary theories. In explaining cooperation, Joseph Grieco (1988) supplemented Waltz's theory with propositions from game theory.

Thus, even though Waltz, like Morgenthau, presented his work as a single stand-alone realist 'theory of international politics', the natural development of scholarly inquiry led to the development of neorealism as a complex sub-school within realism, encompassing many Waltz-inspired theories. What linked the research of these scholars best captured as 'neorealist' was a common bet that Waltz's reformulation of realism was the best place to start inquiry.

Offensive and defensive realism

The advent of neorealism sparked a major debate that still reverberates among scholars. The debate was well under way before the Berlin Wall fell, but the Cold War's end further intensified critical scrutiny of Waltz's ideas. The criticisms added up to a crisis of realism that was easily as consequential as the antirealist storm that had pummelled Morgenthau in the 1960s and 1970s. While the focus at the time was on the theory's deficiencies – neorealism has never recovered the scholarly influence it attained in the 1980s – in hindsight, it is clear that neorealism had caused scholars to think much harder and more clearly about the underlying forces that drive IR. Realists working with Waltz's theory discovered that, depending on how they thought about the core assumptions, and what they saw as the most reasonable expectations about real-world conditions, neorealism could lead to very different predictions. Written in a highly abstract manner, Waltz's neorealism ignored important variations in IR, including geography and technology. Depending on how one conceptualized those factors, the very same neorealist ideas could generate widely disparate implications about the dynamics of inter-state politics. Out of this realization were born two new theoretical sub-schools, each of which built on the basic insights of neorealism: defensive realism and offensive realism.

Building on core ideas presented in *Theory of International Politics* and, arguably even more importantly, on the pioneering work of Robert Jervis (1986) on cooperation under anarchy, defensive realists reasoned that under very common conditions, the war-causing potential of anarchy is attenuated (Taliaferro 2000/2001). The harder conquest is, the more secure all states can be. Anything that makes conquest hard can reduce the security problem. For example, it is hard to contemplate the conquest of states that have the capacity to strike back with nuclear weapons. Thus, even accepting Waltz's arguments about how difficult it is to be secure in an anarchic world, under some conditions, states can still be expected to find ways of defending themselves without threatening others, or can otherwise signal their peaceful intentions, resulting in an international system with more built-in potential for peace than many realists previously thought (Glaser 2010). The result was to push analysts to look inside states for the domestic and ideational causes of war and peace.

Offensive realists, by contrast, were more persuaded by the conflict-generating, structural potential of anarchy itself. They reasoned that, with no authority to enforce agreements, states could never be certain that any peace-causing condition today would remain operative in the future. Even if conquest may seem hard today owing to geography or technology there is no guarantee against another state developing some fiendish device for overcoming these barriers.

Given this uncertainty, states can rarely be confident of their security and must always view other states' increases in power with suspicion. As a result, states are often tempted to expand or otherwise strengthen themselves – and/or to weaken others – in order to survive over the long haul. The result is to reinforce the classic realist argument about the competitive nature of life under anarchy, regardless of the internal properties of states.

Defensive and offensive realism emerged in the 1990s as outgrowths of Waltz's neorealism. In keeping with the tradition established by Waltz and Morgenthau, many of the scholars who developed these theories saw them as articulating *the* realist theory (see, for example Mearsheimer 2001). But it is impossible to put the genie of realism's diversity back into the bottle. It is clear that defensive and offensive realism coexist as distinct sub-schools. And those two sub-schools hardly exhaust realism's diversity, for many other realist theories fall outside either of them.

A telling example of this diversity is the work of Waltz's contemporary Robert Gilpin, whose magisterial *War and Change in World Politics* (1981) is seen by many as a more important and lasting theoretical contribution than Waltz's (Wohlforth 2011; Ikenberry 2014). Written and conceived completely independently from Waltz's *Theory* but certainly no less realist, Gilpin's work provided an elegant theoretical framework to explain the links between shifting power balances, order, and war over centuries. Furthermore, many of the theoretical ideas in Morgenthau's *Politics Among Nations*, especially those relating to the analysis of foreign policy, retained potential relevance, but had fallen by the wayside in Waltz's reformulation of realism. It was the sense that too many important realist ideas had been lost in the transition to neorealism and the closely related sub-schools of offensive and defensive realism that gave rise to the sub-school that eventually came to be called 'neoclassical realism'.

Neoclassical realism

Neoclassical realism embraces rather than denies realism's diversity as well as the complexity of the international system, but clings tenaciously to the goal of rigorous theorizing and careful empirical evaluation. It accepts from neorealism and its descendants the utility of thinking theoretically about the international system as distinct from the internal properties of states. Having carefully specified their assessment of the international conditions particular states face, however, neoclassical realists go on to factor in specific features of a given situation to generate more complete explanations of foreign policy. They seek to recapture the grounding in the gritty details of foreign policy that marked classical realism while also benefiting from the rigorous theorizing that typified neorealism. Their work is characterized by a strong commitment to rigorous historical case studies both to test and develop theoretical propositions.

Neoclassical realist research began as efforts to explain anomalies or puzzles that neorealism could not account for, such as foreign policies seemingly too aggressive or not aggressive enough (Rose 1998). This was partly a reaction to the once common practice of immediately reaching for non-realist theories to account for any phenomenon that seemed inexplicable according to neorealist theory. While retaining the new penchant for careful theorizing of the external system setting, neoclassical realists reached back into classical realism's toolkit for arguments and theories that often provided better explanations for puzzling phenomena. They looked inside states to see how governmental actors registered and processed systemic pressures, tracking how various aspects of domestic politics could alter the effect of a given external incentive on the resulting foreign policy choice (Lobell et al. 2009).

Neoclassical realism is currently in the process of coming into its own as a fully developed realist sub-school. Its advocates have developed a much more fulsome theoretical picture of the international system that builds on and adds more complexity to defensive realism's scheme, a well-developed set of 'intervening variables' (e.g., perception, decision-making, and policy implementation) that mediate the international system's effect, and a more expansive under-standing of the approach's 'dependent variables' to encompass not just specific foreign policy decisions but patterns of outcomes across the international system (Lobell et al. 2016).

Realist theories

Sub-schools within realism help the student figure out the intellectual connections among scholars, how various arguments are related, and how scholarship progresses. Equally important are specific theories about the fundamental constraints and incentives that shape behaviour and outcomes in international politics. When the issue at hand is a real explanatory problem – such as the effort to explain puzzling security dynamics in a particular issue area or regional setting –analysts should take recourse to the specific theories that appear to be relevant, such as theories of the balance-of-power and balance-of-threat, security dilemma, offence-defence balance, hegemonic stability, and power transition. Certainly, there are numerous other realist or realist-related theories, but even this list makes the main point: realist theories, which do the real work of explanation, are far more diverse than any one theoretical sub-school within realism.

Arguably the best-known theoretical proposition about IR is *balance of power theory*. Given the basic problem that, under conditions of anarchy, any state can resort to force to get what it wants, it follows that states are likely to guard against the possibility that one state might amass the wherewithal to compel all the others to do its will and even possibly eliminate them. The theory posits that states will check dangerous concentrations of power by building up their own capabilities ('internal balancing') or aggregating their capabilities with other states in alliances ('external balancing'). Because states are always looking to the future to anticipate possible prob-lems, balancing may occur even before any one state or alliance has gained an obvious power edge.

Balance of threat theory predicts that states will balance against threats, not just power. Threat, in turn, is driven by a combination of three key variables: aggregate capabilities (overall military and economic potential), geography, and perceptions of aggressive intentions. If one state becomes especially powerful, and if its location and behaviour feed threat perceptions on the part of other states, then balancing strategies will come to dominate their foreign policies. Thus, the US began both external and internal balancing after the end of the Second World War, even though the Soviet Union remained decidedly inferior in most categories of power. Ultimately, the Western alliance overwhelmed the Soviet-led alliance on nearly every dimension. Balance-of-threat the-ory holds that it was the location of Soviet power in the heart of Europe, as well as the threat inherent in its secretive government and perceived aggressiveness that produced this outcome (Walt 1987).

Security dilemma theory: the 'security dilemma' is a term coined by John Herz (1951) for the argument that in arming for self-defence, a state might *decrease* its security via the unintended effect of making others insecure, prompting them to arm in response. Robert Jervis (1986) showed how this consequence of anarchy could lead security-seeking states into costly spirals of mistrust and rivalry. He argued that the severity of the security dilemma depends on two variables: the balance between offence and the ability to distinguish offence from defence.

Thus, although anarchy is theoretically a constant, 'there can be significant variation in the attractiveness of cooperative or competitive means, the prospects for achieving a high level of security, and the probability of war' (Glaser 1997: 172). The article prompted a major debate among realists that eventually ended up in the two sub-schools of offensive and defensive realism. Barry Posen (1993) demonstrated how security dilemma theory can be deployed to explain ethnic conflict within states, opening a rich avenue for research relevant to state collapse and civil war.

Offence-defence theory is an offshoot of Jervis's development of security dilemma theory. As developed by Charles Glaser (1994–5), Stephen Van Evera (1999), and others (Lynn-Jones 1995; Glaser and Kaufman 1998; Brown et al. 2004), this is a set of theoretical propositions about how technology, geography, and other factors affect the ease of conquest as opposed to defence, as well as the ease of distinguishing between offensive and defensive postures. Its main prediction is that militarized conflict and war are more likely when offensive military operations have the relative advantage over defensive operations, while peace and cooperation are more likely when defence dominates. Similarly, the easier it is to distinguish offensive from defensive military preparations, the greater the probability of peace and cooperation. If states seek security rather than glory or conquest, they might avoid the security dilemma by creating mainly defensive military postures, thus signalling their benign intent to others and reducing the core problem of uncertainty about intentions that drives the gloomy predictions of defensive realism. The theory also extends to perceptions: when leaders believe offence is relatively easy, war and conflict are more likely, and vice-versa. This has spawned a massive literature that seeks to explain the origins of perceptions and misperceptions of the offence/defence balance (Snyder 1984; Van Evera 1999). Posen (1993) adapted offence–defence theory to help explain the intensity of competition of groups within states when faced with the security problems that may arise when state authority breaks down.

Hegemonic stability theory builds on the observation that powerful states tend to seek dominance over all or parts of any international system, thus fostering some degree of hierarchy within the overall systemic anarchy. It seeks to explain how cooperation can emerge among major powers, and how international orders, comprising rules, norms, and institutions, emerge and are sustained. The theory's core prediction is that any international order is stable only to the degree that the relations of authority within it are sustained by the underlying distribution of power (Gilpin 1982). According to this theory, the current 'globalization' order is sustained by US power and is likely to come undone as challengers like China gain strength.

Power transition theory is a subset of hegemonic stability that seeks to explain how orders break down into war. Building on the premises of hegemonic stability theory, it deduces that dominant states will prefer to retain leadership, that lesser states' preference for contesting that leadership will tend to strengthen as they become stronger relative to the dominant state, and that this clash is likely to come to the fore as the capabilities of the two sides approach parity (Tammen et al. 2000). Applied to the current context, the theory posits that the stronger China gets, the more likely it is to become dissatisfied with the US-led global order. It predicts that a war or at least a Cold War-style rivalry between the US and China is likely unless China's growth slows down or Washington finds a way to accommodate Beijing's preferences.

Contemporary realist scholarship and Security Studies

It has been argued in this chapter that realism is not now and never has been a monolithic and universal 'theory of international politics'. It has always been diverse; even its grandest theories are contingent in scope if not name. The chief development of the last 15 years has been a greater recognition of this fact, as well as an associated decline in realism's centrality to the discipline. With the advent of neoclassical realism, meanwhile, realist research has become more problem-focused, and its interactions with research from other traditions more complex and arguably more productive.

All of this is good news for Security Studies. The accumulation of new and important research by scholars working within the realist tradition has figured centrally in recent scholarship on international security. This includes work that seeks to account for general phenomena, such as the origins of war (Copeland 2000); regional war and peace (Miller 2007); suboptimal under-provision of security by states (Schweller 2006); great-power military interventions (Taliaferro 2004); threat assessment (Lobell 2003); the origins of revisionist state preferences (Davidson 2006); the constraints on peace settlements after major wars (Ripsman 2002); and the dynamics of unipolarity (Wohlforth 1999, 2009; Pape 2005), to mention only a few. It also includes research explaining more discrete events or behaviours, such as US foreign policy in the Cold War (McAllister 2002; Dueck 2005); the end of the Cold War (Schweller and Wohlforth 2000); US, South Korean, and Japanese strategies vis-à-vis the North Korean nuclear crisis (Cha 2000); the evolution of US monetary policy after the demise of the Bretton Woods monetary system (Sterling-Folker 2002); the origins of the Bush administration's approach to foreign policy and the invasion of Iraq (Layne 2005; Dueck 2005); and many others.

These works are eclectic. Most avoid chest-thumping advocacy on behalf of realism. Many expend considerable effort finding fault with other realist works. Nevertheless, if they had to be classified as being in one theoretical school, all would end up in the realist column: they share a sensitivity to realist core insights, a central role for the three key assumptions that define realism, and an appreciation of how neorealism and its successor sub-schools can aid in analysis. At the same time, most are open to the insights of classical realism and lack dogmatic attachment to one theory or the other. While they hardly represent the last word on the respective subjects, in aggregate they stand as testimony to the ongoing contributions of realism to Security Studies.

Conclusion

Realist theories remain an important, if insufficient, part of the Security Studies toolkit. Once we set aside the fruitless debate over which overarching theory trumps all others, the diversity of realist scholarship comes to light. The advent of new sub-schools of realist thought, such as offensive, defensive, and neoclassical realism, helps organize this diversity and makes sense of the many theories that have grown out of the realist tradition. As a result, it is easier for today's security scholars to make sense – and use – of realist theories than it was 10 or 20 years ago. Also, thanks in part to these developments within realism, it is much easier for realists and scholars working in other intellectual traditions to interact productively, as evidenced by a burgeoning literature that bridges realism and constructivism (e.g., Bukovansky 2002; Sterling-Folker 2002; Goddard and Nexon 2005).

Needless to say, today's complex mix of classical, great-power security issues such as the rise of China, Russia, and India, equally classic but newly salient phenomena such as states' failure, civil war, and terrorism, and novel problems like nuclear proliferation presents new challenges to scholars working within and outside the realist tradition. Scholars are energetically deploying the theories discussed herein to address these issues. For example, Charles Glaser (2015) deployed security dilemma theory to propose a way to avoid a US–China confrontation and John Mearsheimer (2014) utilized realist theory to explain the breakdown in relations between Russia and the West.

But work remains to be done. Realist scholarship still has not come fully to terms with research findings on the effects of domestic institutions on international conflict – arguably the most significant development in Security Studies over the last two decades. For their part, democratic peace researchers have yet to take on board the implications of more fine-grained realist theories, which predict much more variation in states' conflict behaviour than neorealism. Both need to grapple with older theories from the classical realist tradition concerning the effect of international systemic conditions on domestic institutions. Realists are still struggling with the implications of nuclear proliferation. They remain unsure of the security implications of the spread of weak and non-survivable nuclear arsenals.

Arguably, the issue that is most ripe for more work is the interaction between international security and the global economy. Decades ago, pioneering scholars such as Robert Gilpin (1975; 1986) and Stephen Krasner (1986; 1991) explored the links between state power, international institutions, and the international political economy. Many of the core ideas they propounded fell by the wayside as scholars studying security and political economy went separate ways. But recent works have begun to re-engage this interaction. Stephen Brooks (2005) shows how the globalization of production by multinational corporations has 'changed the calculus of conflict'. Jonathan Kirshner (2007; see also Kirshner 2006) demonstrates the links between financial interests and states' propensity towards war. As these works demonstrate, in a world of dramatic economic change amid rapidly shifting inter-state power balances, realist scholarship has a lot more to offer Security Studies.

Notes

* This chapter shares some material with Wohlforth (2008) and Wohlforth (2012).
1 Here I follow Gilpin (1996: 7–8). See Donnelly (2000: 7–8) for a good list of representative defining assumptions of realism.
2 Carr's *Twenty Years' Crisis* (1946) does seek to advance IR as a science, but does not explicitly articulate an overarching theory.

References

Brooks, S. (2005) *Producing Security: Multinational Corporations, Globalization, and the Changing Calculus of Conflict*, Princeton, NJ: Princeton University Press.
Brown, M. et al. (eds.) (2004) *Offense, Defense and War*, Cambridge, MA: MIT Press.
Bukovansky, M. (2002) *Legitimacy and Power Politics*, Princeton, NJ: Princeton University Press.
Carr, E. H. (1956) *The Twenty Years' Crisis, 1919–1939: An Introduction to the Study of International Relations*, London: Macmillan.
Cha, V. D. (2000) 'Abandonment, Entrapment, and Neoclassical Realism in Asia: The United States, Japan, and Korea', *International Studies Quarterly* 44(2): 261–91
Copeland, D. (2000) *The Origins of Major War*, Ithaca, NY: Cornell University Press.
Davidson, J. W. (2006) *The Origins of Revisionist and Status Quo States*, New York: Palgrave-Macmillan.
Donnelly, J. (2000) *Realism and International Relations*, Cambridge: Cambridge University Press.
Dueck, C. (2006) *Reluctant Crusaders: Power, Culture and Change in American Grand Strategy*, Princeton, NJ: Princeton University Press.
Gilpin, R. G. (1975) *US Power and the Multinational Corporation*, New York: Basic Books.
Gilpin, R. G. (1982) *War and Change in World Politics*, Cambridge: Cambridge University Press.
Gilpin, R. G. (1986) 'The Richness of the Tradition of Political Realism', in R. O. Keohane (ed.) *Realism and Its Critics*, New York: Columbia University Press, 301–22.

Gilpin, R. G. (1996) 'No One Loves a Political Realist', *Security Studies* 5(3): 3–26.

Glaser, C. (1994–5) 'Realists as Optimists: Cooperation as Self-Help', *International Security* 19(Winter): 50–90.

Glaser, C. (1997) 'The Security Dilemma Revisited', *World Politics* 50(1): 171–201.

Glaser, C. (2010) *Rational Theory of International Politics*, Princeton, NJ: Princeton University Press.

Glaser, C. (2015) 'A US–China Grand Bargain?: The Hard Choice between Military Competition and Accommodation', *International Security* 39(4): 49–90.

Glaser, C. and Kaufmann C. (1998) 'What Is the Offense-Defense Balance and Can We Measure It?', *International Security* 22(1): 44–82.

Goddard, S. and Nexon D. (2005) 'Paradigm Lost? Reassessing *Theory of International Politics*', *European Journal of International Relations* 11(1): 9–61.

Grieco, J. (1988) 'Realist Theory and the Problem of International Cooperation: Analysis with an Amended Prisoner's Dilemma Model', *Journal of Politics* 50: 600–25.

Herz, J. H. (1950) 'Idealist Internationalism and the Security Dilemma', *World Politics* 2(2): 157–80.

Jervis, R. (1986) 'Cooperation under the Security Dilemma', *World Politics* 30(2): 167–214.

Keohane, R. O. (1984) *After Hegemony: Cooperation and Discord in the World Political Economy*, Princeton, NJ: Princeton University Press.

Kirshner, J. (ed.) (2006) *Globalization and National Security*, London: Routledge.

Kirshner, J. (2007) *Appeasing Bankers: Financial Caution on the Road to War*, Princeton, NJ: Princeton University Press.

Krasner, S. (1986) *Structural Conflict: The Third World against Global Liberalism*, Berkeley: University of California Press.

Krasner, S. (1991) 'Global Communications and National Power: Life on the Pareto Frontier', *World Politics* 43(3): 336–66.

Layne, C. (2005) *The Peace of Illusions*, Ithaca, NY: Cornell University Press.

Lobell, S. E. (2003) *The Challenge of Hegemony: Grand Strategy, Trade, and Domestic Politics*, Ann Arbor: The University of Michigan Press.

Lobell, S., Ripsman N., and Taliaferro J. (eds.) (2009) *Neoclassical Realism, the State, and Foreign Policy*, Cambridge: Cambridge University Press.

Lobell, S., Ripsman N., and Taliaferro J. (eds.) (2016) *Neoclassical Realist Theory of International Politics*, Oxford: Oxford University Press.

Lynn-Jones, S. M. (1995) 'Offense-Defense Theory and Its Critics', *Security Studies* 4(3): 660–91.

McAllister, J. (2002) *No Exit: America and the German Problem, 1943–1954*, Ithaca, NY: Cornell University Press.

Mearsheimer, J. (2001) *The Tragedy of Great Power Politics*, New York: W. W. Norton.

Mearsheimer, J. (2014) 'Why the Ukraine Crisis is the West's Fault', *Foreign Affairs* 93(5): 77–89.

Miller, B. (2007) *States, Nations, and the Great Powers: The Sources of Regional War and Peace*, Cambridge: Cambridge University Press.

Morgenthau, H. (1954[1948]) *Politics among Nations: The Struggle for Power and Peace*, New York: Alfred A. Knopf.

Pape, R. (2005) 'Soft Balancing against the United States', *International Security* 30(1): 7–45.

Posen, B. M. (1993) 'The Security Dilemma and Ethnic Conflict' *Survival* 35(1): 27–47.

Ripsman, N. (2002) *Peacemaking by Democracies: The Effects of States' Autonomy on the Post World War Settlements*, University Park: Pennsylvania State University Press.

Rose, G. (1998) 'Neoclassical Realism and Theories of Foreign Policy', *World Politics* 51(1): 144–172.

Schweller, R. (2006) *Unanswered Threats: Political Constraints on the Balance of Power*, Ithaca, NY: Cornell University Press.

Schweller, R. L. and Wohlforth, W. (2000) 'Power Test: Updating Realism in Response to the End of the Cold War', *Security Studies* 9(3): 60–108

Snyder, G. (1997) *Alliance Politics*, Ithaca, NY: Cornell University Press.

Snyder, J. (1984) *The Ideology of the Offensive*, Ithaca, NY: Cornell University Press.

Sterling-Folker, J. (2002) 'Realism and the Constructivist Challenge: Rejecting, Reconstructing, or Rereading', *International Studies Review* 4(1): 73–97.

Taliaferro, J. (2000–1) 'Security Seeking under Anarchy: Defensive Realism Revisited', *International Security* 25(3): 128–61.

Taliaferro, J. (2004) *Balancing Risks: Great Power Interventions in the Periphery*, Ithaca, NY: Cornell University Press.

Tammen, R. et al. (2000) *Power Transitions: Strategies for the 21st Century*, New York: Chatham House.

Tucker, R. (1952) 'Professor Morgenthau's Theory of Political "Realism"', *American Political Science Review* 46(1): 214–24.

Van Evera, S. (1999) *Causes of War: Structures of Power and the Roots of International Conflict*, Ithaca, NY: Cornell University Press.

Walt, S. (1987) *The Origins of Alliances*, Ithaca, NY: Cornell University Press.

Waltz, K. (1959) *Man, the State, and War*, New York: Columbia University Press.

Waltz, K. (1979) *Theory of International Politics*, New York: Random House.

Wendt, A. (1999) *Social Theory of International Politics*, Cambridge: Cambridge University Press.

Williams, M. (2007) 'Introduction', in M. Williams (ed.) *Realism Reconsidered: The Legacy of Hans J. Morgenthau in International Relations*, Oxford: Oxford University Press, 1–17.

Wohlforth, W. C. (1999) 'The Stability of a Unipolar World', *International Security* 21(1): 1–36.

Wohlforth, W. C. (2008) 'Realism', in D. Snidal and C. Rues-Smit (eds.) *Oxford Handbook of International Relations*, Oxford: Oxford University Press.

Wohlforth, W. C. (2011) 'Gilpinian Realism and International Relations', *International Relations* 25(4): 499–511.

Wohlforth, W. C. (2012) 'Realism and Foreign Policy', in S. Smith, A. Hadfield and T. Dunne (eds.) *Foreign Policy: Theories, Actors, Cases*, Oxford: Oxford University Press, 31–48.

2

LIBERALISM: A THEORETICAL AND EMPIRICAL ASSESSMENT

Thomas C. Walker and David L. Rousseau

In the study of politics, liberalism 'has been employed in a dizzying variety of ways' and carries multiple meanings (Bell 2014: 682). Liberalism emphasizes how 'individual freedom, political participation, private property, and equality of opportunity' contribute to political stability (Doyle 1997: 206). In the study of International Relations (IR), liberalism focuses on how human reason, progress, freedom, and individual rights can contribute to peace and security. Born of the Enlightenment, liberalism 'strives for, and believes in, improvement of the human condition and provides a rationale for building cooperative institutions that can facilitate better lives for human beings' (Keohane 2012: 127). While liberals contend that progress toward peace and prosperity is possible, they often disagree over the pace and ease of this progress. Advancing toward a more peaceful world order is a central theme of liberalism and will serve as the focus of this review.

Most liberal theorists posit that international peace and security will increase with democracy, free trade, and membership in international organizations. First, democratic states will be less likely to initiate and escalate conflicts with other democracies (i.e. the inter-democratic peace). Second, international conflict will be reduced among states engaging in international trade. Third, democratic states are more likely to seek cooperative solutions through international institutions. While there are significant differences between liberal thinkers, all share a general faith in the pacifying effects of political liberty, economic freedom, interdependence, and international organizations.

Before proceeding, we must dispel one persistent myth that has clouded understandings of liberalism: the association between liberal internationalism and normative-laden versions of idealism. Howard (1978: 11) once defined 'liberals' as 'all those thinkers who believe the world to be profoundly other than it should be, and who have faith in the power of human reason and human action so to change it'. But liberal theory provides much more than imagining a world as it *should be*. Like realist theory, liberalism provides a coherent set of principles and propositions that explain and predict inter-state relations. By one recent account, quantitative studies testing liberal hypotheses in IR have come to outnumber realist studies published in leading IR journals (Walker and Morton 2005). Given the prevalence of empirical studies testing liberal hypotheses in IR, liberalism cannot be characterized as an exclusively normative, utopian project. We will therefore devote considerable effort to assessing liberal claims in light of the empirical evidence.

Liberalism can be categorized in a number of ways. Zacher and Matthew (1995: 121) present six strands of liberal international theory. Keohane (2002) and Moravcsik (1997) employ the more conventional categories of ideational, commercial, and republican liberalism. In this chapter, drawing from Walker (2008), we begin by comparing Immanuel Kant's *evolutionary liberalism* to Thomas Paine's *revolutionary liberalism* in a first subsection. While Paine's revolutionary liberalism assumes harmonious preferences ensuring cooperation, Kant's evolutionary liberalism recognizes both shared and competing preferences that make cooperation more challenging but still attainable. After surveying the classical origins, we evaluate mounting empirical evidence supporting the core liberal claims that democratic institutions, economic interdependence, and international institutions may all be contributing to the recent decrease in the severity of global wars.

Classical liberals: evolutionary vs. revolutionary liberalism

In this chapter, we trace the most significant liberal claims to the works of Paine and Kant. The pillars of the liberal peace are: (1) democracy reduces military conflict, (2) economic interdependence reduces military conflict, and (3) international institutions reduce military conflict (Russett and Oneal 2001: 35).

Democratic peace and intervention

Just as the balance of power commands realist thought, the democratic peace is central to liberalism. Paine and Kant were among the first to articulate why democratic states may behave more peacefully, especially toward one another. In *Common Sense,* Paine (1776: 80, 95) pointed out that the republics (i.e. democracies) of the world tended to be peaceful. This results from the democratic tendency to 'negotiate the mistake' rather than letting regal pride swell 'into a rupture with foreign powers'. In *Rights of Man,* Paine (1791/2: 47) acknowledged that 'The right of war and peace is in the nation.' By allowing the people to decide, Paine was confident that they would avoid the costs of war and choose peace. Paine's democratic ebullience rests on an extremely optimistic view of human nature. Individuals, once freed from the yoke of oppressive governments, will rapidly rise up to form reasonable, just, and peace-seeking democratic regimes.

Kant published *Perpetual Peace* in 1795, three years after Paine's *Rights of Man* became widely circulated. Kant (1795: 100) took up the same themes, including the democratic peace, proclaiming that if 'the consent of the citizens is required to decide whether or not war is to be declared, it is very natural that they will have great hesitation in embarking on so dangerous an enterprise. For this would mean calling down on themselves all the miseries of war.' Kant, however, did not share Paine's confidence that transitions to democracy and peace would be quick and easy. While Paine (1791/2:119) anticipated the emergence of democracy in all the 'enlightened nations of Europe' within seven years, Kant was sceptical of rapid transitions. As an evolutionary liberal, Kant (1784: 42) envisioned a slow, grinding progress toward democracy. Despite their disagreements over the pace that democratization may take, they both believed, as do all liberals, that free peoples will be rational, cooperative, and transparent in matters of national security. When these attitudes are shared between peoples, peace will occur.

Liberal enthusiasm for democracy can encourage military interventions to spread democracy. These interventions are often cast as 'a core aspect of the foreign policy of liberal states' (Jahn 2012: 685). However, liberals have long disagreed over the question of intervention. Evolutionary liberals are critical of these interventions since democratic institutions develop gradually and cannot be forced by external actors. In one of his 'Preliminary Articles' in *Perpetual Peace*, Kant (1795: 96) determined that 'No state shall forcibly interfere in the constitution and government of another state.' Such an act would be 'a violation of the rights of an independent people'.

Revolutionary liberals like Paine, however, advocate military action to spread democracy. In *Rights of Man*, Part II, Paine (1791/2: 115) pledged to join the French general in a 'Spring Campaign' against Prussia. Such a campaign was justified on national security grounds: 'When France shall be surrounded with revolutions, she will be in peace and safety.' For Paine, the democratic peace would be a peace between democratic states and not a peace enjoyed by any single democracy. Revolutionary liberals cast such interventions in the interests of all democracies. While democratic rule is the core of liberal theory, spreading it through military intervention has been a longstanding source of disagreement.

Peace through trade

The peaceful effect of trade is the second pillar of liberalism. Paine frequently pointed to how economic interactions would reduce misunderstandings that might lead to conflict. He (1791/2: 172) asserted that free trade creates 'a pacific system, operating to cordialize mankind, by rendering nations, as well as individuals, useful to each other ... If commerce were permitted to act to the universal extent it is capable, it would extirpate the system of war.'

While Kant also saw trade leading to peace, his reasoning was somewhat distinct from Paine's. A less utopian and more pragmatic Kant posited that trade may lead to peace because of shared interests of international financiers and businessmen. Kant (1795: 114) claimed that 'the *spirit of commerce* sooner or later takes hold of every people, and it cannot exist side by side with war. And of all the powers (or means) at the disposal of the power of the state, *financial power* can probably be relied on most' (emphasis in original). He (1795: 114) also argued that 'states find themselves compelled to promote the noble cause of peace, though not exactly from motives of morality. And wherever in the world there is a threat of war breaking out, they [trading states] will try to prevent it by mediation.'

International law and organization

While international law and organization constitute a third pillar of liberalism, revolutionary liberals place them in higher regard. Paine (1801: 2) thought it 'absolutely necessary that a *Law of Nations* be formed.' He advocated global governance with power to sanction any state violating international law. Such an organization would also play a key role in global arms reductions, especially in reducing the number of warships.

Evolutionary liberals view international law and organization with more scepticism. They see these organizations as one source of global order, but sovereign states would remain the leading actors. While Kant explored a 'voluntary confederation of republican states' in *Perpetual Peace*, states would maintain their sovereignty. Kant (1795: 113) feared global governance because 'laws progressively lose their impact as the government increases its range, and a soulless despotism ... will finally lapse into anarchy.' Kant (1795: 103) referred to international law proponents like Grotius as 'sorry comforters'.

Empirical tests of liberalism

Over the last quarter century, the three pillars of the liberal peace have come under intense scrutiny from sympathetic liberals and sceptical realists. Empirical tests have ranged from quantitative analysis (Huth and Allee 2002) and laboratory experiments (Geva and Hanson 1999) to historical case studies (Layne 1994) and computer simulations (Rousseau 2005). In the following subsections, we examine the balance of findings for these three central claims. Overall, the empirical literature strongly supports these liberal claims.

Claim 1: democracy reduces military conflict

Liberals predict that democratic states are better able to resolve international disputes without resorting to military force than non-democratic states. Realists disagree and predict that states will balance (e.g. increase defence spending or establish alliances) against all stronger states because these powerful agents represent a threat to a state residing in anarchy. For realists, democracies will behave just like autocracies: they will balance against the strong and use force if the situation calls for it.

Early empirical research on the behavior of democracies seemed to confirm the realist predictions. Wright (1942: 841) concluded that regime type has little impact on the frequency of war because democracies possess attributes that both encourage and discourage war. In an early statistical analysis of the relationship between war and regime type, Small and Singer (1976: 67) concluded that democracies had not been noticeably peaceful over the 1816–1965 period. In the following decade, Chan (1984) and Weede (1984) reached a similar conclusion using quantitative analysis techniques and large cross-national times-series data sets. Although some evidence supporting the democratic peace emerged (Babst 1972; Rummel 1983), the realist position reflected the general consensus in the early 1980s.

The realist consensus came under attack in a series of articles by Doyle (1983; 1986). Doyle reframed the debate by looking at the characteristics of both the initiator of conflict and the target of conflict. After compiling a list of liberal societies from 1700 to 1982 and a list of inter-state wars from 1816 to 1980, Doyle found that no two democracies had engaged in a full scale war against one another. He concluded that 'liberal states have created a separate peace, as Kant argued they would, and have also discovered liberal reasons for aggression, as he feared they might' (Doyle 1986: 1151). Doyle's path-breaking work triggered an avalanche of studies on the democratic peace. According to Levy (1988: 662), 'the absence of war between democratic states comes as close as anything we have to an empirical law in international relations.'

Although there have been some critiques of the claim (e.g. Layne 1994; Gowa 1999; Oren 2003), none has challenged the finding that no two established democracies have gone to war. Most of the empirical analysis has centered on the causal mechanisms: why do democracies behave differently toward one another? When a dispute erupts between two democracies, each side knows that the other faces domestic constraints on the use of force. This expectation limits bluffing, dampens spirals of hostility, and slows the mobilization process. Extensive empirical analysis has been produced for the dyadic, inter-democratic peace (Babst 1972; Doyle 1983, 1986; Maoz and Russett 1993; Russett and Oneal 2001; Rousseau 2005).

A second explanation falls at the state level of analysis and claims that democracies are more peaceful regardless of the opposition (referred to as the 'monadic' democratic peace). Here the causal mechanism does not focus on expectations about the behaviour of the other party in the dispute. Rather, democracies are less likely to initiate disputes and escalate crises because they are constrained by domestic institutions and norms of conflict resolution. The existence of domestic political opposition makes democratic leaders more risk-averse because foreign policy failures (and even costly successes) can be politically costly (Morgan and Campbell 1991; Morgan and Schwebach 1992; de Mesquita and Siverson 1994). Although the early research did not provide much support for this monadic argument, a number of more recent studies have produced strong statistical evidence in support of the hypothesis (Schultz 2001; Huth and Allee 2002; Bueno de Mesquita et al. 2003; Bennett and Stam 2004; Rousseau 2005).

The most persistent critiques of the democratic peace come from those claiming capitalism provides a better explanation (Mousseau 2000; Gartzke 2007). Free market attitudes and integrated economies may explain the peace between democratic states better than the democracy variable. Mousseau (2009), for instance, argues that 'contract-intensive' economies will generate peaceful interaction with similar economic systems. These claims, however, have been challenged by Dafoe et al. (2013). Capitalist peace scholars also cannot easily explain the destructive wars fought between capitalist states engaged in high levels of trade, notably Germany and Britain in 1914. While capitalism is an element of peace, as liberals predict, it does not discredit the strong empirical evidence linking the expansion of political liberty to a reduction in interstate conflict.

Claim 2: economic interdependence reduces military conflict

Economic interdependence is traditionally defined as the degree to which two (or more) states are connected by flows of goods, services, capital, labor, and technology. Liberals predict that these flows will encourage peace. Realists predict that economic interdependence increases the probability of conflict by expanding the number of issue areas under competition (Waltz 1979: 138). For example, Gaddis (1986: 110) argues that economic isolation between the East and West contributed to the 'long peace' during the Cold War.

Liberals posit several causal mechanisms in this relationship. First, decision-makers will calculate the costs of escalating a dispute with a trading partner. If two states are highly interdependent, decision-makers will be less likely to use force. Second, as Kant emphasized, firms and workers benefiting from international trade and investment will pressure government representatives to de-escalate disputes that arise between trading partners. Although research has not decisively disentangled these distinct (but complementary) causal mechanisms, the empirical literature provides significant evidence supporting the interdependence claim (Wallensteen 1973; Gasiorowski 1986; Polachek and McDonald 1992; Mansfield 1994; Russett and Oneal 2001).

Some scholars have qualified the liberal interdependence claim by specifying conditions that restrict the scope of the claim. For example, Keohane and Nye (1977: 10) make a clear distinction between symmetrical interdependence (i.e. both states are equally dependent on each other) and asymmetrical interdependence (i.e., state A is very dependent on state B, but state B is not very dependent on state A). While symmetrical interdependence creates a mutual desire for continued trade and investment, asymmetrical interdependence invites attempts to exploit weakness and manipulate behaviour (also see Hirschman 1945). In a similar vein, Copeland (1996) argues that the expectation of continuing trade is the key conditional variable. Only if state leaders expect trade to continue (or increase) are they less likely to use force. Finally, Ripsman and Blanchard (1996/7) contend that interdependence should only inhibit conflict if the trade involves strategic goods (e.g., oil or nitrates) which cannot be supplied from alternative sources. If substitute goods or markets are readily available, the cost of disrupting the relationship can fall dramatically.

Some argue that the empirical relationship between trade and conflict may be spurious. For example, Gartzke (2007) provides statistical evidence that market openness rather than trade interdependence (or democracy) reduces violence in the post-Second World War era. Similarly, Kim and Rousseau (2005) find that the pacifying impact of trade evaporates when using several different measures of interdependence and a model of reciprocal causation (i.e., simultaneously testing two claims: military conflict decreases trade AND trade decreases military conflict). It should also be noted that the findings from qualitative case studies are often inconsistent with the theoretical expectations. For example, Ripsman and Blanchard (1996/7) find little concern for the costs of interdependence in their analysis of historical crises among great powers during the July Crisis in 1914 and the Remilitarization of the Rhineland Crisis in 1936. Combined with the findings of the capitalist peace, significant empirical evidence supports the liberal claim that trade and interdependence are associated with peace. These findings, however, are less robust than the democratic peace claim.

Claim 3: international institutions reduce military conflict

The third pillar of the liberal peace claims that international institutions decrease the probability of conflict. In contrast, realists tend to view international institutions as either generally ineffective or the instruments of powerful states (i.e., international institutions have no independent causal impact, Mearsheimer 1994/5; Organski 1968). Although most realists and liberals would agree that the number of international institutions has grown exponentially over the last 100 years (e.g., Shanks et al. 1996), they disagree over their impact.

Early studies focused on formal 'international organizations' such as the UN. However, over time the research programme expanded beyond analysis of rules, procedures, and outcomes within formal institutions (e.g., UN voting patterns) and toward 'international institutions' more generally, including broad conceptualizations of 'global governance.' For example, Lipson's analysis of the banking sector's response to the debt crisis in the 1980s emphasizes the 'informal' regime created by banks seeking cooperation with each other (Lipson 1986). Following the lead of Mearsheimer (1994/95: 9), we can define international institutions broadly as a set of rules that govern how actors cooperate and compete with each other within an issue area (see Simmons and Martin 2002). These rules govern behavior in formal institutions such as the World Trade Organization (WTO) and informal institutions such as the debt-crisis banking regime.

These institutions promote cooperation in a wide range of issue areas, from trade and the environment to human rights and gender equality. In the more restricted domain of peace and security, how do international institutions promote peace? First, collective security organizations and alliances can promote peace by deterring aggression or intervening to halt a conflict (Huth and Allee 2002: 278). Second, international and regional institutions can mediate disputes (e.g., the good offices of the UN secretary general) or provide for arbitration (e.g. International Court of Justice). Third, international institutions can monitor compliance with agreements and reduce transaction costs for follow-up accords (Keohane 1984). Fourth, international institutions can promote conflict-reducing norms and alter identities and related interests (Wendt and Duvall 1989; Barnett and Finnemore 1999). Many international institutions reduce conflict through several of these mechanisms simultaneously. For example, the WTO and the Organization for the Prohibition of Chemical Weapons (OPCW) adjudicate disputes, monitor compliance, encourage norms (e.g., promoting economic liberalism in the WTO and banning weapons of mass destruction in the OPCW), and alter cost-benefit calculations (e.g., increasing trade ties in the WTO and collectively punishing of defectors in the OPCW).

Although this pillar of the liberal peace has produced mixed results, extensive evidence supports predictions that international institutions reduce military conflict (Oneal et al. 2003). Despite the intensity of the superpower conflict during the Cold War, new international institutions helped foster a degree of cooperation. In some cases, the link between international institutions and conflict was quite direct. For example, studies have highlighted the role of the International Atomic Energy Agency (IAEA) in curtailing proliferation among rivals such as Brazil and Argentina (Cirincione et al. 2005). In other cases, the role of international institutions was indirect (Dorussen and Ward 2008). For example, most observers credit the General Agreement on Tariffs and Trade (GATT) and the WTO with contributing to the explosive growth in trade during the post-Second World War period (Held et al. 1999: 175). In more general terms, Russett and Oneal (2001: 170–1) find that as two states increase their membership in international organizations, the probability of military conflict declines. Boehmer et al. (2004) argue that international organizations vary with respect to reducing conflict. They demonstrate that organizations with greater institutional structure, particularly those with a security mandate and low levels of member contentiousness, are more likely to reduce interstate conflict. Shifting to the duration of conflict, Shannon et al. (2010) find that international organizations decrease the length of international conflicts. Using network analysis, Dorussen and Ward (2008) demonstrate that membership in international organizations has both a direct and indirect pacifying effect. Although no liberal would claim that international institutions are sufficient for peace, these institutions appear to reduce a wide variety of conflicts.

Patterns of progress: charting the decline in severity of war

Classical liberals provide theories of how the world might progress towards peace, albeit at different rates and degrees of difficulty. Progress remains the bedrock of all liberal approaches to IR and provides a point of contention between realists and liberals. Keohane (2002: 45) noted how 'liberalism believes in at least the possibility of cumulative progress, whereas realism assumes that history is not progressive'. For realists like Mearsheimer (2001: 24, 17), this liberal notion of progress 'clashes with the realist belief that war is an intrinsic element of life in the international system' and there is 'no easy way to escape the harsh world of security competition and war'. While this contention may never be resolved, we can look to recent empirical trends to shed light on questions of progress towards a more peaceful world.

The decline of great-power wars has been widely acknowledged. We are living amidst the longest period of peace between great powers since 1495, when the modern state system emerged (Levy, 1981). Articulating a progressive, liberal explanation for this peace, Mueller (1989: x) argues that 'peoples and leaders in the developing world – where war was once endemic – have increasingly found war to be disgusting, ridiculous, and unwise'. Mueller's explanation coincides with Paine and Kant: reason prevailed and people are beginning to learn to avoid large, costly wars.

With the end of the Cold War and the rise of globalization, liberals were confident that the peace enjoyed between wealthy states would spread to the rest of the world. Realists challenged this liberal optimism. However, in the quarter-century since the end of the Cold War, levels of war and violence in the post-Cold War world have continued to decline, contrary to realist expectations. Relying on data from the Correlates of War Project and the Uppsala Conflict Data Programme, Levy et al. (2001: 22) demonstrate that the 'decade from 1986 to 1995 has been the most peaceful ten-year period since World War II.' They note that 'the common assumption that the spread of ethno-national and civil wars in the 1990s has contributed to an increase in the frequency and severity of war may not be true'. Mack's (2005) report supported the claim that armed conflicts have decreased in the years following the Cold War. Pinker's (2010) far-reaching work also shows a decline in violence across a number of measures. Goldstein (2011) further documents this decline and argues that international peacekeeping efforts are one of the possible causes. Even a realist naysayer of progress like Mearsheimer concedes that there has been a decline in violence. In a review of Goldstein, Mearsheimer (2013: 570) accepts the claim that 'there has been a marked decrease in warfare since 1945, especially since the Cold War ended.' Taken collectively, these studies show that the probability of dying in a political conflict today is far less than at any time for which we have data. This decline is one tangible sign of progress that fits the liberal expectations.

While we should not ignore how this trend toward peace fits liberal expectations, a few important caveats are in order. First, trends are often reversed. World War I, for instance, occurred in the wake of a long, unprecedented period of peace in Europe. Second, this trend is relative. While the probability of death from political conflict has decreased for the world population, bloody conflicts still rage in many parts of the world, terrorist activity is rising, and the absolute numbers of people dying from political conflict remain high. Third, the factors driving this decline in violent wars have not yet been clearly identified. Therefore, instead of engaging in liberal triumphalism, continued analysis of liberalism's three major factors for peace remains in order.

Conclusion

No brief overview can examine all the claims within the broad theory of liberalism. Our discussions of democracy, free trade, and international organization, first articulated by Paine and Kant, reflect the core of the liberal research programme in IR. Several other elements of liberalism, both theoretical and empirical, could have been elaborated. For instance, Lamb (2015) surveyed Paine's influence on contemporary human rights. Williams (2012) critically applied Kant's thought to the evolution of the just war tradition. The idea that democracies will devote less to military budgets, a claim made by both Paine and Kant, has been empirically supported by Goldsmith (2003) and by Fordham and Walker (2005). Reiter and Stam (2002) present evidence that democracies are more likely to win wars, another idea originating in the classical thought of Paine. These studies, along with many others, demonstrate the wide-ranging research within liberalism.

Overall, we have shown that there is strong empirical evidence supporting several claims first articulated by classical liberals. First, the world has seemingly progressed in terms of reducing levels of violent conflict. Recent trends show that the probability of dying as a result of political violence has declined markedly. Second, democratic governance has been associated with this reduction in conflict, especially between democracies. Third, open economies, trade, and interdependence have also contributed to this decline in violence. Fourth, international institutions can reduce conflict but the association is less convincing than democracy and interdependence. Moreover, these three pillars of the liberal peace are interwoven. Empirical research will continue to build upon and challenge the claims made more than 200 years ago by Paine, Kant, and other classical liberals. Liberalism remains a rich research programme and will continue to raise important questions for students of IR.

References

Babst, D. (1972) 'A Force for Peace', *Industrial Research* (April): 55–8.

Barnett, M. and Finnemore, M. (1999) 'The Politics, Power and Pathologies of International Organizations', *International Organization* 49(2): 699–732.

Bell, D. (2014) 'What is Liberalism?', *Political Theory* 42(6): 682–715.

Bennett, D. and Stam, A. (2004) *The Behavioral Origins of War*, Ann Arbor: University of Michigan Press.

Bueno de Mesquita, B. and Siverson, R. (1995) 'War and the Survival of Political Leaders: A Comparative Analysis of Regime Type and Accountability', *American Political Science Review* 89(4): 841–55.

Bueno de Mesquita, B., Smith, A., Siverson, R., and Morrow, J. (2003) *The Logic of Political Survival*, Cambridge, MA: MIT Press.

Chan, S. (1984) 'Mirror, Mirror on the Wall . . . Are the Freer Countries More Pacific?', *Journal of Conflict Resolution* 28(4): 617–48.

Cirincione, J., Wolfsthal J., and Rajkumar, M. (2011[2005]) *Deadly Arsenals: Nuclear, Biological, and Chemical Threats*, Washington, DC: Carnegie Endowment for International Peace.

Copeland, D. (1996) 'Economic Interdependence and War: A Theory of Trade Expectations', *International Security* 20(4): 5–41.

Dafoe, A., Oneal, J., and Russett, B. (2013) 'The Democratic Peace: Weighing the Evidence and Cautious Inference', *International Studies Quarterly* 57(1): 201–14.

Dorussen, H. and Ward, H. (2008) 'Intergovermental Organizations and the Kantian Peace: A Network Perspective', *Journal of Conflict Resolution* 52(2): 189–212.

Doyle, M. (1983) 'Kant, Liberal Legacies, and Foreign Affairs' Parts 1 and 2, *Philosophy and Public Affairs*, 12(3–4): 205–35, 323–53.

Doyle, M. (1986) 'Liberalism and World Politics', *American Political Science Review* 80(4): 1151–69.

Doyle, M. (1997) *Ways of War and Peace: Realism, Liberalism and Socialism*, New York: W. W. Norton.

Fordham, B. and Walker, T. (2005) 'Kantian Liberalism, Regime Type, and Military Resource Allocation: Do Democracies Spend Less?', *International Studies Quarterly* 49(1): 141–57.

Gaddis, J. (1986) 'The Long Peace: Elements of Stability in the Postwar International System', *International Security* 10(4): 99–142.

Gartzke, E. (2007) 'The Capitalist Peace', *American Journal of Political Science* 51(1): 166–91.

Gasiorowski, M. (1986) 'Economic Interdependence and International Conflict: Some Cross-National Evidence', *International Studies Quarterly* 30(1): 23–38.

Geva, N. and Hanson, D. (1999) 'Cultural Similarity, Foreign Policy Actions, and Regime Perception: an Experimental Study of International Cues and Democratic Peace', *Political Psychology* 20(4): 803–27.

Goldsmith, B. (2003) 'Bearing the Defense Burden, 1886–1989: Why Spend More?', *Journal of Conflict Resolution* 47(5): 551–73.

Goldstein, J. (2011) *Winning the War on War: The Decline of Armed Conflict Worldwide*, New York: Dutton.

Gowa, J. (1999) *Ballots and Bullets: The Elusive Democratic Peace*, Princeton, NJ: Princeton University Press.

Held, D., McGrew A., Goldblatt, D., and Perraton, J. (1999) *Global Transformations: Politics, Economics, and Culture*, Stanford, CA: Stanford University Press.

Hirshman, A. (1945) *National Power and the Structure of Foreign Trade*, Berkeley: University of California Press.

Howard, M. (1978) *War and the Liberal Conscience*, New Brunswick: Rutgers University Press.

Huth, P. and Allee, T. (2002) *The Democratic Peace and Territorial Conflict in the Twentieth Century*, Cambridge: Cambridge University Press.

Jahn, B. (2012) 'Rethinking Democracy Promotion', *Review of International Studies* 38(1): 685–705.

Jervis, R. (1978) 'Cooperation under the Security Dilemma', *World Politics* 30: 167–214.

Jervis. R. (1988) 'The Political Effects of Nuclear Weapons', *International Security* 13(2): 80–90.

Kant, I. (1991[1784]) 'Idea for a Universal History with a Cosmopolitan Purpose', in H. Reiss (ed.) *Kant's Political Writings*, Cambridge: Cambridge University Press, 41–53.

Kant, I. (1991[1795]) 'Perpetual Peace', in H. Reiss (ed.) *Kant's Political Writings*, Cambridge: Cambridge University Press, 93–130.

Keohane, R. O. (1984) *After Hegemony: Cooperation and Discord in the World Political Economy*, Princeton, NJ: Princeton University Press.

Keohane, R. O. (2002) *Power and Governance in a Partially Globalized World*, London: Routledge.

Keohane, R. O. (2012) 'Twenty Years of Institutional Liberalism', *International Relations* 26(2): 125–38.

Keohane, R. O. and Nye, J. (1977) *Power and Interdependence: World Politics in Transition*, Boston, MA: Little, Brown.

Kim, H. and Rousseau, D. (2005) 'The Classical Liberals Were Half Right (or Half Wrong): New Tests of the Liberal Peace, 1960–1988', *Journal of Peace Research* 42(5): 523–43.

Lamb, R. (2015) *Thomas Paine and the Idea of Human Rights*, Cambridge: Cambridge University Press.

Layne, C. (1994) 'Kant or Cant: The Myth of the Democratic Peace', *International Security* 19(2): 5–94.

Levy, J. (1981) *War in the Modern Great Power System*, Lexington: University of Kentucky Press.

Levy, J. (1988) 'Domestic Politics and War', *Journal of Interdisciplinary History* 18(3): 653–73.

Levy, J., Walker, T., and Edwards, M. (2001) 'Continuity and Change in the Evolution of Warfare', in Z. Maoz and A. Gat (eds.) *War in a Changing World*, Ann Arbor: University of Michigan Press, 15–48.

Lipson, C. (1986) 'Bankers' Dilemmas: Private Cooperation in Rescheduling Sovereign Debt', in K. Oye (ed.) *Cooperation under Anarchy*, Princeton, NJ: Princeton University Press, 200–25.

Mack, A. (2005) *Human Security Report*, Oxford: Oxford University Press.

Mansfield, E. (1994) *Power, Trade, and War*, Princeton, NJ: Princeton University Press.

Maoz, Z., and Russett, B. (1993) 'Normative and Structural Causes of Democratic Peace, 1946–1986', *American Political Science Review* 87(3): 624–38.

Mearsheimer, J. (1994/5) 'The False Promise of International Institutions', *International Security* 19(3): 9–12.

Mearsheimer, J. (2001) *The Tragedy of Great Power Politics*, New York: W. W. Norton.

Mearsheimer, J. (2013) 'Has Violence Declined in World Politics?', *Perspectives on Politics* 11(2): 570–3.

Morgan, T. and Campbell, S. (1991) 'Domestic Structure, Decisional Constraints, and War', *Journal of Conflict Resolution* 35(2): 187–211.

Morgan, T. and Schwebach, V. (1992) 'Take Two Democracies and Call Me in the Morning: A Prescription for Peace?', *International Interactions* 17(4): 305–20.

Mousseau, M. (2000) 'Market Prosperity, Democratic Consolidation, and Democratic Peace', *Journal of Conflict Resolution* 44(4): 472–507.

Mousseau, M. (2009) 'The Social Market Roots of Democratic Peace', *International Security* 33(4): 52–86.

Mueller, J. (1989) *Retreat from Doomsday: The Obsolescence of Major War*, New York: Basic Books.

Oneal, J. R., Russett, B., and Berbaum, M. L. (2003) 'Causes of Peace: Democracy, Interdependence, and International Organizations, 1885–1992', *International Studies Quarterly*, 47(3): 371–93.

Oren, I. (2003) *Our Enemies and US: America's Rivalries and the Making of Political Science*, Ithaca, NY: Cornell University Press.

Organski, A. F. K. (1968) *World Politics*, New York: Alfred A. Knopf.

Paine, T. (1801) *Compact Maritime of an Association of Nations*, Washington, DC: Smith.

Paine, T. (1986[1776]) *Common Sense*, London: Penguin Books.

Paine, T. (1992[1791/2]) *Rights of Man*, ed. G. Claeys, Indianapolis: Hackett Publishing.

Pinker, S. (2011) *The Better Angels of Our Nature: Why Violence Has Declined*, New York: Viking.

Polachek, S. and McDonald, J. (1992) 'Strategic Trade and Incentives for Cooperation', in M. Chatterji and L. Forcey (eds.) *Disarmament, Economic Conversions and the Management of Peace*, New York: Praeger, 273–284.

Reiter, D. and Stam, A. (2002) *Democracies at War*, Princeton, NJ: Princeton University Press.

Ripsman, N. and Blanchard, J. (1996/7) 'Commercial Liberalism under Fire: Evidence from 1914 and 1936', *Security Studies* 6(2): 4–50.

Rousseau, D. (2005) *Democracy and War: Institutions, Norms, and the Evolution of International Conflict*, Stanford, CA: Stanford University Press.

Rummel, R. (1983) 'Libertarianism and International Violence', *Journal of Conflict Resolution* 27(1): 27–72.

Russett, B. and Oneal, J. (2001) *Triangulating Peace: Democracy, Interdependence, and International Organizations*, New York: W. W. Norton.

Schultz, K. (2001) *Democracy and Coercive Diplomacy*, Oxford: Oxford University Press.

Shanks, C., Jacobson, H., and Kaplan, J. (1996) 'Inertia and Change in the Constellation of International Government Organizations, 1981–1992', *International Organization* 50(4): 593–626.

Shannon, M., Morey, D., and Boehmke, F. J. (2010) 'The Influence of International Organizations on Militarized Dispute Initiation and Duration', *International Studies Quarterly*, 54(4): 1123–41.

Simmons, B. and Martin, L. (2002) 'International Organizations and Institutions', in W. Carlsnaes, T. Risse, and B. Simmons (eds.) *Handbook of International Relations*, London: Sage, 192–211.

Small, M. and Singer, J. (1976) 'The War-Proneness of Democratic Regimes, 1816–1965', *The Jerusalem Journal of International Relations* 1(1): 50–69.

Walker, T. (2008) 'Two Faces of Liberalism: Kant, Paine, and the Question of Intervention', *International Studies Quarterly* 52(3): 449–68.

Walker, T. and Morton, J. (2005) 'Re-Assessing the "Power of Power Politics" Thesis: Is Realism Still Dominant?', *International Studies Review* 7(2): 341–56.

Wallensteen, P. (1973) *Structure and War: On International Relations, 1920–68*, Stockholm: Raben & Sjogren.

Waltz, K. N. (1979) *Theory of International Politics*, Reading: Addison-Wesley.

Weede, E. (1984) 'Democracy and War Involvement', *Journal of Conflict Resolution* 28(4): 649–64.

Wendt, A. and Duvall, R. (1989) 'Institutions and International Order', in E.-O. Czempiel and J. Rosenau (eds.) *Global Changes and Theoretical Challenges*, Lexington, KY: Lexington Books, 51–73.

Williams, H. (2012) *Kant and the End of War: A Critique of Just War Theory*, New York: Palgrave Macmillan.

Wright, Q. (1965[1942]) *A Study of War*, Chicago: University of Chicago Press.

Zacher, M. and Matthew, R. (1995) 'Liberal International Theory: Common Threads, Divergent Strands,' in C. Kegley (ed.) *Controversies in International Relations Theory: Realism and the Neoliberal Challenge*, New York: St. Martin's Press, 107–50.

3

INTERNATIONAL POLITICAL ECONOMY AND SECURITY

Heikki Patomäki

International Studies includes a long and rich tradition of studying both the political economy conditions of war, peace, and security, and the impact of security concerns and war on economic developments. International Studies has also been characterized, however, by an ever more institutionalized division of labour among its sub-fields (Kirshner 1998; Homolar 2010). Hence, several well-known textbooks and basic introductions to international or global political economy omit questions of peace and war, for the most part discussing security only occasionally or just in passing (Frieden and Lake 2014; Ravenhill 2014; Stubbs and Underhill 2005).

Since its inception in 1994, *The Review of International Political Economy* has published a mere handful of substantial articles that explore security-related issues. The few papers that have been published focus on the hegemony of the Unites States and its consequences for international security and global governance (Mawdsley 2007; Pieterse 2007; Stokes 2014; but see also Abdelal 2013; Vlcek 2012). *International Organization* publishes papers both on security and political economy. In the fifteen to twenty years, however, most of its articles have been 'either/or' oriented rather than integrative in their approaches (for a couple of notable exceptions, see Brooks 2013; Rowe 1999). What has been relatively common in political economy textbooks and various edited volumes is to cover security or war and peace in one or two separate chapters (e.g. O'Brian and Williams 2013; Smith et al. 2011). While these kinds of textbooks and anthologies indicate that security is a relevant political economy topic, they also encourage seeing society in terms of rather disjointed sectors, with only limited overlap.

The same applies, *mutatis mutandis*, to Security Studies. Whether we are talking about more narrowly defined strategy (Baylis et al. 2007), Security Studies in the broad sense (Collins 2007) or Critical Security Studies (Booth 2005; Fierke 2007), political economy is either omitted or figures prominently at most in a chapter or two. The best-known Anglo-American journals in the field, such as *International Security* and *Security Studies*, are equally scant of political economy approaches to security issues (for a recent interesting exception, see Solingen 2014), leaving aside occasional discussions on US military-economic capabilities.

The tradition of studying political economy of war and peace and security had begun by the late eighteenth century. In spite of the evident continuities (and repetitively recurring rhetorical moves) in these debates, new arguments and conceptualizations have evolved. Over time, many claims and hypotheses have been subjected to empirical tests, especially during the last few decades. This chapter has four parts. The first gives a short introduction to basic liberalist thought, with free commerce as its centrepiece. The second turns to the nineteenth-century challenges to the Kantian cosmopolitan principles, namely national political economy and Marxist political economy. The third section focuses on classical theories of imperialism, classical realism, and Keynesian thinking on peace and war, outlining dynamic interconnections between economic (mal)developments and major war. In the fourth, I discuss literature that has attempted to test different claims and hypotheses, with emphasis on applying classical thought to the contemporary world.

Liberal theories of markets and interdependence

Since Immanuel Kant's *Perpetual Peace*, the idea of harmony of interests in free markets has been taken as a generator or guarantee of, and thus strategy for, peace. Kant wanted to replace the eighteenth-century idea of 'balance of power' with the more peaceful idea of 'spirit of commerce' (Kant 1983). Kant posited three mechanisms of peace: (i) interdependence through free trade, and the related civilizing effect of commerce, (ii) the republican constitution of states and (iii) prohibition against financing wars by means of state debt.

Of Kant's three mechanisms, it is free commerce that has usually drawn most attention. After Napoleon's wars, liberal reformers started to promote free trade as a pacifying force. In Britain, Richard Cobden (1804–65) advocated laissez-faire and free trade as a means to international peace. Cobden became a celebrated statesman after years of difficulties and struggle. The theoretical basis for his advocacy came from classical political economy. The case for free trade had been put forcefully by David Ricardo in his famous work *Principles of Political Economy and Taxation* (1817). Ricardo professed the benefits of free trade in terms of comparative advantage. International division of labour can be beneficial to all parties even when there is no absolute advantage, that is, capacity of one party to produce particular goods at a lower absolute cost than another. Free trade is a universal good of the whole world.

Following the rise of neoclassical economics, the Ricardian trade theory was reformulated in terms of marginalist methodology as a general equilibrium mathematical model of international trade (Ohlin 1952/1933). The so-called Heckscher-Ohlin model assumes identical production technologies and maintains that different proportions of factors of production (capital and labour) suffice for comparative advantage. Within this framework, it can be admitted that free trade may redistribute wealth and thereby harm particular interests. On the whole, however, free trade is argued to be beneficial to all parties.

Two challenges to liberalism

National political economy

The US was at war with Britain in 1812. After the war British factories were overwhelming American ports with inexpensive goods. Like his US predecessors (such as Henry Clay 1777–1852), Friedrich List (1789–1846) reacted critically to the unique power and economic position of industrialized Britain, which also constituted a potential military threat. List was a classical republican thinker who developed ideas about freedom, democracy, and prosperity of citizens in the modern context of industrializing world economy. List protested against the cosmopolitan principles of classical liberalism and the absolute doctrine of free trade. In his principal work *The National System of Political Economy*, List (1885[1841]) insisted on the special requirements of each nation according to its circumstances and especially to the degree of its development.

List was also arguing for a long-term perspective and systematic economic planning. Adam Smith's 'invisible hand' was neither generalizable nor did it describe accurately the actual practices of the British state. Statesmen should be prepared to take the long view and bring into existence through legislative and administrative action the conditions required for the industrial progress of the nation. This meant, among other things, protective tariffs in the early phases of industrialization; active engagement and public investments in the physical infrastructure (canals, railways, commercial fleet, navy); focused attempts to improve the general level of education and other prerequisites of scientific research and technological development within the country; and active colonialism following the model of the British in India (i.e. creating a core-periphery pattern of trade). It is easy to see how the principles of Listian national economics could lead to a conflict with those who profess the Ricardian idea of free trade as a civilizing force and universal good of the whole world.

Marxian political economy

Marx insisted that the essential conflict in capitalist market society concerns social classes rather than sovereign states. Marx argued that inequalities, property, state-formations, and organized violence have been historically linked, in different historical phases in different ways. Once bourgeois civil society has seized political power in industrializing capitalist market societies, and once the relationship between owners of private capital and wage-labourer has become polarized, state power starts to reflect to a significant degree the interests and visions of private property understood as a power relation, in particular as a relation of command over the labour of workers.

For Marx, the emergent concept of security should be understood as the 'supreme social concept of bourgeois society [. . .] expressing the fact that the whole of society exists only in order to guarantee to each of its members the maintenance of his person, his rights, and his property. By the conception of security bourgeois society does not raise itself above its egoism. Security is rather the confirmation of [or insurance for] its egoism.' (Marx 2008: 46). Marx's key claim was that ultimately security is about the maintenance of life, private property, and possessions. Security is a conservative notion, in the sense of being protective of the already existing and possessed things and values (Marx 2008/1847: 80). International security is an outward extension of the same principle. For Marx, however, the use of force can also be creative in a sense of generating the basis for the expansion of capitalism and world markets (Marx 1906: 823–4).

Gradually, Marx's ideas evolved into a general theory of war and peace. In the absence of God and his commands, Marx envisaged, it is possible to have an organized and peaceful society by abolishing private property and related particular interests. Wages and profit, working class and the class of capitalists, 'stand in the most hostile, in an inverted, relationship towards each other' (Marx 2012: 110). Like Rousseau before him, Marx assumed that as species-beings, humans are cooperative by their nature. It is the emergence of asymmetrical and exploitative institutions that has alienated humans from their true potential for voluntary cooperation. Once that hostility and conflict has been overcome, once harmony has been (re-)established, perpetual peace will follow. Socialism means peace; communism even more so. His ideas inspired subsequent theories of imperialism and war, although many of them attributed the problem to particular sections of private interest, or various fallacies of composition, rather than to the notion of private property per se.

Economics and war

Classical theories of imperialism

John A. Hobson was perhaps the first to systematically articulate connections between underconsumption at home and imperialism, nationalism, militarism, great power hostilities, the armaments race, and the risk of a major war in the world system as a whole. Hobson (1988/1902: 11–13) was also among those few who correctly anticipated the possibility of a major war – and he did so more than a decade before the summer of 1914. Hobson's starting point was the proto-Keynesian notion of underconsumption. Industrialization creates ever more capacity to produce, but wide inequalities suppress consumption at home. Economic downturns aggravate the problem, which makes capitalist states turn forcefully outwards in search for markets for their industrial goods.

Hobson argued that aggressive imperialism tended to foster animosities among competing imperialisms of the modern great powers. The scramble for Africa and Asia evoked the formation of new alliances and drove all the concerned states to expend an ever-growing share of their resources upon military and naval equipment. This led to what Hobson called 'the sliding scale of diplomatic language' with a characteristic new cynical vocabulary of 'sphere of interest', 'sphere of influence', 'suzerainty', 'protectorate', and so on. The process was reciprocal. Imperial Britain was provoking attitudes of enmity in other states and 'since these other nations are not only eager to do their share, but by their jealousy at our undertaking their work continually threatens to wreck the peace in Europe' (Hobson 1988/1902: 70). Imperial expansion had multiplied the number of 'sensitive spots'.

Theories of imperialism take us a long way towards explaining the developments that led to the First World War, yet vary in their accounts of the key causal mechanisms and processes. Apart from Hobson, also Karl Kautsky, V. I. Lenin, Joseph Schumpeter, and Thorstein Veblen proposed different causal hypotheses and told different stories about imperialism and the war, to an extent because of their different ethico-political aims and horizons (for a critical overview and assessment, see Patomäki 2008: 36–58). The diversity of explanatory accounts notwithstanding, the classical theorists of imperialism also agreed on a lot of things. They all saw a specific elite mentality and related practices and institutions, as well as particular vested interests in capitalism, as important components in the complex that produced both imperialism and the war.

Classical political realism: a new critique of the 'harmony of interests' thesis

The Great War was an unprecedented catastrophe, prompting revolutions, national uprisings, and further democratization in many countries. It also created a momentum for liberal peace activists. The establishment of the League of Nations was a step towards realizing Kant's proposal for the conditions and guarantees of a lasting peace in Europe and the world. Its establishment was followed by attempts to restore free trade and the gold standard. Of all the classical theorists of imperialism, this was the heyday of the liberal Schumpeter – except in Russia, where Lenin reigned.

In his analysis of imperialism, Schumpeter accepted the basic conceptions of neoclassical economic theory (which he later criticized in his mature economic theories). The central idea is that perfectly competitive free markets are stable and optimally efficient. Schumpeter also relied upon Ricardo's 'comparative advantage' argument for free trade. Schumpeter's analysis of war and imperialism was thus theory-driven and largely based on the liberalist idea of a harmony of interests in competitive laissez-faire markets (Schumpeter 1989: 100).

However, liberal reformism failed to achieve perpetual peace. During the great depression, world trade collapsed, authoritarian governments rose to power, and Germany, Italy, and Japan left the League. The world was in great depression and a new major war – in effect the continuation of the First World War – was already in sight. According to E. H. Carr (1964/1946: 41–62), the 'harmony-of-interests' thesis of classical liberal political economy described an economy of small producers and merchants that ceased to exist with the industrial revolution.

For Carr, no set of allegedly universal principles, such as the 'invisible hand' of competitive markets, can guarantee domestic or international peace. Actions grounded on assumptions of utopian harmony tend to take part in creating, reinforcing, or deepening conflicts, because universalist utopias often mask particular identities and interests as universal, i.e. as necessarily shared by all. Carr was not opposed to all utopias, however. For Carr, the cosmopolitan world community based on the recognition of equality and rule of law would be a more adequate basis for a global utopia (Carr 1964: 13).

Thus, Carr was advocating the idea of open-ended, peaceful changes to replace various utopian proposals for liberal harmonious order, which he also argued to be ideological. Instead of presumptions of automatic harmony, there would need to be political mechanisms for resolving real conflicts by means of peaceful changes (Carr 1964: 208–23). Carr thus applied the basic republican idea to international relations: in a democratized international society, disputes could be resolved without resorting to the use or threat of coercion.

Keynes on the conditions of international peace

John Maynard Keynes participated in the 1919 Versailles negotiations. Critical of the then-prevailing wisdom, he developed inclusive schemes for rehabilitation of credit and economic life in Europe and even a small-scale 'Marshall Plan' to be implemented after the war. Keynes was especially vocal in opposing the imposition of excessive reparations on Germany. Keynes argued that as the world economy is highly interdependent, 'the European problem is in reality a single whole' (cited in Markwell 2006: 65–72).

Keynes was proved right. The Treaty of Versailles turned out to be catastrophic. It became increasingly clear with the great depression, the rise of fascism, and the Second World War that one-sided punitive justice and reliance on mere free markets can be downright counterproductive. In the early 1940s, Keynes had a new chance. His plan, developed in various steps in 1941–3, addressed the key problem of global economic imbalances between nations. Keynes's starting point was to assume a maximally generalizable perspective on the future global political economy, in order to avoid fallacies of composition and other particularistic illusions. He envisaged the global political economy as a single whole: he wanted to avoid political struggles and asymmetrical situations where specific countries are 'put into a position of particular obligation to others' (Keynes 1980/1941: 46). Obligations should thus be made systemic and financial positions defined against the rest of the world, not against individual countries.

Keynes's proposal for an international clearing union was meant to enable a 'new deal' within every country, including full employment; this also included tentative elements for a global new deal. Thus, global funds should be established for the global common good by means of substantial levies on surplus countries, and by means of creating global money. With common global institutions, the problems that individual states tend to face if left alone could easily be overcome. A crucial part of the design for an international clearing bank was the creation of a central bank currency called a bancor, through which countries would settle their exchange balance. In Keynes's proposal, bancor would have a fixed (but not unalterable) value defined in terms of gold. The central banks of all member states would keep accounts with an international clearing bank 'through which they would be entitled to settle their exchange balances with one another at their par value as defined in terms of bancor' (Keynes 1980/1941: 72). Keynes proposed measures to prevent credit and debit balances piling up, involving a levy on both credits and debits.

However, despite its impartiality and cosmopolitan aspirations, Keynes's own solution was ultimately unstable too. His proposal was based on a variation of the nineteenth-century liberalist dream of a utopian harmony. Keynes argued that although laissez-faire markets do not ensure any

automatic harmony of interests (or collectively optimal outcomes), with proper collective institutional arrangement the international economy can be made a positive–sum game for all parties.
It is important to understand how a particular but mostly implicit theory of justice constituted
Keynes's global vision: justice concerns opportunities, positions, rewards, and punishments. They
are justly distributed if all states are treated equally in Keynes's definition, if socio-economic
inequalities are limited and opportunities sufficiently equal within societies (for a discussion of
problems of different theories of global justice, see Patomäki 2006).

The theory of hegemonic stability

Time and again political economy theories of peace and war have been grounded on the
assumption that harmony can prevail in human society. The presumed harmony is then associated with peace. Nationalists such as List may have been exempt from this assumption, first and
foremost because they have been interested in the development and security of their own nation
only. Carr's assumption of never-ending political conflict, and his republicanism – the combined
ideas of civic virtues and of resolving conflicts by means of peaceful changes – comes closest to
overcoming this assumption in a generalizable fashion. In the 1950s, Karl Deutsch et al. (1957)
developed this Carrian idea into a theory of security community, characterized by the reliable,
institutionally guaranteed possibility of resolving conflicts by means of peaceful changes.

A new variation of the 'harmony-of-interests' thesis evolved in the 1970s in the US. The main
version of the theory of hegemonic stability accepts the basic liberal and economistic account of
the thesis, but argues in line with realpolitik theories that relations between states can be conflictual. The first premise is thus that free trade and maximal openness in investments and finance
are beneficial to everyone, albeit not equally so (Krasner 1976: 318). Liberal international order is
defined as a public good, provided by the leading of a hegemonic state such as Britain or the US.

The global public good was supposed to include the enforcement of property rights, resolution of disputes, stability, and security (Gilpin 1981: 16, 30, 34; Gilpin 1987: 86–7; Kindleberger
1981: 247). The theorists were not united about the nature of the good. Whereas, for instance,
Kindleberger originally stressed moral responsibilities and the need to overcome temporary
asymmetries and counter business cycles, Gilpin has proposed a sort of neo-imperialist interpretation, in which the leading state also collects revenues from others. Not everyone agrees,
however, that a hegemonic state is needed for cooperation. Multilateral cooperation may be possible also by non-hegemonic means (Keohane 1984).

Putting political economy theories to the test

It goes without saying that discussions about the validity of political economy theories of peace
and war, and security more generally, have been complex, interweaving philosophical assumptions, conceptual frames, normative aspirations, historical understandings, and empirical studies
of varying degrees of generality. Attempts to empirically test theories – or hypotheses drawn
from them – have often focused on the connections between commercial liberalism, interdependence, and peace (see also Chapter 2, on liberalism, in this volume). Many of these studies
have taken for granted the categories of neoclassical economics and framed the questions and
operationalized their hypotheses accordingly, in order to test them against data.

Testing different claims and hypotheses

While frequently finding some evidence for the liberal-capitalist thesis, the search for invariant connections (correlations, explanatory factors) has turned out to be hard even within the

liberal-economistic parameters. Further distinctions and auxiliary hypotheses must be made to account for the lack of simple or non-changing regularities. For instance, Schneider (2014) distinguishes between different cases of the freedom of commerce, internally and externally. Internally the distribution of income, and externally the nature of the traded goods, are among the factors that shape the outcome. Moreover, in debates about the merits of the thesis of capitalist peace, many liberal scholars argue that ultimately what matters most for peace is democracy rather than trade (Dafoe et al. 2013; Lee 2013). Because the democratic peace hypothesis is beyond the scope of this overview, suffice it to say that it too has been contested, despite solid empirical support for it (for current assessments of the problems of the democratic peace hypothesis, as well as for criticism of its misuse in political practice, see Barkawi 2015; Ish-Shalom 2013).

On the other hand, unstable industrial growth and trade in capitalist market economies have also been found to be potential causes of conflicts, arms races, and ultimately war. From the 'lateral pressure' theory of Choucri and North (1975) to the reinterpretation of the consequences of the Stolper-Samuelson theorem by Rowe (1999),[1] scholars have found empirical data corroborating assumed connections between capitalist market expansion and war. The most important case supporting these conclusions remains the First World War. The available historical evidence about the war can be plausibly read from the point of view of classical theories of imperialism, by synthesizing their basic insights with explanatory models drawn from post-Keynesian economic theories, theories of path-dependence etc. (Patomäki 2008: Chapters 2 and 3). Likewise the most plausible explanation of the great depression – which enabled the rise of National Socialism in Germany – seems Keynesian too (Galbraith 1972; Minsky 1982), although Friedman and Schwartz (1971) provide a widely cited competing liberal account, blaming erroneous central bank policies for the great crash and consequent depression.

A look into the future

The lessons of history are relevant. It can be argued that the current neoliberal era resembles in some ways both the pre-1914 era and the 1920s (Patomäki 2008).[2] The biggest global financial crisis since the 1930s occurred in 2008–9, indicating the similarity of underlying processes, especially all-encompassing financialization (Rasmus 2012). Kirshner (2014: 47) complements the 'from-economy-to-politics' accounts with the plausible corollary that 'the relatively benign international political environment in 2007–8 compared with the intense security dilemma of the inter-war years were also essential in not making a bad situation worse'. The result of the 2008–9 financial collapse could have been a deep worldwide depression, but since causation works both ways, reasonably co-ordinated responses by contemporary 'big governments' and central banks as lenders-of-last-resort mitigated the worst effects.

One of the widely cited results of recent empirical studies is that income distribution conditions the internal peacefulness of states. This resonates with the basic assumption of underconsumption theorists and post-Keynesian economists, according to which the propensity to consume is higher among the lower-income groups. The well-off can save more of their incomes and accumulate wealth. Thus increasing inequalities imply a lack of sufficient aggregate demand in the system as a whole. Insufficient domestic demand is a problem, which states can subsequently try to export to other states. By thereby relying on a fallacy of composition, however, states risk potential conflicts with other states. Similarly, Piketty (2014; see also Stiglitz 2013) suggests that rising inequalities of income and wealth, particularly in the OECD world but also elsewhere, matter from the point of view of international security.

Piketty maintains that in capitalist market society the trend towards increasing inequalities is difficult to reverse. Historically, only major shocks such as world wars, interwoven with processes of democratization, have been sufficient for invoking progressive taxation and other measures to reduce inequalities. We may also reverse Piketty's question, however: what will the concentration of capital and the rising importance of past and inherited wealth mean for the likelihood of a major politico-economic disaster? Piketty maintains that the developments we are now observing are likely to erode democracy. The concentration of capital can reach very high levels – 'levels potentially incompatible with the meritocratic values and principles of social justice fundamental to modern democratic societies' (2014: 26). Are these high levels also incompatible with democracy? What are the consequences of de-democratization, if that is the outcome of the process of rising inequalities?

There are three main reasons why these developments would increase the likelihood of major economic and political shocks (Patomäki 2014). First, they strengthen the relative power of those actors who are predisposed to disregard Keynesian economic policies needed to ensure full employment and steady economic developments. Famously Kalecki (1943) pointed out that business leaders and capitalists wish to create circumstances in which (i) the success of policies depends on their confidence; (ii) the scope of free markets is maximized; and (iii) hierarchical power relations in the workplace are ensured. When they get what they want, we should expect less economic growth.

Second, within a slackening growth-trend we should also expect to find increasing concentration of capital and wealth, with characteristically Veblenian effects: oligopolization or monopolization of world markets, reducing the scope for democracy; and bigger economic oscillations with larger amplitude. One of the overall upshots is that we should expect a significant increase in the likelihood of major economic crises and shocks, often resulting from boom–and–bust cycles in finance, but equally through other causal mechanisms.

Third, de-democratization and the related tendency for turning political issues into questions of security – repeatedly leading to enemy-construction – are likely to generate and aggravate antagonistic relations with different others. For instance, the 'what is good for us must be good for you' attitude can mean imperial involvement in the development of those regions that are either lagging or falling behind or actively resisting the prevailing direction. However, as Piketty stresses (indirectly echoing the economic nationalism of Clay and List), when countries face the adverse consequences of free market globalization, some of them can also respond by turning to nationalism and protectionism – and to measures which are unacceptable for those who defend free-market globalization and its quasi-constitutional guarantees. These kinds of juxtapositions can all too easily pave the way for the escalation of conflicts, even increasing the likelihood of major political shocks such as a new world war.

In sum, the evidence suggests that there is growing potential for outcomes capable of defeating the liberal hope for perpetual capitalist peace. This concern is related to the debate about the limits to growth and potential for resource wars, even though we know that resource scarcity and environmental problems can also induce cooperation among states (Dinar 2011). Various feedback mechanisms further complicate the picture. For instance, the US has financed its military interventions and wars not with tax raises, but with deficit-spending and debt. This has augmented financial booms and busts, and led to the erosion of good will on the side of the US partners, allies, and creditors (Oatley 2015). Thus, the financial power of the US has supported its military power, while simultaneously destabilizing the world political economy.

Conclusion

Despite tendencies towards specialization and fragmentation in the field of International Studies, research on the political economy of peace and security has not only endured but evolved.

Although it is true that studies on this problematic have been unable to identify any strong and uncontested invariances, or strictly falsify any of the main approaches, these studies have none-theless been informative. We also learn negatively, through failed attempts.

First, various empirical and historical studies have underlined the methodological notion that search for invariant regularities in social sciences is futile. The real world is characterized by multiple, over, and plural determination and thus causation is complex. Moreover, the world is not only complex but – despite continuities at different levels – also changing.

Second, these studies have rendered no unequivocal support for any of the political economy utopias of harmony (liberal, Keynesian, Marxian, neorealist). This negative result has served to strengthen the plausibility of the Carrian approach, according to which politics is about conflicts and power relations, and thus the best chance for peace is to make civilized changes possible through adequate institutional arrangements. Post-Keynesian economic theories may be able to provide good explanations of politico-economic outcomes in many contexts, and the post-Marxian insight about the nature of security may remain valid, but no assumption of ultimate harmony is sustainable.

A cause of concern is the rising trend of inequalities and increasing reliance on free markets, spelling a return of the past. Especially after the end of the Cold War, the international context has been more benign and cooperative than it was in the decades preceding the First World War or during the interwar era. Yet diplomatic discourse has gradually declined, a new geopoliti-cal orientation has gained ground, and military expenditures have once again risen. This is in line with the hypothesis that the capitalist market economy is not inherently peaceful, but can give rise to processes of securitization and enemy-construction. Cooperation among states, and organizations such as the EU, remains possible, but unless the background trends and tendencies are rapidly changed, a new world historical catastrophe looks increasingly likely.

Notes

1 The Stolper-Samuelson theorem is a basic theorem in Heckscher-Ohlin trade theory and concerns income distribution among factors of production. The theorem states that a rise in the relative price of a good will lead to a rise in the return to that factor which is used most intensively in the production of the good, and conversely, to a fall in the return to the other factor. According to Rowe, these changes can also have security implications.
2 There has also been some discussion on the relevance of the pre-1914 analogy especially to the situation in East Asia, where China is seen as the rising power and challenger of the existing order, as Germany was in Europe in 1914. As Graham T. Allison (2012) argues, 'In 11 of 15 cases since 1500 where a rising power emerged to challenge a ruling power, war occurred.' For discussions, see Krause 2014.

References

Abdelal, R. (2013) 'The Profits of Power: Commerce and Realpolitik in Eurasia', *Review of International Political Economy* 20(3): 421–56.
Allison, G. T. (2012) 'Avoiding Thucydides' Trap', *Financial Times*, 22 August 2012.
Barkawi, T. (2015) 'Scientific Decay', *International Studies Quarterly*. Online. DOI: 10.1111/isqu.12204 [accessed 26 May 2015].
Baylis, J., Wirtz, J., Gray, C. S., and Cohen, E. (2007[2000]) *Strategy in the Contemporary World*, Oxford: Oxford University Press.
Booth, K. (ed.) (2005) *Critical Security Studies and World Politics*, Boulder, CO and London: Lynne Rienner.
Brooks, S. G. (2013) 'Economic Actors' Lobbying Influence on the Prospects for War and Peace', *International Organization* 67(4): 863–88.
Carr, E. H. (1964[1946]) *The Twenty Years' Crisis 1919–1939: An Introduction to the Study of International Relations*, New York: Harper & Row.

Choucri, N. and North, R. C. (1975) *Nations in Conflict: National Growth and International Violence*, San Francisco: W. H. Freeman.

Collins, A. (2007) *Contemporary Security Studies*, Oxford: Oxford University Press.

Dafoe, A., Oneal, J. R., and Russett, B. (2013) 'The Democratic Peace: Weighing the Evidence and Cautious Inference', *International Studies Quarterly* 57(1): 201–14.

Deutsch, K. W. et al. (1957) *Political Community and the North Atlantic Area: International Organization in the Light of Historical Experience*, Princeton, NJ: Princeton University Press.

Dinar, S. (ed.) (2011) *Beyond Resource Wars: Scarcity, Environmental Degradation, and International Cooperation*, Cambridge, MA: MIT Press.

Fierke, K. M. (2007) *Critical Approaches to International Security*, Cambridge: Polity Press.

Frieden, J. A. and Lake, D. A. (2014[2002]) *International Political Economy: Perspectives on Global Power and Wealth*, London and New York: Routledge.

Friedman, M. and Schwartz, A. (1971[1963]) *A Monetary History of the United States, 1867–1960*, Princeton, NJ: Princeton University Press.

Galbraith, J. K. (1972[1954]) *The Great Crash, 1929*, Boston, MA: Houghton Mifflin.

Gilpin, R. (1981) *War and Change in World Politics*, Cambridge: Cambridge University Press.

Gilpin, R. (1987) *The Political Economy of International Relations*, Princeton, NJ: Princeton University Press.

Hobson, J. A. (1988[1902]) *Imperialism: A Study*. 3rd edn, London: Unwin Hyman.

Homolar, A. (2010) 'The Political Economy of National Security', *Review of International Political Economy* 17(2): 410–23.

Ish-Shalom, P. (2013) *Democratic Peace: A Political Biography*, Ann Arbor: The University of Michigan Press.

Kalecki, M. (1943) 'Political Aspects of Full Employment', *Political Quarterly* 14(4): 322–31.

Kant, I. (1983) *Perpetual Peace and Other Essays*, Indianapolis, IN: Hackett Publishing.

Kautsky, K. (1970[1914]) 'Ultra-Imperialism', trans. unknown, *New Left Review* (I)59: 41–6.

Keohane, R. O. (1984) *After Hegemony: Cooperation and Discord in the World Political Economy*, Princeton, NJ: Princeton University Press.

Keynes, J. M. (1980[1941]) 'Proposals for an International Currency Union' in J. M. Keynes *The Collected Writings of John Maynard Keynes*. Vol XXV: *Activities 1940–44*, London: MacMillan.

Kindleberger, C. P. (1981) 'Dominance and Leadership in the International Economy: Exploitation, Public Goods and Free Riders', *International Studies Quarterly* 25(2): 242–54.

Kirshner, J. (1998) 'Political Economy in Security Studies after the Cold War', *Review of International Political Economy* 5(1): 64–91.

Kirshner, J. (2014) 'International Relations Then and Now: Why the Great Recession Was Not the Great Depression', *History Of Economic Ideas* 22(3): 47–69.

Krasner, S. D. (1976) 'State Power and the Structure of International Trade', *World Politics* 28(3): 317–47.

Krause, J. (2014) 'Assessing the Danger of War: Parallels and Differences between Europe in 1914 and East Asia in 2014', *International Affairs* 90(6): 1421–51.

Lee, J. L. (2013) 'War on Democratic Peace', *International Studies Quarterly* 57(1): 198–200.

Lenin, V. I. (1998[1917]) *Imperialism, the Highest Stage of Capitalism*. Online. Available HTTP: <http://www.fordham.edu/halsall/mod/1916lenin-imperialism.html> (accessed 6 May 2009).

List, F. (1885[1841]) *The National System of Political Economy*, trans. S. S. Lloyd (1885). Online. Available HTTP: <http://socserv2.socsci.mcmaster.ca/~econ/ugcm/3ll3/list> (accessed 10 July 2015).

Markwell, D. (2006) *John Maynard Keynes and International Relations: Economic Paths to Peace*, Oxford: Oxford University Press.

Marx, K. (2008[1844]) 'On the Jewish Question', in K. Marx *Selected Essays*, Charleston, SC: Bibliobazaar, 27–58.

Marx, K. (2008[1847]) 'Moralizing Criticism and Critical Morality: A Polemic against Karl Heinzen', in K. Marx *Selected Essays*, Charleston, SC: Bibliobazaar, 79–98.

Marx, K. (2012[1845]) 'Proudhon', in K. Marx *Selected Essays*, Auckland: Floating Press, 109–14.

Marx, K. (1906[1867]) *Capital. A Critique of Political Economy*, New York: The Modern Library (Random House).

Mawdsley, E. (2007) 'The Millennium Challenge Account: Neo-Liberalism, Poverty and Security', *Review of International Political Economy* 14(3): 487–509.

Minsky, H. (1982) *Can 'It' Happen Again? Essays on Instability and Finance*, New York: M. E. Sharpe.

Oatley, T. (2015) *A Political Economy of American Hegemony: Buildups, Booms, and Busts*, Cambridge: Cambridge University Press.

Ohlin, B. (1952[1933]) *Interregional and International Trade*, Cambridge, MA: Harvard University Press. (Harvard Economic Studies, 39).

O'Brien, R. and Williams, M. (2013) *Global Political Economy: Evolution and Dynamics*, 4th edn, London: Palgrave Macmillan.

Patomäki, H. (2006) 'Global Justice: A Democratic Perspective', *Globalizations* 3(2): 99–120.

Patomäki, H. (2008) *The Political Economy of Global Security*, London and New York: Routledge.

Patomäki, H. (2014) 'Piketty's Global Tax on Capital: A Useful Utopia or a Realistic Alternative to a Global Disaster?', *Real-World Economics Review*, 69(7 Oct): 51–7. Online. Available HTTP: <http://www.paecon.net/PAEReview/issue69/Patomaki69.pdf> (accessed 2 October 2015).

Pieterse, J. N. (2007) 'Political and Economic Brinkmanship', *Review of International Political Economy* 14(3): 467–86.

Piketty, T. (2014) *Capital in the Twenty-First Century*, trans. A. Goldhammer, Cambridge, MA: The Belknap Press of Harvard University Press.

Rasmus, J. (2010) *Epic Recession: Prelude to Global Depression*, London: Pluto Press.

Ravenhill, J. (2014[2005]) *Global Political Economy*, Oxford: Oxford University Press.

Ricardo, D. (1821[1817]) *Principles of Political Economy and Taxation*, London: John Murray. Online. Available HTTP: <http://www.econlib.org/library/Ricardo/ricP.html> (accessed 2 October 2015).

Rowe, D. M. (1999) 'World Economic Expansion and National Security in Pre-World War I Europe', *International Organization* 53(2): 195–231.

Schneider, G. (2014) 'Peace through Globalization and Capitalism? Prospects of Two Liberal Propositions', *Journal of Peace Research* 51(2): 173–83.

Schumpeter, J. (1989[1951]) *Imperialism and Social Classes*, trans. H. Norden, ed. P. Sweezy, New York: Kelley.

Smith, R., El-Anis, I., and Farrands, C. (2011) International Political Economy in the 21st Century: Contemporary Issues and Analyses, London and New York: Routledge.

Solingen, E. (2014) 'Domestic Coalitions, Internationalization, and War: Then and Now', *International Security* 39(1): 44–70

Stiglitz, J. (2012) *The Price of Inequality*, New York: W. W. Norton.

Stokes, D. (2014) 'Achilles' Deal: Dollar Decline and US Grand Strategy after the Crisis', *Review of International Political Economy*, 21(5): 1071–94.

Stubbs, R. and Underhill, G. R. D. (eds.) (2005) *Political Economy and the Changing Global Order*, Oxford: Oxford University Press.

Veblen, T. (1933[1919]) *The Vested Interests and the Common Man*, New York: Viking Press.

Vlcek, W. (2012) 'Power and the Practice of Security to Govern Global Finance', *Review of International Political Economy*, (19)4/SI: 639–62.

4

THE ENGLISH SCHOOL AND INTERNATIONAL SECURITY

*Barry Buzan**

The 'English school' and 'International Security Studies' are names that are seldom found in the same sentence. Few if any people working within mainstream International Security Studies would think about the English school (ES) as a body of either theory or empirical work relevant to Security Studies. If they thought about it at all, they might well see the ES, with its concerns about order and legitimacy (Bull 1977; Clark 2005) as coming from the opposite, liberal end of International Relations theory, than from the conflict/disorder realist end of the spectrum to which International Security Studies generally relates.

The classic ES approach involves seeing international relations as composed of three elements (Buzan 2004b: 6–10): international system (realism, Hobbes), international society (rationalism, Grotius), and world society (idealism or revolutionism, Kant). These elements are in constant interplay and the nature of international relations depends on the balance among them. In principle, this opens a bridge between the ES and International Security Studies via the realism element in ES theory. In practice, however, the great bulk on ES work has focused on international and world society, and on the rules, norms, and institutions that underpin the social order of international society.

Few within the ES have explicitly addressed the International Security Studies agenda, and the concept of security does not play much role in ES thinking. It is therefore reasonable to ask what a chapter on the English school is doing in a volume on International Security Studies. This chapter contains three answers to this question. The next section sets out the ES as a general theoretical framing for International Security Studies comparable with realism and liberalism and Marxism. The section after that reviews the existing ES literature on international security to show where the overlaps are, and the concluding section opens up some opportunities for how the relationship might be developed further.

The English school as an approach to International Security Studies

As the other chapters in this section make clear, the sub-field of International Security Studies does not stand by itself. Its traditional core of Strategic Studies focuses on state ('national') security and sees threats and responses largely in military terms. As just noted, this traditional core is closely related to realism, whose state-centric, power-political, and conflictual understanding of international relations provides a complementary and close-fitting general framework for

Strategic Studies. Marxism, which also features a power-political and conflictual, if not state-centric, understanding of international relations can also serve as a general theoretical framing for International Security Studies. So can liberalism, though with its emphasis on intergovernmental and transnational institutions, cooperation, and join gains, the framing it provides emphasizes possible ameliorations of and/or exits from the 'permanent' conflicts and security dilemmas of the realist and Marxist worlds. These various theoretical framings have all played their part in the widening and deepening of International Security Studies as a sub-field that has been going on since long before the end of the Cold War (Buzan and Hansen 2009).

The English school has not so far played much of a role in the widening and deepening of International Security Studies, but it could, and probably should, do so. What is distinctive about the ES is its focus on the societal elements of international relations, which it approaches through history, political theory, and law. Constructivists have recently moved onto this ground as well, but their approach to social processes is made mainly through ontology and epistemology. Realism, liberalism, and Marxism all offer a picture of what international society does or should look like. Constructivism generally does not offer such a picture, though Wendt (1999) does give a general sketch of international social orders build around relationships of friend, rival, and enemy. Because the ES comes from historical and normative roots, and makes a feature of the primary institutions of international society,[1] it offers a much more detailed picture of international society and so can more easily serve as a general framing for International Security Studies.

In a nutshell, the ES framing for International Security Studies can be set out as follows. Whereas realism sees a world of enemies and rivals running on a logic of coercion and calculation, the ES agrees with Wendt in allowing enemies, rivals, and friends, and running on a logic of coercion, calculation, and belief. In this sense, the ES incorporates both the realist and liberal framings, and contextualizes them in a range of possible types of international society that offer much more depth and detail than Wendt's general scheme.[2] This spectrum can be envisaged as four general types:

- *Power Political* represents an international society based largely on enmity and the possibility of war, but where there is also some diplomacy, alliance making, and trade. Survival is the main motive, and few values are shared. Institutions will be minimal, mostly confined to rules of recognition and diplomacy. Quite a bit of ancient and classical history looks like this, and the units composing such a society may be empires, city-states, and nomadic barbarians as well as states in the modern sense.
- *Coexistence* is modelled on the exemplar of pre-1945 Europe, meaning the kind of Westphalian system in which the core institutions of international society are the balance of power, sovereignty, territoriality, diplomacy, great power management, war, and international law. The units seek some degree of international order, but remain distinct, self-centred, and not infrequently warlike.
- *Cooperative* means that the units seek a level of order sufficient to pursue some joint projects (e.g. a world economy, human rights, big science). It might come in many guises, depending on what type of values are shared and how/why they are shared, though the standard model here is based on shared liberal values. Cooperation does not require broad ideological agreement, but only instrumental commitments to specific projects. The contemporary commitment to the market is a good example, with many illiberal and nondemocratic countries willing to play by international market rules. Probably war gets downgraded as an institution, and other institutions might arise to reflect the solidarist joint project(s).
- *Convergence* means the development of a substantial enough range of shared values within a set of states to make them adopt similar political, legal, and economic forms, and to aspire

to be more alike. The usual models here are the EU, or democratic peace theory, but in principle any shared ideological base could underpin convergence. The range of shared values simply has to be wide enough and substantial enough to generate similar forms of government (liberal democracies, Islamic theocracies, communist totalitarianisms) and legal systems based on similar values in respect of such basic issues as property rights, human rights, and the relationship between government and citizens.

It is immediately apparent from this spectrum that what type of international society one is in has huge consequences for what the agenda of international security will look like. Life within a power political international society will be extremely different from life in a cooperative or convergence one. It is also clear that these international societies represent forms of social order quite distinct from the materialist sense of order represented by the distribution of power in realism. In a sense, realist assumptions are confined within the power political and coexistence models, and pay attention only to some of the institutions that define those models. The classical ES view of coexistence international societies, like the realist one, stresses great powers, war, and balance of power as key institutions of the social order. But in cooperative and convergence international societies of almost any conceivable sort, war and balance of power will be respectively marginalized or nearly eliminated as institutions. This does not, of course, mean that such societies have no security agenda. As one can see from the contemporary practice of the EU or the liberal international economic order, security concerns move away from the traditional military ones towards economic, societal, and environmental ones, and human security agenda.

International society therefore represents a type of social structure. This structure can vary in form (as above) and also in distribution (it may be universal or partial, and if universal may still have differentiations of degree within it – think of the EU within global international society). Thinking of international society in this way opens the possibility of transposing Walker's (1993) inside/outside perspective to thinking about how an ES approach frames international security. Walker's idea is that thinking about International Relations and international security has been largely framed as a distinction between what goes on inside states (order, progress) and what goes on outside (or between) them (disorder, and a repetitive logic of anarchy). If international society is conceived of as a social structure, then it also has inside/outside qualities, and this points to at least three novel lines of thinking about international security.

1.   What are the security consequences for insiders of being included within the particular set of primary institutions that defines any international society? The primary institutions of international society are the key social framework within which the processes of securitization occur. It makes a difference whether the dominant institutions are, say, dynasticism, human inequality, and suzerainty, or popular sovereignty, human equality, and nationalism. Likewise, the possibilities for securitization are shaped by whether the dominant economic institution is mercantilism or the market. Some institutions have an obvious major impact on what the agenda of international security will look like (e.g. sovereignty, territoriality, colonialism, war, balance of power, human inequality, nationalism, market, environmental stewardship). Will it be a security agenda arising from classic military-political competition among states, or one more centred around interdependence issues such as economy, environment and/or identity?

2.   What are the security consequences for outsiders of being excluded from international society? Insiders have to live with the consequences of being inside as in point 1. Outsiders have the problem of not being recognized as equals, or possibly not being recognized at all. Think of the era of European (or Roman, or Persian, or Chinese) imperialism with the world divided into the civilized, barbarian, and savage, with few or sometimes no restraints

on the 'civilized' from subordinating or even exterminating the 'lesser breeds'. As a few days in Taipei quickly reveals, non-recognition poses real security problems for outsiders. The ES view of inside/outside relating to membership of international society provides a framing for International Security Studies that makes much more sense for constructivist, feminist, and Copenhagen School approaches, and puts the traditionalist, military/political approach into a wider context within which one can see whether its assumptions are appropriate or not.

3   If one puts the inside and outside perspectives together, then the institutions of international society, both individually and collectively, can become the referent objects of security. Since the institutions of international society constitute both the players and the game (think of sovereignty and territoriality and the market for example), threats to those institutions affect both the units and the social order. One of the logics behind the 'war on terrorism' is that violence-wielding outfits such as al-Qaeda threaten the institution of sovereignty. The global market easily becomes a referent object when there are threats to the rule on trade and finance on which its operation rests.

This is how the ES *could* be used as a comprehensive approach to International Security Studies, and the next section will sketch out to what extent this has been done so far.

Existing English school literature on international security

Deciding what is, or is not, 'English school' literature, or indeed what is, or is not, 'international security', is hardly an exact science. Neither is it always clear how they should be linked together. There is, for example some discussion of collective security in classic ES texts (Bull 1977: 238ff.; Hudson 1966), but this has little significance for international security because it is mainly about how to define solidarism, and not really a discussion of collective security in itself. There is also the problem of how to place the work of individuals who sometimes wrote in the ES tradition, but some of whose work is probably more correctly placed outside it: Hedley Bull's works on arms control, for example, or Michael Howard's on war.

Despite these difficulties there is a lot that is pretty clearly both English school and international security. In some cases, ES work is explicitly addressed to security issues, but other cases require an exercise in reading ES work through security lenses. The brief survey that follows is organized along the three lines of thinking about international security within the ES sketched above, albeit not all the literature falls neatly under one or other headings. Limitations of space forbid an attempt to capture all of the literature, but the discussion below is hopefully sufficient to give an accurate sense of its general shape and orientation.

The security consequences of international society for insiders

There are two ways of approaching this topic. The first would be to follow a general set of models of international society like those sketched in the previous section and analyse how their overall social structures impact on the likely agendas of international security. As hinted in that discussion, the impact should be very large: there are huge security implications in the ES idea that a range of international societies is possible along a pluralist-solidarist spectrum. The classical literature had little to say on this question at the global level, but recently it has been taken up in some depth, both generally and through the idea of the security dilemma (Hurrell 2007; Booth and Wheeler 2008). This approach puts into systematic form the general proposition that there is not just one logic of anarchy, as realism suggests, but many (Buzan 1991, 2004b; Buzan et al. 1993; Wendt 1992, 1999; Clark 2005). This idea of multiple possible logics of anarchy is also explored at

the sub-global and regional levels in work on security regimes (Jervis 1985), security communities (Adler and Barnett 1998), and regional security complexes (Buzan 1991; Wæver 1996; Buzan
et al. 1998; Buzan and Wæver 2003) and orders (Lake and Morgan1997; Ayoob 1999).

The second approach is to look at individual primary institutions of international society and
their security consequences. The exemplar here is Mayall's (1990) discussions of how the rise
during the nineteenth century of nationalism and the market as new institutions of international
society not only changed the nature of international politics and security in themselves, but
also transformed the practices associated with other institutions such as war and territoriality.
There has been no systematic attempt to relate the whole possible range of ES institutions to
security issues, though this would be a valuable thing to do. What there has been is quite a lot
of work on some institutions, but not much on others. Much of this work parallels discussions
in International Security Studies, though little of it was done with an international security audience in mind. The ES has devoted a lot of discussion to war (Howard 1966; Bull 1977; Draper
1990; Holsti 1991, 1996, 2004; Windsor 1991; Best 1994; Hassner 1994; Song 2005; Jones
2006), and there is a large body of work specifically on the laws of war by Adam Roberts (2004,
2006, 2007; Roberts and Guelff 2000). There has also been substantial ES work on the balance
of power (Butterfield 1966; Wight 1966; Bull 1977; Hobson and Seabrooke 2001; Kingsbury
2002; Little 2006, 2007), and great power management (Bull 1977; Brown 2004; Little 2006).
Although the security dilemma is not considered to be an institution of international society,
there have been ES reflections on that as well (Butterfield 1951; Booth and Wheeler 2007).

The other big discussions in the ES that relate to International Security Studies are those on
intervention and human rights, which can be read as close to human security. The ES discussion
of human rights is partly a general one about the tensions between human rights and sovereignty
in relation to international order (Bull 1977, 1984b; Vincent 1986; Hurrell 2007: 143–64) and
partly a more particular one about the emergence (or not) of human rights as a norm or institution of international society. There is a lot of discussion of (non)intervention generally (Vincent
1974; Bull 1984a; Roberts 1993, 1996, 1999, 2006; Vincent and Wilson 1993; Makinda 1997,
1998; Mayall 1998; Cronin 2002; Buzan 2004b), and humanitarian intervention in particular
(Wheeler 1992, 2000; Knudsen 1996; Wheeler and Morris 1996; Williams 1999; Ayoob 2001;
Brown 2002; Bellamy 2003; Wu 2006).

The security consequences of international society for outsiders

The only systematic general attempt to think through the security consequences of being
inside or outside international society is Buzan (1996). This remains a pretty preliminary exercise, but did attempt to map out both the specific character of the spectrum of international
societies on a sector by sector basis, and the possible security implications of these for insiders
and outsiders. There has been no specific attempt to follow it up, though both Buzan (2004b)
and Holsti (2004) can be read partly along those lines. Nevertheless, one of the big stories of
the ES, that of the expansion of an initially European international society to global scale, is
essentially about insiders and outsiders, and much of it is about the coercive imposition of
European values and institutions (Bull and Watson 1984; Gong 1984; Zhang 1991; Keene 2002;
Keal 2003). There are many studies in this literature of the encounters between on the one
hand, well-armed Europeans (and later Americans) not hesitant to use force to impose their
values, and on the other, a variety of non-Western cultures (mainly Japan, China, the Ottoman
Empire, Thailand) forced to come to terms with the new Western order. These encounters,
with their stories of unequal treaties and threats of occupation, give a stark insight into the
problems of being outside international society. They also underpin the decline of a core

institution of pre-1945 European international society, colonialism, which became obsolete as international society became global.

The 'expansion of international society' story is not just one of coercion, but also of the spread of particular institutions that frame security issues for all, particularly: sovereignty, territoriality, and nationalism. These institutions were quickly indigenized in many places and used as defence mechanisms against ongoing Western demands. Yet insider/outsider security dynamics are still visible. The intervention literature discussed above is relevant here inasmuch as the politics of intervention is strongly mediated by whether it is understood to be an affair amongst insiders (and therefore subject to the relevant primary institutions) or one between insiders and outsiders (and therefore subject only to whatever rules are thought to be universal). This dynamic plays particularly strongly in relation to institutions that are still more Western than global, most notably human rights and democracy. The West still pressures others to accept these on the grounds that they are universal rights, but there remains much resistance from many quarters to that interpretation. All of this suggests that although the idea of outsiders might appear to have lost much of its interest as international society became global, in fact it is still very much alive. It is perfectly clear, for example, that at the level of 'the street', much of the Islamic world continues to think of itself as a site of resistance to Western values.

In a global international society, of course, all are to some degree insiders, and the idea of outsiders becomes much more relative than it was during the 'expansion' story, when in and out could be pretty clearly drawn. When outsider status is relative, and contingent on one's placement in a differentiated international society (e.g. core or periphery) Wendt's (1999: 247–50) idea that social structures can be held in place by coercion, calculation and/or belief is one useful way of approaching the idea of outsiders in contemporary international society. A contemporary institution like the market is obviously held in place by a mixture: some believe in it (US), some calculate it to be in their interest (China) and others are mainly bullied into it (parts of the third world). Where a particular institution is either contested, or held in place mainly by coercion, that could be seen as marking a form of outsider status.

International society as a referent object of security

This line of thinking features either the international social order as a whole (Bull, 1977: 18), or individual primary institutions, as the referent objects for security. It plays to the English school's focus on social structures, and contrasts with the realist's inclination to privilege the state as the central referent object for all Security Studies. The Copenhagen School has applied its securitization theory to show how the primary (e.g. sovereignty, market) and secondary (e.g. WTO, UN) institutions of international society can be referent object for securitization in their own right (Buzan et al. 1998).

The expansion of international society story discussed above also implicitly features this issue. A consistent theme in the classical ES story of expansion is the consequences of the fact that as European international society expanded, it necessarily moved beyond its foundational cultural base, and absorbed non-European cultures. Much classical ES literature assumes that interstate society necessarily rests on a substrate of shared culture from which it draws the shared values that define and enable its institutions. Modern Europe could be understood as Christendom, and classical Greece could also be understood as a zone of shared culture within which a states-system operated. The concern was that a multicultural foundation would necessarily diminish the pool of shared values available for international society, and thus expansion would equate to weakening. The ongoing tensions over human rights and democracy already noted exemplify the force of this concern, although the readiness with which some institutions, notably sovereignty, nationalism, and territoriality have become accepted and internalized offers some counterweight to it.

If international society can be threatened by a reduction in its cultural coherence, it can also be threatened by the interplay of institutions that pull in contradictory directions. There are several possibilities here, including the market and territoriality, and nationalism and sovereignty, but the one that has been most written about in the ES literature is that between human rights and sovereignty (Bull 1977, 1984; Vincent 1986; Makinda 1998; Bain 2001; Bellamy and McDonald 2004). Here the problem is that if human rights are universal and rooted in the individual, then this brings sovereignty (the absolute right of the state to exercise authority within its territory) into fundamental question. That tension has large implications for the legitimacy of humanitarian interventions, and also ties into the human security agenda of how to harmonize the rights and responsibilities of individuals with those of states (Buzan 2004a; Dunne and Wheeler 2004). In considering this question, Williams (2004) makes the case for linking the more radical concerns with human rights in the ES to the emancipatory themes of Critical Security Studies in order to create a more revolutionist ES approach to security. Morris (2004) and Nardin (2004) address the related, but more general, question of how the structure of international society defines the legitimacy (or not) of the use of force.

Conclusions: opportunities for developing the linkage

It should be clear from the above that in terms of both general framing and specific topics addressed, there is a lot of common ground between the English school and International Security Studies. That said, it is obvious that there is a lack of mutual awareness and interaction between them. The blindness is probably greater on the International Security Studies side, but it is equally true that ES writers need to do more to make the security dimension of ES work explicit, and to address it clearly to issues and debates within International Security Studies. Hopefully, this chapter has shown that the thinness of the contact so far hides quite rich possibilities for synergies. One of these possibilities is to focus attention more specifically on the interplay between the primary institutions of international society and security. How do primary institutions such as nationalism, territoriality, sovereignty, colonialism, human rights, and suchlike both define and frame the whole discourse of security? In what sense can and do such institutions become the referent object for processes of securitization?

Another possible synergy is available in the interplay between the study of regional international societies and regional security. There is some work on this (Ayoob 1999), but so far the ES has not shown much interest in the regional level of international society, having chosen to concentrate on the global level. A good case can be made that there are distinctive regional international societies (think of the EU), and there are some studies that analyse what makes them distinct from the global level, and how that distinctiveness matters (Buzan et al. 2009). In security perspective, for example, it seems clear that within the Middle East, sovereignty is a weaker institution than at the global level, and war a stronger one. Just as a social structural perspective throws interesting light on the analysis of security at the global level, so it does at the regional one. One obvious linkage point here is the Copenhagen School, which has a particular interest in regional security (Buzan and Wæver 2003) and is also open to English school thinking. Can one, for example, theorize a connection between strong security interdependence on the one hand, and the emergence of distinctive regional international societies on the other? Does security interdependence generate the incentives for a degree of international order that underpins international societies? On the face of it, it looks a reasonable hypothesis. It fits with European history, the Middle East case lends further credence to it, and others might as well. The idea of regional international societies also plays into the discussion of intervention above, because the differences represented by regional international society could well define the terms of insider/outsider that would make intervention legitimate or not.

The English school has much to offer to International Security Studies, but it needs to be considerably more proactive than it has been in making this clear to the community of International Security Studies scholars. For their part, some of the International Security Studies community needs to open their eyes to the importance of international society in framing and shaping the agenda of international security.

Notes

★ This is the unrevised version from the first edition of The Routledge Handbook of Security Studies.
1 Primary institutions are deep, organic, evolved ideas and practices that constitute both the players and the game of international relations. They include sovereignty, territoriality, balance of power, war, international law, diplomacy, nationalism, great power management, and the market. This understanding of institutions is quite different from that used by regime theorists and liberal institutionalists who focus mainly on instrumental and constructed organizations and arrangements such as intergovernmental organizations and regimes, which are referred to in the following as secondary institutions. Primary institutions have a history as old as human civilization, whereas secondary ones emerge only in the nineteenth century. See Buzan 2004b, 161–204.
2 The ES has concentrated mainly on international society where states are the central players, and the discussion that follows mainly reflects that focus. World society, which centres mainly on individuals and civil society, is less well developed in ES thinking, and there is some tension as to whether it should be approached via the domestic reform of states or via more cosmopolitan, transnational ways of thinking. There is not space in this short chapter to address this level of complexity.

Further reading

Buzan, B. (2014) *An Introduction to the English School of International Relations*, Cambridge: Polity Press.
Buzan, B. and Zang, Y. (eds.) (2014) *International Society and the Contest over 'East Asia'*, Cambridge: Cambridge University Press.
Knudsen, T. B. (2009) *Humanitarian Intervention and International Society: Contemporary Manifestations of an Explosive Doctrine*, Abingdon: Routledge.
Merke, F. (2011) 'The Primary Institutions of Latin American Regional Interstate Society', Paper for IDEAS Latin America Programme, LSE, 27 January 2011. Online. Available HTTP: <http://udesa. vps31.syncromind.com/files/UAHumanidades/NOTICIAS/MerkePrimaryInstitutionsinLatinAmerica 150211.pdf> (accessed 18 January 2016).
Pejcinovic, L. (2013) *War in International Society*, Abingdon: Routledge.
Ralph, J. (2010) 'War as an Institution of International Hierarchy: Carl Schmitt's Theory of the Partisan and Contemporary US Practice', *Millennium* 39(2): 279–98.
Suzuki, S. (2009) *Civilisation and Empire: China and Japan's Encounter with European International Society*, London: Routledge.
Welsh, J. M. (2011) 'A Normative Case for Pluralism: Reassessing Vincent's Views on Humanitarian Intervention', *International Affairs* 87(5): 1193–204.
Zarakol, A. (2011) *After Defeat: How the East Learned to Live with the West*, Cambridge: Cambridge University Press.

References

Adler, E. and Barnett, M. (eds.) (1998) *Security Communities*, Cambridge: Cambridge University Press.
Ayoob, M. (1999) 'From Regional System to Regional Society: Exploring Key Variables in the Construction of Regional Order', *Australian Journal of International Affairs* 53(3): 247–60.
Ayoob, M. (2001) 'Humanitarian Intervention and International Society', *Global Governance* 7(3): 225–30.
Bain, W. (2001) 'The Tyranny of Benevolence? National Security, Human Security, and the Practice of Statecraft', *Global Society* 15(3): 277–94.
Bellamy, A. J. (2003) 'Humanitarian Responsibilities and Interventionist Claims in International Society', *Review of International Studies* 29(3): 321–40.

Bellamy, A. J. and McDonald, M. (2004) 'Securing International Society: Towards an English School Discourse of Security', *Australian Journal of Political Science* 39(2): 307–30.

Best, G. (1994) *War and Law since 1945*, Oxford: Clarendon Press.

Booth, K. (1991) 'Security in Anarchy: Utopian Realism in Theory and Practice', *International Affairs* 67(3): 527–46.

Booth, K. and Wheeler, N. (2007) *The Security Dilemma: Anarchy, Society and Community in World Politics*, Basingstoke: Palgrave.

Brown, C. (2002) 'Intervention and the Westphalian Order', in R. Norman and A. Moseley (eds.) *Human Rights and Military Intervention*, Aldershot: Ashgate, 153–69.

Brown, C. (2004) 'Do Great Powers Have Great Responsibilities? Great Powers and Moral Agency', *Global Society* 18(1): 5–19.

Bull, H. (1977) *The Anarchical Society. A Study of Order in World Politics*, London: Macmillan.

Bull, H. (ed.) (1984a) *Intervention in World Politics*, Oxford: Clarendon Press.

Bull, H. (1984b) *Justice in International Relations: Hagey Lectures*, Ontario: University of Waterloo.

Bull, H. and Watson, A. (eds.) (1984) *The Expansion of International Society*, Oxford: Oxford University Press.

Butterfield, H. (1951) *History and Human Relations*, London: Collins.

Butterfield, H. (1966) 'The Balance of Power', in H. Butterfield and M. Wight (eds.) *Diplomatic Investigations*, London: Allen and Unwin, 132–48.

Buzan, B. (1991) *People, States and Fear: An Agenda for International Security Studies in the Post-Cold War Era*, Hemel Hempstead: Harvester-Wheatsheaf.

Buzan, B. (1996) 'International Society and International Security', in R. Fawn and J. Larkin (eds.) *International Society after the Cold War*, London: Macmillan, 261–87.

Buzan, B. (2004a) '"Civil" and "Uncivil" in World Society', in S. Guzzini and D. Jung (eds.) *Contemporary Security Analysis and Copenhagen Peace Research*, London: Routledge, 94–105.

Buzan, B. (2004b) *From International to World Society? English School Theory and the Social Structure of Globalisation*, Cambridge: Cambridge University Press.

Buzan, B. and Hansen, L. (2009) *The Evolution of International Security Studies*, Cambridge: Cambridge University Press.

Buzan, B. and Wæver O. (2003) *Regions and Powers*, Cambridge: Cambridge University Press.

Buzan, B., Gonzalez-Pelaez, A., and Jorgensen, K. E. (eds.) (2009) *International Society and the Middle East: English School Theory at the Regional Level*, Basingstoke: Palgrave.

Buzan, B., Jones C., and Little, R. (1993) *The Logic of Anarchy: Neorealism to Structural Realism*, New York: Columbia University Press.

Buzan, B., Wæver, O., and de Wilde, J. (1998) *Security: A New Framework for Analysis*, Boulder CO: Lynne Rienner.

Clark, I. (2005) *Legitimacy in International Society*, Oxford: Oxford University Press.

Cronin, B. (2002) 'Multilateral Intervention and the International Community', in M. Keren and D. A. Sylvan (eds.) *International Intervention: Sovereignty vs Responsibility*, London: Frank Cass, 147–65.

Draper, G. I. A. D. (1990) 'Grotius' Place in the Development of Legal Ideas about War', in H. Bull, B. Kingsbury and A. Roberts (eds.) *Hugo Grotius and International Relations*, Oxford: Clarendon Press, 177–209.

Dunne, T. and Wheeler, N. J. (2004) '"We the Peoples": Contending Discourses of Security in Human Rights Theory and Practice', *International Relations* 18(1): 9–23.

Gong, G. W. (1984) *The Standard of 'Civilization' in International Society*, Oxford: Clarendon Press.

Hassner, P. (1994) 'Beyond the Three Traditions: The Philosophy of War and Peace in Historical Perspective', *International Affairs* 70(4): 737–56.

Hobson, J. M. and Seabrooke, L. (2001) 'Reimagining Weber: Constructing International Society and the Social Balance of Power', *European Journal of International Relations* 7(2): 239–74.

Holsti, K. J. (1991) *Peace and War: Armed Conflicts and International Order 1648–1989*, Cambridge: Cambridge University Press.

Holsti, K. J. (1996) *The State, War and the State of War*, Cambridge: Cambridge University Press.

Holsti, K. J. (2004) *Taming the Sovereigns: Institutional Change in International Politics*, Cambridge: Cambridge University Press.

Howard, M. (1966) 'War as an Instrument of Policy', in H. Butterfield and M. Wight (eds.) *Diplomatic Investigations*, London: Allen and Unwin, 193–201.

Hudson, G. F. (1966) 'Collective Security and Military Alliances', in H. Butterfield and M. Wight (eds.) *Diplomatic Investigations*, London: Allen and Unwin, 176–180.

Hurrell, A. (2007) *On Global Order: Power, Values and the Constitution of International Society*, Oxford: Oxford University Press.

Jervis, R. (1985) 'From Balance to Concert: A Study of International Security Cooperation', *World Politics* 38(1): 58–79.

Jones, C. A. (2006) 'War in the Twenty-First Century: An Institution in Crisis', in R. Little and J. Williams (eds.) *The Anarchical Society in a Globalized World*, Basingstoke: Palgrave, 162–88.

Keal, P. (2003) *European Conquest and the Rights of Indigenous Peoples: The Moral Backwardness of International Society*, Cambridge: Cambridge University Press.

Keene, E. (2002) *Beyond the Anarchical Society: Grotius, Colonialism and Order in World Politics*, Cambridge: Cambridge University Press.

Kingsbury, B. (2002) 'Legal Positivism as Normative Politics: International Society, Balance of Power and Lassa Oppenheim's Positive International Law', *European Journal of International Law* 13(2): 401–36.

Knudsen, T. B. (1996) 'Humanitarian Intervention Revisited: Post-Cold War Responses to Classical Problems', *International Peacekeeping* 3(4): 146–65.

Lake, D. A. and Morgan, P. (1997) *Regional Orders: Building Security in a New World*, University Park: Pennsylvania University Press.

Little, R. (2006) 'The Balance of Power and Great Power Management', in R. Little and J. Williams (eds.) *The Anarchical Society in a Globalized World*, Basingstoke: Palgrave, 97–120.

Little, R. (2007) *The Balance of Power in International Relations: Metaphors, Myths and Models*, Cambridge: Cambridge University Press.

Makinda, S. (1997) 'International Law and Security: Exploring a Symbiotic Relationship', *Australian Journal of International Affairs* 51(3): 325–38.

Makinda, S. (1998) 'The United Nations and State Sovereignty: Mechanism for Managing International Security', *Australian Journal of Political Science* 33(1): 101–15.

Mayall, J. (1990) *Nationalism and International Society*, Cambridge: Cambridge University Press.

Morris, J. (2004) 'Normative Innovation and the Great Powers', in A. J. Bellamy (ed.) *International Society and Its Critics*, Oxford: Oxford University Press, 265–82.

Nardin, T. (2004) 'Justice and Coercion', in A. J. Bellamy (ed.) *International Society and Its Critics*, Oxford: Oxford University Press, 247–64.

Roberts, A. (1993) 'Humanitarian War: Military Intervention and Human Rights', *International Affairs* 69(3): 429–49.

Roberts, A. (1996) 'Humanitarian Action in War', *Adelphi Papers* 305, London: International Institute for Strategic Studies.

Roberts, A. (1999) 'NATO's "Humanitarian War" over Kosovo', *Survival* 41(3): 102–23.

Roberts, A. (2004) 'The Laws of War', in A. K. Cronin and J. M. Ludes (eds.) *Attacking Terrorism: Elements of a Grand Strategy*, Washington DC: Georgetown University Press, 186–219.

Roberts, A. (2006) 'Transformative Military Occupation: Applying the Laws of War and Human Rights', *American Journal of International Law* 100(3): 580–622.

Roberts, A. (2007) 'Torture and Incompetence in the "War on Terror"', *Survival* 49(1): 199–212.

Roberts, A. and Guelff R. (2000[1982]) *Documents on the Laws of War*, Oxford: Oxford University Press.

Song, D. (2005) 'The War Philosophy of the English School: A Grotian Interpretation', *World Economics and Politics* 10: 26–31.

Vincent, J. R. (1974) *Nonintervention and International Order*, Princeton, NJ: Princeton University Press.

Vincent, J. R. (1986) *Human Rights and International Relations: Issues and Responses*, Cambridge: Cambridge University Press.

Vincent, R. J. and Wilson, P. (1993) 'Beyond Non-Intervention', in I. Forbes and M. Hoffman (eds.) *Ethics and Intervention*, London: Macmillan, 122–30.

Wæver, O. (1996) 'Europe's Three Empires: A Watsonian Interpretation of Post-Wall European Security', in R. Fawn and J. Larkin (eds.) *International Society after the Cold War*, London: Macmillan, 220–60.

Walker, R. J. B. (1993) *Inside/Outside: International Relations as Political Theory*, Cambridge: Cambridge University Press.

Wendt, A. (1992) 'Anarchy Is What States Make of It: The Social Construction of Power Politics', *International Organization* 46(2): 391–425.

Wendt, A. (1999) *Social Theory of International Politics*, Cambridge: Cambridge University Press.

Wheeler, N. J. (1992) 'Pluralist and Solidarist Conceptions of International Society: Bull and Vincent on Humanitarian Intervention', *Millennium* 21(3): 463–89.

Wheeler, N. J. (2000) *Saving Strangers: Humanitarian Intervention in International Society*, Oxford: Oxford University Press.

Wheeler, N. J. and Morris, J. (1996) 'Humanitarian Intervention and State Practice at the End of the Cold War', in R. Fawn and J. Larkin (eds.) *International Society after the Cold War*, London: Macmillan, 135–171.

Wight, M. (1966) 'The Balance of Power', in H. Butterfield and M. Wight (eds.) *Diplomatic Investigations*, London: Allen and Unwin, 149–75.

Williams, J. (1999) 'The Ethical Basis of Humanitarian Intervention, the Security Council and Yugoslavia', *International Peacekeeping* 6(2): 1–23.

Williams, P. (2004) 'Critical Security Studies', in A. J. Bellamy (ed.) *International Society and Its Critics*, Oxford: Oxford University Press, 135–50.

Windsor, P. (1991) 'The State and War', in C. Navari (ed.) *The Condition of States*, Buckingham: Open University Press, 125–41.

Wu, Z. (2006) 'John Vincent: Sovereignty, Human Rights and Humanitarian Intervention', in Z. Chen, G. Zhou and B. Shi (eds.) *Open International Society: The English School in IR Studies*, Beijing: Peking University Press, 165–77.

Zhang, Y. (1991) 'China's Entry into International Society: Beyond the Standard of "Civilization"', *Review of International Studies* 17(1): 3–16.

5

CRITICAL
SECURITY STUDIES

David Mutimer

The philosophers have only interpreted the world in various ways; the point is to change it.

(Marx 1888)

This noted aphorism by Karl Marx may be said to mark the origin of modern critical social theory. While the point might be to change the world, it is not the only point. Marx is not suggesting abandoning the philosophers' search for understanding, but rather advocates understanding the world *in order* to change it. It is likely that most, if not all, forms of social theory would accept Marx's point. Even a liberal thinker such as Francis Fukuyama, who argues that the great struggles of history are over, would accept that social theory should seek to understand the operations of our now-eternal liberal democratic present to make things 'better': increase the overall wealth and freedom of the world's people, and include more and more in the virtuous circle of liberal democratic governance and market economies (Fukuyama 1992).

Liberal improvements to the state of the world, however, mark no *fundamental* change in the organization of society. They seek to improve the operation of the system as it is; certainly such improvement is change, but it is not the change sought by those who would identify themselves as critical social theorists. Social critique assumes that there are fundamental features of the world as we find it that must be changed. The job of theory is to identify and interpret those features for the purposes of animating their change. While critical theorists part ways with their liberal counterparts at this point, the conservatives and reactionaries would still be along for the ride. These latter would see the world as having deteriorated from some previous better phase, and the point of conservative theory is to identify the way those problems function in the present, in order to animate a change, returning society to some previous (possibly only perceived) better time.

Critical theories reject the premise that the world was fundamentally better in times past or places distant. Rather, they seek to make changes to the fundamental social organization of the present, so that future social organization frees those presently oppressed by the operation of the world as we find it. This freeing of the oppressed is termed 'emancipation', and the orientation of politics towards future improvement in social life is why this form of politics is sometimes termed 'progressive'.

What, then, are the fundamentals of society that require change in order to produce a progressive politics? Marx's answer was that political identity is determined by the individual's relation to the production process (their social class). Those who own the means of production in any society benefit at the expense of others, and so the 'point' is to reveal this fundamental organization of society, to mobilize the oppressed to change society in their interest. However, what if society is not fundamentally about production, in the way Marx suggests? What if the various identities produced in activities other than production are not subordinate to their class identity? Indeed, perhaps there is no single fundamental nature to social organization in all times and in all places, but rather the various forms of social activity and identity organized differently, contingently at different times and in different places, and so progressive social change must look to multiple sites of fundamental oppression. As industrial capitalism grew and became globalized, and particularly as capitalism became post-industrial, a body of social theory grew that made just such a claim.

What I have sketched, in admittedly a very schematic way, is the broad scope of critical social theory and its primary line of division. Those who follow Marx's theory of a fundamentally class-based society are found on one side of this division. This stream is often termed 'German', in that Marx and a good number of those that followed him were either German or based in Germany – most notably, in the twentieth century, a group of theorists gathered in Frankfurt (the 'Frankfurt school'), who coined the term Critical Theory. On the other side are those who argue that class and production are not fundamental. This second stream is often termed 'French' for the influence of a number of French thinkers in a tradition also usually labelled 'post-structural'. Foremost among these are Jacques Derrida, Michel Foucault, and Jean Baudrillard. There are, of course, near-infinite complexities within these broad areas of social theory, and considerable overlap at their margins. No post-structural thinker, for example, would reject the importance of the basic Marxist critique of capitalist society to understanding (and changing) the present. On the other hand, there is a significant stream of post-Marxist thinking that takes culture and ideology very seriously indeed. My objective in this chapter is to explore what has happened as critical social theory, in its many varieties, has been used on the questions of international security to forge a field of study generally termed Critical Security Studies.

I begin with a short discussion of the origins of Critical Security Studies, as it emerged in the aftermath of the collapse of the Cold War and in response to the problems that collapse revealed with traditional Security Studies. Initially, the leading theoretical position identified with the term Critical Security was constructivism, and so I follow the discussion of origins with a short exploration of the literature on social construction. There is a real question, however, as to whether the constructivist position fits with a commitment to *critical* social theory, and so that section will be followed by two that explore the deployment of first post-Marxist and then post-structural social theory to questions of security. I conclude by considering a recent attempt to bridge the divisions I sketch in the rest of the chapter, revealing in the process some of the ways that some divisions appear inescapable.

Origins

Security Studies was, in its inception and early practice, very much a 'policy science'. As it grew along with the nuclear age, the concern of Security Studies was, in the words of one of its staunchest defenders, 'the study of the threat, use, and control of military force' (Walt 1991). It was concerned with interpreting the world of military strategy, not to change it fundamentally, but to make it better on its own terms. Providing direct policy advice to those in control of states' militaries, particularly to nuclear-armed militaries, was very much a part of the Security Studies understanding of its purpose.

The end of the Cold War and the change that came with it opened what has been termed a 'thinking space' in the study of global security (George 1994). In large part, this thinking space resulted from the manifest failure of political realism, the theory underpinning traditional Security Studies, not only to predict the end of the Cold War, but even to account for it once it had happened (Gusterson 1999). That failure created conditions in which self-consciously critical work to questions of security could be taken seriously in the academy.

What has come to be known as Critical Security Studies grew from this moment in political and intellectual time. The term itself emerged on the margins of a conference held at York University in 1994, and served as the title for the volume produced by that conference. That book, *Critical Security Studies: Concepts and Cases*, is still seen as an important point of origin of the Critical Security Studies idea. The book and label, however, really served as a point around which a number of strands of intellectual development could coalesce. A group of graduate students working with Ken Booth at the University of Wales Aberystwyth were bringing post-Marxist critical theory to bear on questions of security (Booth 2007: xv–xvi). A number of other scholars, mainly at the University of Minnesota and York University, were developing ideas about constructivism in relation to security (Latham 1998; Milliken 2001; Mutimer 1998; Price 1997; Weldes 1999; Williams 1992, 1998). In other places, ideas drawn from French social theory were also being turned to questions of security (Campbell 1992; Dalby 1990).

At the same time, there were at least two other strands of thought that drew on forms of social critique to think about security, but which have not subsequently been captured, by and large, by the 'Critical Security Studies' label. The first is variously known as 'the Copenhagen School' or 'securitization studies' (see Chapter 6 in this volume). Perhaps more interestingly, a range of scholars were thinking about gender and International Relations (IR), including international security (Enloe 1983; Peterson 1992; Sylvester 1994; Whitworth 1998). The Feminist IR scholarship that has grown from this strand of thinking, despite significant overlaps with the work of Critical Security Studies, and severe theoretical divisions within it, continues to exist outside the ambit of Critical Security Studies (see Chapter 8 in this volume).

Security and social construction

The notion of social construction was introduced to the study of international politics just as the Cold War was ending, and was quickly picked up by students of international security (Wendt 1987, 1992). Constructivism builds on the basic notion that social life is a product of social practice. Social construction was very appealing to those seeking to rethink security with the demise of the Cold War. It suggested a context in which the rapid change brought about by the Cold War's end was conceivable (if the Cold War was a construct, it could end, where realism seemed to suggest it could not). It also suggested that the security futures were, at least in part, open, as the constitution of those futures would depend on social practice rather than immutable law.

The appeal of constructivism is reflected in *Critical Security Studies: Concepts and Cases*, and perhaps even more clearly in an article published by one of its editors the following year. In this article, Keith Krause organized the research agenda of the new Critical Security Studies under three rubrics: the construction of threats and responses; the construction of the objects of security; and possibilities for transforming the security dilemma (Krause 1998). The assumption underlying this classification is that security is about the identification of *threats* to a particular *referent object*, and the formulation of policy *responses* to those threats. Traditional Security Studies would accept this notion of security easily, but would give singular answers to each: the threats are military, the referent object is the state, and the responses are the scope of strategic policy. Thinking in terms of social construction opens the prospect of other answers, as it renders the traditional answers contingent. It therefore also opens an important range of what are known as 'how' questions (Doty 1993: 298; Weldes 1999: 15–16). That is, even if the traditional answers are a correct reflection of the world as we find it, how is it that they came to be that way, given that they are constructed, contingent features of the world? These are the questions Krause argues were driving the research in his first two categories (Krause 1998: 308–9).

Krause's third rubric is of a different order. Here the concern becomes normative: how can the way in which security is practised be transformed? This third group of work is normative in at least two ways. Not only is it concerned with a preferred future, but it is grounded in the assumption that social norms are an important part of international political life, even international security. Some early work explored the place of normative constraints on the use of weapons (for example: Price 1997; Tannenwald 2007). There has also been a constructivist interest in the place of norms in the end of the Cold War, and the way norms are produced and institutionalized in contemporary international society to promote security (Tannenwald and Wohlforth 2005; Ghecui 2008). In particular, the place of 'norm entrepreneurs' has been studied, most notably in relation to the creation of the Ottawa Convention banning anti-personnel mines (Price 1988; Finnemore and Sikkink 1998; Price and Reus-Smit 2004; Ulbert and Risse 2005).

As important as constructivism remains in the study of world politics and international security, it is an open question whether it is critical in the sense set out at the beginning of this chapter (cf. Krause 1998: 299f). Clearly, critical social theory accepts the premise of social construction: Were society not produced in and through its practices, transformation would not be possible. However, critical theory is aimed at producing fundamental change of a particular kind, and the possibility, let alone the necessity, of such change is not inherent in the constructivist position (Campbell 1998a: 207–27).[1]

Security and post-Marxism

There can be no doubt as to the commitment to fundamental change of those drawing their primary inspiration for rethinking security from the German, or post-Marxist tradition of critical theory. The nature of that commitment was captured early on in a signal contribution from Ken Booth. In his 1991 article, 'Security and Emancipation', Booth set out the political goal of a post-Marxist informed Critical Security Studies:

> Security means the absence of threats. Emancipation is the freeing of people (as individuals and groups) from those physical and human constraints which stop them carrying out what they would freely choose to do [. . .] Security and emancipation are two sides of the same coin. Emancipation, not power or order, produces true security. Emancipation, theoretically, is security.
>
> *(Booth 1991: 319)*

Booth has spent most of the intervening 20 years working out the implications of thinking about security as emancipation, in the post-Marxist sense of the term. Many of the intellectual foundations for this work were contributed by a colleague of Booth's at Aberystwyth, Richard Wyn Jones, whose 1999 book *Security, Strategy, and Critical Theory* provides an exegesis of Frankfurt school critical theory. His object is 'to lay the conceptual foundations for an alternative critical Security Studies' (Wyn Jones 1999: 165). Those foundations were based on a rethinking of both security and strategy through the intellectual lens provided by the Frankfurt school. He argues that, seen in this way, security is 'deeper', 'broader', 'extended to referents other than the state', and 'focussed, crucially, on emancipation'. And he turns to the work of

Italian philosopher Antonio Gramsci to reconfigure the relationship between security theory and practice in such a way that 'proponents of critical Security Studies can not only interpret the world but also play a role in changing it' (Wyn Jones 1999: 167).

In several iterations, culminating in his *Theory of World Security* (2007), Ken Booth has built on the foundations that Wyn Jones laid to develop a critical theory of world security, which is 'both a theoretical commitment and a political orientation concerned with the construction of world security' (Booth 2007: 30). As a 'theoretical commitment', Booth's theory of world security begins like that of Wyn Jones – with the Frankfurt school and Gramsci. However, he considers these two to be neither sufficient nor in their entirety necessary for his theoretical framework. He therefore engages in what he terms, following Hannah Arendt, *Perlenfischerei* (pearl fishing): 'diving into, first, the critical tradition in social theory, and then the radical tradition in international relations theory. The goal is to find pearls of ideas that might be strung together to make a theory of world security for our time' (Booth 2007: 40).

The theoretical framework Booth develops from his pearls defies easy summary, as it is grand in both scope and execution (Booth 2007: 209–78). He organizes the framework into three levels. The first is 'transcendental theory', or put another way, his ontological claims: 'The transcendental dimension of the overall theoretical framework [...] is constructed out of eight main is-propositions. 'Human sociality' is the best overall label for them, implying as it does the radical possibilities immanent in the biology of being human' (Booth 2007: 210). He conceives human society as being constituted in our interaction, but with the individual as the ultimate referent of security. The second level is epistemological, which he terms 'pure theory', and which is a Frankfurt-inspired take on the constitutive nature of knowledge and the critical possibilities of theory. Finally, his third level is 'practical theory', which he terms 'emancipatory realism' (Booth 2007: 249–77). While the shift in Booth's terminology from 'utopian' to 'emancipatory' realism is in part due to a desire to escape the eschatological overtones of utopia (Booth 2007: 90), the ghost of final goal clearly haunts this project. The goal in question is a communitarian one, which he derives first from Kant (Booth 2007: 80–7) and more recently from Andrew Linklater's elaborations of Jurgen Habermas' ideas (Booth 2007: 54–7). While he explicitly eschews the possibility of blueprints, Booth articulates quite an elaborate vision for an institutionalized world community based on the principles of the Enlightenment (Booth 2007: 124–33 and 427–70).

Theory of World Security stands as the most extensively developed contribution to the post-Marxist (German, Italian, or Welsh) approach to Critical Security Studies. It is long on theoretical development and political desire, but short on engagement with the world of security. This is not to say that there is not an extensive discussion of the state of the world in Booth's text, for there is, but rather that the discussion is not clearly informed by the theory that precedes it, rather than by Booth's own insight and erudition. So, while the post-Marxist approach to critical security is beginning to articulate a political project, it is as yet deficient in turning its critical eye to the concrete questions of contemporary security on which such a project can ultimately be built.

Security and post-structuralism

For all his commitment to theoretical pluralism, there is an oyster bed of international studies into which Booth will not dive in search of his theoretical pearls, and that is the other broad division of critical social theory with which I began: post-structuralism (Booth 2007: 462 and 175–8) (see Chapter 7 in this volume). This work draws on a number of social theorists and philosophers, though a few stand out as being more widely cited than others. These are the French thinkers mentioned at the outset: Foucault, Derrida, and Baudrillard. The range of themes and issues across this literature is similarly broad and varied, but there are, perhaps, four of particular significance to security: the question of identity, that of ethics, and latterly, the biopolitics of security and the subjectivity of the material.

The relationship between identity and security was among the first important themes considered by scholars working in the French tradition. While constructivism had raised the question of identity, those in the post-structural tradition drew on the radical notion of the performative constitution of identity, developed out of the work of Michel Foucault and others, to think about security. David Campbell's work is signal in this regard, with his two major books exploring a range of questions around identity and security (Campbell 1992, 1998b). In *Writing Security*, he examines the ways in which discourses of fear animate a politics of security constitutive of the US, and in particular how difference is produced as 'other' in such discourses. In *National Deconstruction*, Campbell looks at the violent effects of such othering in the case of the war and its aftermath in Bosnia. Bosnia is also the site for a more recent work on a similar theme by Lene Hansen (Hansen 2006) and Elizabeth Dauphinée (Dauphinée 2008; also 2013).

The importance of the wars in the former Yugoslavia to post-structural thinking on security is not accidental. The 'thinking space' brought about by the end of the Cold War into which French philosophy-inspired work entered coincided with the collapse of Yugoslavia and the return of both war and concentration camps to the European continent (George 1994). The latter were particularly important, because the routine criticism of post-structuralism was that it had no politics, and particularly had no way to stand up to 'the worst'. It should be no surprise, then, that the 'ethnic cleansing' in Bosnia, complete with horrifying images of emaciated prisoners behind barbed wire, should capture the attention of post-structural thinkers on questions of security. Nor should it be surprising that the turn to examine Bosnia led these thinkers to ask questions about an ethical politics: how, in a world shorn of grand narratives or a necessary grounding for ethico-political judgements, can you respond to the violent destruction of the other? Answering this question has spawned a rich literature, much of which takes its theoretical cues from the work of Emmanuel Levinas and Jacques Derrida (Campbell 1998b; Campbell and Shapiro 1999; Dauphinée 2008 and 2013; Edkins 2003; Lisle 2006).

If the wars of the former Yugoslavia commanded attention in the 1990s, after the events of 11 September 2001 that attention has tended to shift to the various issues raised by the terror attacks and, in particular, the responses to them. A number of thinkers influenced by post-structural thought have explored concerns around terrorism and security, with many deploying Michel Foucault's concept of biopolitics (Dillon and Lobo-Guerrero 2008). One notable programme of research has been organized under the 'Liberty and Security' label (CHALLENGE 2008). The programme considers the relationship between security and liberty in the European response to terror as a 'technique of government', as Foucault would call it (Bigo 2000, 2006). They explore the means by which governmental practices produce acceptable images of enemy others who can be violently excluded in the name of 'security'. Indeed, the production of the violently excluded other runs through much of the post-structural work on security after 2001, with many scholars drawing on Italian social theorist Giorgio Agamben's work on sovereignty and the exception to think about contemporary practices of security (Edkins et al. 2004; Dauphinée and Masters 2007).

Throughout the Cold War, security was a very abstract concept, as it increasingly centred around building weapons no one expected to use, governed by strategies that were little more than thought-experiments. The past twenty years have reminded us in no uncertain terms about the materiality of security: whether it is the stark return of barbed wire and emaciation in Bosnia, the dust-covered New Yorkers running from collapsed buildings, 'stress positions' and 'water boarding' in Guantanamo Bay, or the use of armed drones in what used to be called assassination but is now more commonly referred to as 'targeted killing.' Security thinkers have recently begun thinking again about the material in this context, often turning to another French thinker for some guidance: Bruno Latour. Latour asks us to think about 'assemblages' of the human and non-human and consider that the agency which produces the effects we want to understand (and judge) is distributed across these assemblages (Latour 2005). To take a relatively clear example, a drone flown against a target in Yemen but controlled in Arizona can be thought of as an assemblage of drone and operator, but also of the strategy and strategists that govern it, as well as the logistic and communication chains that join it. Agency rests not only in the drone operator, and also in other human sites of decision, but crucially in the non-human drones and other technological components in the assemblage (Grondin 2013; Walters 2014). Other scholars have turned this approach to a range of issues of contemporary security, from arms control (Bourne 2012) to torture (van Veeren 2014).

The post-structural work on security is permeated by a concern with the relationship between security and the production of difference as dangerous 'other'. Scholars explore the ways in which representational and other governmental practices produce some as 'secured' and others as 'excluded' from the realm of security, an exclusion that is often effected violently. The politics of such work, therefore, continues in the emancipatory tradition of critical theory: exposing and exploring the production of exclusion for the purposes of informing a transformatory politics in favour of those excluded. The exclusions are produced contingently, in temporally and spatially specific locations, and so 'emancipations' can only be effected in a similarly specific and contingent fashion. The uncertainty of such an approach to political change is most concisely captured by Derrida's notion of democracy that is 'to come' (Campbell 1998b: 165–244). Democracy, in Derrida's sense, is a goal that is always deferred, rather than an institutional framework that can be applied; it is an ethos that informs politics, rather than a politics itself.

Bridging the divides?

In 2006 a group of European scholars committed to the critical study of security attempted to draw together some of the disparate approaches that I have outlined here as quite separate (CASE Collective 2006). The attempt was interesting in a number of ways. The original article was published as a collectively authored piece of work, with a potentially changeable group of authors (CASE Collective 2007), and perhaps just as unusually, it was titled a 'manifesto', making its politics immediately apparent. That politics is set out as breaking down the competitive individualism of contemporary scholarship, and overcoming the divisions that have emerged in critical approaches to security, specifically in the collective's case among the 'Copenhagen', 'Aberystwyth', and 'Paris' schools (CASE Collective 2006: 444–5).

The attempt to overcome internecine divisions and establish a broad research programme that can accommodate the variations of approach that have developed in non-traditional Security Studies is certainly laudable. However, what is particularly notable is that the responses to this initiative, almost without fail, drew attention to the exclusions that were effected by the CASE Collective's attempt at inclusion. Christine Sylvester's 'Anatomy of a Footnote', calls the Collective to account for the exclusion of feminist scholarship (Sylvester 2007). Two others take the Collective to task for its focus on Europe, and the exclusions that it thereby produces (Behnke 2007; Salter 2007). Indeed, Salter went further and joined with his colleague Miguel de Larrinaga to respond at length with 'Cold CASE: a manifesto for Canadian critical Security Studies', reviewing the Canadian contributions to Critical Security Studies (de Larrinaga and Salter 2014; Salter and de Larrinaga 2014).

More recently, Anthony Burke has tried a different tack with the effect of overcoming the divisions in Critical Security Studies. Burke takes an explicitly normative approach to security, drawing on the cosmopolitan tradition in international affairs to provide an improved framework for understanding and responding to global security threats (Burke 2013, 2015). The cosmopolitan tradition has deep roots in liberal political theory, particularly the tradition associated with Immanuel Kant, but has also been elaborated in recent Marxist-inflected International Relations scholarship (Linklater 1988). Burke's own work which has led him to this point is very much in a post-structural tradition (Burke 2007). The responses to his security cosmopolitanism suggest the difficulty of bridging divisions. The liberal overtones concern those who worry about the violence that liberal intervention has brought in the name of universal ends (Cooper and Turner 2013; Bilgin 2015). Others argue that while of course he is right, such a framework does not go nearly far enough (Kaldor 2013; Richmond 2015).

Conclusion

Despite a shared commitment to a security scholarship that informs a politics of fundamental change in the interest of those presently disadvantaged, 'Critical Security Studies' remains riven by variations in approach and attitude. The greatest of those divisions is informed by the split in the wider world of critical social theory between those of a 'German' and those of a 'French' orientation. They are joined, however, by constructivists who seem to fit neither of these geographic markers, by members of the Copenhagen School who seem at times to fit both, and by feminists whose work reaches across and beyond the other divisions.

Attempts at bridging these divides tend rather to fall into them. The problem may perhaps be traced back to the quotation with which I began, in which Marx articulates the point of critical scholarship to be to change the world. It has proved impossible to agree with Marx's assumption that there is a singular 'world', even a singular world of security, which is to be transformed. If the point is to change *worlds*, to achieve *emancipations*, then the multiplicity of approaches is not only to be expected, but to be welcomed. Each in its own way focuses critical thought on different, necessary sites of change, and so they may together inform a politics of multiple transformations. As the CASE Collective learned, however, simply willing such a broad, inclusive Critical Security Study will not make it so.

Note

1 For a clear example of a non-transformatory constructivist theory of world politics, see Wendt (1999).

References

Behnke, A. (2007) 'Presence and Creation: A Few (Meta-)Critical Comments on the C.A.S.E. Manifesto', *Security Dialogue* 38(1): 105–11.

Bigo, D. (2000) 'When Two Become One: Internal and External Securitisations in Europe', in M. Kelstrup and M. C. Williams (eds.) *International Relations Theory and the Politics of European Integration: Power, Security and Community*, London: Routledge, 171–204.

Bigo, D. (2006) 'Security, Exception, Ban, Surveillance', in D. Lyon (ed.) *Theorizing Surveillance: The Panopticon and Beyond*, Portland: Willan Publishing, 46–68.

Bilgin, P. (2015) 'Arguing against Security Communitarianism', *Critical Studies on Security* 3(2): 176–81.

Booth, K. (1991) 'Security and Emancipation', *Review of International Studies* 17(4): 313–26.

Booth, K. (2007) *Theory of World Security*, Cambridge: Cambridge University Press.

Bourne, M. (2012) 'Guns Don't Kill People, Cyborgs Do: A Latourian Provocation for Transformatory Arms Control and Disarmament', *Global Change, Peace and Security* 24(1): 141–63.

Burke, A. (2007) *Beyond Security, Ethics and Violence: War against the Other*, London: Routledge.

Burke, A. (2013) 'Security Cosmopolitanism', *Critical Studies on Security* 1(1): 13–28.

Burke, A. (2015) 'Security Cosmopolitanism: the Next Phase', *Critical Studies on Security* 3(2): 190–212.

Campbell, D. (1992) *Writing Security: United States Foreign Policy and the Politics of Identity*, Minneapolis: University of Minnesota Press.

Campbell, D. (1998a[1992]) *Writing Security: United States Foreign Policy and the Politics of Identity*, Minneapolis: University of Minnesota Press.

Campbell, D. (1998b) *National Deconstruction: Violence, Identity, and Justice in Bosnia*, Minneapolis: University of Minnesota Press.

Campbell, D. and Shapiro, M. (1999) *Moral Spaces: Rethinking Ethics and World Politics*, Minneapolis: University of Minnesota Press.

CASE Collective (2006) 'Critical Approaches to Security in Europe: A Networked Manifesto', *Security Dialogue* 37(4): 443–87.

CASE Collective (2007) 'Europe, Knowledge, Politics: Engaging the Limits: The CASE Collective Responds', *Security Dialogue* 38(4): 559–76.

CHALLENGE (2008) *Liberty and Security*. Online. Available HTTP: <http://www.libertysecurity.org/> (accessed 28 January 2009).

Cooper, N. and Turner, M. (2013) 'The Iron Fist of Liberal Intervention inside the Velvet Glove of Kantian Idealism: A Response to Burke', *Critical Studies on Security* 1(1): 35–41.

Dalby, S. (1990) *Creating the Second Cold War,* London: Pinter.

Dauphinée, E. (2008) *The Ethics of Researching War: Searching for Bosnia*, Manchester: Manchester University Press.

Dauphinée, E. (2013) *The Politics of Exile*, Oxford: Routledge.

Dauphinée, E. and Masters, C. (eds.) (2007) *The Logics of Biopower and the War on Terror: Living, Dying, Surviving*, London: Palgrave-Macmillan.

de Larrinaga, M. and Salter, M. (2014) 'Cold CASE: A Manifesto for Canadian Critical Security Studies', *Critical Studies on Security* 2(1): 1–19.

Dillon, M. and Lobo-Guerrero, L. (2008) 'Biopolitics of Security in the 21st Century: An Introduction', *Review of International Studies* 34(2): 265–92.

Doty, R. L. (1993) 'Foreign Policy as Social Construction: A Post-Positivist Analysis of US Counter-Insurgency Policy in the Phillipines', *International Studies Quarterly* 37(3): 297–320.

Edkins, J. (2003) *Trauma and the Memory of Politics*, Cambridge: Cambridge University Press.

Edkins, J., Pin-Fat, V., and Shapiro, M. J. (eds.) (2004) *Sovereign Lives: Power in Global Politics*, London: Routledge.

Enloe, C. (1983) *Does Khaki Become You? The Militarisation of Women's Lives*, South End: South End Press.

Finnemore, M. and Sikkink, K. (1998) 'International Norm Dynamics and Political Change', *International Organization* 52(4): 887–917.

Fukuyama, F. (1992) *The End of History and the Last Man*, New York: The Free Press.

George, J. (1994) *Discourses of Global Politics: A Critical (Re)Introduction to International Relations*, Boulder, CO: Lynne Rienner.

Ghecui, A. (2008) *Securing Civilization? The EU, NATO and the OSCE in the Post-9/11 World*, Oxford: Oxford University Press.

Grondin, D. (2013) 'The Study of Drones as Objects of Security: Targeted Killing as Military Strategy', in M. Salter and C. E. Mutlu (eds.) *Research Methods in Critical Security Studies: An Introduction*, London: Routledge, 191–4.

Gusterson, H. (1999) 'Missing the End of the Cold War in International Security', in J. Weldes, M. Laffey, H. Gusterson, and R. Duvall (eds.) *Culture of Insecurity*, Minneapolis: University of Minnesota Press, 319–45.

Hansen, L. (2006) *Security as Practice: Discourse Analysis and the Bosnian War*, London: Routledge.

Kaldor, M. (2013) 'Comment on Security Cosmopolitanism', *Critical Studies on Security* 1(1): 42–5.

Krause, K. (1998) 'Critical Theory and Security Studies: The Research Programme of "Critical Security Studies"', *Cooperation and Conflict* 33(3): 298–333.

Latham, A. (1998) 'Constructing National Security: Culture and Identity in Indian Arms Control and Disarmament Practice', *Contemporary Security Policy* 19(1): 129–58.

Latour, B. (2005) *Reassembling the Social: An Introduction to Actor-Network Theory*, New York: Oxford University Press.

Linklater, A. (1998) *The Transformation of Political Community: Ethical Foundations of the Post-Westphalian Era*, Columbia: University of South Carolina Press.

Lisle, D. (2006) *The Global Politics of Contemporary Travel Writing*, Cambridge: Cambridge University Press.

Marx, K. (1888) 'Thesis XI', *Theses On Feuerbach*, The Marx/Engels Internet Archive. Online. Available HTTP: <http://www.marxfaq.org/archive/marx/works/1845/theses/theses.htm> (accessed 12 September 2008).

Milliken, J. (2001) *The Social Construction of the Korean War: Conflict and Its Possibilities*, Manchester: University of Manchester Press.

Mutimer, D. (1998) 'Reconstituting Security: The Practices of Proliferation Control', *European Journal of International Relations* 4(1): 99–129.

Peterson, V. S. (1992) *Gendered States: Feminist (Re)Visions of International Relations Theory*, Boulder, CO: Lynne Rienner.

Price, R. (1988) 'Reversing the Gun Sights: Transnational Civil Society Targets Land Mines', *International Organization* 52(3): 613–44.

Price, R. (1997) *The Chemical Weapons Taboo*, Ithaca, NY: Cornell University Press.

Price, R. (2004) 'Emerging Customary Norms and Anti-Personnel Landmines' in R. Price and C. Reus-Smit (eds.) *The Politics of International Law*, Cambridge: Cambridge University Press, 106–30.

Richmond, O. (2015) 'Security Cosmopolitanism or "Securitopia": an Ontological Trap and a Half-Hearted Response to Structural War?', *Critical Studies on Security* 3(2): 182–9.

Salter, M. (2007) 'On Exactitude in Disciplinary Science: A Response to the Network Manifesto', *Security Dialogue* 38(1): 113–22.

Salter, M. and de Larrinaga, M. (2014) 'Special Issue on Canadian Security Studies', *Critical Studies on Security* 2(1): 1–19.

Sylvester, C. (1994) *Feminist Theories and International Relations in a Postmodern Era*, Cambridge: Cambridge University Press.

Sylvester, C. (2007) 'Anatomy of a Footnote', *Security Dialogue* 38(4): 547–58.

Tannenwald, N. (2007) *The Nuclear Taboo: The United States and the Non-Use of Nuclear Weapons since 1945*, Cambridge: Cambridge University Press.

Tannenwald, N. and Wohlforth, W. (eds.) (2005) 'Ideas, International Relations and the End of the Cold War', Special Issue of *Journal of Cold War Studies* 7(2).

Ulbert, C. and Risse, T. (2005) 'Deliberately Changing the Discourse: What Does Make Arguing Effective?', *Acta Politica* 40(3): 351–67.

Van Veeren, E. (2014) 'Materializing US Security: Guantanamo's Object Lessons and Concrete Messages', *International Political Sociology* 8(1): 20–42.

Walt, S. (1991) 'The Renaissance of Security Studies', *International Studies Quarterly* 35(2): 211–39.

Walters, W. (2014) 'Drone Strikes, *Dingpolitik* and Beyond: Furthering the Debate on Materiality and Security', *Security Dialogue* 45(2): 101–18.

Weldes, J. (1999) *Constructing National Interests: The United States and the Cuban Missile Crisis*, Minneapolis: University of Minnesota Press.

Wendt, A. (1987) 'The Agent-Structure Problem in International Relations Theory', *International Organization* 41(3): 335–70.

Wendt, A. (1992) 'Anarchy is What States Make of It: The Social Construction of Power Politics', *International Organization* 46(2): 391–425.

Wendt, A. (1999) *Social Theory of International Politics*, Cambridge: Cambridge University Press.

Whitworth, S. (1998) 'Gender, Race and the Politics of Peacekeeping', in E. Moxon-Browne (ed.) *A Future for Peacekeeping?*, Basingstoke: Macmillan, 176–91.

Williams, M. C. (1992) 'Rethinking the "Logic" of Deterrence', *Alternatives* 17(1): 67–94.

Williams, M. C. (1998) 'Identity and the Politics of Security', *European Journal of International Relations* 4(2): 207–28.

Wyn Jones, R. (1999) *Security, Strategy, and Critical Theory*, Boulder, CO: Lynne Rienner.

6

CONSTRUCTIVISM AND SECURITIZATION STUDIES

Juha A. Vuori

Social constructivism is concerned with how our social realities come about: how is it that ontologically subjective and epistemologically objective mental representations like identities, states, or security turn into reciprocally institutionalized roles and come to be taken as real and as indisputable as the physical reality we can touch, smell, and see? Social constructivism is interested in how deontic powers such as 'rights, duties, obligations, requirements, permissions, authorizations, entitlements, and so on' (Searle 2011: 9) are brought about. From such a general viewpoint, 'ideas matter' when they are used to assign and eliminate deontological modalities, i.e., partake in 'the creation of commitments, the assignment and elimination of rights and entitlements or obligations, the legitimation of expectations, and the like' (Sbisà 1999: 11).

Social constructivism was a crucial position in debates about ontology and epistemology in the field of International Relations (IR) in the 1980s and 1990s. Indeed, social constructivism can be considered a metatheory rather than a specific theory of international politics (although there are also operative constructivist theories in IR) and there are many shades of constructivism in terms of ontological, epistemological, and normative views and commitments (Hacking 1999). While there are 'conventional constructivist' approaches to security (e.g., Katzenstein 1996), the theory of *securitization* has taken the constructivist insights to their most elaborate form.

Accordingly, this chapter introduces the main elements and assumptions of the theory in three main parts. The first part looks at the notion of securitization and the core elements of the model at the heart of the theory. The second part looks at the aspect of 'securitization' more closely, considering meanings of security, the normative underpinnings of securitization theory, and what 'successful' securitization entails. The third part tackles the question of what kind of 'theory' securitization theory is, paying particular attention to the distinction between a theory and a theoretical framework, and how securitization theory can be applied to different empirical cases.

The theory of securitization: the basics

The notion of securitization captures the performative power politics of the concept 'security' and has shown how issues acquire the status of security through intersubjective socio-political processes. Although many things can threaten the existence of valued referent objects, such threats do not come with labels – they require political action to gain the deontic rights, duties, obligations, requirements, and authorizations that come about by 'performing and getting others to accept' (Searle 2011: 85) securitization speech acts. The aim of securitization studies is to gain an increasingly precise understanding of who (securitizing actors) can securitize (political moves via speech acts) which issues (threats), for whom (referent objects), why (perlocutionary intentions/how-causality), with what kinds of effects (inter-unit relations), and under what conditions (facilitation/impediment factors) (Vuori 2011a: 7).[1]

Securitization theory was an answer to the broadening and deepening debates about security in the late 1980s; it is possible to widen the study of security without rendering everything as security by fixing on the form of security speech and by viewing security as a status and modality. For Ole Wæver, the original developer of securitization theory (Wæver 1989a, 1995), 'one could "throw the net" across all sectors and all actors and still not drag in everything with the catch, only the security part' (Wæver 2011: 469). This was achievable through a focus on particular speech acts, where securitizing actors claimed existential threats to valued referent objects so that audiences would accept, or at least not oppose, extraordinary measures that would otherwise not be acquiesced.

Such social construction of threats, and remedies for them, was considered an effective means to gain legitimacy for unpalatable policies that broke the rules of everyday politics. In this sense, the approach combines the study of what securitization does (what it 'triggers') with political constellations, or who or what does securitization (what 'triggers' it) (Guzzini 2011: 336–7). The effects of securitization on society, process, and polity can be studied in three stages (Wæver 2014: 28), where

1. Aspirations of actors are related to societal conditions;
2. Political codifications that constitute particular relationships are analysed through speech act theory;
3. Effects on political, legal, and socio-psychological life are examined.

The theory of securitization models the way we have learned to understand what security is and what counts as security, as well as how something becomes security and what security does. The theory allows for different kinds of analysis of the distinct political move: the 'causal analysis' of its consequences, the 'sociological analysis of social patterns that condition political possibilities', and the political theorization of 'life under different arrangements' (Wæver 2014: 31). In this way, the notion of securitization denotes the process of creating social facts, statuses, and modalities of security. The model contains several important elements (Buzan et al. 1998): the general script or plot of security entails priority and utmost importance of the particular issue; the existence of a valued referent object is at stake and under threat. The model as such has seven variables:[2]

1. A securitizing actor (that which or who makes the move towards a new, or to alter an existing, issue of security in accordance with particular conventions and grammars);
2. A referent object (that which is to be secured);
3. A threat (that which threatens the referent object);
4. An audience (the necessary relation needed to produce the deontic modality of security or those who have to be 'convinced' for securitization to be satisfied);
5. Felicity conditions (rules and conventions of the speech act and its consequences);
6. Facilitation factors (factors that can facilitate or impede the acceptance of the securitization move; social conditions that relate to social positions of the actor and audience as well as the threat);
7. Functional actors (actors that are neither the securitizing actor, the threat, nor the referent object, but still have some bearing on the process).

The model has *speech act theory* at its core: the theory of securitization 'was built from the start on speech act theory, because it is an operative method' (Wæver 2014: 27). This is an opportune foundation for a theory of social construction, as speech acts are taken to be the basic form of human communicative interaction in speech act theory (Searle and Vanderveken 1985). The basic idea here is that people do things by talking, that they perform different kinds of acts by speaking (Austin 1975).[3] Language is not used merely to convey information; it is for example used to explain (assertives), order (directives), threaten (comissives), thank (expressives), and declare things, e.g. war (declarations) (Searle and Vanderveken 1985). Such acts can be analysed through three types or aspects of speech acts (Austin 1975):

- Locutionary (an act *of* saying something with a sense and a reference);
- Illocutionary (an act *in* saying something);
- Perlocutionary (an act *by* saying something).

Speech act theory suggests that people interact with the language they use by infusing it with illocutionary forces, which are used to produce (perlocutionary) effects in other people that can affect the feelings, attitudes, and subsequent behaviour of the hearer(s). Such forces have broader universality across languages than certain verbs of a particular language. Yet illocutions, unlike perlocutions, are conventional: they are done conforming to conventions that are historicized and dependent on social and cultural factors (Austin 1975).[4]

What is securitization?

Securitization as a keyword or notion has become very enticing, even to the degree that it is used in articles to do things without any references to the securitization studies literature. There seems to be something self-explanatory in the term as such, which may partly explain some of the confusion in the critical literature on it. Other alternative terms that engage similar phenomena, such as security framing or threat politics, do not appear to have the same appeal as securitization. Intuitively, securitization is about how security comes about.

As such, security means different things to different societies, as the core fears of any group or nation are unique and relate to vulnerabilities and historical experiences (Wæver 1989b: 301). Yet, despite this historical contingency, security tends to be portrayed as something 'good', as being or feeling safe from harm or danger, which corresponds with its everyday (non-expert) meaning as something of positive value. Perhaps paradoxically, in the realm of international politics, security is often understood as a more negative concern, since it is about blocking unwanted developments. Concomitantly, security arguments in effect reproduce insecurities; security arguments tend to promise more than they can deliver.

Securitization and the 'negative' side of security

Securitization studies have highlighted this negative side of security and participated in elucidating how, rather than being positive or good for all, the increase of security for some means its sacrifice for others. Some have suggested that this kind of a critical view entails an 'escape' from security as such. Yet the approach does not aim at a 'rejection' of security altogether, but merely to make security speech unable 'to function in the harmonious self-assured standard-discourse of realism' (Wæver 1989a: 38). Rather than a total escape from security, the point is to alter 'security' from the inside by unmasking its operative logic and stripping away its innocent appeal. Such a 'cynical' (Wæver 1989a: 52) or 'sceptical' (Wæver 2012a: 53) view of security turns security issues into political ones, and makes their theorization 'critical'. The intention is to handle security problems by revealing their contingent nature and open them up for the evaluation of political responsibility.

The normative push and political recommendation of such an approach is 'less security, more politics' and the development of 'possible modalities' for the desecuritization[5] of politics (Wæver 1989a: 52): it is generally (which can only be assessed in practice though) more conducive to treat identities as identities, religion as religion, the environment as the environment, and so on, and to engage their politics through the particular modalities and rationalities of those fields rather than those of security. This however does not entail a preference for insecurity: security is a situation where there is a threat with measures against it, whereas insecurity is a situation where there is a threat and no certain measures to counteract it (Wæver 1995: 56). What is desirable is desecuritization, which leads back to (or keeps an issue within; Bourbeau and Vuori 2015) a-security or non-security – a situation where there is no threat and thus no need for restrictive measures.

Such preferences link up with visions of the political and of politics (Huysmans 2014). In terms of how politics is understood and what kinds of political effects the theory of securitization has, there have been multiple positions: those that take politics as the production of meaning, those that treat it as a modern institutional organization, and those that view it as ethical science (Gad and Petersen 2011). For Wæver (2011: 470), the theory of securitization combines a Schmittian concept of security with an Arendtian concept of politics, as it is 'strung between Schmittian (anti)political exceptions and an Arendtian co-creation' (Greenwood and Wæver 2013: 501). In other words, 'the political conception of securitization theory is *inspired by Arendt, implemented through speech act theory*' (Wæver 2014: 27, emphasis in original). This means that while security tends to produce a depoliticizing effect, political and social contexts cannot close off securitization or desecuritization. While many security issues and policies are path-dependent (Bourbeau 2014), there is always a possibility that something unexpected will take place. This is why scholars and theories should not explain away the openness and 'in-betweenness' of politics (Wæver 2014).

The preference for less security and more politics stems from the particular security politics of the late 1980s in Europe: to speak about national security did particular things that were problematic in light of democracy (and has continued to do so, even as the claimed threats have changed). Accordingly, part and parcel of securitization studies has been the genealogical study of how security has come to have such performative power (Wæver 1989a: 14, 2012b, Stritzel and Vuori 2016). Indeed, security has not had a uniform meaning or power even in Europe.

The contemporary usage dates to the early-to-mid twentieth century when 'national security' combined two favourable notions, and became political vogue after the Second World War. In the US, 'reasons of state' combined with sovereign immunity had meant that any state documents could be deemed secret and there was no possibility to sue the state. By restricting state secrets to issues of national security, what the new illocutionary power of security did politically was to limit and specify state power. It is at this conjunction that 'speaking security' began to do things it had not done before (Wæver 2012b); the previous speech acts of 'national interest' and 'necessity' ceased to work as effectively while 'security' attained a new (illocutionary) force and entailed a new kind of status transformation with concomitant deontic rights, responsibilities, and political functions. It is because of such features that securitization (and not security as such) can be considered a 'speech act' (Wæver 1989a, 1995, Vuori 2011a). If securitization moves are successful, the speaker is able to 'break the rules' (i.e., the regular deontic rights and responsibilities of a particular field) that normally constrict behaviour and policies, and shift the issue into the depoliticized area of utmost priority and urgency – to the high politics of survival.[6]

Successful securitization and its consequences

What 'success' means has been one point of contestation within securitization studies. Views have differed between whether it is enough to garner potential support for security measures, or whether actual measures need to be implemented. An 'if {a,b,c}, then securitization happens, and with it the defined effects {x, y, z}, typically involving some exceptional measures' causal diagram of securitization (Patomäki 2014) is, however, problematic in Wæver's (2014) view. This is because securitization is neither necessary, nor sufficient, to achieve 'security' understood as a policy or some means to repel an existential threat: threat perceptions, securitizations, and security actions are indeterminate (see Vuori 2011a: 136–40 for the full argument). Yet, various combinations of these three variables entail different costs for decision makers or securitizing actors.

For example, security action without legitimization in the form of securitization may be costly in terms of trust or popular support. Indeed, securitization is akin to raising a bet (Wæver 1995: 80), not in the sense of betting being a speech act, but in securitization raising the political stakes of an issue to a principled level of survival, or some other most vital interest (Wæver 1989a: 43). Even successful securitization has its costs: securitization is a 'political move because it has a price' (Wæver 1989a: 45). The difference between betting and securitization becomes apparent with the realization that it is impossible to make a bet without betting, but it is possible to do security without securitization speech acts. Thus, the core point of interest is the intersubjective establishment of a security status for an issue: threat perceptions, whether something is really a threat, or measures to bring about security are not the main concern, even though they may be of interest in the overall investigation that follows an examination of securitization.[7]

This is why it is necessary to separate 'success' as the 'happiness' or 'satisfaction' of securitization speech acts (i.e. securitization moves) and the concomitant status transformation of an issue (if the moves have such an effect) from the 'success' of the politics of securitizing something: happy securitization and the establishment of a security issue may yet lead to very unfortunate political outcomes. At the same time, securitization speech acts can always fail: securitization is 'equally constituted by its possible success and its possible failure – one is not primary and the other derived' (Wæver 1989a: 45).[8] Success relates to how the audience is conceptualized (Balzacq 2005, Léonard and Kaunert 2011).

In theoretical terms, securitization reconfigures the (necessary) relationship of the speaker and audience (Wæver 2014: 29). Here, the audience has to be such that this reconfiguration can provide the speaker with what the particular strand of securitization (Vuori 2008, 2011a) seeks to gain in terms of deontological modalities and statuses: securitization can be about raising an issue onto the agenda, legitimating future or past acts, control, or deterrence. In practical terms, successes and failures of such acts are on a continuum (as in speech act theory): it is highly unlikely that entire audiences will ever be fully and uniformly convinced by any political speech acts, including securitization. Indeed, the questions of what suffices to bring about a security status transformation, and what counts as assuaging rhetoric that convinces people need to be distinguished. Someone (e.g., a leader of a social movement or opposition party) may convince thousands of the security status of an issue (with securitization moves to raise the issue onto the agenda, Vuori 2008, 2010) yet fail to gain a deontic status transformation for it. Indeed, audiences that grant moral support for security policies may differ from those that can grant deontic powers (Balzacq et al. 2015b).

What kind of theory is securitization theory?

As securitization is a theoretical notion, it becomes necessary to consider what kind of a theory the 'theory' of securitization is, or should be: a meta-theory, a philosophical theory, a constitutive or ontological theory, or an empirical theory (Balzacq and Guzzini 2014: 2–3). Different views on this have produced positions that argue for varying emphases. Which kind of an understanding of theory and which version is selected to guide the framework of a securitization study has a major heuristic bearing on how a particular study is conducted (Vuori 2014).

In the debate between linguistic/discursive and practice-oriented approaches some positions emphasize the technocratic mundane practices and techniques of security professionals that enact and modulate limits of the secure and insecure (e.g. Bigo 2002; Huysmans 2014), rather than the speech act spectacles of high politics. The positional divides have also been phrased as those between philosophical and sociological views (Balzacq 2011), where the latter focus on different aspects of the context and structures of securitization processes in a sociological vein while the original formulations of the theory were closer to a post-structuralist position that highlighted the performativity and creativity of speech acts, and contained both 'internal' and 'external' aspects in the 'event' of securitization (Stritzel 2007: 366).

The constitutive (Buzan and Hansen 2009: 215) approach has organized the theory around the illocutionary aspect of securitization as a transformative event where the relationship of rights and duties is reconfigured (Wæver 2014), while the non-positivist causal mechanism approach of interpretivist process-tracing has investigated the how-causality of why certain moves can be expected, some gain receptive audiences, and why certain action-complexes may follow from securitization (Guzzini 2011; Patomäki 2014). Finally, securitization has also been viewed as a theory of politics that allows for the combination of philosophical and sociological investigation (Williams 2014) as well as an ethical theory of security that can deem when securitization is justified (Floyd 2011).

If and when security is considered to be a social construction, would it not suffice to study such processes like any other social construction of X? Or, as such processes resemble framing (Watson 2012), could securitization not be studied as the framing of X? Is securitization not just 'an ideal-typical model of a particular and limited-scale social mechanism' (Patomäki 2014: 38), or 'a distinct theory of discourse' (Stritzel 2014: 51)? Why is there a need for a specific theory of securitization?

The theory of securitization is more than the framing of threat politics. Securitization theory is a theory of the event when a security status comes about, i.e., a theory about when the deontic modality or status function of an issue is transformed (which can be a very prolonged and gradual process).[9] Yet, the theory is about more than just the social mechanisms involved in such processes: Wæver's (1989a, 1995) project has been to produce a theory of the politics of speaking security, about the 'power politics of a concept' (Buzan et al. 1998: 32), which takes the approach beyond discourses and rhetoric 'to a theory of political co-production between multiple actors of social states' (Wæver 2014: 28). Political status transformations should be studied 'neither in or by single actors nor as socially determined and thereby unpolitical' (Wæver 2014: 28): 'politics is a sphere of re-presentation of the social – it is not the social, nor can it ever be' (Wæver 1989a: 11). Securitization as just the social construction, frame, or discourse of X would lose sight of the political aspects of securitization theory, which must be avoided even when the theory is combined with approaches to framing (e.g., Paltemaa and Vuori 2006), social mechanisms (Guzzini 2011), or resonant values and threat images (Stritzel 2007, 2014).

Theory or theoretical framework?

It is important here to distinguish between a theory and a theoretical framework, as it seems that the two have at times been confused in the various debates around securitization studies. Individual theories are often formulated to explain, predict, understand, or to criticize certain phenomena or social structures. But a 'theory on its own never predicts or explains' (Wæver 2014: 30); it is used as a basis for comparing empirical instances and to generate specific hypotheses; 'when theories are applied to the world, their elements require specification', and no conclusions of the social world can 'be derived from a theory in the absence of such intermediate steps' (Kaplan 2014: 52). Indeed, particular theories can be used to do many things in different situations. Theoretical frameworks on the other hand tend to be particular to individual studies or pieces of research. A framework can contain several theories and concepts, which together are used to deal with specific research aims, problems, and questions. Indeed, theoretical frameworks are generally not readily available in the literature, but need to be put together for particular studies.

That Buzan et al. (1998) precisely presented a ready-made framework for analysis rather than merely a singular theory may explain some of the success of the approach. Yet, it is not the only option for how to study securitization (e.g., Balzacq 2015b).[10] What is problematic is that elements of this particular framework are often assumed to be elements of the theory, and the proposal of a different framework is claimed to develop the core theory. However, to argue for the insertion of framework–elements into the theory is to confuse how theory development works. Every application of a theory is different, whereby each unique setup and empirical finding cannot claim to alter the theory.

The theory of securitization is general in the sense that it does not define particular sectors or levels of security, types of political actor that could bring about securitization, nor criteria for when securitization would be achieved in a practical sense.[11] The theory names the relations of the qualities of its various elements, but does not mention what these particular elements are, as this would 'reduce theory to an unlimited assembly of unrelated propositions' (Kaplan 2014: 56). When a theory 'is used to take real-world initial and boundary conditions into account, it directs attention to the most relevant factors' (Kaplan 2014: 188). But, the identification of practically relevant conditions is the task of the applier of the theory. Initial conditions (like features of the political system where the study takes place) and boundary conditions (like domestic and international political situations and historical events) affect what is existentially valuable, the plausibility of linking threats and referent objects, and whether security issues can be dismantled.[12] Yet, we have to keep in mind that such conditions cannot close the success and failure of securitization off: securitization is a political process, and not purely a social mechanism.

Varied applications of securitization theory/frameworks

While securitization studies with its various frameworks and research designs allow for great variation in types of questions and inquiries, it is important to maintain the corporate identity of the core theory. This can be achieved by keeping the philosophical (Balzacq 2011) or illocutionary theory (Wæver 2014) of securitization as the core, and by adding other elements (e.g., sociological approaches) into a framework of research that is guided by this theory (e.g. Vuori 2011a, 2011b). In other words, once we have thrown in the net of securitization theory, we can trace processes and examine effects, but these are part of the framework of particular studies that are guided by specific research questions and problems.

Securitization studies contains a number of relevant questions that may not all be answerable in each and every situation with the same research design: for example, not all political systems operate in the same way, which makes different actors relevant, and may have implications for the kinds of research materials that are available or can be produced for investigation (Vuori 2014). The theory has to be translated for each particular study as part of its framework. To use a theoretical model in empirical research is to contextualize it: 'all theories are analogues when applied to the world' (Kaplan 2014: 48), and no process of securitization is identical to another. Indeed, it does not make sense to include all the variety of political and social situations that exist in a theory of securitization. This is why it is necessary for an applier of a general theory to take the initial and boundary conditions into account when the theory is used to do research. For example, so-called external facilitation factors are boundary conditions that cannot be predefined in the theory; 'Boundary conditions that limit the scope of a theory are not part of the axiomatic account of a theory' (Kaplan 2014: 62).

Similarly important is not to stretch the concept of securitization. While the theory was developed for specific purposes (desecuritization) in a particular place (Europe) in a particular time (late Cold War), it was intended for application around the world (Wæver 1989a: 26).[13] The problem is that one cannot move from a general definition of securitization to the criticism of securitization in a particular society by simply adjusting for context: 'the meanings of the concepts that are employed depend upon how they are incorporated in a system' (Kaplan 2014: 98). If this is ignored, the original concept will become 'stretched'. The introduction of 'strands of securitization' (Vuori 2008, 2011a) that are derived from illocutionary logic, i.e. the logic of the operative theory at the heart of securitization theory, actually develop the theory of securitization (rather than present another framework) in a way that allows for broader empirical investigation without stretching the concept.

Neither the contexts nor the purposes of theories remain static; rather, they change with each application. The question then is not only who initially developed a theory and for which purpose, but who uses it, where, and for what purpose. Theories have politics installed in their set-ups, but these become effectual in their application to particular instances (Wæver 2011: 469). This requires reflection and careful consideration on the part of the applier of a theory (Vuori 2014).

Conclusion

This handbook-entry has not done justice to all the numerous debates within securitization studies. These debates, in addition to both critics' and originators' statements, indicate the academic success of this critical approach to security. Securitization studies have been multifaceted in what, where, and how issues of security have been investigated and critiqued. Some see this as resulting in a too contradictory whole (Stritzel 2014). It is therefore important to distinguish the core theory from the numerous studies with varying frameworks: a theory needs to have internal consistency, but its applications will always be unique in some aspect.

How politics is approached can serve as an example here. As argued above, the theory of securitization is partly a political and critical theory. Yet, not every applier will subscribe to the same political agenda: securitization studies contain different points and gradients of the approach (Hacking 1999; Vuori 2014). Different scholars abide by different theories of politics; some view politics as an activity, while others see it as an arena. It is possible to limit the theory of securitization to one theory of politics, as Wæver (2014) does with Arendt. But securitization theory can also be used to elucidate phenomena and practices in accordance with a variety of approaches to politics. This is made possible by a minimal core theory and an adaptive combination of other features in a broader framework for each particular study.

For example, the speech act approach to securitization can be used to investigate how identities are produced in processes of securitization, yet it can also be used to investigate how securitization operates in bureaucratic battles of resource allocation. That there is variety in the elements and aims of theoretical frameworks within securitization studies means that all such elements need to be carefully reflected on when designing research. Indeed, such frameworks and studies need to display plurality, because a single theory cannot answer all the questions of interest critical scholars pose in regard to security.

Notes

1 For original questions, see Buzan et al. 1998: 32.
2 These formulations differ somewhat from the original ones (Buzan et al. 1998) and they represent a synthesis of various criticisms (e.g. Balzacq 2005; Stritzel 2007; Vuori 2011a; Wæver 2014).
3 Yet the theory is not limited to speech: for example non-verbal communication and visual images can also be used to commit speech acts. Accordingly, 'visual securitization' has become its own strand of investigation within securitization studies (for a review, see Andersen et al. 2015).
4 Different interpretations and versions of speech act theory have a bearing on securitization studies debates too. Most prominently, Thierry Balzacq (2005), by drawing on Bourdieu and Habermas, presents securitization as a 'pragmatic' or strategic act that aims to influence audiences in favour of the securitizing actor, whereas Wæver (2011, 2014), drawing on Sbisá, considers securitization an illocutionary act that has conventional effects. Vuori (2011a: 164) argues that some strands of securitization have conventional effects or consequences while others do not.
5 Space does not allow for a proper treatment of desecuritization, which has become a strand of its own within securitization studies (see e.g. Hansen 2012). This literature has mainly focused on three sets of questions: what counts as desecuritization (identification of the phenomenon), why should there be desecuritization (ethics and normativity), and how can desecuritization be achieved (transformative practice) (Balzacq et al. 2015a).
6 The more sociological approaches have emphasized the mundane everydayness of security practices and techniques (Bigo 2002; Huysmans 2014) as well as the possibility of security practice remaining below issues of survival (Balzacq 2011). Securitization may come about in the exceptional manner of high politics, but it can also be produced diffusely through techniques, technologies, and practices (Huysmans 2014).
7 E.g. was securitization justified (Floyd 2011), what were its inter-unit effects (Caballero–Anthony et al. 2006), how can the process be traced within a polity (Léonard and Kaunert 2011).
8 Although securitization studies have been interested in the failure of securitization, in, e.g., the GDR in 1989 (Wæver 1995), from the start there has been a selection bias towards successful securitization in empirical investigations (Salter 2011).
9 Securitizations that consist of singular speech act situations are quite specific and need to be strongly codified (Guzzini 2011: 335). Indeed, strands of securitization that have conventional effects or consequences tend to be codified into laws (Vuori 2011a: 164). The approach does not preclude the study of gradual processes (Vuori 2010).
10 Particularly if the research interest concerns expert routines (Bigo 2002) or everyday enactments (Huysmans 2014) of security rather than politics at a 'principled' international level (Wæver 1989a).
11 'Different initial conditions produce differences in types of systems' (Kaplan 2014: 160), whereby the initial conditions of securitization in a democratic or a dictatorial political system are different (which is also pointed to by empirical appliers, e.g., Jackson 2006; Wilkinson 2007). If securitization theory was a systems theory, the result would be comparative theories of securitization in different political systems, rather than a general theory of securitization. We would for example have a democratic, a dictatorial, a revolutionary (yet, see Holbaard and Pedersen 2012), an authoritarian, and a totalitarian theory of securitization, or a theory of securitization for each sector and level of security (yet, see Buzan and Wæver 2009), or even for each particular state.
12 See Hayes (2013: 4–7) for a discussion of boundary conditions in relation to securitization studies.
13 The issue of 'theory travel' (Vuori 2014), and which kinds of problems the application of the approach to non-European socio-political contexts produces is another example of debates in securitization studies. Beyond the issue of theoretical application in different contexts, the varying distal and proximate contexts of securitization (Balzacq 2011) in terms of resonant values (Stritzel 2007), on- and back-stage discussions of experts (Salter 2008), and translation of threat images (Stritzel 2014) have also been discussed.

References

Andersen, R. S., Vuori, J. A., and Mutlu, C. E. (2015) 'Visuality', in C. Aradau, J. Huysmans, A. Neal, and N. Voelkner (eds.) *Critical Security Methods: New Frameworks for Analysis*, New York and London: Routledge, 85–117.
Austin, J. L. (1975[1962]) *How to Do Things with Words*, Oxford: Oxford University Press.

Balzacq, T. (2005) 'The Three Faces of Securitization: Political Agency, Audience and Context', *European Journal of International Relations* 11(4): 171–201.

Balzacq, T. (2011) 'A Theory of Securitization: Origins, Core Assumptions, and Variants', in T. Balzacq (ed.) *Securitization Theory: How Security Problems Emerge and Dissolve*, London and New York: Routledge, 1–30.

Balzacq, T. and Guzzini, S. (2014) 'Introduction: "What Kind of Theory – If Any– Is Securitization?"', *International Relations*, OnlineFirst (October), 2–7.

Balzacq, T., Depauw, S., and Léonard, S. (2015a) 'The Political Limits of Desecuritization: Security, Arms Trade, and the EU's Economic Targets', in T. Balzacq (ed.) *Contesting Security: Strategies and Logics*, London and New York: Routledge.

Balzacq, T., Léonard, S., and Ruzicka, J. (2015b) '"Securitization" Revisited: Theory and Cases', *International Relations*, OnlineFirst: 1–38.

Bigo, D. (2002) 'Security and Immigration: Toward a Critique of the Governmentality of Unease', *Alternatives* 27(1): 63–92.

Bourbeau, P. (2014) 'Moving Forward Together: Logics of the Securitisation Process', *Millennium – Journal of International Studies* 43(1): 187–206.

Bourbeau, P. and Vuori, J. A. (2015) 'Security, Resilience, and Desecuritization: Multidirectional Moves and Dynamics', *Critical Studies of Security* 3(3): 1–16.

Buzan, B. and Hansen, L. (2009) *The Evolution of International Security Studies*, Cambridge: Cambridge University Press.

Buzan, B. and Wæver, O. (2009) 'Macrosecuritization and Security Constellations: Reconsidering Scale in Securitization Theory', *Review of International Studies* 35(2): 253–76.

Buzan, B., Wæver O. and de Wilde, J. (1998) *Security: A New Framework for Analysis*, Boulder, CO: Lynne Rienner.

Caballero-Anthony, M., Emmers, R., and Acharya, A. (eds.) (2006) *Non-Traditional Security in Asia: Dilemmas in Securitisation*, Aldershot: Ashgate.

Floyd, R. (2011) 'Can Securitization Be Used in Normative Analysis? Towards Just Securitization Theory', *Security Dialogue* 42(4–5): 427–39.

Gad, U. P. and Petersen, K. L. (2011) 'Concepts of Politics in Securitization Studies', *Security Dialogue* 42(4–5): 315–28.

Greenwood, M. T. and Wæver, O. (2013) 'Copenhagen–Cairo on a Roundtrip: A Security Theory Meets the Revolution', *Security Dialogue* 44(5–6): 485–506.

Guzzini, Stefano (2011) 'Securitization as a Causal Mechanism', *Security Dialogue* 42(4–5): 329–41.

Hacking, I. (1999) *The Social Construction of What?*, Cambridge, MA: Harvard University Press.

Hansen, L. (2012) 'Reconstructing Desecuritisation: The Normative-Political in the Copenhagen School and Directions for How to Apply It', *Review of International Studies* 38(6): 525–46.

Hayes, J. (2013) *Constructing National Security: US Relations with India and China*, New York: Cambridge University Press.

Holbaard, M. and Pedersen, M. A. (2012) 'Revolutionary Securitization: an Anthropological Extension of Securitization Theory', *International Theory* 4(2): 165–97.

Huysmans, J. (2014) *Security Unbound: Enacting Democratic Limits*, London and New York: Routledge.

Jackson, N. J. (2006) 'International Organizations, Security Dichotomies and the Trafficking of Persons and Narcotics in Post-Soviet Central Asia: A Critique of the Securitization Framework', *Security Dialogue* 37(3): 299–317.

Kaplan, M. A. (2014) *Transcending Postmodernism,* Houndmills and New York: Palgrave.

Katzenstein, P. J. (ed.) (1996) *The Culture of National Security: Norms and Identity in World Politics*, New York: Columbia University Press.

Léonard, S. and Kaunert, C. (2011) 'Reconceptualizing the Audience in Securitization Theory', in T. Balzacq (ed.) *Securitization Theory: How Security Problems Emerge and Dissolve*, London and New York: Routledge, 57–76.

Paltemaa, L. and Vuori, J. A. (2006) 'How Cheap Is Identity Talk? A Framework of Identity Frames and Security Discourse for the Analysis of Repression and Legitimization of Social Movements in Mainland China', *Issues and Studies* 42(3): 47–86.

Patomäki, H. (2014) 'Absenting the Absence of Future Dangers and Structural Transformations in Securitization Theory', *International Relations*, OnlineFirst (October), 33–40.

Salter, M. B. (2008) 'Securitization and Desecuritization: A Dramaturgical Analysis of the Canadian Air Transport Security Authority', *Journal of International Relations and Development* 11(4): 321–49.

Salter, M. B. (2011) 'When Securitization Fails: The Hard Case of Counter-Terrorism Programs', in T. Balzacq (ed.) *Securitization Theory: How Security Problems Emerge and Dissolve*, London and New York: Routledge, 116–31.

Sbisà, M. (1999) 'Act', *Journal of Linguistic Anthropology* 9(1–2): 9–11.

Searle, J. R. (2011[2010]) *Making the Social World: The Structure of Human Civilization*, Oxford: Oxford University Press.

Searle, J. R. and Vanderveken, D. (1985) *Foundations of Illocutionary Logic*, Cambridge: Cambridge University Press.

Stritzel, H. (2007) 'Towards a Theory of Securitization: Copenhagen and Beyond', *European Journal of International Relations* 13(3): 357–83.

Stritzel, H. (2014) *Security in Translation: Securitization Theory and the Localization of Threat*, Houndmills and New York: Palgrave.

Stritzel, H. and Vuori, J. A. (2016) 'Security', in F. Berenskoetter (ed.) *Concepts of World Politics*, Thousand Oaks: Sage.

Vuori, J. A. (2008) 'Illocutionary Logic and Strands of Securitisation: Applying the Theory of Securitisation to the Study of Non-Democratic Political Orders', *European Journal of International Relations* 14(1): 65–99.

Vuori, J. A. (2010) 'A Timely Prophet? The Doomsday Clock as a Visualization of Securitization Moves with a Global Referent Object', *Security Dialogue* 41(3): 255–77.

Vuori, J. A. (2011a) *How to Do Security with Words: A Grammar of Securitisation in the People's Republic of China*, Turku: University of Turku Press.

Vuori, J. A. (2011b) 'Religion Bites: Falungong, Securitization/Desecuritization in the People's Republic of China', in T. Balzacq (ed.) *Securitization Theory: How Security Problems Emerge and Dissolve*, London and New York: Routledge, 186–211.

Vuori, J. A. (2014) *Critical Security and Chinese Politics. The Anti-Falungong Campaign*, London and New York: Routledge.

Wæver, O. (1989a) 'Security and the Speech Act: Analysing the Politics of a Word', *Working Paper No. 1989/19*, Copenhagen: Centre for Peace and Conflict Research.

Wæver, O. (1989b) 'Conflicts of Vision – Visions of Conflict', in O. Wæver, P. Lemaitre, and E. Tromer (eds.) *European Polyphony: Perspectives beyond East–West Confrontation*, London: MacMillan, 283–325.

Wæver, O. (1995) 'Securitization and Desecuritization', in R. D. Lipschutz (ed.) *On Security*, New York: Columbia University Press, 46–86.

Wæver, O. (2011) 'Politics, Security, Theory', *Security Dialogue* 42(4–5): 465–80.

Wæver, O. (2012a) 'Aberystwyth, Paris, Copenhagen: The Europeanness of New "Schools" of Security Theory in an American Field', in A. B. Tickner and D. L. Blaney (eds.) *Thinking International Relations Differently*, London and New York: Routledge, 48–71.

Wæver, O. (2012b) 'Security: A Conceptual History for International Relations', Paper Presented at the History of the Concept of 'Security': from the Roman Republic to the Risk Society of Today Conference, 26–28 November 2012, organized by the Centre for Advanced Security Theory.

Wæver, O. (2014) 'The Theory Act: Responsibility and Exactitude as Seen from Securitization', *International Relations*, OnlineFirst (October), 26–32.

Watson, S. D. (2012) '"Framing" the Copenhagen School: Integrating the Literature on Threat Construction', *Millennium – Journal of International Studies* 40(2): 279–301.

Wilkinson, C. (2007) 'The Copenhagen School on Tour in Kyrgyzstan: Is Securitization Theory Useable outside Europe?', *Security Dialogue* 38(5): 5–25.

Williams, M. C. (2014) 'Securitization as Political Theory: The Politics of the Extraordinary', *International Relations*, OnlineFirst (October), 19–25.

7

POSTSTRUCTURALIST APPROACHES TO SECURITY

Claudia Aradau and Rens van Munster

Since the early 1990s, the field of Security Studies has witnessed the growth of poststructuralist approaches to security (Buzan and Hansen 2009). Drawing largely on ideas and concepts from political theory, continental philosophy, and sociology, poststructuralist approaches have inspired an understanding of security not as 'a noun that names things' but 'as a principle of formation that does things' (Dillon 1996: 16), where the central objective is not to define what security is but to interrogate security as a form of productive power that makes reality intelligible and actionable in particular ways. The central point of departure in poststructuralist approaches to security is that representations of threats define the relationship between self and other as antagonistic, which in turn justifies violent practices and calls for the restriction of democratic principles and political agency. For these reasons, poststructuralists are generally critical of security and instead want to stimulate a wider process of reflection and action leading to different understandings of social and political relations, which do not imply a self/other antagonism. One of the main concerns for poststructuralist thinkers has therefore been how to resist security, unmake its practices, and challenge its exclusionary logic (Huysmans 2014).

This chapter aims to provide a broad (although necessarily simplified) account of the ways in which the poststructuralist literature has engaged the question of security. We begin with a brief discussion of the poststructuralist problematization of Security Studies as a field of knowledge that undergirds and legitimizes a range of violent practices enacted in the name of the sovereign state. We then go on to consider how poststructuralists have conceptualized and theorized security as a form of productive power. First, we turn to understandings of security as a sovereign form of power. Here, poststructuralists have drawn upon the work of Carl Schmitt and especially that of Giorgio Agamben to suggest that practices of security constitute political community by delineating friend and enemy. Second, we examine poststructuralist understandings of security that are based on Michel Foucault's work on governmentality and biopolitics. These scholars have pointed out that security does not just concern the sovereign decision upon the enemy, but also the biopolitical question of managing the well-being and life chances of populations. Here, the power of security lies in its potential to inscribe limits, divisions, and hierarchies between different categories of the population. Concerned with the violence and insecurity that security fosters in the constitution of political communities, the final section focuses on poststructuralist challenges to security and points to the different ways in which security practices are resisted and their power unmade.

Challenging Security Studies: discourse, power, materiality

'The most far-reaching contribution of post-structural approaches to security', writes Anthony Burke (2013: 77), 'is to have brought the very idea of security under critical scrutiny'. Until the mid-1980s, Security Studies as a field had predominantly understood security as the defence of the state against the threat of other states under conditions of anarchy. Security was conceptualized as national security and intimately linked to the study of war and peace (for an overview, see Buzan and Hansen 2009).

Poststructuralists increasingly took issue with these assumptions and pointed out that they rested on particular ontological and epistemological foundations. Drawing on post-positivist approaches to science, they claimed that knowledge produced in Security Studies should not be taken for objective reflections on reality 'out there'; rather, analyses of security were said to partake in the very constitution and reification of social reality. Our access to the world is mediated through interpretative practices, including scientific ones, which in turn shape the social reality on the basis of which actors understand and behave towards themselves and each other. Security is effectively a 'regime of truth' whose emergence and stabilization is made possible through the reiteration of (scientific) discourses, the deployment of power relations, and mobilization of methods.

The attribution of insecurity to certain individuals or groups, places or activities happens only through historical processes, discourses, and practices. Moreover, these ascriptions of danger have performative power, and they come to inscribe social and political relations, subjectivities, and institutions. Poststructuralists both explore the conditions under which it is possible to make authoritative claims about security and the effects of such claims on reality. They have drawn attention to the mutual constitution of self and other through the antagonistic logic of war and foreign policy (Campbell 1992; Hansen 2006). Security discourses depend upon and sustain particular representations of the world. David Campbell's (1992) study of American foreign policy and identity has explored how discourses of danger divide the world between a clear inside and outside, where identity is located within the political community with security practices attempting to exclude difference, heterogeneity, and otherness.

Since security cannot be thought about without a prior account of what entity or political community needs securing, representations of threat and insecurity are also always political statements about the desirable nature of the political community (Walker 1997). In his seminal analysis of strategic studies, Bradley Klein (1994) forcefully showed how that field, by taking the state as its 'natural' point of departure, actively contributed to the process of state formation while reproducing an image of the international arena as an anarchic system of states where security can only be achieved at the expense of other states' security. It presupposes trust and identity between members of a community, while it relegates indeterminacy, fear, and anarchy outside the social order.

The performative power of security emerges not just through discursive practices, but also through particular methods of knowledge production. Poststructuralist analyses have tended to focus on discourse and power, but more recently materiality has been shown to undergird questions of truth, security, and politics. The distinction between discourse and materiality has been the subject of much writing in social sciences and has informed poststructuralist approaches as well (e.g. Coole and Frost 2010; Lundborg and Vaughan-Williams 2014). The main focus has been on how security not just enacts sociality but also materiality in particular ways. For instance, critical infrastructure protection assumes a stable materiality and silences debates about decaying infrastructure and privatization of infrastructure under neoliberalism (Aradau 2010). At the same time, materiality has underpinned discussions of methods. The focus on methods – e.g. graphs, visualizations, diagrams, and statistics – as inscription devices shows that method debates are as much about politics as knowledge-making (Aradau and Huysmans 2014). It is the authority of statistics that allows 'professional *managers* of unease' to produce a regime of truth about what constitutes security and what not (see Bigo 2006).

The next two sections offer a brief overview of how poststructuralist approaches have analysed security as a regime of truth underpinned by particular power relations.

Security, sovereign power, and exceptionalism

Poststructuralist approaches have reformulated the relation between security and the sovereign. Instead of deriving security from a taken-for-granted *raison d'état*, these approaches have shown how sovereignty and security are co-constitutive. This understanding of security has drawn on the work of the Copenhagen School, which defines security as a speech act by means of which an actor presents an issue as an existential threat that justifies extraordinary measures to neutralize that threat (Buzan, Wæver and de Wilde 1998). Upon this view, security is a modality that elevates issues above politics and everyday haggling by investing them with a sense of intensity and urgency.

This definition shares important traits with Schmitt's rendering of the political as the exceptional decision that constitutes the border between friend and enemy (Huysmans 1998; Williams 2003). According to Schmitt, this situation is best captured by the metaphor of 'war', for although war need not be actually present between friends and enemies, 'the ever present possibility of combat' grounds the domain of the political and constitutes the authentic self-delineation of a political community (Schmitt 1996: 32).

Agamben's (1998, 2005) reworking of the state of exception has inspired many poststructuralists to further develop our understanding of security as sovereign power. First, his work adds the important insight that the state of exception does not just produce sovereignty but also its mirror image of bare life, i.e. life that can be killed with impunity. Underpinned by sovereign power, security is understood as an exceptional practice that draws boundaries between political life (*bios*) and abject, disqualified, or bare life (*zoe*). For Agamben, the concentration camp exemplifies the space where we find the most extreme form of bare life, in as far as prisoners do not enjoy legal protection against the atrocities of the guards who act as sovereigns.

Agamben's observations have informed a range of analyses of the war on terror and contemporary security policies. The war in Iraq (Diken and Laustsen 2005; van Munster 2004), refugee camps and airport holding zones (Noll 2003; Salter 2008), humanitarian intervention (Dauphinée and Masters 2007; Edkins, Pin-Fat, and Shapiro 2004), detention centres of terrorist suspects (Neal 2006), shoot-to-kill policies of the London police (Vaughan–Williams 2007) have all been recognized as exceptional practices by means of which the life of some people is reduced to that of bare life. Second, Agamben's work points to the antagonistic relationship between democracy and security on the one hand and law and security on the other. For Agamben, the state of exception is explicitly linked with fascism, which raises the profound question to what extent security practices instil forms of non-democratic politics at the heart of contemporary liberal societies based on the rule of law (see e.g. Bigo and Tsoukala 2008; Honig 2009).

Despite its wide application in poststructuralist approaches, Agamben's theory of the exception has been criticized for offering a simplified and ahistorical picture of security. Whatever the spatial and temporal transformations of practices, security is ultimately always found to constitute a binary relation of inclusion/exclusion, friend/enemy, democracy/state of exception and *bios/ zoe*. The understanding of security as something exceptional, however, downplays other, more routine forms of power and knowledge. Vivienne Jabri (2006) has argued that the metaphor of 'war' associated with security has become a transnational strategy of control that targets states, communities, and individuals. Rather than referring to a generalized state of affairs, the state of exception is inscribed differently upon various sectors of society and experienced differently by particular categories of populations.

Similarly, Didier Bigo (2002, 2006), who focuses on the security experts that manage 'unease' within society on a daily basis, points out that exceptional security practices can be understood in the context of ongoing processes of bureaucratic and market-driven routinization. Moreover, recent analyses of exceptional spaces show that even these are not devoid of agency, rules, and regulation. For instance, Guantánamo Bay is imbued with knowledge and technologies of governance: from ration cards and hygiene education to psychological therapy. They are not empty spaces of 'bare life', as they are governed by bureaucratic technologies and regulations that are often reminiscent of practices with a distinct colonial or other political history (Johns 2005; Neal 2006). Rather than the limit of social and political relations, or the excluded inclusion of bare life, camps can be seen as veritable laboratories of governance, where particular technologies of governance are experimented with and deployed (e.g. Bulley 2014).

Governmentality and the biopolitics of security

Security practices are heterogeneous and historically variable. Poststructuralist scholars have particularly drawn on Michel Foucault's analyses of how different regimes of power function in heterogeneous ways that go beyond the sovereign question of territoriality and centralized legitimate authority. Foucault argues that during the eighteenth century sovereign power gradually transformed into and became complemented by new forms of power: discipline and biopolitics. Disciplinary power focuses on the individual, while biopolitics takes populations and their lives as the object of governance, while the advent of the biopolitical state brings about a change in the development of the modern state from the 'city-citizen' game to that of pastoral care of life and the living (Foucault 2007). A governmental mode of analysis unpacks security as a specific type of ordering of the *polis*, of governing circulation and managing populations. Biopolitics implies that security is neither a form of war nor a form of surveillance, as descriptions of the Panopticon have commonly held. As emphasized by Bigo, security as biopolitical 'is related to normality and liberty, not with war and survival, nor with coercion and surveillance' (Bigo 2008: 107).

In liberal societies security practices are directly related to the promotion and protection of the mobility and circulation of populations, goods, and services rather than the protection of territories (Dillon and Lobo-Guerrero 2008; Dillon and Reid 2001; Duffield 2007). This is not to say the boundaries are no longer relevant or that individuals and populations are not normalized. Practices of managing circulation and preventing risky events ultimately produce categories of individuals who are to be protected at the expense of the exclusion and elimination of others. As racial boundaries delimit and divide the life of the species between life worth living and life which is to be curtailed (Foucault 2004), security practices are exposed as *insecuring*, dividing categories of populations, and preparing some for elimination, disciplining or therapy. In Dillon's (2005: 41) words, the 'continuous biopolitical assaying of life proceeds through the epistemically driven and continuously changing interrogation of the worth and eligibility of the living across a terrain of value that is constantly changing'. The effects of security therefore need to be unpacked through concrete and historically situated analyses of practices.

The biopolitical management of populations also introduces a specific temporal element in the analyses of security. The governmentality of populations and the conjoint betterment of life already contained an implicit temporal element. Temporality becomes explicitly problematized when scenarios of danger concern the occurrence of events in the future life of populations and sovereignties. Security practices intervene to 'tame' the future and to recuperate the temporality of progress and linearity. Whether understood through statistical calculations of probability (Lobo-Guerrero 2007), scenarios of preparedness (Anderson 2010; Collier and Lakoff 2008; Lakoff 2006), speculation (de Goede 2012), or imaginations of catastrophe (Aradau and van Munster 2007, 2011), security practices do not only work upon space but also upon time and are increasingly turned towards unpredictable and unknowable futures. These anticipatory practices bear important political effects for law, rights claims, justice, and democracy, in that they reduce the importance of experience, memory, narratives of the past, evidence, and proof (de Goede and de Graaf 2013; Kessler 2011; Krasmann 2012).

Unmaking security

These various analyses diagnose the political effects of security as troubling. As an exceptional practice, security works against democracy, foretells of violence, and enacts exclusions. As a governmental and biopolitical practice, security is entwined with bureaucratic modes of regulation that divide life to be bettered from life less worth living. For many poststructuralists, the question of how security practices can be resisted or 'unmade' (Huysmans 2006) has emerged as an important question. Drawing on diverse strands of continental philosophy, they have offered diverging and sometimes competing answers. However, all approaches share an interest in transforming the relationship between self and other. For Rob Walker (1997: 78), a critical discourse about security depends upon 'emerging accounts of who we might become, and the conditions under which we might become other than we are now without destroying other, ourselves, or the planet on which we all live'. At least three approaches to unmaking of security can be discerned: ethics/responsibility, resistance/agency, and emancipation.

Ethics and responsibility

A first group of poststructuralist thinkers has sought to unmake security through the notion of ethics and responsibility. They stress the interdependence between self and other as crucial, because it undermines the exclusionary logic of security by pointing at the need to recognize the fundamental ambivalence, heterogeneity, and difference that contaminates all identities. Whereas discourses of danger portray the other as the condition of impossibility for the existence of a secure, homogeneous identity, these ethical positions stress that alterity is deeply enmeshed with the subject. Rather than homogeneous and separate, self and other are inextricably entwined. Upon this view, an '*ethical relation* in which our responsibility to the other is the basis for reflection' can replace the inimical and antagonistic relations that security brings about (Campbell and Shapiro 1999: x).

Lene Hansen (2006) has already drawn attention to the complexity of self/other relations and the degrees of difference that are constitutive of identity. But there are different ways in which poststructuralist authors have confirmed and sought to reformulate securitized relationships as radically interdependent. Some, like David Campbell, have drawn on the work of Derrida and Levinas. According to Levinas' philosophy, the ethical relationship with the other is defined by responsibility towards the other. Although security may define our relationship to the other in terms of abjection, violence, and domination, the structure of responsibility nevertheless summons us to recognize 'the structural condition of alterity prior to subjectivity and thought' (Campbell 1999: 41). Even if we can never fully respond to the calls of others at all times, the understanding of subjectivity in terms of responsibility helps us resist discourses of security that depend on the other's suppression and domination in favour of forms of belonging that respond to the ethical call of the other.

Judith Butler (2003: 15) comes to similar conclusions, but she grounds subjectivity in the practice of mourning and corporeal vulnerability: 'The body implies mortality, vulnerability, agency: the skin and the flesh expose us to the gaze of others, but also to touch, and to violence, and bodies put us at risk of becoming the agency and instrument of all these as well'. Bodily vulnerability experienced in the loss of the other's life (for example, as a result of disease, death, or violence) can have a transformative impact on the self who, constituted in relation to the other, no longer is the same after the loss. For Butler, the experience of fragility in the context of a loss is not just a private matter but a political principle around which to reinvent and rearticulate social ties on the basis of bodily suffering: 'To grieve, and to make grief itself into a resource for politics is not to be resigned to inaction, but it may be understood as the slow process by which we develop a point of identification with suffering itself' (Butler 2003: 19).

Both the principles of responsibility and mourning ethically reconfigure the antagonistic logic of security, in which the other is not encountered as grievable life but as an enemy who is not worth mourning over. The ethical imperative is to recognize vulnerability and to inquire and deconstruct into the social and political conditions by means of which some forms of life appear (non-)grievable. For example, Edkins' (2003) writings on trauma and Zehfuss' work (2007) on memory critically examine how traumatic events related to war and suffering have entered collective memory, pointing out the significance of remembering an identity that does not derive simply from the desire to secure oneself in the face of the other.

Resistance and agency

Poststructuralist approaches have sometimes been criticized for their quasi-exclusive concern with 'we', the subject. The 'other' is often envisaged as derivative of the constitution of 'us'. Different others succeed one another, subjected to the need of identity reproduction. In Campbell's analysis of how American identity is reproduced through re-writings of dangers, the others are 'faceless faces', substitutable to one another. The other only exists as a constitutive outside, as the limit to the domain of subjectivity. The weak or the other, Barkawi and Laffey (2006) argue, appear as only bearers of rights and objects of emancipation rather than wilful agents.

By focusing on the '"unliveable" and "uninhabitable" zones of social life which are nevertheless populated by those who do not enjoy the status of the subject' (Butler 1993: 3), several scholars have attempted to recuperate the other as something more than a blank space defined only through negation. Here, the constitution of the subject through discourses of danger comes up against the intransigence of political agency and the resistance of political subjects. Isin and Rykiel (2007: 184) have argued that a distinction needs to be drawn between the camp as a space of abjection, where subjects were eliminated after having been stripped of citizenship and 'abject spaces' – spaces where people are rendered inexistent, invisible, and inaudible. The difference has profound political implications: abject spaces are simultaneously spaces of resistance, where abjection is challenged and sovereign practices rendered ineffective.

Agency is not only present in the refugee camp (Puggioni 2006), but informs other exceptional spaces and practices (Mezzadra 2006; Nyers 2006). Migrants and refugees, for example, engage in daily practices of resistance against securitization. Focusing on the agency of the other, Nyers (2003) rethinks cosmopolitanism from the standpoint of migrants, the cast-offs of the global order. Arguing that the migrant is the cosmopolitan figure per se, he calls for a move away from an understanding of cosmopolitanism that aims at the constitution of world citizens behind the horizon of contemporary politics towards an understanding of cosmopolitanism that is located in concrete struggles. The "No One Is Illegal" initiative and other anti-deportation campaigns are examples of abject cosmopolitanism in action insofar as they radically call into question claims to sovereignty and principles of border control. Local struggles are the concrete situations where a democratic cosmopolitanism is enacted and establishes new forms of relationality with the other.

Emancipation

At first sight, emancipation appears to be in tension with poststructuralist approaches, particularly given the criticism of universality that underpins emancipatory ideas. However, several authors have brought together a poststructuralist analysis of security with emancipatory concerns. In our reading, emancipation configures resistance to security through an 'unconditional principle', drawing on political stakes that are set at a distance, referring to a *de jure* universality, equality, or freedom as the reference point for emancipation. Drawing particularly on the work of Jacques Rancière and Alain Badiou, recent literature on emancipation and security shifts the political concerns of danger and risk towards those of equality and freedom. Thus, this literature develops a different understanding of emancipation than the one associated with Ken Booth's (1991) approach to 'security as emancipation'. Rather than thinking order, this literature attends to ruptures, interruptions, and disorders that challenge the ways in which security practices constitute communities and govern populations.

Rancière's (1999) view of universal rights as something simultaneously present (as written inscriptions) and non-present (not enacted) points at an irresolvable *aporia* that functions as the necessary background condition for any emancipatory politics of equality (rights are out there to be taken). For example, most states claiming that human rights and freedom are universal values have also securitized their borders when it comes to the circulation of the poor, who today move under the name of 'economic refugees', 'illegal immigrants', or '*bogus* asylum seekers'. According to Rancière, the *de facto* denial of mobility to large parts of the people of the world is one of the most significant denouncements of equality in our time, that draws our attention to the fact that the universal right to the freedom of movement is only a right of those who make something of that universal inscription. Rens van Munster (2009) has drawn attention to how undocumented immigrants in France, the *sans-papiers*, have appropriated for themselves the European inscription of the freedom of movement. As Madjiguène Cissé (1997 emphasis added), one of the spokespersons for the movement, argued: 'When these rights are under threat, it is legitimate to struggle to have them reinstated . . . Freedom of movement is not something invented. It *confirms* an existing situation.'

Equality is the other principle that informs emancipatory political action. Equality can be understood as a claim in tension with the hierarchical practices that security presupposes. In particular, Aradau (2008a, 2008b) has pointed out that equality as a presumption can help to unmake the hierarchical logic that security entails, while at the same time furnishing a principle upon which a different relationality with the other can be conceived.

Conclusion

With its emphasis on the importance of representation, performativity, and power, poststructuralism has entered Security Studies as a means by which to challenge the common-sense assumptions of realist and constructivist approaches about the reality of security. Yet, poststructuralism is not a unified body, let alone a theory. There are different, sometimes irreconcilable, interpretations of security and its political effects which in turn inform different views of politics and security. Nonetheless, at a time where security literally seems to be everywhere, poststructuralist approaches have proved a significant intellectual reservoir for interrogating the concept of security. What unites the approaches analysed here under the rubric of poststructuralism is a commitment to critique as a condition of possibility for alternative political practices.

This chapter has engaged with some of the strands and representatives of poststructuralist thought and the challenges that these have posed to Security Studies. Unpacking security as an exceptional or governmental practice has led to complex analyses of its functioning and political effects. As security draws limits and divisions among categories of the population, mobilizes knowledge and culture to render some forms of life 'bare', inferior or less worth living, the question of 'unmaking security' has emerged as one of the most innovative areas of research. The discontent with the proliferation of security issues, the effects of practices upon political communities, the constitution of the subject and democracy will lead to increasing interest in transformation, resistance, ethics, or emancipation over order and discipline.

References

Agamben, G. (1998) *Homo Sacer: Sovereign Power and Bare Life*, trans. D. Heller-Roazen, Stanford, CA: Stanford University Press.

Agamben, G. (2005) *State of Exception*, trans. Kevin Attell, Chicago: Chicago University Press.

Anderson, B. (2010) 'Preemption, Precaution, Preparedness: Anticipatory Action and Future Geographies', *Progress in Human Geography* 34(6): 777–98.

Aradau, C. (2008a) 'Forget Equality? Security and Liberty in the "War on Terror"', *Alternatives: Global, Local, Political* 33(3): 293–314.

Aradau, C. (2008b) *Rethinking Trafficking in Women: Politics out of Security*, Basingstoke: Palgrave Macmillan.

Aradau, C. (2010) 'Security that Matters: Critical Infrastructure and Objects of Protection', *Security Dialogue* 41(5): 491–514.

Aradau, C. and Huysmans, J. (2014) 'Critical Methods in International Relations: The Politics of Techniques, Devices and Acts', *European Journal of International Relations* 20(3): 596–619.

Aradau, C. and van Munster, R. (2007) 'Governing Terrorism through Risk: Taking Precautions, (Un)knowing the Future', *European Journal of International Relations* 13(1): 89–115.

Aradau, C and van Munster, R. (2011) *Politics of Catastrophe: Genealogies of the Unknown*, London: Routledge.

Barkawi, T. and Laffey, M. (2006) 'The Postcolonial Moment in Security Studies', *Review of International Relations* 32(2): 329–52.

Bigo, D. (2002) 'Security and Immigration: Toward a Critique of the Governmentality of Unease', *Alternatives* 27(1): 63–92.

Bigo, D. (2006) 'Globalized (In)Security: The Field and the Ban-Opticon', in Collection Cultures & Conflicts (eds.) *Illiberal Practices of Liberal Regimes: The (In)Security Games*, Paris: L'Harmattan, 5–49.

Bigo, D. (2008) 'Security: A Field Left Fallow', in M. Dillon and A. Neal (eds.) *Foucault on Security and War*, Basingstoke: Palgrave Macmillan, 93–114.

Bigo, D. and Tsoukala, A. (eds.) (2008) *Terror, Insecurity and Liberty: Illiberal Practices of Liberal Regimes after 9/11*, Abingdon: Routledge.

Booth, K. (1991) 'Security and Emancipation', *Review of International Relations* 17(4): 313–26.

Bulley, D. (2014) 'Inside the Tent: Community and Government in Refugee Camps', *Security Dialogue* 45(1): 63–80.

Burke, A. (2013) 'Post-Structural Security Studies', in L. Shepherd (ed.) *Critical Approaches to Security*, Abingdon: Routledge, 77–88.

Butler, J. (1993) *Bodies that Matter: On the Discursive Limits of 'Sex'*, London: Routledge.

Butler, J. (2003) 'Violence, Mourning, Politics', *Studies in Gender and Sexuality* 4(1): 9–37.

Buzan, B. and Hansen, L. (2009) *The Evolution of Security Studies*, Cambridge: Cambridge University Press.

Buzan, B., Wæver, O., and de Wilde, J. (1998) *Security: A New Framework for Analysis*, Boulder, CO: Lynne Rienner.

Campbell, D. (1992) *Writing Security: United States Foreign Policy and the Politics of Identity*, Manchester: Manchester University Press.

Campbell, D. (1999) 'The Deterritorialization of Responsibility: Levinas, Derrida, and Ethics after the End of Philosophy', in D. Campbell and M. Shapiro (eds.) *Moral Spaces: Rethinking Ethics and World Politics*, Minneapolis: University of Minnesota Press, 29–56.

Campbell, D. and Shapiro, M. (1999) 'Introduction: From Ethical Theory to the Ethical Relation', in D. Campbell and M. Shapiro (eds.) *Moral Spaces: Rethinking Ethics and World Politics*, Minneapolis: University of Minnesota Press, vii–xx.

Cissé, M. (1997) *The Sans-Papiers: The New Movement of Asylum Seekers and Immigrants without Papers in France: A Woman Draws the First Lesson*, London: Crossroads.

Collier, S. and Lakoff A. (2008) 'Distributed Preparedness: The Spatial Logic of Domestic Security in the United States', *Environment and Planning D, Society and Space* 26(1): 7–28.

Coole, D. and Frost, S. (2010) *New Materialisms: Ontology, Agency, and Politics*, Durham, NC: Duke University Press.

Dauphinée, E. and Masters, C. (2007) 'Introduction: Living, Dying, Surviving I', in E. Dauphinée and C. Masters (eds.) *The Logics of Biopower and the War on Terror: Living, Dying, Surviving*, Basingstoke: Palgrave Macmillan, vii–xix.

de Goede, M. (2012) *Speculative Security: The Politics of Pursuing Terrorist Monies*, Minneapolis: University of Minnesota Press.

de Goede, M. and de Graaf, B. (2013) 'Sentencing Risk: Temporality and Precaution in Terrorism Trials', *International Political Sociology* 7(3): 313–31.

Diken, B. and Laustsen, C. B. (2005) *The Culture of Exception: Sociology Facing the Camp*, London: Routledge.

Dillon, M. (1996) *The Politics of Security. Towards a Political Philosophy of Continental Thought*, London: Routledge.

Dillon, M. (2005) 'Cared to Death: The Biopoliticised Time of Your Life', *Foucault Studies* 2: 37–46.

Dillon, M. and Lobo-Guerrero, L. (2008) 'Biopolitics of Security in the 21st Century: An Introduction', *Review of International Studies* 34(2): 265–92.

Dillon, M. and Reid, J. (2001) 'Global Liberal Governance: Biopolitics, Security and War', *Millennium – Journal of International Studies* 30(1): 41–66.

Duffield, M. (2007) Development, Security and Unending War: Governing the World of Peoples, Cambridge: Polity Press.

Edkins, J. (2003) *Trauma and the Memory of Politics*, Cambridge: Cambridge University Press.

Edkins, J., Pin-Fat, V., and Shapiro, M. J. (eds.) (2004) *Sovereign Lives: Power in Global Politics*, London: Routledge.

Foucault, M. (2004) *Society Must Be Defended*, trans. D. Macey, London: Penguin Books.

Foucault, M. (2007) *Security, Territory, Population*, Basingstoke: Palgrave.

Hansen, L. (2006) *Security as Practice: Discourse Analysis and the Bosnian War*, London: Routledge.

Honig, B. (2009) *Emergency Politics: Paradox, Law, Democracy*, Princeton, NJ: Princeton University Press.

Huysmans, J. (1998) 'The Question of the Limit: Desecuritisation and the Aesthetics of Horror in Political Realism', *Millennium* 27(3): 569–89.

Huysmans, J. (2006) *The Politics of Insecurity: Fear, Migration and Asylum in the EU*, London: Routledge.

Huysmans, J. (2014) *Security Unbound: Enacting Democratic Limits*, Abingdon: Routledge.

Isin, E. F. and Rykiel, K. (2007) 'Abject Spaces: Frontiers, Zones, Camps', in E. Dauphinée and C. Masters (eds.) *The Logics of Biopower and the War on Terror: Living, Dying, Surviving*, Basingstoke: Palgrave Macmillan, 181–204.

Jabri, V. (2006) 'War, Security and the Liberal State', *Security Dialogue* 37(1): 47–64.

Johns, F. (2005) 'Guantanamo Bay and the Annihilation of the Exception', *The European Journal of International Law* 16(4): 613–35.

Kessler, O. (2011) 'The Same as It Never Was? Uncertainty and the Changing Contours of International Law', *Review of International Studies* 37(5): 2163–82.

Klein, B. (1994) *Strategic Studies and World Order: The Global Politics of Deterrence*, Cambridge: Cambridge University Press.

Krasmann, S. (2012) 'Law's Knowledge: On the Susceptibility and Resistance of Legal Practices to Security Matters', *Theoretical Criminology* 16(4): 379–94.

Lakoff, A. (2006) 'From Disaster to Catastrophe: The Limits of Preparedness', *Social Science Research Council*, 11 June. Online. Available HTTP: <http://understandingkatrina.ssrc.org/Lakoff/> (accessed 12 August 2015).

Lobo-Guerrero, L. (2007) 'Biopolitics of Specialized Risk: An Analysis of Kidnap and Ransom Insurance', *Security Dialogue* 38(3): 315–34.

Lundborg, T. and Vaughan-Williams, N. (2014) 'New Materialisms, Discourse Analysis, and International Relations: a Radical Intertextual Approach', *Review of International Studies* 41(1): 3–25.

Mezzadra, S. (2006) *Diritto di fuga. Migrazioni, cittadinanza, globalizzazione*, Verona: Ombre Corte.

Neal, A. W. (2006) 'Foucault in Guantanamo: Towards an Archaeology of the Exception', *Security Dialogue* 37(1): 31–46.

Noll, G. (2003) 'Visions of the Exceptional: Legal and Theoretical Issues Raised by Transit Processing Centres and Protection Zones', *European Journal of Migration and Law* 5(3): 303–42.

Nyers, P. (2003) 'Abject Cosmopolitanism: The Politics of Protection in the Anti-Deportation Movement', *Third World Quarterly* 24(6): 1069–93.

Nyers, P. (2006) 'Taking Rights, Mediating Wrongs: Disagreements over the Political Agency of Non-Status Refugees', in J. Huysmans, A. Dobson, and R. Prokhovnik (eds.) *The Politics of Protection: Sites of Insecurity and Political Agency*, London: Routledge, 48–67.

Puggioni, R. (2006) 'Resisting Sovereign Power: Camps in-between Exception and Dissent', in J. Huysmans, A. Dobson, and R. Prokhovnik (eds.) *The Politics of Protection: Sites of Insecurity and Political Agency*, London: Routledge, 68–83.

Rancière, J. (1999) *Disagreement: Politics and Philosophy*, trans. J. Rose, Minneapolis: University of Minnesota Press.

Salter, M. B. (2008) 'When the Exception Becomes the Rule: Borders, Sovereignty, and Citizenship', *Citizenship Studies* 12(4): 365–80.

Schmitt, C. (1996) *The Concept of the Political*, trans T. B. Strong, Chicago: University of Chicago Press.

van Munster, R. (2004) 'The War on Terrorism: When the Exception Becomes the Rule', *International Journal for the Semiotics of Law* 17(2): 141–53.

van Munster, R. (2009) *Securitizing Immigration: The Politics of Risk in the EU*, Basingstoke: Palgrave.

Vaughan-Williams, N. (2007) 'The Shooting of Jean Charles de Menezes: New Border Politics?', *Alternatives: Global, Local, Political* 32(2): 177–95.

Walker, R. B. J. (1997) 'The Subject of Security', in K. Krause and M. C. Williams (eds.) *Critical Security Studies: Concepts and Cases*, London: UCL Press, 61–81.

Williams, M. C. (2003) 'Words, Images, Enemies: Securitization and International Politics', *International Studies Quarterly* 47(4): 511–31.

Zehfuss, M. (2007) *Wounds of Memory: The Politics of War in Germany*, Cambridge: Cambridge University Press.

8

DEBATES IN FEMINIST SECURITY STUDIES

Annick T. R. Wibben

> Until women have control over their own security a truly comprehensive system
> of security cannot be devised.
>
> *(Tickner 1992: 30)*

When feminist scholars began to make their mark on the field of International Relations (IR) in the 1980s, security was at the top of their agenda. IR feminists drew on a long history of writing about issues of peace, war, and violence largely in the form of historical or cross-cultural case studies (Gioseffi 2003). These writings, and the associated feminist activism, form the basis for Feminist Security Studies (FSS) today. Since 1915, the Women's International League of Peace and Freedom (WILPF) has been actively involved in security debates (Confortini 2012);[1] in the 1960s, women (and WILPF) helped create the International Peace Research Association. Despite their efforts, peace research became a male-dominated field, with gender noticeably absent even from debates about structural violence, where gender should be a central category. Still, feminist peace researchers were, by the late 1960s, analysing power and emphasizing empowerment over coercion; by the 1970s, they had moved on to developing notions of security with an adversary and broadened security to include security against want, security of human rights, and the security of an empowered civil society.[2] In the 1980s, they focused on the linkages between war and patriarchy (Boulding 1992: 56–7).

In the early 1990s, feminists began to phrase their insights on peace, war, and violence in terms of security, thus engaging debates in IR's sub-field of Security Studies more directly. The advent of FSS is traced to Ann Tickner's 1992 *Gender in International Relations: Feminist Perspectives on Achieving Global Security* (Blanchard 2003). In 1993, feminist peace researcher Betty Reardon wrote *Women and Peace: Feminist Visions of Global Security*. Both books, notable in their emphasis on global security (rather than national security), draw on the long tradition of feminist engagements with issues of peace, war, and violence – now framing them explicitly as security issues. Feminist insights on alternative conceptions of power, cooperative security, and non-state-centric perspectives (Brock-Utne 1989; Stiehm 1972) have also influenced Security Studies through alternative approaches, such as Critical Security Studies (Booth 1997; cf. Tickner 2001).

Since the turn of the century, a veritable explosion of feminist work in Security Studies has ensued, with FSS emerging as an important field at the intersection of Security Studies and feminist IR. This chapter provides an overview of this multifaceted literature in three main parts. First, I discuss the commonalities, and even more crucially, the differences between FSS researchers and their scholarship. Thereafter, I turn to outline some key contributions of FSS to the study of security. Finally, the theoretical diversity within FSS, which is ground for sustained debate, is shown.

Debates in Feminist Security Studies

A decade after the publication of the first special issue on gender and security in the journal *Security Dialogue* (2004), no singular feminist position on security has emerged, as recent debates among feminist scholars make abundantly clear (see Sjoberg and Lobasz 2011; Shepherd 2013). Nonetheless, the label FSS has flourished 'as the marker for a growing body of work that explicitly engages in feminist research questions, approaches, and politics (albeit to varying degrees)' (Stern and Wibben 2014: 2). Importantly, FSS is interdisciplinary – with scholars trained in peace research and Security Studies, but also in anthropology, history, literary theory, philosophy, or sociology. Feminist (methodological) commitments unite these scholars: They (1) ask feminist research questions; (2) base their research on women's experiences; (3) adopt a (self-)reflexive stance; and (4) have an emancipatory agenda (Tickner 2006: 22–9). Whereas IR, like many traditional sciences, assumes gender neutrality, feminists make gender (the socially constructed femininity/masculinity distinction) a central category of analysis – it is 'a socially imposed and internalized lens through which individuals perceive and respond to the world' (Peterson 1992b: 194). Consequently, FSS scholars argue that concepts and ideas about security, as well as security practices and institutions, are shaped by gender. To analyse these, 'FSS includes approaches, for instance, that pay attention to the workings of gender in order to ask questions about security; it also includes scholarship that refuses any line of distinction that separates "security" from the workings of gender' (Stern and Wibben 2014: 2).

Adopting a bottom-up approach to security, feminist scholars pay close attention to the impact of security policies, including war, on the everyday lives of people (Sylvester 2013), departing from a large part of traditional Security Studies research. FSS scholars challenge the notion that wars are fought to protect vulnerable populations (such as children and women) and show that civilians are often explicitly targeted (especially in ethno-nationalist wars) (Enloe 1998; Hansen 2000, 2001). Rather than offering security for all their citizens, states often threaten their own populations through direct or structural violence reflected in war-fighting priorities and embedded in institutions (Enloe 1993, 2000; Peterson 1992a; Reardon 1985; Tickner 1992; Tobias 1985; Young 2003). Feminists assert that the increasing technologization of war, from nuclear strategy to the current revolution in military affairs, depersonalizes killing, offers the illusion of clean warfare, and obscures accountability (Blanchard 2003; Cohn 1989; Masters 2005; Molloy 1995). Finally, FSS scholars also directly engage traditional theories of security (Sjoberg 2013) and policy questions familiar to any security scholar (Hudson et al. 2008/9; MacKenzie 2015).

Feminist contributions to Security Studies are varied, and it is not currently possible to trace a dominant position in FSS with a progressive history. However, significant debates about the scope and direction of this body of work have emerged. The first of these, 'The State of Feminist Security Studies: A Conversation', published in *Politics & Gender* (edited by Sjoberg and Lobasz 2011) represents a varied set of short pieces. Carol Cohn's contribution queries the 'inherent ambiguity in the label [Feminist Security Studies] itself, related to which two of the three words one sees as most closely linked' (2011: 581). She proposes that 'if the two words most closely linked are "security" and "studies," then the pre-existing field of Security Studies is the subject, and the question – both grammatical and epistemological – is in what way the adjective "feminist" modifies it' (2011: 581). This question is important because FSS, as Maria Stern and I argue, 'signals a commitment to feminism as a reflexive, many-faceted, and expansive field of inquiry and ethico-politics that is intertwined with the interrogation of security' (2014: 2).

A set of replies to these concerns, published in 2013 in *International Studies Perspectives* (edited by Shepherd) raised concerns about the fact that all authors featured were US-based and that citation practices replicated Anglo-American dominance in IR. In the opening essay, Laura Shepherd asks that 'we remain attentive to the question of who gets to be part of the conversation, and ask whose contestations are seen as legitimate challenges to dominant ways of knowing both within and outside of FSS' (2013: 2). This sentiment is echoed by Swati Parashar who asks, 'just where are these conversations taking place, where are the disagreements, and what are the compromises?' (2013a: 441). These debates are crucial for the politics of FSS: 'Given the proliferation of feminist security scholarship, which is based on a variety of feminisms, feminist scholars should begin to debate the content and scope of their research [. . .] there are some real differences in feminist scholarship – and these differences matter' (Wibben 2011b: 591).

Contributions of Feminist Security Studies

Asking 'where are the women (in security)?', feminists have subverted traditional approaches to Security Studies which do not include women. 'There are states and they are what is' Elshtain quips, asserting that 'professionalized IR discourse [. . .] is one of the most dubious of many dubious sciences that mask the power plays embedded in the discourse and the practices it legitimates' (1987: 91). Why do IR and Security Studies fail to notice diplomats' wives who provide safe spaces for back-room manoeuvres; barmaids and sex workers who serve military personnel (cf. Enloe 2000, Moon 1997); and women who fight for national causes, even in combat roles (cf. Goldman 1982; Herbert 1998; Lorentzen and Turpin 1998; MacKenzie 2015; Solaro 2006; Stiehm 1996)? Why these silences when women's existence is central to the workings of IR and security politics?

Contrary to generalized narratives of women as peacemakers or as victims needing rescue and protection, feminists document broader involvement of women in matters of international security. They reveal how armed forces need men and women to function in gender-specific ways that underline and reinforce skewed cultural norms and structural inequalities (Belkin 2012; Enloe 1998, 2000; Herbert 1998; Whitworth 2004). For example, states mobilize women to support wars, drawing on them as mothers (Bayard de Volo 2001; Haq 2007; Nikolic-Ristanovic 1998), as symbols of the nation or bearers of tradition (Yuval-Davis 1997), or by employing them in factories while men are deployed (Woollacott 1998). Women's acceptance of these roles, deemed acceptable for them, glamorizes the role of men as just warriors and positions women as the rebuilders after men's wars (Boulding 1988; Elshtain 1987). For many feminists, therefore, women and men 'share complicity in warfare and militarism through their participation in the dual mythology of masculinity and femininity' (Burguieres 1990: 8).

Feminists have also probed the topic of women as aggressors (Alison 2009; Hamilton 2007; MacKenzie 2012; Nacos 2005; Parashar 2013b; Sjoberg and Gentry 2007; Stiehm 1996; Sylvester 1987, 1989), presenting evidence that many women are violent (just as many men are peaceful), shattering the often-assumed affinity between women and peace – what some have called the women and peace thesis. These scholars highlight the need to examine the relationship of both women and men to violence and the gendering of violence itself, particularly its association with masculinity. This should not obscure the fact that women are still predominantly victims of war (and of militarized societies). One gendered form of victimization, the rape of conquered women, has long been considered a normal aspect of war (and peace, as True 2012 highlights). More recently, due to its use as a tactic of ethnic cleansing in the former Yugoslavia (e.g., Nikolic-Ristanovic 2000; Stiglmayer 1993), rape as a strategy of war has achieved renewed attention. While researchers have found evidence of rape as a strategy of war in a variety of conflicts, more recently researchers have begun to question this singular focus and caution that more careful attention to the varied context within which such violence takes place is needed. In their research on sexualized violence in the Democratic Republic of the Congo, Maria Eriksson-Baaz and Maria Stern (2013) found that soldiers raped for a variety of reasons and that there was not enough evidence to support the widely accepted narrative of rape as a strategy of war. Their research also highlights a phenomenon that feminist scholars/activists have observed more broadly – that there is a continuum of violence between peace and wartime (Cockburn 2004; Cuomo 1996; Reardon 1993).

More specifically, in the case of the former Yugoslavia, Zorica Mrsevic raises the following question: 'Did the civil war [. . .] cause an increase in domestic violence, or did domestic violence cause the war?' (Mrsevic 2001: 41). She argues that the high prevalence and tolerance of domestic violence in Yugoslav society before the war 'contributed significantly to the "ease" with which young men suddenly changed from apparently decent boys to brutal perpetrators of violent acts' – the underlying cause being patriarchal society where 'aggressive masculinity is not only tolerated, but encouraged' (Mrsevic 2001: 42).[3] Exploring the linkages of patriarchal societies and aggressive masculinities with violence and militarism has been an important theme of FSS (Cockburn 2004; Cockburn and Zarkov 2002; Duncanson 2013; Enloe 1987, 1998; Higate 2003; Reardon 1985; Whitworth 2004). When performing feminist gender analysis, men and masculinity need to be analysed alongside women and femininity – and, Cockburn cautions, 'we need to observe the functioning of gender as a relation [. . .] of power that compounds other power dynamics' (2004: 25). The relationship between masculinity and violence, however, is culturally specific and always changing because gender hierarchies are constructions that intersect with hierarchies of class, nation, race, or religion.

Theoretical commitments of Feminist Security Studies

Epistemologically and politically, FSS scholars are diverse. Feminist empiricists, for example, address the security puzzle by strictly adhering to mainstream scientific norms and inserting women as data. Standpoint feminists theorize from the position of subjugated women to bring their silenced perspectives into the conceptualization of security. Feminist poststructuralists decry 'universal (or universalizing) claims about the existence, nature, and powers of reason, science, language, and the "subject/self"' (Harding 1986: 28), questioning the entire framework of Security Studies. Postcolonial feminists study gender subordination as one of many intersecting forms of oppression women face; they critique the myopias of Western feminists' theorizing, such as in the case of Afghanistan, where the 'feminist focus on women under the Taliban rang with superior tones of enlightenment and righteousness, singling out the most exotic and distant situations, and representing the women of Afghanistan as passive victims' (Young 2003: 230).

These differences among feminist (security) scholars provide an impetus for continual engagement in the conversation and for a continual questioning essential to feminist approaches. This variety is at odds with traditional Security Studies, which prefers a single coherent narrative of security with immutable answers (cf. Wibben 2011a).[4] While some commitments, such as the liberal feminist goal of achieving equality also by integrating women into the armed forces, and the anti-war feminist analysis of militaries as a central element of patriarchal control, are directly at odds with one another, most feminists see disagreement as a necessary and productive element of scholarly debate (Sylvester 1987) and debate differing political implications. 'Any feminist perspective would argue that a truly comprehensive system of security cannot be achieved until gendered relations of domination and subordination are eliminated' (Tickner 1992: 23). The commitment to theorizing on the basis of women's experiences to achieve meaningful security arrangements is common to all feminists (Wibben 2011a).[5]

Due to the centrality of women's experiences in feminist research, the most fundamental and far-reaching debate among feminists is about essentialism, or the question of whether or not women and men have underlying, universal essences – a uniquely female or male nature – that is more fundamental than any variations among them. Feminists presupposing this essence point to biological roots: gender difference follows sex difference. Conservatives use claims about women's biology to argue that only men should fight wars and women should support them in home-front, feminine roles. Cultural feminists similarly conclude that women, as natural peacemakers, should resist war and seek power in world affairs to make the world less violent. Liberal feminists argue that women can surmount biology's limits and train to become more like men to gain equal access to public affairs and institutions like the military (cf. MacKenzie 2015; Solaro 2006). Feminist poststructuralists sceptical of essentialism argue that gender is mutable and socially, or even performatively (Butler 1990) constructed, even in the military; thus, women joining the military conform to, and simultaneously challenge, institutional gender stereotypes. Postcolonial feminists, concerned with the deeply gendered implications of colonialism, illuminate how contemporary military endeavours still rely on colonial tropes; they vehemently resist the recruitment of colonial subjects into militaries of the colonizer (Riley et al. 2008; Smith 2006).

These debates are key – the way feminists conceptualize gender shapes their entire analytical endeavour. When gender is the main category of analysis, what one sees depends on the gender-lens adopted. Consider the women and peace thesis already mentioned, which stereotypes women as peaceful, whether due to biology or to their social role as mothers, and which casts men as the violent sex. Burguieres (1990: 2–9) outlines three feminist lenses used to address this thesis: (1) accept binary male and female stereotypes, but try to subvert them to a feminist purpose (cultural feminism); (2) reject the female stereotype to argue that women should seek equality by becoming more like men (liberal feminism); (3) reject both male and female stereotypes as historically inaccurate and supportive of peaceful mother/violent man constructions of patriarchy and militarism (poststructuralist feminism). These lenses have different political implications and shape feminist recommendations on peace, war, and security issues accordingly: 'Broadly, the goal of the first approach is peace grounded in feminine values; the second has equality with men as its main objective; and the third approach aims at peace based on a new world order centred around new gender relations and structures' (Burguieres 1990: 9).

FSS encompasses all three positions; however, essentialism is increasingly scarce and the focus tends towards studying women's everyday lives and intersections between gender, class, race, religion, or nation. The latter move, a result of influences on FSS from transnational and postcolonial feminists, examines how these intersections produce particular subject positions and distinct forms of oppression. 'Embracing an intersectional approach, which emerges from a critical political stance as a "vision of generating counter-hegemonic and transformative knowledge production, activism, pedagogy, and non-oppressive coalitions" requires scholars to pay attention to specific contexts and their politics' (Wibben 2014: 754, citing Bilge). As Sylvester warns, 'the differing lived experiences and multiple fractured identities women have in the contemporary era, and the many political struggles to which these identities give rise' (1987: 500) need to be taken seriously. Without addressing the specificities of particular struggles within which narratives of identity politics are articulated, feminist scholarship mimics hegemonic representations of identity in which some, usually already marginalized members, are repeatedly excluded from belonging (Yuval-Davis 1997).

When heeding these warnings, the contribution of FSS and its addressing of the lacunae in traditional Security Studies is clear: 'feminists contest the possibility of a perfectly controlled, coherent security policy that could handle every international contingency' (Blanchard 2003: 1290). They question the quality of survival from a feminist standpoint that moves beyond survival (of the state) as the unitary and ultimate goal of security efforts, incorporating the historically complex relationship of women to states. They look beyond questions of military capabilities – and how to maintain or achieve peace through war (relying on 'power over') – advocating violence if at all only as a last resort and seeking common ground and pathways to negotiating the end of (armed) conflicts. The origins and implications (in peacetime) of wartime violence can thus both be located on a continuum and can be understood from the vantage points of the struggles of everyday life, a positionality that unravels stark distinctions of before and after war (Cuomo 1996; Wibben 2011a). The contributions of FSS are considerable – they shine a light on issues that traditional security scholarship and practice continuously fail to consider.

Conclusion

Since the publication of the first edition of this Handbook, feminist scholars have conducted ground-breaking research probing these questions, making crucial practical, political, and theoretical interventions (e.g. Detraz 2015; Gentry and Sjoberg 2015; MacKenzie 2012, 2015; Parashar 2013a; Pratt and Richter-Devroe 2014; Sjoberg 2013; Sylvester 2013; Wibben 2011a).[6] As Steve Smith noted, 'the contribution of feminist writers to Security Studies is [. . .] both considerable and ultimately destabilizing for the subfield [. . .] looking at security from the perspective of women alters the definition of what security is to such an extent that it is difficult to see how any form of traditional Security Studies can offer an analysis' (2005: 48). As feminist scholars are addressing questions that traditional scholarship misses, they are keenly reflexive in their research practices (Wibben 2016) and their work has important policy implications.

One example, the Women, Peace & Security (WPS) Agenda, which arose out of United Nations Security Council (UNSC) Resolution 1325 and was specified in subsequent resolutions, has led to a veritable explosion of research on its policy consequences.[7] A historic milestone, 1325 was the first resolution of the UNSC to specifically address women in war and to recognize women not simply as victims but as agents 'in building peace and guaranteeing security' (Pratt and Richter-Devroe 2014: 2). The WPS Agenda has been promoted primarily by mainstreaming gender, urging the incorporation of a gender perspective into all policies and programmes related to peace and security at the UN (Cohn et al. 2004; Hudson 2009), but also mandates National Action Plans (Gumru and Fritz 2009). While the need for further analysis of this process remains, the mainstreaming of gender and the inclusion of women in the security sector is significant.

More broadly, feminist scholars have begun to debate the politics of FSS (Wibben 2011b), challenging both traditional and critical security scholars, particularly for their lack of engaging with the political implications of their work. Transnational and more radical feminist scholarship made important contributions here (see Riley et al. 2008) by challenging the parameters of traditional Security Studies and its Anglo-American exceptionalism that commonly supports US imperialism. The 'war on terror' has accentuated the need to examine epistemic violence embedded in the appeal to women's liberation as a justification for intervention and to recognize the importance of looking at violence (and war) as part of a historically and culturally situated continuum (see Wibben 2016). As Ayotte and Husain summarize: 'While the physical and structural violence inflicted upon women must remain a central component of feminist theory and criticism, the war on terrorism in Afghanistan also demonstrates that the Western appropriation and homogenization of third-world women's voices perform a kind of epistemic violence that must be addressed along with material oppressions' (2005: 112–13).

Given the state of global politics, a move toward intersectional approaches that recognize the fundamental simultaneity of gender, race, nation, and more, and their impact on research practices and findings, is desperately needed in FSS. An intersectional approach is less 'concerned with the institutional success of the knowledge it produces [and more focused on] institutional and social change through counter-hegemonic knowledge production' (Bilge 2012: 409). FSS must, therefore, remain true to its origins by constantly engaging in a critique of the ways in which (also its own) theoretical and methodological practices might lend themselves to perpetuating physical, structural, and epistemic violence.

Notes

1 Of course, not all women are also feminists, nor are all feminists women – but WILPF is representative of a particular, anti-war feminist stance also to be found in FSS today (cf. Cohn and Ruddick 2002). More recently, WILPF created an academic network to strengthen the activist–academic conversations (http://www.wilpfinternational.org/academic-network/).
2 Much as human security does today (Hamber et al. 2006; Hoogensen and Stuvøy 2006; Hudson 2005).
3 Sharoni (1994) makes eerily similar observations for the Israeli–Palestinian conflict.
4 These epistemological and methodological choices of feminists also have important ethical and political implications; it matters how we study issues of peace, war, violence, and security and whether our aim is to challenge existing power relations or simply to describe the status quo. Once we take people's experiences in all their multiplicity and specificity seriously, rather than focus solely on states, different ethical commitments must follow (cf. Introduction in Wibben 2016).
5 It is important that theorizing on the basis of women's experience does not imply an essentialized construction. Instead, women are identified in particular contexts (usually by others). Womanhood, therefore, is always a question of social positioning. As such, we cannot think woman without examining gender, race, class, and other intersections simultaneously.
6 The Feminist Security Studies Network (http://groups.yahoo.com/neo/groups/FeministSecurityStudies/) aims to connect these scholars also via Facebook (https://www.facebook.com/groups/48680787483/).
7 There is also a Women Peace and Security group on Facebook (https://www.facebook.com/groups/160475027434631/).

References

Alison, M. (2009) *Women and Political Violence: Female Combatants in Ethno-National Conflict*, London: Routledge.
Ayotte, K. and Husain, M. E. (2005) 'Securing Afghan Women: Neocolonialism, Epistemic Violence and the Rhetoric of the Veil', *Feminist Formations* 17(3), 112–33.
Bayard de Volo, L. (2001) *Mothers of Heroes and Martyrs: Gender Identity Politics in Nicaragua, 1979–99*, Baltimore, MD: Johns Hopkins University Press.
Belkin, A. (2012) *Bring Me Men: Military Masculinity and the Benign Facade of American Empire, 1898–2001*, Oxford: Oxford University Press.
Bilge, S. (2012) 'Intersectionality Undone: Saving Intersectionality from Feminist Intersectionality Studies', *Du Bois Review* 10: 405–24.
Blanchard, E. M. (2003) 'Gender, International Relations, and the Development of Feminist Security Theory', *Signs* 28(4): 1289–1312.
Booth, K. (1997) 'Security and the Self: Reflections of a Fallen Realist', in K. Krause and M. C. Williams (eds.) *Critical Security Studies*, Minneapolis: University of Minnesota Press, 83–119.
Boulding, E. (1988) 'Warriors and Saints: Dilemmas in the History of Men, Women and War', in E. Isaksson (ed.) *Women and the Military System*, London: Harvester-Wheatsheaf, 225–47.
Boulding, E. (1992) 'Women's Experiential Approaches to Peace Studies', in C. Kramarae and D. Spender (eds.) *The Knowledge Explosion*, New York: Teachers College Press, 54–63.
Brock-Utne, B. (1989) *Feminist Perspectives on Peace and Peace Education*, New York: Pergamon Press.
Burguieres, M. K. (1990) 'Feminist Approaches to Peace: Another Step for Peace Studies', *Millennium* 19(1): 1–18.

Butler, J. (1990) *Gender Trouble: Feminism and the Subversion of Identity*, New York: Routledge.

Cockburn, C. (2004) 'The Continuum of Violence: A Gender Perspective on War and Peace', in W. Giles and J. Hyndman (eds.) *Sites of Violence*, Berkeley: University of California Press, 24–44.

Cockburn, C. and Zarkov, D. (eds.) (2002) *The Postwar Moment: Militaries, Masculinities, and International Peacekeeping*, London: Lawrence and Wishart.

Cohn, C. (1989) 'Sex and Death in the Rational World of Defense Intellectuals', in L. R. Forcey (ed.) *Peace: Meanings, Politics, Strategies*, New York: Praeger, 39–72.

Cohn, C. (2011) 'Feminist Security Studies: Toward a Reflexive Practice', *Politics and Gender* 7: 581–6.

Cohn, C. and Ruddick, S. (2002) 'A Feminist Ethical Perspective on Weapons of Mass Destruction', in S. Lee and S. Hashmi (eds.) *Ethics and Weapons of Mass Destruction: Religious and Secular Perspectives*, Princeton, NJ: Princeton University Press, 405–35.

Cohn, C., Kinsella, H., and Gibbings, S. (2004) 'Women, Peace and Security: Resolution 1325', *International Feminist Journal of Politics* 6(1): 130–40.

Confortini, C. (2012) *Intelligent Compassion: Feminist Critical Methodology in the Women's International League for Peace and Freedom*, New York: Oxford University Press.

Cuomo, C. J. (1996) 'War is Not Just an Event: Reflections on the Significance of Everyday Violence', *Hypatia* 11(4): 30–45.

Detraz, N. (2015) *Environmental Security and Gender*, New York: Routledge.

Duncanson, C. (2013) *Forces for Good? Military Masculinities and Peacebuilding in Afghanistan and Iraq*, London: Palgrave Macmillan.

Elshtain, J. B. (1987) *Women and War*, New York: Basic Books.

Enloe, C. (1987) 'Feminist Thinking about War, Militarism and Peace', in B. B. Hess and M. M. Ferree (eds.) *Analyzing Gender: A Handbook Of Social Science Research*, Newbury Park: Sage, 526–47.

Enloe, C. (1993) *The Morning After: Sexual Politics at the End of the Cold War*, Berkeley: University of California Press.

Enloe, C. (1998) 'All the Men Are in the Militias and All the Women Are Victims: The Politics of Masculinity and Femininity in Nationalist Wars', in L. A. Lorentzen and J. Turpin, (eds.) *The Women and War Reader*, New York: NYU Press, 50–62.

Enloe, C. (2000) *Maneuvers: The International Politics of Militarizing Women's Lives*, Berkeley: University of California Press.

Eriksson Baaz, M. and Stern, M. (2013) *Sexual Violence as a Weapon of War? Perceptions, Prescriptions, Problems in the Congo and Beyond*, London: Zed Books.

Gentry, C. E. and Sjoberg, L. (2015) *Beyond Mothers, Monsters, Whores: Thinking About Women's Violence in Global Politics*, London: Zed Books.

Gioseffi, D. (ed.) (2003[1988]) *Women on War: An International Anthology of Writings from Antiquity to the Present*, New York: Feminist Press at CUNY.

Goldman, N. L. (ed.) (1982) *Female Soldiers – Combatants or Noncombatants?* Westport: Greenwood Press.

Gumru, B. and Fritz, J. M. (2009) 'Women, Peace And Security: An Analysis of the National Action Plans Developed in Response to UN Security Council Resolution 1325', *Societies without Border* 4(2): 209–25.

Hamber, B., Hillyward, P., Maguire, A., McWilliams, M., Robinson, G., Russell, D., and Ward, M. (2006) 'Discourses in Transition: Re-Imagining Women's Security', *International Relations* 20(4): 487–502.

Hamilton, C. (2007) 'Political Violence and Body Language in Life Stories of Women ETA Activists', *Signs* 32(4): 911–32.

Hansen, L. (2000) 'The Little Mermaid's Silent Security Dilemma and the Absence of Gender in the Copenhagen School', *Millennium* 29(2): 285–306.

Hansen, L. (2001) 'Gender, Nation, Rape: Bosnia and the Construction Of Security', *International Feminist Journal of Politics* 3(1): 55–75.

Haq, F. (2007) 'Militarism and Motherhood: The Women of the Lashkar-I-Tayyabia in Pakistan', *Signs* 32(4): 1023–46.

Harding, S. G. (1986) *The Science Question in Feminism*, Ithaca, NY: Cornell University Press.

Herbert, M. S. (1998) *Camouflage Isn't Only for Combat: Gender, Sexuality and Women in the Military*, New York: NYU Press.

Higate, P. (2003) *Military Masculinities: Identity and the State*, New York: Praeger.

Hoogensen, G. and Stuvøy, K. (2006) 'Gender, Resistance and Human Security', *Security Dialogue* 37(2): 207–28.

Hudson, H. (2005) '"Doing" Security as though Humans Matter: A Feminist Perspective on Gender and the Politics of Human Security', *Security Dialogue* 36(2): 155–74.

Hudson, N. F. (2009) *Gender, Human Security and the UN: Security Language as a Political Framework for Women*, London: Routledge.

Hudson, V. M., Caprioli, M., Ballif-Spanvill, B., McDermott, R., and Emmett, C. F. (2008/9) 'The Heart of the Matter: The Security of Women and the Security of States', *International Security* 33(3): 7–45.

Lorentzen, L. A. and Turpin, J. (eds.) (1998) *The Women and War Reader*, New York: NYU Press.

MacKenzie, M. (2012) *Female Soldiers in Sierra Leone: Sex, Security, and Post-Conflict Development*, New York: New York University Press.

MacKenzie, M. (2015) *Beyond the Band of Brothers: The US Military and the Myth that Women Can't Fight*, Cambridge: Cambridge University Press.

Masters, C. (2005) 'Bodies of Technology: Cyborg Soldiers and Militarized Masculinities', *International Feminist Journal of Politics* 7(1): 112–32.

Molloy, P. (1995) 'Subversive Strategies or Subverting Strategy? Toward a Feminist Pedagogy for Peace', *Alternatives* 20(2): 225–42.

Moon, K. H. S. (1997) *Sex among Allies: Military Prostitution in US–Korea Relations*, New York: Columbia University Press.

Mrsevic, Z. (2001) 'The Opposite of War Is Not Peace – It Is Creativity', in M. R. Waller and J. Rycenga (eds.) *Frontline Feminisms*, New York: Routledge, 41–55.

Nacos, B. L. (2005) 'The Portrayal of Female Terrorists in The Media: Similar Framing Patterns in the News Coverage of Women in Politics and in Terrorism', *Studies in Conflict & Terrorism* 28(5): 435–51.

Nikolic-Ristanovic, V. (1998) 'War, Nationalism, and Mothers in the Former Yugoslavia', in L. A. Lorentzen and J. Turpin (eds.) *The Women and War Reader*, New York: NYU Press, 195–210.

Nikolic-Ristanovic, V. (ed.) (2000) *Women, Violence and War: Wartime Victimization of Refugees in the Balkans*, Budapest: CEU Press.

Parashar, S. (2013a) 'Feminist (In)Securities and Camp Politics', *International Studies Perspectives* 14(4): 440–3.

Parashar, S. (2013b) *Women and Militant Wars: The Politics of Injury*, London: Routledge.

Peterson, V. S. (1992a) *Gendered States: Feminist (Re)Visions of International Relations Theory*, Boulder, CO: Lynne Rienner.

Peterson, V. S. (1992b) 'Transgressing Boundaries: Theories of Knowledge, Gender and International Relations', *Millennium* 21(2): 183–206.

Pratt, N. and Richter-Devroe, S. (eds.) (2014) *Gender, Global Governance and International Security*, London: Routledge.

Reardon, B. (1985) *Sexism and the War System*, New York: Teachers College Press.

Reardon, B. (1993) *Women and Peace: Feminist Visions of Global Security*, Albany: SUNY Press.

Riley, R., Mohanty, C. T., and Pratt, M. B. (eds.) (2008) *Feminism and War: Confronting US Imperialism*, London: Zed Books.

Sharoni, S. (1994) 'Homefront as Battlefield: Gender, Military Occupation and Violence against Women', in T. Mayer (ed.) *Women and the Israeli Occupation*, New York: Routledge, 121–37.

Shepherd, L. (ed.) (2013) 'The State of the Discipline: A Security Studies Forum', *International Studies Perspectives* 14(4): 436–62.

Sjoberg, L. (2013) *Gendering Global Conflict: Toward a Feminist Theory of War*, New York: Columbia University Press.

Sjoberg, L. and Gentry, C. E. (2007) *Mothers, Monsters, Whores: Women's Violence in Global Politics*, London: Zed Books.

Sjoberg, L. and Lobasz, J. K. (eds.) (2011) 'The State of Feminist Security Studies: A Conversation', *Politics & Gender* 7(4): 573–604.

Smith, A. L. (2006) 'Heteropatriarchy and the Three Pillars of White Supremacy: Rethinking Women of Color Organizing', in A. L. Smith, B. E. Richie, and J. Sudbury (eds.) *Color of Violence: The INCITE! Anthology*, Boston, MA: South End Press, 66–73.

Smith, S. (2005) 'The Contested Concept of Security', in K. Booth (ed.) *Critical Security Studies and World Politics*, Boulder, CO: Lynne Rienner, 27–62.

Solaro, E. (2006) *Women in the Line of Fire: What You Should Know about Women in the Military*, Emeryville, CA: Seal Press.

Stern, M. and Wibben, A. T. R. (2014) 'A Decade of Feminist Security Studies Revisited', *Security Dialogue*, Special virtual issue, 1–6. Online. Available HTTP: <http://sdi.sagepub.com/site/Virtualspecialissues/Introduction_Feminist_Virtual_Issue.pdf> (accessed 29 June 2015).

Stiehm, J. H. (1972) *Nonviolent Power: Active and Passive Resistance in America*, Lexington, MA: Heath.

Stiehm, J. H. (1996) *It's Our Military, Too! Women and The US Military*, Philadelphia: Temple University Press.

Stiglmayer, A. (ed.) (1993) *Mass Rape: The War against Women in Bosnia-Herzegovina*, Lincoln: University of Nebraska Press.

Sylvester, C. (1987) 'Some Dangers in Merging Feminist and Peace Projects', *Alternatives* 12(4): 493–509.

Sylvester, C. (1989) 'Patriarchy, Peace, and Women Warriors', in L. R. Forcey (ed.) *Peace: Meanings, Politics, Strategies*, New York: Praeger.

Sylvester, C. (2013) *War as Experience: Contributions from International Relations and Feminist Analysis*, London: Routledge.

Tickner, J. A. (1992) *Gender in International Relations: Feminist Perspectives on Achieving Global Security*, New York: Columbia University Press.

Tickner, J. A. (2001) *Gendering World Politics: Issues and Approaches in The Post-Cold War Era*, New York: Columbia University Press.

Tickner, J. A. (2006) 'Feminism Meets International Relations: Some Methodological Issues', in B. A. Ackerly, M. Stern, and J. True (eds.) *Feminist Methodologies for International Relations*, Cambridge: Cambridge University Press, 19–41.

Tobias, S. (1985) 'Toward a Feminist Analysis of Defense Spending', *Frontiers* 8(2): 65–8.

True, J. (2012) *The Political Economy of Violence against Women*, Oxford: Oxford University Press.

Whitworth, S. (2004) *Men, Militarism and UN Peacekeeping*, Boulder, CO: Lynne Rienner.

Wibben, A. T. R. (2011a) *Feminist Security Studies: A Narrative Approach*, London: Routledge.

Wibben, A. T. R. (2011b) 'Feminist Politics in Feminist Security Studies', *Politics and Gender* 7(4): 590–5.

Wibben, A. T. R. (2014) 'Researching Feminist Security Studies', *Australian Journal of Political Science* 49(4): 743–55.

Wibben, A. T. R. (ed.) (2016) *Researching War: Feminist Methods, Ethics and Politics*, London: Routledge.

Woollacott, A. (1998) 'Women Munition Makers, War, and Citizenship', in L. A. Lorentzen and J. Turpin (eds.) *The Women and War Reader*, New York: NYU Press, 126–31.

Young, I. M. (2003) 'Feminist Reactions to the Contemporary Security Regime', *Hypatia* 18(1): 223–31.

Yuval-Davis, N. (1997) *Gender and Nation*, London: Sage Publications.

9

POSTCOLONIALISM: INTERROGATING NATIONAL SECURITY AND DRONE WARFARE

*Sheila Nair**

Postcolonialism is a relative newcomer to the debates on national security. In part this may be due to International Security Studies' (ISS) problematic incorporation of the non-West and in association the 'insecurities' that are intrinsic to dominant national security tropes produced by the West in relation to postcolonial selves and states. Bilgin suggests that one important reason for this occlusion is not that a 'blind spot' exists in Security Studies in regard to the non-Westerner, but rather that it underscores a 'historical absence' in ISS of the non-Western subject/object, which is 'constitutive' of Security Studies as theory and practice (Bilgin 2010: 616). The constitutive-ness of this absence may also be understood as reproducing the dominance of a mainstream security paradigm that relegates the non-West to a space of lawlessness, difference, exceptionalism, and subalternity.[1] Thus, the other must be resisted or annihilated, or alternatively seen as needing protection, redemption, saving, and education. Further, the reproduction of the self-other binary in mainstream security discourse and the absence it implies is a condition of possibility for conventional Security Studies whose emphasis on a 'high politics' of 'national' security is contrasted to a 'low politics' associated with concerns around human security, gender, development, or the environment (cf. Tickner 1992; Enloe 1996; Bilgin 2010). These latter concerns are typically relegated to the margins of the security discourse instead of being viewed as intrinsic to its privileging of national security.

Postcolonial critiques of international security are not only attentive to 'low politics', but as this chapter will show, they focus our gaze on the erasures, silences, and omissions of mainstream national security discourse. A postcolonial approach in the study of International Relations (IR) and international security utilizes an intersectional lens bringing into view race, gender, class, sexuality, and other axes of difference as constitutive of the hierarchical and colonizing ordering of IR (cf. Chowdhry and Nair 2002. The wilful neglect in Security Studies of not merely the 'low politics', but more significantly, the construction and reproduction of high politics presumes the negation of the non-Western subject and its objectification in dominant national security tropes. In that vein, this chapter adds to the groundwork laid by a small but growing number of studies on postcolonial insecurity such as Muppidi (1999), Krishna (1999), Barkawi and Laffey (2006), and Biswas (2014). However, the purpose of this chapter is not to 'survey' the evolution of the small sub-field of postcolonial Security Studies, as it were. Instead, I explore how a postcolonial approach assists in understanding representations of US national security with specific reference to drone warfare and its targets. We know that since 11 September 2001 hundreds of thousands of civilian deaths have resulted from the US-led wars and occupation of Iraq and Afghanistan and the destabilization of neighbouring countries. Yet these deaths have been rationalized as an unfortunate consequence of the pursuit of a just and righteous cause.

A postcolonial approach disrupts such certainties and challenges assumptions about what is ethically sanctioned and legally justifiable in these wars. The chapter has three main parts. In the first part, drone warfare is problematized by showing how the victims of drone strikes become voiceless, faceless, and disembodied. In the second, I show how 'targeted' killings are rationalized and in the last part, I offer a postcolonial critique as an explanation for this rationalization.

Drone warfare and 'heartbreaking tragedies'

The use of drones in waging the 'Global War on Terror' begun under George W. Bush has been expanded by his successor, Barack Obama. Despite the intensification of this programme over the last decade, there has been little public protest or discussion of its ethics, logic, or implications. Laurie Calhoun, writing in the journal *Peace Review*, argues that the US justification for the attack shows a blatant disregard by the world's pre-eminent superpower not only for the norms of international law but its own federal legal armature, which it holds up as an exemplar to the world (Calhoun 2003). After all, Calhoun asks, aren't such wanton killings, and the impunity associated with them, a hallmark of tyrannical regimes the US has long distinguished itself from? Calhoun's piece draws attention to the moral equivalencies being formulated by the US state including, among other things, the need to balance the arbitrary taking of lives by drones with claims that possible harm will result if they aren't used. Calhoun's indictment is apposite:

> The dust of innocent people does indeed bear an uncanny resemblance to the dust of terrorists, and the same vehicle driven by the head of a family or the head of a terrorist cell would have left precisely the same scrap metal remains. But perhaps we should not agonize too much over this disturbing possibility . . . no one knows with certainty who those people were . . . only that their deaths were effected by predator drone.
>
> *(Calhoun 2003: 209)*

As Calhoun's stark assessment illustrates, in the post-9/11 world Muslim bodies and spaces have been marked, managed, and obliterated, leaving behind minimal traces of lives cut short in the deserts, valleys, cities, and mountains where alleged terrorists purportedly hang out and do business.

Rationalizations over the acceptability of predator drones, with code names such as RQ-1 Predator,[2] suggest that this type of collateral damage is an unfortunate outcome of a war that is being waged in response to the attacks of 9/11 and the worldwide threat that al-Qaida, its affiliates, and new jihadist organizations pose (*John Brennan Delivers Speech* 2012). Even the deaths of children and other non-combatants have not triggered much criticism of US policy and in the mainstream media the attention to drone-related killings has been episodic at best. More recently, even the spotty coverage of death by drone or the trauma it engenders has been displaced by the beheadings and threats by militant non-state entities such as the Islamic State of Iraq and al-Sham (ISIS), rallying public support for further US military intervention in the region.

From the vantage point of sovereign authority, the collateral damage of drone 'surgical strikes' is limited to perhaps a few thousand as opposed to hundreds of thousands of civilian deaths. These deaths are typically presented as an unfortunate but unintended consequence, while the need for the attacks themselves is unquestionably portrayed as a necessary evil in US security discourse.

For example, US President Barack Obama acknowledges the civilian casualties as 'heart breaking tragedies' that will 'haunt him and those in the chain of command "for as long as we live"' but not surprisingly defends armed drones as the 'most discriminating aerial bombers available in modern warfare' (Coll 2014). Despite the stated normative underpinnings of a war that began as retribution for the deaths of a few thousand Americans and others on home ground, many of those targeted by drones are guilty by proximity. Children running in a yard may be obliterated by a predator drone, but they are voiceless, faceless, and disembodied in a security discourse that hails drone warfare as simultaneously 'defensive' and 'offensive' and integral to the US' survival. Meanwhile the deaths of US soldiers on a combat mission are grieved by honouring them in moments of silence as their humanizing portraits flash across television screens. The difference in treatment may be (simplistically) attributable to the way people personalize loss – one of 'us' as opposed to one of 'them'. But as Judith Butler has pointed out, this accords with 'the differential allocation of grievability that decides what kind of subject is and must be grieved, and which kind of subject must not' (Butler 2006: xiv–xv). How this difference is finely honed in the US security narrative in the case of drone warfare is shown in the next section.

Rationalizing 'targeted' killings

Predatory drones and *predator unmanned aerial vehicles* (UAVs) have entered popular discourse in a manner that might have been unanticipated a few years ago; public officials, journalists, and commentators talk about these machines in ways that underscore their instrumental role in waging the Global War on Terror under the Obama administration, although their use has declined somewhat since 2010 in Pakistan.[3] In his speech, President Obama defends drones as 'the most discriminating aerial bombers available in modern warfare – preferable to piloted aircraft or cruise missiles' (Coll 2014). He claims that these machines are less expensive and expansive while allowing for precision targeting and killing of individuals suspected by the US of being involved in 'terrorist' activity, nowadays broadly conceived, although originally the principal Global War on Terror target was al-Qaida.[4] He further suggests that 'jets and missiles cannot linger to identify and avoid non-combatants before striking, and [...] they are likely to cause "more civilian casualties and more local outrage"' (Coll 2014).

Importantly, however, drone warfare does not discriminate between those suspected of such activity that happen to be nationals of other countries or American citizens, but it is the latter and not the deaths of the former that energize mainstream drone critics in the US. So, for example, the controversial death by drone of an American cleric, Anwar Al-Awlaki, and his son in Yemen was not something that most commentators loudly condemned (ostensibly because of the victims' alleged terrorist credentials and affiliations) but it was used to illustrate the unbridled and unlimited scope of executive power. It was an instance of what might be possible in the new age of unmanned warfare, fixating those concerned about the possibility of American drones targeting 'ordinary' Americans in their own backyards or in a cafe down the street. A leaked memo, outlining the conditions under which an American citizen might be killed by the US government, led to the most sustained discussion yet in the media and the US Congress about the use of drones since 2011 (Klaidman 2013). The outrage accompanying the memo, which implies that a kill list maintained by the executive arm of the US government may include Americans, has dominated the headlines, overshadowing a substantive discussion of the horror inflicted by drones in war zones.

Estimates of deaths by drone are inexact given the official secrecy. However, organizations such as The Bureau of Investigative Journalism (TBIJ) report that 'from June 2004 through mid-September 2012, available data indicate that drone strikes killed 2,562–3,325 people in Pakistan, of whom 474–881 were civilians, including 176 children' (2012: iv). Another account suggests that 'more than 800 innocent civilians and only 22 al-Qaida commanders have been killed by these aerial attacks' since 2010 (Shaukat 2013). Despite the certainty of at least some collateral damage, there remains an unquestioning acceptance of the use of drones in the national security arsenal of the US. Public opinion surveys illustrate the overwhelming support for drone warfare even if evidence surfaces that civilians including children have been killed. The *Huffington Post* reports that in a 'HuffPost/YouGov survey of a representative sampling of 1,000 Americans, 54 per cent of respondents support killing individuals who are suspected of being high-level members of al-Qaida, while 18 per cent oppose the idea. Those opinions shift to 43 per cent in support and 27 per cent against if the suspect is an American citizen – but in both cases opposition is low' (Grim and Siddiqui 2013). In another earlier poll done in February by the *Washington Post*-ABC News, 'eight in ten Americans (83 per cent) approved of the Obama administration's use of unmanned drones against suspected terrorists overseas . . . 59 per cent strongly approving of the practice' showing strong bipartisan support (Cillizza 2013). Drones are popular '[B]ecause they are perceived to be effective in reducing the threat of terrorism without endangering American lives . . . there is little public appetite for an extended look at how unmanned attacks fit into our broader national security policy. Minds are made up on the matter' (Cillizza 2013).

The 'fog of war' analogy is also frequently used to rationalize the deaths, since at any given time decision makers (and especially those who operate the machines) may have imperfect information. Unfortunate as it may seem, according to this narrative, a few children and other civilians will invariably be harmed, since the drones can hardly be expected to 'linger' when enacting a human toll (see Coll 2014). And while it may 'haunt' some US policymakers for the rest of their lives, the haunting has clearly not brought about a halt to drone warfare, but rather its expansion to terror targets in Syria and Iraq (Coll 2014). Drones target the bad guys, but when 'non-combatants' are killed they should not have been close to the targets in the first place. In other words, 'guilt by proximity' explains many of these deaths in official accounts (Balko 2012; Becker and Shane 2012). The deaths of children in schoolyards can thus be presented as accidental and unfortunate, but they underscore the lack of accountability, and impunity, of the US state.

The intensification of the US security drone programme should not come as a surprise given these rationales, even if it continues to unsettle some media and academic commentators. Mainstream scholarly critiques of drones generally assert some moral outrage, but by situating their critiques in reference to 'just war' notions they further rationalize drone warfare. Just war's legal criteria – 'the laws of war' – are the gold standard against which drone warfare's harm is measured (Vogel 2010). In other words, by subjecting drone warfare to notions of proportionality or military necessity and other criteria embedded in laws of war or armed conflict is to make sense of it, and harmonize it with legal definitions and rationalizations for war. According to McKelvey 'the fact that drones represent a vastly superior tool . . . does not make the use of drones inherently disproportionate . . . (since) the laws of war do not require parties to fight with equal strength or ability – only with equal respect for and compliance with the rules' (2011: 127). A challenge to this argument is that drone warfare's constitutionality is suspect and that it fails to pass the basic test of 'due process' rights enshrined in American law and under 'just war' doctrine.

Braun and Brunstetter (2011) also explore the ethical implications of drone warfare in the context of 'just war' theory and the technological advances that shift understandings about what constitutes just war. Yet Braun and Brunstetter fail to interrogate the expansion and limits of security, and sovereign power and authority, and reinforce the hegemonic assessments of the strategies and tactics utilized in drone warfare. While drone warfare may be subject to critical scrutiny, the hierarchical ordering of IR that enables its use in the first place is dismissed and remains unaccounted for.

A postcolonial critique

This subsection situates a postcolonial critique as a counter critique to the predominantly liberal and Western-centred national security and drone warfare discourses presented above.

Security and hegemony

One reason for the elision of drone warfare as a tool of Western imperialism and colonization may lie in what Dalby (1997) calls the 'politics of security discourse' and its rootedness in Western triumphalist claims in the post-Cold War era. He suggests that a 'nagging ethnocentric doubt' remains about the 'whole discursive enterprise of international Security Studies', which reveals a 'mode of hegemony' whereby the United States 'constructed a geopolitical order in terms of "us" and "them", friend and foe' (Dalby 1997: 19).

Similarly, calling attention to the Eurocentric origins of Security Studies, Barkawi and Laffey (2006) highlight the need to reframe the field so that international security asymmetries are not naturalized but rather disassembled. In doing so they ask how and why being attentive to the 'postcolonial rupture' challenges dominant or mainstream (and even some critical) understandings of international security and security relations in order to generate a counter narrative of security that takes as its point of departure a questioning of the underlying (and sometimes explicit) impulse to 'liberate' and 'emancipate' the other. They also point to the inadequacy of 'critical and human security approaches' that 'revolve around the concept of emancipation, an idea derived from the European Enlightenments' (*sic*).

In this literature, the agent of emancipation is almost invariably the West, whether in the form of Western-dominated international institutions, a Western-led global civil society, or in the 'ethical foreign policies of leading Western powers' (Barkawi and Laffey 2006: 350). Likewise, Biswas notes that Security Studies, including its critical sub-field, has not given adequate attention to the analysis of the 'connections between global power, hierarchies, and neocolonialism', a neglect that postcolonial scholars seek to ameliorate (2014: 15). In her critical study of the nuclear non-proliferation regime, Biswas draws attention to its embeddedness in a colonial order that rationalizes the production and consumption of hegemonic rationality, sovereignty, and security while normalizing the status quo, an order nevertheless resisted by those states desiring nuclear power. A postcolonial critique provides an opportunity to revisit long-standing debates in the field of Security Studies and more carefully engage the discursive production of Euro-American vulnerability and the long shelf lives of third-world threats and the insecurities they engender (cf. Agathangelou 2010).

From a postcolonial perspective, the use of drones by the US and its allies in the context of threats posed by nameless and faceless others in regions of the world that allegedly spawn terror invalidates notions of sovereign accountability and sovereign authority under 'just war' theory and the corpus of international humanitarian and human rights laws. The question is not so much about whether there can be *any* justification at all for targeted killings but whether such killings signal a special and exceptional existence where the reasonableness and justness of drone deaths become part of the dominant narrative even if they complicate the US' self-professed bedrock democratic principles and adherence to 'rule of law'.

Sauer and Schornig (2012) point to the irony of liberal democracies 'being so intrigued by unmanned weapons systems and particularly drones'. What is it about democracies, they ask, that makes drones not only the 'liberal weapon of choice' but also their 'silver bullet'? The authors contend that, among other things, casualty aversion among liberal democratic publics plays a role. Significantly, they also attribute drone desire to a 'normative hierarchy' that places greater value on 'our' soldiers' lives over those of other populations. According to Sauer and Schornig, the necessity for 'self-protection' against an alleged enemy opponent who has no regard for the 'rules of war' becomes a part of the rationale. Complicating this argument, though, is the corresponding 'desire to enforce and export universal human rights or militarily uphold international law' (Sauer and Schornig 2012: 369).

As Gregory (2011), citing Der Derian (2009), has argued, 'the development of a precision-strike capability, the cultural turn towards a counter-insurgency that places the local population at the centre of its operation, and the refinement of the legal armature that regulates armed conflict have all contributed to . . . "virtuous war"' (2011: 188). Virtuous wars where fighting an enemy that is seemingly far less technologically adept and sophisticated is presented as much more acceptable in terms of collateral damage, including limiting the loss of military personnel (since drones can be operated from a control room in Nevada), promotes the educative mission of the 'democratic state' (Gregory 2011). Further, in US field manuals, rules and codes of military engagement establish a 'kill-chain'. Underpinning the kill chain are binaries such as 'militant'/'civilian', 'good Muslim'/'bad Muslim', 'soccer mom'/'terrorist', and a range of other associated terms and meanings, which reproduce the disposability and dispensability of Muslim bodies.

American exceptionalism and its others

A postcolonial perspective would also question the assertion of American 'exceptionalism' grounded in gendered, classed, sexed, and racialized terms against enemies such as 'rogue' states and 'terrorist' non-state entities. The other is thus a non-white, anti-capitalist, infantilized, hyper-sexualized, and feminized object in US national security discourse (Hunt 2009). In a provocative analysis of US exceptionalism, Puar (2007) ties the concept 'homonationalism' to the US' production of 'terrorist assemblages'. Puar situates the construction of the terrorist in US security discourse in relation to binaries underpinning orientalized imageries and representations of the other where some forms of queerness become the norm and others constitute a deviancy from that norm. Thus homonationalism renders others deviant in the framework of dominant or accepted national understandings of homosexuality and difference, thereby securing support even amongst formerly marginalized 'queer' citizens who might otherwise challenge or disrupt the dominant narrative of exceptionalism.

It is also illustrative of homonationalism that drone warfare may be waged without regard to the US constitution or legal limits, and is sustained by an imaginative, and perhaps imaginary, construction of US exceptionalism. Such an invocation of US exceptionalism is comparable to the argument against torture by another US senator who ascribes its use to foreign others who do not possess the same values as 'us'/US. John McCain plays on the notion that a 'civilized' nation cannot torture. In condemning torture McCain is arguing that it is not consistent with American exceptionalism; it is not 'who we are' (McCain 2014).

These beliefs about American exceptionalism and its corollary nationalism circulating in political rhetoric are reflective of a broader societal consent around the construction of oppositions (*us/US/self* and *them/foreign/other*) in the dominant security discourse. That the self exhibits qualities of valor, virtù, and sacrifice for God and 'mother' country that are woven into the fabric of military service is also taken for granted. The emergence of the 'security mom' in national security discourse after 9/11 captures this assumption well. Grewal (2006) shows how the post 9/11 other is simultaneously racialized, gendered, classed, and sexualized, while being positioned as threatening not only to the state, but on a very personal/intimate level as threatening to the subject/self, who develops a pathological fear of the 'stranger within' as demonstrated in the writings (or better yet, 'ranting') of the neo-conservative Asian American syndicated columnist, Michelle Malkin.

Grewal cites Malkin's rhetoric as an example of the ostensibly 'deracialized' security mom whose 'ideas of security and safety' are situated 'within imperial and transnational contexts of neoliberalism and geopolitics, and the production of a subject in relation to rearticulations of outsiders and insiders, home, and homeland'. Consequently, '(If) the question is whether the security mom is a new subject or an older national one, we can see that it is a new subject that is created on the foundation of historically embedded subjects. The specificities and the histories of this subject become visible as an assemblage of disparate and connected forms of power; new strategies and technologies; deeply sedimented American notions of home; and domesticity, imperialism, and feminism' (Grewal 2006: 28). Grewal concludes that in this cultural imaginary, fear of the other looms large and anchors the subject/self in the dominant national security narrative as under siege.

Drones and the violence of sovereign power

Extending these insights to a postcolonial analysis of drone warfare I argue that the normalization of othering in national security and sovereignty discourses enables the US and its allies to counter 'threat' and 'terror' by adopting measures that explicitly contradict the self's presumed 'exceptionalism' and yet are deemed necessary to preserving that identity. The enemy is depicted not only in hypermasculinized terms – typical of this is how the Taliban are portrayed as systematically oppressing women whose liberation is presented as an objective of US occupation – but are also rendered as effeminate, dirty, inscrutable, irrational, and uncivilized. The subaltern status of such groups in security discourse – designated by the global movement of capital and imperialism to the margins of political, economic, cultural, intellectual, and social life – is nevertheless audible in other ways, even if their speech is rendered unintelligible (see Spivak in Biswas 2014: 171). Edward Said (1997) explores, for example, the depiction of Islam and its adherents in film, literature, and popular media in *Covering Islam* and presciently anticipates the post-9/11 caricatures of Muslims and especially Muslim men, and their denigration in security discourse. These depictions make these groups intelligible and audible within the framework of a security discourse that sees them as an existential threat to the West.

Giorgio Agamben's work on the exception and bare life, which calls attention to the distinction between bare life – *homo sacer* or 'sacred man', which is 'life that cannot be sacrificed and yet may be killed' – and ordinary political life, also complements a postcolonial critique of security (Agamben 1998: 82). In Agamben's words:

> What defines the status of *homo sacer* is therefore not the original ambivalence of the sacredness that is assumed to belong to him, but rather the particular character of the double exclusion into which he is taken and the violence to which he finds himself exposed.
>
> *(Agamben 1998: 82)*[5]

The notion of bare life is a useful way of thinking about the marginality of postcolonial people who have been targeted by drones and the 'zones of indistinction' they occupy in IR. The reproduction of sovereignty, sovereign power, and *homo sacer* operate in and through a colonial logic that reproduces hierarchical relations of rule, power, and violence and renders drone warfare rational under 'just war' and 'due process' arguments. Bare postcolonial lives are imbricated in a colonial order informed by racialized, sexed, classed, and gendered constructions of sovereignty

101

and sovereign power (Nair 2011). While exceptions are generally conceived in exclusionary terms but not consistently so,[6] sovereign power's reach through the use of drones may be seen as attaching itself to an inclusive exclusion in the elimination of politically excluded life. Further, as Pugliese (2011) argues, such an anomic violence relies on the 'prosthetics of law' creating a 'robotic' distance between the executioner and its human targets.

Postcolonial critiques of security are indebted to Foucault's work on govermentalities, biopolitics, and power and recent scholarship that is attentive to these connections. For example, Shaw (2013) illuminates how the US 'Predator Empire', expansive and overwhelmingly powerful in its reach and capacity to kill at will, discursively constructs 'peripheral' and 'ungoverned spaces' marked by 'persistent insecurity and chaos' that are a hallmark of national security policy under Obama (2013: 7). He concludes that the 'digitizing' of space, where the distance being traversed by drones is in effect compressed through the use of 'real-time technologies', renders immediate and intimate the gaze of the predator operators as they target people. The intimacy that is implied in this compression is very similar to the ways colonial and postcolonial binaries work to eviscerate difference while establishing its immutability in security discourse and governmentality.

Foucault describes governmentality as the 'ensemble of institutions, procedures, analyses, and reflections, the calculations and tactics that allow the exercise of the very specific albeit complex form of power' with its target population and as 'its essential technical means apparatuses of security' (Foucault 1991: 102). Governmentality, evident in the workings of bureaucratic agencies, petty officials, and non-state entities with power over decisions to take out life, can thus be understood as intrinsic to the execution of drone warfare. The high-value targets chosen for elimination by the Pentagon or US Central Intelligence Agency (CIA) personnel operate within such 'apparatuses of security' and enjoy the impunity of 'petty sovereigns' whom Butler (2006) invokes as indispensable cogs in the wheels of sovereign power. But governmentality, instead of devitalizing the state (as a form of power), reanimates it, allowing for the sovereign to suspend the law and negate political life (Butler 2006: 53–61).

Further, as Butler argues: 'it seems important to recognize that one way of 'managing' a population is to constitute them as the less than human without entitlement to rights, as the humanly recognizable. This is different from producing a subject who takes the norm of humanness to be its constitutive principle' (2006: 97). Shaw suggests that it is precisely this denial of humanity that is at work in the Predator Empire's reach and in the technologies that collapse time and space and generate a 'pre-emptive, future-oriented biopolitics that exists in an exceptional space outside centuries of international humanitarian law' (2013: 13). Thus, the actions of petty sovereigns such as the CIA agent who shoots and kills two unarmed motorcyclists at a traffic stop in a city in Pakistan because he presumes they were going to attack him first, reinforce the 'lawlessness' of postcolonial others and spaces of international relations.

Conclusion

A postcolonial perspective on security addresses the invisibilities and silences embedded in mainstream Security Studies that effectively reproduce binaries of self and other, making the latter a legitimate object and target of coercive, sovereign power, for example, of the US state. It thereby calls attention to the constitutive practices and erasures, buttressed by normative and legal claims and justifications that inform these binaries and enable state violence and power to be enacted with little resistance from mass publics in the West. Reflecting on postcolonial vulnerabilities in this context the chapter re-centres the margins by critically addressing the rationalizations around drone warfare. A postcolonial approach might enable us to better understand the plight of, and terror inflicted on, marginalized, subaltern peoples targeted by drones. It helps reveal what is erased and omitted in mainstream Security Studies, which rest also on the peripheralization of non-Western geopolitical spaces and zones in national security discourse. One of the key questions a postcolonial interrogation raises is how might mainstream Security Studies approach these omissions and erasures in a productive engagement with it, and how might postcolonial scholarship be responsive? Are debates in the field doomed to be mere 'debates'? Is it feasible or even possible to have a dialogue in Security Studies that might lead to an intervention that can seriously speak to and meaningfully address the tragedies that Obama alludes to? Unfortunately, the lack of clear answers may have a lot to do with the mutual unintelligibility of mainstream and postcolonial approaches to security.

Notes

* A much earlier version of this paper was presented at the European Conference on Politics and Gender in Barcelona in 2013. My thanks to the editors, Myriam and Thierry, for their comments and very helpful suggestions for changes. I would also like to thank Himadeep Muppidi for taking the time to read it and provide feedback. I alone am responsible for any shortcomings.
1 This concept borrowed from Antonio Gramsci has been critical to the project of the South Asian Subaltern Studies collective whose work has been influential in postcolonial theory (e.g. Ranajit Guha 1989; Spivak 1988). While there are important differences and dissonances among these perspectives, the notion of subalternity attached to the subaltern classes – including peasants, aboriginal peoples, other marginalized groups, and women among them – is central to how postcolonial theory engages the notion of the margins and the peripheral in international security.
2 'R' is the Department of Defense's (DoD) code for reconnaissance aircraft while the 'Q' designates that it is unmanned.
3 http://counterterrorism.newamerica.net/drones
4 Cole notes that '"Al Qaeda" is a vague term somewhat arbitrarily applied by the Washington regional groups involved in local fundamentalist politics, as with the Partisans of Sharia, the Yemeni militants who have taken over the city of Zinjibar, or expatriate Arab supporters in Pakistan of the Haqqani of Pashtun fighters – former allies of the United States in their struggle against the Soviet occupation of Afghanistan' (2012).
5 Agamben explains the relationship of the exception and zone of indistinction as one where: 'the state of exception is neither external nor internal to the juridical order, and the problem of defining it concerns precisely a threshold, or a zone of indifference where inside and outside do not exclude each other but rather blur with each other' (Agamben 2005: 23).
6 Alternatively, Ong suggests that the exception 'can also be a positive decision to include selected populations and spaces as targets of "calculative choices and value orientations"' (2006: 5).

References

Agamben, G. (1998) *Homo Sacer: Sovereign Power and Bare Life*, Stanford, CA: Stanford University Press.
Agamben, G. (2005) *State of Exception*, Chicago: University of Chicago Press.
Agathangelou, A. M. (2010) 'Bodies of Desire, Terror and the War in Eurasia: Impolite Disruptions of (Neo)liberal Internationalism, Neoconservatism and the 'New' Imperium', *Millennium – Journal of International Studies* 38(3): 693–722.
Akhtar, N. (2011) 'Pakistan and US Partnership: Cost or Benefit?', *International Journal on World Peace* 28(4): 7–31.
Balko, R. (2012) 'US Drone Policy: Standing near Terrorists Makes You A Terrorist', *Huffington Post*, 29 May. Online. Available HTTP: <http://www.huffingtonpost.com/2012/05/29/drone-attacks-innocent-civilians_n_1554380.html> (accessed 20 April 2015).
Barkawi, T. and Laffey, M. (2006) 'The Postcolonial Moment in Security Studies', *Review of International Studies* 32(2): 329–52.
Becker, J. and Shane, S. (2012) 'Secret "Kill List" Proves a Test of Obama's Principles and Will', *The New York Times*, 29 May. Online. Available HTTP: <http://www.nytimes.com/2012/05/29/world/obamas-leadership-in-war-on-al-qaeda.html> (accessed 20 April 2015).

Bilgin P. (2010) 'The "Western-Centrism" of Security Studies: "Blind Spot" or Constitutive Practice?', *Security Dialogue* 41(6): 615–22.

Biswas, S. (2014) *Nuclear Desire: Power and the Postcolonial Nuclear Order*, Minneapolis: University of Minnesota Press.

Brunstetter, D. and Braun, M. (2011) 'The Implications of Drones on the Just War Tradition', *Ethics & International Affairs* 25(3): 337–58.

Butler, J. (2006) *Precarious Life: The Powers of Mourning and Violence*, New York: Verso.

Calhoun, L. (2003) 'The Strange Case of Summary Execution by Predator Drone', *Peace Review* 15(2): 209–14.

Chowdry, G. and Nair S. (eds.) (2002) *Power and Postcolonialism in International Relations: Reading Race, Gender and Class*, London: Routledge.

Cillizza, C. (2013) 'The American Public Loves Drones', *The Washington Post*, 6 February. Online. Available HTTP: <http://www.washingtonpost.com/blogs/the-fix/wp/2013/02/06/the-american-public-loves-drones/> (accessed 4 April 2015).

Cole, J. (2012) 'The Age of American Shadow Power', *Nation* 294(18): 25–7.

Coll, S. (2014) 'The Unblinking Stare: The Drone War In Pakistan', *The New Yorker*, 24 November. Online. Available HTTP: <http://www.newyorker.com/magazine/2014/11/24/unblinking-stare> (accessed 3 April 2015).

Dalby, S. (1997) 'Contesting an Essential Concept: Reading the Dilemmas in Contemporary Security Discourse', in K. Krause and M. C. Williams (eds.) *Critical Security Studies*, Minneapolis: University of Minnesota Press, 3–31.

Der Derian, J. (2009) *Virtuous War: Mapping the Military-Industrial-Media-Entertainment Network*, London: Routledge.

Enloe, C. (1996) 'Margins, Silences and Bottom Rungs: How to Overcome the Underestimation of Power in the Study of International Relations', in K. Booth, S. Smith, and M. Zalewski (eds.) *International Theory: Positivism and Beyond*, Cambridge: Cambridge University Press, 186–202.

Foucault, M. (1991) 'Governmentality', in G. Burchell, C. Gordon, and P. Miller (eds.) *The Foucault Effect: Studies in Governmentality*, Chicago: University of Chicago Press, 87–104.

Gregory, D. (2011) 'From a View to a Kill: Drones and Late Modern War', *Theory, Culture & Society* 28(7–8): 188–215.

Grewal, I. (2006) 'Security Moms in the Early Twentieth-Century United States: The Gender of Security in Neoliberalism', *Women's Studies Quarterly* 34(1–2): 25–39.

Grim, R. and Siddiqui, S. (2013) 'Democrats Confront Obama on Drone Policy during Closed-Door Gathering with Senators', *The Huffington Post*, 3 March. Online. Available HTTP: <http://www.huffingtonpost.com/2013/03/12/democrats-drone-policy_n_2862544.html?> (accessed 3 April 2015).

Guha, R. (1989) 'On Some Aspects of the Historiography of Colonial India', in R. Guha and G. Spivak (eds.) *Selected Subaltern Studies*, Oxford: Oxford University Press, 37–44.

Hunt, M. (2009) *Ideology and US Foreign Policy*, New Haven and London: Yale University Press.

John Brennan Delivers Speech on Drone Ethics, 2012. Online. Available HTTP: <http://www.npr.org/templates/transcript/transcript.php?storyId=151778804> (accessed 4 April 2015).

Klaidman, D. (2013) 'Obama's Drone Debacle', *The Daily Beast*, 9 March. Online. Available HTTP: <http://www.thedailybeast.com/articles/2013/03/09/obama-s-drone-debacle.html> (accessed 5 April 2015).

Krishna S. (1999) *Postcolonial Insecurities: India, Sri Lanka, and the Question of Nationhood*, Minnesota: University of Minnesota Press.

McCain, J. (2014) 'Floor Statement by Senator John McCain on Senate Intelligence Committee Report on CIA Interrogation Methods', 9 December. Online. Available HTTP: <http://www.mccain.senate.gov/public/index.cfm/2014/12/floor-statement-by-sen-mccain-on-senate-intelligence-committee-report-on-cia-interrogation-methods> (accessed 22 May 2015).

McKelvey, B. (2011) 'Due Process Rights and the Targeted Killing of Suspected Terrorists: The Unconstitutional Scope of Executive Killing Power', *Vanderbilt Journal of Transnational Law* 44: 1353–84.

Muppidi, H. (1999) 'Postcoloniality and the Production of International Insecurity: The Persistent Puzzle of US–Indian Relations', in J. Weldes, M. Laffey, H. Gusterson, and R. Duvall (eds.) *Cultures of Insecurity: States, Communities and the Production of Danger*, Minneapolis: University of Minnesota Press, 119–46.

Muppidi, H. (2012) *The Colonial Signs of International Relations*, New York: Columbia University Press.

Nair, S. (2011) 'Sovereignty, Security and the Exception: Towards Situating Postcolonial *Homo Sacer*', in G. Delanty and S. Turner (eds.) *Handbook of Contemporary Social and Political Theory*, New York and London: Routledge, 386–394.

Ong, A. (2006) *Neoliberalism as Exception: Mutations in Citizenship and Sovereignty*, Durham, NC: Duke University Press.

Puar, J. K. (2007) *Terrorist Assemblages: Homonationalism in Queer Times*, Durham, NC and London: Duke University Press.

Pugliese, J. (2011) 'Prosthetics of Law and the Anomic Violence of Drones', *Griffith Law Review* 20(4): 931–61.

Robertson, J. (2013) 'Judges Shouldn't Decide about Drone Strikes', *The Washington Post*, 15 February. Online. Available HTTP: <http://www.washingtonpost.com/opinions/judges-shouldnt-decide-about-drone-strikes/2013/02/15/8dcd1c46–778c-11e2-aa12-e6cf1d311> (accessed 3 April 2015).

Said, E. W. (1979) *Orientalism*, New York: Vintage Books.

Said, E. W. (1997) *Covering Islam: How the Media and the Experts Determine How We See the Rest of the World*, New York: Vintage Books.

Sauer, F. and Schörnig, N. (2012) 'Killer drones: The "Silver Bullet" of Democratic Warfare?', *Security Dialogue* 43(4): 363–80.

Shaukat, S. (2012) 'Killing Civilians: Obama's Drone War in Pakistan', *Global Research*, 14 December. Online. Available HTTP: <http://www.globalresearch.ca/killing-civilians-obamas-drone-war-in-pakistan/5315661> (accessed 10 April 2015).

Shaw, I. G. (2013) 'Predator Empire: The Geopolitics of US Drone Warfare', *Geopolitics* 18(3): 536–59.

Spivak, G. C. (1988) 'Can the Subaltern Speak?', in C. Nelson and L. Grossberg (eds.) *Marxism and the Interpretation of Culture*, Urbana: University of Illinois Press, 271–313.

Tickner, J. A. (1992) *Gender in International Relations: Feminist Perspectives on Achieving Global Security*, New York: Columbia University Press.

Vogel, R. J. (2011) 'Drone Warfare and the Law of Armed Conflict', *Denver Journal of International Law and Policy* 39(1): 101–38.

10

HUMAN SECURITY: LESSONS LEARNED FROM AFGHANISTAN

Gunhild Hoogensen Gjørv

Human security made its big debut in a nineteen-page chapter in the 1994 United Nations Development Programme (UNDP) Human Development Report, expanding the notion of security to include dimensions of food, health, community, environmental, economic, personal, and political security, with the vague and noble intention to address some of the glaring weaknesses of security policy, and shed light on the importance of the security of people. The UNDP report defined human security as 'freedom from fear, freedom from want', and claimed it consisted of four essential characteristics: it was universal, interdependent, easier to ensure through early prevention, and people-centred (UNDP 1994). It additionally encompassed seven categories: political, personal, food, health, environment, economic, and community security (UNDP 1994). Therefore, human security can be simply understood as security in everyday life.

More than twenty years later, academic and policy literature are still uncertain about a definition (Breslin and Christou 2015). The human security concept has been subject to much discussion and debate, including arguments about 'how the concept is difficult for policy makers to operationalize when it is defined too broadly, how it is meaningless to focus upon individuals per se, as well as how it is such a necessary concept that finally brings non-state actor voices into the security debate' (Hoogensen Gjørv 2014b: 61). At the same time, one can question where the power behind the concept now lies – is it an empowering tool? Do human security analyses focus on the lives of ordinary people and their (in)security challenges, and potentially thereafter affect policy (bottom-up approach)? Or do we find that states have co-opted the concept for their own devices, not least in claims and justifications for military intervention, a critique more and more frequently heard?

This chapter will look at these questions, engaging with common critiques of human security and bringing forward a new understanding of human security emerging at the civil–military interface. It has three parts. In the first, I discuss some of the consequences of the hijacking of 'human security' by the world of states, and then point out that civil–military interactions are a site to study interactions between top-down (state) and bottom-up (human) security. This is further elaborated in the second sub-section, in which I show how a multi-actor security perspective, based on positive security notions, helps us to observe and assess conflict and post-conflict settings. In the third, I share observations from my research in Afghanistan to offer insights into how we can support human security in civil–military operations and reduce the 'virtuous imperialist' footprint at the same time.

Human security – a state agenda in sheep's clothing?

Until the end of the Cold War, security was largely confined to the militarized and elite notion of state security bound within an anarchic international system regulated by superpowers (Hough 2008; Walt 1991). These traditional approaches have focused on the state as the primary security referent (or target) for security, as well as the primary security actor (creating security). It became clear in the 1990s, however, that the fixation on the state and its existence often had little to do with the way security was experienced 'on the ground'.

The development of 'human security' as a concept was in large part a response to a lack of acknowledgement of the personal experience of security in those 'traditional' approaches to security. It had also become increasingly clear that the state was by no means the sole security actor, particularly in conditions of weak or failed states, where civilians (and non-civilians) have had to rely on other sources, including themselves, to establish some semblance of security to manage their day-to-day existences. The concept thus draws attention to the security dynamics taking place at the level of civilians/non-combatants/non-state actors (Tadjbakhsh and Chenoy 2007; UNDP 1994; Wibben 2008). Understanding the needs and capacities of persons, and how they understand and manage their security needs, is crucial for any other security actor who will operate in the same environment.

Even though the 'human security agenda' was proposed in the early 1990s as a global initiative focusing on the security of individuals, it thereafter seemed to be largely adopted as a foreign policy approach by a number of global North countries, practising a 'new' way of understanding and providing assistance to the global South. The co-optation of human security by states, particularly those engaging in military interventions, comes with several consequences, addressed in the first sub-section. In the second, I suggest examining the experiences of civil–military interaction as a theoretically and analytically fruitful lens for the analysis of human security and how it is operationalized or practised.

Virtuous imperialism

Oz Hassan assesses the development of human security through the category of political security, which he claims has dominated the debates with its focus on 'the prevention of government repression, systematic violation of human rights, and threats from militarization' (Hassan 2015: 86). Though the apparent original intention was a focus on civilians, Hassan shows how political security has been subjected to tensions with the dominance of the state, whereby the state determines threats to political security, in particular through 'Responsibility to Protect' (R2P), which is a policy platform that has strong roots in human security (Abiew 2010; Bellamy 2009; ICISS 2001). Humanitarian interventions, which play a significant part in R2P, then become a primary vehicle for human security, but based on threats towards civilians that were largely identified by states, for state security. As Michael Pugh claims, 'rational, civilized "humanitarian intervention" may be a part of the packaging in which Western security culture, self-perception, and self-interest are wrapped' (Pugh 2005: 50).

Beyond identifying and perhaps 'solving' human security crises abroad as a foreign policy platform, human security also seemed to become a way of identifying the 'other' as a source of insecurity for those living in the global North, both as individuals and communities but also state security (Hoogensen Gjørv 2014b). The concept can be understood to entrench linear and elitist thinking with regard to security and lead to the perpetuation of the superior–subordinate relationship in North–South relations (Chandler 2008; Hoogensen Gjørv 2014b).

Although the human security concept appeared to break the apparent stranglehold that a narrow state-based conception had managed to co-opt since the Second World War and particularly through the Cold War, the prevailing assumption about human security is that it is a concept only relevant for particular regions of the world. It perpetuates ahistorical claims about the state and sovereignty, uncritical assumptions that state security trickles down to individuals and provides security at the community and individual level, that state security is well established in global North states. These sorts of claims have often been rooted in the realist tradition that assumes that 'strong states provide better security' (Wibben 2011: 70). Through this logic, the global North is composed of 'strong' states, having eradicated its own human security issues, and is well placed to assist the South in eradicating the same. This understanding of security is also very state-based, assuming that security is addressed by state actors alone, rather than being a process that involves multiple actors, state and non-state (Hoogensen Gjørv 2012). The result becomes an imbalance in perceptions and explanations of what occurs within and across regions and the globe, as well as disguising the contributions and competencies of different actors in providing security at different levels (Hoogensen Gjørv 2012; Stuvøy 2009).

I have described elsewhere the co-optation of human security for state security purposes as 'virtuous imperialism', whereby global North states engage in humanitarian interventions or other proclaimed human security measures for the purposes of ensuring that unrest in the global South does not find ways to extend to northern states through migration or terrorism (Hoogensen Gjørv 2014b). David Chandler raised this point as well, noting that human security was just a vehicle for state-security agendas (Chandler 2008). A state-security based orientation and implementation of human security renders non-state actors passive, and further renders invisible any human insecurities and vulnerabilities that are not identified by states. It assumes that community and individual voices are fully represented and attended to by a state actor, and it disguises, if not prevents, possible shared human security concerns and experiences between peoples across communities and regions, let alone states. The question is, whose expressions of security are actually 'heard' by those who have the power to act on these articulations (Hansen 2000)? If speech acts of security are made by marginalized or even 'everyday' people, but not recognized by those with the choice and power to respond, does that mean these are no longer articulations of security or insecurity?

Narrowing the focus: human security and civil–military engagement

Although the above criticisms of a state-based human security approach need to be taken seriously, this attempt to 'hijack' the original (though vague) human security agenda, to put it bluntly, is not so black-and-white. I want to suggest that tensions exist between state and individual/people-based security whereby it is clear that states are not the only game in town, and that bottom-up/community/individual perspectives on security can be influential in the creation and maintenance of state security, not only the other way around. The past two decades have illustrated these tensions well, as they have been characterized by expensive, personnel/troop heavy operations that have relied upon close military contact with civilian actors (local populations as well as civilian organizations and local to national authorities). Here, a new site for human security emerges.

Civil–military contact can be perceived in different ways, not least as either a militarization of civilian space whereby the military encroach upon and make use of civilian resources and information, or as a recognition by state and military actors that awareness and support for human security issues (well-being of populations affected by and within areas of operations) is crucial to the end goal of stabilization and security, or a combination of both, which I will argue here. Though military activities have largely always affected civilian populations, there has been an alarming trend since the end of the Cold War where there has been an enormous increase in civilian casualties as compared with military. The spaces between civilian and military have become much more narrow, and more often than not overlap. The recognition of these developments has resulted in a field of theory and practice called civil–military interaction: 'Civil–military interaction speaks to that untidy place where the ethics, ideals, practicalities, and realities regarding the relations between militaries and civilians meet up and often struggle with each other's goals and mandates. Civil–military interaction refers to the range and nature of contact, coordination, and/or cooperation between national (local) and international (foreign) civilians (ranging from government officials to NGOs both humanitarian and development, to local populations) and military actors in crisis situations' (Hoogensen Gjørv 2014a: 7).

A new framework for analysis

The security of civilian actors, including non-governmental agency aid workers and government employees, as well as the general population, lies at the core of the civil–military interface. Though militaries act at the behest of their governments, linking military strategy and goals to state security, their efforts on the ground affect, and are affected by, the state of human security in the area of operations. An analysis of human security in the local spaces where operations are taking place requires broader insights into security than what is offered by traditional state-based approaches. In what follows, I use a multi-actor security perspective that helps to refocus attention to new sites of human security and include feminist perspectives for the evaluation of power and authority in these sites.

From negative to positive security

The notions of positive and negative security can be used to reflect upon the human security distinction between 'freedom from want' and 'freedom from fear' and the measures by which security can be achieved. Negative security relies considerably upon state actors and use of force/violence, and is rooted in fear, whereas positive security makes space for non-violent measures and non-state actors. Positive and negative security can contribute to theorizing about what human security perspectives might imply for civil–military interaction (Hoogensen Gjørv 2012; Knight 2008; UNDP 1994).

Positive and negative security both reflect the tensions within the ways the concept of security in general has been conceptualized, who provides security and how, and how scholars and practitioners themselves place a 'value' on security. Negative security relates to the treatment of security as a concept we wish to avoid, one that should be invoked as little as possible. We value it negatively because it represents the use of force. On the other hand, the concept of security has also been known to represent something that is positively valued, or as something that is good or desired, providing a foundation to pursue our needs and interests and enjoy a full life (Hoogensen Gjørv 2012; Roe 2008).

Negative security can thus be understood as 'security from' (a threat) and positive security as 'security to' or enabling. Negative security is often associated with what is called traditional security that assumes a universally defined actor called 'the state' with state-centric security issues, addressed by a universally agreed-upon tool of security – the military. This is often understood to be the more dominant understanding of security, a type of "big S" security, given its dominance in relation to other security perspectives. The focus upon identification of threats and the use of violence affects the way we understand and practice "big S" security. The identification of danger and enemies legitimizes or justifies the use of force. It reduces the possibilities for recognizing multiple actors because we do not *want* multiple actors employing violence.

Thus negative security has been dominated by a 'uni-actor' approach, whereby the term 'security' ought to be a limited, one-actor, state-centric concept, linked to the state's assumed monopoly of force. Negative security thus invokes the deployment of the most extreme measures (usually the military) to address issues of immediate and existential danger. When the state invokes security-producing measures to protect the state, however, these same measures may or do have a deleterious effect on other actors, such as individuals and communities, who may feel inclined to respond to ensure their own security.

Positive security, on the other hand, reflects a central foundation for enabling, the foundation of trust. Trust is established largely through non-violent means, through negotiation, compromise, and dialogue. This is often framed as 'everyday' security (associated with individuals and communities), which reflects positive security, assumes the existence of trust created through good governance, respect for the law, cooperation, and an open society. Positive security allows the security analyst to ask how, for whom, and by whom, security is produced, exposing the values and contexts behind a diversity of practices of security. Positive security makes visible as well as prioritizes non-state actors, attempting to 'know' security that affects individuals every day.

Positive security therefore has much in common with some of the human security literature that recognizes individuals and communities as security actors (Hoogensen and Stuvøy 2006; Scharffscher 2011; Stern 2006). These non-state actors endeavour to seek security, not just in relation to avoiding threats, but also to building their capacities. Many of the practices to avoid threats and build capacities are non-violent in character, including measures ranging from humanitarian and development aid, to economic, education, environmental, and other social network supports. These measures and practices are crucial to providing secure environments. Thus when the state disappoints (which is not insignificant, as the state will always play a crucial role for providing certain measures for its citizens), individuals and communities often employ their own non-violent practices to ensure security, building upon whatever resources they might have at their disposal at the time. These are practices in positive security.

Understanding the core assumptions within positive and negative security allows us to observe and assess the field where multiple actors play a role in conflict and post-conflict settings. The ways in which conflict has 'developed' have a direct bearing upon how we will perceive and operationalize civil–military interaction. Although insurgencies and guerrilla warfare have been present throughout history, state-based perceptions involving large scale, professional armies have dominated. This dominant view has increasingly had to share space with the complex conflict formations we have seen over the past two decades, moving from large armies fighting against each other to a complex combination of a variety of actors vying to gain control (host nation military, intervention militaries, combating political opponents, criminals), while other 'civilian' or non-combatant actors are actively engaging within the same area of operations (Kaldor 2007).

The increased recognition of diverse actors as well as the complexities behind interventions (consent-based or support to one 'side') also affects the ways in which third parties or international organizations are able to interact with other actors as well as how they are perceived, rendering now-classical notions such as 'peacekeeping' less relevant (Soderlund et al. 2008). In many instances combatants have no intention of responding to diplomatic efforts or laying down arms at the behest of international actors which claim a moral authority on behalf of the international community (Soderlund et al. 2008).

All of these actors embody a set of values that they prioritize and wish to see survive into the future; these values inform their vision of the political, of which perceptions of security are an important part (Wibben 2011). Some actors, both military and civilian, engage in positive-security oriented projects or activities. These contribute to practices and experiences of security that support insecure populations with capacities to build upon and stabilize their lives once again. The same or other actors might also create insecurity (for example, political and military actors using force for regime-changing or state-building goals) with a purpose to generate a new system that prioritizes their own values and political projects, creating a different vision of the political, a different framework for security. Thus one's understanding of security depends upon the political agenda or political vision of the relevant actors.

A multi-actor security perspective

We should ask whether or not it should suffice to think of security largely in terms of military action and the protection of the state, and leave other actors out of the security picture. Although there are some who might argue this, experience has shown that both military and their political leadership need to be aware of who else is influencing security and security perceptions in their area of operations, and that this includes many non-state actors who traditionally have not been acknowledged. Civil–military interaction is about recognizing this multitude of actors, and about operationalizing a multi-actor security perspective, by including, if not prioritizing, the roles and security perceptions of people.

People across the political spectrum (from humanitarian to government to local populations) are 'everyday' security actors, and function alongside the 'traditional' (read: dominant or big 'S' security) tool of security: the military. 'Everyday' security has interacted with and been influential on big 'S' security. In past and current complex operations, we see the operationalization of negative security or (in)security which expresses vulnerabilities and sources of fear, as well as positive security focusing on capabilities and enabling, whereby people, societies, and groups have been able to create or build their security by a variety of means, to ensure that life continues, and to ensure a good life can be found (Bajpai 2004; CHS 2003; Hoogensen 2005; Hoogensen Gjørv 2012). Using an actor-based security framework, various actors, from communities and individuals to researchers, policy makers, state-based security practitioners (military and police actors), and private security agencies/NGOs/industry, are made visible, and are recognized as participants who express their perceptions of threats and assess their capacity to cope, in concert with others.

In other words, the state and the military are not the only 'security' actors, particularly where human security is concerned (Hasegawa 2007). Government, military, and policy-makers are neither always the leading actors in providing or identifying security, nor need to intervene at all levels of identified human (in)security as they may not have the competency to do so; however they can act as important conduits for the facilitation of knowledge between communities and actors, as well as respond to human in/securities when communities can no longer effectively respond to threats (UNDP 1994).

Questions of legitimacy and authority

The various actors within a security dynamic will be perceived as having differing forms of legitimacy and authority according to their roles. Questions about the legitimacy and authority of the host nation (questioned either by the host population and/or external actors) are used to justify decisions to intervene in a complex emergency, at which time political and/or legal legitimacy and authority transfers, ideally temporarily, to external actors, both military and civilian. This can create relationships of dependency by local populations upon external actors (where external actors become service-providers of everything from schooling and medical aid to veterinary care), particularly upon long-term actors such as non-governmental organizations (NGOs) and international organizations (IOs), and at times militaries. Over time, external actors working in the host nation might still have authority, but their legitimacy is reduced if the popular feeling is that there is not a timely transfer of authority to 'more legitimate' institutions such as the host government, if local populations see the external actors as potentially threatening their security (physical as well as identity), or if local populations do not see an increase or an improvement in their own security. In other words, legitimacy and authority are not static, and change over time depending on the circumstances (Hoogensen Gjørv 2014a).

Local populations find themselves in the unique situation of, in part, being a target for the efforts of many if not all of the other security actors and their efforts, as well as actors themselves that can influence the security dynamic. The military, as well as government/ministerial, NGO, and local community leaders attempt to exercise forms of control over populations, either to win their trust, or to protect them, or both. This is particularly the case in the civil–military relationship, where different actors vie for control through the use of force or claims to competence to argue for the legitimacy and authority of their roles in relation to civilian populations: 'sometimes competing claims for control over populations (between militaries and NGOs, for example) will work to disenfranchise or depower local populations, even if that is not the intended consequence' (Hoogensen Gjørv 2014a: 44). External actors such as international militaries and NGOs/IOs need to constantly be vigilant over how their own legitimacy functions in relation to other actors, and where legitimacy and authority ought to rest ultimately. Ideally legitimacy ends up in the hands of local populations and more specifically given local leaders or potential leaders. Finding out who is a risky task in itself and is an equally important part of the security dynamic and the possibilities for a long-term and stable security for the future.

Civil–military interaction is thus influenced by a mix of moral, political, and legal authority. International and national/host militaries act with political and legal authority, but may often lack moral authority and legitimacy amongst affected constituents (local populations, NGOs), such that they might meet with resistance. NGOs are often considered to have a legal (international humanitarian law (IHL)) and moral authority, particularly when acting on the basis of a humanitarian mandate to help people in need, but may also suffer legitimacy issues if they have not convinced their potential beneficiaries of their merit (Hilhorst 2003), or where their relationships with donor countries and the challenges of national/international aid systems come into question (Tvedt 2007).

Governments, both host nation and donor/troop contributing nation, engage political and legal authority, but also to some degree moral authority, when making claims and pronouncements regarding the need to protect civilians from harm and suffering. The extent of government authority is connected to legitimacy with the local population, but is not always dependent upon it. At times, the political authority of the host government, despite its weaknesses, might hold more weight with communities than does the moral authority of NGOs, if in the long run the host nation government means greater long-term stability and independence. Thus legitimacy and authority to act are important components of the civil–military relationship and depend greatly upon the context of the crisis situation.

Bringing in feminist perspectives

In the realm of interactions between different actors at different political and social scales, feminist approaches have been ground-breaking and trail-blazing for security theoretical perspectives. Feminist security theories have had a strong people-centred focus and have been developing in parallel, as well as in concert with, human security theorizing (Hoogensen and Rottem 2004; Sylvester 2010): 'security narratives limit how we can think about security, whose security matters, and how it might be achieved' (Wibben 2011: 65).

The extensive research in Feminist Security Studies, spanning over 20 years, can be used to further inform the dynamics of the civil–military interface, as well as human security theories (Blanchard 2003; Hoogensen and Stuvøy 2006). Feminist Security Studies looks theoretically and empirically at how security is created from the position of marginalized voices, exposing those security processes that are happening 'on the ground' whether they are recognized by state authorities or not. Feminist security theory brings to light "Everyday" security, making visible the processes and actors that are also primary in the civil–military spaces existing at the 'tactical level', or rather, at the level where people actually live and survive, if not thrive.

Instead of feeding into dominant approaches to Security Studies that focus on a very small portion of the security grid and from the top down (big 'S' security), gender analysis takes its starting point from the bottom up; in concert with human security, but with an increased awareness of the impact of gender socialization on personal relations and security perceptions. Acknowledging that the personal is political, these analyses reach down to the individual's experience, claiming that they are relevant, not just at the level of the individual, but also in relation to the community, the state, and the global order. By identifying the articulation of security needs by those who are least secure or in positions of non-dominance, security is reoriented away from elite interests (Hoogensen and Stuvøy 2006). Feminist approaches have had a long and established tradition of highlighting marginalized realities faced on a daily basis by, arguably, the majority of the world's population, from economic insecurity and domestic violence, to rape as an institutionalized strategy of large-scale warfare, as well as from the gendered roots of war itself.

Practising human security in a complex space:
the case of Afghanistan

The claim of human security, through R2P or humanitarian intervention, as well as from aid organizations, is that the most important actors 'on the ground' are the people who live in the 'host' nation, or that nation where international actors deploy to support in the provision of assistance and establishment of security. In today's complex operations, troop-contributing/donor nations and NGOs claim to be acting on behalf of the welfare of host-nation people where the complex emergency is occurring.

The protection of the host-nation civilians may not be always the primary reason for an intervention (at least by foreign governments), but often local population security and well-being, their human security, is invoked by donor/troop-contributing nations as a key concern of those who choose to engage themselves in complex emergencies. Civilians of the host nations are often used as the *raison d'être* behind ethical foreign policies and principles such as R2P. These are the people who are labelled as 'beneficiaries' of NGOs (national, local, or international), or are the 'local population' with whom militaries will interact. Not all civilians are beneficiaries of course, nor will all civilians have direct contact with governmental or military personnel. However, many if not most might be impacted by these external actors in either direct or indirect ways.

Often the civilians of the host nation are portrayed as those who need help or protection. What is important to remember first and foremost is that they are people who are the frontline of effort and support for their own communities when crisis arises, as they themselves must find ways to cope and survive, sometimes with little to no resources and supplies, before any NGO, military, or official presence arrives in their area. These civilians are by far the best 'experts' on their culture and customs, and while foreigners (militaries and international NGOs) may compete about 'who has been in the area the longest' or who can best identify local population needs when making claims about competency and expertise, these civilians have been on site and are aware of their own needs, though these might be competing. These same civilians are a mix (as any population) of people who are biased, politically motivated, restricted/influenced/coloured by the knowledge-base and skills available to, and developed by, their communities and cultures, and play roles in complex power arrangements based on gender, class, ethnicity, and other social classifications.

As such, it was not surprising that amongst the Afghan citizens I spoke with during my own research on the relevance of human security to civil–military interaction, I was met with a wide range of opinions and thoughts about the future of their families, their communities, and of Afghanistan. To even write about 'civilians' in this sense, the people living in and amongst complex emergencies (in Afghanistan or otherwise), is extremely difficult. There are no unified principled or political positions here, as people's expectations for the future, and their sense of security, vary according to the diverse values they hold. There may be some uniformity of values along religious and/or ethnic lines (though not always), and education access and levels can also play a significant role (and cause simplistic divides between the 'educated' and 'non-educated'). It is thus difficult to try to capture the 'civilian position' in a complex emergency, but this group of civilians have the most to gain or lose in the civil–military interface, and play a crucial role, if not the most crucial role, in a multi-actor security dynamic. A number of individuals, many operating at the local level as local leaders, also have considerable influence on security.

The importance of local 'acceptance' and willingness to work with other actors (military or NGO) has been long acknowledged to be relevant to the creation, development, and maintenance of security – at both local (human) and regional as well as state levels. This impact is hotly debated as well. On the one hand it is recognized that local community acceptance is necessary for other actors – from NGOs to warring parties such as Afghan government forces and NATO ISAF forces, as well as opposition forces such as the Taliban (in the Afghan case) – to gain power in the region in question. Government and military forces want to gain legitimacy with local populations because local community support means solidification of authority and power. Part of the process for establishing legitimacy with local populations is ensuring the provision of human security – ensuring the security of everyday lives, from health care to education to job opportunities to local physical security. The delivery of services plays a crucial role in human security perspectives at the local level, and when these are delivered in cooperation with local community authorities, they can contribute to the establishment of stability in their region.

Different interpretations arise regarding these legitimization processes and the creation of security. These interpretations take us back to the tensions within the human security agenda, where the security needs of people are set against the security needs of the state. On the one hand, claims by many aid organizations or NGOs are that they work with local communities (and their authorities) to gain access and acceptance to be able to deliver needs-based services to that community. Emphasis is placed on the legitimacy that they gain by negotiating through local authorities. The process is framed in such a way that we see how non-state actors work together to provide crucial basic services that contribute to human security – the everyday lives of local populations.

At the same time it is acknowledged that part of the process, particularly in such politically tense and conflict-filled environments, implies that the acceptance of NGO involvement by local authorities also might mean that these same authorities use the NGO delivery of services for their own purposes to gain legitimacy with their own populations (ANSO 2010). These local authorities may not be state-based actors or support the current state leadership, but they may be allied with those who are attempting to gain power at the state level (such as the Taliban). Thus the acceptance and legitimacy provided by local populations, in conjunction with the potential that this also means greater legitimacy for the local powerbrokers, can have a significant effect on security at the local, regional, and even national levels (Hoogensen Gjørv 2014a). On the other hand, similar processes taking place by other actors (state or state-supporting international actors) such as ISAF militaries and/or ISAF civilian actors who attempt to negotiate acceptance with communities and offer services for the fulfilment of human security needs, have been heavily criticized as 'hearts and minds' operations whereby local community acceptance and legitimacy is 'bought' by offering different services or products desired by the community (Gompelman 2011).

In both cases we see different arguments employed – where the delivery of crucial services to communities is consistent with community needs and driven by 'bottom-up' needs and processes, or where the state/powerbrokers use human security needs for their own solidification of state-based security. The latter argument is particularly levelled against the Western forces that have been largely active in Afghanistan up until December 2014. The 'hearts and minds' critique reflects the arguments against the human security agenda where human security is just a virtuous framing of standard state interests and security.

Conclusion

What the case illustrates is that human security, and the complex multitude of actors that are involved in creating security (which we see exemplified in the civil–military interface through different forms of interaction), cannot be understood as 'either/or'. Human security approaches indeed do expose the activities and processes that are taking place 'on the ground', creating spaces of security, often fragile, but in constant development. We see the efforts made locally, by women and men according to varying capacities. We see also how these efforts and processes can be and are influential to perceptions of security beyond the individual and community level, where these processes can influence balances of power for competing interests. And where the powers behind these competing interests indeed understand that local community perceptions and experiences of security can be decisive for their own purposes.

The lessons we should take away therefore are that human security perspectives emanating from the community and individual levels, from the bottom up, are not irrelevant or side issues to the so-called traditional or big 'S' security articulated by state actors. Particularly in situations where state authorities are weak, fragile, or virtually non-existent, the relevance of community needs and interests can be even more crucial to security at multiple levels. At the same time we have to be on constant vigil for the ways in which human security agendas can be and are abused, insofar as 'everyday' security is not prioritized or is devalued for purposes considered separate or more important than ensuring human security.

References

Abiew, F. K. (2010) 'Humanitarian Intervention and the Responsibility to Protect: Redefining a Role for "Kind-Hearted Gunmen"', *Criminal Justice Ethics* 29(2): 93–109.

ANSO (2010) *ANSO Quarterly Data Report* Q.3, Kabul: ANSO.

Bajpai, K. (2004) 'An Expression of Threats Versus Capabilities across Time and Space', *Security Dialogue* 35(3): 360–1.

Bellamy, A. J. (2009) *Responsibility to Protect: The Global Effort to End Mass Atrocities*, London, Polity Press.

Blanchard, E. M. (2003) 'Gender, International Relations, and the Development of Feminist Security Theory', *Signs: Journal of Women in Culture and Society* 28(41): 1289–1312.

Breslin, S. and Christou, G. (2015) 'Has the Human Security Agenda Come of Age? Definitions, Discourses and Debates', *Contemporary Politics* 21(1): 1–10.

Chandler, D. (2008) 'Human Security: The Dog That Didn't Bark', *Security Dialogue* 39(4): 427–38.

CHS (2003) *Human Security Now*, New York: United Nations Publications.

Gompelman, G. (2011) *Winning Hearts and Minds? Examining the Relationship between Aid and Security in Afghanistan's Faryab Province*, Medford, MA: Tufts University Press.

Hansen, L. (2000) 'The Little Mermaid's Silent Security Dilemma and the Absence of Gender in the Copenhagen School', *Millennium – Journal of International Studies* 29(2): 285–306.

Hasegawa, Y. (2007) 'Is a Human Security Approach Possible? Compatibility between the Strategies of Protection and Empowerment', *Journal of Refugee Studies* 20(1): 1–19.

Hassan, O. (2015) 'Political Security: From the 1990s to the Arab Spring', *Contemporary Politics* 21(1): 86–99.

Hilhorst, D. (2003) *The Real World of NGOs*, London: Zed Books.

Hoogensen, G. (2005) 'Gender, Identity, and Human Security: Can We Learn Something from the Case of Women Terrorists?', *Canadian Foreign Policy* 12(1): 119–40.

Hoogensen, G. and Rottem S. V. (2004) 'Gender Identity and the Subject of Security', *Security Dialogue* 35(2): 155–71.

Hoogensen, G. and Stuvøy, K. (2006) 'Human Security, Gender and Resistance', *Security Dialogue* 37(2): 207–28.

Hoogensen Gjørv, G. (2012) 'Security by Any Other Name: Negative Security, Positive Security and a Multi-Actor Security Approach', *Review of International Studies* 38(4): 835–59.

Hoogensen Gjørv, G. (2014a) *Understanding Civil–Military Interaction: Lessons Learned from the Norwegian Model*, London: Ashgate.

Hoogensen Gjørv, G. (2014b) 'Virtuous Imperialism or a Shared Global Objective? The Relevance of Human Security in the Global North', in G. Hoogensen Gjørv, D. R. Bazely, M. Goloviznina, and A. J. Tanentzap (eds.) *Environmental and Human Security in the Arctic*, London and New York: Routledge, 58–79.

Hough, P. (2008) *Understanding Global Security*, London: Routledge.

ICISS (2001) *The Responsibility to Protect: Report of the International Commission on Intervention and State Sovereignty (ICISS)*, Ottawa: International Development Research Centre.

Kaldor, M. (2007) *New and Old Wars: Organized Violence in a Global Era*, 2nd edn, Stanford, CA: Stanford University Press.

Knight, A. (2008) 'Civil–Military Cooperation and Human Security', in C. Ankersen (ed.) *Civil–Military Cooperation in Post-Conflict Operations: Emerging Theory and Practice*, Abingdon: Routledge, 15–30.

Pugh, M. (2005) 'Peacekeeping and Critical Theory', in A. J. Bellamy and P. Williams (eds.) *Peace Operations and Global Order*, New York and London: Routledge, 39–58.

Roe, P. (2008) 'The "Value" of Positive Security', *Review of International Studies* 34: 777–94.

Scharffscher, K. S. (2011) 'Disempowerment through Disconnection: Local Women's Disaster Response and International Relief in Post-Tsunami Batticaloa', *Disaster Prevention and Management* 20(1): 63–81.

Soderlund, W. C., Briggs, E. D., Hildebrant, K., and Sidahmed, A. S. (2008) *Humanitarian Crises and Intervention: Reassessing the Impact of Mass Media*, Sterling: Kumarian Press.

Stern, M. (2006) *Naming Security – Constructing Identity: 'Mayan-Women' in Guatemala on the Eve of Peace*, Manchester: Manchester University Press.

Stuvøy, K. (2009) 'Security under Construction: A Bourdieusian Approach to Non-State Crisis Centres in Northwest Russia', Ph.D. dissertation, University of Tromsø.

Sylvester, C. (2010) 'Tensions in Feminist Security Studies', *Security Dialogue* 41(6): 607–14.

Tadjbakhsh, S. and Chenoy, A. M. (2007) *Human Security. Concepts and Implications*, London and New York: Routledge.

Tvedt, T. (2007) 'International Development Aid and Its Impact on a Donor Country: A Case Study of Norway', *The European Journal of Development Research* 19(4): 614–35.

UNDP (1994) *Human Development Report 1994: New Dimensions of Human Security*, New York: United Nations Development Programme.

Walt, S. M. (1991) 'The Renaissance of Security Studies', *International Studies Quarterly* 35(2): 211–39.

Wibben, A. T. R. (2008) 'Human Security: Toward an Opening', *Security Dialogue* 39(4): 455–62.

Wibben, A. T. R. (2011) *Feminist Security Studies: A Narrative Approach*, London: Routledge.

11

RISK AND SECURITY

Karen Lund Petersen

In Security Studies, *risk* has become a forceful description of current trends in the American and European governance of security, portrayed in the management of global threats such as terrorism, climate change, organized crime, and nuclear proliferation. These policies are often described by concepts of risk, resilience, and precaution. But what exactly is the relation between Security Studies, risk, and these seemingly new practices of governance? And how do these concepts challenge the conventional understandings of risk and security?

The one thing uniting these concepts and debates is a preoccupation with the unknowable, the new threat, the uncertain future, and the subsequent difficulty of management and prevention. Ulrich Beck and Anthony Giddens talk about an increasing 'ambiguity of knowing' in today's approaches to risk, Zygmunt Bauman about the vision of unnamed and unanticipated threats, and Frank Furedi about the 'crisis of causality' and a following idiom of fear (Baumann 2006: 11; Beck 1992: 183; Furedi 2009: 202; Giddens 1992: 85). In these statements, each scholar tries to grasp a changing temporality: a changing understanding of the relation between present and future in the management of threat. The argument is that we are no longer able to control, predict, or even manage the future and that, consequently, traditional risk management strategies cannot be upheld. In this context, resilience and precaution have become the dominant neologisms describing the impossibility of possible management: the new hybrids between practices of risk and security.

On the face of it, risk in Security Studies is about the management of new and possible catastrophic threats; about an increasing concern for how security politics is being bureaucratically managed in the everyday mundane practices of governments, civil groups, and private companies. In this debate, we ask how the unknown has become the baseline for decision-making. How the idea of the unknown – the ambiguity of knowledge – is constituted as an object of knowledge in the practice of security. Thus, at the meta-theoretical level, the debate on risk in Security Studies is about how we handle the paradox of asserting knowledge in a world of unknowns, about defining 'the thing' that potentially can provide a basis for decision-making.

This chapter tells the story of how the concepts of risk and security increasingly merge in Security Studies and how contemporary security practices of resilience and precaution write and rewrite classical notions of risk.

The first part of the chapter briefly introduces past and current debates on the concept of risk, discussing how it relates to current trends in Security Studies.[1] The second part presents the two ways in which the concept of uncertainty has figured as a counter-concept to risk, while the third part shows how we are currently engaging these concepts of uncertainty – two different under-standings of knowledge – in the current perceptions of precaution and resilience. The final part of the chapter takes up some of the central discussions in Security Studies on riskification and secu-ritization and discusses how we should theoretically develop future studies on risk and security.

Risk in Security Studies: a partial history

As we understand it today, the concept of risk came into being in the early modern era, around the same time that the nation-state was established as the main political unit. Just as state forma-tion was an answer to the ongoing religious wars, risk became a powerful secular alternative to religious visions of fate. Where destiny could determine fate, risk designated a belief in the pos-sibility for human progress and control over the future. Risk thus became the antithesis to destiny (cf. Bernstein 1998; Douglas 1990; Giddens 1991; Luhmann 1991).

While the concept of risk, associated with risk management as an organizational decision-making practice, is still very much about control and the management of possible futures, uncer-tainty has become the absolutely most defining counter-concept to risk. Frank Knight's work from 1921 addressing the distinction between risk and uncertainty has become iconic in risk studies. He defined risk as the 'known chance' (related to probability) and uncertainty as the unknown; uncertainty thus designating the impossibility of classification, quantification, and, to some extent, also prevention (Best 2008; Knight 1921: 245; Runde 1998). Where rational behav-iour can help us manage or even possibly eliminate risk, uncertainty refers to indeterminacy between the actions of today and the events of tomorrow.

In International Relations (IR), the Cold War debates on security largely escaped this debate on management. Focused on the study of war and national security, IR was generally more con-cerned with political order, identity, and social contract. Uncertainty (in the form of anarchy) was largely the premise upon which the international system operated, and thereby also the basis of any decision-making. In 'a balance of power vision', the only certainty that existed was the reoccurrence of war.[2] In comparison with the individual economic ontology[3] expressed in most risk thinking during the twentieth century, the 'management' of security was inextricably linked to the idea of a social contract, to the idea of national interest and politics.

In the 1980s, this realist conception of security, tied to the organization of the nation-state, became increasingly questioned. It was argued that a concept of (international) politics defined by order and territory could not capture the new developments, that the aim of security politics was more than just avoiding the reoccurrence of war, and that it was embedded in every political decision in the everyday bureaucratic management of the nation's security (Bigo 2000; Buzan et al. 1998).

Almost parallel to this development in Security Studies, sociologists and anthropologists pointed to the political nature of risk and criticized the rather instrumentalist understanding expressed in conventional risk management practices. Most prominently, Ulrich Beck (1992) has linked different conceptions of risk to the evolution of the industrial society and Mary Douglas has focused on the political choices involved in the societal selection of which risks to prioritize (Douglas and Wildavsky1982). In the French poststructuralist camp, scholars pointed to the disciplining effects and neoliberal character of the dominant economic practices of risk analysis (Ewald 2001; O'Malley 2004; Rose 1993). Common for these scholars was a focus on the politics of risk analysis and its historical and cultural heritages.[4]

Although the concepts of risk and security are shaped by their respective disciplinary histories, the recognition that security is also about the 'internal' management of security and that risk management is fundamentally political did bring the debates together. Yet this unity of interest in the governance of new, uncertain, and often catastrophic threats also exposes the limits of the two disciplinary perspectives. While we might agree to the political nature of risk management and the fact that security is more than 'merely' military security, Security Studies still struggles with how to understand and theoretically comprehend security as a bureaucratic practice of state agencies, civil organizations, and private enterprises. Likewise, risk studies increasingly struggles to understand 'security matters' as threats that cannot be delimited in space or time (cf. Beck 2003).

In this environment where concepts of risk and security constantly meet, neologisms of resilience and precaution have come to define a political and hybrid practice of 'security risk management'. These concepts, as I will argue, draw upon different understandings of uncertainty to bring out the 'securityness' of risk.

Risk as uncertainty: the ambiguity of knowing

There are basically two ways in which the concept of uncertainty figures a counter-concept to risk: one where uncertainty is positioned as a different category of knowledge and one where uncertainty prescribes a fundamental ambiguity of life. These two concepts of uncertainty, I will later argue, correspond to the current practices of precaution and resilience, respectively.

The *first* understanding follows Knight and defines uncertainty as a category of threats that are distinct from normal (measurable and controllable) risk. Accordingly, uncertainty is observable and can be dealt with politically: it is possible to locate and categorize and, on that basis, define strategies for dealing with these uncertainties. This understanding can be found in every conventional approach to risk management, in scenario analysis, and in likelihood-impact analysis. In scenario analysis, the explicit purpose is to identify possible uncertain futures and translate them into manageable risks – to make the future present (Bradfield et al. 2005; Postma and Liebl 2005).

In the *second* understanding, uncertainty is a fundamental premise of life and possible wealth; it is not a category of threats that can be seized and managed. We simply cannot categorize uncertainty since 'we don't know what we don't know'. In this version (as represented in the works of J. M. Keynes, for example), uncertainty is a condition of social affairs, distinct from steering and control in political and social affairs. In this second form, uncertainty exceeds control and risk analysis. Uncertainty cannot be categorized, but is a fundamental fact of social life (Best 2008: 356; Runde 1998). This understanding of uncertainty, I will later argue, can be found in resiliency strategies focusing on business continuity and emergency planning, and in responsibilization strategies such as awareness campaigns.

These different concepts of uncertainty are not, however, merely descriptions of the ways in which we, as researchers, observe others' observations; they are also evoked for the sake of arguing that the contemporary concept of risk is qualitatively different than previously, that there is a historical and structural shift in our understanding of risk.[5] This argument is presented clearly in Ulrich Beck's work (1992, 1999). In his distinction between first and second modernity, he makes the case for how societies have increasingly become aware of possible global catastrophes and how this awareness has changed our perception of risks. In the first modernity, a decision was based on the idea of progress. The object of fear was a *definable* Other (God, class, or nations). A decision could therefore rest on calculation and the vision that it was possible to control the future. In the second 'reflexive' modernity, decisions are often based on what *we do not know*. We have become reflexive about our own production of risk, as we are acknowledging the existence of a fundamental uncertainty about the relationship between present action and future consequences. The object of fear is the 'end of the world' or the catastrophe that might occur.

Another prominent scholar describing a similar development is François Ewald. In his analysis of the history of insurance and the concept of precaution, he shows how the concept of risk has been highly central to the internal organization of society throughout modern history.

The understanding of risk as locatable and calculable legitimizes the so-called internal order of society, he argues. Risk has come to govern our understanding of modern politics and become 'naturalized' as a principle of political governance that defines the meanings of responsibility and legality (Ewald 1991).

That said, Ewald also shows how this modern logic of decision is being confronted today. He observes what can be called a 'culture of precaution' – an understanding of risks as non-risks (or as 'uncertainty' in the sense defined by Knight). I quote: 'While the language of risk, against the background of scientific expertise, used to be sufficient to describe all types of insecurities, the new paradigm (precaution) sees uncertainty in the light of an even newer science . . . science that is consulted less for the knowledge it offers than the doubt it insinuates' (Ewald 2001: 274). In describing a precautionary logic, Ewald draws a distinction between the modern form of risk and that of uncertainty. For society and political order, the consequences of this shift described by both Beck and Ewald are huge, as responsibility no longer refers to the consequences of a decision, but to the decision itself. In this world, uncertainty of knowledge is no longer 'innocent', but the mere existence of suspicion commits one to take precautionary steps. Moral obligations are, as Ewald (2001: 285) puts it, 'swallowed up in public ethics', an ethics based on *doubt* rather than exact science.[6]

Beck and Ewald have some striking observations on what is involved in reflexive and/or precautionary risk decisions and how these reflections have become a precondition for how we approach and act in social affairs; how we can no longer describe uncertainty as 'just' a category of knowledge that can possibly be transformed into manageable risks. For these authors, uncertainty and doubt have become a fundamental fact of life.

The question, however, remains: how are these concepts of uncertainty reflected in what are argued to be the new risk-mitigating practices – precaution and resilience? Do these risk-mitigating practices envision risk and uncertainty as categories of knowledge or, in the vision of these concepts, is politics based on the idea of fundamental uncertainty?

Precaution and resilience as risk practices

Precaution and resilience appear increasingly frequently in academic writings as well as in policy documents as descriptions of *the* new risk management practices that can help us manage possible catastrophes and unforeseen security threats. In the following, I will go through the debates on these concepts and try to come to terms with the newness of these visions.

Precaution

As a political concept, the precautionary principle became popular as a legal and political instrument with the Brundtland Report and the UN Rio summit in 1992. In the Rio Declaration, precautionary action became established as an approach to risk mitigation, because 'where there are threats of serious or irreversible damage, lack of full scientific certainty shall not be used as a reason for postponing such measures' (UN 1992, principle 15). The emphasis on a lack of scientific evidence (uncertainty) together with emphasis on the possible catastrophic character of the threat defined the meaning of precaution.

While scientific *uncertainty* became the most powerful discourse in the debates on the precautionary principle, freedom of choice was not considered a valuable position. Rather, precaution came to designate 'a special kind' of decision-making. Precaution came to refer to (scientific) uncertainty as a 'category of knowledge'; as something that can be targeted, comprehended, and therefore also possibly managed (similar to Knight 1921). It designated the 'possibility of possible' management: a 'vision of movement' from uncertainty to risk and management.

This concept of precaution as 'possible management' is, however, not only represented in the literature on environmental matters (e.g. Kahan et al. 2010) but also present in the entire literature on black swans (Taleb 2007) and the general literature on scenario building (Bradfield et al. 2005; Chermack 2011; Postma and Liebl 2005). In IR we find this understanding of precaution in the debates on the US–EU trade relations and the disagreement on what can and should form the basis for risk regulation at the international level (Lee et al. 2009; Stirling 2007; Vogel 2012).

There is also, however, another concept of precaution present in Security Studies, one that draws on the second vision of uncertainty (uncertainty as a fundamental premise of life). Drawing on the observations made by Beck and Ewald about decision-making in late modernity, critical scholars have observed how a changed understanding of threats has triggered a shift in the rationale behind the governance of security risks. A new rationale of precaution, based on a fundamental uncertainty, has been injected into today's management of security and left us with a paradox of defining moral obligations of doubt within a paradigm of management, it is argued (Aradau and van Munster 2007; Kessler and Werner 2008; Kessler 2010; Rasmussen 2009).

Within this line of thinking, de Goede (2008) and Furedi (2009) have raised a distinct criticism of the first concept of precaution, arguing how scenario thinking works to translate imagined futures into current management and control, and how such a process of remediation potentially escalates fear.

Resilience

The concept of resilience, Walker and Cooper write, 'has infiltrated vast areas of social science, becoming a regular, if under-theorized, term of art in discussions of international finance and economic policy, corporate risk analysis, the psychology of trauma, development policy, urban planning, public health and national security' (2011: 143). Yet the meaning of the term and the associated practices are much debated (cf. Dunn Cavelty et al. 2015a).

Especially the metaphorical status of the concept, originating in biology, renders it both debated and politically powerful. The 'original' description of resilience, designating the ability of complex eco-systems to adapt and persist, is figuratively and metaphorically linked to the need for organizational adaptation and recovery in the face of new and possibly catastrophic threats. The political concept of resilience thus takes over the idea of a 'normal' state of affairs or, as some scholars argue, an unquestioned 'equilibrium' that we must constantly preserve or strive towards (Prior and Hagmann 2013; Stark 2014) – in health policies, climate policies, and security. In security, homeland security in particular, resilience has come to describe the capacity of organizations or systems to endure and survive in the face of new threats, and thus the ability of organizations and citizens to mobilize to adapt to new global and transcending threats.

Resilience therefore does more than merely describe a certain logic of decision-making; it also designates a state of affairs or the preferred condition of an organization or system.[7] The metaphorical status of the concept is what makes it powerful, as it fixes and naturalizes the meaning of political mobilization and leaves little room for choice and hence contestation and debate.[8] Like the 'invisible hand', 'becoming resilient' is described as a natural process that is given by the use of metaphor. There is simply no choice but to adapt!

In many ways one can argue that resilience is a transcending form of securitization, as it assumes a need for immediate action/adaption. Yet the relation between means and ends is only vaguely defined and remains somewhat metaphorical. In conventional risk management, the future is a preferred future and the goal is to get there; in a resiliency paradigm, the goal is to sustain what we have already achieved. Thus, contrary to conventional risk analysis, the construction of resilience as a metaphor makes preservation, rather than progress, the natural political ideal. The concept of resilience thus lacks vision!

How is this need for adaption described in Security Studies? Similarly to the concept of precaution, the concept of resilience relies on an understanding of the future as increasingly uncertain. Yet the concept of resilience does more than defend a decision climate that celebrates the ability to adapt by acting in a precautionary manner (Stark 2014). Rather, resilience describes a need for preserving essential societal functions and designing adaptable institutions.[9] The means to resilience are emergency management, business continuity planning, awareness raising, and responsibilization of citizens and companies.

In many ways, the description of resilience (as being used in Security Studies and by policy-makers) breaks with the consequentialist thinking of conventional risk analysis. In the context of resilience, risk mitigation is not a matter of making the unknown known; rather, the premise is that we will never know. This way of thinking about risks thus installs 'radical' uncertainty as a general principle upon which decisions are made and describes a demand of some kind of identification of the existing uncertainties. In that way, we should adapt by preparing for a fast recovery.

The concept of resilience generally presumes a fundamental uncertainty in social life: one that we cannot escape; one that relies on doubts, worst-case thinking, and a wish for preserving that which we already have. It is an 'approach to risk management that foregrounds the limits of predictive knowledge and insists on the prevalence of the unexpected' (Walker and Cooper 2011: 147). Yet compared to precautionary approaches, 'resilience' involves a different temporality: its metaphorical status makes it a strategy about the 'means' only, not the 'ends'. The concept of resilience presupposes a description of a preferred political order, an equilibrium, and calls for means of preservation rather than new visions.

As I have argued elsewhere, this deontological form of risk management is increasingly present in the security practices of private companies. Corporate security management is no longer based so much on the idea of assessing the threats external to the organization as about preparing for the worst and being morally obliged to our own morality (Petersen 2012b: 127–8). In this version of risk, risk management is not about defining the future in the present but about the present of the present. Michael Power (2007) makes a similar observation, talking about the 'implosion of risk management' in private financial companies. He argues that auditing has become the means for making the company accountable to its own morality (not the law). Consequently, such practices tend to install doubt and suspicion as the baseline for decision-making and leave us with a deontological ethic whereby moral obligations are 'swallowed up in public ethics'.

Conclusion

As argued in the introduction to this chapter, risk in security is about how to know and act on the unknown. Two conceptual meanings of uncertainty have dominated risk thinking since the mid-twentieth century: meanings which can be found in the new risk-mitigating strategies in security governance, precaution, and resilience. In one understanding, uncertainty is a category of knowledge that we constantly seek to control and can possibly be transformed into manageable risks. This understanding of risk is still very much alive in the current debates on precaution, scenario-building, and black swans as attempts to make the unknowable future known.

In the second version of uncertainty, risk management has moved beyond the possibility of management. Uncertainty is a fundamental premise of life that transcends all other forms of management. The first concept of uncertainty (uncertainty as possibly manageable) dismantles previous consequentialist thinking and celebrates a deontological vision of decision-making. In many ways, the concept of resilience repeats this vision of knowledge in its celebration of preservation by adaption.

What, then, is the place of this debate in Security Studies? One of the most powerful approaches in Europe is found in securitization theory, developed by Ole Wæver,[10] and much of the debate on how to place risk in Security Studies tries to link up to this debate. One set of scholars argues that the risk perspective is substantively different from securitization: risk designates a different way of governing security, one that escapes the existential character of security and is therefore more fundamental to everyday (Aradau et al. 2013; Hagmann and Dunn Cavelty 2012; Petersen 2012b).

From a completely different perspective, Corry and Clapton have proposed that we expand securitization theory with a theory of riskification (Clapton 2011; Corry 2012). Riskification is, according to Corry, the 'construction of conditions of possibilities of harm (a risk) to a governance object' (249). The main point is that risk, contrary to security, is concerned with potential threats (contrasted to immediate threats) and therefore leads to precautionary action.[11] According to Corry and others, in this risk perspective, the unknown threats are localizable and thereby potential objects of management.

There are at least two remarks to be made regarding this risk agenda in critical Security Studies: one that rests on mere empirical observations and the other that relates to the limits of possible critique. First, to identify risk as riskification may render us blind to the many concepts of risk practices in daily life and to the fact that these two concepts increasingly merge in the daily practices of organizations, companies, and governments. As we have just seen, this trend can be observed in the practices associated with resilience and precaution. These neologisms, while drawing on different concepts of uncertainty, do not take a specific form, but rather open up different decision logics and political solutions. Although these neologisms centre on how to handle new and uncertain threats, the claims to knowledge expressed in these concepts are very different. We need to recognize the actual negotiations of meaning going on in the practice of security. These conceptual constructions are deeply political, as they construct responsibility and possible political action differently.

Second, we need to ask about the possibility of critique – not only regarding the possibility of a critical examination of the political effects of the many policy innovations in the area of security but also in relation to the theories we produce. For analytical and normative reasons, it is important to single out the performativity of the different conceptual uses and expose the scientific limits and enable an evaluation of each analysis. Scholars have criticized the Copenhagen School concept of securitization for being overly formalistic; for ignoring or marginalizing the political power of new institutional arrangements and discourses within the field of security (Huysmans 2006). Yet while we might question the validity of the concept in today's practice of security, the theorization that this approach represents is preferable on the grounds that it enables scientific critique and debate concerning the usefulness of what we do.

In sum, we should not give up on the ability to see new forms of security governance, nor should we attempt to escape theory. Maybe we should not stick to either securitization or riskification but instead constantly widen our horizons to envision and theorize new forms of security . . . and risk?

Notes

1 The conceptual analysis presented is inspired by Reinhart Koselleck's approach to conceptual history. A focus on the constellation of concepts and counter concepts, and how they prescribe meaning and political action, is essential (Koselleck 1985).
2 Felix Berenskoetter (2011) argues that the idea of future uncertainties has played little or no role in constructivist analysis.

3 The social welfare argument has, however, been a strong component in the twentieth-century understanding of risk (see Ewald 2001), yet the purpose of much of the thinking on, e.g., insurance was to calculate and individualize risks to the benefit of society as a whole.

4 For an overview of these debates, see Petersen 2012b.

5 In the actual risk practice of organizations and companies, these two forms are often not considered exclusive; even if uncertainty is accepted as a fundamental fact, politics and management are always about control; about making political decisions and selecting threats and risks.

6 Michael Power (2007) has a similar observation when talking about an increasing 'implosion of risk management'. Analyzing corporate decision-making, he argues that we currently see more and more businesses acting towards an increasingly uncertain risk environment and that this has led to an increase in internal auditing and control, self-control and moral action being the one thing that can be controlled. This development is also reflected in some of the debates on Corporate Social Responsibility (see e.g. Thompson 2012).

7 Or as Dunn Cavelty, Kaufmann, and Kristensen write, resilience has become 'an organizing principle in political life', designating a meaning of uncertainty as complexity as well as idea about responsible subjects (2015: 6–8).

8 Pendal et al. (2010) argue that the metaphorical translation into politics makes the concept vague and therefore not very powerful.

9 These functions aimed at maintenance are sometimes referred as 'societal security', as the social value and norms to be upheld (Lindberg and Sundelius 2012).

10 For an overview of the debate, see Gad and Petersen (2011).

11 In this perspective, there is no sensitivity regarding the difference between conventional risk thinking (consequentiality, causality) and precautionary decision logics, as described above.

References

Aradau, C., Lob-Guerrero, L., and van Munster, R. (2008) `Security, Technologies of Risk, and the Political: Guest Editors' Introduction', *Security Dialogue* 39(2 -3): 147 -54.

Aradau, C. and van Munster, R. (2007) `Governing Terrorism through Risk: Taking Precautions, (Un) Knowing the Future', *European Journal of International Relations* 13(1): 89 -115.

Bauman, Z. (2006) *Liquid Fear*, Cambridge: Polity Press.

Beck, U. (1992) *Risk Society: Towards a New Modernity*, New Delhi: Sage.

Beck, U. (2003) 'The Silence of Words: On Terror and War', *Security Dialogue* 34(3): 255–6.

Berenskoetter, F. (2011) 'Reclaiming the Vision Thing: Constructivists as Students of the Future', *International Studies Quarterly* 55(3): 647–68.

Bernstein, P. L. (1998) *Against the Gods*, New York: Wiley.

Best, J. (2008) 'Ambiguity, Uncertainty, and Risk: Rethinking Indeterminacy', *International Political Sociology* 2(4): 355–74.

Bigo, D. (2000) 'When Two Becomes One: Internal and External Securitisations in Europe', in M. Kelstrup and M. Williams (eds.) *International Relations Theory and the Politics of European Integration: Power, Security and Community*, London: Routledge, 171–204.

Bradfield, R., Wright, G., Burta, G., Cairnsb, G., and Der Heijden, K. (2005) 'The Origins and Evolution of Scenario Techniques in Long Range Business Planning', *Futures* (37): 795–812.

Buzan, B., De Wilde, J., and Wæver, O. (1998) *Securitization: A New Framework for Analysis*, Boulder, CO: Lynne Rienner.

Chermack, T. J. (2011) *Scenario Planning in Organisations: How to Create, Use and Assess Scenarios*, San Francisco, CA: Berrett-Koehler.

Clapton, W. (2011) 'Risk in International Relations', *International Relations* 25(3): 280–95.

Corry, O. (2012) 'Securitisation and Riskification: Second Order Security and the Politics of Climate Change', *Millennium* 40(2): 235–58.

de Goede, M. (2008) 'Beyond Risk. Premediation and the post-9/11 Security Imagination', *Security Dialogue* 39(2–3): 155–76.

Douglas, M. (1990) 'Risk as a Forensic Resource', *Daedalus* 119(4): 1–16.

Douglas, M. and Wildavsky, A. (1982) *Risk and Culture: An Essay on the Selection of Technical and Environmental Dangers*, Berkeley: University of California Press.

Dunn Cavelty, M., Kaufmann, M., and Kristensen, K. S. (2015) 'Resilience and (In)Security: Practices, Subjects and Temporalities', *Security Dialogue* 46(1): 3–14.

Ewald, F. (1991) 'Insurance and Risk', in G. Burchell, C. Gordon, and P. Miller (eds.) *The Foucault Effect: Studies in Governmentality*, Chicago: University of Chicago Press, 197–201.

Ewald, F. (2001) 'The Return of Descartes' Malicious Demon: An Outline of a Philosophy of Precaution', in T. Baker and J. Simon (eds.) *Embracing Risk: The Changing Culture of Insurance and Responsibility*, Chicago and London: University of Chicago Press, 273–302.

Furedi, F. (2009) 'Precautionary Culture and the Rise of Possibilistic Risk Assessment', *Erasmus Law Review* 2(2): 197–220.

Gad, U. P. G. and Petersen, K. L. (2011) 'Concepts of Politics in Securitization Studies', *Security Dialogue* 42: 315–28.

Giddens, A. (1991) *Modernity and Self-Identity*, Cambridge: Polity Press.

Giddens, A. (1992) 'Risk, Trust, Reflexivity', in U. Beck (ed.) *Risk Society: Towards a New Modernity*, New Delhi: Sage.

Hagmann, J. and Dunn Cavelty, M. (2012) 'National Risk Registers: Security Scientism and the Propagation of Permanent Insecurity', *Security Dialogue* 43(1): 79–96.

Huysmans, J. (2006) *The Politics of Insecurity: Fear, Migration and Asylum in the EU*, Abingdon: Routledge.

Kahan, D. M., Jenkins-Smith, H., and Brama, D. (2010) 'Cultural Cognition of Scientific Consensus', *Journal of Risk Research* (September): 1–28.

Kessler, O. (2010) 'Risk', in P. J. Burgess (ed.) *Routledge Handbook of New Security Studies*, Abingdon: Routledge, 17–27.

Kessler, O. and Werner, W. (2008) 'Extrajudicial Killing as a Risk Management', *Security Dialogue* 39(2–3): 289–308.

Knight, F. (1921) *Risk, Uncertainty and Profit*, Boston, MA: Hart, Schaffner & Marx.

Koselleck, R. (1985) *Futures Past: On the Semantics of Historical Time*, New York: Columbia University Press.

Lee, K., Sridha, D., and Patel, M. (2009) 'Bridging the Divide: Global Governance of Trade and Health', *The Lancet* 373: 416–22.

Lindberg, H. and Sundelius, B. (2012) 'Whole of Society Disaster Resilience: The Swedish Way', in D. G. Kamien (ed.) *McGraw-Hill Homeland Security Handbook*, McGraw-Hill Company: 1295–1319.

Luhman, N. (1991) *Soziologie des Risikos*, Berlin: Walter de Gruyter.

O'Malley, P. (2004) *Risk, Uncertainty and Government*, London: Glasshouse Press.

Pendal, R., Foster, K., and Cowell, M. (2010) 'Resilience and Regions: Building Understanding of the Methaphor', *Cambridge Journal of Regions, Economy and Society* 3: 71–84.

Petersen, K. L. (2012a) *Corporate Risk and National Security Redefined*, Abingdon, Oxon: Routledge.

Petersen, K. L. (2012b) 'Risk: A Field within Security Studies', *European Journal of International Relations* 18(4): 693–717.

Postma, T. J. B. M. and Liebl, F. (2005) 'How to Improve Scenario Analysis as a Strategic Management Tool', *Technological Forecasting & Social Change* 72(1): 161–73.

Power, M. (2007) *Organized Uncertainty: Designing a World of Risk Management*, Oxford: Oxford University Press.

Prior, T. and Hagmann, J. (2013) 'Measuring Resilience: Methodological and Political Challenges of a Trend Security Concept', *Journal of Risk Research* 17(3): 281–98.

Rasmussen, M. V. (2009) *The Risk Society at War: Terror, Technology and Strategy in the Twenty-First Century*, Cambridge: Cambridge University Press.

Rose, N. (1993) 'Government, Authority and Expertise in Advanced Liberalism', *Economy and Society* 22(3): 283–99.

Runde, J. (1998) 'Clarifying Frank Knight's Discussion of the Meaning of Risk and Uncertainty', *Cambridge Journal of Economics* 22(5): 539–46.

Stark, A. (2014) 'Bureaucratic Values and Resilience: An Exploration of Crisis Management Adaption', *Public Administration* 92(3): 692–706.

Stirling, A. (2007) 'Risk, Precaution and Science: Towards a More Constructive Policy Debate', *EMBO Report* 8(4): 309–15.

Taleb, N. N. (2007) *The Black Swan: The Impact of the Highly Improbable*, New York: Random House.

Thompson, G. (2012) *Constitutionalisation of the Global Corporate Sphere*, Oxford: Oxford University Press.

Vogel, D. (2012) 'The Transatlantic Shift in Regulatory Stringency', in D. Vogel (ed.) *The Politics of Precaution: Regulating Health, Safety, and Environmental Risks in Europe and the United States*, Princeton, NJ: Princeton University Press, 1–21.

Walker, J. and Cooper, M. (2011) 'Genealogies of Resilience: From Systems Ecology to the Political Economy of Crisis Adaptation', *Security Dialogue* 42(2): 143–60.

12

SECURITY AS PRACTICE

*Christian Bueger**

Practice theoretical perspectives are a relative newcomer in Security Studies. Drawing on many of the insights of poststructuralism and broader cultural theory, the main reference point is the practice turn across the social sciences (Adler and Pouliot 2011; Bueger and Gadinger 2014; Schatzki et al. 2001; Spiegel 2005). The core claim of this turn is to take 'practices' as the smallest unit of analysis. It is neither actors (politicians, professionals, states, etc.), nor structures (the international system, regions, etc.) which are in focus, but organized forms of doing and saying, and the relations established therein. Turning to practices is seen as beneficial for several reasons. First, it allows transcending many of the dichotomies that have haunted Security Studies for decades, such as those between agency and structure, the ideational and the material, or the exception and the everyday (Adler and Pouliot 2011; Bueger and Gadinger 2014; Neumann 2002). Second, it promises new methodological strategies geared at proximity to those engaging in the production of security, and hence allows the enriching of the empirical basis of Security Studies. Third, and perhaps most importantly, the move to practice has the objective to produce knowledge of practical value that can speak to societal and political concerns.

Practice theory is, however, not a unified perspective. It is best understood as a family of different frameworks and attempts to develop new vocabularies which centre on practices as the main unit of analysis. In Security Studies three approaches have become particularly influential:

1. Accounts that draw on the work of Pierre Bourdieu and study security as a distinct field of practice;
2. The security community of practice approach, which argues that security is embedded in community structures; and
3. Relationalist perspectives which study the relations that produce security.

This chapter has four main parts. Before we revisit the features of each approach, I will introduce the basic premises of the practice theoretical perspective. Drawing on this discussion, I show how the three approaches develop these insights and use them to study security-related phenomena. I end with a brief discussion of some of the future challenges of the security-as-practice agenda.

Understanding the practice turn

Practice theories are developed in various social science disciplines. Notably, the fields of science and technology studies, organization studies, anthropology, and social theory have spearheaded the discussion. The denominator 'practice theory' emerged in the 1980s (Ortner 1984), yet a common signpost became the 2001 volume *The Practice Turn in Contemporary Theory* (Schatzki et al. 2001). The book not only announced that a new 'turn' was under way, it also documented how far advanced and varied practice theorizing is.

Practice theories are developed from a range of traditions (Hillebrandt 2014; Miettinen et al. 2009). Appreciating these traditions gives us a first approximation of the core concerns of practice theory. One reference point is the early work of Karl Marx. In his *Theses on Feuerbach* he pointed to the importance of practice as the fundamental category of human life (Marx 1845[2002]). As he argued, 'all social life is essentially practical. All mysteries which lead theory to mysticism find their rational solution in human practice and in the comprehension of this practice' (Marx 1845[2002]). He made two important arguments: first, that also theorizing should be understood as a practical activity; second, that practices are material and 'sensuous' activities, and hence one needs to appreciate the reciprocity of ideational and material dimensions of action.

A second source is the relational thinking of pragmatists such as John Dewey and the late Ludwig Wittgenstein. Dewey and Wittgenstein argued that rule-following is to be understood as a practice. Knowing how to follow a rule requires knowledge which is not contained in the rule itself. Instead a practical knowledge of how to follow a rule is necessary (Miettinen et al. 2009; Pritzlaff and Nullmeier 2011).

A third source is notably important in methodological terms, that is, the ethno-methodological research tradition established by Harold Garfinkel. Ethno-methodology is centred on the study of everyday production of meaning and how actors create a stable social order through their everyday activities (Gad and Bruun Jensen 2014).

A fourth source is poststructuralist thought, and in many ways practice theories can be understood as a further advancement of this perspective (Neumann 2002). Practice theories advance the core claim of poststructuralism that essentialist understandings need to be overcome and that the contingent nature of the world and the ways by which it is produced need appreciation. Themes such as the links between theory and practice and between the material and the ideational, as well as contingency and practical knowledge, are hence crucial for practice-theoretical thinking.

Situating practice theory

If practice theory draws on these traditions, how can it be situated in the theory landscape? German social theorist Andreas Reckwitz (2002) developed a useful overview which gives us a good understanding of how practice theory differs from other approaches to security. Reckwitz suggested that there are three different ways to think about action: rational choice theory, norm constructivism, and cultural theories.

Rational choice theories take the strategic interaction of interest-driven individuals as the main explanatory factor. We find such thinking for instance in deterrence theory (Knopf 2010; Quackenbush 2011). Norm constructivists assume that individuals are driven by norms and that a normative consensus can explain the coordination of individual actions (see, in Security Studies for instance, Farell 2002; Katzenstein 1996). Both perspectives have significant limits, as Reckwitz (2002) argues, since they can neither fully grasp where interests and norms actually come from, nor the collective dimensions of action. This is exactly the strength of what Reckwitz calls cultural theories. They focus on the underlying knowledge and symbolic orders that make action possible in the first place.

Practice theories are one branch of cultural theory. To understand their distinctiveness, Reckwitz suggests differentiating them from two other types of theories, namely mentalism and textualism. All three differ in where they locate knowledge and meaning. For mentalist theories, knowledge is to be located in the mind of people. In Security Studies, such theories for instance study the belief systems of elites or processes of threat perceptions and frames (Hudson 2005; Noreen and Sjöstedt 2004; Stein 2013). The other type of theories, Reckwitz labels as textualism. Here the focus is on external structures of meaning. We find expressions of textualist perspectives for instance in works on security discourses (for instance Campbell 1992; Hansen 2006; Herschinger 2010).

Practice theories differ: 'The focus is neither solely on the internal (inside the head of actors), nor on the external (in some form of structure)' (Bueger and Gadinger 2015: 6). Practices are in-between the inside and the outside. Practice theorists hence 'identify the social in the mind (since individuals are carriers of practices), but also in symbolic structures (since practices form more or less extra-subjective structures and patterns of action)' (Bueger and Gadinger 2015: 6). It is important not to overplay these differences, since in many ways practice theorists advance mentalist and textualist perspectives, and there are no clear intellectual boundaries.

What is a practice?

There is a variety of definitions of practice. These definitions, however, agree more or less on three core elements of which a practice is composed: first, bodily movements in the form of doing and saying; second, practical knowledge which might be tacit or explicit; and third, objects (artefacts and things) used in a practice. Consider the practice of cooking. Cooking requires basic bodily movements such as cutting or stirring, but also more complex cooking techniques such as steaming, barbecuing, or deep frying. Advanced cooking is usually conducted by a team of chefs; these have to communicate – hence also sayings are involved. Various objects and artefacts are handled in the practice of cooking. One uses ingredients (things), but also artefacts specifically designed for the practice of cooking, such as knives, ovens, pots, or pans.

Also, different types of knowledge matter. Recipes and cookbooks provide explicit knowledge. Yet, as anyone who has tried to make a mayonnaise by recipe might have experienced, more knowledge is required. Practical experience on timing and when to throw in what ingredient, or how fast to stir, will be needed for a good mayonnaise. One also requires a sense of what is tasty and what is disgusting. To cook a tasty meal all these elements need to be carefully arranged in a certain way. The example is also telling since, I think, it is easy to agree that in order to understand cooking, it would make little sense to study only texts and cookbooks or rely on abstract principles of gastrosophy. This is why practice theorists often accuse other cultural theorists of over-intellectualizing social life. Sometimes matters are more mundane and practical than academics are trained to assume.

Practical configurations

A practice does not develop out of nowhere. When a new practice emerges, it draws on elements of prior practices. Think about microwave cooking: it is a new practice and changes how we cook, notably by its speed, but much of the food and recipes stay the same. One wouldn't discard the global history of food just because a new practice enters the game. Practices hence form chains across time and space, and should not be seen in isolation but as part of larger practical configurations.

Theorists have developed different terms to speak about these larger configurations. The most established ones, to which we shall come back, are the concepts of 'fields', 'community', 'actor-network', and 'assemblage'. Although practices are always part of larger configurations, it is important to recognize that these do not structure or even determine a practice. Practice theorists develop a very distinct understanding of the relation of micro and macro. A practice is dependent on enactments in concrete situations. To come back to the practice of cooking: there are some overarching features of the practice, yet, the practice is dependent on what happens at restaurants and home kitchens around the world where the practice is enacted. Any act of cooking will differ. My mayonnaise is certainly different from yours. Yet, any mayonnaise making will rely on a broader configuration (ingredients, equipment, recipes, skills, tastes, etc.) on how to make it, how we eat it, and why we like (or dislike) it.

In summary, bodily movements, practical knowledge, objects, and practical configurations are the basic categories of practice theories. Yet, as we will see in the formulations of practice theory in Security Studies, there is quite some variance over how these are interpreted and emphasized.

Bourdieu in Security Studies

Pierre Bourdieu is, along with Anthony Giddens, the most famous advocate of practice theory. It is hence unsurprising that Security Studies has paid special attention to his concepts when the practice turn was introduced to the field. Scholars drawing on Bourdieu's work are sometimes known as the Paris School. The idea of a Paris School was invented by Ole Wæver in order to signify that there was a remarkable body of research that differed in its arguments from securitization research and to initiate a debate between the Paris and Copenhagen Schools (Wæver 2004). We shall come back to the differences between securitization research and the security-as-practice agenda later. Wæver's label of a Paris School was perhaps as much a misfit as the term Copenhagen School. Although Didier Bigo, a core advocate of Bourdieusan approaches, was based in Paris, many others advancing the perspective, such as Jef Huysmans, Michael Williams, or Trine Villumsen Berling, were not.

Within a broader International Relations (IR) context Richard Ashley (1987) and Stefano Guzzini (2000) had already pointed prominently to the value of Bourdieu's work. Yet, it was Bigo (e.g. 1994, 2002) who was one of the first to demonstrate how the Bourdieusan framework could be utilized empirically to study security. Bigo's core argument was that we need to study the practices by which security is made and issues become known as threats. Drawing on case study work on the relation between migration and security in Europe, he argued that it was pivotally the practices of experts, professionals, and bureaucrats working in governments, international organizations, think tanks, or universities that mattered (Bigo 2002). These actors form a field of security practice which determines the meaning of security, what should count as threats, and what responses would be required. Bigo (2002) opposed the idea that security was the outcome of a public spectacle. Rather it was made in everyday practices, such as producing statistics or threat assessments.

To understand Bigo's argument it is useful to very briefly investigate Bourdieu's version of practice theory. Bourdieu's practice theory is relatively complex and places emphasis on practical knowledge and larger configurations.[1] Four terms are crucial. With the terms 'doxa' and 'habitus' Bourdieu grasps practical knowledge. 'Habitus' refers to the practical knowledge which is inscribed in individual bodies on the basis of collective experiences across time and space. The term 'doxa' refers to the practical knowledge of larger practical configurations, which Bourdieu described as 'fields'.

Bourdieu drew on a gambling metaphor to explore the relations between these concepts. The 'field' constitutes the game; the 'doxa' of the field are the explicit and tacit rules of that game; and 'habitus' is the experience that the players bring to that game. Within fields actors compete against each other and struggle for status and resources ('capital') useful for dominating the game, policing its boundaries, and excluding actors from playing in it. Bourdieu developed these concepts mainly through studies of French society and argued to understand society as composed of various fields (e.g. the economic, artistic, or academic fields). With his interest in domination and exclusion as core mechanisms of fields, his calls for emancipation and under-standing theory as a form of practice, Bourdieu's theory follows visibly a Marxist tradition of practice theory (Joas and Knöbl 2009).

Security Studies scholars drawing on Bourdieu tend to emphasize one of these concepts. Advancing the line of reasoning of Bigo's perspective on experts and professionals, the concept of 'doxa' is, for instance, crucial in Berling's work (2012, 2015). Arguing that European security constitutes a distinct field, she sets out to understand the 'doxa' of that field by following the work of security intellectuals, theorists, and experts, paying attention to think tanks in particular. As she demonstrates, such an account can more fully explain the transformations that occurred in the European security landscape of the 1990s. With her emphasis on theorizing as a key practice in the field, she also shows how the Marxist and Bourdieusan concerns over theory as practice can be turned into a productive empirical agenda which has little to do with self-contemplation.

Others prioritize the 'field' as the core category. Huysmans (2002), for instance, discussed NATO's transformation during the 1999 Kosovo crisis, by arguing that NATO had entered a new international field of practice, the humanitarian field. Williams (2012) draws on the concept of fields to argue that there is a new economy of security. Following Bourdieu's argument that competition between actors is the core driver of fields, he diagnoses that the rise of private secu-rity companies has radically increased competition in the security field.

If the European discussions have a core interest in the power dimension and the emancipa-tory and critical potential of Bourdieu, this is less of a concern in the North American debate. Habitus has been the core concept in this debate, not the least because the concept allows for easier links to norm-oriented and mentalist versions of constructivism. Vincent Pouliot (2008) and Ted Hopf (2010), for instance, drew on the habitus to argue for the importance of practical knowledge and the way it conditions security relations.

Security communities of practice

A second version of practice theory draws on the writings of the organizational sociologist Etienne Wenger and his framework of communities of practices (Lave and Wenger 1991; Wenger 1998). This approach centres on the collective character of practice and suggests grasping practi-cal configurations as communities. The communities of practice approach (CPA) was introduced to Security Studies by Emanuel Adler. In the introduction to his 2005 book, Adler pointed to the usefulness of the approach and the new paths it opens, in particular for the study of security communities. In two following articles he specified how the framework provides new directions for security community research (Adler 2008; Adler and Greve 2009).

The core question that Wenger tried to address in developing CPA was how to understand when and how learning occurs. The initial book, co-authored with Lave, argued that learn-ing has to be grasped as socialization into a practical configuration (Lave and Wenger 1991). Learning hence should not be understood as an individual mental affair, but as a collective process, and moreover, following up on the general tenets of practice theory, as a bodily activity. Learning is thus taken as equivalent to the acquisition of practical, collectively shared knowledge and the capacity to enact it. Lave and Wenger described this process as a movement in which a learner starts out at the periphery of a practical configuration, then moves closer to the centre and becomes a master in the practical skills required to perform well. In his second book, Wenger (1998) generalized the concept of communities of practice and theorized it as a basic social category which is driven by learning, everyday interaction, and shared repertoires of practice.

Security communities were introduced in the literature as a concept that refers to a group of states which have overcome the security dilemma and among whose members war has become an unthinkable option. Frequent interactions between states and a shared identity or culture were identified as mechanism for the emergence of such communities (Adler and Barnett 1998; Deutsch et al. 1957). These two mechanisms provided the anchoring points for reconceptualizing security communities as practical configurations, that is, communities which achieve coherence through practice.

As Adler (2008) argued in drawing on the case of NATO, security communities are driven by practices of self-restraint. They develop a shared repertoire of practices, such as cooperative security, shared understandings of security, and partnership projects. Adler offers a powerful practice-based reinterpretation of security institutions and regimes centred on the identification of types of practices which make war unthinkable. The importance of shared understandings in the repertoires of communities, moreover, enables a direct link to securitization. A security community implies that members securitize together (Buzan and Wæver 2009). Such an interpretation also makes the approach productive to study how looser transnational community structures develop in response to a distinct threat, such as piracy (Bueger 2013).

Relational security approaches

If the first two approaches are clearly associated with the work of a distinct theorist, this becomes fuzzier when we consider the third approach, namely relationalist practice theory.[2] Relationalist approaches draw on a broad repertoire and seek inspiration in particular from actor-network theory and assemblage theory, associated with names such as Bruno Latour, John Law, Michel Callon, Annemarie Mol, or Gilles Deleuze. In their emphasis on relations, this account comes very close to poststructuralist concerns. Indeed, Law (2009) argued that one should understand such approaches as providing micro-oriented and empirical versions of poststructuralist ideas.

The importance of objects and technology is foregrounded much more strongly than in the other approaches. The starting point is to investigate how practical configurations emerge, how they are maintained, and when and how they erode in the face of controversy. The terms 'actor-network', 'agencement', or 'assemblage' are used to signify practical configurations. As Law (2012: 157) argues, practices are from this perspective 'detectable and somewhat ordered sets of material-semiotic relations'. And as he further develops this argument, the analytical and empirical task is in

> exploring possible patterns of relations, and how it is that these get assembled in particular locations. It is to treat the real as whatever it is that is being assembled, materially and semiotically in a sense of analytical interest. Realities, objects, subjects, materials, and meanings, whatever form they take these are all explored as an effect of the relations that are assembling and doing them. Practices, then, are assemblages of relations.
> *(Law 2012: 157)*

With this definition of tasks, Law points to two core tenets of the approach. That is, first, conceptual parsimony. If Bourdieu and Wenger elaborate quite a nuanced and complex conceptual apparatus in order to study practice, relationalists want to do analysis with a range of basic concepts, such as relations and assemblage. They focus on empirical descriptions of situations and employ further concepts only in so far as they have been identified in the actual practical configuration.

Second, a position is taken which wants to put equal weight on the ideational and the material as well as the human and the non-human. This has been called a 'symmetrical' position. The concept of an 'actant' gathered from semiotics is important to achieve this symmetry. An actant is any element in an assemblage that has the capacity to act. According to this idea, agency should not be seen as the property of humans, but as the effect of relations. In consequence, also non-humans, such as technologies, can in principle carry agency. It is, however, important to emphasize that this is not an argument for prioritizing non-humans. The argument is for symmetry, after all.

Core ideas of relationalism were introduced to IR by Patrick Jackson and Daniel Nexon (1999) and Xavier Guillaume (2007). In Security Studies these arguments were, however, dormant for quite some time, until a wave of scholars started to become concerned about the role of science, technology, and expertise. Bueger and Villumsen (2007) provided one of the first articles in Security Studies to draw on Latour's actor-network theory. They argued that the approach is particularly useful to understand how scientific expertise enters the domain of foreign and security policy. Studying how an actor-network was woven around the fact that democracies do not wage war against each other, they showed that relationalism is particularly important to understand the rise of new practical configurations. Bueger and Bethke (2014) continued this line of reasoning. Employing the actor-network theory approach more fully, they showed how the concept of the 'failed state' emerged and argued that a significant network of various allies was required to turn the 'failed state' into a core security problematique.

Another line of reasoning focuses on the role of technology in security, in particular surveillance and weapon technology. Per Schouten, for instance, studies the airport as a relational configuration. He shows how security is assembled at this location by relations of all sorts of things and activities, including checkpoints, passengers, screening technology, or patrols (Schouten 2014). Walters (2014) analyses drone strikes from this perspective and shows how the military and drone technology is assembled. The studies of Schouten and Walters, however, do not only provide powerful examples of how relationalist approaches rethink the materiality of security. They also show that in contrast to the two other approaches, which understand practices as routines, repertoires, and stability, relationalist accounts are better equipped to analyse change, contention, and political controversy.

The security-as-practice agenda: conclusion

Approaches developed from Bourdieu, Wenger, and relationalist ideas provide us with three different accounts of how the core ideas of practice theory can be translated into research frameworks for the study of security. They offer three different versions of how to conceptualize practical configurations as a rather structured field, as coherent community structures, or as looser heterogeneous networks. They also emphasize core elements of practice differently (Bueger and Gadinger 2014). If in relationalism bodies and artefacts achieve a central role, the two other approaches emphasize knowledge (habitus, learning) much more strongly.

The security-as-practice agenda is growing and new theoretical ideas and other approaches continue to be introduced. The field will hence widen over the coming years. The agenda is in the meantime well established. This is not least because the practice perspective succeeds in integrating concerns of other approaches such as securitization theory or constructivist approaches. Indeed, the security-as-practice perspective develops core insights from traditional securitization theory further. There are two core points of departure. Practice theorists aim at going beyond the focus on linguistic practices of traditional securitization research. The aim is to include material aspects, stretching from the role of the body to artefacts and technologies, in the analysis. Practice theory, moreover, switches emphasis towards the everyday production of security. In many ways, making security is a matter of routine and reproduction. This does not question the claims of traditional securitization theory. Rather it is to claim that the speech acts described in the traditional securitization account are the exception rather than the norm. Both practice theory and securitization theory share the emphasis on performativity, yet in practice theory the emphasis is on routinized performances. With discursive approaches increasingly moving beyond text and starting to rethink their concepts of action and materiality (Aradau et al. 2014), there is also an increasing convergence with this field of research. This conversation will also spur conceptual innovation and new research puzzles (Balzacq et al. 2010). Also the question of how to conceptualize the normativity of practice and hence relate the practice agenda to the concerns of norm constructivism and international political theory is a promising research avenue.

It is important to note, however, that the security-as-practice perspective is in the first place an empirical agenda. Although many efforts have focused on developing concepts, practice approaches, notably relational ones, place a heavy burden on empirical work. This essentially implies going beyond text, since it is difficult to reconstruct practices on the basis of documents. The intent is to explore the broader spectrum of ethnographic methods (Bueger and Mireanu 2014; Gad and Bruun Jensen 2014). In the face of the cultures of secrecy and violence that much of Security Studies deals with, the methodological implications of the practice perspective and how practice theoretical concepts can be put to good empirical use will drive the future agenda and ultimately decide on the future direction of research.

Notes

* For comments and suggestions I am grateful to Jan Stockbruegger, Trine Villumsen Berling, Médéric Martin-Mazé, Myriam Dunn Cavelty, and Thierry Balzacq.
1 For detailed discussions on these concepts and their importance for Security Studies, see the contributions in Adler-Nissen (2013).
2 All practice theories emphasize the importance of relations, yet in those approaches which can be clustered around the term 'relationalist approaches' relations become the primary category and understanding of practice.

References

Adler, E. (2008) 'The Spread of Security Communities: Communities of Practice, Self-Restraint, and NATO's post-Cold War Transformation', *European Journal of International Relations* 14(2): 195–230.

Adler, E. and Barnett, M. N. (1998) 'Security Communities in Theoretical Perspective', in E. Adler and M. N. Barnett (eds.) *Security Communities*, Cambridge: Cambridge University Press, 3–28.

Adler, E. and Greve, P. (2009) 'When Security Community Meets Balance of Power: Overlapping Regional Mechanisms of Security Governance', *Review of International Studies* 35(1): 59–84.

Adler, E. and Pouliot, V. (eds.) (2011) *International Practices*, Cambridge: Cambridge University Press.

Adler-Nissen, R. (ed.) (2013) *Bourdieu in International Relations*, London: Routledge.

Aradau, C., Martin, C., Eva, H., Owen, D. T., and Voelckner, N. (2014) 'Discourse/Materiality', in C. Aradau, J. Huysmans, A. Neal, and N. Voelckner (eds.) *Critical Security Methods: New Frameworks for Analysis*, London: Routledge, 57–84.

Ashley, R. K. (1987) 'The Geopolitics of Geopolitical Space: Toward a Critical Social Theory of International Politics', *Alternatives: Global, Local, Political* 12(4): 403–34.

Balzacq, T., Basaran, T., Bigo, D., Guittet, E., and Christian, O. (2010) 'Security Practices', in R. A. Denemark (ed.) *International Studies Encyclopedia Online*, Blackwell Publishing. Online. Available HTTP: <http://www.isacompendium.com/> (accessed 1 July 2015).

Berling, T. V. (2012) 'Bourdieu, International Relations, and European Security', *Theory and Security* 41(5): 451–478.

Berling, T. V. (2015) *The International Political Sociology of Security. Rethinking Theory and Practice*, Abingdon: Routledge.

Bigo, D. (1994) 'The European Internal Security Field: Stakes and Rivalries in a Newly Developing Area of Police Intervention', in M. Anderson and M. den Boer (eds.) *Policing across Nations*, London: Pinter Publications, 161–73.

Bigo, D. (2002) 'Security and Immigration: Toward a Critique of the Governmentality of Unease', *Alternatives* 27(1), 63–92.

Bueger, C. (2013) 'Communities of Security Practice at Work? The Emerging African Maritime Security Regime', *African Security* 6(3–4): 297–316.

Bueger, C. and Bethke, F. (2014) 'Actor-Networking the Failed State: An Enquiry into the Life of Concepts', *Journal of International Relations and Development* 17(1): 30–60.

Bueger, C. and Gadinger, F. (2014) *International Practice Theory: New Perspectives*, Basingstoke: Palgrave MacMillan.

Bueger, C. and Gadinger, F. (2015) 'The Play of International Practices', *International Studies Quarterly* 59(3): 449–460.

Bueger, C. and Mireanu, M. (2014) 'Proximity', in C. Aradau, J. Huysmans, A. Neal, and N. Voelckner (eds.) *Critical Security Methods: New Frameworks for Analysis*, London: Routledge, 118–41.

Bueger, C. and Villumsen, T. (2007) 'Beyond the Gap: Relevance, Fields of Practice and the Securitizing Consequences of (Democratic Peace) Research', *Journal of International Relations and Development* 10(4): 417–48.

Buzan, B. and Wæver O. (2009) 'Macrosecuritisation and Security Constellations: Reconsidering Scale in Securitisation Theory', *Review of International Studies* 35(2): 254–76.

Campbell, D. (1992) *Writing Security: United States Foreign Policy and the Politics of Identity*, Minneapolis: University of Minnesota Press.

Deutsch, K. W., Burell, A. S., Kann, R. A, Lee, M., Lichtermann, M., Lidgren, R. E., Loewenheim, F. L., and Van Wagenen, R. W. (1957) *Political Community and the North Atlantic Area: International Organization in the Light of Historical Experience*, New York: Greenwood Press.

Farell, T. (2002) 'Constructivist Security Studies: Portrait of a Research Programme', *International Studies Review* 4(49): 49–72.

Gad, C. and Bruun Jensen, C. (2014) 'The Promises of Practice', *The Sociological Review* 62(4): 1–21.

Guillaume, X. (2007) 'Unveiling the "International": Process, Identity and Alterity', *Millennium – Journal of International Studies* 35(3): 741–58.

Guzzini, S. (2000) 'A Reconstruction of Constructivism in International Relations', *European Journal of International Relations* 6(2): 147–82.

Hansen, L. (2006) *Security as Practice. Discourse Analysis and the Bosnian War*, Milton Park and New York: Routledge.

Herschinger, E. (2010) *Constructing Global Enemies: Hegemony and Identity in International Discourses on Terrorism and Drug Prohibition*, Milton Park and New York: Routledge.

Hillebrandt, F. (2014) *Soziologische Praxistheorien. Eine Einführung*, Wiesbaden: Springer VS.

Hopf, T. (2010) 'The Logic of Habit in International Relations', *European Journal of International Relations* 16(4): 539–61.

Hudson, V. M. (2005) 'Foreign Policy Analysis: Actor-Specific Theory and the Ground of International Relations', *Foreign Policy Analysis* 1(1): 1–30.

Huysmans, J. (2002) 'Shape-Shifting NATO: Humanitarian Action and the Kosovo Refugee Crisis', *Review of International Studies* 28(3): 599–618.

Jackson, P. T. and Nexon, D. H. (1999) 'Relations before States: Substance, Process and the Study of World Politics', *European Journal of International Relations* 5(3): 291–332.

Joas, H., and Knöbl, W. (2009) *Social Theory: Twenty Introductory Lectures*, Cambridge: Cambridge University Press.

Katzenstein, P. J. (ed.) (1996) *The Culture of International Security: Norms and Identity in World Politics*, New York: Columbia University Press.

Knopf, J. (2010) 'The Fourth Wave in Deterrence Research', *Contemporary Security Policy* 31(1): 1–33.

Lave, J. and Wenger, E. (1991) *Situated Learning: Legitimate Peripheral Participation*, Cambridge: Cambridge University Press.

Law, J. (2009) 'Actor Network Theory and Material Semiotics', in B. S. Turner (ed.) *The New Blackwell Companion to Social Theory*, Oxford: Blackwell, 141–58.

Law, J. (2012) 'Collateral Realities', in F. D. Rubio and P. Baert (eds.) *The Politics of Knowledge*, Abingdon: Routledge, 156–78.

Marx, K. (2002 [1845]) *Theses on Feuerbach*, The Marx/Engels Internet Archive. Online. Available HTTP: <https://www.marxists.org/archive/marx/works/1845/theses/theses.htm> (accessed 1 July 2015).

Miettinen, R., Samra-Fredericks, D., and Yanow, D. (2009) 'Re-Turn to Practice: An Introductory Essay', *Organization Studies* 30(12): 1309–27.

Neumann, I. B. (2002) 'Returning Practice to the Linguistic Turn: The Case of Diplomacy', *Millennium – Journal of International Studies* 31(3): 627–51.

Noreen, E. and Sjöstedt, R. (2004) 'Estonian Identity Formations and Threat Framing in the post-Cold War Era', *Journal of Peace Research* 41(6): 733–50.

Ortner, S. B. (1984) 'Theory in Anthropology since the Sixties', *Comparative Studies in Society and History* 26(1): 126–66.

Pouliot, V. (2008) 'The Logic of Practicality: A Theory of Practice of Security Communities', *International Organization* 62(2): 257–88.

Pritzlaff, T. and Nullmeier, F. (2011) 'Capturing Practice', *Evidence & Policy* 7(2): 137–54.

Quackenbush, S. L. (2011) 'Deterrence Theory: Where Do We Stand?', *Review of International Studies* 37(2): 741–76.

Reckwitz, A. (2002) 'Toward a Theory of Social Practices: A Development in Culturalist Theorizing', *European Journal of Social Theory* 5(2): 243–63.

Schatzki, T. R., Knorr-Cetina, K., and Von Savigny, E. (eds.) (2001) *The Practice Turn in Contemporary Theory*, London: Routledge.

Schouten, P. (2014) 'Security as Controversy: Reassembling Security at Amsterdam Airport', *Security Dialogue* 45(1): 23–42.

Spiegel, G. M. (ed.) (2005) *Practicing History: New Directions in Historical Writing after the Linguistic Turn*, New York: Routledge.

Stein, J. G. (2013[2004]) 'Threat Perception in International Relations', in L. Huddy, D. O. Sears, and J. S. Levy (eds.) *The Oxford Handbook of Political Psychology*, Oxford: Oxford University Press.

Wæver, O. (2004) 'Aberystwyth, Paris, Copenhagen: New 'Schools" in Security Theory and Their Origins between Core and Periphery', Paper presented at the Annual Convention of the International Studies Association, Montreal. Copenhagen: Copenhagen University.

Walters, W. (2014) 'Drone Strikes, Dingpolitik and beyond: Furthering the Debate on Materiality and Security', *Security Dialogue* 45(2): 101–18.

Wenger, E. (1998) *Communities of Practice: Learning, Meaning and Identity*, Cambridge: Cambridge University Press.

Williams, M. C. (2012) 'The New Economy of Security', *Global Crime* 13(4): 312–19.

PART II

Security challenges

13

TERRORISM AND COUNTERTERRORISM

Oldrich Bures

Following the tragic events of 11 September 2001 (9/11), terrorism has become one of the major security threats. The fight against terrorism has, correspondingly, become a key priority for national governments and national security agencies, as well as an important part of the agenda of various international organizations. As a consequence, there has also been a proliferation of academic literature analysing various aspects of terrorism and counterterrorism. Although research on these interrelated topics did not start *de novo* after 9/11, a lot of the (counter-) terrorism literature has only been written since 2001. In this chapter, only the key debates and findings that go beyond the academic ivory towers are presented.

The chapter has six main parts, structured along important debates. In the study of terrorism, the first debate concerns the very definition of the term terrorism; the second is about the emergence of 'new' terrorism (e.g. answers to the question of whether al-Qaida represents a new *sui generis* threat); the third is about the 'root' causes (e.g. answers to the macro-level question of why terrorism occurs), and the fourth, the radicalization debate, presents the answers to the more micro-level question of what makes an individual susceptible to radical views to the extent that s/he eventually becomes a terrorist.

The fifth part then turns to a survey of the key factors that explain both the commonalities and differences in the design of counterterrorism policies. The sixth identifies two ideal-type approaches to counterterrorism (the criminal model and the war model) and discusses their strengths and shortcomings, including the difficult search for a balance between security and liberty. The chapter concludes with a few notes on the current state of the art in terrorism and counterterrorism research.

The definitional debate

The study of terrorism has been complicated by a seemingly never-ending dispute about the definition of terrorism. To some extent, this is a consequence of the fact that scholars from a relatively wide array of social sciences, including political science, criminology, psychology, and law have defined terrorism in accordance with their specific research agendas.

Nevertheless, the mainstream view is that the inability of Terrorism Studies to reach a consensus on a definition of the object under investigation is a serious shortcoming of this growing field. Moreover, beyond academe, the persisting lack of universal agreement on a legal definition is also considered to be an obstacle to international counterterrorism cooperation. In this regard, it is also important to note that many countries did not have an official definition of terrorism in their national legal codes prior to 9/11 and, to this day, even the United States has several operative definitions that do not fully overlap.

As there is not enough space here to offer even a brief comparative analysis of the existing definitions of the term terrorism, the reader is recommended to consult some of the extensive academic accounts of the definitional debate. A useful starting point in this regard is the *Routledge Handbook of Terrorism Research* (2011) whose editor, Alex P. Schmid, has devoted a considerable part of his career to the search for a consensus academic definition of terrorism and an internationally acceptable legal definition in the UN General Assembly. The former describes terrorism as 'a doctrine about the presumed effectiveness of a special form or tactic of fear-generating, coercive political violence and, on the other hand, [as a] conspiratorial practice of calculated, demonstrative, direct violent action without legal or moral restraints, targeting mainly civilians and non-combatants, performed for its propagandistic and psychological effects on various audiences and conflict parties'. The latter states that an act of terrorism is 'the peacetime equivalent of a war crime' (Schmid 2011: 86–7).

Although some would certainly challenge either of these definitions, at least within Western academic circles, the key definitional disputes have receded to the margins of Terrorism Studies. Terrorism has by now been clearly distinguished as a specific type of political violence and it is no longer conflated with other forms of violence, such as guerilla warfare or civil wars, which in the past hampered both uniform data collection and the identification of more generalizing explanations. Most scholars now also use a different terminology, including 'genocide' or 'ethnic cleansing', to describe various types of government atrocities against civilians, thus sidelining the once-vexing debate about state terrorism. Even the often-cited adage 'one man's terrorist is another man's freedom fighter' no longer dominates the academic discourse, which has become less normatively based: 'people are generally deemed terrorists whenever they attack civilians to instill fear in the population for a given political goal regardless of its nature or perceived legitimacy' (Foley and Abrahms 2011). In other words, rather than interpreting how people choose to label their horrible acts of violence, it is the meaning of particular violence that is now subject to interpretation and virtually all terrorism scholars agree that its meaning is at the very least political (Sageman 2014a: 616). In the realm of politics, however, the aforementioned adage still arguably captures the single most important obstacle to the agreement on an internationally binding legal definition of terrorism in the UN General Assembly.

The 'new' terrorism debate

In the aftermath of the 9/11 terrorist attacks, which many saw as historically unprecedented both in terms of their execution and impact, a new debate has emerged both within academic and policy-making circles: can we place al-Qaida in the same class of phenomena as traditional 'old' terrorist groups such as the Red Army Faction and Irish Republican Army, or does it represent a 'new' *sui generis* type of terrorism?

Most policy-makers and many scholars have initially advanced the latter view. They have argued that al-Qaida constitutes a qualitatively distinct terrorist threat because it uses violence for the sake of violence rather than as a means to achieve a set of specific political goals (Benjamin and Simon 2003; Laqueur 2003; Morgan 2004). As such, al-Qaida has been portrayed as an apocalyptic movement with an elusive global goal of re-establishing Islamic rule in all Muslim lands. In addition to unprecedented lethality due to the desire to cause large numbers of civilian casualties, possibly via the use of a weapon of mass destruction (Allison 2004), the 'new' terrorists are allegedly also more transnational and religious than most of the 'old' terrorist groups (Duyvesteyn 2004). al-Qaida's looser, decentralized, network-like organizational structure, with various 'affiliated' or 'associated organizations' cropping up in various parts of the world, has also been singled out as a new unique feature (Sageman 2004).

More recently, however, the empirical basis behind the new terrorism argumentation has been disputed and many scholars have pointed out that along all of the three aforementioned dimensions (goals, methods, structure), there is more continuity than change. According to David Rapoport (2004), the history of terrorism is composed of four generational 'waves' and the current wave is but one discrete religiously-inspired episode that had already begun in the late 1970s. According to Martha Crenshaw (2007: 77), the difference between old and new terrorism is 'one of degree rather than kind' and the fundamental process of terrorism has not changed.

As such, the 'new' terrorism can be seen as just one manifestation of a larger methodological problem – the difficulty of studying constantly evolving clandestine terrorist organizations (which fortunately still manage to execute only a relatively small number of violent attacks). Moreover, the difficulty of studying extremely low base rate events is further compounded by the lack of availability of comprehensive and reliable data, most of which is classified as top secret by national governments. As a consequence, academics have to rely primarily on a few data sets (most notably the RAND–St. Andrews Chronology of International Terrorism, the US Department of State's Patterns of Global Terrorism, and the National Consortium for the Study of Terrorism and Responses to Terror's Global Terrorism Database). They contain only crude descriptions of terrorist incidents based on press reporting, which is not always reliable. This is particularly the case in non-democratic countries, where much of the press is either owned or controlled by the state. Moreover, while a database entry can very crudely describe a terrorist incident, it usually gives no details on the plots. From such data, 'one can make statements about the frequency and distribution of terrorist attacks, but little about how people turn to political violence, which requires far more detailed, comprehensive, and reliable data' (Sageman 2014a: 672).

The 'root' causes debate

Another major debate in Terrorism Studies concerns the hitherto unsuccessful quest to identify the 'root' causes of terrorism. There is a vast body of literature devoted to this topic and different scholars have singled out a wide variety of factors which, in their opinion, help to answer the crucial question of why terrorism occurs. The arguments range from the role of poverty, unemployment, (lack of) education, political leaning, perceptions of grievance and threat, rise of modernity, aggressive imposition of Western culture, (lack of) democracy, to a search for identity, personality factors, and religion, without any single factor providing a fully satisfactory answer. Moreover, as Max Taylor (2014: 584) pointed out, in the search for 'root causes' scholars 'at times seem not to understand the difference between correlation and causation, and where causation is claimed, rarely question or explore direction, and significantly we see too often confusion between the necessary conditions for something to occur and sufficient explanations'. Nevertheless, even if one settles with correlation, the empirical evidence provided in support of even the most frequently cited 'root' cause explanations of terrorism is at best inconclusive.

The presence of an extremist ideology justifying and legitimizing violence has been a particularly popular 'root' cause explanation of terrorism in the recent past. While most attention has been paid to religious extremism, secular extremist ideologies have been noted as well (Peters 2006: 115). In the aftermath of 9/11, almost all attention has nonetheless been paid to radical

Islamists, who often claim to be solely guided by the Quran, and the assumption that 'there was some mysterious process of indoctrination or brainwashing that transformed "vulnerable" or "at risk" naive young people into fanatic killers or true believers' (Sageman 2014b: 667). This explanation has, however, been challenged on empirical grounds. A study by Olivier Roy (2008), for example, found that al-Qaida members typically have a limited knowledge of the basic tenets of Islam (see also Coolsaet and de Swielande (2008)). According to Sageman (2008: 157), it is therefore possible to argue that 'Radical Islamic theology is not the main source of appeal for the vast majority of global Islamist terrorists.'

Another disputed 'root' cause of terrorism is (ir-)rationality. Many earlier studies of terrorism claimed that people who turn to terrorism are irrational or downright crazy. The alleged discoveries of personality pathology, however, did not stand up to subsequent empirical scrutiny (Sageman 2014b; Victoroff 2005). Therefore, there is a consensus nowadays that terrorists do not suffer from any major mental illness. In fact, as Richardson (2006: 14) noted, 'Interviews with current and former terrorists as well as imprisoned terrorists confirm that the one shared characteristic of terrorists is their normalcy.' Similarly, at the organizational level of analysis, several studies have shown that terrorist organizations behave in a rational manner, although they disagree on their incentive structure (Bloom 2005; Pape 2005).

This in turn suggests that terrorists may actually be rational actors whose resort to violence can be understood via the standard rational actor model. In this view, terrorists are strategic political utility maximizers who (a) are motivated by stable and consistent political preferences, (b) evaluate the political payoffs of their available options, and (c) elect to participate in terrorist groups because their political effectiveness is superior to alternative forms of protest. All of these assumptions of the rational model, however, have also been empirically disputed (Foley and Abrahms 2011). First, it is a mistake to assume that being a terrorist is a stable attribute of any person (Sageman 2014b: 667). Second, anonymous terrorism accounts for around 70 per cent of all attacks worldwide and specific policy demands are rarely forthcoming, even when the terrorist group divulges its identity to the target country (Foley and Abrahams 2010). Third, there is now empirical evidence proving that a vast majority of terrorist groups do not even partially succeed in accomplishing their political ends by attacking civilians. According to a large study by RAND, which examined 648 terrorist groups since 1968, only 4 per cent achieved their policy demands (Jones and Libicki 2008:15, 33).

Other often cited 'root' cause explanations of terrorism are similarly contested. Some studies advance the claim that terrorism is a response to political oppression, which may force some members of opposition groups to resort to violence because of the lack of alternatives and state repression, which in turns fuels the perception of injustice (Crenshaw 2007: 71). Going a step further, an often-invoked popular explanation of terrorism suggests that terrorism is a weapon of the weak and oppressed. Academic studies have nonetheless shown that (a) only a small percentage of individuals from aggrieved minorities go on to become terrorists, (b) terrorists rarely come from the oppressed people they claim to represent, and (c) terrorism is conspicuously absent from the most politically oppressive societies (Foley and Abrahms 2011).

Poverty has also fallen out of favor as a 'root' cause explanation of terrorism because both qualitative case studies and large-*n* quantitative studies have demonstrated that (a) the most recent high-profile terrorist attacks have been perpetrated by upper-middle-class individuals (including the 9/11 attacks), (b) terrorists do not tend to hail from countries with poor economies, and (c) they are often wealthier than the average citizen in their country of residence (Krueger 2007; Piazza 2006). Similarly, the available evidence does not support another often-cited explanation of terrorism – lack of education (Krueger and Maleckova 2003).

The radicalization debate

In the absence of an agreement on the root causes of terrorism at the macro-level, much attention has recently been paid to the topic of radicalization at the micro-level, e.g. answering the vexed question of what makes an individual susceptible to radical views, to the extent that s/he eventually becomes a terrorist. Radicalization processes have in particular been debated in Europe in the aftermath of the terrorist attacks in Madrid (2004) and London (2005), which were carried out by 'homegrown perpetrators – young people who had grown up in the West and conducted terrorist operations in their own backyard' (Sageman 2014b: 668). Due to its post-9/11 origins, the debate has thus far been almost exclusively focused on Islamist radicalization.

Within the academic debate, the shift of emphasis to understanding the bottom-up process of radicalization, from an inconclusive search for universal top-down root causes of terrorism, also reflects an acknowledgement that humans are complex: 'They catch the fire of terrorism in myriad ways – some environmental, some individual (or more likely, in most cases, a mix of the two); and unlike metals, they are strategic – they interact with the environment (including government counter-measures) and adapt in unpredictable ways' (Stern 2014: 607–8). There is, therefore, no universal pathway to terrorism and the reasons why some people are radicalized to the extent of catching the terrorist fire are bound to 'vary greatly across historical eras, regions of the world, and ideologies' (Schanzer 2014: 599).

Moreover, radicalization leading to acts of terrorism is a non-linear and multi-stage process of varying duration, and many radicals do not resort to violence in the pursuit of their goals. Several experts have therefore already noted that we need to differentiate between violent and non-violent radicalization, pointing out that only the latter amounts to catching the terrorist fire (Coolsaet and de Swielande 2008: 158; Schanzer 2014: 599). Taking these caveats into account, the following paragraphs offer a summary of relevant trends, manifestations, and dynamics of radicalization processes potentially leading to acts of terrorism.

When looking at the available literature as whole, a number of specific contributing factors have been singled out as facilitators of radicalization and/or motivations for terrorism. According to some scholars, they can be divided into the *internal* and *external* categories. Others have argued for a *local* versus *global* division, but the final lists of specific factors are quite similar under both approaches:

- failing, weak, and rogue states;
- unresolved conflict, social upheaval, economic stagnation, and high unemployment in Islamic countries;
- globalization and social-economic factors, alienation, propagation of an extremist worldview;
- proliferation of weapons of mass destruction, poverty, abuse of human rights, environmental degradation, international crime, and irrational fundamentalism;
- global inequity and global malaise due to worldwide religious revival and rise of identity politics, leaving no middle ground for tolerance and political compromise; and
- the rise of modernity, the aggressive imposition of Western culture, the lack of democracy in the Middle East.

Virtually all existing studies of radicalization focused on the *external/global* factors also emphasize the recent wars in Iraq and Afghanistan, along with the continuing Israeli–Palestinian conflict and the decades-old separatist longings in a number of countries with large Muslim minorities (such as Chechnya or Thailand), and long-term neglect of whole communities (such as the Bedouin in the Sinai), arguing that they have had a strong impact on the thinking of young Muslims all around the world to the extent that each new conflict between the West and the Muslim world fuels radical activities (Coolsaet and de Swielande 2008; Neumann and Brook 2007).

The most frequently cited internal/local factors contributing to Islamist radicalization are the Internet, mosques, refugee camps, and prisons. According to some studies, the list is actually much longer, but even when it comes to the alleged top place of radicalization, there is no consensus about the specifics. Dittrich (2007: 57), for example, believes that the Internet 'plays a key role in the radicalization process'.

In contrast, a study by the British Change Institute (2008: 4) concluded that the Internet 'may contribute to 'radicalization, including self-radicalization' but that it is likely 'to be secondary to face-to-face interaction in real settings'. Other studies have also highlighted the importance of pre-existing friendship and kinship, along with the shared experiences from Afghanistan, Iraq, and nowadays Syria, which have provided both a training ground and a magnet for Islamist terrorists (Sageman 2004; Roy 2008).

Several recent accounts of radicalization may offer a possible bridge between the aforementioned local/global explanations. In the tradition of French sociology, several authors have argued that radicalization occurs as 'individuals seek to reconstruct a lost identity in a perceived hostile and confusing world' (Dalgaard-Nielsen 2010: 799). Especially vulnerable are second- and third-generation Muslim immigrants in Europe, who suffer from a double sense of non-belonging – they have become Westernized to the extent of no longer feeling part of the community of their parents' home countries, while they simultaneously experience various forms of discrimination and socio-economic disadvantage in European societies. Extremist Islamism offers them the solution in the form of 'substitute identity, a feeling of community, and a vehicle for reclaiming the right to self-definition and dignity' (Dalgaard-Nielsen 2010: 801). Nevertheless, not all individuals will necessarily turn to radicalism in their search for a substitute identity. This is because the process of radicalization always takes place at the intersection of a particular personal history and a particular enabling environment, and some kind of a trigger is always necessary to start it off.

Another set of explanations informed by social movement theory and network theory therefore stresses that radicalization is essentially about 'whom you know' at the meso-level of analysis: 'radical ideas are transmitted by social networks and violent radicalization takes place within smaller groups, where bonding, peer pressure, and indoctrination gradually change the individual's view of the world' (Dalgaard-Nielsen 2010: 801). According to Wiktorowicz (2004), the process of emergence of a radical therefore consists of several specific steps: personal crisis, search for meaning, establishing contact with a group (often through existing personal relationships and networks), participation in lectures and recruitment sessions, acceptance of the group's message, more intensive socialization process, and active participation based on personal beliefs (Wiktorowicz 2004). Even these accounts, however, do not fully explain the specific link(s) between the many possible individual/group/mass/local/global factors of radicalization.

Counterterrorism

As with responses to other contemporary security threats, the existing counterterrorism policies reflect the opinions of their drafters concerning the definition, nature, and causes of terrorism. Thus, although not all scholars who study terrorism make explicit recommendations regarding the counterterrorism implications of their findings, it is clear that the aforementioned debates about the definition of terrorism, its contemporary nature, and its macro-level root causes, as well as the micro-level processes of radicalization, imply the adoption of rather different types of counterterrorism policies.

In other words, responses to the terrorist threat depend on how it is interpreted in the first place: as an unprecedented, imminent, large-scale, deadly risk linked to fanatical foreigners who hate us for what we are, or, as a crime committed by a group with distinct ethnic and social characteristics, radicalized by identifiable and resolvable social and political grievances, and motivated by both short- and long-term goals (Edwards and Meyer 2008: 6). In this social constructivist view, the subjective aspect of the threat is as important as the objective aspect, and the extent to which terrorism is seen as a grave security threat depends on a process of social construction, which is inherently intersubjective and takes place *among* various actors and audiences. The differences in perception of both the nature and salience of the threats posed by contemporary terrorism therefore represent a key variable in explaining the different approaches to counterterrorism. In this light, it is also not surprising that the counterterrorism literature primarily offers case studies of individual states' responses to terrorism, which usually start with the analysis of the terrorist threat(s) facing a particular country before moving to its counterterrorist response(s) (see, for example, Alexander 2002; Art and Richardson 2007; Charters 1994; Forest 2007; Reinares 2000; Schmid and Crelinsten 1993; von Hippel 2005).

From this literature, it is possible to identify both a set of factors explaining the differences in national counterterrorism policies and the most common counterterrorism measures and approaches. Regarding the former, it is clear that prior history of terrorism, as well as counterterrorism, matters. While for some states terrorism is nothing new, for many it represents a relatively novel security threat. In Europe, for example, only six countries (Spain, France, Greece, Germany, Italy, and the United Kingdom) account for almost 90 per cent of all terrorist attacks perpetrated since 1968. Different societies have also faced different types of terrorist groups. In Europe, over 90 per cent of all terrorist incidents are still perpetrated by ethno-separatist groups (Bures 2011).

Additional variables explaining the divergence of adopted counterterrorism policies are related to the social acceptability of the risk of terrorism. In addition to its familiarity (how unexpected and unusual is it?) they include control (what means are available to minimize or avoid it?); catastrophic potential (what is the worst-case scenario?); equity (who is affected in what way?); knowledge (what do we know about the phenomenon?); collective lessons learnt from previous events that are seen or intentionally portrayed as similar; the exact impact of media coverage on public opinion; and the trust in experts and political actors as objective evaluators of risks (Meyer 2009).

Regarding the last factor, it is important to note that, especially since 9/11, the terrorist threat may have been exaggerated for instrumental and strategic reasons by officials from various intelligence agencies. As noted by one scholar who had the opportunity to also work within the US intelligence community, 'its constant focus on potential terrorist plots and its exposure to a deluge of daily threats, the overwhelming majority being false alarms, create a sense of complacency among old analysts or, worse, a sense of imminent threat, extraordinarily out of proportion to the real threat' (Sageman 2014b: 675). It is therefore useful to point out that in quantitative terms, the risk of falling victim to a terrorist attack in Europe is '33 times smaller than dying of meningitis, 822 times than being murdered for non-political reasons and 1,833 times less likely than being killed in a car accident' (Edwards and Meyer 2008: 17).

At the same time, however, it is important to keep in mind the insights from the pre-9/11 literature on terrorism, which reminds us that the actual numbers of terrorist attacks and their victims are only of secondary importance, because what really matters is the 'irrational anxiety' (Nicholson 2003), which makes individuals believe that they will be the next victim of a terrorist attack, even though statistically speaking it indeed may be enormously more likely that they will be killed in a traffic accident. No government can therefore afford to ignore the threat of terrorism which often targets civilians going about their normal lives.

Approaches to counterterrorism: two models

Although the particular responses to the threat of terrorism differ from country to country due to the aforementioned factors, they usually include a mixture of legislative and operational responses. The latter have traditionally been carried out by national police forces and intelligence agencies, whose operations have long been seen as the most important counterterrorism instruments in most countries around the world. In contrast, before 9/11, military responses to terrorism were generally considered both ineffective and inappropriate, with the exception of the use of special forces in hostage crises (Wilkinson 2001: 133–6). After 9/11, however, the use of military power became the key ingredient of a new US counterterrorism policy. The declaration of a 'global war on terror' by the G. W. Bush administration reflected not only its perception of al-Qaida in line with the aforementioned 'new' terrorism argumentation, but also a perception of failure of the hitherto dominant criminal model of counterterrorism.

These two understandings of terrorism have led to two distinct approaches to counterterrorism over time: the war and the criminal model. The war model thinks of terrorism in the context of an enemy to be defeated in war, and vests the military with the primary authority to combat it. The role of the government and the other security agencies is limited to disrupting the terrorist networks and harassing their supporters. The war model is proactive in that it takes the fight to wherever the terrorists are located, regardless of national borders. In contrast, the criminal model thinks of terrorism as a heinous crime and thus primarily a law-enforcement problem. As with other types of crime, it is the job of the police (with the help of intelligence services) to find the terrorists, put them in detention, and assemble evidence for prosecution in courts, and the job of judges and juries to try them later. The criminal model is therefore rather reactive in that the whole law enforcement process can start only once some terrorist attacks have been executed, or at least seriously contemplated.

Both of the aforementioned ideal-type approaches to the fight against terrorism suffer from important pitfalls, which is also one reason why, in practice, most countries utilize a mixture of all available instruments. The criminal model, for example, is severely limited by the national remit of police and judiciary jurisdictions, and thus needs to be complemented by international cooperation, which is not always forthcoming (Bures 2011). The war model, and its post-9/11 US variant in particular, has been criticized for being too open-ended, since the notion of victory is unclear; for a futile attempt to fight what amounts to a tactic of combat; and for substantial financial, material, and human costs. Moreover, it has been argued that the war model also opens the door for authorities to use propaganda and to abrogate civil liberties.

However, attempts to privilege security over liberty in the name of counterterrorism are not only restricted to the war model: Schmid and Crelinsten (1993), for example, have argued that it was primarily through the criminal justice – not the military – route that Western states' responses to terrorism had moved away from democratic acceptability. There is also a substantial body of legal literature examining the plethora of legal instruments adopted since 9/11 to fight terrorism, which also points to an uneasy relationship between security and justice beyond the US war on terror (Cameron 2003; Tappeiner 2005).

An important assumption in these security and/or/versus liberty debates is that we know how to assess the effectiveness of existing counterterrorism policies. Unfortunately, this assumption is not warranted, as there is a remarkable lack of analyses of the impact of adopted counterterrorism measures at all levels. As a consequence, 'it remains largely a matter of faith that anti-crime and anti-terror efforts have some impact beyond the immediate operational outcomes' (Levi 2007: 264). Despite the billions spent annually on counterterrorism, we still lack an adequate performance evaluation baseline to figure out what 'works' and why. To some extent, this is due to the methodological difficulties regarding the quality and quantity of data, as well as in finding the right proxy indicators that would complement the readily available, yet inherently limited, quantitative criteria (such as the number of arrests, requests for assistance, or amounts of frozen terrorist money) that do not shed much light on the actual effects of counterterrorism measures on specific cultures, groups, and individuals.

Methodologically explicit empirical works on counterterrorism effectiveness therefore represent a much-needed addition to the case studies and thematic policy discussions that tend to dominate the existing counterterrorism literature. Apart from further large-*n* studies, more qualitative research should also be done to improve our understanding of how multiple variables combine to produce counterterrorist outcomes. At the same time, it is important to note that the standard of comparison clearly matters when it comes to evaluating the effectiveness of any type of policy. Some experts have therefore argued that the 'critics of antiterrorist efforts should remain realistic . . . and bear in mind that terrorists enjoy crucial advantages. They chose the targets, means and dates of their attacks. Moreover . . . [g]overnments have to be lucky all the time and the terrorists need to be lucky only once' (Neuhold 2006: 42).

Concluding remarks: glass half full or half empty?

In a recent provocative article, Marc Sageman (2014a: 565) claimed that '[d]espite over a decade of government funding and thousands of newcomers to the field of terrorist research, we are no closer to answering the simple question of "What leads a person to turn to political violence?".' His lamenting about the 'Stagnation in Terrorism Research' triggered a lively debate among the leading researchers of terrorism and counterterrorism, most of whom have argued that despite many shortcomings, 'Terrorism Studies has never been in better shape than now' (Schmid 2014: 587).

Although the succinct literature reviews presented in this chapter do not (and cannot) resolve this important debate, they do confirm the lack of clear-cut answers to several key questions, including the one posed by Sageman. Further theoretically- and empirically-informed research is certainly needed to explore the causes and consequences of terrorism, as well as the effectiveness of counterterrorism. At the same time, this chapter also highlighted the key methodological difficulties that go a long way towards explaining the existing state of the art in the research of terrorism and counterterrorism. The reader is therefore encouraged to further explore the field of Terrorism Studies in order to judge whether the glass is half full or half empty.

References

Alexander, Y. (2002) *Combating Terrorism: Strategies of Ten Countries*, Ann Arbor: University of Michigan Press.
Allison, G. T. (2004) *Nuclear Terrorism: The Ultimate Preventable Catastrophe*, New York: Times Books.
Art, R. J., and Richardson, L. (2007) *Democracy and Counterterrorism: Lessons from the Past*, Washington, DC: US Institute of Peace Press.
Benjamin, D., and Simon, S. (2003) *The Age of Sacred Terror: Radical Islam's War against America*, New York: Random House.
Bloom, M. (2005) *Dying to Kill: The Allure of Suicide Terrorism*, New York, Columbia University Press.
Bures, O. (2011) *EU Counterterrorism Policy: A Paper Tiger?*, Aldershot, Ashgate.
Cameron, I. (2003) 'UN Targeted Sanctions, Legal Safeguards and the European Convention on Human Rights', *Nordic Journal of International Law* 72(2): 159–214.
Change Institute (2008) 'Studies into Violent Radicalisation; Lot 2: The Beliefs, Ideologies and Narratives'. Online. Available HTTP: <http://ec.europa.eu/justice_home/fsj/terrorism/prevention/docs/ec_radicalisation_study_on_ideology_and_narrative_en.pdf> (accessed 11 May 2010).

Charters, D. A. (1994) *The Deadly Sin of Terrorism: Its Effect on Democracy and Civil Liberty in Six Countries*, Westport, CT: Greenwood Press.

Coolsaet, R. and de Swielande, T. S. (2008) 'Epilogue: Zeitgeist and (De-)Radicalisation', in R. Coolsaet (ed.) *Jihadi Terrorism and the Radicalization Challenge in Europe*, Aldershot: Ashgate, 154–81.

Crenshaw, M. (2007) 'Terrorism and Global Security', in C. A. Crocker, F. O. Hampson, and P. Aall (eds.) *Leashing the Dogs of War: Conflict Management in a Divided World*, Washington, DC: USIP Press, 67–82.

Dalgaard-Nielsen, A. (2010) 'Violent Radicalization in Europe: What We Know and What We Do Not Know', *Studies in Conflict & Terrorism* 33(9): 797–814.

Dittrich, M. (2007) 'Radicalisation and Recruitment: The EU Response', in D. Spence (ed.) *The European Union and Terrorism*, London: John Harper Publishing, 54–70.

Duyvesteyn, I. (2004) 'How New is the New Terrorism?', *Studies in Conflict & Terrorism* 27(5): 439–54.

Edwards, G. and Meyer, C. O. (2008) 'Introduction: Charting a Contested Transformation', *Journal of Common Market Studies* 46(1): 1–25.

Foley, F. and Abrahms, M. (2011) 'Terrorism and Counterterrorism', in R. Denemark (ed.) *The International Studies Encyclopedia*, London: Blackwell Online. Available HTTP: <http://www.isacompendium.com/public/> (accessed 6 June 2016).

Forest, J. (2007) *Countering Terrorism and Insurgency in the 21st Century: International Perspectives*, Westport, CT: Praeger Security International.

Jones, S. G. and Libicki, M. C. (2008) *How Terrorist Groups End: Lessons for Countering al Qa'ida*, Washington, DC: RAND.

Krueger, A. B. (2007) *What Makes a Terrorist: Economics and the Roots of Terrorism*, Princeton, NJ: Princeton University Press.

Krueger, A. B. and Maleckova, J. (2003) 'Education, Poverty and Terrorism: Is there a Causal Connection?', *Journal of Economic Perspectives* 17(4): 119–44.

Laqueur, W. (2003) *No End to War: Terrorism in the Twenty-First Century*, New York: Continuum.

Levi, M. (2007) 'Lessons for Countering Terrorist Financing from the War on Serious and Organized Crime', in T. J. Biersteker and S. E. Eckert (eds.) *Countering the Financing of Terrorism*, London: Routledge, 260–88.

Meyer, C. O. (2009) 'International Terrorism as a Force of Homogenization? A Constructivist Approach to Understanding Cross-National Threat Perceptions and Responses', *Cambridge Review of International Affairs* 22(4): 647–66.

Morgan, M. J. (2004) 'The Origins of the New Terrorism', *Parameters: US Army War College* 34(1): 29–43.

Neuhold, H. (2006) 'International Terrorism: Definitions, Challenges and Responses', in D. Mahncke and J. Monar (eds.) *International Terrorism. A European Response to a Global Threat?*, Brussels: Peter Lang, 23–46.

Neumann, P. R. and Brook, R. (2007) *Recruitment and Mobilisation for the Islamist Militant Movement in Europe*. Online. Available HTTP: <http://ec.europa.eu/justice_home/fsj/terrorism/prevention/docs/ec_radicalisation_study_on_mobilisation_tactics_en.pdf > (accessed 18 May 2010).

Nicholson, M. (2003) 'An Essay on Terrorism', *American Diplomacy* 19(8): 8.

Pape, R. A. (2005) *Dying to Win, The Strategic Logic of Suicide Terrorism*, New York: Random House.

Peters, G. B. (2006) 'Forms of Informality: Identifying Informal Governance in the European Union', *Perspectives on European Politics and Society* 7(1): 25–40.

Piazza, J. A. (2006) 'Rooted in Poverty? Terrorism, Poor Economic Development and Social Change', *Terrorism & Political Violence* 18(1): 159–77.

Rapoport, D. C. (2004) 'The Four Waves of Modern Terrorism', in A. K. Cronin and J. M. Ludes (eds.) *Attacking Terrorism. Elements of a Grand Strategy*, Washington, DC, Georgetown University Press, 46–73.

Reinares, F. (2000) *European Democracies against Terrorism: Governmental Policies and Intergovernmental Cooperation*, Aldershot: Ashgate.

Richardson, L. (2006) *What Terrorists Want: Understanding the Enemy, Containing the Threat*, New York: Random House.

Roy, O. (2008) 'Al-Qaeda: A True Global Movement', in R. Coolsaet (ed.) *Jihadi Terrorism and the Radicalization Challenge in Europe*, Aldershot: Ashgate, 109–14.

Sageman, M. (2004) *Understanding Terror Networks*, Philadelphia: University of Pennsylvania Press.

Sageman, M. (2008) *Leaderless Jihad: Terror Networks in the Twenty-First Century*, Philadelphia: University of Pennsylvania Press.

Sageman, M. (2014a) 'Low Return on Investment', *Terrorism & Political Violence* 26(4): 614–20.

Sageman, M. (2014b) 'The Stagnation in Terrorism Research', *Terrorism & Political Violence* 26(4): 665–80.

Schanzer, D. H. (2014) 'No Easy Day: Government Roadblocks and the Unsolvable Problem of Political Violence: A Response to Marc Sageman's "The Stagnation in Terrorism Research"', *Terrorism & Political Violence* 26(4): 596–600.

Schmid, A. P. (2011) *The Routledge Handbook of Terrorism Research*, Abingdon: Routledge.

Schmid, A. P. (2014) 'Comments on Marc Sageman's Polemic "The Stagnation in Terrorism Research"', *Terrorism & Political Violence* 26(4): 587–95.

Schmid, A. P. and Crelinsten, R. D. (1993) *Western Responses to Terrorism*, London: Frank Cass.

Stern, J. (2014) 'Response to Marc Sageman's "The Stagnation in Terrorism Research"', *Terrorism & Political Violence* 26(4): 607–13.

Tappeiner, I. (2005) 'The Fight against Terrorism: The Lists and the Gaps', *Utrecht Law Review* 11(1): 97–125.

Taylor, M. (2014) 'If I Were You, I Wouldn't Start from Here: Response to Marc Sageman's "The Stagnation in Terrorism Research"', *Terrorism & Political Violence* 26(4): 581–6.

Victoroff, J. (2005) 'The Mind of the Terrorist: A Review and Critique of Psychological Approaches', *Journal of Conflict Resolution* 49(1): 3–42.

Von Hippel, K. (2005) *Europe Confronts Terrorism*, London: Palgrave Macmillan.

Wiktorowicz, Q. (2004) *Islamic Activism: A Social Movement Theory Approach*, Bloomington: Indiana University Press.

Wilkinson, P. (2001) *Terrorism versus Democracy: The Liberal State Response*, London: Frank Cass.

14

ORGANIZED CRIME

Adam Edwards

'Organized crime' is now a major focus for public policy, as exemplified in the United Nations Convention Against Transnational Organized Crime (Edwards and Gill 2003; UNODC 2004) and, in Europe, its prominence on the EU's agenda for creating an 'Area of Freedom, Security and Justice'. In turn, this agenda has generated a whole new genre of policy-oriented learning, the 'threat assessment' of organized crime, which endeavours to provide policy-makers with an understanding of current organized crime patterns, in particular concerns about 'transnational' crimes resulting from the greater mobility of people and goods across borders, and to inform the targeting and coordination of efforts at prevention (EU OCTA 2006 and *passim*; EU SOCTA 2013; EU iOCTA 2014). As such, threat assessments of organized crime exemplify the more profound logic of security, to anticipate and prevent especially serious threats to public safety, as contrasted with the retrospective logic of criminal justice which seeks guilt for predicate offences after the fact of their commission. This policy shift from criminal justice to security, from prosecution on the facts to the prevention of threats yet to be realized, is controversial both for its challenge to principles of due process and because of concerns over the unintended consequences of pre-emptive interventions.

In the social science research community, however, the very concept of organized crime is controversial. Some consider it to be little more than a political construct, used by policy elites in the liberal democracies to depict themselves as primarily the victims of 'alien' threats from a familiar rogues' gallery of organized crime groups (OCGs): 'Cosa Nostra', 'Columbian cartels', 'Chinese triads', 'Russian Mafiya', etc. (Woodiwiss 2003; Woodiwiss and Hobbs 2009). Others identify a self-referential bureaucratic politics at play in the construction of organized crime threats as problems of law enforcement implying law enforcement solutions, including innovations in confiscating the proceeds of crime (Sheptycki 2003; van Duyne and Vander Beken 2009).

Counterpoised to the threat assessment industry and its sceptics, however, is an emerging field of research which focuses analysis on the organization of serious crimes, including the opportunities for their commission and the social relations which these imply (Edwards and Levi 2008). This analytical shift has generated an energetic research programme concerned with the 'crime scripts' or *modus operandi* employed by criminal organizations to commission different types of crime (Cornish and Clarke 2002; Levi and Maguire 2004), the 'scenarios' which are more or less conducive to the organization of these crimes (Vander Beken and Verfaillie 2010), the normative, as well as empirical, inquiry into the 'social harms' that qualify certain types of crime as 'serious'

Table 14.1 Organised crime policy trends and their analytical focus

Trend	Analytical Focus
The actor-orientation (1): conspirators	Organised crime groups (OCGs)
The actor-orientation (2): illegal entrepreneurs	Illicit networks
The actor-orientation (3): poly-criminals	'Potpourri' of 'threat indicators':
	OCGs
	SOCs (Serious organised crime areas)
	CRFs (Crime-relevant factors)
	Effects of OCGs + SOCs on EU society
Organisation of serious crimes: commissioning	Scripts, scenes, and scenarios

priorities for governmental action (Greenfield and Paoli 2010), and the conditions or 'scenes' in which these scripts are played out.

This analytical shift has had an impact on policy trends, partly influencing the European Council's 2006 decision on the remit of Europol (the European Policing agency) to shift the scope of its work from 'organized crime' to 'serious crime' (Dorn 2008). The primary location of this shift in thinking has, however, been in the academy and its pressure on policy-makers, as in the Royal United Services Institute's programme of research on organized crime (RUSI 2013). To place this more recent trend in context and as a precursor to discussing its implications for the policy–research relationship, it is possible to distinguish three other dominant policy trends, each with their own distinctive analytical focus (see Table 14.1). This chapter has four main parts, one on each trend.

The actor-orientation (1): conspirators

Histories of the definition of 'organized crime' as an official category and focus for policy identify its origins in American law enforcement (Woodiwiss 2003). One of the earliest uses of the concept has been traced back to the 1896 report of the New York Society for the Prevention of Crime into racketeering, gambling, and prostitution. Both here, and in the US National Commission on Law Observance and Enforcement (the Wickersham Commission 1929–31), the problem is defined in terms of the political and economic conditions generating racketeering, including the corruption and collusion of public officials in municipal government (Smith 1991; Woodiwiss 2003).

Post-Second World War, however, historians identify a major shift in policy discourse. 'What' questions about the kinds of crime that were being organized and how they were organized became less important than questions about 'who' was doing the organizing, in particular concerns about the influence of foreign career criminals (Smith 1991). Critics of this analytical shift refer to the new concept of organized crime as an 'alien conspiracy theory', epitomized by the proceedings of the 1950 Kefauver Senate Investigating Committee (on 'organized crime in interstate commerce') which was preoccupied with the organization of criminal conspiracies around ethnic groups, in particular those emanating from the Italian-American community. Whilst the Kefauver Committee continued the Wickersham Commission's concern with the role of officialdom in the facilitation of criminal enterprises, it promoted the now familiar distinction between the 'upper world' of legitimate commerce and government and the 'underworld' of criminal conspiracies (Paoli and Fijnaut 2004).

The Kefauver Committee popularized the idea of 'a nationwide crime syndicate known as the Mafia, whose tentacles are found in many large cities' (United States Senate 1951: 131).

Mafia imagery subsequently dominated policy discourse in the US. The concept of organized crime as the consequence of ethnically based syndicates with international connections was given academic credibility through Donald Cressey's contribution to Lyndon Johnson's 1967 Presidential Task Force on Organized Crime. Cressey's (1969) landmark text, *Theft of a Nation*, represented organized crime in the US as a shadow state, mirror-imaging the hierarchically-organized rational bureaucracies of the law enforcement agencies charged with tackling 'it'.

These core aspects of the Cressey model also clarify the purposes of the principal law enforcement instrument that came out of the Johnson Task Force, the Racketeer Influenced and Corrupted Organizations (RICO) statute of 1970, to prosecute membership of criminal enterprises involved in predicate offences. The analytical preoccupation with OCGs received a 'pluralist' revision in Ronald Reagan's Presidential Commission on Organized Crime, which retained a focus on the threat posed by ethnically based conspiracies but broadened the scope beyond the Mafia to accommodate the perceived impact of 'Colombian cartels', the Japanese Yakuza, and Russian groups, etc. It was also under the auspices of the Regan Commission that a strict dichotomy between the upper world of legitimate finance and public administration, and the underworld of criminal conspiracies was consolidated, with negligible attention given to the role of corporations and officialdom in the facilitation of organized crime (Potter 1994).

The lineage of the alien conspiracy theory continues through to present representations of 'transnational' organized crime in other regions, particularly in Europe post-Soviet Union, and can be discerned in the EU's threat assessments (see below). Within the American 'home' of the concept of organized crime, however, this theory has been challenged by those arguing that much illegal market activity, particularly in the narcotics markets, operates in a 'disorganized way' and is better conceptualized in terms of marketplace dynamics (Naylor 1997; Reuter 1983).

The actor-orientation (2): illegal entrepreneurs

Conceptualizing organized crime in terms of illicit enterprise has also been a defining character-istic of much European policy activity in relation to organized crime. The analytical concern with enterprise has the advantage of shifting policy change and learning away from the blunt, ethno-centric, and potentially bigoted focus on ethnically defined groups (without denying that ethnicity and kinship can be employed as resources for organizing illicit markets). It accommodates looser partnerships of co-offenders and consequently acknowledges the phenomenon of project crimes arranged by networks of illicit entrepreneurs brought together by 'criminal contact brokers' for the purposes of commissioning particular offences (Hobbs 2001; Klerks 2003). The use of social net-work analysis to conceptualize and explain such project crimes has become a key focus of academic research, for example on human trafficking (Campana 2015) or gun crime (Oatley and Crick 2015).

Even so, analysis of the structural properties of organized crime problems, in particular their accomplishment through social networks of entrepreneurs, still privileges a focus on particular co-offenders rather than the assemblage of these actors and the necessary resources for organizing serious crimes in conditions that are conducive. As a consequence, there is a danger of repeating the reductionist explanation of conspiracy theorists only this time reducing the policy problem to the structural properties of 'the network' of entrepreneurs rather than 'the syndicate' of alien conspirators.

In addition, the looser definition of organized crime as illicit entrepreneurship has attracted criticism for simply adding to the ambivalence of a policy construction that accommodates activities ranging from tax fraud through to drugs trafficking and terrorist activity and actors as diverse as the Italian Cosa Nostra through to youth gangs (Fijnaut et al. 1998). Paoli and Fijnaut (2004: 41) conclude their history of the concept of organized crime by arguing:

Its very plurality of meanings, explaining its recent success in world public debate, and making it a catchy label to signify popular anxieties and foster legislative changes, hinders the full transformation of organized crime into a clear-cut legal category. Despite the definitional efforts made by several domestic governments and international organizations, organized crime [. . .] remains a vague and ambiguous catchphrase, the application of which inevitably entails varying – but usually high – degrees of arbitrariness.

The actor-orientation (3): poly-criminals

One response to this definitional problem has been to replace the search for an all-encompassing definition with evolving content definitions of emerging threats and risks. This approach can be discerned in the United Nations Convention against Transnational Organized Crime and, more explicitly still, in the European Union's annual Organized Crime Threat Assessments (the 'OCTA'), which commenced in 2006 and concluded in 2011 before being replaced by the current EU Serious and Organized Crime Threat Assessment (the 'SOCTA'), first published in 2013 covering the 2013–2017 period with an 'interim assessment' expected in 2015.[1]

Reviewing the journey from OCTA to SOCTA provides a means of tracing the evolution of thinking about organized crime in elite European policy-making circles over the past decade and, within this thinking, the particular importance of the threat assessment as a new genre of policy-making. The replacement of the EU Organized Crime Situation Reports (OCSR) by the OCTA in 2006 was justified on the grounds that transnational OCGs were outwitting and outflanking the capacities of national police and intelligence agencies, and this warranted both a transnational response from European-wide agencies such as Europol and one that aimed to anticipate and pre-empt, not simply react to, problems of transnational organized crime. In these terms the ambition of the OCTA was to inform the anticipatory governance of transnational organized crime problems and to justify pre-emptive interventions. As such it is a significant shift in governmentality from 'criminal justice', the retrospective detection and prosecution of suspects 'on the facts' of offences already committed, to 'security' and the justification of pre-emptive interventions against suspects yet to offend. Given the gravity of this shift for due process and allied risks of miscarriages of justice, it is worth reflecting on developments in threat assessment and the fitness for purpose of this policy genre in warranting pre-emptive intervention.

Whilst adding to the range of factors considered in threat assessments, this policy trend has continued the tendency in other actor-oriented accounts to treat organized crime as a collective noun, a singular thing, rather than a variegated process. As a consequence, more elaborate content definitions of this thing have only resulted in a 'potpourri' of factors to be considered, rather than their assemblage into something that realist social scientists would recognize as resembling an explanation with a clear explanandum (the thing to be explained) and related explanans (the premises that explain 'the thing' and their antecedent conditions) (Keat and Urry 1981: 10, 248–9).

The absence of clear explanatory thinking in the policy process for security strategies premised on pre-emptive intervention ought to provoke considerable concern. It would be disconcerting enough if, in Paoli and Fijnaut's (2004) terms, policy-oriented learning about retrospective law enforcement continued to be 'arbitrary', but in the context of legitimating the *pre*judice of security strategies it is surely indefensible. If the building of predictive machines to warrant pre-emptive intervention is to remain a possible and desirable policy goal then the methodology of threat assessment is justifiably a core concern for anyone interested in the politics and jurisprudence of security strategies.

From OCTA to SOCTA

The journey from OCTA to SOCTA can be characterized as one in which actors, the OCGs, remain central but are represented as more sophisticated 'poly-criminals' in that they diversify into a range of criminal activities that can complement one another, such as trafficking in people as well as narcotics, and enabling illegal migration as well as shipping forced labour into the vice markets and sweatshops of Western Europe.

This first threat assessment argued that, whilst the OCSR that preceded the OCTA provided a descriptive account, the OCTA 'puts an emphasis on the qualitative assessment of this complex and multi-faceted phenomenon', noting 'a need for a close attention on key criminals […] asking the question what they are doing and how, rather than who they are' (OCTA 2006: 6). In these terms the OCTA recognizes different kinds of organized groups, including 'flexible and fluid patterns of association between individual criminals', and emphasizes the importance of understanding 'the conditions under which patterns of criminal association and co-offending emerge and exist' (OCTA 2006: 12).

Reference is also made to the principal activities of these groups, specifically drug trafficking, trafficking in human beings and illegal immigration, fraud, Euro counterfeiting, commodity counterfeiting and intellectual property theft, and money laundering. The OCTA (2006: 17–22) also identifies 'key facilitating factors with regard to criminal markets' – such as problems of globalization and ease of movement across borders – which provide OCGs with opportunities for commissioning serious crimes, including document forgery and identity theft, misuse of the transport sector, and exploitation of the financial sector.

Even so, the assessment proceeds from an identification of OC actors to their activities and their consequences, rather than taking the accomplishment of particular criminalized activities as the analytical focus, in which the mobilization of different actors is but one part. The admixture of the indicators, categories, regional patterns, principal activities, and facilitating factors used to define the threats posed by organized crime groups has been criticized for producing a confused analytical tool (cf. van Duyne and Vander Beken 2009: 274).

Mindful of the confused picture emerging out of the OCTA, the first assessment notes that, 'Weighting crime areas against one another is inherently difficult. This too, has less to do with analytical insights than value statements, reflecting different priorities in the MS [Member States of the European Union] and beyond' (2006: 25). It is acknowledged that, ultimately, the intelligence on which the OCTA is premised is gleaned from, 'years of political and law enforcement experience' (2006: 26), a dependence that is reinforced by the key methodological instrument of threat assessments: surveys of police forces' perceptions of organized crime activity (Gregory 2003; van Duyne and Vander Beken 2009).

Without wishing to dismiss the relevance of political and law enforcement-based assessments of threat, there is a danger that these bracket-off other kinds of expertise about organized crime (for consequences see Edwards and Levi 2008: 372–4). Whilst cataloguing OCG actors and activities, threat assessments remain very obtuse and abstract about the explanation of organized crime problems and consequently how remediable they are. There is little sense of how serious crimes are actually organized and what this tells us about the possibilities for crime reduction. Whilst subsequent iterations of the annual OCTA have refined the discussion of its core concepts, the ramifications of its law enforcement-centred strategy remain.

SOCTA 2013–2017

The establishment of the EU SOCTA for the 2013–17 period was promoted by the incumbent Director of Europol, Rob Wainwright, as a significant development in thinking that takes policy-making about organized crime beyond the OCTA. The SOCTA is premised on 'a new methodology' that was developed over the course of 2011–12 (SOCTA 2013: 42), which contains the refining of indications of OCGs and augmenting these with indices of serious organized crime areas (SOCs), their effects on EU society, and the identification of various crime-related factors (CRFs) in the environment which can either facilitate or inhibit OCGs and SOCs.

In a novel development, the SOCTA methodology is also accompanied by a response from three academic researchers interested in organized crime (SOCTA 2013: 44–5). These academics identify key challenges in the methodological conundrum of prediction in future-oriented approaches to threat assessment. As predictive models are invariably premised on the extrapolation of historical data, they condemn analysts to fight the last battle rather than genuinely anticipate and effectively intervene against novel criminal practices. As a response to this conundrum they suggest, but don't explain, the need for 'continuous crime trend scanning, extending the SOCTA approach to support a more proactive approach' (SOCTA 2013: 45). They also note a conceptual need to recognize the mobility of multi-commodity poly-criminal actors across national and administrative boundaries, and the need to avoid the kind of mirror-imaging that has debilitated previous security strategies (see also Sheptycki 2003). They argue that global crime problems require global policy responses, otherwise security agencies bound by national and other administrative boundaries are destined to be outflanked by the increasingly 'flat' networked and distributed organization of criminal activity. Finally, the experts discuss the implications of these future trends for the process, as well as the content, of threat assessment, arguing that it will have to be more dynamic, flexible, and responsive than previous exercises that were too slow and bureaucratized to keep pace with adaptations in criminal organization. The last point echoes a long-established criticism of the policy response to organized crime by researchers noting the 'proteiform' qualities of serious crime in which adaptations are fuelled by an ongoing 'arms race' between perpetrators and preventers to outwit and outflank each other (Dorn 2003; Ekblom 2003).

However, it is not clear if the indices of OCGs, SOCs, effects and CRFs defined in the SOCTA methodology actually tell us much about the drivers of serious crime or, more prosaically, how serious crimes are actually organized (cf. RUSI 2014). The failure to pose this basic question remains the most remarkable characteristic of the politics and jurisprudence of security in this policy area. Indeed it can be argued that it is the jurisprudential preoccupation with criminal law enforcement rather than crime and harm reduction that explains much of this basic theory failure in the policy response to organized crime. In this regard, and notwithstanding the preoccupation with the flat, networked, and distributed organization of criminal activity, the actor-oriented legacy of Kefauver and Cressey remains strong in SOCTA 2013. Whilst not wishing to doubt the importance of the criminal prosecution of serious offenders for heinous crimes, realizing the difference between criminal law enforcement on the one hand and crime and harm reduction on the other remains important for innovations in the future development of the policy–research relationship.

The organization of serious crimes: commissioning processes

The distinction between law enforcement and crime reduction does not preclude the role of the former in the latter, only the treatment of the two as synonymous. If crime reduction is more than law enforcement, what else is it? Concepts taken from volume crime reduction, of household burglary and automobile thefts for example, have been used by criminologists to rethink the organization of serious crimes (Cornish and Clarke 2002; Ekblom 2003; Felson 2006; Levi and Maguire 2004; Levi 2007, see also Greenfield and Paoli 2010; Vander Beken and Verfaillie 2010). Although marginal to the policy process, which remains dominated in Europe, North America, and the UN by the various actor-oriented accounts considered above, it is possible to identify a number of core propositions about the commissioning of serious crimes, whose synthesis provides an alternative conceptual framework in which the dilemmas of security responses, particularly pre-emptive intervention, to organized crime could be re-thought.

Reducing serious crimes entails an analytical focus on the commissioning of offences

The attributes of perpetrators, in particular their ethnicity, are of concern only in so far as they help explain the commissioning process, such as the use of kinship networks as vehicles for the production and exchange of illicit goods and services, and as insulation against law enforcement operations, as in the trafficking of Moroccan hashish from the Rif into Western European capitals (Edwards 2005). By contrast, the offence-focus implies a concern with specific types of crime and a presumption (to be corroborated and refined through comparative empirical research) that different types of crime necessitate different commissioning processes or, to use a criminological term, they necessitate different 'crime scripts'[2] which break down any crime into the particular sequence of activities through which it is accomplished. For example, the scripts entailed in the production and distribution of crystal methamphetamine from the sourcing of precursor chemicals, the construction of drug manufacturing labs, the storage and distribution of the product, the collection and reinvestment of proceeds from the sale of the product, and so on (Chiu et al. 2011).

Understanding the commissioning of serious crimes entails an analytical concern with the interactions of offenders, victims, and guardians in specific social contexts

Contrary to the dramatic focus on the pursuit and prosecution of 'crime bosses', 'kingpins', and 'core nominals', a concern with the commissioning process also reveals the routine interactions between offenders, their targets, and the presence or absence of capable guardians that consequently create opportunities for serious crime. A concern with these interactions can broaden understanding of the social contexts of commissioning to include transnational markets and e-commerce through the Internet, and help to anticipate future 'scenarios', including the likely consequences of different policy responses for escalating or reducing crime rates. Renowned examples include the impact of law enforcement operations against drug dealers generating violent turf wars for the share of markets freed-up by the successful removal of particular dealers, and the likely consequences of decriminalizing illicit drug use for public health and safety (Vander Beken and Verfaillie 2010).

The harmful effects, the 'seriousness', of serious crime entails normative as well as empirical analysis and interpretation, as well as measurement in the prioritization of the policy response

Another implication of the distinction between law enforcement and crime reduction is to shift the focus of policy outcomes from successes or failures in the prosecution of offenders for predicate offences – the volume of their criminal assets that are confiscated, or the volume of illicit goods that are captured – towards reductions in the harmful consequences of these offences. The presumption here is that incapacitation or disruption of particular offenders does little to alter or debilitate the commissioning process or its harmful impact, particularly in highly lucrative markets such as the trade in narcotics, where there are many recruits waiting to step into the shoes of incarcerated or otherwise incapacitated offenders.

Establishing the relative harm of different types of serious crime entails challenges that are both normative ('what constitutes a harm and from whose perspective?') and empirical (whether to calculate harms in terms of gross figures or net of possible benefits, for example the therapeutic benefits that are believed to accrue from cannabis use for those suffering neurological complaints, see Greenfield and Paoli 2010: 8–9). As such, attempts have been made to develop a 'risk assessment matrix' that ranks harms according to their 'severity' (on a scale from negligible to catastrophic) and their 'probability' (from unlikely to frequent). Although not without some interpretative flexibility, this matrix at least provides the analyst with a systematic starting point for prioritizing the seriousness of certain activities relative to others from one extreme (frequent and catastrophic) to another (unlikely and negligible) (Greenfield and Paoli 2010: 16).

Analysis of the scripts, scenarios, and harmful effects of organizing serious crimes implies a more concrete identification of weak points or 'vulnerabilities' in the commissioning process for specific types of crime and their prioritization in policy responses

Emerging work in this field identifies border controls, shipping routes, and visa applications as notable weak points in trafficking human beings and transporting stolen vehicles (Levi and Maguire 2004: 428–9). Other examples of weak points identified through script analysis include the ease with which payment card fraud could be commissioned prior to the introduction of 'chip and pin' cards (Levi and Maguire 2004: 433–8), or the ease with which vehicle identification numbers (VINs) could be switched from legal but wrecked automobiles to stolen vehicles for the purposes of resale (Tremblay et al. 2001: 568). Allied to the harm-reduction framework, the analysis of commissioning informs a policy response that can prioritize the investment of resources in targeting weak points and in accordance with judgements about the severity and probability of any given crime type, which is likely to be attractive in an 'age of austerity' in public expenditure and limited resources for crime prevention.

A crime reduction strategy premised on the targeting of weak points in the commissioning process implies a broadening of the policy response from law enforcement to include other public authorities, the involvement of private organizations, and public-private partnerships

The identification of crime promoters, as well as intentional co–offenders (conspirators, entrepreneurs, and poly-criminals), in the commissioning process broadens the scope of crime reduction beyond law–enforcement measures targeting known offenders. Allied to normative and empirical judgements about the harms associated with different crimes, this approach begins to suggest a rationale for a division of labour amongst public and private sector 'preventers', and opportunities for public–private partnerships in which the effort and costs of sustainable crime reduction are shared (Levi and Maguire 2004: 417–23). In addition to charging public authorities other than the police (such as vehicle licensing authorities) and private organizations (such as solicitors and accountants) with surveillance and enforcement duties in relation to the commission of serious crimes, this policy trend generates a wider repertoire of policy choices. It might, for example, be argued that scarce public resources are better concentrated on crimes that are more frequent and more critical (if not catastrophic) for a higher proportion of the public (Greenfield and Paoli 2010). Whilst highly controversial, not least because of its explicit prioritization of policy responses and targets, the harm-reduction approach provides a normative, as well as an empirical, framework for the politics and jurisprudence of group offending. It enables deliberation about the necessary prioritization of alternative policy agendas for criminal, restorative, and social justice and for risk management and their relationship to sustainable public protection in contexts of austere public expenditure (Edwards and Hughes 2012; Edwards et al. 2013).

> *This broadening of the policy response also implies a concern with the conditions or 'scenes' in which scripts are played out, resulting in more or less harmful scenarios. The concept of scenes alerts us to the importance of an analytical concern with the conditions that can enable or frustrate security scripts and their rewriting*

Continuing the dramaturgical metaphor, it can be acknowledged that scenes provide possibilities for improvisation in the script and are not crudely deterministic of performance. Even so, they suggest a certain narrative progression in the script which actors are disciplined to follow and do not completely rewrite each time they perform. Disambiguating improvisation and narrative in serious crime scenes is in part a question for 'concrete', empirical research, requiring access to the accounts that can be elicited through qualitative interviews with offenders, victims, control agents, and other researchers and their construct validation, including the scripts, scenarios, and scenes that emerge from cross-examination in court proceedings (Levi 2008). As a precursor to this it is, however, it is also possible to engage in abstract research entailing thought experiments about the necessary and contingent social relations that render serious crimes possible (Edwards and Levi 2008; also Felson 2006).

Conclusion

There is a need to challenge the language and assumptions of crime 'analysts' allied to the policy process and to rehabilitate an older language of social research that renders explicit the different practices necessary at various stages of social scientific work (Keat and Urry 1981: 248–9). Researching, rather than 'analysing', the organization of serious crimes alters the relationship between social scientists and the policy community. This shifts the policy-research relationship away from a view that social scientists ought to be enrolled into agendas set by policy-makers to service their technical refinement or better communication to broader publics. Conversely, the language of research locates social scientists as constructive critics of these agendas, inhabiting a culture of organized scepticism that can pose alternative visions of control. These alternatives may, for example, entail counter-intuitive (for law enforcement agencies) forms of non-enforcement, such as triggering self-regulation (Edwards and Gill 2002).

Notes

1 Unreleased at the time of writing this chapter.
2 A concept initially developed by Cornish and Clarke (2002) to augment rational choice analyses of organized crimes, and subsequently elaborated and applied by Levi and Maguire (2004) to understand other practices in the modi operandi of organizing and preventing serious crimes. The concept is employed in this chapter in this later, broader, sense.

References

Campana, P. (2015) 'The Structure of Human Trafficking: Lifting The Bonnet on a Nigerian Transnational Network', *British Journal of Criminology*. Online. Available HTTP: <http://bjc.oxfordjournals.org/content/early/2015/06/09/bjc.azv027.1> (accessed 29 October 2015).

Chiu, Y.-N., Leclerc, B. and Townsley, M. (2011) 'Crime Script Analysis of Drug Manufacturing in Clandestine Laboratories', *British Journal of Criminology* 51: 355–74.

Cornish, D. B. and Clarke, R. (2002) 'Analyzing Organized Crimes', in A. Piquero and S. Tibbetts (eds.) *Rational Choice and Criminal Behaviour*, London: Routledge, 41–64.

Cressey, D. (1969) *Theft of a Nation*, New York: Harper and Row.

Dorn, N. (2003) 'Proteiform Criminalities' in A. Edwards and P. Gill (eds.) *Transnational Organised Crime: Perspectives on Global Security*, London: Routledge, 227–40.

Dorn, N. (2008) 'The End of Organised Crime in the European Union', *Crime, Law and Social Change* 51: 283–95.

Edwards, A. (2005) 'Transnational Organised Crime', in J. Sheptycki and A. Wardak (eds.) *Transnational and Comparative Criminology in a Global Context*, London: Glasshouse Press, 211–25.

Edwards, A. (2011) 'The Organisation of Serious Crimes: Key Trends in Policy and Research', in J. Rafailovich, S. Gabova, and S. Popov (eds.) *Organized Crime, Civil Society and the Policy Process: Conference Proceedings*, Sofia: RiskMonitor Foundation, 32–44.

Edwards, A. and Gill, P. (2002) 'Crime as Enterprise? The Case of Transnational Organised Crime', *Crime, Law and Social Change* 37(3): 203–33.

Edwards, A. and Gill, P. (eds.) (2003) *Transnational Organised Crime: Perspectives on Global Security*, London: Routledge.

Edwards, A. and Hughes, G. (2012) 'Public Safety Regimes: Negotiated Orders and Political Analysis in Criminology', *Criminology and Criminal Justice* 12(4): 433–58.

Edwards, A. and Levi, M. (2008) 'Researching the Organisation of Serious Crimes', *Criminology and Criminal Justice* 8(4): 363–88.

Edwards, A., Hughes, G., and Lord, N. (2013) 'Urban Security in Europe: Translating a Concept in Public Criminology', *European Journal of Criminology* 10(3): 260–83.

Ekblom, P. (2003) 'Organised Crime and the Conjunction of Criminal Opportunity Framework', in A. Edwards and P. Gill (eds.) *Transnational Organized Crime: Perspectives on Global Security*, London: Routledge, 241–63.

Felson, M. (2006) *The Ecosystem for Organized Crime*, HEUNI Paper 26, Helsinki, The European Institute for Crime Prevention and Control.

Fijnaut, C., Bovenkerk, F., Bruinsma, G., and Van de Bunt, H. (1998) *Organised Crime in the Netherlands*, The Hague: Kluwer Law International.

Greenfield, V. and Paoli, L. (2010) *If Supply-Oriented Drug Policy is Broken, Can Harm Reduction Help Fix It? – Melding Disciplines and Methods to Advance International Drug Control Policy*, United States Naval Academy, Department of Economics Working Paper 2010–30.

Gregory, F. (2003) 'Classify, Report and Measure: the UK Organised Crime Notification Scheme', in A. Edwards and P. Gill (eds.) *Transnational Organized Crime: Perspectives on Global Security*, London: Routledge, 78–96.

Hobbs, D. (2001) 'The Firm: Organizational Logic and Criminal Culture on a Shifting Terrain', *British Journal of Criminology* 41: 549–60.

iOCTA (2014) *European Union Internet Organised Crime Threat Assessment*, The Hague: Europol.

Keat, R. and Urry, J. (1981) *Social Theory as Science*, London: Routledge.

Klerks, P. (2003) 'The Network Paradigm Applied to Criminal Organisations: Theoretical Nitpicking or a Relevant Doctrine for Investigators? Recent Developments in The Netherlands', in A. Edwards and P. Gill (eds.) *Transnational Organized Crime: Perspectives on Global Security*, London: Routledge, 97–113.

Levi, M. (2007[1994]) 'Organised Crime and Terrorism', in M. Maguire, R. Morgan, and R. Reiner (eds.) *The Oxford Handbook of Criminology*, Oxford: Oxford University Press.

Levi, M. (2008) 'Organized Fraud and Organizing Frauds: Unpacking Research on Networks and Organization', *Criminology and Criminal Justice* 8(4): 389–419.

Levi, M. and Maguire, M. (2004) 'Reducing and Preventing Organized Crime: an Evidence-Based Critique', *Crime, Law and Social Change* 41: 397–469.

Naylor, T. (1997) 'Mafia, Myths and Markets: On the Theory and Practice of Enterprise Crime', *Transnational Organized Crime* 3(3): 1–45.

Oatley, G. and Crick, T. (2015) 'Measuring UK Crime Gangs: A Social Network Problem', *Social Network Analysis and Mining* 5(33): 1–16.

OCTA (2006) *European Union Organised Crime Threat Assessment 2006*, The Hague: Europol.

Paoli, L. and Fijnaut, C. (2004) 'Introduction to Part I: The History of the Concept', in C. Fijnaut and L. Paoli (eds.) *Organised Crime in Europe: Concepts, Patterns and Control Policies in the European Union and Beyond*, Dordrecht: Springer, 21–46.

Potter, G. (1994) *Criminal Organizations: Vice, Racketeering and Politics in an American City*, Prospect Heights: Waveland.

Reuter, P. (1983) *Disorganised Crime: The Economics of the Visible Hand*, Cambridge, MA: MIT Press.

RUSI (Royal United Services Institute) (2013) 'Organised Crime'. Online. Available HTTP: <https://rusi. org/projects/organised-crime> (accessed 21 October 2014).

RUSI (Royal United Services Institute) (2014) 'Assessing the Threat of Organised Crime: The First National Strategic Assessment', RUSI Analysis, 23 May. Online. Available HTTP: <https://rusi.org/commentary/ assessing-threat-organised-crime-first-national-strategic-assessment> (accessed 21 October 2014).

Sheptycki, J. (2003) 'Global Law Enforcement as a Protection Racket: Some Sceptical Notes on Transnational Organised Crime as an Object of Global Governance', in A. Edwards and P. Gill (eds.) *Transnational Organized Crime: Perspectives on Global Security*, London: Routledge, 42–58.

Smith, D., Jr (1991) 'Wickersham to Sutherland to Katzenbach. Evolving an "Official" Definition for Organised Crime', *Crime, Law and Social Change* 16(2): 135–54.

SOCTA (2013) *European Union Serious and Organised Crime Threat Assessment 2013*, The Hague: Europol.

Tremblay, P., Talon, B., and Hurley, D. (2001) 'Bodyswitching and Related Adaptations in the Resale of Stolen Vehicles: Script Elaborations and Aggregate Crime Learning Curves', *British Journal of Criminology* 41: 561–79.

United States Senate (1951) *Third Interim Report of the Special Committee to Investigate Organized Crime in Interstate Commerce (Kefauver Committee)*, Washington DC: United States Government Printing Office.

UNODC (2004) *United Nations Convention against Transnational Organized Crime and the Protocols Thereto*, Vienna: United Nations Office on Drugs and Crime.

van Duyne, P. and Vander Beken, T. (2009) 'The Incantations of the EU Organised Crime Policy Making', *Crime, Law and Social Change* 51: 261–81.

Vander Beken, T. and Verfaillie, K. (2010) 'Assessing European Futures in an Age of Reflexive Security', *Policing and Society* 20(2): 187–203.

Woodiwiss, M. (2003) 'Transnational Organised Crime: The Global Reach of an American Concept', in A. Edwards and P. Gill (eds.) *Transnational Organized Crime: Perspectives on Global Security*, London: Routledge, 13–27.

Woodiwiss, M. and Hobbs, D. (2009) 'Organized Evil and the Atlantic Alliance: Moral Panics and the Rhetoric of Organized Crime Policing in America and Britain', *British Journal of Criminology* 49(1): 106–28.

15

MIGRATION AND SECURITY

Jef Huysmans and Vicki Squire

Today, migration, mobility, and borders are familiar themes in the study of international politics.[1] That was not always the case, however, and particularly not in Security Studies. In the 1970s and 80s you would have been hard pressed to find any analysis focusing on migration in Security Studies. While it was previously considered to be a social and economic phenomenon belonging to the fields of socio-economic history, historical sociology, and anthropology, migration is now pivotal in debates surrounding global politics (Castles and Davidson 2000; Castles and Miller 1993; Sassen 1996).

Many things have changed since the 1980s, but four have played a central role in understanding how migration has emerged as a concern for scholars of Security Studies specifically:

1. The end of the Cold War and the rise of new security issues in Security Studies;
2. The development of new approaches to security;
3. The rise of international human security agendas; and
4. Developments in counter-terrorism policy in the wake of 9/11.

As a sub-discipline of International Relations (IR), largely oriented towards the US and Europe, Security Studies fell into a crisis after 1989–91, as both security institutions and security scholars lost their international bearing. What to do now that the insecurities that had dominated European and US agendas for decades no longer demanded priority? In reply, a discourse and institutionalisation of 'new' insecurities took centre stage. Moreover, the increasing use of the term 'Security Studies' was itself instrumental in opening up the military-focused bipolar security agenda to include new areas of study (Buzan 1991; Tickner 1995). In this context, the cross-border movement of people was a key issue that entered Security Studies (Heisbourg 1991; Widgren 1990). Simultaneously, migration and borders became a central area for the development of constructionist understandings of security, an approach that does not take security as a given, but analyses the processes through which a phenomenon is politically reframed as a security issue. Moreover, in the 1990s refugee policy became linked to the global human security agenda, while mass migration was defined as a key human security concern by the United Nations Development Programme. In the wake of 9/11, these developments were intensified and reconfigured through counterterrorist policies, as well as through analyses concerned with the effects of such policies on human mobility, immigrants, and borders.

These developments of a migration/security nexus opened up a contested terrain within Security Studies (Bigo 2002; Guild and van Selm 2005; Wæver et al. 1993). The immediate questions in this context were:

- To what extent can migration be considered a serious security threat for states?
- What kind of insecurities does migration raise, and for whom or what?

In parallel, another set of questions emerged. They were not oriented towards strategic policy development aimed at defending the state, but concerned with the consequences and legitimacy of securitizing migration:

- Is it legitimate to govern migration through security policies?
- Through which political processes is migration framed as a security question, and what alternative framings exist or are possible?
- What are the consequences of politicizing migration as a security issue?
- How can a critical political analysis of mobility be developed out of the nexus of migration and security?

In charting the terrain through which these questions have emerged, this chapter draws attention to the complexity of current debates surrounding migration and security. The first section shows how the analysis of the migration/security nexus has been approached both from a traditional security perspective, through a focus on the security of the state, and from a human security perspective, through a focus on the security of individual migrants. Drawing attention to the normative dilemmas posed by the framing of migration as a security issue, it emphasizes the critical importance of the conceptual framing of the *relation* between migration and security.

This feeds into the second section, which charts a diverse body of critical work. Here, security is not a condition of the state or the individual, but refers to knowledges, discourses, technologies, and/or practices that mediate the relation between the social processes of human mobility and the search for governmental control and steering capacity over them. Considering how this body of work can be developed in terms that open up the migration/security nexus to a richer analysis of the relation between mobility and politics, the final section claims that security questions should not be allowed to dominate the terrain of migration, but should be examined in relation to a range of political and socio-economic questions.

Strategic and humanitarian approaches to the migration/security nexus

In this section, we specifically show how analysts from both migration studies and Security Studies tend to approach the migration/security nexus in traditional terms, through conceptualizing security as a value to be achieved by means of national security policies and/or humanitarian actions. We conclude the chapter by introducing challenges from Critical Security Studies, which make a case for a reframing of migration and security.

Migration in traditional Security Studies

Many of the leading works introducing migration into the area of Security Studies have done so by defining migration as a central dimension of a rounded security agenda. Thus, it has been argued that migration needs to be factored into the calculations of national security strategy, and that national security needs to be factored into the calculations of migration policy (Rudolph 2006; Weiner 1995). Such strategic approaches, which are important in giving migration studies greater legitimacy within the US mainstream of IR and strategic studies, treat security as a condition that is affected by migration and, thus, by migration policies.

These strategic analyses calculate the extent to which migratory and demographic developments bear upon national security questions. Such considerations range from fears of refugees and immigrants becoming violent political actors (Loescher 1992) to the effect of migration on social cohesion and the availability of a sufficient work force (Rudolph 2006). In this regard, scholars at the nexus of migration and security have opened up the area of migration studies beyond its classical economic focus on the state's selection of skilled and unskilled migrants for economic purposes (cf. Constant and Zimmerman 2005). This has contributed to a wider process through which the relationship between migration studies and refugee studies has been reconfigured (cf. Scheel and Squire 2014).

Strategic analysts also draw attention to the ways that security concerns impact on a state's migration policies. However, not all strategic analyses of the migration/security nexus define migration as a threat to national security (Rudolph 2006: 31). Migration can equally importantly become a condition of national security, thus supporting arguments for a less restrictive migration policy. What defines this approach is that it understands the migration/security nexus as a calculus of how migration impacts, positively as well as negatively, on the security of a state.

Human security and migration

Analysts of human security focus attention on the security of the person rather than that of the state and bring into view the protection of humans who migrate. This humanitarian approach has been reaffirmed in relation to refugees and asylum seekers (Nadig 2002), as well as in relation to the trafficking of (primarily women and children) migrants (Jonsson 2009).

Despite its widespread pragmatic and normative appeal, a focus on human security is of limited effect in radically reframing migration. Human security is largely incorporated as a dimension that is internal to global migration management (Koser 2005). This is evident, for example, in the growing linkage between migration and development, which does not effectively transcend a migration-control framework due to the predominance of political and institutional concerns over security (Lavenex and Kunz 2008).

Notwithstanding these limitations, some analysts have made a pragmatic case for human security and humanitarianism in the attempt to ensure that liberal democratic states move 'closer to realizing the values they claim to live by now' (Gibney 2004: 260). A pragmatic humanitarianism may be critical as a normative approach that holds the liberal democratic state to account in the face of excessively restrictive migration controls. However, it is less critical as a political approach that challenges the securitization of migration. Humanitarianism is essentially concerned with the protection of vulnerable populations and with redressing harmful practices. In this regard, it tends to approach the migrant as a disempowered victim rather than as a political actor. As such, humanitarianism does not escape a framework of security, but is integral to an approach through which migrants are either politicized as 'threatening' subjects to be feared, or are depoliticized as 'vulnerable' subjects to be pitied (see Aradau 2004; Pallister-Wilkins 2015; Squire 2015a). A shift from fear to pity here does not decouple migration and security, but intensifies security concerns in both international and domestic debates over migration. Indeed, debates regarding the migration/security nexus involve the coarticulation of both human and national security concerns. Rather than featuring as two discrete and mutually exclusionary approaches, strategic and human security approaches largely come together through their mutual securitization of migration.

A critique

So how precisely do strategic and human security approaches come together in terms that securitize migration? These approaches share the potential reification of migration as a 'threat'. By approaching security as a value or a condition to aspire to, analysts from each approach tend to assume that migration policy can be developed either in terms that increase the security of states, or in terms that increase the security of migrants, or indeed in terms that increase the security of both states and migrants. In so doing, they bring free movement firmly into the field of security, thus consolidating the articulation of migration as a security 'threat'. This legitimizes exclusionary distinctions that have become particularly widespread across Europe, North America, and the Asia-Pacific in terms that identify 'undesirables' such as 'illegal immigrants' and 'asylum seekers' as necessitating intensified controls. Both strategic and human security approaches thus potentially consolidate what critical Security Studies scholars have defined as the securitization of migration and free movement (Bigo 2002; Huysmans 2006; Squire 2009).

For this reason, strategic and human security approaches are limited in terms of their ability to open up the intellectual terrain at the nexus of migration and security in all its sociological, political, and normative richness. Strategic approaches not only eliminate the normative questions regarding how securitizing migration produces exclusion, violence, and inequality; they also reduce the political and social complexity of migration to the strategic interaction between states. Migration becomes a factor in the calculation of power and the national security of states (e.g. as an economic resource or as a cultural factor affecting social cohesion). Human security approaches open up normative questions and shift attention beyond the state, but do not go far enough in considering how framing migration in terms of two conflicting security claims – human versus national security – produces particular effects. Most notably, human and strategic security perspectives render the management of threats (whether to the person or to the state) the defining stake of migration policy, while conferring legitimacy on policy-making assemblages of security agencies, development experts, human rights lawyers, migration experts, NGOs and humanitarian organizations. It is in a context of exclusionary and technical or bureaucratic relations that a critical and political analysis of the social processes involved in the linkage of migration and security is required.

Critical analyses of the migration/security nexus

One way in which a less strategic and more critical political sociological approach to the migration/security nexus can be developed is in the analysis of the effects that the political framing of migration as a threat has on public perception and opinion formation. Over recent years, public opinion regarding migration in many countries within the global North has become hostile toward 'asylum seekers', 'illegal migrants', and sometimes migration more generally. An analysis of the discrepancy between perceptions of migration and the objective threat that migration poses, as well as between threat perceptions of migration in the political elite and in the wider public is of political interest in this regard (Lahav 2004).

Social materiality

However, focusing on threat perceptions underplays the social materiality of the securitizing processes – security in this literature seems to exist primarily in the mind. By contrast, critical scholars suggest that the securitization of migration implies more than simply perceptions. Of particular importance are the societal circulations of security discourses, the application of security technologies, the development of legal categories through material practices such as form-filling, and professional routines that construct and sustain actions through which migration is governed as a security 'threat'.

A continuous and intensive circulation of discourses of immigration 'floods', for example, can change dominant language through which migration is approached. Such changes usually go together with changes in institutional locations of migration policy. A language that employs metaphors such as 'floods' legitimates a stronger focus on border controls and a more crucial position of border police, as opposed to employers' interests, for example (Garrelli et al. 2013). What matters here is not so much what people believe, but the nature and the available palette of languages that publics, policy-makers, and professional organizations can draw upon when speaking about migration, as well as the skills and knowledge that border police bring to the management of migration compared to the skills and knowledge of employer organizations and unions (see Andreas 2009).

It is here that Critical Security Studies opens up the analysis of the migration/security nexus to its political and social richness, while at the same time maintaining critical distance from objectivist accounts in which 'undesirable' migrants are identified as 'threatening'. Rather than a value or a fact, security is understood in terms of a language, knowledge, and professional skill-set linked to particular organizations, which is always shaped in relation to other knowledges, discourses, technologies, or practices that contest it.

The question is not whether migration is indeed a security issue or not, but rather how the migration/security nexus has gained potency as a method of governing migration in certain situations. In shifting attention to the social and political processes that construct phenomena as a security issue, these critical approaches avoid taking insecurities as given. The policy question is not what needs to be done to reduce insecurities provoked by (particular categories of) migration. Rather, consideration is paid to the consequences of governing migration by means of security policies or practices, and to how the negative consequences of this, and the securitization of migration more broadly, can be avoided.

Sites, agencies, technologies

Critical Security Studies scholars have examined these questions in relation to various sites, agencies, and technologies at the intersection of migration and security. Important sites in this regard are camps in which migrants are detained (Ilcan 2013; Johnson 2013; Le Cour Grandmaison et al. 2007). The border areas or zones through which migrants pass, such as airports, embassies, and customs are also important sites of investigation (Infantino and Rea 2012; Muller 2005; Salter 2008).

In terms of agencies, critical scholars, among others, have looked at the increasing role of security professionals, including private agencies, in the regulation of movement (Bigo 1996a; Guiraudon 2000). Such research also examines various security technologies employed in the regulation of migration, such as visas, asylum procedures, biometrics, and surveillance (e.g. Amoore, 2006; Bellanova and Fuster, 2013).

All of these approaches share the idea that security practices involve a specific strategy or technique of governing and (de)politicizing migration. Politically speaking, migration and mobility are one of the key areas in which the legitimacy of security measures is heavily contested. Such a focus therefore does not simply invite sociological investigations into how issues become securitized, but also demands a political analysis of (a) the ways in which the process of securitizing migration confers political legitimacy on particular groups or actions (for example, nationalist movements and parties); and of (b) different contestations of security knowledges, discourses, technologies, or practices (for example debates on data protection and privacy in relation to demands for a more intensive gathering and storage of data from refugees, migrants, and mobile people more generally). Critical analysts thus focus on the precise nature and effects of using security instruments, knowledges, and discourses in the area of migration, as well as on the institutions sustaining such processes (e.g., Pilkington 1998; van Munster 2009).

The presence of security policies in the migration area is thus explained not only by the political use of security language in the migration field and by the use of references to migration-related issues in security debates like counterterrorism. The process of securitizing migration includes the presence and relative power of security professionals and experts in the migration policy field (Bigo 1996a; Boswell 2007; Guiraudon 2000). It also includes the transfer of security practices and instruments between different policy areas concerned with controlling mobility. For example, in the European Union there have been significant transfers between the policing of football hooligans through travel restrictions and the control of migration (Tsoukala 2004). Similarly in the North American context, scholars have considered how a range of separate issues become associated with migration through security and policing knowledges, discourses, technologies, and practices (Andreas 2009).

Inclusions/exclusions

In undertaking such analyses, critical scholars of the migration/security nexus highlight the exclusionary and violent effects of security knowledges, discourses, technologies, and practices on particular groups of migrants (Guild 2009; Le Cour Grandmaison et al. 2007; Walters 2002). There has been a proliferation of critical scholarship over recent years that examines the political effects of profiling and surveillance techniques on mobile people. This includes a focus on fingerprinting, data storage and mining, camps, visas, passports, etc. (Bigo and Guild 2005; Bonditti 2004; Muller 2005).

Beyond the field of critical Security Studies, related concerns have emerged in debates regarding the role of border walls as markers of a waning (or resurgent) sovereignty in a post-9/11 context (Brown 2010). The concern here has not only been with the exclusionary articulation of borders and identity (Epstein 2007). The political and practical characteristics of exclusionary and violent knowledges, discourses, technologies, or practices have been debated, in particular in terms of their exceptional or routine status (e.g. Basaran 2008). These debates are important for the field of critical Security Studies and the migration/security nexus, because they prompt consideration of how the securitization of migration might be challenged, or transformed from a security question to a non-security issue.

Moving beyond the migration/security nexus

Critical Security Studies scholars conceive security as having various meanings and as constituting social and political techniques of governing that effectively shape human mobility. In other words, security is not conceived of as a value to aspire to or a condition of insecurity that needs addressing but as a *constitutive mediator* of the relation between mobility and politics. This brings to the fore the normative nature of writing security, where security knowledge easily slips into a securitizing knowledge.

In this regard, one of the important questions for critical studies of the migration/security nexus is whether it is possible to perform Security Studies without contributing to the process of securitization. This has led to significant debates surrounding the desecuritization (Wæver 1995) of issues such as migration. Sociological analyses of desecuritization aim to study how in a situation of securitized migration, migration can be taken out of the security policy area and governed through non-security instruments. Such process includes delegitimizing the role of security professionals and discourses, taking migration out of the realm of 'the exceptional', changing routine governmental techniques of managing migration, and so on. Yet although such an approach has often been called for, such analyses are hard to find in Security Studies, critical or not.

A more fruitful approach, at least in terms of the existing literature, has been to displace the focus on security by developing an analysis of the politics of mobility. Security knowledges, discourses, technologies, and practices through which migration is governed often remain significant in these analyses, but they are placed within a wider understanding of the political significance and contestations of mobility (Guild 2009; Ilcan 2013). Security, along with its linkages to migration, then becomes one of several issues that affects, shapes, and constrains mobility, rather than the defining concern. Important here, then, is that security is not privileged either as a value or as a governing practice in the analysis of migration.

A growing literature looks at the political agency of migrants. Such studies take issue with analyses that overstate the capacity of restrictive and humanitarian security policies to destroy the agency of migrants. They mostly study situations in which exclusionary techniques of governing, including security practices, imply an impoverishment of the political agency of specific migrants (for example, by approaching migrants as victims requiring 'treatment' rather than as autonomous people making specific claims about their rights, ambitions, and/or equal standing as human beings). Yet, rather than focusing on the details of the methods of control and their effects in terms of discriminations, objectifications of subjects, and destitution of political agency, they study what migrants are actually doing and how their actions gain political significance (e.g. Aradau 2008; Johnson 2014; Mezzadra 2011). This is more in line with a rights-based approach, which has been posed as an alternative to a security-oriented approach in relation to forced migration (Goodwin-Gill 2001); trafficking (Jordan and Duvell 2002); and 'illegal immigration' (Cholenewski 2000).

However, rather than focusing on the inherent rights of individuals, these critical analysts have shown how mobility can serve as a mode of 'becoming political' in a context of global inequality (see Chimni 2000; Jordan and Duvell 2002). Analysts of migration and security have moved in this direction in recent years, such as by considering citizenship claims as claims to being political through demands to the right to hold rights. Such claims are seen as significant politically because they are 'mis-placed' or irregular according to an exclusionary and de-politicizing frame of security (e.g. Andrijasevic 2010; McNevin 2006; Nyers and Moulin 2007). Others have looked more closely at how what are sometimes defined as 'abusive' actions by migrants – such as their 'tricking' of the system – are forms of resistance rather than simply opportunistic practices. These interpretations look less at rights claims and more at the everyday practices of mobility and how they resist through escaping or appropriating the governmental techniques of control (Bagelman 2013; Papadopoulos et al. 2008; Scheel 2013; Squire 2015b).

Another method by which the migration/security nexus has been opened to a wider political analysis of mobility has been to foreground the question of violence that is committed against the body of migrants and its political legitimacy. Refugees fighting the government in their country of origin from abroad or the violence exercised upon the body of migrants are in this sense not reduced to a question of matters of human security and national security. Instead of security, the political nature of violence takes the foreground. For example, some have opened up the question of what the exercise of violence against the body of refugees (e.g. in detention centres), as well as what the forms of resistance that involve self-imposed violence (e.g. lip or eye sewing, hunger strikes or suicide attempts) tell us about the nature of the modern state and international politics and the political role of violence in it (Edkins 2005; Le Cour Grandmaison et al. 2007; Nyers 2006: 97–122).

Others have pointed to the significance of indirect forms of violence enacted through material forces such as the desert or the sea, raising the question of how such violence plays into the legitimization of restrictive measures (Doty 2011; Squire 2014; Sundberg 2011). Like the literatures foregrounding migrant agency, these studies take key political issues at stake in the governance of mobility – in this case the nature and political significance and legitimacy of violence – rather than the techniques of security practice as the main object of analysis. Security or securitization is then part of, but not presumed to be central to, the analysis of migration or mobility (see Boswell 2007; Squire, 2016). Rather, the central focus concerns the wider political questions that are articulated in relation to mobility and migration policies.

Conclusion

In the first section of this chapter we considered how the migration/security nexus is developed and sustained through the interplay of national and human security concerns. In Security Studies each is represented by a discrete set of analyses, one focusing on how migration raises issues of national security and the other focusing on how current conditions and policies endanger individual migrants or people in an interconnected world. As a result very few analyses look at how both are interconnected in practice and jointly sustain the governing of migration through security techniques.

We then moved on to examine how critical Security Studies scholars have unpacked the social and political processes through which migration is made into and sustained as a matter of security. The migration/security nexus in these terms is then not seen as the result of threats to national security and to migrants as such, but in relation to changes in the governing of migration. In other words, the nexus is seen as a consequence of a political and governmental reframing of migration.

The chapter concluded with a proposal to study the migration/security nexus indirectly. Instead of homing in on security threats or the processes of securitization, we highlight the significance of analyses that situate the securitization of migration within a wider analysis of practices of citizenship, violence, or political subjectivities. Such political analysis of the migration/security nexus has developed an understanding of how security knowledges, discourses, technologies, and practices operate across a political field where various approaches to human mobility are contested through struggles over the definition of (legitimate) political agency, the role of violence, competing conceptions of rights or justice, etc. These readings of the migration/security nexus thus shift research away from simply refining our understanding of the security dimensions of migration and the implications of its securitization. It embeds securitizing processes in social and societal negotiations of central political questions, which are rarely engaged exclusively in security terms.

Note

1 Our presentation starts from developments in Security Studies in IR. Analysts from disciplines such as sociology, anthropology, criminology, and social history have studied aspects of the nexus between migration and security, independent of the focus on migration that emerged in Security Studies towards the end of twentieth century. The importance of this point is not that Security Studies in IR comes late to these issues, but rather to be clear on the disciplinary angle that informs our overview. Given its inherently multidisciplinary dimensions, migration remains one of these terrains in Security Studies that is particularly open, or at least has great potential, to be a productive meeting ground for various disciplinary foci.

References

Amoore, L. (2006) 'Biometric Borders: Governing Mobilities in the War on Terror', *Political Geography* 25(3): 336–51.
Andreas, P. (2009) *Border Games: Policing the US–Mexico Divide*, Cornell: Cornell University Press.
Andrijasevic, R. (2010) *Migration, Agency and Citizenship in Sex Trafficking*, Basingstoke: Palgrave.

Aradau, C. (2004) 'The Perverse Politics of Four Letter Words: Risk and Pity in the Securitisation of Human Trafficking', *Millenium – Journal of International Studies* 33(2): 251–77.

Aradau, C. (2008) *Rethinking Trafficking in Women. Politics out of Security*, Basingstoke: Palgrave.

Bagelman, J. J. (2013) 'Sanctuary a Politics of Ease?', *Alternatives: Global, Local, Political* 38(1): 49–62.

Basaran, T. (2008) 'Security, Law, Borders: Spaces of Exclusion', *International Political Sociology* 2(4): 339–54.

Bellanova, R. and Fuster, G. G. (2013) 'Politics of Disappearance: Scanners and (Unobserved) Bodies as Mediators of Security Practices', *International Political Sociology* 17(2): 188–209.

Bigo, D. (2002) 'Security and Immigration: Toward a Critique of the Governmentality of Unease', *Alternatives: Global, Local, Political* 27: 63–92.

Bigo, D. and Guild, E. (eds.) (2005) *Controlling Frontiers: Free Movement into and within Europe*, Aldershot: Ashgate.

Bonditti, P. (2004) 'From Territorial Space to Networks: A Foucaultian Approach to the Implementation of Biopolitics', *Alternatives: Global, Local, Political* 29: 465–82.

Boswell, C. (2007) 'Migration Control in Europe after 9/11: Explaining the Absence of Securitization', *Journal of Common Market Studies* 45(3): 589–611.

Brown, W. (2010) *Walled States, Waning Sovereignty*, New York: Zone Books.

Buzan, B. (1991[1983]) *People, States and Fear: An Agenda for International Security Studies in the post-Cold War Era*, London: Harvester Wheatsheaf.

Castles, S. and Davidson, A. (2000) *Citizenship and Migration. Globalization and the Politics of Belonging*, New York: Routledge.

Castles, S. and Miller, M. J. (1993) *The Age of Migration: International Population Movements in the Modern World*, London: MacMillan.

Chimni, B. S. (2000) 'Globalization, Humanitarianism and the Erosion of Refugee Protection', *Journal of Refugee Studies* 13(3): 243–64.

Cholenewski, R. (2000) 'The EU Acquis on Irregular Migration: Reinforcing Security at the Expense of Rights', *European Journal of Migration and Law* 2(3–4): 361–405.

Constant, A. and Zimmerman, K. F. (2005) 'Immigrant Performance and Selective Immigration Policy: A European Perspective', *National Institute Economic Review* 194(1): 94–105.

Doty R. L. (2011) 'Bare Life: Border-Crossing Deaths and Spaces of Moral Alibi', *Environment and Planning D: Society and Space,* 29(4): 599-612.

Edkins, J. (2005) 'Through the Wire: Relations of Power and Relations of Violence', *Millennium – Journal of International Studies* 34(1): 1–24.

Epstein, C. (2007) 'Guilty Bodies, Productive Bodies, Destructive Bodies: Crossing the Biometric Borders', *International Political Sociology* 1(2): 149–64.

European Council (2005) *Presidency Conclusions of the Brussels European Council*. Online. Available HTTP: <http://www.consilium.europa.eu/ueDocs/cms_Data/docs/pressData/en/ec/92202.pdf> (accessed 3 October 2008).

Garrelli, G., Sossi, F., and Tazzioli, M. (2013) *Spaces in Migration: Postcards of a Revolution*, London: Pavement Books.

Gibney, M. (2004) *The Ethics and Politics of Asylum*, Cambridge: Cambridge University Press.

Goodwin-Gill, G. (2001) 'After the Cold War: Asylum and the Refugee Concept Move on', *Forced Migration Review* 10: 14–16.

Guild, E. (2009) *Security and Migration in the 21st Century*, Cambridge, Polity Press.

Guild, E. and van Selm, J. (eds.) (2005) *International Migration and Security. Opportunities and Challenges*, London: Routledge.

Guiraudon, V. (2000) 'European Integration and Migration Policy: Vertical Policy-Making and Venue Shopping', *Journal of Common Market Studies* 38(2): 251–71.

Hall, A. (2012) *Border Watch: Cultures of Immigration, Detention and Control*, London, Pluto Press.

Heisbourg, F. (1991) 'Population Movements in post-Cold War Europe', *Survival* 33(1): 31–43.

Huysmans, J. (2006) *The Politics of Insecurity: Fear, Migration and Asylum in the EU*, London: Routledge.

Ilcan, S. (2013) 'Paradoxes of Humanitarian Aid: Mobile Populations, Biopolitical Knowledge, and Acts of Justice in Osire Refugee Camp', in S. Ilcan (ed.) *Mobilities, Knowledge and Social Justice*, Quebec: MacGill University Press, 177–206.

Infantino, F. and Rea, A. (2012) 'La mobilisation d'un savoir pratique local. Attribution des visas Schengen au Consulat Général de Belgique à Casablanca', *Sociologie pratiques* 24: 67–77.

Johnson, H. L. (2013) 'The Other Side of the Fence: Reconceptualising the 'Camp' and Migration Zones at the Borders of Spain', *International Political Sociology* 7(1): 75–91.

169

Johnson, H. L. (2014) *Border, Asylum and Global Non-Citizenship: The Other Side of the Fence*, Cambridge, Cambridge University Press.

Jonsson, A. (2002) 'Human Rights or Wrongs? The Struggle for a Right-Based Response to Trafficking in Human Beings', *Gender and Development* 10(1): 28–37.

Jonsson, A. (2009) (ed.) *Human Trafficking and Human Security*, London, Routledge.

Jordan, B. and Duvell, F. (2002) *Irregular Migration: The Dilemmas of Transnational Mobility*, Cheltenham: Edward Elgar.

Koser, K. (2005) 'Irregular Migration, State Security and Human Security', *Paper for the Global Commission on International Migration*. Online. Available HTTP: <www.gcim.org> (accessed 10 August 2008).

Lahav, G. (2004) *Immigration and Politics in the New Europe*, Cambridge: Cambridge University Press.

Lavenex, S. and Kunz, R. (2008) 'The Migration–Development Nexus in EU External Relations', *Journal of European Integration* 30(3): 439–57.

Le Cour Grandmaison, O., Lhuilier, G., and Valluy, J. (eds.) (2007) *Le Retour Des Camps? Sangatte, Lampedusa, Guantanamo . . .*, Paris: Editions Autrement.

Loescher, G. (1992) 'Refugee Movements and International Security', *Adelphi Papers, 268*, London: International Institute for Strategic Studies.

McNevin, A. (2006) 'Political Belonging in a Neo-Liberal Era: The Struggle of the *sans papiers*', *Citizenship Studies* 10(2): 135–51.

Mezzadra, S. (2011) 'The Gaze of Autonomy: Capitalism, Migration and Social Struggles', in V. Squire (ed.) *The Contested Politics of Mobility. Borderzones and Irregularity*, London, Routledge, 121–42.

Muller, B. (2005) 'Borders, Bodies and Biometrics: Towards Identity Management', in E. Zureik and M. B. Salter (eds.) *Global Surveillance and Policing: Borders, Security, Identity*, Milton: Willan Publishing, 83–96.

Nadig, A. (2002) 'Human Smuggling, National Security, and Refugee Protection', *Journal of Refugee Studies* 15(1): 1–25.

Nyers, P. (2003) 'Abject Cosmopolitanism: The Politics of Protection in the Anti-Deportation Movement', *Third World Quarterly* 24(6): 1069–93.

Nyers, P. (2006) *Re-thinking Refugees*, London: Routledge.

Nyers, P. and Moulins, C. (2007) '"We Live in the Country of UNHCR": Refugee Protests and Global Political Society', *International Political Sociology* 1(4): 356–72.

Pallister-Wilkins, P. (2015) 'The Humanitarian Politics of European Border Policing: Frontex and Border Police in Evros', *International Political Sociology* 9(1): 53–69.

Papadopoulos, D., Stephenson, N., and Tsianos, V. (2008) *Escape Routes. Control and Subversion in the 21st Century*, London, Pluto Press.

Pilkington, H. (1998) *Migration, Displacement and Identity in Post-Soviet Russia*, London: Routledge.

Rudolph, C. (2006) *National Security and Immigration*, Stanford, CA: Stanford University Press.

Salter, M. B. (2003) *Rights of Passage. The Passport in International Relations*, Boulder, CO: Lynne Rienner.

Salter, M. B. (2008) 'Imagining Numbers: Risk, Quantification and Aviation Security', *Security Dialogue* 39(2): 243–66.

Sassen, S. (1996) *Losing Control? Sovereignty in an Age of Globalization*, New York: Columbia University Press.

Scheel, S. (2013) 'Autonomy of Migration Despite its Securitisation? Facing the Terms and Conditions of Biometric Rebordering', *Millennium – Journal of International Studies* 4(3): 575–600.

Scheel, S. and Squire, V. (2014) 'Forced Migrants as Illegal Migrants', in E. Fiddian-Qasmiyeh, G. Loescher, K. Long, and N. Sigona (eds.) *The Oxford Handbook of Refugee and Forced Migration*, Oxford University Press: Oxford, 188–99.

Squire, V. (2009) *The Exclusionary Politics of Asylum*, Basingstoke: Palgrave.

Squire, V. (2014) 'Desert "Trash": Posthumanism, Border Struggles, and Humanitarian Politics', *Political Geography,* 39: 11–21.

Squire, V. (2015a) *Posthumanitarian Border Politics between Mexico and the US: People, Places, Things*, Basingstoke: Palgrave-Macmillan.

Squire, V. (2015b) 'Acts of Desertion: The Ambiguities of Abandonment and Renouncement across The Sonoran Borderzone', *Antipode* 47(2): 500–16.

Squire, V. (2016) 'The Securitization of Migration in the EU: An Absent Presence?', in G. Lazaridis and K. Wadia (eds.) *The Securitization of Migration in the EU*, Basingstoke: Macmillan, 19–36.

Sundberg, J. (2011) 'Diabolic Caminos in the Desert and Cat Fights on the Río: A Posthumanist Political Ecology of Boundary Enforcement in the United States–Mexico Borderlands', *Annals of the Association of American Geographers*, 101(2), 318–36.

Tickner, J. A. (1995) 'Re-Visioning Security', in K. Booth and S. Smith (eds.) *International Relations Theory Today*, Cambridge: Polity Press, 175–97.

Tsoukala, A. (2004) 'Les nouvelles politiques de contrôle du hooliganisme en Europe: de la fusion sécuritaire au multipositionnement de la menace', *Cultures & Conflicts* 51: 83–96.

Ullman, R. (1983) 'Redefining Security', *International Security* 8(1): 129–53.

van Munster, R. (2009) *Securitizing Immigration: The Politics of Risk in the EU*, Basingstoke: Palgrave.

Wæver, O. (1995) 'Securitisation and Desecuritisation', in R. Lipschutz (ed.) *On Security*, New York: Columbia University Press, 46–86.

Wæver, O., Buzan, B., Kelstrup, M., and Lemaitre, P. (1993) *Identity, Migration and the New Security Agenda in Europe*, London: Pinter.

Walters, W. (2002) 'Deportation, Expulsion, and the International Police of Aliens', *Citizenship Studies* 6(3): 265–92.

Watson, S. (2011). 'Back Home, Safe and Sound: The Public and Private Production of Insecurity', *International Political Sociology* 5(2): 160–77.

Weiner, M. (1995) *The Global Migration Crisis: The Challenge to States and to Human Rights*, New York: Harper Collins.

Widgren, J. (1990) 'International Migration and Regional Stability', *International Affairs* 66(4): 749–66.

16
CYBER-SECURITY

Ronald Deibert

Cyberspace refers to the environment of global digital electronic telecommunications. Broader than the 'Internet' it includes the entire spectrum of networked information and communication systems and devices. Cyberspace is pervasive today and growing relentlessly. It now permeates all aspects of society, economics, and politics to the point of being widely recognized as 'critical infrastructure' by governments, the private sector, and civil society. Network downtime, even for a few minutes, can trigger huge financial losses, and disrupt political organization or government services deemed essential. The security of cyberspace is, therefore, one of the critical questions of global politics in the twenty-first century (Deibert 2013).

Reflecting this importance, cyberspace is entering into a period of intense contests and potential chaos, as a multitude of different actors (states, civil society, businesses, militants, and organized criminal groups) compete to shape the domain in their strategic interests. Many governments are now confronting a wide range of new threats related to cyberspace, including crime, espionage, militant extremism, and warfare. Adding to the rising tumult, since June 2013 a steady stream of reports have emanated from the disclosures of former National Security Agency (NSA) contractor, Edward Snowden, about advanced cyber espionage, exploitation, and surveillance operations undertaken by the United States' NSA and its allies in the 'Five Eyes' community (United Kingdom's GCHQ, Canada's CSE, New Zealand's GCSB, and Australia's ASD). Snowden's disclosures have blown open an extraordinary covert effort to shape, control, mine, subvert, and even sabotage cyberspace at all levels, from the code to satellites and everything in between. Reactions to these revelations have been intense, causing diplomatic rifts, corporate backlash, and legal, technical, and policy changes worldwide (Schneier 2015).

The *securitization* of cyberspace – its transformation into an object of security – is perhaps the most important force shaping global communications today. *Cyber-security* is the field of practice that covers both threats *to* and *through* cyberspace (Deibert and Rohozinski 2010). Policymakers around the world are rushing to develop cyber-security strategies to deal with what they perceive as a growing range of cyber-related threats. Some are following the lead of the United States, setting up within their armed forces dedicated cyber commands and laying out formal doctrines for cyberspace foreign policy and security. Others are adopting more unconventional security strategies, such as providing tacit support for patriotic or militant groups to engage in offensive cyber-attacks. In some cases, the excuse of cyber-security is being used to implement far-reaching surveillance measures through 'anti-terror' or 'cyber-crime' laws that critics worry infringe on human rights and civil liberties. As cyber-security programmes grow, governments are building up an advanced suite of information controls, ranging from filtering and surveillance to computer network exploitation, serviced by a growing cyber-security private sector (Deibert 2013; Harris 2014).

Together, these cyber-security developments reflect a major sea change the world over in the way governments approach cyberspace. Whereas, ten years ago, states were either oblivious to the Internet or took a laissez-faire approach, today they are moving swiftly to assert their power and shape the domain in ways that suit their strategic domestic and foreign-policy interests. As this process unfolds, the character of cyberspace will invariably change.

The growing assertion of states and state power in cyberspace is happening at the same time as information and communication technologies are continuing to deeply permeate social, political, and economic life, and merge together into a single ecosystem of communications, sometimes referred to as the universe of 'Big Data' (Schneier 2015). The rise of social networking, cloud computing, mobile connectivity, and 'The Internet of Things' has produced profound social shifts. Huge and growing volumes of data now follow us around like a digital exhaust, entrusted to a multitude of private companies who monetize the bits and bytes that represent our habits, preferences, social networks, movements, and even our most intimate thoughts.

Never before in human history has so much of our lives been turned inside out and routinely shared, wittingly and unwittingly, with third parties. Naturally, such huge databases are irresistible targets for state and criminal exploitation. Massive data breaches of millions of user accounts are now common. But more broadly speaking, this epochal shift in the communications environment has fundamentally shifted the nature of public policy and security: states looking to control, secure, or otherwise shape cyberspace must now enlist companies to assist in the process, through legal measures, informal pressures, transfer of revenues for services rendered, and/or appeals to patriotism, including, at times, controlling infrastructure beyond their national borders.

There are countervailing forces, however, that may mitigate some dangerous outcomes: major stakeholders across governments, the private sector, and civil society recognize the value of developing norms of mutual restraint that protect and preserve cyberspace as a shared resource. Many are actively working on 'rules of the road' that will mitigate misunderstanding and conflict (Lewis 2013). Others are pushing to replace the existing rather haphazard infrastructure with more secure and robust protocols and standards (Schneier 2013). The Snowden disclosures have spurred on some of these activities, encouraging the development of privacy-enhancing tools, digital security training, and assertions of corporate social responsibility. At the same time, the trends towards a greater degree of nationalized controls and offensive capabilities (some of them also spurred on by Snowden's disclosures) are deep and powerful and will be difficult to reverse.

This chapter addresses these issues in three parts. In the first, the details of the securitization of cyberspace are described. It is shown how much the perception of 'what needs to be protected' differs among governments – but that there is overall convergence when it comes to approaches dealing with cyber-threats: greater state control over cyberspace. In the second part, the chapter discusses the major impetus for this development: mounting (feelings of) insecurity, which goes hand in hand with a thriving cyber-security market. The third addresses international governance attempts.

The securitization of cyberspace

The object of cyber-security

Government perceptions vary widely in terms of what they consider to be the 'objects' of cyber-security (that which is to be protected) and the scope and nature of the threats

(Deibert 2002). These variations in perceptions around cyber-security have generated significant global tensions. The United States and other liberal democracies favour open communication networks, the projection of ideas, and see cyberspace (with some exceptions) primarily as a shared resource or mixed public-private commons. China, Russia, and most authoritarian and non-democratic countries, on the other hand, place more emphasis on 'information security', which is generally equated with regime security. These governments are more comfortable asserting territorialized controls over cyberspace, and see primary threats coming both from other states and from organized anti-regime movements. They also tend to see an imbalance biased towards the US and its allies' interests in existing cyberspace governance arrangements, which has traditionally led to tension in international Internet and other governance forums.

However, such a tidy division of the world should not be stretched too far as there are numerous examples where the similarities are as striking as the differences, and many grey areas where rhetoric and practice do not align. For example, China and other authoritarian countries depend on an open Internet for economic and social reasons and must continuously walk a fine line asserting state controls without alienating their populations, scaring off private sector investment, or fuelling international instability (Lindsay 2015). China is now home to the world's largest number of Internet users, and several of the top Internet companies in software and hardware development are China-based. Likewise, as the Snowden disclosures have shown, the US and its allies in the liberal-democratic core have exerted enormous efforts to compel national-based companies to collude around information controls, and have proved capable themselves of disrupting, subverting, and blocking networks when what they see as national or corporate security considerations warrant it.

Perceptions of threats that are enabled *through* cyberspace also vary, depending on the country concerned, and include everything from anonymous hacktivists, content deemed offensive (like pornography) or illegal (such as that which violates copyright), the online activities of radical, extremist militant groups, and organized anti-regime mobilization. In spite of these different perspectives on what constitutes a threat stemming from underlying ideology or political system, however, governments are converging around a similar set of approaches to dealing with these varied threats.

It is now increasingly common for governments to take strong measures to attempt to control the services, tools, and platforms used by whatever they perceive to be threatening adversaries. These can include laws forbidding the publication of certain types of content, enforced typically through take-down notices issued to companies to remove offending content. They may involve national-level Internet and increasingly mobile content filtering systems that target a range of content to prevent citizens from accessing it. Many governments are requiring telecommunications, mobile, application, and Internet Service Provider (ISP) companies to put in place special 'back doors' to enable state law enforcement and intelligence to access user data directly. Interestingly, many politicians in authoritarian (e.g., China, Iran, Pakistan, Russia) and liberal-democratic (e.g., United Kingdom, Canada) countries alike favour banning certain types of encryption, though not without considerable backlash from civil libertarians, engineering communities, and others.

In spite of their different rhetoric and underlying political philosophies, in other words, most governments are moving in the same general direction: greater state control over cyberspace within national territorial boundaries, typically involving greater responsibilities on the private sector to assist in policing their networks. The securitization of the Internet may mean that the image of it that many still have in mind – as a highly distributed, non-territorial space – represents only a brief period in time now past (Deibert and Rohozinski 2011).

Internet filtering and beyond

The worldwide growth of Internet filtering is one of the main characteristics of cyberspace securitization (Deibert et al. 2010). Early in the Internet's history, it was widely assumed that the Internet was difficult for governments to manage and would bring about major changes to authoritarian forms of rule. Over time, however, these assumptions have been called into question as governments, often operating in coordination with national telecommunications companies and ISPs, have erected information controls not only on the Internet, but on other platforms and devices as well (e.g., mobile devices and applications).

It is fair to say that there is a growing norm worldwide for nationwide blocking of Internet content, although the rationales for implementing filtering vary from country to country, as does the content targeted for blocking. Some justify Internet filtering to control access to content that violates copyright, concerns the sexual exploitation of children, or promotes hatred and violence. Other countries filter access to content related to minority rights, religious movements, political opposition, and human rights groups. For example, in response to a controversial video considered defamatory to Islam, Pakistan has for several years blocked Internet access to the entire YouTube platform, as well as political, human rights, and security-related content. Thailand filters any content considered offensive or insulting to the royal family under broad *lèse majesté* laws. Canadian ISPs are required by law to filter access to content related to the sexual exploitation of children, and new anti-terror legislation may open up filtering to content related to radical extremism. In the United Kingdom, citizens must 'opt in' to receive unfiltered Internet connections that otherwise block access to pornography.

Countries vary widely in terms of their transparency and accountability around such processes, and in terms of the methods by which they carry out filtering. In China, Internet connections to banned content are interrupted by the 'Great Firewall of China' with packet resets which terminate the connection, making it appear to the user that something is wrong with the Internet (Crandall et al. 2007). Invariably, the private sector actors who own and operate the vast majority of cyberspace infrastructure, including Internet search engines, are being compelled or coerced to implement controls on behalf of states (see section on application controls below). Many authoritarian regimes employ Western-made technology to filter the Internet. For example, the Canadian company Netsweeper is the Internet content filtering system of choice for Pakistan, Somalia, Yemen, Afghanistan, United Arab Emirates, and others (Citizen Lab 2013).

The trajectory of greater government intervention into cyberspace has developed beyond Internet filtering. Governments have shown a greater willingness to employ a broader range of means, including covert and offensive-minded tactics, to shape cyberspace in their strategic interests. For example, there have been a growing number of incidents where states have disrupted or tampered with communication networks for political purposes, including around elections and public demonstrations (Howard et al. 2011). Both Egypt and Libya severed all Internet access for brief periods of time during the so-called Arab Spring, a tactic that has also been employed in Nepal, China, Pakistan, Nigeria, Belarus, Burma, and other countries at various times. During the so-called Green Revolution in Iran, the government was suspected of ordering Internet ISPs to tamper or 'throttle' bandwidth, and the use of certain protocols associated with censorship circumvention and anonymity tools, as a means to control opposition movements. Cambodia ordered a ban on all SMS messaging two days prior to national elections.

These 'just-in-time' methods of blocking access to services or websites are not exclusive to non-democratic regimes. During riots in the United Kingdom in 2011, some British parliamentarians discussed implementing similar controls on mobile devices and social networking platforms, and the Bay Area Rapid Transit (BART) authority in San Francisco, United States, disabled cellular networks on its transit system in 2011 to prevent its use by protesters. Such drastic moves show that some governments may be willing to sacrifice a lot to prevent the Internet from being used as a tool for mobilization.

Policing cyberspace through internet intermediaries

Regimes aiming to control popular uprisings fuelled by cyberspace technologies are turning to the private sector to identify, isolate, and contain organizers and participants. These actions, in turn, have generated fear, intense scrutiny, and often widespread condemnation and criticism of the companies compelled or encouraged to collude with the regimes (Mackinnon 2011). For example, in Egypt in 2008, one of the country's largest cellphone carriers, Vodafone, turned over information on users who employed the service to organize food protests. Later, in 2011, the company admitted that it had sent messages on behalf of state security services, encouraging Egyptians to take to the streets to counter the mass uprising in that country. Both cases caused public outrage and calls for boycotts against the company from human rights and privacy advocates.

The public pressure on companies to be more transparent about the extent to which they cooperate with governments has led some, such as Google, Microsoft, Yahoo!, Twitter, and others to produce 'transparency reports' that give statistics on government requests to take down information or turn over information about users to government agencies. One of the most remarkable of these transparency reports was released by Vodafone, which provided an extraordinary picture of the pressures that company faced from state security services worldwide.

Nowhere is the government pressure on the private sector more apparent than through the Snowden disclosures, where reams of documents reveal that US companies were legally compelled to turn over user data and install sophisticated data-mining equipment at key network chokepoints, all the while being legally compelled not to talk about it. Some companies, like Twitter, sued the US government, arguing that such National Security letters (as the gag orders are called) violate their First Amendment rights contained in the US constitution. Of course, one can only infer that other countries compel corporations based in their jurisdictions to do something similar.

Mobile devices and their many millions of applications represent a new frontier where information controls are implemented. Research by groups like the Citizen Lab at the University of Toronto has shown that many popular applications used in China, such as Tom Skype, WeChat, and Weibo, are designed with built-in content filtering and surveillance capabilities (Citizen Lab 2013b). Remarkably, the research has documented variation among filtering and surveillance practices across applications, which suggests that while the Chinese government sets broad expectations about what content should be subject to blocking or monitoring, the actual decisions about targeted content are taken by individual companies. As billions of users now connect to cyberspace from mobile devices, the downloading of filtering and surveillance practices to mobile applications represents a considerably more fine-grained and potentially powerful tool of state control.

Cyber insecurities

Cyber-crime and espionage

A major impetus behind the push to secure cyberspace is the growing problem of cyber-crime. While precise estimates are notoriously difficult to pin down given the subterranean nature of the phenomenon, most researchers agree that the scope, scale, and impact of cyber-crime are increasing. In recent years, cyber-security researchers have observed the growing *industrialization* of cyber-crime that includes chains of specialized professionals ranging from coders to attackers to money launderers, all of whom manage themselves as professional businesses, independent contractors in a highly competitive arena (Goodman 2015). Not surprisingly, there have been a series of high-profile data breaches of major businesses, defence contractors, and government agencies worldwide in recent years that appear to be continuing unabated.

Cyber-crime is growing at such an accelerated pace for several reasons. First, the number of users coming online, including individuals, businesses, organizations, and governments is growing at an exponential rate, creating a growing baseline of potential targets. Second, the ways in which we communicate and share information online have changed fundamentally over the last years, with the growth of social networking, cloud computing, and mobile forms of connectivity (Goodman 2015). We share more data with each other, entrust it to third parties outside our immediate control, and click on links and documents over social networking platforms and services with a greater degree of frequency. Cyber-crime also thrives because of the lack of deterrence. Law-enforcement agencies tend to operate in national jurisdictions, and numerous constraints exist that prevent coordination across borders. Cyber-criminals can act globally, but hide locally in jurisdictions where either such activities are tolerated or police lack resources and capabilities (Goodman 2015).

But one of the major reasons for the explosion in cyber-crime is the blurring of cyber-crime, espionage, and even warfare (Deibert 2013). It is well known among cyber-security researchers who study cyber-crime and cyber-espionage that the techniques, exploits, and overall tradecraft are largely generic to both worlds. For example, China's aggressive cyber-espionage campaigns, now well known and widely studied and reported on over many years targeting industry, government, military, and civil society targets, involve largely the same command and control infrastructure, software exploits, and social-engineering techniques as those pioneered in cyber-crime (Citizen Lab 2014). Likewise, Russia's use of information operations in armed conflicts from Estonia to Georgia have likely depended on the enrolment of Russian hackers from the worlds of organized crime, said to be among the world's most skilled (Deibert et al. 2012). Studies of the Syrian civil war have shown how Syrian intelligence agencies have used widely available cyber-crime toolkits to infiltrate Syrian opposition forces, often with lethal effect (Galperin et al. 2013).

Recent Snowden disclosures have shown that the NSA, GCHQ, and Canada's CSE all capitalize on the discovery of poorly protected China-based cyber-espionage networks for their own benefit. The disclosures also show evidence that superpower (i.e. NSA, GCHQ, CSE, as well as China and Russia) cyber espionage networks actually have an incentive to hoard strategically exploitable vulnerabilities in software (known as 'zero days' if they are not known to the larger public), furthering cyber-insecurity under the rubric of national security. Protecting the integrity of communications systems is a mission imperative, but so is building 'back doors', which is a kind of insecurity-by-design. Such programmes are designed to proactively weaken *information* security and are justified on the basis of strengthening *national* security (Deibert 2014).

The combination of enabling conditions, including a lack of law-enforcement resources, a growing number of victims, more valuable data being placed online, and major incentives among state intelligence agencies and illicit actors to exploit the wares of the cyber-criminal, means that we can expect the underworld of cyber-crime to grow and expand into areas critical to global security worldwide.

Cyber-warfare

In addition, cyberspace is emerging as a new domain of war fighting. Cyberspace is now explicitly recognized in United States strategic doctrine as equal in importance to land, air, sea, and space (US Department of Defense 2006), and a dedicated strategic command has been established in the United States military around cyberspace. Although estimates vary widely, several dozen states are actively developing military doctrines for cyberspace operations (Hughes 2010), while others may be employing unconventional cyberspace strategies. There is an arms race looming on the horizon in cyberspace that suggests a period of intense hostility operating within and through this domain. Questions of whether and how traditional concepts of strategic thought, such as deterrence, apply in the cyber domain are now very much alive in the strategic studies literature (Committee on Deterring Cyberattacks 2010).

While the rhetoric of cyber-war is often heated and exaggerated to serve policy ends (Walt 2010; Rid and Lee 2014), there are recent cases of international conflict in which cyberspace has played a prominent and important role. During the 2006 war in South Lebanon, for example, Hezbollah was able to dominate the information environment by exploiting the Internet and other technologies as part of its distributed communication infrastructure. Likewise, in Estonia (2007), the state's banking and public administration systems were brought to a standstill as millions of computers from around the world were hijacked and harnessed together as a botnet to flood the country's national backbone. During the Russia–Georgia 2008 war over the disputed territory of South Ossetia, Georgian government ministries came under a massive distributed denial-of-service attack (Deibert et al. 2012).

The definitive case of military action in cyberspace may be the so-called Stuxnet attack on Iranian nuclear enrichment facilities, organized jointly by the United States and Israeli intelligence. The highly evolved attack employed several combined zero day exploits and was the product of numerous months and many millions of dollars of research and advanced preparation. Although it brought nuclear enrichment programmes only to a limited halt, it is widely seen as the first act of sabotage undertaken in cyberspace, and crossed a Rubicon in terms of the evolution of cyber-warfare (Zetter 2014). Now the precedent has been set and is widely reported on, it is likely that other countries' armed forces will seek to catch up.

The political economy of cyber-security

One by-product of the huge growth in military and intelligence spending on cyber-security has been the fuelling of a global market for sophisticated surveillance and other security tools. Cyberspace securitization includes a political economy dimension: there is a growing cyber-industrial complex around security products and services that both responds to, but also shapes, the policy marketplace. Corporate giants of the Cold War, like Northrup Grumman, Boeing, and General Dynamics, are repositioning themselves for lucrative cyber-security defence contracts, alongside an array of subterranean niche companies that offer computer network exploitation products and services.

The global cyber-arms trade now includes malicious viruses, computer exploits, and massive botnets (Deibert 2013). States that do not have an in-house capacity on the level of the NSA and its allies can now buy advanced capabilities directly from private contractors. These capabilities are proving particularly attractive to many regimes that face on-going insurgencies and other security challenges, as well as persistent issues around popular protests and street-level demonstrations. As the advertised end-uses of these products and services include many legitimate needs, such as network traffic management or lawful intercept, it is difficult to prevent abuses and difficult even for the companies themselves to know to what ends their products and services might ultimately be directed – a situation leading many to employ the term 'dual-use' to describe them.

Research by the University of Toronto's Citizen Lab has uncovered numerous cases of human rights activists targeted by advanced digital spyware, manufactured by Western companies – spyware that once implanted on a target's device can extract files and contacts, send emails and SMS messages, turn on the microphone and camera, and track the location of the user (Marquis Boire et al. 2013). The Citizen Lab's global scan of the command and control servers of these products – the computers used to send instructions to infected devices under control – has produced disturbing evidence of a global market that knows no boundaries. Citizen Lab researchers found one product, Finspy, marketed by a UK company, Gamma Group, in a total of twenty-five countries, including countries with such dubious human rights records as Bahrain, Bangladesh, Ethiopia, Qatar, and Turkmenistan. A subsequent Citizen Lab report found that twenty-one governments are current or former users of a spyware product sold by an Italian company called Hacking Team, including nine who receive the lowest ranking, 'authoritarian', in the *Economist*'s 2012 Democracy Index.

Meanwhile, a 2014 Privacy International report on surveillance in Central Asia finds that many of the countries in the region have implemented far-reaching surveillance systems at the base of their telecommunications networks, using advanced US and Israeli equipment, and supported by Russian intelligence training. Products that provide advanced deep-packet inspection, content filtering, social-network mining, cellphone tracking, and even computer attack are being developed by Western firms, and marketed worldwide to regimes seeking to limit democratic participation, isolate and identify opposition, and infiltrate meddlesome adversaries abroad (Deibert 2013).

Governance

Cyber-arms control

Some researchers and policy-makers are now debating the merits of 'cyber-arms control.' While it is clear that there is a growing need for mutual restraints on growing hostilities and threats in cyberspace, not everyone agrees that arms control accords apply to the domain. Information – the central ingredient of warfare in cyberspace – is thought to be impossible to control in today's digitally networked and highly distributed environment. Moreover, attackers can hide their tracks and muddy attribution, making verification of any arms-control agreement difficult. However, lessons can be derived from arms-control regimes that do not restrict classes of weapons per se but rather actor behaviour in entire domains instead (e.g. the Outer Space Treaty, the Chemical Weapons Convention, the Antarctic Treaty).

There is also an informal and influential cyber-security 'epistemic community', which cuts across public and private sectors. They secure cyberspace in an ad hoc but occasionally very coordinated fashion that could be thought of as a form of cyber-security 'arms control.' For example, in April 2011, the FBI and the US Justice Department, working with the non-profit Internet Systems Consortium, dismantled the Coreflood botnet, a network of compromised computers which had been used to steal user credentials and an estimated $100 million from victims. With a court order permitting them to set up what is known as a 'sinkhole', officials replaced the botnet's command and control servers and sent code directly to compromised machines, stopping them from communicating and effectively disabling the botnet without users' permission. Government filings claimed that the commands sent would not cause any damage to compromised machines and would not provide officials with access to any user data.

However, some questioned how certain investigators would not disrupt sensitive equipment, while others questioned whether this would open the floodgates to other requests to disrupt the computers of individuals engaged in questionable activity. The Coreflood takedown, and others like it, may be seen as part of a new form of distributed cyber-security in which governments, the private sector, and civil society work to contain and mitigate unwanted behaviour in cyberspace. A critical question will be whether such mitigation is done in a transparent and accountable way or not, and avoids the risk of cyber-vigilantism.

One important facet of the control of threats to cyberspace is the impartiality of national computer emergency response teams (CERTS). Formed in the early days of the Internet, CERTs were seen as neutral and technical responses to threats to the Internet, run by engineers whose only allegiance was to the network's health, regardless of state boundaries. Over time, CERTs expanded internationally, and were federated together through a global organization, the Forum for Incident Response and Security Teams (FIRST). As cyber-security concerns have grown, however, and states' law enforcement and intelligence agencies have become more assertive about controlling cyberspace, CERTs have been affected. Their neutrality and impartiality has been gradually eroded as they are institutionalized into secretive national security structures, which in turn has impacted their ability to share information with each other transnationally. Restoring impartiality and trust to CERTs (perhaps through a model along the lines of the Red Cross, as some have proposed) faces major hurdles and powerful countervailing trends, but will be essential to the health of cyberspace on a global level (Hollis and Maurer 2015).

International governance and cyberspace security

Cyberspace is a complex domain that encompasses a variety of media (e.g. the Internet, telecommunications, cable, satellite, cellular phones). All of these media have their own sites of governance, with overlapping but still distinct groups of stakeholders, norms, principles, and rules. Cyberspace governance is thus diffuse and heterogeneous. There is no one central organization of cyberspace governance around which cyber-security issues might be coordinated, but instead a complex set of nested cyber-security regimes (Nye 2014).

Cyber-security governance has been debated at the United Nations in various forums going back at least a decade. One of the principal forums has been the UN Group of Governmental Experts on Cyber-Security, or GGE. At the time of writing four GGEs have been convened that include experts from as many as fifteen to twenty countries. While GGE reports have set markers around 'rules of the road' for cyberspace, including asserting that international law applies to state relations in cyberspace, the forum stalled in the wake of the Snowden disclosures and the diplomatic rivalries it engendered.

Outside of the United Nations, governance of cyber-security is coordinated among states in regional settings (e.g., NATO, Shanghai Cooperation Organization, ASEAN, Gulf Cooperation Council) as well as in technical and standard-setting bodies, such as ICANN, the IETF, and the International Telecommunications Union, and in major international conferences, such as the London Cyber Conference process, which started in 2011 and continues annually in different host countries. While discussions in these forums are important and can set normative terrain that influences the shape of cyber-security, they also reflect major trends in domestic practices and the preferences of the world's most powerful states.

Conclusion

The next decade will be critical for the future of cyberspace. There are several trajectories of possible development, depending on how the domain is secured and what contingencies may arise as the future unfolds. Cyberspace is entering into a period of potential chaos and instability, as cyber-crime continues its growth in an unabated fashion, an arms race in cyberspace escalates, served by a growing cyber-security industrial complex, and new, potentially lethal weapons are developed to target critical infrastructures. When these factors are considered alongside growing trends of territorialization, the future of cyberspace as an open commons of information may be in peril.

However, there are countervailing forces that might be marshalled to check and constrain some of the more dangerous possible outcomes, while protecting and even furthering the gains in freedom and individual empowerment that have been made over the last decade because of open networks. Major stakeholders across governments, the private sector, and civil society recognize the value of constituting cyberspace as a shared resource that is both open and secure, and are actively working on norms, rules, principles, and technological infrastructure to support it as such.

Moving forward, it will be critical to find ways to secure cyberspace and address all of the vexing threats that exist without undermining the benefits of open networking and liberal-democratic principles, such as access to information, freedom of speech, and privacy, and the enormous gains that have been made in advancing democracy and liberty through open networking. Here, liberal-democratic governments have a special role to play in this process, ensuring that the same principles that are promoted internationally are respected in domestic settings. When liberal-democratic countries download policing functions to the private sector without proper oversight and accountability, hoard security vulnerabilities, rather than disclose them to the public, as 'weapons' in their arsenals, allow companies based in their jurisdictions to profit from tools and services that enable widespread censorship and surveillance abroad, authoritarian and other governments find legitimacy for their own policies (Deibert 2013). A consistent, comprehensive strategy to secure cyberspace in a way that deals with mutually perceived threats while at the same time ensuring that basic human rights, such as freedom of speech, access to information, and privacy, are bedrock pillars of global cyberspace will be the major challenge for the next decade.

References

Citizen Lab (2013a) 'O Pakistan, We Stand on Guard for Thee: An Analysis of Canada-Based Netsweeper's Role in Pakistan's Censorship Regime', *Citizen Lab Research Brief No. 18*, June.

Citizen Lab (2013b) 'Asia Chats: Analyzing Information Controls and Privacy in Asian Messaging Applications', *Citizen Lab Research Brief No. 26*, November.

Citizen Lab (2014) 'Communities @ Risk: Targeted Digital Threats against Civil Society', *Citizen Lab Report No. 48*, November.

Committee on Deterring Cyberattacks (2010) *Letter Report from the Committee on Deterring Cyberattacks: Informing Strategies and Developing Options for US Policy*, Washington, DC: National Research Council.

Crandall, J. R. et al. (2007) 'ConceptDoppler: A Weather Tracker for Internet Censorship', *14th ACM Conference on Computer and Communications Security*, October 29–November 2.

Deibert, R. (2002) 'Circuits of Power: Security in the Internet Environment', in J. P. Singh and J. Rosenau (eds.) *Information Technologies and Global Politics: The Changing Scope of Power and Governance*, New York: SUNY Press: 115–42.

Deibert, R. (2013) *Black Code: Surveillance, Privacy and the Dark Side of the Internet*, Toronto: Random House.

Deibert, R. (2014) 'The Cyber-Security Syndrome', *OpenCanada.org*, 25 November. Online. Available HTTP: <http://opencanada.org/features/the-cyber-security-syndrome/> (accessed 25 November 2014).

Deibert, R. and Rohozinski, R. (2010) 'Risking Security: Policies and Paradoxes of Cyberspace Security', *International Political Sociology* 4(1): 15–32.

Deibert, R. and Rohozinski, R. (2011) 'Contesting Cyberspace and the Coming Crisis of Authority', in R. Deibert, J. G. Palfrey, R. Rohozinski and J. Zittrain (eds.) *Access Contested: Securing, Identity, and Resistance in Asian Cyberspace*, Cambridge, MA: MIT Press, 21–41.

Deibert, R., Crete-Nishihata, M., and Rohozinski, R. (2012) 'Cyclones in Cyberspace: Information Shaping and Denial in the 2008 Russia–Georgia War', *Security Dialogue* 43(2): 3–24.

Deibert, R., Palfrey, J. G., Rohozinski, R., and Zittrain, J. (eds.) (2010) *Access Controlled: The Shaping of Power, Rights, and Rule in Cyberspace*, Cambridge, MA: MIT Press, 21–41.

Galperin, E., Marquis-Boire, M., and Scott-Railton, J. (2013) 'Quantum of Surveillance: Familiar Actors and Possible False Flags in Syrian Malware Campaigns', *Citizen Lab and Electronic Frontier Foundation Research Brief No. 29*, December 23.

Goodman, M. (2015) *Future Crimes: Everything is Connected, Everyone is Vulnerable and What We Can Do about It*, New York: Random House.

Harris, S. (2014) *@War: The Rise of the Military–Internet Complex*, Boston, MA: Eamon Dolan/Houghton Mifflin Harcourt.

Hollis, D. and Maurer, T. (2015) 'A Red Cross for Cyberspace', *Time*, February 19.

Howard, P. N., Agarwal, S. D., and Hussain, M. M. (2011) 'The Dictators' Digital Dilemma: When Do States Disconnect Their Digital Networks?', *Issues in Technology Innovation* (13): 1–11.

Hughes, R. (2010) 'A Treaty for Cyberspace', *International Affairs* 86(2): 523–41.

Lewis, J. (2013) *Conflict and Negotiation in Cyberspace*, Washington: Center for Strategic and International Studies.

Lindsay, J. (2015) 'The Impact of China on Cybersecurity: Fiction and Friction', *International Security* 39(3): 7–47.

MacKinnon, R. (2011) 'Corporate Accountability in Networked Asia', in R. Deibert, J. G. Palfrey, R. Rohozinski, and J. Zittrain (eds.) *Access Contested: Securing, Identity, and Resistance in Asian Cyberspace*, Cambridge, MA: MIT Press, 195–215.

Marquis-Boire, M., Marczak, B., Guarnieri, C., and Scott-Railton, J. (2013) 'For Their Eyes Only: The Commercialization of Digital Spying', *Citizen Lab*, April 30.

Nye J. S., Jr (2014) 'The Regime Complex for Managing Cyber Activities', *Global Commission on Internet Governance Paper Series*, May.

Rid, T. and Lee, R. (2014) 'OMG Cyber!', *The RUSI Journal* 159(5): 4–12.

Schneier, B. (2013) 'The US Government Has Betrayed the Internet. We Need to Take it Back', *The Guardian*, September 5. Online. Available HTTP: < http://www.theguardian.com/commentisfree/2013/sep/05/government-betrayed-internet-nsa-spying > (accessed 29 October 2015).

Schneier, B. (2015) *Data and Goliath: The Hidden Battles to Collect Your Data and Control Your World*, New York and London: W. W. Norton.

US Department of Defense (2006) *National Military Strategy for Cyberspace Operations*, Washington, DC: US Joint Chiefs of Staff.

Walt, S. (2010) 'Is the Cyber-Threat Overblown?', *Foreign Policy*, March 30. Online. Available HTTP: <http://walt.foreignpolicy.com/posts/2010/03/30/is_the_cyber_threat_overblown> (accessed 6 October 2010).

Zetter, K. (2014) *Countdown to Zero Day: Stuxnet and the Launch of the World's First Digital Weapon*, New York: Crown Publishing.

17

WAR

Christopher Coker

War is possibly the oldest human activity, certainly the most persistent. According to one source, 14,500 wars broke out between 3500 BC and the late twentieth century, leaving only 300 years of peace (Henderson 2010). According to another, all but 5 per cent of human societies have engaged in at least occasional warfare, and most have fought constantly (Keeley 1996).

War is an extension of human ambition. For millennia it has offered the greatest scope for political and social change. It is perfectly possible to argue that cooperation, not conflict, has been even more important in history, but it is also important to recognize that war and peace are not different coins: they are two sides of the same coin. War Studies and Peace Studies are usually taught separately and appeal to different people, but that is a mistake. After all, as Aristotle tells us in the *Politics*, the only purpose of war is peace.

War's future, however, invites very different opinions. Some writers stick with the old verities (Gray 2005; Keegan 1993). For them war has not changed and is unlikely to any time soon. Other writers think it is changing fast – that what we are seeing across the developing world are 'new wars' (Kaldor 1992; van Creveld 1996). And still others claim that it may be coming to an end; it is degenerating fast, mutating into a criminal activity, unstructured by the old rules, and unanchored to any ethical principles or rules – the so-called laws of war (Horgan 2012; Mueller 2011). My own conclusion is that war is an *evolutionary phenomenon* whose origins can be traced back to the very beginning of humanity, and which, like all evolved systems, descends through modification; and that we will not live at peace with each other permanently until it has exhausted its evolutionary possibilities.

Whenever looking at the future of any human behavioural pattern, the ethnologist Nikolaas Tinbergen suggests that we should ask four questions (Pepperberg 2013: 383):

1. What is its origin? How did it first arise?
2. What is the mechanism? How does it work?
3. What is the ontogeny? How do we observe it develop over time?
4. What is its function? What are all the possible reasons it is done?

I will discuss war with respect to all four questions in four parts. In the first section, I contrast literature that situates the origins of war in evolutionary biology with literature that argues for cultural (and social) determinants, showing that socialization in early hunter-gatherer societies marked the beginning of warfare and violent 'othering'. In the second section, I introduce war as 'an evolved cultural performance' (Allen 2004: 69–70), with tremendous influence on human behaviour through the ages. In the third, I look at the evolution of weaponry and technology and show different ways of warfare (or cultural change). In the fourth section, I discuss the idea that war has been good for progress and that it will continue to evolve rather than become obsolete.

The origins of war

How did war first arise? Are we the only species that does war? What about ants, which seem to be in conflict with each other most of the time? Genuine coalitional aggression, writes Doyne Dawson, emerged in the line of primates that ended in us, and before that among the ants. This is noteworthy, because cooperative behaviour is normally restricted to kinship groups. Ants are the only social animal to have broken that barrier by creating closely related kin groups of enormous size (a tropical ant hill may number 20 million ants (Dawson 2001: 25)). Robert O'Connell writes that virtually all the prerequisites for war are present in ant society: armies, 'politics' and lasting societal results; but the practitioners are automata just a few millimetres long. Individually, they are genetically predestined for a martial existence, since they share three-quarters of their genes with their sisters. As such they sacrifice for the group because it is the best chance to perpetuate their own genes. Death in battle, he adds, is trivial if compared with the success of an army made up of near-replicates (O'Connell 1996: 346).

But there's the rub. Echoing the opening lines of Virgil's epic poem the *Aeneid*, the Harvard sociobiologist Edward Wilson writes 'I sing of ants and the man' in his novel about the world's two dominant species: humans and ants (Wilson 2011: 1). However, ants do not really lend themselves to epic poetry – the collective impulse to kill kills the heroic. And the fact that we have poetry makes all the difference. Wilson, though, argues that evolutionary selection and gene expression set limits on the influence that culture has on human behaviour, summed up in a famous claim that 'cognition is translated into circuitry' (Wilson 1975). It was the biologist Stephen J. Gould who challenged that argument:

> Genes make enzymes and enzymes control the rates of chemical processes. Genes do not make 'novelty seeking' or any other complex and overt behaviour. Predisposition via a long chain of complex chemical reactions, mediated through a more complex series of life circumstances, does not equal identification or even causation.
>
> *(Gould 2001: 282)*

Culture, therefore, appears to be the key. We have it – ants do not. Primatologists, however, argue that chimpanzees have it too, if in a rudimentary form; they also argue that they war against each other. *Chimpanzee Politics* is the title of a famous book by the primatologist Frans De Waal (De Waal 1982). We share all but 1.5 per cent of our genetic makeup with them. That 1.5 per cent is all-important, however: over 600,000 different nucleotides allow plenty of room for important variations. If we consider the whole DNA, there may 32 million substitutions, or differences, between ourselves and our near-cousins. And even that does not capture the real difference: for the gene alone is not important. What *is* important is the rest of the genome, the rest of the cell, and above all its interaction with the larger world (Allen 2004: 209).

This also applies to the important question of tool use. We have observed (at least since 1840) chimpanzees using basic tools: hollowing out wood to access termites, or using a rock to crack shells. However, as Adriaan Kortlandt warns, we must not chimpomorphize *Homo sapiens* and its ancestors. To do so would be a case of vulgar paleo-anthropomorphism. Kortlandt agrees that chimps can imitate human behaviour. He believes that the chimps of Bossu in Eastern Guinea acquired their nut-cracking abilities from watching humans, since the use of rocks is an innovation known to be partly contextual, and suitable rocks were non-existent until exposed by agriculture (Kortlandt 1986: 126). But the real point is that the use of tools invokes more than the ability to crack open a shell for us: every tool we use involves new cognitive skills that are passed on over the generations – ever faster thanks to language, then writing, and now digital media.

There are seven species of Great Ape on the planet; six of them live in nature. One cannot live without artifice. Despite innate biological deficits, we have evolved by developing tools, and later technology. Both allowed the weakest ape of all eventually to come out on top (Taylor 2010). The first spears have been found at a *Homo erectus* site in Southern Germany. War, then, probably predates *Homo sapiens*. For what makes us different from the other apes is that projectile weapons allowed smaller, less muscular or powerful males not only to kill other animals but each other, including the Alpha male. As Hobbes famously wrote in *Leviathan* the strong man has no defence against a weaker man, armed and dangerous.

With the invention of weapons came gracilization – skeletal structures became less robust. As the selective advantage of size diminished over time, so did aggression – social intelligence became more important, and with the growth of social intelligence came a significant growth in socialization. The earliest evidence we have of warfare coincides with rising cooperation among our ancestors. In-group cohesion became more valued, not only for the security it offered, but for the identity it permitted as shared symbols of belief came into being. War became a way of life for our hunter-gatherer ancestors. Most likely, it was they who began the tradition of identifying the out-group as distinctly 'other', or in effect non-human (Wilson 2004: 113).

Not agreeing with this thesis, some anthropologists and historians argue that war as collective violence is not to be found before the Mesolithic period, and then as a result of complex social organizations, higher population density, and competition for resources (Wuketis 2007). The key here is social substitutability – massing people in armies involves a greater displacement of vengeance than does a blood feud (or headhunting); it involves non-family members many times removed from the members held accountable for a particular outrage. The emergence of social substitutability creates what Rousseau called 'accidental soldiers' – enemies that are not held personally responsible for aggression, and can be taken prisoner and repatriated after a conflict is over. It allows for more lethal violence because it is organized by a group, but also for more selective targeting (Kelly 2000: 71).

The mechanism of war

How does war work? Or, a closely related question, what societal purpose does it serve? War may appear highly maladaptive until one goes back to some of its functions. For a start, it enhances group survival: by promoting collective behaviour it allows groups to compete and gain an advantage over others. Thereby, it promotes communal bonding, reinforces social solidarity, and involves a large repertoire of social practices that put people in touch with the larger communities, including the ancestors.

War also channels human aggression into collective purposes (Gat 2007). What bond us to each other are social practices and customs: ceremonies and rituals and etiquettes, including what the historian Geoffrey Parker calls 'etiquettes of atrocity' (the norms of war); all of these are performative (Parker 2002). Life itself is essentially a performance – and war, too is an evolved cultural performance (Allen 2004: 69–70). Furthermore, there is memory. Some wars are 'remembered' because of what they say about the techniques (the brilliance of design) or the cleverness of a strategy, or even the guile of a stratagem. Herodotus invented history so that the names of the actors in the wars between the Greeks and Persians would never be forgotten. These memories become part of a cultural architecture with archetypal figures (e.g. Hannibal and his elephants, Alexander on the Indus). These are what some scientists call 'memes', an element of culture that can be passed on by non-genetic means. They can be said to resemble genes in that they produce cultural change in a process similar to natural selection; those passed on by imitation and learning dominate social life (Dawkins 1976: 192).

Finally, war has become increasingly complex over time. It encourages specialization; domestication of talents; and it increases cerebration while it decreases emphasis on physical stamina – all drivers for cultural evolution. It also became open to philosophical and political analysis in ancient China and Greece, moving to the centre stage of human learning. Philosophers like Aristotle began to tease out the general principles: the difference between offence/defence; war and peace; nature and character of war (Coker 2010; Gelven 1994). War, the pre-Socratic philosopher Heraclitus tells us, is 'the father of everything': it changes society, and society changes the conduct of war: think of the Greek hoplite and the city-state; the Swiss pike men and the republic; standing armies and absolute monarchies; conscription and the nation-state. And we can add to the list today's market-states and private security companies (Bobbitt 2007).

Indeed, 'force and the threat of force' writes Colin Gray, 'had a greater impact upon the many contexts for human behaviour than has any other source of influence' (2007: 265). The complexity of war really inheres in the main role of cultural evolution: the awakening of human faculties (Midgley 1995: 145). We are born with an innate predisposition for language, realized over time. We strive to make more of ourselves. As the philosopher Mary Midgley writes, we are more persistent, cooperative, pugnacious, and acquisitive; not just more intelligent. We are more curious about the world and ourselves, and our place in it. This tendency to use every faculty is what led us to outdistance our nearest cousins, the chimpanzees. We are at the top of the food chain not because we are survival specialists but because for us survival is not enough. What we aim for in cultural evolution is not survival, but ever-higher levels of complex social existence which often put our survival at risk. The moral of the story, if evolution has a moral, is that survivors are those that remain at the bottom of the great chain of being, like amoebae or, for that matter, ants, who have all been around much longer than we have and will almost certainly survive us.

The ontogeny of war

Technological evolutions

How did war develop over time? War throws up new technological possibilities that we explore, but do not always exploit. Most recently, we have used science, before that technology, and even before that, tools (Stephenson 2013). War is driven by an internal logic that drives from the simple to the complex, from the general to the specific, from the instinctual to the intellectual. We were able to develop skills in the use of weapons that demanded knowledge: to use a longbow took years of training; to use a sword for a samurai was the work of a lifetime. Anyone can use a gun (it requires minimal training). Anyone can, in theory, be a drone pilot, or at least those who have the requisite motor skills. Technology allowed us to go one stage beyond the tools: to outsource our intelligence and share it with others. Even a fighter pilot does not need to know how his plane actually works. He relies on the engineers. Science has been the dominant force in war since 1700, but 'we exploit science to make war because we are warlike creatures. If science did not exist, we would still be killing one another' (Smith 2007: 29).

Weapons have consistently augmented physical strength and thus extended the scope of our ambition. Physical enhancement begins with social learning. If you are a hunter-gatherer you can observe two people making hand axes by 'chipping' or 'flaking' them out of large pieces of stone. And, if you are clever enough, you can improve upon the design. When you notice that a club can be combined with a hand axe, you are on the way to making the first hafted axe. When someone tied a vine to the ends of a bent stick, the first bow came into existence, and the first arrow soon followed (Pagel 2012: 47). Furthermore, there are striking examples of cultural convergence in history: the first arrow was invented around 8,000 BC in Europe. But it emerged everywhere else as well, even in the Americas, which had been cut off from the Old World 3,000 years earlier, showing how archery is one of those inventions that, given time, will emerge spontaneously in every culture.

The first bows appeared in the Neolithic era, and provided a revolutionary increase in the range and volume of firepower. They more than doubled the range of the spear, and since arrows were lighter and easier to carry, they increased the volume of firepower. Then came the sling: slingers would put a rock or lead ball in a leather pouch attached on two sides by a long strand of rope. They would swing it around in increasingly wider and faster circles and then release one end of the rope. Leap thousands of years to the Bronze Age, writes Malcolm Gladwell, and the heavily armed Goliath had as much chance as any Bronze Age warrior with a sword would have had against an opponent armed with a .45 automatic pistol (Gladwell 2013: 12).

Fast forward a thousand years or more to another lethal weapon: the longbow, which gave the English a decisive 'edge' over their rivals for almost three hundred years. It was less sophisticated than the crossbow but more lethal; but its use was also far more physically demanding than the gun. However, it represented an evolutionary dead-end. The longbow was replaced by guns once they had greater velocity and penetrative power; more important still, their use did not require training or practice from childhood (Black 2014: 82–3). The gunpowder age did not arrive overnight, however, and its impact must not be exaggerated. A Roman legion was as effective as a European Army in 1500 despite the fact that the Romans did not have firepower. However, by 1800, the smooth-bore muzzle-loaded musket, explosive shells, and, later, machine guns would have given a European army a decisive advantage. Today, adds Ian Morris, a single jet bomber has half a million times the killing capacity of a Roman legion (2014: 334).

The example of artillery offers perhaps the most vivid illustration of how increases in human reach are part and parcel of increases in the speed of information processing. The invention of artillery is usually dated to the siege of Motya in Sicily in 399 BC. During the assault, Syracusian engineers developed non-torsion crossbows that could hurl iron bolts and spears. Half a century later, Macedonia was the first to employ true torsion catapults which had a propulsion power that allowed bolts and stones to be shot with accuracy at 300 yards (Hanson 2013: 237). With the invention of gunpowder, ballistics became more mature. The process was slow, but that is not the point: there was a steady progression from platform-centric to system-centric warfare, to the effect-centric model of today.

In the eighteenth and nineteenth centuries, artillery involved direct-fire weapons which were not easily moved and had to be sited prior to the battle. On the battlefields of the First World War, indirect fire started to play an important role. Gunners now acquired their targets by using forward observers who relayed targeting information back to the battle lines. Come the Second World War, and artillery evolved again: it was now more mobile and thus more rapid and effective. The introduction of portable radios enabled continuous fire support for the first time. The Cold War years saw even more impressive advances – the introduction of artillery systems that could offer operational and even strategic effects. The US Army was one of the first to adapt guided missiles, both targeted and free-flight, with impressive ranges, while the introduction of computers allowed for a degree of precision guidance that would have been unthinkable before the 1970s. Digital command, control, and communication systems allowed militaries to reduce collateral damage.

GPS use ushered in a third age of artillery, which became effect-centric, described by one author as 'the biggest revolution since the invention of the cannon' (Osborne 2007: 17). It involves the 'intelligent' use of firepower. Intelligence here is not defined as common sense or intellectual ability: it is what evolutionary theorists understand by the term – the processing of information. Instead of talking of the 'survival of the fittest' these days we refer to the survival of the best informed. As a species, we survived and thrived thanks to our superior situational awareness. Information translates into effective decision-making (the flight or fight dynamic) and translates into a competitive advantage over time.

Ways of warfare

The ontogeny of war, however, is illustrated not only by technological progress, but also by cultural change – the emergence of 'ways of warfare'. In the *Anti-Dühring*, Engels develops some of the themes that both he and Marx had set out in the *German Ideology*. The book is important because it posits that we produce ourselves through labour. We have neither a fixed nor an unchallenged nature that is biological (today we would say genetic) or spiritual. There is instead a dialectically conceived relation between our nature as determined by our conditions of life and the practical transformation of those conditions (Marx 1996: 21).

Engels claimed that material factors in war are important: all theories, forms of consciousness, religions, and morals arise from the mode of production. He highlights Clausewitz's claim (a writer whom he much admired): every era fights wars in its own fashion. Clausewitz famously sketches the history of war from classical times to the present, involving the nomads (Tartars); the city-states of the ancient world; the feudal kingdoms of medieval Europe; the eighteenth-century European states that were usually in a perpetual state of war with each other, and the embryonic nation-states of his own day. It follows that for Engels as for Clausewitz everything must be studied within its own cultural context (Clausewitz 1976; Engels 2001).

Take one of the great mysteries of war: numbers. Numbers do make a difference: military historians are often impressed by how small numbers of men can often prevail against larger numbers; an army that is severely outnumbered can sometimes emerge as the victor. In such cases, winning involves turning quantity into quality. The Mongols overcame considerably higher than a two to one inferiority in numbers as they conquered a large part of the known world. The key to their success was the application of a Napoleonic formula, centuries before it was formulated. The strength of an army, like the quantity of motion in mechanics, is estimated by the mass multiplied by the velocity, and the Mongols achieved this by moving at twice the speed of their opponents (Chambers 1979: 65). They not only conducted war differently; they thought about it differently, in terms of the economy of force, the unity of command, and the capacity to concentrate. All these features, which appeared in nineteenth-century manuals on war, were known to the Mongols seven hundred years earlier.

Of course, Engels' claim begs almost as many questions as there are answers. Is there a 'way of warfare' distinctive to a culture, as some historians argue? Is there still a distinctly Western one, or is there now merely an 'American' one, and what, if anything, is distinctive about it? A 'way of war' is a set of attitudes towards war which is culturally conditioned, or framed. Attitudes, we are told by philosophers, are structured arrangements of feelings; they involve thought and they generate rules. Every organization, business, and even university cultivates attitudes in those who work for it or those it trains (Hanson 2003).

It is fairly telling that the West has been supreme in war for the past two centuries, and was supreme for a time long before that when Greek armies were led by Alexander the Great and the Roman legions by a succession of highly professional commanders. Victor Davis Hanson writes that the Greeks introduced three concepts into war that, in Engels' terms, enabled them to translate quantity into quality. One is the decisive battle which is distinguished by the overwhelming use of force at a critical moment. In the third Philippic, Demosthenes bemoaned the fact that of all the arts the Greeks had taken the art of war in a new direction – decisiveness. And decisiveness required shock battle (Hanson 2002: 93) such as the Greek phalanx meeting the Persians in hand-to-hand combat, the German blitzkrieg of the Second World War, and, more recently, America's striking 'shock and awe' campaign in Iraq.

Second, Hanson claims, the West has managed to field armies with a high degree of primary group cohesion. Here too, we may be able to trace a linear progression from the republican armies of Rome which could often field citizens for seventeen years at a time (the longest rate of mobilization of any society in history) to the US army, whose primary group cohesion gives it a cutting edge: the degree of attachment soldiers have to their comrades, their unit, and their country (Wong 2002: 21).

Third, there is the use of technology as a force multiplier, especially since 1870, when Western technological superiority first became pronounced. The essence of technology, Heidegger tells us, is not technological. The essence is how we see it and use it, and the purposes it serves. Both are conditioned by cultural factors. For Hanson 'scientific method, unfettered research, and capitalist production' which, he claims, all first developed in the West, explains why Western societies have enjoyed such a decisive technological lead (2002: 360).

However, Hanson's thesis has drawn fire from many critics. Some argue that it is an exercise in orientalism; it stereotypes and even demeans other cultural achievements (Bracken 1999; Porter 2009). Others contend that the Chinese were the first to equip a 'modern' army funded by a sophisticated tax base, the first to employ gunpowder in battle (Lorge 2008). It was South East Asia that lagged behind: Vietnam had been subdued by Ming artillery long before the Europeans arrived on the scene. Other writers insist that in our preoccupation with the Western way of war we have simply forgotten others. To be sure, Cortes overcame the Aztecs, but they did not go under without a fight, and historians are now inclined to attribute the Spanish success not to the fact that they found themselves fighting a Bronze Age culture so much as to their own willingness to adapt – instead of fighting by their own rules (as they would have done back home) they took part in a Meso-American style of war, giving their own allies who did most of the fighting a decisive advantage in the form of guns, horses, and dogs, which the Indians did not have (Watson 2011).

The point I am making is this: there seems to be a profound and complex need for war in all human societies and at all times. It is because the need is real that war has a nature; it is because it is complex that it reflects the culture engaged in it. Which is only to say that what is universal as a need is experienced differently: every war has its own cultural grammar which expresses the needs and emotions of the two (or more) sides staking part. Those from the same culture will play by the same rules (or try to change them usually only under duress, and often too late). When war pits two different cultures against each other, there will be clash of styles – the ultimate 'culture shock'.

The functions of war

Finally, what is war good for? War is not in our genes and evolutionary history is certainly not destiny. Therefore, war survives only because (and as long as) it serves a purpose. A number of writers have waded into answering the question of what war is good for, including Ian Morris. On the basis of considerable analysis, Morris claims that it has made the world safer. It has been good in the productive latitudes (the agricultural heartlands that extend from Asia to the New World). By the end of the first century AD, the Roman world's social development, thanks to 400 years of constant warfare, was roughly at a level that would not be reached again in Western Europe until the early eighteenth century. And thanks to war, the Han Dynasty which ruled China until the third century AD reached a position which Europe would not attain until the late sixteenth century.

War has been good for progress because it has pacified the violent – the unruly, the barbarians, the savages – or whatever civilization prefers to name them. Usually it tamed them permanently by bringing them within an imperial system; empire is by far the oldest and most successful political unit we have devised. What Morris is arguing is that war has contributed enormously to our 'future fitness'. Morris' book is not making out an evolutionary case (such as group selection) which has its exponents (Coker 2014; Sober and Wilson 2009; Turchin 2011) but it does have an evolutionary theme. He insists that the world will soon move out of the shadow of the Pax Americana into the sunlight of a Pax Technologica (Morris 2014). In the new era, war will no longer serve a useful purpose.

However, nothing in his book actually suggests that war has yet exhausted its evolutionary possibilities: no one can, surely, 'declare peace' until it has finally broken out. More recently, writers like John Mueller who forecast the end of war suggest that it serves no economic end; it no longer pays dividends on belief (Mueller 2011; Tetrais 2011). The problem with arguments that war has become anachronistic, anomalous, or surplus to requirements is that they tend to be teleological. War is the way by which we discover what we share in common; even Herbert Spencer, the father of Social Darwinism, believed that war had given us a competitive advantage, before finally being overcome by peace interest (Wright 2001: 64).

War seems to be evolving fast. Evolution, we must remember, is blind, and it is driven by its own needs, not our own. Take cyber-warfare. Not everyone is agreed that a cyber-war is possible (Rid 2013). But other writers suggest that cyber-power – the ability to control and manipulate the cyber-domain, which is increasingly merging with the physical, is not only a force multiplier but a new form of power and influence (Hoffman 2013). The fifteen countries with the largest defence budgets are already figuring out how to integrate cyber-military capabilities into military operations. We now confront all manner of cyber-prefixed threats from 'cyber-espionage' to 'cyber-terror' and even 'cybergeddon', and these in turn have engendered other cyber-prefixed neologisms such as 'cyber-security', 'cyber-power', and 'cyber-strategy'.

Furthermore, there is space, which promises some highly dangerous possibilities, mostly in terms of anti-satellite warfare. Space is what strategists call the ultimate high ground (Dolman 2002/12; Gray 2005). In 2011 the US Defense Department published the first document establishing the use of space weapons with the goal of 'charting the path for the next decade to respond to the current and projected space strategic environment' (DoD 2011). Also, there is nano-tech to come – where military applications are endless from smaller computers, smaller sensors, micro-robots for reconnaissance using propulsion principles known from larger technical systems, propellers, and wings or biometric ones (hopping and wriggling) (Altman 2004).

Conclusion

So, what is war still good for? The civilizing process; asocial sociability; empire-building: all or none of the above? All we know is that what it is really good for is tribalism – it is the heart of group selection, and the imperative still holds. We have waged it for millennia, because it is what we do, and we do it very well. Less bloodily since we left our hunter-gatherer condition ('the common denominator' of the human condition in the words of Claude Levi-Strauss) but more lethally (with the inventions of weapons of mass destruction – a term first coined in the Spanish Civil War). It is precisely because we are so inventive that we have not yet come near to exhausting war's evolutionary possibilities. And it is because we remain aggressive that the world is so divided religiously and socially, and because we are so fearful of the future that we may still find plenty of reasons to go to war again. Steven Pinker is no doubt right: we are less violent than we once were (Pinker 2013). But human beings, as historians since Thucydides have told us, have a tendency to revert back when times get tough, and times could well get tougher.

References

Allen, B. (2004) *Knowledge and Civilisation*, Boulder, CO: Westview.
Altman, J. (2004) 'Military Uses of Nanotech: Perspectives and Concerns', *Security Dialogue* 35(6): 61–79.
Aristotle, (2005[4th century BC]) *The Politics*, New York: Rowman & Littlefield.
Black, J. (2013) *War and Technology*, Bloomington: Indiana University Press.
Bobbitt, P. (2009) *Terror and Consent: The Wars of the Twenty-First Century*, London: Allen Lane.
Bracken, P. (1999) *Fire in the East: The Rise of Asian Military Power*, London: Harper Collins.
Chambers, J. (1979) *The Devil's Horseman: The Mongol Invasion of Europe*, London: Phoenix.
von Clausewitz, C. (1976) *On War*, ed. and trans. by Peter Paret and Michael Howard, London: J. M. Dent.
Coker, C. (2010) *Barbarous Philosophers: Reflections on the Nature of War from Heraclitus to Heisenberg*, London: Hurst.
Coker, C. (2014) *Can War Be Eliminated?*, Cambridge: Polity Press.
Dawkins, R. (1976) *The Selfish Gene*, Oxford: Oxford University Press.
Dawson, D. (2001) *The First Armies*, London: Cassell.
De Waal, F. (1982) *Chimpanzee Politics*, New York: Harper Collins.
Dolman, E. (2002) *Astropolitik: Classical Geopolitics in the Space Age*, London: Frank Cass.
Dolman, E. (2012) *Pure Strategy: Power and Policy in the Space and Information Age*, London: Frank Cass.
Engels, F. (2001) *Anti-Duhring*. Online. Available HTTP: <https://www.marxists.org/archive/marx/works/download/Engels_Anti_Duhring.pdf> (accessed 29 October 2015).
Gat, A. (2007) *War in Human Civilization*, Oxford: Oxford University Press.
Gelven, M (1994) *War and Existence: A Philosophical Inquiry*, University Park: Pennsylvania State University.
Gladwell, M. (2013) *David and Goliath: Underdogs, Misfits and the Art of Battling Giants*, London: Allen Lane.
Gould, J. (2001) *The Lying Stones of Marrakech*, London: Vintage.
Gray, C. (2005) *Another Bloody Century: Future Warfare*, London: Weidenfeld and Nicolson.
Hanson, V. D. (2002) *Culture and Carnage: Landmark Battles in the Rise of Western Power*, New York: Anchor.
Hanson, V. D. (2003) *Ripples of Battle*, Doubleday: New York.
Hanson, V. D. (2013) *Culture and Carnage*, New York: Knopf Doubleday.
Henderson, C. (2010) *Understanding International Law*, London: John Wiley.
Hoffman, F. (2013) 'You May Not Be Interested in Cyberwar but It Is Interested in You', *War on the Rocks*, 7 August. Online. Available HTTP: <http://warontherocks.com/2013/08/you-may-not-be-interested-in-cyber-war-but-its-interested-in-you/> (accessed 29 October 2015).
Horgan, J. (2012) *The End of War*, San Francisco: McSweeney Books.
Kaldor, M. (1992) *New Wars*, Cambridge: Polity Press.
Keegan, J. (1991) *A History of Warfare*, London: Hutchinson.
Keeley, L. H. (1996) *War before Civilization*, Oxford: Oxford University Press
Kelly, R. (2000) *Warrior Societies and the Origins of War*, Ann Arbor: University of Michigan Press.
Kortlandt, A. (1986) 'The Use of Stone Tools by Wild-Living Chimpanzees and Earliest Hominids', *Journal of Human Evolution* 15(2): 77–132.
Lorge, P. (2008) *The Asian Military Revolution*, Cambridge: Cambridge University Press.
Marx, K. (1996) *The German Ideology*, London: Lawrence and Wishart.
Midgley, M. (1995) *Beast and Man: the Roots of Human Nature*, London: Routledge.
Morris, I. (2014) *War – What Is It Good For?*, London: Profile.
Mueller, J. (2011) *War and Ideas: Essays*, London: Routledge.

O'Connell, R. (1996) 'Origins of War,' in R. Cowley and G. Parker (eds.) *The Osprey Companion to Military History*, New York: Houghton Mifflin.

Osbourne, K. (2007) 'Demand Source for Precision Artillery', *Defence News*, 13 August.

Pagel, M. (2012) *Wired for Culture: The Natural History of Human Cooperation*, London: Allen Lane.

Parker, G. (2002) *Empire, War and Faith in Early Modern Europe*, London: Penguin.

Pepperberg, I. (2013) 'Tinbergen's Questions', in J. Brockman (ed.) *This Explains Everything*, New York: Harper.

Pinker, S. (2012) *The Better Angels of Our Nature*, London: Allen Lane.

Porter, P. (2009) *Military Orientalism*, London: Hurst.

Rid, T. (2012) *Cyberwar Will Not Take Place*, London: Hurst.

Smith, D. (2007) *The Most Dangerous Animal*, New York: St. Martin's Press.

Sober, E. and Wilson, D. S. (2009) *Unto Others: The Evolution and Psychology of Unselfish Behaviour*, Cambridge, MA: Harvard University Press.

Stepheson, M. (2013) *The Last Full Measure: How Soldiers Die in Battle*, London: Duckworth.

Taylor, T. (2010) *The Artificial Ape: How Technology Changed the Course of Human Evolution*, New York: St. Martin's Press.

Tetrais, B. (2011) 'The Demise of Ares? The End of War as We Know It', *Washington Quarterly* 35(3): 7–22.

Turchin, P. (2007) *War, Peace and War: The Rise and Fall of Empires*, London: Penguin.

US Department of Defense (Office of the Director of National Intelligence) (2011), *National Security Space Strategy*, Washington, DC.

Van Creveld, M. (2009) *The Transformation of War*, New York: Simon and Schuster.

Watson, P. (2011) *The Great Divide: History and Human Nature in the Old World and the New*, London: Weidenfeld and Nicolson.

Wilson, E. O. (1975) *Socio-Biology: The New Synthesis*, Cambridge, MA: Harvard University Press.

Wilson, E. O. (2004) *On Human Nature*, Cambridge, MA: Harvard University Press.

Wilson, E. O. (2011) *Anthill: A Novel*, New York: W. W. Norton.

Wong, L. (2002) *Why They Fight: Combat Motivation in the Iraq War*, Carlisle, PA: US Army War College, Strategic Studies Institute.

Wright, R. (2001) *Non-Zero: The Logic of Human Destiny*, London: Vintage.

Wuketis, F. (ed.) (2007) *Handbook of Evolution: The Evolution of Human Societies and Cultures*, London: Wiley.

18

ETHNIC AND RELIGIOUS VIOLENCE

Delphine Alles

The current period seems to be characterized by a growing number of ethnic and/or religious tensions, in parallel with the mobilization of collective identity narratives during violent conflicts – whether these narratives legitimate, motivate, or denounce the resort to violence. Most domestic conflicts do have an ethnic or religious dimension which tends to become increasingly salient as the conflict persists, notwithstanding the variety of root-causes that may be involved in these processes. Yet, the terms of the interrelationship between ethnicity and religion on the one hand, and ethnicity, religion, and violence on the other, are far from settled.

The lack of consensus on this interrelationship largely results from the burgeoning yet relatively recent scholarly interest for this subject, due to a combination of academic and contextual factors. Social sciences have long been dominated by the modernization-as-secularization thesis, which considered religion as an irrelevant factor in modern politics. More broadly, identity-based mobilizations were perceived as the remnants of a world that was bound to disappear. Violence supported by ethnic and religious narratives was hence seen as a distinctive feature of archaic societies living in failed states, in contrast with a 'modern' world of stable nation-states – at the risk of failing to make sense of significant exceptions such as the violence between Catholics and Protestants in Northern Ireland.

In the post-Cold War context, the increasing salience of 'new wars', characterized by (among other features) the violent contestation of state legitimacy and political control by non-state actors wielding identity labels (Kaldor 2007[1999]), and the parallel globalization of informal violence justified on religious grounds (Keohane 2002), exemplified by the 9/11 attacks, has called for new frameworks of analysis. Ethnicity and religion may be invoked in the context of structural or indirect violence as much as in direct physical or personal violence. The notion of 'cultural violence', which encompasses elements deriving from ethnicity and religion as it refers to 'any aspect of a culture that can be used to legitimize violence in its direct or structural form' (Galtung 1990: 291), is appealing, for it unites the different expressions of violence under a single concept. Yet, the very comprehensiveness of the notion tends to impede its analytic and normative clarity. The scope of this chapter is hence reduced to physical violence, although it acknowledges that structural violence shapes the broader contexts within which acts of violence are perpetrated (Galtung 1969).

This chapter first clarifies the notions of ethnic and religious violence and the debates surrounding the agency of identity labels in conflict settings. It then analyses the contextual and systemic factors most frequently invoked to explain the occurrence of such violence. The subsequent developments explore the consequences of the mobilization of ethnic or religious narratives on patterns of violence, and the specific difficulties they introduce for conflict resolution and peacebuilding strategies.

The changing boundaries of ethnic and religious narratives

Definition issues could be sidestepped by arguing that episodes of violence involving actors who explicitly found their behaviour on ethnic or religious narratives can be characterized as such. Completing this approach, Jonathan Fox has developed a useful taxonomy, relying on combinable criteria which determine whether a conflict can be considered religious (a reasoning that could be expanded to ethnic dimensions): the fact that actors are motivated by religious beliefs and ideologies; the involvement of religious institutions (to mobilize violence, or to support conflict resolution); whether the use of religious language or symbols has an influence on the conflict's outcome; and the role played by religious identity (Fox 2002). Yet, while ethnic and religious narratives both refer to individual and group identities, it is essential to distinguish their respective characteristics, which rest on two specific conceptions of group membership and otherness. A reflection on the place of these narratives as a dependent or independent variable is also necessary, as this option directly orientates the analysis of their relationship with violence, hence shaping different conflict resolution strategies.

Two overlapping yet distinct concepts

At the analytical level, ethnic and religious violence tend to be reified in the context of violent confrontations involving people belonging to different groups. They are also often seen as overlapping concepts, because they are mutually reinforcing as collective identity markers (Marty and Appleby 1997) and often mobilized in situations of inter-communal violence. It is hence common to talk about ethno-religious violence without necessarily distinguishing the political and strategic implications of these two notions, which are characterized by contingent contours and contested definitions.

While religion is one of the traits that may define ethnicity, not all ethnic identities have a religious component, and most religions do not have an ethnic dimension – the Jewish or Armenian cases, where nation and religion nearly coincide, constitute exceptions. Ethnicity refers to a category that singles out a group of individuals under a specific name (for instance Tutsi, Javanese, or Croat). Ethnic boundaries may be constructed by the group itself or ascribed to its members from the outside, by other groups or by administrative norms, based on varying criteria which include a common history, kinship, social practices, a common language, and a reference to a territory presented as their homeland (Smith 2001). The weight of this combination of factors on actors' self-perceptions and behaviours towards 'Others' may vary among individuals and groups, but ethnicity tends to be reified as primordial by individuals because it is entrenched within their ordinary experiences (Geertz 1973).

By contrast, the definition of religion – whether it should be based on its function or its contents, and the extent to which it shapes group identities and patterns of behaviours – is heavily contested. While Durkheim addresses religion as a source of social integration (Durkheim 1912), Geertz defines it as '(1) a system of symbols which acts to (2) establish powerful, pervasive and long-lasting motivations in men (3) by formulating conceptions of a general order of existence and (4) clothing these conceptions with such an aura of factuality that (5) the moods and motivations seem uniquely realistic' (Geertz 1973: 90). Juergensmeyer (1993) and Fox (2002) assimilate religion to a type of ideology which, among other characteristics, provides 'a meaningful framework for understanding the world' although it has the specificity of being derived from an external framework (Fox 2002: 14). For Juergensmeyer, who theorizes the continuity between symbolic and real acts of religious violence, religious worldviews may hence justify the resort to violence by providing a symbolic core to the idea of a world divided into warring camps (Juergensmeyer 2003).

A key to dynamically analysing the relationship between religion, ethnicity, and violence is to address these concepts as socially and/or politically constructed rather than given. The definitions of ethnic and religious identities indeed evolve across time. Membership criteria vary, groups can be subjected to sub-divisions or assimilation in larger wholes, and overlapping religious or ethnic identities may be mobilized in different ways at different times. These changing boundaries have been considered as a characteristic of ethnicity (Gurr 1993; Horowitz 2000) and a similar observation can be made for religion. Religious groups appropriate and redefine what they consider as the 'truth', although the transformations of religious narratives – for theological or political purposes – are more likely to produce scissions (the Christian schisms, or the division between Shi'ite and Sunni Muslims), especially when the definition of the doctrine is monopolized by formal institutions. These evolutions complicate the analysis of violence involving ethnic and religious narratives.

Beyond their commonalities, ethnicity and religion can be distinguished by the nature of the political demands they found and by their membership (Fox 2002), which generate two conceptions of 'otherness'. While both are exclusive identities, the definition of ethnic boundaries sets the demographic limits of group membership and is ascribed as a label, unrelated to the notion of personal adhesion or consent. Ethnic identities are, however, subject to transformation and hybridization, for instance through intermarriage or migration. Religion, by contrast, sets strict membership criteria and requires an exclusive adhesion, but does not prevent the group membership from expanding, since individuals may join a religious group by conversion. This difference opens two conceptions of the relationship with territoriality and political authority.

While ethnic identities are constructed in relation with a territory, most religions are not geographically confined, since they are conceived as true and given, regardless of time and place. One of the repercussions of this feature, in the context of a conflict, is that the involvement of external supporters may be triggered by the mobilization of a religious narrative. Religious and ethnic narratives may also challenge the state's monopoly over the definition of legitimacy and the use of physical violence, by justifying the use of violence against actors or authorities presented as threats to the core of the group's identity. These two identity narratives nevertheless hold different relationships with political institutions. While ethnic narratives are attached to a territorial reference, religious discourses are founded on an external source of legitimacy. When religions are perceived as a primordial source of identity, they are therefore more difficult to combine with an overarching political framework. This facilitates their mobilization by violence entrepreneurs and makes them more difficult to appease through negotiated peace settlements.

The agency of ethnic and religious identities

The study of the relationship between violence and ethnic or religious narratives has long suffered from the reductionism of two opposing categories of analytical frameworks – primordialism and culturalism on the one hand, functionalism and instrumentalism on the other.

For primordialists, belonging to an ethnic group is seen as a natural characteristic of human life, reinforced through socialization mechanisms that derive from common cultural practices (Smith 1981; Horowitz 2000). In this view, violence and conflicts are seen as a consequence of the irreconcilable demands resulting from the intrinsic characteristics and interests of ethnic or religious groups. Conflicts are thereby analysed as a function of difference, and any group may potentially, at some point, seek independence and encounter the opposition of the others. The culturalist approach addresses the substance of ethnic or religious identities. It considers social behaviours to be prescribed by values proceeding from identities and, hence, from cultures, some of which are inherently inclined to resort to violence.

These approaches seem to respond to the common-sense observation that most contemporary conflicts mobilize ethnic or religious narratives. However, they fail to critically address this linkage and to take into account the changing boundaries of ethnic or religious narratives, as well as the possibility of their strategic mobilization. An important body of literature, resting on both qualitative and quantitative research, demonstrates that ethnic and religious diversity are neither necessary nor sufficient conditions for violence to occur. As diversity is present everywhere as a rule, the same groups may be opposed in certain times and places while they cohabit in others, and violence remains exceptional by comparison to peaceful coexistence (Bates and Yackolev 2002; Fearon and Laitin 1996, 2000; Habyarimana et al. 2008).

The opposite claim, that ethnicity or religion are never relevant as independent variables or as the root cause of violence, derives from the constructivist school which considers these identities as socially constructed and 'imagined' (Anderson 1991[1983]). This approach, focusing on the changing boundaries of identities and their mobilization by groups or political elites, has given way to two distinct yet compatible perspectives. Functionalists, on the one hand, consider violence to proceed from more determining social, economic, or political conditions, which may provide the backdrop of a mobilization of identity narratives legitimizing the use of violence. Violence and its justifications are nevertheless considered as a function of this more general context. Instrumentalist perspectives rather focus on the role of manipulative elites seeking material or political gains. They perceive identity narratives as instruments to mobilize masses, rather than inherent sources of violent behaviours.

A possible compromise would be to follow Geertz's approach in considering that, despite the constructed and contingent nature of ethnic or religious identities, the fact that they are in practice reified as primordial by certain individuals provides them with the ability to shape worldviews and behaviours. Although violence is never essentially religious or ethnic, identity narratives intervene in shaping conflict settings, legitimizing or framing the resort to violence, and influencing behaviours. This perspective calls for multilevel and multi-causal analyses, which can form the basis of inclusive conflict-resolution frameworks.

Contextual and systemic factors

Beyond the previously mentioned cleavage, the eruption of ethnic or religious narratives legitimizing violence, as well as the forms and success of their mobilization, can be tied to contextual or systemic evolutions.

Contextual dimensions and politico-institutional triggers

Ethnic or religious violence is favoured in politico-institutional contexts which shape and reify identity-based categories and differences, particularly through ethno-nationalist discourses, laws, institutions, or policies that ascribe individuals to these groups. Such contexts provide a basis for the construction and perception of collective identities, thus determining their political mobilization. It is particularly the case when ethnic or religious categorization accounts for discriminatory policies, granting certain groups control of political or material resources which materialize in horizontal inequalities (Stewart 2008). The deriving sense of collective exclusion and relative deprivation opens the path to contestation and potentially violent mobilization (Gurr 1970), especially when minorities cannot expect ever to achieve political representation and influence. Colonial systems based on a 'divide and rule' logic, and the political institutions which have retained these characteristics (Rwanda or, to a lesser extent, Malaysia), are particularly predisposed to this tendency.

As ethnic or religious narratives supporting violence challenge the state's monopoly over the legitimate use of force and contradict the obligations derived from national allegiance and citizenship, their mobilization by identity entrepreneurs is more prone to meet grassroots support where the state is weak or contested. This is clearly the case in contexts where the nation-state model has been imported after the Second World War, without enabling the emergence of a social contract based on the integration of different identities in a national model and the constitution of an autonomous political space (Badie 1992). In the presence of fragile political legitimacy, the mobilization resulting from a collective sense of exclusion is triggered by institutional weaknesses (Easterly 2001), as weak institutions fail to provide the basis of cross-group relations and references. They hence reinforce the individuals' tendency to rely on communal solidarities, favouring the perception of a security dilemma by groups who feel that they cannot count on an overarching authority to provide security guarantees (Kauffman 1996).

While the resort to violence is never automatic, it is also favoured when minorities' expectations are repressed and their survival appears threatened. Policies directly affecting them as a group – discrimination or the use of violence by political rulers to consolidate their power (Collier et al. 2008) – constitute additional factors. Violent mobilizations are particularly likely to meet grassroots support when the minority elites answer these frustrations with an ideology that echoes the people's grievances (Gurr 1993).

Contemporary developments and systemic factors

The forms taken by the expression of narratives legitimizing violence are, to a large extent, shaped by the contemporary evolutions of the international system. Globalization has multiplied individuals' potential referents and allegiances, along with the destabilization of the territorial nation-state as the primary source of legitimacy and object of loyalty. It has thus transformed the patterns of violence as well as the narratives that legitimize it. This phenomenon has increased identity-related uncertainties and fears of standardization or dissolution through transnational contacts and processes (Appadurai 1998, 2006).

Addressing religious-based violence, Juergensmeyer pursues his argument on the systemic factors of religious resurgence. He analyses the rise of religious violence in a context where the Enlightenment project and secular nationalism have lost some of their appeal, while global insecurity rises. The resulting emergence of religious nationalist movements, which combine traditional communitarian values with the state reference, is seen as particularly prone to induce violence (Juergensmeyer 2008). David C. Rapoport also attributes a decisive importance to the political and global context in his approach to terrorism justified on religious grounds, which he analyses as the fourth wave of terrorism (Rapoport 2004).

Consequences on violence patterns

Beyond the controversies over the sources of ethnic or religious violence, or the very relevance of these notions, scholars on the subject focus on the impact of ethnic and religious narratives on patterns of contemporary violence.

On the extent of the conflict

The academic production reflects a divergence over the impact of religious and ethnic dimensions on the intensity of conflicts. While several quantitative and qualitative studies have observed that the involvement of religious narratives impacts the level of violence (Basedau et al. 2011; De Soysa and Nordas 2007; Henne 2012; Fox 2002, 2003, 2004; Toft 2007), others have drawn opposite conclusions (Collier and Hoeffler 2002; Lacina 2006; Pearce 2005).

Studies belonging to the first category refer to the fact that ethnic and religious narratives involve primordial references that are tied to the core of actors' identities and hence to their existential survival. When these identities are threatened (in real or perceived terms), the feeling that the constructed Other's very existence is a constituent of this threat may trigger mass violence, which aims at destructing the perceived threat rather than simply changing the terms of a balance of power.

On the other hand, several works contest the existence of a statistically significant impact of ethnicity and religion on the degree of violence. They highlight the presence of a counter-intuitive correlation between a high lethality and ethnically homogeneous contexts (Lacina 2006) – which does not debunk the possibility of a temptation to annihilate the potential threats to group homogeneity. Taking into account the relevance of religious narratives, Collier and Hoeffler (2002) have also relativized the significance of the apparent statistical correlation between religious issues and violence, by showing that the latter does not seem to depend on the former in practice.

The transnational spillover of violence based on identity narratives

The transnational implantation of several ethnic groups contributes to the internationalization of their causes, which may even transform the balance of power in their favour (Gurses 2014). The issue is, however, particularly salient with religion, whose transnational nature facilitates the 'contagion' of conflicts that are interpreted along religious lines (Fox 2004). Religious narratives are particularly prone to provoke a transnational spillover effect when they are constructed as the prominent explicative variable of a conflict. Religion indeed exerts a form of soft-power (Haynes 2012), which calls on individuals' exclusive allegiances by answering their demands for identity and integration with an all-inclusive narrative that provides them with a feeling of belonging and a source of engagement.

The spillover effect results from the attraction of resources and militants who primarily identify with the religious dimensions of a cause, to conflict terrains where violence was initially a function of multiple factors. As internal conflicts prolong in time and draw external support on the basis of this dimension, religious interpretations tend to trump other aspects of the conflict. This effect can be sought by local actors in search of international support (Afghanistan Mujahidin during the 1980s) but it may also result from the self-involvement of external actors who analyse a conflict along religious lines, sometimes against the intentions of its initial protagonists (the Free Aceh Movement from 1976 to 2005). Such developments impede conflict resolution by reifying the religious dimensions of a conflict, obliterating rational arguments in favour of its interpretation as a struggle for non-negotiable moral values or a 'cosmic war' (Juergensmeyer 2003).

Globalization has also facilitated the spread of problem-perception frameworks and behaviour patterns, by violence entrepreneurs who publicize them on international media or via spectacular actions (religious-based terrorism). This phenomenon complicates the analysis of violence legitimized by identity-based narratives, as it contributes to its propagation on terrains where the major politico-institutional factors of violence are seemingly irrelevant. Such a transposition results from the adhesion of individuals who endorse what they perceive as the cause of a group with whom they identify. It leads to the reification of religious violence through these actors' discourses, as well as the importation of violent behaviours legitimized by these narratives (the transposition of the Israeli–Palestinian conflict by French citizens of Jewish and Arab descent (Hecker 2012), or the endorsement of Daech's rhetoric and actions by European residents).

Dealing with ethnic and religious violence

The spread of religious and ethnic narratives legitimizing violence contributes to the entrenchment of these conflicts and to the reification of their identity dimensions by drawing in external actors who are primarily mobilized on this basis. This phenomenon hinders the negotiation of peace settlements, calling for conflict-resolution strategies which take into account the role and specificity of ethnic or religious actors and narratives.

Impacts on peace-reconstruction strategies

A strong presence of identity narratives impacts the nature and the efficiency of conflict-resolution measures. The reification of a conflict as ethnic or religious first complicates its resolution through a negotiated settlement, as negotiations are likely to succeed only if they focus on non-identity issues (Svensson 2007; 2012; Svensson and Harding 2011; Toft 2007). Inflicted or experienced violence also tends to reinforce the feeling of insecurity and the exclusiveness of identity narratives, entrenching them in individual and collective worldviews. This weights on the establishment of peacebuilding strategies, largely restraining the efficiency of international involvement and the use of force as the underlying dimensions of these conflicts cannot be transformed by coercive interventions (Kaufman 1996; Lake and Rotchild 1998).

Peacebuilding strategies depend on the understanding of the sources of violence. Analyses resting on primordialist or culturalist frameworks tend to consider a complete separation or a consociational political system (such as the one instituted by the Lebanese constitution) as the only reliable options. The efficiency of such measures has, however, been contested (Pischedda 2008), especially as they may lean toward 'balkanization' or ethnic purification. Constructivist approaches rather focus on the necessity to understand identity construction and violence-mobilization processes, in order to create the preconditions of a transformation (Isajiw 2000). For functionalists, the goal would be to understand the contingencies of each situation and to transform the socio-economic or political context, in order to foster inter-group cooperation, protect minorities, and/or reduce the incentives to engage in conflict (Collier et al. 2003; Habyarimana et al. 2008). Instrumentalist perspectives on peacebuilding rather require engaging the ethnic or religious elites, through cooptation or support for the moderates, in order to incite them to induce their followers to support peaceful solutions (Alles 2015b; Byman 2002). In sum, the success of peacebuilding strategies depends upon their ability to take into account the specificities of violence legitimized by identity narratives, bringing back the issue of the interpretation of the role played by these identities.

Challenges to conflict resolution and peacebuilding

Taking into account ethnic and religious references, actors, or traditions may be a necessary condition to transform a conflict, notwithstanding its primary causes, once it has been reified as ethnic or religious. To this end, addressing identity narratives as constructed and changeable opens the possibility of transforming violent interactions into peaceful exchanges. But whether ethnicity and religion are seen as primordial or as socially constructed, it is essential not to undermine the legitimacy of the conflict-transformation attempt. This requires peacemakers to take seriously the involvement of actors who define and legitimate their engagement on ethnic or religious grounds, and to speak a language they will understand.

Relying on ethnic or religious actors, as well as local cultural references, may be an option to increase the audience of a more peaceful and inclusive interpretation of the identity narrative. Seeking to transmute these conceptions, instead of promoting their marginalization, has the advantage of engaging the populations to transform narratives which sustain their identity by promoting its most inclusive aspects. It thus prevents the risk of leaving the parties with the impression that a compromise was imposed on them – which, in the context of exclusive identities, opens the possibility for violence to resurge by creating frustration and resentment. Conflict-resolution strategies relying on the spread of inclusive identity narratives may take different forms, which are not mutually exclusive. They form the basis of a growing research field, which would still deserve more conceptualization as well as case study analyses (Hertog 2010).

The involvement of religious peacemakers tends to facilitate the dialogue with actors whose motivations and perceptions of legitimacy are voiced in spiritual rather than material claims. Appleby (2000) hence considers them as critical to peace construction and the emergence of a context of dialogue, reconciliation, and bridges between groups, while Bercovitch and Kadayifci-Orellana (2009) stress their specific legitimacy and leverage. External religious mediators derive their credibility from their standing and willingness to engage with religious communities, as opposed to traditional states' representatives who are rarely willing to speak the language of spiritual claims and are not at ease with open a dialogue on these issues (Bartoli 2009).

Religious teachings and local practices may also be relied upon as a resource for conflict transformation, by providing the basis of peacebuilding strategies or cooperative mechanisms. The idea of promoting them as tools for peaceful cooperation is increasingly developed, both in theory and as a practice. Along this line, Marc Gopin (2000) develops the constructive role that can be played by religion in building a global community of shared moral commitments. The pacifist engagement of Gandhism and its integration of Hindu teachings is a case in point (Juegensmeyer 2005), but most religious traditions also have a discourse on peace and coexistence which may be relied upon (Galtung 2000; Ter Haar and Busuttil 2004).

Another option may also consist in valorizing the interpretation or concrete practices of a culture or religion that facilitate peaceful cooperation, in order to support a peacebuilding narrative by showing that it is not alien to the identity and references of the seemingly antagonistic actors. It can take the form of promoting local social practices, such as inter-communal pacts, which may have been forgotten prior to or in the context of the episodes of violence, to provide the basis of new inter-group interactions (Alles 2015a).

A difficulty, however, especially in the presence of religious or ethnic groups that are not organized around a central source of authority and legitimacy, is to not discredit the attempt or the proponent of a reinterpretation of religion or tradition. The risk is particularly salient when the initiative comes from external peacebuilders or by contested national authorities, who may open a new cleavage. This observation calls for the involvement of 'change agents' who hold enough legitimacy to provoke the adhesion of a large range of followers. Such a strategy may involve co-opting religious or ethnic elites to encourage them to favour inter-group dialogue or non-violence, or empowering moderate leaders to promote the most peaceful forces in a society (Alles 2015b).

The involvement of religious actors is also one of the aspects of the 'de-radicalization' strategies conducted with the aim of changing the mindsets of terrorism convicts, through inter-religious dialogue or exchanges with clerics or reinserted militants. These programmes, which have become increasingly established since 2001, are still under scrutiny as data remains too limited to assess their results on a large scale (Horgan and Braddock 2010). They have, however, been criticized both on their principles and on their efficiency.

Conclusion

This chapter has sought to underline that, while there are no systematic causalities, it is possible to identify conditions under which ethnic or religious narratives are more likely to support violent mobilizations. These conditions are largely impacted by the transformations resulting from globalization and the evolution of the contemporary international system, which reshape the expressions of violence while complicating their analysis. The transnational diffusion of violence narratives contributes to their reification in terrains where the previously evoked preconditions are not necessarily reunited. This phenomenon has led to a securitization of ethnic and religious issues and identities, which can be the basis of discriminatory behaviours or policies (Fox and Akbaba 2015; Shani 2014) – themselves contributing to reinforcement of the minorities' sense of communal identity, and potentially nourishing further contestation of state legitimacy.

The legitimation of violence by ethnic or religious narratives also impacts the forms of the conflict as well as peacebuilding strategies. Identity-based narratives, especially when they call on transnational references and solidarities, tend to prolong conflicts by facilitating the involvement of external supports and resources. They also complicate conflict resolution, by accentuating the non-negotiable dimensions of a conflict and its perception as a threat to the core of an individual's and/or group's identity. This decreases the chance for a traditional negotiation or mediation to succeed, and requires peacebuilders to speak the language of ethnic or religious mobilizations. The latter observation calls for the development of further research on the interplay between the root causes of violence and its interpretation along ethnic or religious lines, in order to analyse the conditions of this shift. Situations where inter-ethnic or inter-religious regulation or conflict-transformation mechanisms worked well, especially without external intervention, would also deserve to be considered by future research agendas dealing with ethnic and religious violence.

References

Alles, D. (2015a) 'Le dialogue interreligieux en Indonésie: de la réinvention d'une tradition à sa projection internationale' [Interfaith dialogue in Indonesia: from the revival of tradition to its international projection], *Champs de mars* 26: 136–51.

Alles, D. (2015b) *Transnational Islamic Actors and Indonesia's Foreign Policy: Transcending the State*, London: Routledge.

Anderson, B. (1991[1983]) *Imagined Communities*, London: Verso.

Appadurai, A. (1998) 'Dead Certainty: Ethnic Violence in the Era of Globalization', *Development and Change* 29(4): 905–25.

Appadurai, A. (2006) *Fear of Small Numbers: An Essay on the Geography of Anger*, Durham, NC: Duke University Press.

Appleby, R. S. (2000) *The Ambivalence of the Sacred: Religion, Violence, and Reconciliation*, Oxford: Rowman & Littlefield.

Badie, B. (1992) *L'État importé. Essai sur l'occidentalisation de l'ordre politique*, Paris: Fayard.

Bartoli, A. (2009) 'NGOs and Conflict-Resolution', in J. Bercovitch, V. Kremenyuk, and W. Zartman (eds.) *The Sage Handbook of Conflict-Resolution*, London: Sage: 392–412.

Basedau, M., Strüver, G., Vüllers, J., and Wegenast, T. (2011) 'Do Religious Factors Impact Armed Conflict?', *GIGA Working Papers Series*, 168.

Bates, R. H. and Yackolev, I. (2002) 'Ethnicity, Capital Formation, and Conflict: Evidence from Africa', in C. Grootaert and T. Van Bastelaer (eds.) *The Role of Social Capital in Development*, New York: Cambridge University Press, 310–40.

Bercovitch, J. and Kadayifci-Orellana, A. S. (2009) 'Religion and Mediation: The Role of Faith-Based Actors in International Conflict Resolution', *International Negotiation* 14(1): 175–204.

Byman, D. L. (2002) *Keeping the Peace: Lasting Solutions to Ethnic Conflicts*, Washington DC: Johns Hopkins University Press.

Collier, P. E., Bates, R. H., Hoeffler, A., and O'Connelle S. A. (2008) 'Endogenizing Syndromes', in N. J. Benno, S. A. O'Connell, R. H. Bates, P. Collier, and S. C. Chukwuma (eds.), *The Political Economy of Economic Growth in Africa, 1960–2000*, Cambridge: Cambridge University Press: 391–420.

Collier, P. E., Elliott, V. L., Hegre, H., Hoeffler, A., Reynal-Querol, M., and Sambanis, N. (2003) *Breaking the Conflict Trap: Civil War and Development Policy*, Washington, DC; New York: World Bank; Oxford University Press.

Collier, P. E. and Hoeffler, A. (2002) `On the Incidence of Civil War in Africa', *Journal of Conflict Resolution* 46(1): 13 -28.

De Soysa, I. and Nordas, R. (2007) 'Islam's Bloody Innards? Religion and Political Terror, 1980–2000', *International Studies Quarterly* 51(4): 927–43.

Durkheim, E. (1968[1912]) *Les formes élémentaires de la vie religieuse*, Paris: Presses Universitaires de France.

Easterly, W. (2001) 'Can Institutions Resolve Ethnic Conflict?', *Economic Development and Cultural Change* 49(4): 687–706.

Fearon, J. D. and Laitin, D. D. (1996) 'Explaining Interethnic Cooperation', *American Political Science Review* 90(4): 715–35.

Fearon, J. D. and Laitin, D. D. (2000) 'Violence and the Social Construction of Ethnic Identity', *International Organization* 54(4): 845–77.

Fox, J. (2002) *Ethnoreligious Conflict in the Late Twentieth Century: A General Theory*, Lanham, MD: Lexington Books.

Fox, J. (2003) 'Ethnoreligious Conflict in the Third World: The Role of Religion as a Cause of Conflict', *Nationalism and Ethnic Politics* 9(1): 101–25.

Fox, J. (2004) 'Is Ethnoreligious Conflict a Contagious Disease?', *Studies in Conflict & Terrorism* 27(2): 89–106.

Fox, J. and Akbaba, Y. (2015) 'Securitization of Islam and Religious Discrimination: Religious Minorities in Western Democracies, 1990–2008', *Comparative European Politics* 13: 175–97.

Galtung, J. (1969) 'Violence, Peace, and Peace Research', *Journal of Peace Research* 6(3): 167–91.

Galtung, J. (1990) 'Cultural Violence', *Journal of Peace Research* 27(3): 291–305.

Galtung, J. (2000) *Conflict Transformation by Peaceful Means: The Transcend Method. Participants' and Trainers' Manual*, Geneva: United Nations Disaster Management Training Programme.

Geertz, C. (1973) *The Interpretation of Cultures*, New York: Basic Books.

Gopin, M. (2000) *Between Eden and Armageddon: The Future of World Religions, Violence, and Peacemaking*, Oxford: Oxford University Press.

Gurr, T. R. (1970) *Why Men Rebel*, Princeton, NJ: Princeton University Press.

Gurr, T. R. (1993) *Minorities at Risk: A Global View of Ethnopolitical Conflicts*, Washington DC: United States Institute of Peace Press.

Gurses, M. (2014) 'Transnational Ethnic Kin and Civil War Outcomes', *Political Research Quarterly*: 1–12.

Habyarimana, J., Humphreys, M., Posner, D., and Weinstein, J. (2008) 'Is Ethnic Conflict Inevitable? Parting Ways over Nationalism and Separatism', *Foreign Affairs* 87(4): 138–41.

Haynes, J. (2012) *Religious Transnational Actors and Soft Power*, Farnham: Ashgate.

Hecker, M. (2012) *Intifada française? De l'importation du conflit israélo-palestinien*, Paris: Ellipses.

Henne, P. S. (2012) 'The Ancient Fire: Religion and Suicide Terrorism', *Terrorism and Political Violence* 24(1): 38–60.

Hertog, C. (2010) *The Complex Reality of Religious Peacebuilding: Conceptual Contributions and Critical Analysis*, Lanham, MD: Lexington Books.

Horgan, J. and Braddock, K. (2010) 'Rehabilitating the Terrorists? Challenges in Assessing the Effectiveness of De-radicalization Programs', *Terrorism and Political Violence* 22(2): 267–91.

Horowitz, D. L. (2000[1985]) *Ethnic Groups in Conflict*, Berkeley: University of California Press.

Isajiw, W. W. (2000) 'Approaches to Ethnic Conflict Resolution: Paradigms and Principles', *International Journal of Intercultural Relations* 24(1): 105–24.

Juergensmeyer M. (1993) *The New Cold War? Religious Nationalism Confronts the Secular State*, Berkeley: University of California Press.

Juergensmeyer M. (2003[2000]) *Terror in the Mind of God: The Global Rise of Religious Violence*, Berkeley: University of California Press.

Juergensmeyer M. (2005) *Gandhi's Way – A Handbook of Conflict Resolution*, Berkeley: University of California Press.

Juegensmeyer M. (2008) *Global Rebellion : Religious Challenges to the Secular State, from Christian Militias to al Qaeda*, Berkeley: University of California Press.

Kaldor, M. (2007[1999]) *New and Old Wars: Organized Violence in a Global Era*, Stanford, CA: Stanford University Press.

Kaufman, S. J. (1996) 'Spiraling to Ethnic War: Elites, Masses, and Moscow in Moldova's Civil War', *International Security* 21(2): 108–38.

Keohane R. O. (2002) 'The Globalization of Informal Violence, Theories of World Politics, and the "Liberalism of Fear"', *Dialogue IO* 1(01): 29–43.

Lacina, B. (2006) 'Explaining the Severity of Civil Wars', *Journal of Conflict Resolution* 50(2): 276–89.

Lake, D. A. and Rotchild, D. (eds.) (1998) *The International Spread of Ethnic Conflict: Fear, Diffusion, and Escalation*, Princeton, NJ: Princeton University Press.

Marty, M. E. and Appleby, R. S. (eds.) (1997) *Religion, Ethnicity and Self-Identity: Nations in Turmoil*, London: University Press of New England.

Pearce, S. (2005) 'Religious Rage: A Quantitative Analysis of the Intensity of Religious Conflicts', *Terrorism and Political Violence* 17(3): 333–52.

Pischedda, C. (2008) 'Partition as a Solution to Ethnic Conflict', *The International Spectator: Italian Journal of International Affairs* 43(4): 103–22.

Rapoport. D. C. (2004) 'The Four Waves of Modern Terrorism', in A. Kurth Cronin and J. M. Ludes (eds.) *Attacking Terrorism: Elements of a Grand Strategy*, Washington, DC: Georgetown University Press: 46–73.

Shani, G. (2014) *Religion, Identity and Human Security*, New York: Routledge.

Smith, A. D. (1981) *The Ethnic Revival*, New York: Cambridge University Press.

Smith, A. D. (2001) *Nationalism: Theory, Ideology, History*, Cambridge: Polity Press.

Stewart, F. (ed.) (2008) *Horizontal Inequalities and Conflict: Understanding Group Violence in Multiethnic Societies*, Basingstoke: Palgrave Macmillan.

Svensson, I. (2007) 'Fighting with Faith: Religion and Conflict Resolution in Civil Wars', *Journal of Conflict Resolution* 51(6): 930–49.

Svensson, I. (2012) *Ending Holy Wars: Religion and Conflict Resolution in Civil Wars*, Brisbane: University of Queensland Press.

Svensson, I. and Harding, E. (2011) 'How Holy Wars End: Exploring the Termination Patterns of Conflicts with Religious Dimensions in Asia', *Terrorism and Political Violence*, 23(2): 133–49.

Ter Haar, G. and Busuttil, J. J. (eds.) (2004) *Bridge or Barrier: Religion, Violence and Visions for Peace*, Leiden: Brill.

Toft, M. D. (2007) 'Getting Religion? The Puzzling Case of Islam and Civil War', *International Security* 31(4): 97–131.

19
ENERGY SECURITY

Robert W. Orttung

Oil price volatility, fears of instability in the Middle East, Russia, Venezuela, and other energy-producing regions, rapidly changing technology, and concerns about global warming have moved energy security to the top of the international political agenda. Oil in particular has evolved from being the world's most important traded commodity to a powerful tool in the political and economic relations among countries: whether a country produces oil and gas for the global market or must rely on fuel imports, energy helps define its position in international politics.

Energy is redefining the international security structure, as rapid price swings rebalance power on energy markets. China's maturing economy, marked by slowing growth, is scrambling expectations about future demand on the market, as the country seems to need less energy than once anticipated. State-controlled companies in resource-rich countries seek to use their resources as a weapon to promote state interests. However, behemoths like Gazprom are starting to falter, due to their own inefficiency and pushback from customers seeking to diversify their supplies.

While the unpredictability of the constantly changing international energy market contains the potential for conflict, we argue that the current situation may also present opportunities for global cooperation. Also, as new technologies and alternative energies develop, the relative importance of traditional sources of energy will change and again transform international power relations. Both energy exporters and importers are essentially interested in a stable energy system with functioning market mechanisms. They also have a common interest in ensuring that energy use does not destroy the Earth's environment in terms of climate change, air pollution, and water issues (Brown and Dworkin 2011).

This chapter first examines the various definitions of energy security. Second, it provides a brief overview of the history of energy security. Third, it examines the many sources of change currently affecting the international energy system. Fourth, it analyses the impact of energy on international politics, showing how the search for energy security can alternatively foster conflict and cooperation. The final section looks at challenges for the future.

Differing definitions and strategies

Countries have different perspectives on energy security depending on whether they import or export energy (SIPRI 1974: 17–20). Importing countries emphasize reliable supplies of ample energy, affordable prices, a diversity of producers, and adequate infrastructure to transport oil and gas (Kalicki and Goldwyn 2005: 9–10). Traditional energy importers include the US, Europe, and Japan. These countries have more recently been joined by rising powers, such as China and India, whose growing economies have outstripped domestic energy production.

Energy exporting countries list other priorities when defining energy security (Yergin 2006): they prefer high prices and stable demand, typically provided by a diversity of customers; maintaining maximum control over their energy industries, while obtaining sufficient domestic or foreign investment to maintain or increase output; and ensuring that their economies are sufficiently diversified so that they are not reliant on fluctuating energy commodity prices. The Middle East, Venezuela, and Russia control the world's largest oil reserves, and Canada joins these ranks if tar sands, an unconventional form of oil, are included. The Organization of Petroleum Exporting Countries (OPEC) controls three-quarters of the world's oil deposits. Russia and Saudi Arabia are the biggest oil exporters. Russia, Iran, and Qatar have the largest natural gas reserves. In addition to the US, they are currently the largest producers (British Petroleum 2015).

The evolution of technology and developing economies is shifting roles among importers and exporters. Consumption is moving from West to East, while supply sources are moving from East to West (Kalicki and Goldwyn 2013: xxv). Although the US has relied on extensive imports to meet its growing energy needs since the 1970s, the shale revolution has dramatically increased domestic production of oil and gas. In 2014, the US overtook Russia as the largest producer of these fuels and is even considering the possibility of launching exports (British Petroleum 2015). Deep-water drilling is also producing new sources not imagined previously. China and India began importing energy in the 1990s, much later than the West, but now their enormous need for all kinds of energy has transformed the market. China surpassed the US as the largest oil importer in 2013. However, slowing growth, beginning in 2014, meant that Chinese markets would not prove as lucrative for exporters as previously expected. European import dependence varies from country to country, but the continent as a whole relies heavily on oil from the Middle East and natural gas from Russia.

Definitions of energy security are largely driven by national interests, particularly by the question of whether a country depends on foreign energy imports or on the income it derives from exports. Importers have sought to keep energy prices relatively low through the development of a highly competitive market for energy resources. This approach favours open access to oil and gas fields, free-flowing investment by private corporations to develop resources, and the use of military force to ensure that supply lines remain open. Exporters seek to maximize the return they receive from selling their energy assets on the market. Accordingly, they have resorted to strategies of asserting state control over assets, blocking foreign companies from exploiting their resources, and even reducing energy supplies if that will increase their profitability.

The strategies of consumers and producers differ in their reliance on market or statist solutions, and the result is increased friction. Whereas consumers favour competitive markets to ensure low-priced, reliable supplies, producers are increasingly asserting control through state-owned companies to maximize their profits. Western companies are more frequently being squeezed out of countries that want to take control of their own resources. At the same time, petrostates find that they now have more money, which makes them important players on the world stage and allows them to assert their interests. However, Russia's state-owned natural gas monopoly Gazprom has lost market share in the lucrative European market and faces an EU lawsuit aimed at what the consumers allege are illegal practices (Aslund 2010; Noel 2013). Another difference between consumers and producers is that importing states are constantly seeking to reduce their demand for foreign energy, whether through domestic sources, increased efficiency, or the development of alternative sources. Currently hydroelectricity and renewable sources make up 9.3 per cent of global energy use (British Petroleum 2015), but that number is expected to rise dramatically in the future. To the extent that consumers actually succeed in reducing demand, it will undermine the position of the exporters.

Despite these differences, producers and consumers share an interest in maintaining the stability of the current international energy system. If prices rise too high or supplies become too scarce, energy costs could undermine economic growth, thereby hurting the economic interests of all countries. The fact that the producers and consumers share similar interests is important, because it makes possible a web of interconnecting trade ties among countries that helps to preserve international stability. Both producers and consumers have an interest in insuring that the energy pipelines and transportation routes are secure from terrorist attack, extreme weather such as hurricanes, and excessive costs imposed by transit country governments (Deutch and Schlesinger 2006: 9).

Historical background

In the twentieth century, oil fuelled Western economic growth and sustained armies worldwide. The control of oil became a key question of national military strategy when First Lord of the Admiralty Winston Churchill, on the eve of the First World War, decided to shift the British navy from domestic sources of coal to foreign sources of oil (Yergin 2006). Oil also played an extremely important role in the Allied defeat of the Axis powers in the Second World War, as Germany ran short of fuel for its offensives in Russia and Africa, and Japan lacked the energy to keep its military machine running (Singer 2008). In the aftermath of the Second World War, the direct influence of oil on military affairs declined, but the control of oil has remained a strategic goal ever since.

The most prominent use of energy as an economic weapon was the Arab oil embargo of the US and several European countries. The Arab countries sought to end US support for Israel after the 1973 Yom Kippur War by slashing energy shipments to the US. This led to a fourfold increase in oil prices, and ultimately imposed some pain not only on the US, but on Western consumers in general. Ultimately, however, the US did not change its foreign policy, and the embargo did not achieve its goal. Higher prices drove down US oil consumption, causing prices to fall and leading to overproduction and a glut on the market. The subsequent era of relatively cheap oil (under US$30 per barrel) lasted through to the end of the 1990s. The oil embargo had a powerful, but short-term, impact on thinking about energy security. Until that crisis, politicians and analysts had assumed that energy supplies would remain relatively cheap and accessible. In the years after the crisis, Western countries began making plans for dealing with future energy crises. However, the return of cheap energy in the early 1980s took away the impetus for this kind of action, and the topic received little attention until the dramatic rise in prices beginning in 2002.

Immediately following the 1973 embargo, the major powers set up international institutions to coordinate their energy policies better. The embargo was possible because the oil-producing countries were organized through OPEC, which was established in 1960 and brought together many of the key oil producers. In 1974, the Western countries set up the International Energy Agency (IEA) to coordinate Western energy policies, prevent oil supply disruptions, advocate alternative energy solutions, and provide information about the energy situation. A major limitation on the IEA is that countries must be members of the Organization for Economic Cooperation and Development (OECD) to join, and therefore the new consuming countries like China and India are not members. The only energy-focused organization that includes all major producers and consumers is the International Energy Forum (IEF), which was established in 2003 in an effort to promote dialogue between producers and consumers at the ministerial level. Despite its inclusive character, this organization has had little practical impact. Unfortunately, none of these organizations is designed to address the problems of the twenty-first century, which include climate change, sustainability, energy poverty, and adaptation; so, most likely, bilateral relations will be the most useful way to build broader international support in dealing with modern energy challenges (Ramsay 2013).

Beyond the reformed institutional structure, the West also set up strategic reserves of oil, and began to diversify its sources of energy away from the Middle East. At the same time, the US entered into a bargain with Saudi Arabia in which the US offered protection from Iraqi or Iranian aggression, while Saudi Arabia provided spare capacity, which it used to maintain sufficient supplies during crises, such as the Iraqi invasion of Kuwait in 1990, followed by the US-led effort to repel the threat. With President Barak Obama's efforts to improve US–Iranian relations, and a shift in export markets to Asia, the special US–Saudi relationship is beginning to fray.

Key trends and themes in energy security today

Today, it is widely accepted that the existing energy system is no longer sustainable and that extensive changes are inevitable. First, and most importantly, oil prices are now extremely volatile, rising rapidly following decades of stability from around US$30 in 2002 to a record high over US$140 in the middle of 2008, but then falling again well below US$50 by the end of the year, and rising and falling again by 2015. There are contradictory pressures on oil prices, making it extremely hard to predict what the price will be. On the upside, global demand for energy will continue to grow as China and India modernize their economies and expand access to cars, appliances, and larger homes for their citizens. Additional upward pressure comes from fewer investment opportunities for international oil companies, as governments take over fields in many of the key producing countries; insufficient investment in developing new fields as old ones begin to run dry; and production obstacles in countries like Libya, Iraq, Iran, and Nigeria. However, there are substantial downward pressures as well. As Chinese growth slows, demand is also dropping. Global consumption increased just 0.9 per cent in 2014, the slowest rate of growth since the 1990s. Similarly, supplies are increasing as the US boosts production and the treaty with Iran improves prospects that Iranian oil will return to international markets at previous levels following the lifting of sanctions. Other supply comes from exporters such as Saudi Arabia, which has continued to pump oil, despite low prices, in order to make US shale production unprofitable, and Russia, whose economy is heavily dependent on energy export revenue.

Second, with price volatility as a defining feature, both consumers and producers now realize that they are vulnerable to the market. Over the last forty years, power seesawed between the two sides. Western consumers benefited after the failure of the Arab oil embargo left Saudi Arabia with excess capacity and Western countries as the only customer, leading to an era of cheap energy. The advantage shifted to the producers between 2002 and the summer of 2008, when growing demand in Asia erased the excess capacity and the rise of new customers meant that producers could sell to consumers outside the West. More recently, consumers have been able to take advantage of greater supply on the market. Although energy producers have always benefited financially from their sales, the enormous influx of energy money due to higher prices meant that producing countries, such as Russia and Venezuela, felt that they could play a more assertive role in international politics. By 2015, countries that relied heavily on energy exports were facing a decline in their economic power: the producers no longer look as powerful, while consumers benefit from low energy prices even as other parts of their economy might continue to struggle.

Third, the Western-based international oil companies (IOCs) that once controlled most of the world's energy reserves have lost much of their past power to national oil companies (NOCs). Until the Arabs started privatizing their oil industries in the 1960s, privately owned Western oil companies, once defined as the 'Seven Sisters,' controlled 85 per cent of oil and gas reserves. These companies were the dominant players until the rise of OPEC (Sampson 1975). In 2011, NOCs controlled 'approximately 90 percent of the world's oil reserves and 75 percent of production (similar numbers apply to gas), as well as many of the major oil and gas infrastructure systems' (Tordo et al. 2011). The rise of the NOCs means that producer countries now have much greater control over how their reserves are used and gain a greater share of the profits than in the past. China's NOCs have also caused concern in the US, though sober analysis sees much of their alleged aggression as more myth than reality (Downs 2010).

In the face of the rising power of NOCs, Western countries have imposed sanctions to force these countries to change behaviour. In the case of Iran, the US and EU imposed crippling restrictions on Iranian energy sales abroad, which cut that country's exports by 400,000 barrels per day by mid-2012 (Kalicki and Goldwyn 2013: 5) and may have led Iran to agree to negotiations on its nuclear weapon capacity, leading to a deal in 2015. After Russia's annexation of Crimea, Western countries imposed sanctions on companies selling technology necessary for Russia to develop potential Arctic resources, but these restrictions have not induced Russia to end its occupation (Oxenstierna and Olsson 2015). As these cases illustrate, consumers are much more likely to impose energy sanctions than oil exporters (Shaffer 2009: 4). Russia, however, has frequently limited gas supplies to countries it does not favour, most prominently Ukraine and Georgia.

A fourth change is the type of fuel dominant in the international system. Traditionally, oil has been the most important fuel, particularly in the US, and will remain an important fuel source for many decades to come (Vaitheeswaran 2007: 24). Although oil is a finite resource, new technology is making production possible where previously the costs had been prohibitive. Peak oil theory suggested that once oil production hit its apogee, output would drop off sharply (Hubbert 1956), with potentially catastrophic economic consequences for oil-consuming countries if they did not take proper preventive action (Hirsch 2005). Expectations that the world had passed or would soon pass peak production (Deffeyes 2006) or that non-OPEC oil production would peak by 2010 (Pagnamenta 2008), proved incorrect. With the addition of non-conventional sources of oil, current global reserves are approximately 5 trillion barrels – to put this number in perspective, the world has burned about 1 trillion barrels since the beginning of the nineteenth century (Yergin 2011: 239). From 2012 to 2014, the US increased its oil production by more than a million barrels per day each year.

Fifth, even as oil prices remain volatile, consumer countries are looking for new types of energy. In the near future, natural gas will become increasingly important, particularly with the extension of the liquefied natural gas infrastructure. Nuclear power in 2014 provided 4.4 per cent of total global energy production. The 2011 Fukushima accident, the worst since Chernobyl, raised questions about the safety of existing plants, but construction continued in some areas. New technologies are bringing down the price of alternative fuels, such as solar and wind power, making them competitive with fossil fuels (*New York Magazine* 2015). However, such sources currently make up just 2.5 per cent of total energy consumption and their widespread implementation remains a question for the future.

Finally, a growing awareness of climate change provides another source of change in the international energy system (Solomon 2007). Fears that continued use of hydrocarbon-based energy at current or accelerating rates would lead to catastrophic environmental changes have altered the way that many individuals view their energy habits.

Impact of energy on international security

Energy became a matter of national security when countries began to depend on imports in order to secure the continued operation of their economies. Since energy is now essential to most aspects of civilized life, it has become a central issue in politics at both the international and national levels (Proninska 2007). If managed poorly, energy resources can provide the basis for tensions and potentially even violent conflict within and among states. If managed wisely, however, energy can stimulate international cooperation and the development of a conflict-inhibiting environment.

Pessimistic scenarios suggest that competition over increasingly scarce energy supplies will inevitably lead to more frequent international conflicts (Klare 2001). In the most straightforward example of such a 'resource war', Saddam Hussein invaded Kuwait in 1990 to gain control of its oil. Because of the size of its population and resulting energy needs, China is frequently portrayed as potentially fomenting conflict over resources in part because it is willing to invest in areas of the world shunned by the West, such as Sudan, Iran, and Zimbabwe, to secure the energy it needs to fuel its rapid growth. Additionally, disputes over energy exist in a variety of areas, such as the Caspian, Central Asia, the Middle East, Africa, and Latin America (Heinberg 2005: 210–20). Expanded offshore oil drilling has led to greater maritime conflict over time (Nyman 2015).

Given energy's centrality to economic life, the most extreme theorists of resource wars expect struggles over energy to override all other considerations (Klare 2008: 7). They argue that states will increasingly use their powers to ensure that they have sufficient supplies of energy. Oil will no longer be a commodity to be bought and sold on the international market, but will be an object of armed confrontation. Likewise, energy-deficient countries will seek to ensure their energy supplies by building alliances with energy producers through massive arms transfers, particularly to unstable regions in Africa, the Middle East, and the Caspian basin (Klare 2008: 239). A more nuanced version of the resource wars thesis argues that resource stress is an indirect cause of violence that interacts within a complex web of factors by causing social dislocations that include widening gaps between rich and poor, increased rent-seeking by elites, weakening of states, and ethnic cleavages (Homer-Dixon 2008). Jeff D. Colgan provides greater nuance to our understanding of the connections between energy and international conflict by arguing that petrostates are more likely to be aggressive towards their neighbours following a revolution than other states because the income from oil sales provides the means for aggression after a domestic revolution has eliminated any domestic political constraints on the leader's behaviour (Colgan 2013).

In addition to contributing to international conflict, energy supplies are a source of instability in the countries that produce them. According to an extensive literature on the 'resource curse', since the 1970s, when producing states wrested control of energy income from the Western IOCs, the extensive wealth generated by the exploitation of natural resources has had a negative impact on these countries' growth tempo (Sachs and Warner 1995), has given authoritarian leaders the ability to resist global democratizing trends, has created more opportunities for men than women (Ross 2012), and has greatly stimulated the prevalence of corruption (Kang 1999: 46). Oil wealth has a particularly corrosive effect on a country's institutions if the state plays a dominant role in the petroleum sector (Jones Luong and Weinthal 2010). One additional consequence of the resource curse is that oil-producing countries are much more prone to civil wars and internal conflict than countries without such resources (Ross 2008: 2). Besides disrupting a county's economics and politics, oil makes it easier for insurgents to fund their uprisings and intensifies ethnic grievances. In places like Iraq and Nigeria, insurgents have sold oil on the black market to continue their war-fighting efforts.

Such predictions of resource wars are not universally accepted, however (Hamilton 2003; Tompson 2006; Victor 2007). The resource wars literature basically argues that energy consumers are fighting over a shrinking supply of energy in what amounts to a zero-sum game. However, if countries view energy as just another commodity, then the problem becomes how best to build efficient markets to deliver this commodity, regardless of its physical location. In that sense, the zero-sum game is transformed into a mutually advantageous task where energy-consuming countries have a common interest in managing markets effectively (Victor 2007).

Cooperation could be facilitated by recognition of common interests on the part of energy consumers. The US and China, the world's two largest energy consumers, could work together on alternative sources of energy that are environmentally friendly and reduce oil dependence (Zha and Hu 2007: 111). The two countries could also develop new ways of saving energy in industrial and residential applications.

Such cooperative efforts need not be limited to energy consumers. Net energy producers such as Saudi Arabia and Russia are consuming increasing amounts of energy and have a strong interest in increasing their energy efficiency in order to prolong existing supplies of fossil fuels and develop alternative sources when those limited supplies run out. Therefore, both consumers and producers share an interest in developing new technologies for solar and wind energy, efficient building design, electric cars, and a host of other technologies. The problem is that these common interests first need to be articulated on a political level in order to facilitate cooperation among consumers and producers.

Challenges for the future

The quest for energy security in the future faces a number of challenges. First, a key challenge for the West will be addressing potential threats posed by possible instability among energy exporters. The crises that disrupted energy supplies after the Second World War usually happened 'unexpectedly,' as Daniel Yergin has pointed out (2011: 4). As a result of high energy prices, Western countries have transferred a significant amount of wealth to countries that do not support Western foreign policy interests, such as Iran, Russia, and Venezuela. On one hand, the enormous transfer of wealth from energy-consuming to producing countries is creating a new situation where states can play a much larger role on international financial markets than they ever did in the past, potentially using their growing leverage for political purposes (Teslik 2008). On the other hand, low energy prices make it difficult for the leaders of energy exporting countries to fulfil promises made to their populations, such as maintaining rising standards of living. For example, as economic conditions worsened inside Russia, President Vladimir Putin took the previously unimaginable step of invading his western neighbour and annexing part of its territory.

Second, in order to address challenges posed by climate change, both energy producers and energy consumers will have to reorganize their societies over the coming decades to increase energy efficiency and find new sources of energy in order gradually to transform the existing fossil-fuel-based energy system into one that is sustainable over the long term. Since increased energy efficiency will reduce the rate of consumption growth and eventually absolute demand, it will likely favour consumers more than producers. For the foreseeable future, an interdependent energy market is a fact of life and likely a stabilizing influence in the world. In general, the international energy market supplies importers with stable supplies of relatively cheap energy while generating economic growth in producers (Verrastro and Ladislaw 2007: 99). The energy market also sets constraints on the amount of violence in the system. Even at the height of the Cold War, the Soviet Union reliably supplied energy to Europe, and Venezuela still supplies oil to the US despite strong anti-US rhetoric on the part of Venezuelan leader Hugo Chavez and his successor Nicolas Maduro. Likewise, for all of its upheavals, the Middle East has been a generally reliable energy supplier to the West (Fattouh 2007).

Third and finally, future research should focus on addressing the key technological and policy challenges that must be overcome to transform existing energy usage patterns into more sustainable practices that will serve the security interests of current energy producers and consumers. There are several key technological challenges facing energy scientists today. One example is the development of cheap photovoltaic cells along with distribution and storage systems that can efficiently convert sunlight into electricity, move the voltage from where it is produced to where it is needed, and store it until the final customer wants to consume it (Woods 2008). There are similarly important technical challenges in the field of wind energy and biofuels. Technologies considered 'near at hand' can improve recovery of natural gas from shales, improve solar photovoltaics, expand grid-scale electricity storage, stimulate production of electric cars and LED lighting, and greatly increase the energy efficiency and effectiveness of US military energy use (Shultz and Armstrong 2014).

In addition to addressing the technical issues, researchers also need to define energy policies that will encourage greater energy efficiency and the use of alternatives to fossil fuels. Researchers particularly need to define how governments can best intervene, through tax incentives, mandates, and other measures, to encourage more sustainable energy usage when markets do not provide these kinds of incentives.

To be sustainable over the long term, any new policies must meet the differing needs of countries that import energy and those that export it. While policies that improve efficiency and promote alternative sources have obvious applications for today's energy importers, they also benefit energy exporters. Many of the exporters are trying to diversify their economies away from a reliance on energy and therefore are beginning to consume more energy as they develop other industries. Since energy-rich countries are among the most inefficient energy users in the world, they too will benefit from the development of new technologies. A gradual evolution away from fossil fuels has the potential to preserve the cooperative aspects of the current energy system, while moving it in an environmentally sustainable direction.

References

Aslund, A. (2010) 'Gazprom: Challenged Giant in Need of Reform', in A. Aslund, S. Guriev, and A. C. Kuchins (eds.) *Russia after the Global Economic Crisis*, Washington: Peterson Institute for International Economics, 151–68.

British Petroleum (2015) *BP Statistical Review of World Energy*, June. Online. Available HTTP: <http://www.bp.com/en/global/corporate/about-bp/energy-economics/statistical-review-of-world-energy.html> (accessed 10 September 2015).

Brown, M. A., and Dworkin, M. (2011) 'The Environmental Dimension of Energy Security', in B. K. Sovacool (ed.) *The Routledge Handbook of Energy Security*, London: Routledge, 176–90.

Colgan, J. D. (2013) *Petro-Aggression: When Oil Causes War*, Cambridge: Cambridge University Press.

Deffeyes, K. S. (2006) *Beyond Oil: The View from Hubbert's Peak*, New York: Hill and Wang.

Deutch, J. and Schlesinger, J. R. (2006) *National Security Consequences of US Oil Dependency*, New York: Council on Foreign Relations.

Downs, E. (2010) 'Who's Afraid of China's Oil Companies?', in C. Pascual and J. Elkind (eds.), *Energy Security: Economics, Politics, Strategies, and Implications*, Washington: Brookings Institution Press, 73–102.

Fattouh, B. (2007) 'How Secure are Middle East Oil Supplies?', Oxford: Oxford Institute for Energy Studies. Online. Available HTTP: <http://www.oxfordenergy.org/pdfs/WPM33.pdf> (accessed 16 December 2008).

Hamilton, A. (2003) 'Resource Wars and the Politics of Scarcity and Abundance', *Dialogue* 1(3): 27–38.

Heinberg, R. (2005[2003]) *The Party's Over: Oil, War and the Fate of Industrial Societies*, Gabriola Island, BC: New Society Publishers.

Hirsch, R. L., Bezdek, R., and Wendling, R. (2005) 'Peaking of World Oil Production: Impacts, Mitigation, and Risk Management', Washington, DC: Department of Energy. Online. Available HTTP: <http://www.netl.doe.gov/publications/others/pdf/Oil_Peaking_NETL.pdf> (accessed 16 December 2008).

Homer-Dixon, T. (2008) 'Straw Man in the Wind', *The National Interest Online*, 2 January. Online. Available HTTP: <http://www.nationalinterest.org/PrinterFriendly.aspx?id=16522> (accessed 16 December 2008).

Hubbert, M. K. (1956) 'Nuclear Energy and the Fossil Fuels', Paper Presented at the Spring Meeting of the Southern District, Division of Production, American Petroleum Institute, San Antonio, TX, 7–9 March. Online. Available HTTP: <http://www.hubbertpeak.com/hubbert/1956/1956.pdf> (accessed 16 December 2008).

Jones Luong, P. and Weinthal, E. (2010) *Oil Is Not a Curse: Ownership Structure and Institutions in Soviet Successor States*, New York: Cambridge University Press.

Kalicki, J. H. and Goldwyn, D. L. (2005) *Energy and Security: Toward a New Foreign Policy Strategy*, Baltimore, MD: Johns Hopkins University Press.

Kalicki, J. H., and Goldwyn, D. L. (eds.) (2013) *Energy and Security: Strategies for a World in Transition,* 2nd edn, Washington: Woodrow Wilson Center Press.

Kang, D. (1999) *Crony Capitalism,* New York: Cambridge University Press.

Klare, M. T. (2001) *Resource Wars: The New Landscape of Global Conflict,* New York: Henry Holt.

Klare, M. T. (2008) *Rising Powers, Shrinking Planet: The New Geopolitics of Energy,* New York: Metropolitan Books.

New York Magazine (2015) 'The Sunniest Climate-Change Story You've Ever Read', 7 September. Online. Available HTTP: <http://nymag.com/daily/intelligencer/2015/09/sunniest-climate-change-story-ever-read.html#> (accessed 27 October 2015).

Noel, P. (2013[2005]) 'European Gas Supply Security: Unfinished Business', in J. H. Kalicki and D. L. Goldwyn (eds.) *Energy and Security: Strategies for a World in Transition*, Washington: Woodrow Wilson Center Press, 169–86.

Nyman, E. (2015) 'Offshore Oil Development and Maritime Conflict in the 20th Century: A Statistical Analysis of International Trends', *Energy Research and Social Science* 6: 1–7.

Oxenstierna, S. and Olsson, P. (2015) *The Economic Sanctions against Russia: Impact and Prospects of Success,* Stockholm: FOI.

Pagnamenta, R. (2008) 'IEA Warns non-OPEC Oil Could Peak in Two Years', *The Times* (London), 21 July. Online. Available HTTP: <http://business.timesonline.co.uk/tol/business/industry_sectors/natural_resources/article4368523.ece> (accessed 16 December 2008).

Proninska, K. (2007) 'Energy and Security: Regional and Global Dimensions', SIPRI Yearbook. Online. Available HTTP: <http://yearbook2007.sipri.org/chap6 (accessed 16 December 2008).

Ramsay, W. C. (2013) 'Energy Sector Governance in the 21st Century', in J. H. Kalicki and D. L. Goldwyn (eds.), *Energy and Security: Strategies for a World in Transition*, Washington: Woodrow Wilson Center Press, 140–56.

Ross, M. L. (2008) 'Blood Barrels: Why Oil Wealth Fuels Conflict', *Foreign Affairs* 87(3): 2–9.

Ross, M. L. (2012) *The Oil Curse: How Petroleum Wealth Shapes the Development of Nations,* Princeton, NJ: Princeton University Press.

Sachs, J. D. and Warner, A. M. (1995) 'Natural Resource Abundance and Economic Growth', *NBER Working Paper 5398.*

Sampson, A. (1975) *The Seven Sisters: The Great Oil Companies and the World They Shaped,* New York: Viking.

Shaffer, B. (2009) *Energy Politics*, Philadelphia: University of Pennsylvania Press.

Shultz, G. P. and Armstrong, R. C. (2014) *Game Changers: Energy on the Move,* Stanford, CA: Hoover Institution Press.

Singer, C. (2008) *Oil and Security,* Stanley Foundation Political Analysis Brief, January.

Solomon, S., Qin, D., Manning, M., Chen, Z., Marquis, M., Averyt, K. B., Tignor, M., and Miller, H. L. (eds.) (2007) *Climate Change 2007: The Physical Science Basis – Contribution of Working Group I to the Fourth Assessment Report of the Intergovernmental Panel on Climate Change,* New York: Cambridge University Press.

Stockholm International Peace Research Institute (SIPRI) (1974) *Oil and Security,* New York: Humanities Press.

Teslik, L. H. (2008) 'Backgrounder: Sovereign Wealth Funds', Washington, DC: Council on Foreign Relations, 18 January. Online. Available HTTP: <http://www.cfr.org/publication/15251> (accessed 16 December 2008).

Tompson, W. (2006) 'A Frozen Venezuela? The 'Resource Curse' and Russian Politics', in M. Ellman (ed.) *Russia's Oil: Bonanza or Curse?*, London: Anthem.

Tordo, S., Tracy, B. S., and Arfaa, N. (2011) 'National Oil Companies and Value Creation', *World Bank Working Paper No. 218.* Online. Available HTTP: <http://siteresources.worldbank.org/INTOGMC/Resources/9780821388310.pdf> (accessed 29 October 2015).

Vaitheeswaran, V. V. (2007) 'Think Again: Oil', *Foreign Policy* 163(November–December): 24–30.

Verrastro, F. and Ladislaw, S. (2007) 'Providing Energy Security in an Interdependent World', *The Washington Quarterly* 30(4): 95–104.

Victor, D. G. (2007) 'What Resource Wars?', *National Interest Online*, 12 November. Online. Available HTTP: <http://www.nationalinterest.org/PrinterFriendly.aspx?id=16020> (accessed 16 December 2008).

Woods, R. (2008) 'How China's Thirst for Oil Can Save the Planet', London: *The Sunday Times*, 6 July. Online. Available HTTP: <http://www.thesundaytimes.co.uk/sto/business/article104256.ece> (accessed 29 October 2015).

Yergin, D. (2006) 'Ensuring Energy Security', *Foreign Affairs* 85(2): 69–82.

Yergin, D. (2011) *The Quest: Energy, Security, and the Remaking of the Modern World,* New York: Penguin.

Zha, D. and Hu, W. (2007) 'Promoting Energy Partnership in Beijing and Washington', *The Washington Quarterly* 30(4): 105–15.

20

RESOURCES, THE ENVIRONMENT, AND CONFLICT

Ole Magnus Theisen and Nils Petter Gleditsch

Since the Second World War, around 250 armed conflicts in over 150 countries and territories have claimed some 10 million lives in battle-related violence.[1] The current number of armed conflicts has declined markedly since the early 1990s, despite a recent upswing. Persons killed in battle have shrunk dramatically since the Second World War and mortality from violence overall is on a long-term decline (Pinker 2011). However, the thirty-plus ongoing armed conflicts continue to represent a crucial component of human insecurity. In addition to the direct loss of life in battle, armed conflict claims high human costs through disease, refugee flows, and the destruction of infrastructure (Gates et al. 2012). Reducing armed conflict makes a major contribution to improving human security. Can we look forward to a continued reduction in global violence?

A number of potential hurdles to a continued decline of violence have been proposed. One of them is increasing resource scarcity. A common perspective is to view scarce renewable resources as a motive for fighting – be it with your neighbour, another group, or even the state. Increasing concern with the condition of the world's environment in the 1970s led many to believe that environmental degradation might become sufficiently serious to lead to violence. Many saw the role of resources as filling the explanatory gap as armed conflict continued even after the decline of ideological conflicts associated with the Cold War. This perspective has been identified as neo-Malthusian.

Climate change has now arguably replaced classical neo-Malthusian concerns as the most debated model of 'environmental conflict'. Since the social mechanisms in the causal model linking resource scarcity to conflict are largely unchanged, we refer to both as the 'ecoviolence' perspective. This view in turn has been fundamentally challenged by environmental optimists,[2] as well as by political ecologists and liberals.[3]

This chapter has three major parts. First, we review the main strands of thought in the debate before providing a brief survey of the empirical state of the art. We find the more dramatic version of the ecoviolence model to have little empirical foundation, particularly if scarcity in and by itself is expected to produce conflict. We round off by pointing out some of the main problems of the empirical literature and discuss future priorities.

Schools of thought

Ecoviolence

The original model of Malthus (1993[1798]) assumed that any human population would grow at a geometrical ratio, while food production could only grow arithmetically – resulting in recurrent demographic collapses. Important elements of this model survive in current ecoviolence models. Natural resources are seen as limited on 'spaceship Earth' and so is human rationality under stressful conditions. Population growth, increasing consumption, and harmful methods of extraction combine to deplete or depreciate resources. The resulting scarcity can lead to competition and eventually armed conflict.

Moderate ecoviolence scholars argue that this generally happens through increased grievances or by weakening the state (Homer-Dixon 1999), but also by making the alternatives to legal labor more attractive, ranging from petty theft to joining an insurgent movement (Burke et al. 2009). This line of thinking is found in the Club of Rome's *The Limits to Growth* (Meadows et al. 1972), in the report by the Brundtland Commission (1987) on the environment and development, and in several scholarly works (e.g. Homer-Dixon 1999; Myers 1993; see Kahl 2006 for a modification). It is also reflected in the literature of most environmental pressure groups, many environment ministries, and other official bodies, as well as in the justification for awarding the Nobel Peace Prize for 2004 to Wangari Maathai and for 2007 to Al Gore and the Intergovernmental Panel on Climate Change (IPCC).

Scarce resources considered important enough to fight for include land, fresh water, and food; these resources are thought to become even scarcer due to population growth. For instance, a great deal of public attention has been given to the prospects of 'water wars', where upstream countries would dam or consume river water and provoke water-constrained downstream countries to go to war (Starr 1991). A favourite case is Egypt's anger with Ethiopia's damming of the Blue Nile potentially spilling over into conflict. For developing countries, ecoviolence scholars foresee a decline in food production. More recently, climate change with increasing temperatures, shifting precipitation patterns, an increased frequency of extreme weather events, melting ice-sheets, and sea-level rise has taken centre stage within the ecoviolence argument, often leading to very dire projections (Hsiang et al. 2013, though see Buhaug et al. 2014 for a rebuttal).

Environmental optimists

Environmental optimists stress that natural resources are generally more abundant than realized in ecoviolence models. Resources can be substituted and recycled when necessary, and technological progress makes it possible to consume less. In this view, the relative importance of renewable resources decreases as technological advance is driven by human ingenuity and demands from the market economy. The optimists seldom comment on conflict (see Simon 1989 for a rare exception), but their views have clear implications: if resources are globally abundant and can be priced, substituted, and traded to avoid serious scarcities, and if the increase in population can be held in check, there is no obvious reason why groups or countries should fight over natural resources. If resources are scarce to the point where people will fight for them, it is because politics has interfered. To avoid waste, inefficiency, and local scarcity, resources must be properly priced and trading allowed.

Ecoviolence scholars counter these points by stating that markets and institutions are frequently dysfunctional in developing states, and they thus fail to alleviate scarcities. New technologies (as illustrated by desalination of salt water or the Green Revolution) are usually too expensive for poor farmers and frequently lead to further degradation. Moreover, some resources, such as water, are non-substitutable. Finally, environmental degradation often follows a non-linear pattern, complicating detection and making preventive measures harder to apply (Homer-Dixon 1999; Kahl 2006).

Environmental optimists are somewhat divided on the demographic issue. Boserup (1965) argues that population growth is conducive to rural economic growth[4] and Simon (1996) argues that human ingenuity is the only scarce resource. Thus, continued population growth will provide an advantage in the indefinite future. Most environmental optimists, however, argue that the second demographic transition (lower fertility) is now cancelling out the effects of the first (lower mortality). A recent UN population projection (UN 2012) indicates that world population is likely to increase from its current level of 7 billion to close to 11 billion at the end of the twenty-first century, with Africa experiencing a fourfold increase (Gerland et al. 2014). UN population projections have been criticized by Lutz et al. (2014) for not accounting properly for the effects of education and for over-looking recent survey material on fertility for pivotal countries. These scholars project that world population will peak at 9.4 billion in 2070 and then gradually decline. In any case, neither projection implies a 'population explosion', although some regions still have high population growth.

Figure 20.1 shows the trend in food prices for the period 1960–2014. The long-term development up to the year 2000 lends little support to a prediction of a global food crisis. The most recent decade and a half, however, has seen a rise in food prices, which has been linked to climate extremes and which in turn has been said to cause social unrest. According to this view, the Arab spring was caused by increases in food prices triggered by drought in China's wheat-growing region. In turn, this led to major purchases of wheat in the global market, doubling the price of wheat, with important political implications for Egypt, the world's largest importer of grain (Sternberg 2012). However, the IPCC's Fifth Assessment Report (IPCC 2014: 495) states that even though prices may have become more sensitive to extreme weather in recent years, the effect of oil on prices is increasing. Thus, it is difficult to attribute global price fluctuations to weather phenomena. Disregarding the impact of climate, some analyses have found a link between food production or prices and different forms of political instability (Arezki and Brückner 2014; Maystadt et al. 2014), while others have failed to do so (Buhaug et al. 2015).

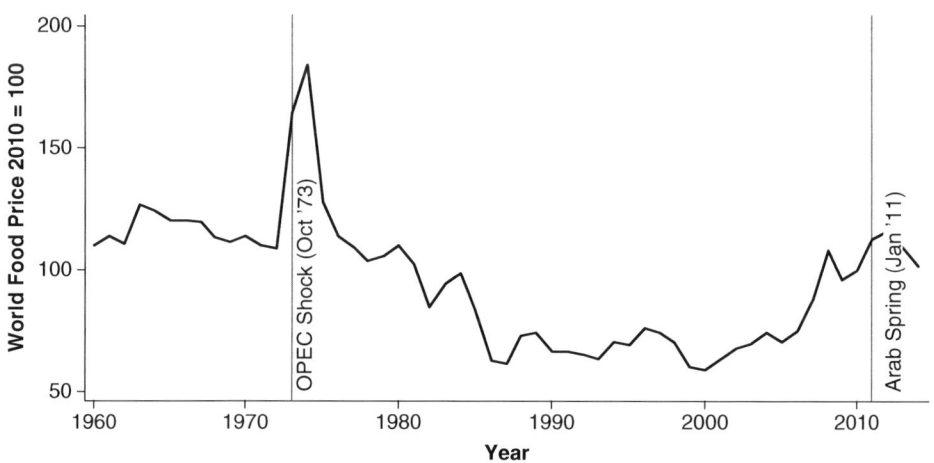

Figure 20.1 International food prices 1960–2014

Note: Global food prices weighted by the Manufactures Unit Values Index (World Bank 2015).

The role of institutions: liberals and political ecologists

Liberal conflict theory rests primarily on the role of cooperation and the role of democracy. It argues that an emerging resource scarcity may stimulate cooperation as well as violent conflict. Fighting over a shared resource may be more costly than working out ways to share it. Low-level conflict may serve as a warning signal that prompts states or groups into cooperation (Lonergan 2001; Wolf 2007).

Democracy is relevant to resource conflict in two ways. First, liberal theorists argue that democracy is likely to promote resource conservation (Gleditsch and Sverdrup 2002; Payne 1995) or at least environmental commitment (Neumayer 2002). Sen (1989) points out that famines rarely, if ever, occur in democracies, because press freedom and other features of democracy provide warning signals and mobilize countermeasures when food shortages occur. Second, stable democracies are very unlikely to fight each other (Gleditsch and Hegre 1997) or to suffer serious internal violence (Hegre 2014; Hegre et al. 2001). If democracies very rarely fight internally or among themselves for any other reason, they are not likely to do so because of resource scarcity.

Political ecology, the fourth general strand of thought, refutes any strong *direct* linkage between renewable resource scarcity and conflict (Turner 2004). If scarcity appears to promote conflict, there is most likely a third factor causing both. Issues of distribution, power, and institutions are therefore more important than absolute resource scarcity as they mediate the actors' access to more or less scarce resources. While political ecologists do not generally side with the optimists, they are critical of ecoviolence models (see Hartmann 2014; Peluso and Watts 2001). Liberals share with many environmental optimists a belief in the beneficial effects of the market. With political ecologists, they share a focus on institutions, which they see as more important than the physical state of the environment. While liberals tend to focus on democracy and cooperation, political ecologists usually emphasize questions of distribution. Hence, these two schools often have divergent views of the effects of trade liberalization on livelihoods in the developing world.

The state of research

Theoretical shortcomings

The argument between the different schools of thought has generated much heat. Can we adjudicate this debate by means of systematic empirical evidence? The existing empirical literature suffers from several methodological problems. We will first deal with the case-based literature. We then turn to contemporary large-*n* research, which has recently grown too rapidly to permit a discussion study by study.

Case studies from the ecoviolence tradition, primarily represented by Homer-Dixon (1999) and his associates, as well as Bächler (1999) and Kahl (2006), have been criticized for lack of detail. The lack of archival research, detailed field research, and opinion surveys makes it difficult for the reader to identify the conflict actors and trace their motivations. Surprisingly few studies show clearly 'who did what to whom when and why' in conflicts where scarce renewable resources are said to play a role (Deligiannis 2012: 86). Moreover, studies that do contain such detailed information have only recently started to inform theoretical arguments in quantitative analyses. The lag has arguably occurred because such studies frequently belong to political ecology, anthropology, and geography – fields international relations scholars and economists are not very familiar with. Although some high-quality studies have been published in the last few years (e.g. Adano et al. 2012), case studies without sufficient detail still dominate the field, risking leading large-*n* researchers astray as processes driving complex conflicts are sometimes compared to aggression in baseball (see Raleigh et al. 2014 for a critique).

Homer-Dixon (1999) and his associates limited their studies to cases with armed conflict. Such a design provides a good starting point for a research programme, but makes it impossible to judge whether the conflict cases suffer from more severe scarcities than the peaceful cases, or what contextual factors matter. An improved research design was used by Bächler (1999), who studied twenty-one conflict and twenty-one non-conflict cases, and who reached more moderate conclusions regarding the role of renewable resources.

Another issue is how to measure scarcity. The concept of environmental scarcity (Homer-Dixon 1999) includes *supply-induced scarcity*, referring to the absolute supply of a resource, the ways of extracting it, and its vulnerability; *demand-induced scarcity*, which is driven by increasing consumption per capita; and *structural scarcity,* the distribution of a resource.[5] This operationalization has been criticized for lumping together quite disparate processes that could be seen as causes or effects of each other rather than supplements. For instance, scarcity of farmland (i.e. demand-induced scarcity) is frequently seen as a motivation for more intensive crop methods and economic diversification, while severe pollution or degradation (i.e. supply-induced scarcity) is much less likely to produce the same outcome (Fairhead 2001: 219).

Finally, scholars across methodological divides frequently refer to future wars as evidence. The statement by Ehrlich (1968: 11) that the battle to feed humanity has been lost is one example, the many references to 'climate wars' another (Schwartz and Randall 2003). While there may well be a potential for future conflict, pessimistic predictions must be accompanied by a solid theoretical argument for why future societies will be sufficiently different from the present to bring about such dramatic changes.

Large-n studies

The vast expansion of the quantitative literature on resource scarcity and conflict inspired hopes of discovering strong and robust relationships. If scarcities increase in the future, it could then be plausibly argued that we should expect more scarcity-based conflict. Although both methods and data are improving, the field is far from reaching agreement on linkages that are robust to different methods, operationalization of key concepts, time periods, or types of conflict (Bernauer et al. 2012; Buhaug et al. 2014; IPCC 2014; Meierding 2013; Scheffran et al. 2012).

An early review by Theisen (2008) shows that there is little consensus on the neo-Malthusian idea that scarcity of land and water is an important driver of civil conflict at the national level. Studies at sub-national levels are somewhat more supportive of land pressure and different forms of violence (e.g. André and Platteau 1998; Raleigh and Urdal 2007; Tadjoeddin et al. 2012). A number of studies have investigated the 'water wars' argument. Gleditsch et al. (2006) found that sharing a river increases the risk of low-level interstate conflict, although water scarcity does not appear to be very important. Brochmann and Gleditsch (2012), however, found with new data that it was difficult to distinguish between the effects of being neighbours and sharing a river. Hensel et al. (2006) analyzed specific river claims and found that water scarcity in the challenger state increases the risk of militarization of a river claim, while specific river institutions decrease the risk of a militarized outcome. Wolf (2007) found very few violent skirmishes in modern times but a very strong record of cooperative behaviour over water issues.

From an initial concern with slower-moving processes such as land pressure, the literature has shifted to a focus on shorter-term phenomena such as drought, temperature spikes, and natural disasters. Two studies in particular have generated heated debates. Miguel et al. (2004) used year-on-year changes in rainfall as an instrument for economic shocks, concluding that loss of rainfall increases conflict through its effect on economic growth. Although not targeted at the climate–security debate, the study has served as inspiration for several such studies. The study has been criticized for its conflict coding (Jensen and Gleditsch 2009) as well as for its measure of climate anomalies (Ciccone 2011). Several other studies have failed to find a robust link between rainfall as an instrument for growth on the one hand, and civil conflict as an outcome (Koubi et al. 2012; van Weezel 2014). Studies testing the direct effect of precipitation on civil conflict have found that less rainfall increases risk (Hendrix and Glaser 2007) and has no effect on conflict (Theisen et al. 2012), or decreases conflict risk (Hendrix and Salehyan 2012; Salehyan and Hendrix 2014). Over ten studies have analyzed rainfall and civil conflict in sub-Saharan Africa, without reaching consensus (Theisen et al. 2013).

A highly publicized study of temperature and conflict (Burke et al. 2009) found civil war in sub-Saharan Africa to be significantly more likely during warmer years, leading to an increase in civil war incidence of about 50 per cent by 2030 on current climate emission trajectories. This finding was challenged by Buhaug (2010), who demonstrated that their results are sensitive to the choice of estimation technique, sample period, and the choice of conflict data. While the jury is still out on the methodological divide, Burke et al. (2010) concede that temperature is unrelated to African civil war if more recent years are added to the analysis. Other recent studies fail to find robust effects of temperature on civil conflict (Couttenier and Soubeyran 2013; Klomp and Bulte 2013; Salehyan and Hendrix 2014).

A 'coming anarchy'?

The failure of the research community to reach a consensus begs the question whether there are any systematic relationships outside specific contexts. Most quantitative studies have focused on the role of scarcity in the form of droughts, heat waves, or natural disasters as motivations behind violent collective action. In this they have relied heavily on ecoviolence studies, or less tenable assumptions derived from psychology, which might be problematic, as they often overlook relevant literature that could point out other potential effects of contemporaneous or near-contemporaneous weather. Detailed research on farmer–herder conflicts in the Sahel (Turner 2004) or cattle raiding in East Africa (Adano et al. 2012) has shown that such fights are rarely motivated by a sudden fall in access to water or pasture. The immediate effects of weather in these contexts generate tactical responses that bear more resemblance to how the weather has affected tactical considerations in the conduct of conventional warfare (Winters 2001), than causing spontaneous fights over dwindling resources. Thus, analysis of contemporaneous relationships between weather and conflict run the risk of conflating tactical considerations about when to fight (or remain peaceful) with underlying motivations for fighting (see Landis 2014; Salehyan and Hendrix 2014 for recent discussions of this). Lagging the effect of resource variables by a few time-units would reduce this risk, but it would then deprive the researcher of the ability of analysing 'shocks' as potential triggers of violence.

In the search for the possible effects of scarce renewable resources on grievances, the potentially contradictory effects of adverse weather and land value in the short term often go unnoticed. As a drought sets in with the concomitant fall in food production, land prices tend to fall, and cattle prices even more so (Sen 1982). Thus, the motivation for fighting over scarce food – more valuable in drought years – might increase, while land and cattle – comparatively *less* valuable in drought years – could provide less of a motivation for fighting.[6] Conversely, in climatically good times the value of land and cattle rises and could provide greater motivation for contest.

Spatial factors also need more attention. Recently several studies have heeded the call of analysing potential local effects of resource scarcity (e.g. Theisen et al. 2012), but very few studies have been able to capture long-distance effects of weather or climate on resource scarcity. As the discussion of the Arab Spring in Egypt shows, suggested causes and effects may be thousands of miles apart and involve several steps between the ultimate cause and the final outcome. Moreover, geographically disaggregated analyses aiming at capturing local scarcity may suffer from myopia by conflating the actual locality of the fighting with the area where grievances have their origin (Detges 2014).

Based on this review of the literature, the more drastic apocalyptic scenarios forecasting global scarcities, mass deprivation, and major interstate and intrastate violence should be viewed with scepticism. However, local and regional scarcities are still possible, and in some cases even plausible. A major war over shared water resources seems very unlikely, while local and smaller armed clashes and military posturing cannot be ruled out. Resource scarcity is also likely to interact with factors such as economic development and political institutions in increasing the risk of conflict. Two channels, food security and migration (Bernauer et al. 2012), often feature as the most plausible links between climate change and violence. Some research has been carried out on food prices and different forms of violence (see above), but data constraints have impeded cross-national research on environmentally induced migration and violent conflict. The 'environmental migration' literature tends to overlook conventional explanations of migration and therefore overemphasizes environmental factors (Doevenspeck 2011). Similarly, alarmist claims about widespread conflicts over food caused by crop failures often overlook essential insights into how starvation and famines arise through processes of entitlement loss (Sen 1982).

Could drastic shifts change this picture? Human-induced climate change is often presented as the ultimate ecoviolence scenario. Figure 20.2 shows the Northern Hemisphere temperature patterns for the last 1500 years. This is the famous 'hockey stick', with the recent rise in temperature as the blade of the stick. Earlier versions of this graph have been criticized for underestimating extremes in the pre-1850 period.[7] Moreover, the last fifteen years have seen slower growth. Historically, this is a short period and the causes of the slowdown of global warming are not clear (IPCC 2013:194). There is broad scientific agreement that globally the past thirty to fifty years are warmer than any other period of that length during the last 800 years, and that this is mainly attributable to anthropogenic emissions (IPCC 2013: 386).

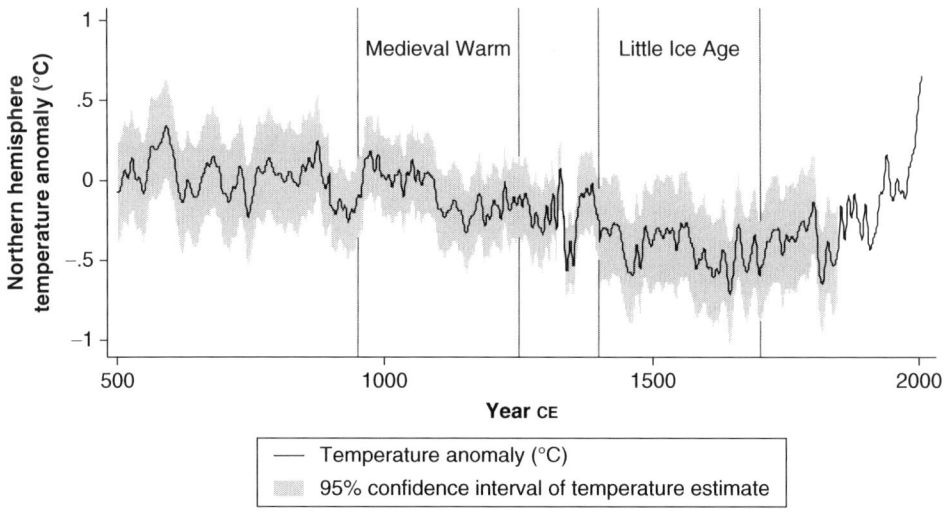

Figure 20.2 Northern Hemisphere temperature anomalies 500–2006 CE

Note: The graph shows the Northern Hemisphere mean temperature. Data from Mann et al. (2008).

The rise in temperatures plays a key role in some ecoviolence scenarios which foresee that some parts of the world will be more prone to violent conflict (e.g. Burke et al. 2009). But can year-to-year variations in weather – by far the most frequently used way to capture climatic effects on conflict – yield relevant information about social effects of long-term climate change? Climate is generally interpreted as the average weather over a longer period, typically thirty years (IPCC 2013). Critics, including the authors of Chapter 18 of the most recent IPCC assessment of the social effects of climate change, warn against conflating weather anomalies with climate change.[8] Studies using annual or monthly deviations from a period mean assume stationarity in the longer-term climate, which is unlikely (Busby et al. 2012), although for the short to medium term for Africa, the most studied region, 'observed rainfall variability is *greater* than changes [in levels] suggested by climate models for the next 50–100 years' (Adger et al. 2003: 187, italics in original). Analyses of climatic changes over the centennial and even millennial scale are more in line with the conventional definition of climate. Such studies have consistently found that periods with a climate less suitable for agricultural production, i.e. a *colder* climate in the temperate zone, see more upheavals and wars (e.g. Tol and Wagner 2010; Zhang et al. 2011), although an increasingly industrialized and globalized economy makes it hard to generalize these findings to the modern era.

Thus, we cannot be very specific about the implications of longer-term climate change on the risk of future violent conflict. Even within the generally accepted scenarios of a human-induced rise in global average temperature of 2–4 °C in the twenty-first century, we are unable to account reliably for the negative and positive effects on human affairs. While the Maldives and substantial parts of Bangladesh may be flooded by sea-level rise, Siberia may bloom from rising temperatures. Drastic climatic change will require adaptation which, while costly, may also lead to innovation. However, if nations act in unison to combat climate change and its adverse consequences, it could also have a rallying effect and lead to more cooperation and less conflict. Environmental and resource factors in conflict certainly warrant our attention; but our knowledge is limited. Only by mobilizing considerable hubris can we take for granted that man's domination of his environment is as benevolent as envisaged by the optimists or as malevolent as outlined in ecoviolence scenarios.

Notes

* We thank the Research Council of Norway for financial support (grant 240315/F10), and several colleagues at PRIO and NTNU for commenting on this chapter or the earlier version (Gleditsch and Theisen 2010). Replication data for the two graphs can be found at www.prio.no/cscw/datasets.
1 Based on the UCDP/PRIO conflict data, which include all armed conflicts with more than 25 battle-related deaths in a given year (Gleditsch et al. 2002; Themnér and Wallensteen 2014). The figures for battle deaths are from Lacina and Gleditsch (2005) and include civilian as well as military fatalities.
2 Also called cornucopians, Private Prometheans, or technological optimists.
3 We leave out the 'resource curse' hypothesis, as it focuses on locally abundant but globally scarce (primarily) non-renewable resources (Basedau and Lay 2009).
4 In the Machakos District in Kenya both the area's population and development level increased, resulting in higher yields per hectare and labor shortage (Tiffen et al. 1994).
5 A similar operationalization was applied by Kahl (2006).
6 See Adano et al. (2012) for argument along these lines concerning cattle. See Toulmin (1991) for a discussion of cattle and grain prices in response to drought.
7 For supplementary information on the data and the hockey-stick debate, cf. note 1 above.
8 Cf. Gleditsch and Nordås (2014: 5).

References

Adano, W. R., Dietz, T., Witsenburg, K., and Zaal, F. (2012) 'Climate Change, Violent Conflict and Local Institutions in Kenya's Drylands', *Journal of Peace Research* 49(1): 65–80.

Adger, W. N., Huq, S., Brown, K., Conway, D., and Hulme, M. (2003) 'Adaptation to Climate Change in the Developing World', *Progress in Development Studies* 3(3): 179–95.

André, C. and Platteau, J. P. (1998) 'Land Relations under Unbearable Stress: Rwanda Caught in the Malthusian Trap', *Journal of Economic Behavior and Organization* 34(1): 1–47.

Arezki, R. and Brückner, M. (2014) 'Effects of International Food Price Shocks on Political Institutions in Low-Income Countries', *World Development* 61(1): 142–53.

Bächler, G. (1999) *Violence through Environmental Discrimination*, Dordrecht: Kluwer Academic.

Basedau, M. and Lay, J. (2009) 'Resource Curse or Rentier Peace? The Ambiguous Effects of Oil Wealth and Oil Dependence on Violent Conflict', *Journal of Peace Research* 46(6): 757–76.

Bernauer, T., Böhmelt T., and Koubi, V. (2012) 'Environmental Changes and Violent Conflict', *Environmental Research Letters* 7(1): article no. 015601.

Boserup, E. (1965) *The Conditions of Agricultural Growth: The Economics of Agrarian Change under Population Pressure*, London: Allen and Unwin.

Brochmann, M. and Gleditsch, N. P. (2012) 'Shared Rivers and Conflict – A Reconsideration', *Political Geography* 31(8): 519–27.

Brundtland, G. H. et al. (1987) *Our Common Future*, Oxford: Oxford University Press, for the World Commission on Environment and Development.

Buhaug, H. (2010) 'Climate Not to Blame for African Civil Wars', *Proceedings of the National Academy of Sciences* 107(38): 16477–82.

Buhaug, H. et al. (2014) 'One Effect to Rule Them All?', *Climatic Change* 127(3–4): 391–7.

Buhaug, H., Benjaminsen, T. A., Sjaastad, E. O., Theisen, O. M. (2015) 'Climate Variability, Food Production Shocks, and Violent Conflict in Sub-Saharan Africa', Environmental Research Letters 10(12):125015

Burke, M. B., Miguel, E., Satyanath, S., Dykema, J. A., and Lobell, D. B. (2009) 'Warming Increases the Risk of Civil War in Africa', *PNAS* 106(49): 20670–4.

Burke, M. B., Miguel, E., Satyanath, S., Dykema, J. A., and Lobell, D. B. (2010) 'Climate Robustly Linked to African Civil War'. *PNAS* 107(51): E185

Busby, J. W., Gulledge, J., Smith, T., and White, K. (2012) 'Of Climate Change and Crystal Balls: The Future Consequences of Climate Change in Africa', *Air & Space Power Journal: Africa & Francophonie* 3(3): 4–44.

Ciccone, A. (2011) 'Economic Shocks and Civil Conflict: A Comment', *American Economic Journal: Applied Economics* 3(4): 215–27.

Couttenier, M. and Soubeyran, R. (2013) 'Drought and Civil War in Sub-Saharan Africa', *Economic Journal* 124(575): 201–44.

Deligiannis, T. (2012) 'The Evolution of Environment-Conflict Research: Toward a Livelihood Framework', *Global Environmental Politics* 12(1): 78–100.

Detges, A. (2014) 'Close-up on Renewable Resources and Armed Conflict', *Political Geography* 42: 57–65.

Doevenspeck, M. (2011) 'The Thin Line between Choice and Flight', *International Migration* 49(S1): e50–e68.

Ehrlich, P. R. (1968) *The Population Bomb*, New York: Ballantine.

Fairhead, J. (2001) 'International Dimensions of Conflict over Natural and Environmental Resources', in N. L. Peluso and M. Watts (eds.) *Violent Environments*, Ithaca, NY and London: Cornell University Press, 213–36.

Gates, S., Hegre, H., Nygård, H. M., and Strand, H. (2012) 'Development Consequences of Armed Conflict', *World Development* 40(9): 1713–22.

Gerland, P., Raftery, A. E., Ševčíková, H., Li, N., Gu1, D., Spoorenberg, T., Alkema, T., Bailey, K., Fosdick, J. C., Lalic, N., Bay, G., Buettner, T., Heilig, G. K., and Wilmoth, J. (2014) 'World Population Stabilization Unlikely This Century', *Science* 346(6206): 234–7.

Gleditsch, N. P. and Hegre, H. (1997) 'Peace and Democracy: Three Levels of Analysis', *Journal of Conflict Resolution* 41(2): 283–310.

Gleditsch, N. P. and Nordås R. (2014) 'Conflicting Messages? The IPCC on Conflict and Human Security', *Political Geography* 43(November): 82–90.

Gleditsch, N. P. and Sverdrup, B. O. (2002) 'Democracy and the Environment', in Redclift, M. and Page, E. A. (eds.) *Human Security and the Environment*, Cheltenham: Edward Elgar, 45–70.

Gleditsch, N. P. and Theisen, O. M. (2010) 'Resources, the Environment, and Conflict', in Dunn Cavelty, M. and Mauer, V. (eds.) *The Routledge Handbook of Security Studies*, London: Routledge. 221–31.

Gleditsch, N. P., Furlong, K., Hegre, H., Lacina, B., and Owen, T. (2006) 'Conflicts over Shared Rivers: Resource Scarcity or Fuzzy Boundaries?' *Political Geography* 25(4): 361–82.

Gleditsch, N. P., Wallensteen, P., Eriksson, M., Sollenberg, M., and Strand, H. (2002) 'Armed Conflict 1946–2001: A New Dataset', *Journal of Peace Research* 39(5): 615–37.

Hartmann, B. (2014) 'Converging on Disaster: Climate Security and the Malthusian Anticipatory Regime for Africa', *Geopolitics* 19(4): 757–83.

Hegre, H. (2014) 'Democracy and Armed Conflict', *Journal of Peace Research* 51(2): 159–72.

Hegre, H., Ellingsen, T., Gates, S., and Gleditsch, N. P. (2001) 'Towards a Democratic Civil Peace? Democracy, Political Change, and Civil War, 1816–1992', *American Political Science Review* 95(1): 17–33.

Hendrix, C. S. and Glaser, S. M. (2007) 'Trends and Triggers: Climate Change and Civil Conflict in Sub-Saharan Africa', *Political Geography* 26(6): 695–715.

Hendrix, C. S. and Salehyan, I. (2012) 'Climate Change, Rainfall, and Social Conflict in Africa', *Journal of Peace Research* 49(1): 35–50.

Hensel, P., Mitchell, S. M., and Sowers, T. E. (2006) 'Conflict Management of Riparian Disputes', *Political Geography* 25(4): 383–411.

Homer-Dixon, T. (1999) *Environment, Scarcity, and Conflict*, Princeton, NJ: Princeton University Press.

Hsiang, S. M., Burke, M., and Miguel, E. (2013) 'Quantifying the Influence of Climate on Human Conflict', *Science* 341(6151): 1212ff.

IPCC (2013) *Climate Change 2013: The Physical Science Basis. Contribution of Working Group I to the Fifth Assessment Report of the Intergovernmental Panel on Climate Change*, Cambridge: Cambridge University Press.

IPCC (2014) *Climate Change 2014: Impacts, Adaptation, and Vulnerability. Contribution of Working Group II to the Fifth Assessment Report of the Intergovernmental Panel on Climate Change*, Cambridge: Cambridge University Press.

Jensen, P. S. and Gleditsch, K. S. (2009) 'Rain, Growth, and Civil War: The Importance of Location', *Defense and Peace Economics* 20(5): 359–72.

Kahl, C. (2006) *States, Scarcity, and Civil Strife in the Developing World*, Princeton, NJ: Princeton University Press.

Klomp, J. and Bulte, E. (2013) 'Climate Change, Weather Shocks, and Violent Conflict: A Critical Look at the Evidence', *Agricultural Economics* 44, supplement: 63–78.

Koubi, V., Bernauer, T., Kalbhenn, A., and Spilker, G. (2012) 'Climate Variability, Economic Growth, and Civil Conflict', *Journal of Peace Research* 49(1): 113–27.

Lacina, B. and Gleditsch, N. P. (2005) 'Monitoring Trends in Global Combat: A New Dataset of Battle Deaths', *European Journal of Population* 21(2–3): 145–66.

Landis, S. T. (2014) 'Temperature, Seasonality and Violent Conflict: The Inconsistencies of a Warming Planet', *Journal of Peace Research* 51(5): 603–18.

Lonergan, S. C. (2001) 'Water and Conflict: Rhetoric and Reality', in P. F. Diehl and N. P. Gleditsch (eds.) *Environmental Conflict*, Boulder, CO: Westview, 109–24.

Lutz, W., Butz, W., and Samir, K. C. (2014) *World Population and Global Human Capital in the 21st Century*, Oxford: Oxford University Press.

Malthus, T. (1993[1798]) *An Essay on the Principle of Population*, Oxford: Oxford University Press.

Mann, M. E. et al. (2008) 'Proxy-Based Reconstruction of Hemispheric and Global Surface Temperature Variations over the Past Two Millennia', *PNAS* 105(36): 13252–7.

Maystadt, J. F., Tan, J. F. T., and Breisinger, C. (2014) 'Does Food Security Matter for Transition in Arab Countries?' *Food Policy* 46(2): 106–15.

Meadows, D., Randers, J., and Behrens, W. (1972) *The Limits to Growth: A Report for the Club of Rome on the Predicament of Mankind*, New York: Universe.

Meierding, E. (2013) 'Climate Change and Conflict: Avoiding Small Talk about the Weather', *International Studies Review* 15(2): 185–203.

Miguel, E., Satyanath, S., and Sergenti, E. (2004) 'Economic Shocks and Civil Conflict: An Instrumental Variable Approach', *Journal of Political Economy* 112(4): 725–53.

Myers, N. (1993) *Ultimate Security: The Environmental Basis of Political Stability*, New York: W. W. Norton.

Neumayer, E. (2002) 'Do Democracies Exhibit Stronger Environmental Commitment? A Cross-Country Analysis', *Journal of Peace Research* 39(2): 139–64.

Payne, R. A. (1995) 'Freedom and the Environment', *Journal of Democracy* 6(3): 41–55.

Peluso, N. L. and Watts, M. (2001) 'Violent Environments', in N. L. Peluso and M. Watts (eds.) *Violent Environments*, Ithaca, NY: Cornell University Press, 3–38.

Pinker, S. (2011) *The Better Angels of Our Nature: The Decline of Violence in History and Its Causes*, New York: Penguin.

Raleigh, C., Linke, A., and O'Loughlin, J. (2014) 'Extreme Temperatures and Violence', *Nature Climate Change* 4: 76–7.

Raleigh, C. and Urdal, H. (2007) 'Climate Change, Environmental Degradation, and Armed Conflict', *Political Geography* 26(6): 674–94.

Salehyan, I. and Hendrix, C. (2014) 'Climate Shocks and Political Violence', *Global Environmental Change* 28: 23 –50.

Scheffran, J., Brzoska, M., Kominek, J., Link, P. M., and Schilling, J. (2012) 'Climate Change and Violent Conflict', *Science* 336(6083): 869–71.

Schwartz, P. and Randall, D. (2003) *An Abrupt Climate Change Scenario and Its Implications for United States National Security*, Washington, DC: Environmental Media Services.

Sen, A. (1982) *Poverty and Famines*, Oxford: Clarendon Press.

Sen, A. (1989) `Food and Freedom', *World Development* 17(6): 769–81.

Simon, J. L. (1989) 'Lebensraum: Paradoxically, Population Growth May Eventually End Wars', *Journal of Conflict Resolution* 33(1):164–80.

Simon, J. L. (1996) *The Ultimate Resource 2*, Princeton, NJ: Princeton University Press.

Starr, J. R. (1991) 'Water Wars', *Foreign Policy* 82: 17–36.

Sternberg, T. (2012) 'Chinese Drought, Bread and the Arab Spring', *Applied Geography* 34: 519–24.

Tadjoeddin, M. Z., Chowdhury, A., and Murshed, S. M. (2012) 'Routine Violence in Java, Indonesia: Neo-Malthusian and Social Justice Perspectives', in J. Scheffran et al. (eds.) *Climate Change, Human Security and Violent Conflict*, Berlin: Springer, 633–50.

Theisen, O. M. (2008) 'Blood and Soil? Renewable Resource Scarcity and Internal Armed Conflict', *Journal of Peace Research* 45(6): 801–18.

Theisen, O. M., Gleditsch, N. P., and Buhaug, H. (2013) 'Is Climate Change a Driver of Armed Conflict?', *Climatic Change* 117(3): 613–25.

Theisen, O. M., Holtermann, H. and Buhaug, H. (2011/2012) 'Climate Wars? Assessing the Claim that Drought Breeds Conflict', *International Security* 36(3): 79–106.

Themnér, L. and Wallensteen, P. (2014) 'Armed Conflicts, 1946–2013', *Journal of Peace Research* 51(3): 541– 54.

Tiffen, M., Mortimore, M., and Gichuki, F. (1994) *More People, Less Erosion: Environmental Recovery in Kenya*, Chichester: Wiley.

Tol, R. S. J. and Wagner, S. (2010) 'Climate Change and Violent Conflict in Europe over the Past Millennium', *Climatic Change* 99(1–2): 65–79.

Toulmin, C. (1991) 'Tracking through Drought: Options for Destocking and Restocking', in I. Scoones (ed.) *Living with Uncertainty*, London: Intermediate Technology Publications, 95–115.

Turner, M. D. (2004) 'Political Ecology and the Moral Dimensions of "Resource Conflicts"', *Political Geography* 23(7): 863–89.

Weezel, S. van (2014) 'Economic Shocks and Civil Conflict Onset in Sub-Saharan Africa, 1981–2010', *Defence and Peace Economics* 26(2): 153–77.

Winters, H. A. G., Galloway, G. E., Jr, Reynolds, W. J., and Rhynel, D. W. (2001) *Battling the Elements: Weather and Terrain in the Conduct of War*, Baltimore, MD: Johns Hopkins University Press.

Wolf, A. T. (2007) 'Shared Waters: Conflict and Cooperation', *Annual Review of Environment and Resources* 32: 241–69.

World Bank (2015) *Prospects Commodity Markets,* Washington, DC: World Bank. Online. Available HTTP: <http://go.worldbank.org/4ROCCIEQ50> (accessed 06 November 2015).

Zhang, D. D., Lee, H. F., Wang, C., Li, B., Pei, Q., Zhang, J., and An, Y. (2011) 'The Causality Analysis of Climate Change and Large-Scale Human Crisis', *PNAS* 108(42): 17296–301.

21

PANDEMICS
AND GLOBAL HEALTH

Simon Rushton and Sonja Kittelsen

On 25 April 2009, on the basis of the outbreak and spread of a novel influenza virus with pandemic potential, the World Health Organization (WHO) Director-General, Margaret Chan, announced a Public Health Emergency of International Concern (PHEIC) – the first declaration of its kind following the entry into force of the revised International Health Regulations (IHR) in 2007. Shortly thereafter, on 11 June 2009, the WHO elevated its pandemic alert level to Phase 6, indicating that the circulating influenza A (H1N1) virus had entered a pandemic phase.

The declaration sparked controversy, as, by this point, experts already recognized that the impact of the H1N1 influenza virus was relatively mild compared to what had initially been feared. The WHO's decision to raise the pandemic alert level led to criticisms by some that the threat posed had been overstated, and to speculation regarding the extent to which the WHO's decision-making was politically motivated or unduly influenced by industry interests (Council of Europe Parliamentary Assembly 2010; Fidler 2009: 768). Managing H1N1 thus presented the WHO with not only an epidemiological challenge, but also a political one.

The 2009 H1N1 influenza outbreak and the controversy surrounding it is only one manifestation of the increased government, public, and media attention that has been paid to the threat of pandemics in recent years, especially since the turn of the millennium. The emergence of new viruses such as human immunodeficiency virus (HIV) in the 1980s and the Severe Acute Respiratory Syndrome (SARS) coronavirus in the early 2000s, the resurgence of old viruses in more volatile forms, and the possibility of biological agents being used to cause deliberate harm, have all drawn attention to the threat that the microbial world poses to individuals, states, and the global population.

Yet, this is in no sense new. History is replete with examples of the disruption disease has caused to militaries, societies, and economies. What distinguishes contemporary manifestations of the security–health link is the impact that globalization has had on the spatial and temporal dimensions of insecurity, and the consequences that this has had for how governments respond to the threat of disease emergence and spread. The past two decades have witnessed the rise of new forms of government action aimed at strengthening national and international capacities to rapidly detect and respond to an outbreak, in the full knowledge that in a globalized world an outbreak event is unlikely to be confined to one state alone.

As the controversy surrounding the 2009 H1N1 influenza pandemic demonstrates, determining what constitutes a health security threat and how we should respond to it is not just a technical matter, but a highly political (and politicized) one. The aim of this chapter is to exam-ine the political nature of this relationship between pandemics, global health, and security in three parts. The first part provides an overview of the concept of health security, addressing both how sources of insecurity are identified, and who or what is recognized as being threatened. The second part examines some of the most common contemporary responses to pandemic threats and discusses some of the controversial issues that they have raised. Following on from this dis-cussion, the third part looks at some of the political issues generated by the increasing tendency of some governments (especially those in industrialized Western countries) to approach pandem-ics in national security terms – in particular how the type of exceptional emergency responses that often characterize efforts to address immediate security threats can bring public health into conflict with other political, economic, and social values.

Pandemics, global health, and 'health security': security for whom and from what?

Neither 'global health' nor 'health security' are unified concepts. As Andrew Lakoff has noted, what global health entails differs depending on the actors involved in its promotion: 'different projects of global health imply starkly different understandings of the most salient threats facing global populations, of the relevant groups whose health should be protected, and of the appro-priate justification for health interventions that transgress national sovereignty' (Lakoff 2010: 59). In a similar vein, William Aldis (2008) has noted the absence of an agreed definition of health security. How that concept of health security is understood invariably determines how sources of insecurity are identified, who or what is recognized as threatened, and how responses are shaped. For example, whether one takes the individual, the state, or the global population as a whole as the referent object of health security inevitably has a bearing on how sources of health insecurity are identified and framed.

The various conceptualizations of the notion of health security that have emerged over the past couple of decades can broadly be categorized according to two lines of thinking – which Sara Davies has labelled 'statist' and 'globalist' approaches to health security (Davies 2009). As Davies has noted, the statist approach primarily focuses on the threat of disease to the economic, political, and military stability of the state and, in much of the academic literature, has often been associated with securitization theory. In contrast, the globalist perspective takes the individual as the referent object of security. Its starting point is the recognition of health as a fundamental human right and, in this regard, it has much in common with the concept of human security and with critical security theory (Davies 2009: 13–14; Davies 2010: 1170–1). Sources of health insecurity in a globalist mode are generally more broadly cast to encompass not only the threat of disease, but also the structural conditions that determine health outcomes.

While these modes of thinking about health security differ in conceptual terms, in prac-tice the distinction between them is often blurred. Independent of whether the referent object of security is seen as the individual or the state, both statist and globalist perspectives share a recognition of an increased vulnerability to a broadening array of health challenges, due to a growing interconnectedness associated with processes of globalization. Both approaches, moreo-ver, acknowledge a role for the state in providing for health security, albeit to varying degrees. Nevertheless, the distinction between these competing modes of thinking about health security is politically significant, as the different rationales for intervention underpinning them have direct bearing on how global health priorities are set. This includes determining what health challenges fall into and out of focus, as well as the appropriate means of responding to identified sources of insecurity.

Whilst the concept of human security has gained support from a variety of actors – within the UN System, global civil society, and academia – it is the more statist approaches to health security that have tended to have a tangible policy impact. Increasing media and political attention on so-called 'Emerging Infectious Diseases' (EIDs) through the 1990s led to infectious diseases rising up the security agendas of key states – not least the United States (King 2002; Weir and Mykhalovskiy 2010).

The HIV/AIDS pandemic, for example, gained particular prominence as a security issue. In addition to having devastating consequences for individuals and communities affected by the disease, the scale and spread of HIV/AIDS, particularly in sub-Saharan Africa, led academics and policy-makers alike to focus on the possible impact of the pandemic on state and regional stability (Altman 2003; National Intelligence Council 2002; Singer 2002). This included the possible impact of the virus on peacekeeping forces and the armed forces of the state. In a seminal move in July 2000, the United Nations Security Council (UNSC) passed Resolution 1308 recognizing HIV/AIDS as a 'risk to stability and security' in Africa on the basis of the vulnerability of peacekeeping forces to HIV/AIDS and the possibility of these forces serving as vectors in spreading the disease further (UNSC 2000). While the causal links between some of these claims have since come under scrutiny (Barnett and Prins 2006; McInnes and Rushton 2010), the HIV/AIDS pandemic continues to hold resonance as a security issue in some quarters. In 2011, the Security Council reiterated the potential security implications of HIV/AIDS in Resolution 1983 (UNSC 2011).

In addition to the HIV/AIDS pandemic, this statist view of health security threats has been bolstered by the experience of SARS in 2002–3, the resurgence of the H5N1 avian influenza virus in 2004–5, the H1N1 influenza pandemic in 2009, and most recently, the Ebola outbreak in West Africa in 2014–15. In these cases the link between infectious disease and national/international security has been argued along three broad lines: (1) that disease can threaten international stability (for example through negatively impacting the global economy, through the instigation of migration flows or impacting on the operational capacity of militaries and peacekeeping forces); (2) that it can disrupt the economic and political stability of states; and (3) that disease can create high rates of morbidity and mortality (McInnes and Lee 2012: 148–54). The scale of the Ebola outbreak, for example, raised international alarm not only on the basis of the clear devastation that it caused for those individuals and communities affected, but also due to the risk that it was thought to pose to state and regional stability. On 18 September 2014, the UNSC passed Resolution 2177, declaring the Ebola outbreak a 'threat to international peace and security' on precisely these grounds (UNSC 2014).

The possibility of a biological agent being released for the purposes of deliberate harm, highlighted by the 2001 anthrax attacks in the United States, marks another prominent manifestation of the security–health link – raising the possibility that future pandemics may not always be naturally occurring. While the threat of biological attack is not a new security concern, the 2001 anthrax attacks underscored the utility of a robust public health capacity in not only detecting and containing naturally emerging diseases, but also in defending against the possibility of a deliberate biological attack (Heymann 2003: 202).

However, while global health in general has received increased political attention since the turn of the millennium, many scholars have argued that the focus on the security implications of infectious diseases (and, overwhelmingly, on the national and international, rather than human security implications) has meant that a select set of diseases have been successfully propelled into the realm of 'high politics' at the expense of a more holistic view of the threats to health that people around the world face on a day-to-day basis. It is thus not surprising that, despite the changes that globalization (and, in many countries, the neoliberal 'rolling back' of the state) has wrought, governments remain at the heart of contemporary efforts to address those health issues that have most commonly been identified as security threats – not least pandemics. The next section of this chapter will examine how health security is pursued in more detail, by focusing on some of the most notable national and global responses to disease-based security threats.

Common responses to pandemic threats

Governments seek to respond to pandemics in a variety of ways, which can vary according to a range of factors including the nature of the outbreak; the society, economy, and political system of the state; and the extent to which the government in question perceives the outbreak to represent a threat to its national security or other vital interests.

Emergency powers of various kinds are often used to address major disease outbreaks, including measures such as the use of forcible quarantine (in which those who appear to be well but may have been exposed to a disease have their movements restricted); compulsory vaccination or medical treatment; and the conscription of medical professionals to assist in tackling the emergency (Colmers and Fox 2003: 398). Other common emergency responses include 'social distancing' measures (for example closing schools and transport infrastructure), introducing health checks at borders, refusing to allow air travel from particular destinations, or preventing the import of certain types of goods. Emergency healthcare measures, such as the creation of temporary isolation facilities, are also often put in place at hospitals and medical centres in order to allow them to treat a higher than normal number of people and to control the spread of infection. Typically these emergency powers will be exercised for a limited time only, with things returning to normal once the situation has been brought under control.

Alongside these short-term emergency responses, governments concerned by the security implications of disease have also sought to take longer-term approaches to preparing for pandemics. Four examples of such strategies are: preparedness planning; investing in research and development for 'medical countermeasures'; stockpiling pharmaceuticals and other medical supplies; and seeking to enhance international cooperation to improve the coordination of global responses to health security threats. Here we briefly examine each of these forms of response.

Preparedness

The concept of 'preparedness' has increasingly entered the policy discourse in many states in recent years, partly in response to infectious disease threats, but also to other security challenges, including natural disasters and climate change. The aim of public health preparedness is to help prevent, mitigate, and recover from a health emergency (Nelson et al. 2007). The range of specific activities that fall under the rubric of preparedness is wide (e.g. CDC 2011), including developing the laboratory capacity to promptly detect and diagnose outbreaks; improving the ability of the public health infrastructure to deal with a major outbreak; ensuring that different levels and branches of government share information and coordinate their responses; and putting in place plans and systems to enable the different emergency services to work together.

Research and development

Some countries – the United States being by far the most active in this regard – have also sought to increase the range of medical responses available through funding and conducting research and development into 'medical countermeasures' (which includes pharmaceuticals and biologics such as vaccines, antibodies, and antimicrobials, as well as diagnostics and other medical technologies) to prevent and mitigate the effects of disease outbreaks, whether naturally occurring or manmade. In the US case it is the possibility of biological weapons being used by terrorist groups, 'lone wolf' individual terrorists, or 'rogue states' that has primarily driven this effort. In the decade following the 2001 9/11 attacks and the subsequent 'Amertithrax' anthrax letter attacks, the US government spent approximately US$60 billion on biodefence programmes (Hayden 2011), a large proportion of which was dedicated to scientific research into detecting, diagnosing, and treating pathogens.

These programmes have caused significant controversy. Some have argued that, despite the focus on biological weapons threats, these research efforts have had significant knock-on benefits for public health more broadly (e.g. Burnett et al. 2005) – not least in better equipping us to deal with pandemic disease threats. Others, however, believe that the real effect of this investment has been to promote and enrich a 'biodefence industrial complex' (Fidler and Gostin 2007); that the money which has been spent has been used ineffectively; that the prioritization of programmes focusing on a narrow range of biological agents has diverted attention from naturally occurring disease threats (Scientists Working Group on Biological and Chemical Weapons 2010); and that the massive scale-up of biodefence research could actually increase rather than reduce the security threat.

Stockpiling

The creation of national strategic stockpiles of medicines and other supplies has also been prioritized by some governments seeking to ensure that they have the resources available and ready to be deployed in the case of a major health emergency. Again, these preparedness efforts have not been uncontroversial. In some countries there have been public debates around the resource implications of maintaining large stocks of medicines that may never be needed, coupled with doubts around the efficacy of some of the commonly stockpiled medicines – as seen in debates over the UK's and US' stockpiling of Tamiflu (van Noorden 2014). Some have suggested that commercial interests may have influenced the adoption of these resource-intensive preparedness strategies (Cohen and Carter 2010), whilst some countries in the global South have complained that the West's stockpiling of such drugs (as well as other initiatives such as making advance purchase agreements with pharmaceutical manufacturers) has led to the health security of rich, industrialized countries being protected at the expense of poorer parts of the world, who are as a result unable to acquire the medicines they need – either because they are priced out or because global supplies are limited.

Global coordination

Finally, one of the notable features of the discourse around health security is that, even where that security has been understood in statist terms, there has been a strong emphasis on the need for international cooperation, and for disease-based threats to be addressed at the global level. The IHR (WHO 2005) – the WHO-led global framework through which countries share information about disease outbreaks of potential international significance, as well as coordinate the global response – is the centrepiece of this international cooperative effort. These regulations were significantly updated in 2005 in order to tackle some of the problems with the previous arrangements (in particular that they applied only to a small number of specified diseases, and that – as we discuss in the next section – governments often failed to report outbreaks for fear of the economic and political consequences of doing so).

It is undoubtedly the case that an increasing awareness amongst governments of the global nature of health security was crucial in generating the political momentum that led to this new international agreement. But again it has led to some tensions between the global North and some states in the global South who have argued that the updated IHR impose significant costs upon them (in particular the requirement that they strengthen their domestic public health surveillance infrastructure) without sufficient support from the developed world (who are primarily the ones who see the strengthening of global disease surveillance as a security imperative) (Davies et al. 2015; Rushton 2011).

Balancing health security with other values

Each type of response to pandemic disease threats, then, has generated controversy – and those controversies are yet to be resolved. But aside from these specific debates there are some other big political questions that are raised by the move towards understanding pandemics in security terms. In particular, the types of exceptional response that often characterize attempts to address perceived security threats can have the consequence of bringing public health into conflict with other social, political, and economic values. This raises deeply political questions about 'how much' health security we want or need (as individuals, or as nations), and what we are prepared to sacrifice in order to get it.

In this section we examine three areas in which trade-offs frequently have to be made between infectious disease control and other values: how to limit the progress of pandemics without causing international travel and trade to grind to a halt; how to balance the human rights and civil liberties of individuals with the need to protect the health of the wider community; and the extent to which a focus upon pandemic disease threats may distort the policy agenda, drawing much-needed attention and resources away from other pressing global issues (including other global health issues). In each of these three cases we see 'what is best for health security' being balanced against other things that we value as societies: free travel and trade; individual rights and freedoms; and opportunity costs.

Disease containment vs. travel and trade

The problem of new diseases being imported through travel and trade has been present throughout history, and many public health innovations (such as the introduction of quarantine practices in fourteenth-century Venice (Gensini et al. 2004)) have developed as a response to disease threats associated with trading with other societies. As mentioned, globalization has exacerbated this problem, increasing both the overall volume of international travel and trade as well as its rapidity.

Closing borders to imports from a country affected by a major disease outbreak has been a common response – and it is equally common that travellers decide (or are advised) not to visit an affected city, region, or country. The SARS outbreak of 2003 was one of the most dramatic recent examples of this, with the virus spreading rapidly across continents and significantly affecting international travel and trade. Indeed the SARS outbreak was thought at the time to pose a catastrophic threat to the global economy (although later analyses found that economies recovered to their pre-outbreak levels relatively soon after SARS was contained (Keogh-Brown and Smith 2008)).

As a result of these consequences, governments have in some cases been unwilling to alert the outside world to the existence of an outbreak. There have been many cases – including SARS, where China initially attempted to cover up the outbreak – where governments have deliberately withheld information from the international community, hampering the international response and increasing the likelihood of a localized outbreak becoming a global pandemic for which the world is unprepared. Some of the innovations in the 2005 IHR were intended to address precisely this problem, including giving authority to the WHO to take action on the basis of non-government reports of an outbreak and establishing a stronger role for the WHO in recommending travel and trade measures.

The stated purpose of the IHR is 'to prevent, protect against, control, and provide a public health response to the international spread of disease in ways that are commensurate with and restricted to public health risks, and which avoid unnecessary interference with international traffic and trade' (WHO 2005: Art.2). Given both the centrality of international travel and trade to the contemporary global economy and the increasing degree to which infectious diseases are seen as security threats, striking this balance is perhaps more politically difficult now than in any previous period. There is a clear trade-off between the two potentially competing values: it is impossible to entirely eliminate the risk of diseases travelling across borders (in other words to be completely 'secure') so long as people and goods do.

Disease containment vs. human rights and civil liberties

Efforts to protect public health have also long involved a trade-off between the rights and freedoms of individuals and the protection of the community as a whole from infectious disease threats. From the practice of 'shutting up' infected houses during the plague in seventeenth-century London (McKinlay 2009) to the enforced quarantine procedures put in place in West Africa to attempt to control the spread of Ebola (Eba 2014), individuals with (or suspected of having been exposed to) a serious infectious disease have often found their freedom of movement restricted in the name of public health.

It is not only in response to rapidly spreading infections like Ebola that we have seen individual rights and liberties compromised. HIV/AIDS has triggered a particularly vigorous debate over the rights of People Living with HIV and AIDS (PLWHA) since HIV was first identified in the early 1980s. This was in part a result of the fact that many of those communities most affected (such as men who have sex with men, sex workers, and intravenous drug users) had long been victims of discrimination and denial of rights even before HIV came on the scene. Yet the responses of many governments to HIV were highly controversial and were frequently justified on the grounds of protecting population health.

This problem has not gone unrecognized. For instance, 'The Siracusa Principles' (UN Commission on Human Rights 1984) set out the conditions under which it is permissible for governments to derogate from the International Convention on Civil and Political Rights – including in cases of public health emergency (see Amon 2014). Whilst non-binding in terms of international law, these principles nevertheless set clear standards for the restriction of individual rights against which national policies during pandemics can be tested.

In addition to being problematic on ethical and human rights grounds, there is evidence to suggest that approaches to disease control which unduly infringe rights and liberties can also undermine the efficacy of the response. During the 2014 Ebola outbreak, for example, there was at least one documented case of a 'break out' from an enforced quarantine facility, and many cases of people, distrustful of the authorities, seeking to conceal cases of infection. Studies of PLWHA affected by travel restrictions also found evidence of potential negative health consequences, for example cases where PLWHA would cease taking medications when they visited the US (which for many years refused entry to PLWHA) due to concerns that the discovery of AIDS drugs in their luggage could lead to them being turned back at the border (Mahto et al. 2006).

Here again we see health security being balanced against other values. In pure public health terms, separating those individuals who have a disease (or who may have a disease but are not yet displaying symptoms) from the rest of the community who are uninfected is the most effective form of containment. But both ethical and practical considerations also weigh upon decision making, meaning that hard choices often have to be made about how much individual freedom we are prepared to trade for security – choices that are often made even harder by the conditions of emergency and uncertainty that frequently characterize pandemic response.

Addressing security threats vs. distorting the health agenda

Finally, as with all resource allocation decisions, there are trade-offs between investing in preparing for and responding to pandemic disease threats and the opportunity costs of not being able to use those resources in pursuit of other objectives. If, as the Copenhagen School suggests, the result of securitization is to prioritize those issues seen as 'security threats' above others, then it naturally follows that those that are not seen as security issues may be under-prioritized in comparison. These prioritizations play out at both the national and international levels.

Nationally, there have been a number of debates in recent years over the preparedness plans put in place (particularly by governments in the West) in relation to potential future pandemics, with disagreements centring on whether this is an effective use of resources (which could otherwise be used to address other health issues) and the effectiveness of some of the preparedness measures that have been adopted. For example, as we discussed above, there have been debates over the extent to which pharmaceutical stockpiles offer value. In a context in which health system expenditure on pharmaceuticals and other medical technologies continues to increase rapidly, and even in the most wealthy countries political debates over the affordability and rationing of drugs for cancer and myriad other conditions are ongoing, some have been concerned that the perception of pandemics as security threats has allowed drugs intended to treat certain types of conditions to break free of the financial restrictions that would otherwise apply – even though (given that pharmaceuticals have a shelf life, and the likelihood or nature of future pandemics is in any case unknown) there is a real possibility that the drugs stockpiled in the name of pandemic preparedness may never actually be used.

A similar debate plays out at the global level over the impact that the securitization of a select group of diseases has had on the overall global health agenda – not least as it pertains to international aid. Given that pandemics (with the notable exception of HIV/AIDS) are responsible for relatively few deaths globally each year compared with big global killers such as ischaemic heart disease, stroke, lower respiratory infections, and chronic obstructive lung disease – the top four on the WHO's current list of causes of death worldwide (WHO 2014) – there are questions over the extent to which pandemics are prioritized and – more conceptually – over the way in which statist national security-based approaches (some would argue Western national security-based approaches) to disease threats have crowded out globalist human security considerations. If we look at the day-to-day health issues that are most threatening to human well-being around the world, after all, pandemic diseases scarcely register. On the other hand, the potential devastation that a major pandemic could cause, not only in terms of human life and well-being but also economic cost, is incalculable. Again, therefore, we see the trading-off of investment in addressing potential future health risks against investment in other health threats – or in strengthening health systems.

Conclusions

All of these political trade-offs highlight the difficulties of responding to pandemic events in ways that address security concerns over the impact of pandemic diseases whilst at the same time being commensurate with other goals and interests. Achieving these balances is further complicated by the fact that decisions about how to respond to a pandemic are often taken in emergency situations characterized by a lack of clear information about the scale and nature of the threat; media and public pressure for the authorities to 'do something'; risk aversion (although governments can be criticized not only if they have failed to prepare, but also if they are perceived to have over-hyped a threat); and in some cases an absence of effective 'medical countermeasures' – for example in the case of emerging and re-emerging infectious diseases where it can often be the case that no effective vaccines or treatments exist.

This has led some to question whether the securitization of pandemics is ultimately a good thing. On the one hand, securitization can be beneficial in galvanizing both political attention and resources to address a number of disease challenges. Certainly the investment in prepared-ness over the course of the past decade (which has not just come from the health sector, but from security budgets) can at least in part be attributed to a perceived security imperative. On the other hand, as the discussion on pandemic response has illustrated, the convergence of the realms of health and security also raises concerns on ethical, practical, and political grounds. These concerns relate not only to what global health issues receive the attention of governments and the international community (raising questions about how those priorities are set, and in whose interests), but also to the extent to which a securitized response to the threat of disease – whether in the short or longer term – disproportionately or unnecessarily interferes with other rights, priorities or values.

The effects of securitizing pandemic diseases have been profound, affecting not only health policy but also how security is practised – what Stefan Elbe has described as the 'medicalization of security' (Elbe 2010). The emphasis placed on medicalized responses to the security threat posed by pandemics, such as epidemiological surveillance or pharmaceutical stockpiling, has clear implica-tions for global health, drawing attention away from 'upstream' efforts to prevent disease outbreaks (for example by grappling with the thorny questions of the social and economic determinants of health) in favour of short-term emergency responses to emerging but transient threats. The securiti-zation of pandemics may even have wider political consequences for the international system. With an increased focus on global health security comes the expectation that governments will monitor and effectively manage disease spread within their populations (Elbe 2010: 173). Those that fail (or are simply unable) to do so could find themselves being seen by their peers as pariah states.

Given this link between disease control and legitimate governance, the rise of health security, particularly in its statist form, may ultimately provide a legitimating argument for more powerful states to breach the sovereignty of others in the event of an outbreak that garners international concern (Elbe 2011: 220–1). The political relationship between pandemics, global health, and security, then, not only has effects on security policy and health service provision, but also speaks to fundamental questions of power and interest in the international system.

References

Aldis, W. (2008) 'Health Security as a Public Health Concept: A Critical Analysis', *Health Policy and Planning* 23(6): 369–75.
Altman, D. (2003) 'AIDS and Security', *International Relations* 17(4): 417–27.
Amon, J. J. (2014) 'Health Security and/or Human Rights?', in S. Rushton and J. Youde (eds.) *The Routledge Handbook of Global Health Security*, Abingdon: Routledge, 293–303.
Barnett, T. and Prins, G. (2006) 'HIV/AIDS and Security: Fact, Fiction and Evidence – a Report to UNAIDS', *International Affairs* 82(2): 359–68.
Burnett, J. C., Panchal, R. G., Aman, M. J., and Bavari, S. (2005) 'The Rapidly Advancing Field of Biodefense Benefits Many Other, Critical Public Health Concerns', *Discovery Medicine* 5(28): 371–7.
Centers for Disease Control and Prevention (2011) *Public Health Preparedness Capabilities: National Standards for State and Local Planning*, Atlanta, GA: CDC.
Cohen, D. and Carter, P. (2010) 'Conflicts of Interest: WHO and the Pandemic Flu "Conspiracies"', *British Medical Journal* 340(7759): 1274–9.

Colmers, J. M. and Fox, D. M. (2003) 'The Politics of Emergency Health Powers and the Isolation of Public Health', *American Journal of Public Health*, 93(3): 397–9.

Council of Europe Parliamentary Assembly (2010) *Handling of the H1N1 Pandemic: More Transparency Needed*, Resolution 1749. Final version.

Davies, S. E. (2009) *Global Politics of Health*, Cambridge: Polity Press.

Davies, S. E. (2010) 'What Contribution Can International Relations Make to the Evolving Global Health Agenda?', *International Affairs* 86(5): 1167–90.

Davies, S. E., Kamradt-Scott, A., and Rushton, S. (2015) *Disease Diplomacy: International Norms and Global Health Security*, Baltimore, MD: Johns Hopkins University Press.

Eba, P. M. (2014) 'Ebola and Human Rights in West Africa', *The Lancet* 384: 2091–2.

Elbe, S. (2010) *Security and Global Health: Toward the Medicalization of Insecurity*, Cambridge: Polity Press.

Elbe, S. (2011) 'Should Health Professionals Play the Global Health Security Card?', *The Lancet* 378(9787): 220–1.

Fidler, D. P. (2009) 'H1N1 after Action Review: Learning from the Unexpected, the Success and the Fear', *Future Microbiology* 4(7): 767–9.

Fidler, D. P. and Gostin, L. O. (2007) *Biosecurity in the Global Age: Biological Weapons, Public Health, and the Rule of Law*, Palo Alto, CA: Stanford University Press.

Gensini, G., Yacoub, M., and Conti, A. (2004) 'The Concept of Quarantine in History: From Plague to SARS', *Journal of Infection* 49(4): 257–61.

Hayden, E. C. (2011) 'Biodefence since 9/11: The Price of Protection', *Nature* 477(7363): 150–2.

Heymann, D. (2003) 'The Evolving Infectious Disease Threat: Implications for National and Global Security', *Journal of Human Development* 4(2): 191–207.

Keogh-Brown, M. and Smith, R. D. (2008) 'The Economic Impact of SARS: How Does the Reality Match the Predictions?', *Health Policy* 88(1): 110–20.

King, N. B. (2002) 'Security, Disease, Commerce: Ideologies of Post-Colonial Global Health', *Social Studies of Science* 32(5/6): 763–89.

Lakoff, A. (2010) 'Two Regimes of Global Health', *Humanity* 1(1): 59–79.

Mahto, M., Ponnusamy, K., Schuhwerk, M., Richens, J., Lambert, N., Wilkins, E., Churchill, D. R., Miller, R. F., and Behrens, R. H. (2006) 'Knowledge, Attitudes and Health Outcomes in HIV-infected Travellers to the USA', *HIV Medicine* 7(4), 201–4.

McInnes, C. and Lee, K. (2012) *Global Health and International Relations*, Cambridge: Polity Press.

McInnes, C. and Rushton, S. (2010) 'HIV, AIDS and Security: Where Are We Now?', *International Affairs* 86(1): 225–45.

McKinlay, A. (2009) 'Foucault, Plague, Defoe', *Culture and Organization* 15(2): 167–84.

National Intelligence Council (2002) *The Next Wave of HIV/AIDS: Nigeria, Ethiopia, Russia, India, and China*, ICA 2002-04D, September.

Nelson, C., Lurie, N., Wasserman, J., and Zakowski, S. (2007) 'Conceptualizing and Defining Public Health Emergency Preparedness', *American Journal of Public Health* 97(Suppl. 1): S9–S11.

Rushton, S. (2011) 'Global Health Security: Security for Whom? Security from What?', *Political Studies* 59(4): 779–96.

Scientists Working Group on Biological and Chemical Weapons (2010) 'Biological Threats: A Matter of Balance', *Bulletin of the Atomic Scientists*, February 2.

Singer, P. W. (2002) 'Aids and International Security', *Survival* 44(1): 145–58.

United Nations Commission on Human Rights (1984) *The Siracusa Principles on the Limitation and Derogation Provisions in the International Covenant on Civil and Political Rights*, 28 September 1984, E/CN.4/1985/4. Online. Available HTTP: <http://www.refworld.org/cgi-bin/texis/vtx/rwmain?docid=4672bc122> (accessed 10 August 2015).

United Nations Security Council (2000) *Resolution 1308*, S/RES/1308, 17 July.

United Nations Security Council (2011) *Resolution 1983*, S/RES/1983, 7 June.

United Nations Security Council (2014) *Resolution 2177*, S/RES/2177, 18 September.

van Noorden, R. (2014) 'Report Disputes Benefit of Stockpiling Tamiflu', *Nature*, 10 April. Online. Available HTTP: <http://www.nature.com/news/report-disputes-benefit-of-stockpiling-tamiflu-1.15022> (accessed 4 June 2014).

Weir, L. and Mykhalovskiy, E. (2010) *Global Public Health Vigilance: Creating a World on Alert*, New York: Routledge.

World Health Organization (2005) *International Health Regulations (2005)*, Geneva: WHO.

World Health Organization (2014) *The Top 10 Causes of Death*, Fact Sheet No. 310, May. Online. Available HTTP: <http://www.who.int/mediacentre/factsheets/fs310/en/> (accessed 10 August 2015).

PART III

Regional (in)security

22

CHINA'S RISE: COUNTERPRODUCTIVE FEARMONGERING

Jiun Bang and David C. Kang*

Can China rise peacefully? For many, the answer is clearly *no*. In fact, John Mearsheimer (2014: 410–11) admits that his assessment is 'downright depressing' and hopes that actual developments will 'contradict my theory and prove my predictions wrong'. For others like Zhu Feng (2008: 54), 'China is a satisfied, cooperative, and peaceful country'. Indeed, China's four decades of unprecedented economic growth and diplomatic dynamism have prompted tremendous diverging speculation about the regional and global implications (Goh 2007/8; Kang 2007; Ross 2006; Womack 2006). Although two balance-of-power blocs are unlikely to characterize contemporary East Asia, neither has China regained its place at the top of the regional hierarchy. Perhaps the most important question, then, regarding China's emergence is whether contemporary China – operating in a Western-derived, Westphalian world order – can find a place for itself within this larger order that is both stable and legitimate.

The real tragedy here, of course, is that time has passed considerably since the first fearmongering about China's ascent, and yet we are still stuck asking the same misleading question. *China has, in fact, already risen.* In this chapter, we show what this power transition entails in three parts. In the first, we describe Chinese regional dominance in general terms. In the second, we look at the aspect of armament in the region, a main factor for fears of instability in East Asia. We show that, contrary to many predictions, there is no arms race happening, and that the power transition, overall, is taking place peacefully. In the third, we focus on China's regional and global economic impact, which further cements the picture of an overall peaceful power transition.

Power transition: general aspects

Although China has not passed the United States (US) on a global scale, by many measures China has already completed an Asian regional power transition. China's share of regional Gross Domestic Product (GDP) in 1988 was 7.4 per cent; today it is 46 per cent, while Japan has fallen from 72 per cent of regional GDP in 1988 to 24 per cent today (Figure 22.1). In 1988, China's share of East Asian trade was 6.6 per cent, while Japan's share was 47 per cent (World Bank 2013). Today, China's share of regional trade is 40 per cent, and Japan's share is 12 per cent. Furthermore, despite decades of pessimistic predictions about the end of Chinese economic growth, China continues to grow at a higher rate than its neighbours (Goldstone 1995; Chang 2001).

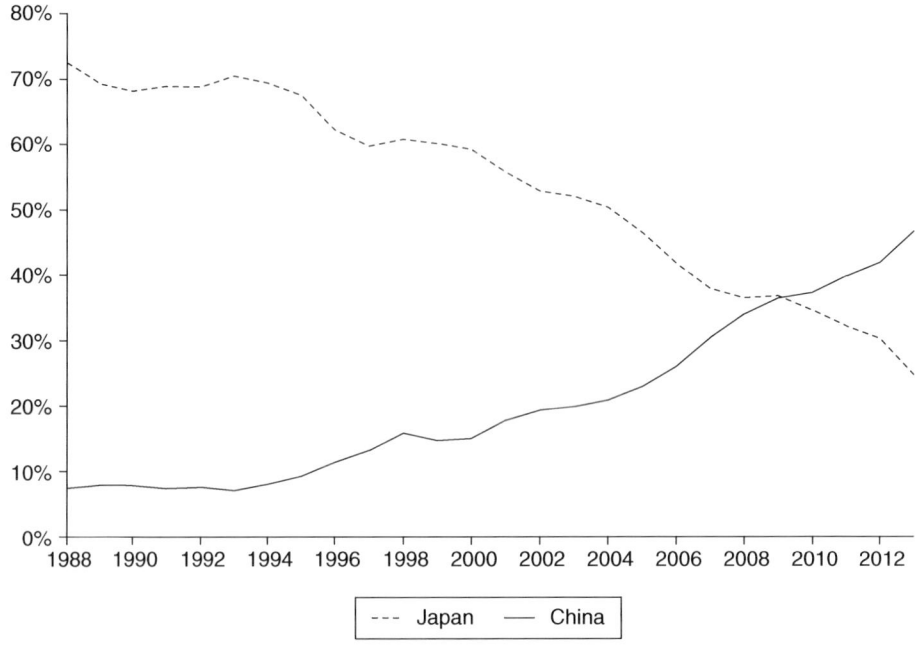

Figure 22.1 China's and Japan's share of East Asian GDP, 1988–2013. Countries: Australia, China,
        Indonesia, Japan, Malaysia, Philippines, Singapore, South Korea, Taiwan, Thailand, Vietnam

Source of data: World Bank development indicators.

As for US–China relations, at almost any time since 1978 the US could have identified China as the most likely challenger to US hegemony, prompting a preventive war by the US. After all, China in 1988 produced 5.8 per cent of US GDP and today produces 55 per cent. Within less than thirty years, China has become second globally to the US in GDP and military expenditure. This growth was transparent, obvious, and massive.

China has already risen to regional dominance, and has done so without major war. Three decades of leaders in these countries have seen China's military and economic growth and have decided year after year not to contest that growth and not to prepare their militaries for war. It is probably unrealistic to argue that the US and East Asian governments have been so myopic that a generation of their foreign policy, political, and military leaders have been unable to see China's growth as a dominant East Asian actor and a potential challenger to the US. In short, while 'just wait' for East Asian balancing might have been a credible expectation in the mid-1980s or even the 1990s, that regional power transition is now complete. There is no doubt about which country will be the most powerful or have the largest economy. Rather, the only question in the region is *how big* that gap between China and its neighbours will become. If East Asian states were going to compete with China and attempt to keep up, they should have started long ago. Those who still expect a balancing or containment coalition to arise against China in the future instead need to explain why this has not yet occurred.

Although China's ascent carries global implications, its impact is felt most directly, and most immediately, in East Asia. While China may have achieved regional pre-eminence, it clearly has not yet become a global force similar to that of the US. Not surprisingly, some notable scholars in China have had no problems with roughly equating China's regional strategy to that of its grand strategy given its 'very limited global interests' (Zhang and Tang 2005: 48). It is easy to play up China as a donor of aid – particularly to countries in Africa – and easy to forget its dual role as a recipient. In fact, China is eligible for World Bank lending as one of twenty-four developing countries identified in East Asia and the Pacific (alongside Fiji, North Korea, and Palau), and has loans from the International Bank for Reconstruction and Development (IBRD) totalling a sum (original principal) of $571.5 million in the three-month period ending on 31 March 2015 (World Bank Group 2015).

Nevertheless, while US leaders might have ignored China's growth for the time being, it is now clear that China is the most likely long-run challenger to the US. One reason that a preventive war or even major tensions between China and the US have not occurred lies in the fact that the two are negotiating a different issue from those typically identified by rationalists. Although, in theory, states can negotiate over any issue that involves revising the status quo, Powell (2002: 8) notes that it is 'usually about territory'. The US and China do not have territorial disputes, nor do they debate the gains from trade (Gartzke 2007; Lake 2010/11; Powell 1999). While the US and China might bicker about economic issues such as China's monetary and trade policies, the US has made no attempt to sanction China, nor has it attempted to slow Chinese economic growth in any way. In fact, the US has been an important element in supporting China's generation-long economic growth. The only major issue between the US and China involves *status* – which country is the East Asian leader? Which country is the global hegemon? What status is, how it is measured, and how it is achieved is much more nebulous than disputes that are normally studied in the context of war.

What arms race?

East Asia has numerous factors that many pundits and scholars identify as dangerous for rivalry and war. In fact, there is increasing discussion that East Asia is experiencing an arms race, that the regional security dilemma is intensifying, and that balancing against China is in the offing. Coupled with a muscular US rebalancing effort toward the Pacific, many view the developments in the region to be unsettling and ripe for rivalry (Friedberg 2011; Goldstein 2013; Liff and Ikenberry 2014; Mearsheimer 2010, 2014).[1] Indeed, the debate over whether China's rise will provoke fear in its East Asian neighbours and concomitant balancing behaviour has been raging for at least two decades (Acharya 2007, 2014; Betts 1993; Fravel 2012; Friedberg 1993; Johnston 2012, 2013; Swaine and Fravel 2011; Taylor 2014; Womack 2009).

On the one hand, there are the traditional power transition theorists, who have described American strategic thinking as 'stale' for being too consumed by the conflicts in Iraq and the Middle East, when it really is the US–China dyad that has the singular potential for major war (Tammen and Kugler 2006). This is coupled with threat-based arguments as espoused by Friedberg (1993, 2011), Goldstein (2013b), and Mearsheimer (2010, 2014) that give structural reasons for why China inevitably will challenge the status quo, the US, and regional peace and security architecture.

There is strong belief in a steadfast positive correlation between expansion in material capabilities and national interests in ways that may raise the likelihood of a US–China confrontation, so that 'Today's environment might be even more dangerous [than the Cold War]' (Goldstein 2013a). Though less emphatic, others, like Betts (1993), still choose to emphasize the importance of the balance of power and assess potential scenarios for instability that are based on the number of 'poles' present (unipolarity, bipolarity, and multipolarity), and Tellis (2014: 17) cautions against the internal factors that could be disruptive, such as pernicious nationalism.

Nonetheless, there are a number of scholars who see more possibility for continued regional and global stability. They focus on the choices that China and other countries will make, rather than structural characteristics of size or some endogenous destabilizing quality possessed by the actor. For example, Acharya (2003/04; 2014) believes that tendencies such as market liberalism, economic interdependence, and security multilateralism (along with the US hub-and-spokes model) have been quite underestimated, and these dynamics are what differentiates the current security landscape from that of the immediate aftermath of the Second World War.[2]

Johnston (2003, 2008, 2013) makes a lucid argument for why China actually has limited aims and is increasingly a status quo power despite accusations to the contrary, which is in part echoed by others like Swaine and Fravel (2011) who weigh in on the 'assertive or not' debate with their finding that there has not been much alteration in China's long-standing strategy on maritime sovereignty disputes: 'such actions have not constituted unilateral attempts to resolve a particular issue by force or otherwise reject a preference for negotiation. When possible, Beijing has attempted to maintain an emphasis on bilateral negotiation and avoid conflict'.

On several occasions, Fravel (2010, 2011, 2012) has used the rationalist logic to make it clear that China's strategic goals for its military are largely conservative rather than expansionist, mostly because the likely benefits from expansion are low, and so in the end, it does not really pay for China to engage in aggression. Some (Huang 2013a, 2013b) have chosen a more norms-driven framework by examining the process of socialization and avenues for status-enhancing, which may serve to tame China's ambitions and mediate potentially disruptive outcomes.

One way to begin adjudicating between these two approaches is to explore what East Asian states are actually doing in response to China's rise. If East Asian states are not, in fact, arming themselves as much as is widely believed, and if they are thus not in fact balancing China, then major

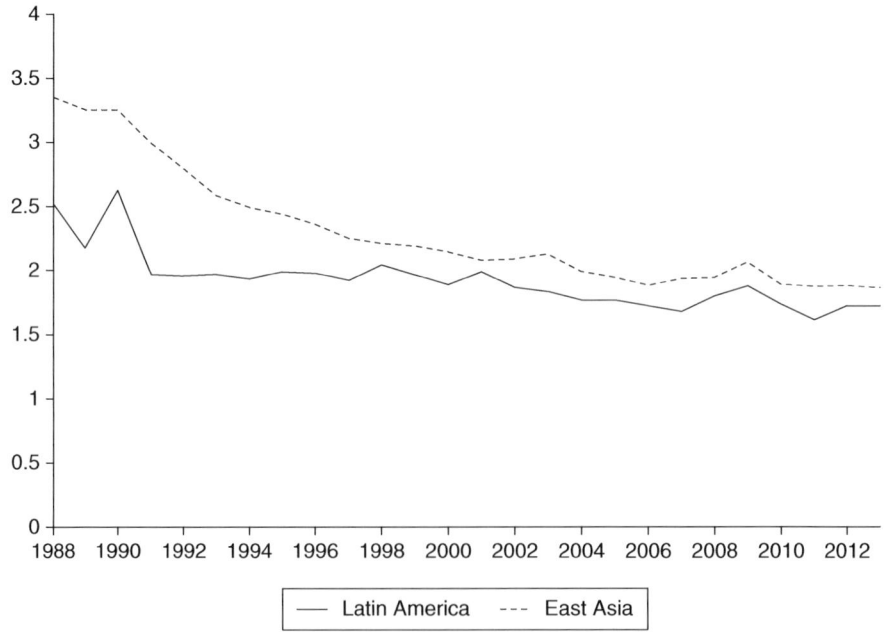

Figure 22.2 East Asian and Latin American defence spending, 1988–2013 (% of GDP). East Asia: Australia, China, Indonesia, Japan, Malaysia, Philippines, Singapore, South Korea, Taiwan, Thailand, Vietnam. Latin America: Argentina, Bolivia, Brazil, Chile, Columbia, Ecuador, Peru, Uruguay, Venezuela

Source of data: Information from the Stockholm International Peace Research Institute (SIPRI), http://www.sipri.org/databases/milex, 2014.

contours of the debate about China's rise and East Asian security need to be seriously re-evaluated. It so happens that data on the East Asian defence effort reveals that East Asian military expenditures have declined fairly significantly over the past quarter-century. As shown in Figure 22.2, the eleven major East Asian countries (including China) devoted an average of 3.35 per cent of their economies to military expenditures in 1988, but by 2013 that average was 1.86 per cent of GDP (SIPRI 2014). Furthermore, the gap between East Asian and Latin American spending has narrowed considerably. In 2013, Latin American countries devoted an average of 1.72 per cent of their economies to the military.

Even measured in absolute terms, recent Japanese defence expenditures rose only 27 per cent over 25 years when adjusted for inflation, and Japanese Prime Minister Abe's proposed increases will total only 5 per cent by 2018 (Figure 22.3). In fact, Japan (−0.2 per cent), Taiwan (−2.6 per cent), and Australia (−3.5 per cent) all *decreased* defence spending slightly in 2013, despite the knee-jerk reaction to assume some military build-up is ongoing. Vietnam's increase in 2013 was 2.4 per cent, Singapore's 2.1 per cent.

A common explanation for low military expenditures and threat perceptions in East Asia emphasizes the reassuring character of the US security presence in the region. It is widely believed that US military presence in the Pacific dampens regional conflicts, reassures allies, and deters regional states from seeking hegemony. For example, Brooks, Ikenberry, and Wohlforth (2012: 37) argue that US retrenchment would lead to greater regional insecurity, which 'could well feed proliferation cascades, as states such as Egypt, Jordan, South Korea, Taiwan, and Saudi Arabia all choose to create nuclear forces'. Stephen Walt (2006) argues for less US commitment abroad precisely because he believes US allies are spending less than they would otherwise.

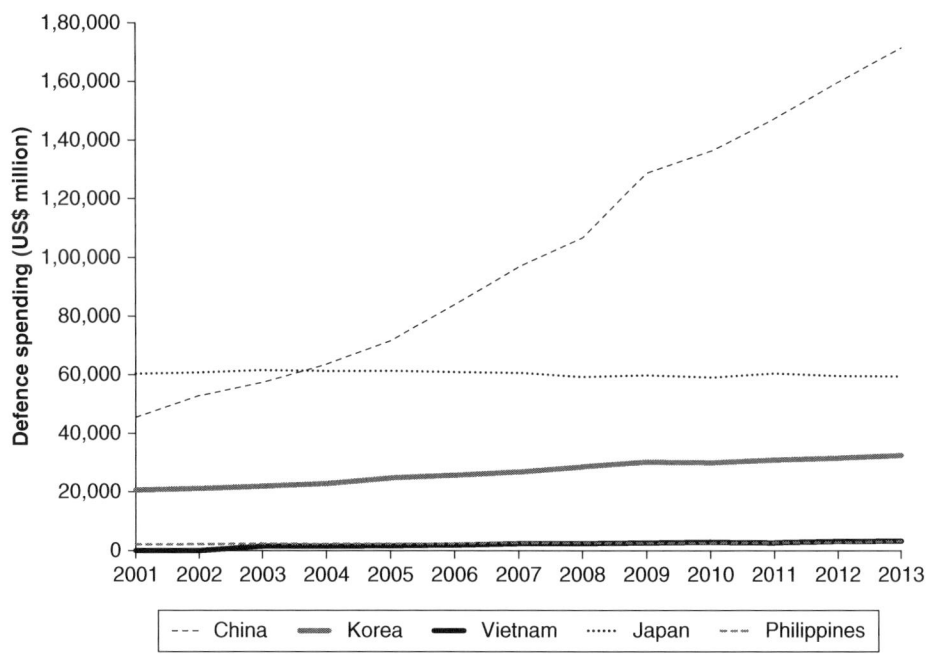

Figure 22.3 China's rivals 2001–2013

Source of data: SIPRI 2014.

With that said, is there empirical evidence that US allies are under-spending because a US security umbrella allows them a free ride on defence? If this were the case, we would expect that non-US allies would spend more on their militaries than US allies. However, East Asian countries with a US alliance (as identified by the US State Department) and those lacking a US alliance have similar military expenditures (Figure 22.4). While there was a notable difference in defence spending at the end of the Cold War in the late 1980s, defence expenditures quickly became similar.

While it is plausible that the US would defend its treaty allies from direct threats to their national survival, it is far less clear that the US would engage in a major war with China over maritime disputes in which it has no direct stake. This arises because of moral hazard in alliances: too clear a US commitment to its allies may embolden them to take risky actions because they believe the US will support them, drawing the US into a war that it does not want to fight (Kelly 2014). The US is thus careful about clarifying or extending its security guarantees to its alliance partners.

This point is also picked up by Hugh White (2012), who has suggested a 'third way' rather than either unconditional US support or retreat from the region, by creating a power-sharing scheme as represented by a 'Concert of Asia' that resembles the Concert of Europe that existed from the 1800s to the early 1900s. From the perspective of East Asian states, the US alliance system may be reassuring about national survival, but it is unlikely to ever be a complete military guarantee against all contingencies. The fact that there are voices within the US that call for negotiating a 'grand bargain' that involves the US ending its commitment to defend Taiwan against possible Chinese aggression in return for a peaceful resolution of the land and maritime disputes in the South China and East China Seas, along with Chinese acceptance of a long-term US military role in East Asia, is testament to the illusion of blanket guarantees (Glaser 2015).

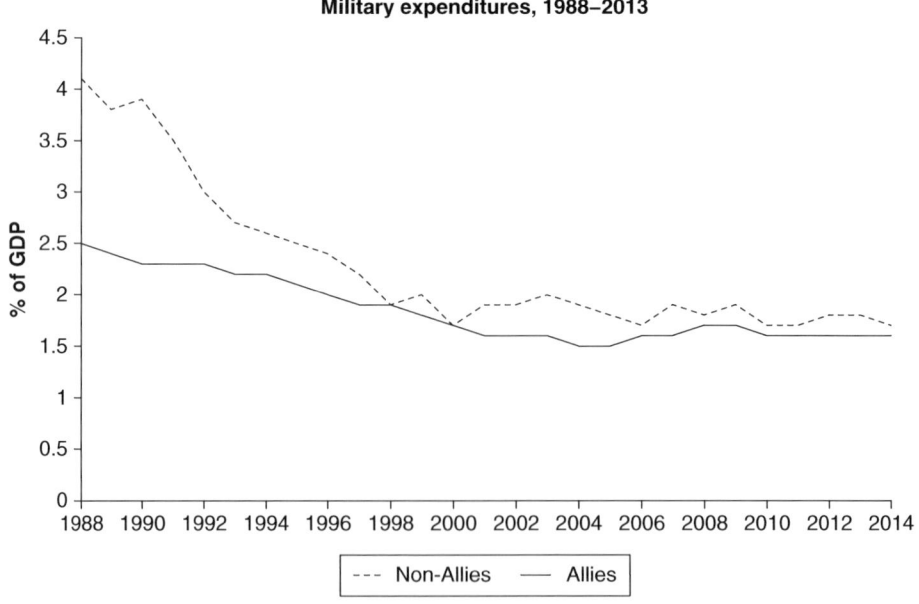

Figure 22.4 US allies and non-allies. Allies: Australia, Japan, Korea, Philippines, Thailand, non-allies: China, Indonesia, Malaysia, Taiwan, Vietnam

Source of data: SIPRI 2014.

In sum, the data reveal that, measured as a proportion of their economy, the East Asian defence effort in 2013 was almost half of what it was in 1988. With rapid economic growth outpacing other regions of the world over the past generation, East Asian absolute expenditures on defence have increased. Yet East Asian governments appear to have chosen to increase their expenditures at a lower rate than Latin America, despite achieving higher economic growth. The real surprise in the data, however, is the *lack* of response by China's regional neighbours. In short, by almost any measure, East Asia looks like Latin America in terms of military expenditures.

The explanation for continued low military expenditures and a peaceful power transition in East Asia is actually quite simple: few states fear for their survival, and hence they are not arming as if they do. Competing maritime claims in the South China Seas do not deny the right of any state in the region to exist, except for Taiwan. The US and China may be facing off over regional hegemony, but few other states feel the necessity to choose sides. Given that the stakes are actually fairly low, it is not surprising that few states appear willing to make the costly domestic and economic trade-offs that would be required for major and sustained investments in militaries. In fact, some (Christensen 2006: 120) have even noted that in the wake of 9/11, 'US–Indian strategic cooperation has apparently catalysed Sino-Indian cooperation and confidence building', because China takes a proactive and accommodating position on economic interaction. Hence, it is misleading to think that states are necessarily forced into different camps or that such alignments may automatically entail negative implications.

China's global economic impact

Compared to the Soviet challenge of the twentieth century, which posed an ideological and economic alternative to the West, China poses at most a potential military challenge, and one that will occur far in the future. In fact, even the most pessimistic of predictions regarding China's military intentions do not envision a direct threat to the US itself. Rather, those who see a military conflict between the US and China envision disputes over interests in the western Pacific. This is not to discount the potential military threat that China poses to the US and to its ability to project power in East Asia – that potential is real. Rather, compared to the military threat presented by the Soviet Union, China as yet does not pose the same type of threat.

Economically, China has become what it is today by embracing essentially a free market system, beginning with the 1978 economic reforms in which Deng Xiaoping declared that 'to get rich is glorious'. China experienced over thirty-five years of astounding economic growth, not by competing with capitalism, but rather by embracing it. As such, although there is some discussion of a 'Beijing consensus', the reality is that a fundamental reliance on market forces and decentralized production and consumption – the roots of market capitalism – is what drives the Chinese economy (Pei 1994).

Most importantly, neither the Chinese state, nor even the Chinese Communist Party, presents an alternative ideological or normative belief system in contrast to the reigning Western orthodoxy. Communism remains the state ideology in name only. Perhaps the greatest issue facing the Chinese leadership and people in the future will be the articulation of a set of values and beliefs that can animate both domestic politics and its foreign policies, and that other countries and peoples find legitimate. Today, China's beliefs do not exist in any coherent form (Gill and Huang 2006).

Is Chinese power rising in economic and social relations? During the Cold War, the US placed an embargo on trade with the Soviet Union because it felt there were security externalities to trade – that is, international trade would benefit the Soviet Union. In the case of China and its neighbours, the opposite has occurred: all regional countries are rapidly increasing their economic relations with China. In fact, what is most surprising is not that China has become the largest trading partner of South Korea, Japan, and Taiwan, but the speed with which the transition took place. Less than twenty years ago Chinese trade was little more than 3 per cent of South Korean trade, whereas by 2011 it had become over 20 per cent of total trade. In contrast, US shares of Korean total trade dropped from 28 per cent in 1990 to under 10 per cent by 2011, with similar declines in Japan's share of Korea's total trade. The Japanese and Taiwanese patterns are just as dramatic: Japanese trade with China was 3 per cent in 1990 and over 20 per cent by 2011; while US trade with Japan dropped from 28 per cent in 1990 to less 12 per cent in 2011. Taiwan shows a similar pattern, and again, China's share of trade has come directly at the expense of the US and Japan. Japan's trade deficit with China in 2013 – US$52 billion – is expected to grow even larger in 2014.

Investment, trade, and financial flows between north-east Asian countries and China continue to increase rapidly, despite political rivalry that dominates the headlines. Over one million Taiwanese now conduct business in mainland China – almost 5 per cent of the entire Taiwanese population (Richburg 2010). Thus, while there is fear about potential Chinese economic domination, regional firms and individuals have clearly voted with their feet, and there is no hint of any move in South Korea to limit or retard economic interactions between the two countries.

The movement of people is also illuminating. For instance, South Koreans flock to the US to study, but they are increasingly also going to China. In 2012, 33 per cent of all foreign students in China came from South Korea, or 62,855 South Korean students; this number is close to the 72,000 South Korean students currently studying in the US (Yonhap New Agency 2013). Although the overall number of Japanese students studying abroad has declined during the past two decades, according to Japan's Ministry of Education, Culture, Sports, Science, and Technology (MEXT) (2015), from a total of 60,138 Japanese nationals studying overseas in 2012, 21,126 were studying in China (an increase of 2,637 from the previous year) compared to a slightly lower figure of 19,568 in the US (a decrease of 398). According to the Japan National Tourism Organization (JNTO), a record 13.4 million foreign tourists travelled to Japan in 2014 (up from 10.8 million the previous year), with visitors from China representing 2.4 million, which marks an increase of 83 per cent. In fact, there were so many Chinese tourists flocking to Japan that Laox, a Chinese-owned duty-free chain catering to Chinese visitors to Japan, witnessed an increase of 1,400 per cent on its stock since 2012 (Minter 2015).

Yet China's global economic role is not limited to East Asia. Perhaps, most dramatically, founding members of the China-led Asian Infrastructure Investment Bank (AIIB) included India, Vietnam, the Philippines, Australia, the United Kingdom, and Germany. While India and China have not resolved their border dispute, they also have a complex and multifaceted relationship. Both are facing similar pressures, being placed in the top five annual net importers of oil, with China surpassing the US to become number one in 2014, and India at fourth (US Energy Information Administration 2015). China, out of sheer necessity, will need to navigate its relations beyond its immediate regional neighbourhood, especially as it has diversified its sources of crude oil imports, so that the six countries that make up just over 60 per cent of China's total imports represent different parts of the world: Saudi Arabia (19 per cent), Angola (13 per cent), Russia (11 per cent), Oman (10 per cent), Iraq (9 per cent), and Iran (9 per cent) (US Energy Information Administration 2015). Even as South African president Jacob Zuma was cancelling his scheduled appearance at the Asian-African Conference in Indonesia (19–24 April 2015) to address ongoing anti-immigration riots at home, China was emphasizing the spirit of trans-continental cooperation at the summit, as well as lodging a protest with the South African police and asking them to ensure the safety of the Chinese people (Mkhize 2015). Like it or not, China will be pulled in multiple directions, reinforcing the incentive to figure out its role and impacts on a global platform.

Conclusion: power transitions and post-hoc arguments

Although China remains more a regional than global actor, China is increasingly the gravitational centre of East Asia. In many areas, East Asia looks more politically stable, economically prosperous, and integrated than it did a quarter-century ago. However, while the longer-term regional trends are all positive, the point of disconnect needs to be identified. First, regional multilateral architecture has developed, providing greater confidence in the region's ability to manage differences in the post-Cold War era. Second, China's phenomenal economic growth has propelled it into the role of regional hub of economic investment and trade, and this has produced even greater and less costly opportunities for the economies of Asia. The evidence on military spending leads to the conclusion that although the region does contain potential flashpoints, countries are seeking ways to manage relations with each other that emphasize institutional, diplomatic, and economic solutions rather than purely military solutions. However, identifying whether and when this rather reassuring vision of the region may erode will be important.

For China, sceptics have been predicting an end to rapid Chinese economic growth ever since it began under Deng Xiaoping in the late 1970s (Chang 2001). There is no doubt that China's economic model faces tremendous challenges, and Minxin Pei wrote in 2012 that, 'The latest news from Beijing is indicative of Chinese weakness: a persistent slowdown of economic growth, a glut of unsold goods, rising bad bank loans, a bursting real-estate bubble, and a vicious power struggle at the top, coupled with unending political scandals'. East Asia remains in flux, and far from having deeply stable relations among all the countries in the region.

Today, as China increasingly appears poised to 're-emerge' as the most materially powerful country in East Asia, there is a corresponding question about whether or not China can enjoy the normative power that it once held. China has a long way to go before becoming a leader. Although China may already be – or may soon become – the largest economic and military power in East Asia, it has virtually no cultural or political legitimacy as a leading state. The difference between China at the height of its hegemony five centuries ago and China today is most clearly reflected in the fact that nobody today thinks that China is still the civilizational centre of the world: few contemporary East Asian states or peoples look to China for cultural innovation or for practical solutions to present problems.

Given the changes in the international system and the central place of the US, there is almost no chance that China will become the East Asian regional hegemon, much less challenge the US globally. Too much has changed for that to happen, and the US – even as it adjusts to changing circumstances – is not going to disappear from the region. Perhaps the more important question is whether the US and China can come to some type of accommodation and agreement on each other's roles and their relations with each other. While, to date, both the US and China are working to accommodate each other and stabilize their relations, that process is far from complete. How these two countries manage East Asian leadership, the status they accord each other, and how other regional countries come to view them will be central aspects of whether or not the future of East Asian international relations is one of increasing stability.

Admittedly, there are countries in the region that are starting to feel that they are having to make decisions on mutually exclusive issues that have come to represent 'sides', e.g. the case of South Korea, regarding the deployment of the Terminal High Altitude Area Defense (THAAD) by the US and joining the Asian Infrastructure Investment Bank (AIIB) led by China. It may be that some day East Asian countries will make a clear choice and openly ask for US primacy, and begin outright to balance against China. China and the US may indeed divide up the region into two blocs. But neither has yet happened, and until it does, scholars might be wise to consider carefully the possibility that the future of East Asia may lie between these two extremes.

The more solemn voices may be right, and – just wait – the region may be heading towards a classic bipolar confrontation where containment, blocs, and military deterrence are at the forefront. However, the evidence on military spending leads to the conclusion that although the region does contain potential flashpoints, countries are seeking ways to manage relations with each other and with China that emphasize institutional, diplomatic, and economic solutions, rather than purely military ones. It may be useful to end with some caution on the follies of mischaracterizing the dynamics surrounding China and the region and reading too much into something that is not necessarily there. As Fravel and Twomey (2015: 183) have nicely pointed out, 'the tendency of "memes" [on China] to reverberate in a charged domestic political echo chamber in the US is large and counterproductive'. The same goes for those that abound at the international level.

Notes

* Research was partially supported by the MacArthur Foundation and Korea Foundation.
1 For a counter-argument, see Fu (2015).
2 Short of claiming that there will be peace of the 'positive' variant, he does state that there is potential for constraining the power-maximizing behaviour of China while restraining extreme balancing/containment by the US and its allies.

References

Acharya, A. (2003/04) 'Will Asia's Past Be Its Future?', *International Security* 28(3): 149–64.
Acharya, A. (2007) 'The Emerging Regional Architecture of World Politics', *World Politics* 59(4): 629–52.
Acharya, A. (2014) 'Power Shift or Paradigm Shift? China's Rise and Asia's Emerging Security Order', *International Studies Quarterly* 58(1): 158–73.
Betts, R. K. (1993) 'Wealth, Power, and Instability: East Asia and the United States after the Cold War', *International Security* 18(3): 34–77.
Brooks, S., Ikenberry, J. G., and Wohlforth W. (2012) 'Don't Come Home, America: The Case against Retrenchment', *International Security* 37(2): 7–51.
Chang, G. (2001) *China's Coming Collapse,* New York: Random House.
Christensen, T. (2006) 'Fostering Stability or Creating a Monster? The Rise of China and US Policy toward East Asia', *International Security* 31(1): 81–126.
Feng, Z. (2008) 'China's Rise Will Be Peaceful: How Unipolarity Matters', in R. S. Ross. and Z. Feng (eds.) *China's Ascent: Power, Security, and the Future of International Politics*, Ithaca, NY: Cornell University Press, 34–54.
Fravel, M. T. (2010) 'International Relations Theory and China's Rise: Assessing China's Potential for Territorial Expansion', *International Studies Review* 12(4): 505–32.
Fravel, M. T. (2011) 'China's Strategy in the South China Sea', *Contemporary Southeast Asia* 33(3): 292–319.
Fravel, M. T. (2012) 'All Quiet in the South China Sea: Why China is Playing Nice (for Now)', *Foreign Affairs*, March 22. Online. Available HTTP: <https://www.foreignaffairs.com/articles/china/2012-03-22/all-quiet-south-china-sea> (accessed 6 June 2016).
Fravel, M. T. and Twomey, C. P. (2015) 'Projecting Strategy: The Myth of Chinese Counter-Intervention', *The Washington Quarterly* 37(4): 171–87.
Friedberg, A. (1993) 'Ripe for Rivalry', *International Security* 18(3): 5–33.
Friedberg, A. (2011) *Contest for Supremacy: China, America, and the Struggle for Mastery in Asia*, New York: W. W. Norton.
Fu, R. T. (2015) 'Correspondence: Looking for Asia's Security Dilemma', *International Security* 40(2): 181–204.
Gartzke, E. (2007) 'The Capitalist Peace', *American Journal of Political Science* 51(1): 166–91.
Gill, B. and Huang, Y. (2006) 'The Sources and Limits of Beijing's Soft Power', *Survival* 48(2): 17–36.
Glaser, C. L. (2015) 'A US–China Grand Bargain? The Hard Choice between Military Competition and Accommodation', *International Security* 39(4): 49–90.
Goh, E. (2007/08) 'Great Powers and Hierarchical Order in Southeast Asia: Analyzing Regional Security Strategies', *International Security* 32(3): 113–57.

Goldstein, A. (2013a) 'China's Real and Present Danger', *Foreign Affairs* 92(5): 136.

Goldstein, A. (2013b) 'First Things First: The Pressing Danger of Crisis Instability in US–China Relations', *International Security* 37(4): 49–89.

Goldstone, J. (1995) 'The Coming Chinese Collapse', *Foreign Policy* 99: 35–42.

Japan Ministry of Education, Culture, Sports, Science and Technology (MEXT) (2015) 'The Number of Japanese Nationals Studying Overseas and the Annual Survey of International Students in Japan', 27 February. Online. Available HTTP: <http://www.mext.go.jp/english/topics/1357495.htm> (accessed 20 May 2015).

Japan National Tourism Organization (JNTO) (2014) 'Foreign visitors and Japanese departures'. Online. Available HTTP: <http://www.jnto.go.jp/eng/ttp/sta/PDF/E2014.pdf> (accessed 20 May 2015).

Johnston, A. I. (2003) 'Is China a Status Quo Power?', *International Security* 27(4): 5–56.

Johnston, A. I. (2008) *Social States: China in International Institutions, 1980–2000*, Princeton, NJ: Princeton University Press.

Johnston, A. I. (2012) 'What (if Anything) Does East Asia Tell Us about International Relations Theory?', *Annual Review of Political Science* 15: 53–78.

Johnston, A. I. (2013) 'How New and Assertive is China's New Assertiveness?', *International Security* 37, 4: 7–48.

Kang, D. C. (2007) *China Rising: Peace, Power, and Order in East Asia*, New York: Columbia University Press.

Kelly, R. E. (2014) 'Moral Hazard: Japan–South Korea Relations and International Relations Theory', *The Interpreter*, 16 January. Online. Available HTTP: <http://www.lowyinterpreter.org/post/2014/01/16/Entrapment-vs-moral-hazard-in-US-alliances-in-Asia.aspx?COLLCC=976462795&> (accessed 20 May 2015).

Lake, D. (2010/11) 'Two Cheers for Bargaining Theory: Assessing Rationalist Explanations of the Iraq War', *International Security* 35(3): 7–52.

Liff, A. and Ikenberry, J. (2014) 'Racing toward Tragedy?: China's Rise, Military Competition in the Asia Pacific, and The Security Dilemma', *International Security* 39(2): 52–91.

Mearsheimer, J. (2010) 'The Gathering Storm: China's Challenge to US Power in Asia', *Chinese Journal of International Politics* 3: 381–96.

Mearsheimer, J. (2014)[2003]) *The Tragedy of Great Power Politics*. New York: W. W. Norton.

Minter, A. (2015) 'Why Chinese Tourists Love Japan', *Bloomberg View*, 25 March. Online. Available HTTP: <http://www.bloombergview.com/articles/2015–03–25/why-chinese-tourists-love-japan> (accessed 20 May 2015).

Mkhize, D. (2015) 'Update: 4-Anti-Immigrant Unrest Hits S. Africa as Zuma Condemns Violence', *Reuters*, 16 April. Online. Available HTTP: <http://www.reuters.com/article/2015/04/16/safrica-violence-idUSL5N0XD2MF20150416> (accessed 15 May 2015).

Pei, M. (1994) *From Reform to Revolution: The Demise of Communism in China and the Soviet Union*, Cambridge, MA: Harvard University Press.

Powell, R. (1999) *In the Shadow of Power: States and Strategies in International Politics*, Princeton, NJ: Princeton University Press.

Powell, R. (2002) 'Bargaining Theory and International Conflict', *Annual Review of Political Science* 5: 1–30.

Richburg, K. (2010) 'Despite a Government Standoff, People of China and Taiwan Increasingly Mingle', *Washington Post*, 20 July. Online. Available HTTP: <http://www.washingtonpost.com/wpdyn/content/article/2010/07/19/AR2010071905247.html> (accessed 20 May 2015).

Ross, R. (2006) 'Balance of Power Politics and the Rise of China: Accommodation and Balancing in East Asia', *Security Studies* 15(3): 355–95.

Stockholm Institute for Peace Research (SIPRI) (2014) 'SIPRI Military Expenditure Database'. Online. Available HTTP: <http://www.sipri.org/databases/milex> (accessed 20 May 2015).

Swaine, M. and Fravel, M. T. (2011) 'China's Assertive Behavior, Part Two: The Maritime Periphery', *China Leadership Monitor* 35: 1–29.

Tammen, R. and Kugler, J. (2006) 'Power Transition and China–US Conflicts', *Chinese Journal of International Politics* 1: 35–55.

Taylor, B. (2014) 'The South China Sea Is Not a Flashpoint', *Washington Quarterly* 37(1): 99–111.

Tellis, A. J. (2014) *Balancing without Containment: An American Strategy for Managing China*, Washington, DC: Carnegie Endowment for International Peace.

US Department of State (n.d.) 'US Collective Defense Arrangements'. Online. Available HTTP: <http://www.state.gov/s/l/treaty/collectivedefense/> (accessed 20 May 2015).

US Energy Information Administration (2015) 'China', 14 May. Online. Available HTTP: <http://www.eia.gov/countries/cab.cfm?fips=ch> (accessed 20 May 2015).

Walt, S. (2006) *Taming American Power: The Global Response to US Primacy*, New York: W. W. Norton.

White, H. (2012) *The China Choice: Why America Should Share Power*, Sydney: Black.

Womack, B. (2006) *China and Vietnam: The Politics of Asymmetry*, Cambridge: Cambridge University Press.

Womack, B. (2009) *China among Unequals*, Singapore: World Scientific.

World Bank (2013) 'World Development Indicators Online'. Online. Available HTTP: <http://data.worldbank.org/data-catalog/world-development-indicators> (accessed 20 May 2015).

World Bank Group Finances (2015) 'Country Profile on China'. Online. Available HTTP: <https://finances.worldbank.org/en/countries/China> (accessed 20 May 2015).

Yonhap New Agency (2013) 'S. Korean Students in China Quadruple in 11 Years', 2 October. Online. Available HTTP: <http://english.yonhapnews.co.kr/national/2013/10/02/25/0302000000AEN2013 1002002500315F.html> (accessed 20 May 2015).

Zhang, Y. and Tang, S. (2005) 'China's Regional Strategy', in D. Shambaugh (ed.) *Power Shift China and Asia's New Dynamics*, Berkeley: University of California Press, 48–68.

23

INDIAN SECURITY POLICY

Sumit Ganguly

India's security policy is in a state of transition as the country attempts to secure its position as an emergent power in Asia and beyond. The willingness on the part of Indian policy-makers to accept the use of force as a critical element of national power represents a profound shift from the ideational outlook that had influenced Indian policy-making in the immediate post-independence era. The task before them now involves making judicious choices about military commitments, deployments, and accordingly appropriate levels of defence spending.

The scholarship on India's security policy is limited and mostly dated (Cohen and Dasgupta 2012; Gordon 1995; Kavic 1967; Thomas 1986; 1978). Such a lacuna in the literature is puzzling because of India's overt acquisition of nuclear weapons in 1998, its abandonment of its commitment to non-alignment after the Cold War, and its growing significance as an Asian power (Ganguly 2006). Despite the profound changes of late, scholarship on Indian security policy continues to be dogged by a lack of attention.

This chapter will trace the origins, evolution, current state, and future directions of the country's security policy since its emergence as an independent state following the collapse of the British Indian Empire in 1947. It will look at the impact of critical political choices on the part of the country's leadership, the role of regional security threats, and India's relative lack of importance to the global rivalry during much of the Cold War era. The chapter will deal with the intellectual rationale for India's initial security policies, their re-evaluation and transformation in the aftermath of the 1962 Sino-Indian border war, its conflicts with Pakistan, its quest for nuclear weapons, its responses to internal uprisings, and its attempts to extend its reach beyond the confines of the subcontinent.

Post-independence concerns

In the immediate aftermath of India's emergence as an independent state in 1947 following the end of the British colonial empire in South Asia, Indian policy-makers adopted an ideational foreign policy which sought to de-emphasize military preparedness. A number of factors shaped India's defence policies in the post-independence era. Most importantly, Prime Minister Jawaharlal Nehru, the principal architect of India's foreign and security policies, was acutely concerned about the significant opportunity costs of defence spending (Cohen 1971). Simultaneously, he feared that a large military establishment could also encourage Bonapartist ambitions and undermine India's nascent democracy (Ganguly 1991). Finally, he also hoped to contribute to a world order where the use of force was proscribed in international politics.

Nehru's wishes notwithstanding, almost immediately after its independence, India found itself embroiled in a war with Pakistan over the status of the state of Jammu and Kashmir (Ganguly 2001). The war ensued because of Pakistan's attempts to exploit a tribal rebellion in the western reaches of this state (Hodson 1969; Khan 1975). In keeping with their faith in multilateral institutions and acting on the advice of Lord Louis Mountbatten, the last viceroy, India's political leadership referred the Kashmir dispute to the United Nations Security Council (Gupta 1966). The war came to a close on 1 January 1949, when the Security Council imposed a cease-fire as multilateral negotiations to resolve the dispute began.

The Indian military possessed sufficient capabilities to cope with the threat from Pakistan. However, it was fundamentally ill-equipped to deal with the threat that arose from the People's Republic of China (PRC) over a disputed border along much of India's Himalayan frontier (Hoffmann 1990). Prime Minister Nehru and his defence minister, V. K. Krishna Menon, believed that the threat from the PRC could be contained through diplomacy and conciliation. To that end, India made significant concessions to the PRC. It resorted to the mildest criticism of the Chinese invasion and occupation of Tibet in 1950, even though China's move meant the end of a strategic buffer (Sen 1960). Specifically, at the behest of the PRC, the Indian government eschewed all extra-territorial rights in Tibet that it had inherited as holdovers from the British colonial period.

More to the point, Nehru was convinced that the great powers would not remain passive in the event of a Sino-Indian conflict and thereby moved to promptly contain the tensions. As it turned out, this assumption proved to be completely flawed. Negotiations aimed at resolving the border dispute broke down in 1960. Worse still, India, despite its inadequate military capabilities, embarked upon a strategy of compellence. This strategy involved sending in lightly armed Indian troops in 'penny packets' to display India's resolve to hold territory that the Chinese had claimed. When the PRC chose to attack these Indian packets, they proved no match for the battle-hardened People's Liberation Army (PLA). The Indian troops lacked adequate clothing, firepower, and logistical support. Worse still, the Indian military reinforcements that were abruptly moved from the plains were not acclimated to high-altitude warfare and, consequently, faced multiple and crippling health hazards. This short but brutal war proved to be a military and diplomatic debacle for India. Militarily, the Indian armed forces suffered a stinging defeat, and diplomatically India found itself bereft of support apart from some limited assistance from the US and the UK.

The aftermath of 1962

In the wake of this conflict, India's policy-makers were forced to re-evaluate India's military preparedness to cope with ongoing threats from both Pakistan and, more importantly, the PRC. Since India had acquitted itself adequately against Pakistan in the 1947–8 war, the principal threat it had to contend with involved the PRC. To that end, Indian policy-makers chose to embark on the creation of a 45-squadron air force equipped with supersonic aircraft, a million-man army with ten new mountain divisions trained in high-altitude warfare, and a modest programme of naval modernization (Thomas 1978).

The Indian fixation on countering the potential security threat from the PRC and the concomitant rearmament programme provoked Pakistani anxieties. From the Pakistani standpoint, India's increased military capabilities could make a crucial difference in a future Indo-Pakistani conflict. Fearing that a window of opportunity might be closing to reclaim the disputed territory of India's Jammu and Kashmir state through the use of force, the Pakistani politico-military elite fashioned an elaborate strategy to seize Kashmir militarily (Ganguly 1989). The plan had two distinct phases. In the first phase, code-named 'Operation Gibraltar', Pakistani troops disguised as locals would infiltrate the Kashmir Valley and seek to sow discord amongst the population. Exploiting these disturbances that they had successfully stirred, Pakistan would launch a full-scale invasion of Kashmir ('Operation Grand Slam') and seize it in a short war.

To the dismay of the Pakistani war planners, none of their assumptions proved tenable. Though some Kashmiris were discontented with Indian rule, they nevertheless evinced little interest in assisting the Pakistani infiltrators. Instead, they alerted Indian authorities who promptly moved to seal the Cease-Fire Line. Despite the loss of strategic surprise, the Pakistani leadership went ahead with its war plans and launched an assault on Kashmir in early September 1965. The Indian forces were prepared for this attack and succeeded in blunting the Pakistani onslaught. The war lasted for about three weeks and was brought to a close through a United Nations Security Council resolution. Since the US demonstrated little interest in promoting a post-war accord, the Soviet Union stepped into the breach. Moscow persuaded the adversaries to return to the status quo ante and also to abjure the use of force to settle the Kashmir dispute (Brines 1968).

Despite this commitment to refrain from the use of force to settle bilateral disputes, India and Pakistan became involved in a third war in 1971. This conflict stemmed from the exigencies of Pakistani domestic politics and the emergence of Bengali sub-nationalism in East Pakistan (Jahan 1972; Zaheer 1994). However, after negotiations in the wake of Pakistan's first free and fair national elections broke down, the Punjabi-dominated Pakistani military resorted to a brutal crackdown in East Pakistan. In the face of widespread repression, close to ten million Bengalis fled to India. Burdened with this significant refugee influx, Indian policy-makers, having exhausted the diplomatic alternatives, fashioned a politico-military strategy designed to break up Pakistan (Jackson 1975; Jacob 1997). Indian military planners trained, armed, and provided sanctuaries to an indigenous guerrilla movement, the 'Mukti Bahini' (literally 'liberation force') and ultimately provoked the Pakistani regime to launch a military assault on India in early December 1971. Indian forces, which had been carefully arrayed to respond with a 'blitzkrieg strategy', managed to bring the war to a successful close within three weeks (for a discussion of the Indian blitzkrieg strategy, see Mearsheimer 1983). The war led to the break-up of Pakistan and the creation of the independent state of Bangladesh. Following this war, India emerged as the pre-eminent military power in the subcontinent. Also, given India's military preponderance, a long peace ensued on the subcontinent until the outbreak of an indigenous insurgency in India's disputed state of Jammu and Kashmir in 1989.

The nuclear conundrum

Contrary to many analyses,[1] the origins of the Indian nuclear weapons programme can be traced quite clearly to the country's perception of the threat emanating from the PRC. Within two years of India's disastrous defeat at the hands of the PRC, the Chinese had tested their first nuclear weapon at Lop Nor. The Chinese nuclear test set off a firestorm of controversy in the Indian parliament (Mirchandani 1968). Segments of the Indian right wing wanted the country to abandon non-alignment and seek a nuclear guarantee against the PRC from the Western world. Others wanted India to develop its own nuclear weapons capabilities to cope with this emergent threat from the PRC. After considerable debate, the leadership chose neither to dispense with non-alignment nor to pursue a nuclear weapons programme. Instead, it made a feeble effort to seek a nuclear guarantee from the great powers, notably the UK, the Soviet Union, and the US. In the event, all three states rebuffed India (Noorani 1967).

In the wake of this failure to obtain a nuclear guarantee, India embarked upon the Subterranean Nuclear Explosions Project (SNEP). Simultaneously, at the international level, it maintained its spirited opposition to the drafting of the Nuclear Nonproliferation Treaty (NPT) in the Eighteen Nation Disarmament Committee (ENDC) in Geneva. India's opposition was straightforward: it contended that the treaty was inherently inequitable. It sought to prevent the *horizontal* spread of nuclear weapons while urging good-faith efforts to curb *vertical* proliferation (Kapur 1976).

Not surprisingly, India chose not to accede to the NPT when it was passed and entered into force on 1 January 1970. As a consequence of its refusal to join the NPT regime, India found itself isolated from global nuclear commerce. Despite its inability to participate in international nuclear activities, India went ahead with both its peaceful and its military nuclear programmes. In May 1974, it tested its first nuclear weapon in the Rajasthan desert and promptly faced a series of bilateral and multilateral sanctions (Ganguly 1982). Given the country's parlous economic conditions, its leaders chose not to carry out further tests, but work on the nuclear weapons programme proceeded apace, even though individual Indian governments chose to either retard or accelerate the programme (Tellis 2000).

Crossing the nuclear Rubicon

In the late 1990s, as a consequence of developments at the global, regional, and national levels, India chose to dispense with its policy of nuclear ambiguity and crossed the nuclear Rubicon in May 1998. Specifically, four factors influenced the Indian decision to end its nuclear restraint. The first two factors were located at the global level. First, at the NPT Review Conference in May 1995, the US managed to persuade the vast majority of UN members to extend the NPT indefinitely and unconditionally. Second, it sought to pass the Comprehensive Test Ban Treaty (CTBT) in 1998, despite vigorous objections from India and a handful of other states to one particular clause in the CTBT that required forty-four states with ongoing nuclear power programmes to ratify the treaty before September 1998 to enable it to enter into force.

The significance of the indefinite and unconditional extension of the NPT and the requirement that a sub-set of states ratify the CTBT to enable its entry into force was not lost on Indian policy-makers. They correctly concluded that the widespread global support for the NPT in the wake of the 1995 Review Conference placed India in an extremely isolated position and thereby subjected it to potentially acute pressures to accede to this global regime. Additionally, they realized that inexorable pressure would mount on them to sign and ratify the CTBT before September 1998.

Apart from these two global considerations, two other factors played critical roles in compelling India's policy-makers to depart from their commitment to nuclear abstinence. First, with the end of the Cold War and the Soviet collapse, India's policy-makers realized that they could no longer count on the Soviet security guarantee that was embedded in the twenty-year Indo-Soviet treaty of 'peace, friendship, and cooperation', even if it were to be renewed (Horn 1982; Racioppi 1994). Consequently, India could no longer expect Russia to act as a brake on possible Chinese revanchism. Second, they also concluded that in the late 1980s and early 1990s, the PRC had made Pakistan its virtual strategic surrogate in South Asia through the transfer of nuclear weapons and ballistic missile technology (NTI 2008).

Given these global and regional considerations, India's policy-makers determined that they could not afford to abandon the nuclear weapons option. With the seemingly inexorable movement toward the conclusion of a CTBT, Indian policy-makers feared that their ability to carry out nuclear tests would be foreclosed, leaving India in a strategically vulnerable position.[2] In the aftermath of the nuclear tests, India faced widespread international condemnation and a new raft of US-initiated sanctions. However, through patient and deft diplomacy, it managed to get the bulk of them lifted within a span of about two years (Talbott 2004). Despite its failure to persuade India (and Pakistan) to foreswear their nascent nuclear weapons capabilities, the Clinton administration left office convinced that nuclear weapons in the region were a deeply destabilizing force.

A seismic policy shift

A significant policy shift occurred under the administration of George W. Bush. Initially, it was concerned about Pakistan's nuclear weapons programme. However, in the aftermath of the terrorist attacks of 11 September 2001, the US needed to engage Pakistan. Apart from its interest in ensuring the security and safety of the Pakistani nuclear weapons infrastructure, the Bush administration evinced little interest in rolling back Pakistan's capabilities. Simultaneously, it did little to pressure or persuade India to abandon its nuclear weapons programme. On the contrary, in 2005, the Bush administration started negotiations with India on a comprehensive civilian nuclear agreement that would enable India to maintain its nuclear arsenal and also participate in global nuclear commerce (Ganguly and Mistry 2006). Protracted and difficult negotiations ensued over the next three years. In October of 2008, after considerable spirited debate in both the US and India, a deal was finally agreed. Under the terms of this agreement, India can now engage in normal nuclear commerce without being subjected to the bilateral and multilateral sanctions that had been imposed on it in the aftermath of its first nuclear test in 1974 (Mistry 2014).

Is the region more stable as a consequence of the acquisition of nuclear weapons by India and Pakistan? There is a growing and vigorous debate on this subject (for arguments for nuclear stability, see Ganguly and Hagerty 2004; for an alternative view, see Kapur 2007). The proponents of stability contend that the mutual possession of nuclear weapons has all but eliminated the prospect of full-scale war in the region as both sides understand the consequences of the nuclear revolution (on the significance of the nuclear revolution, see Jervis 1989). Others contend that given Pakistan's revisionist ambitions, the region has actually become more war-prone. They contend that Pakistani decision-makers are more likely to provoke India, secure in the knowledge that India has no viable conventional military options because of Pakistan's possession of nuclear weapons and the concomitant fears of escalation to the nuclear level. Given their fundamentally divergent premises about the effects of nuclear weapons on the likelihood of war, the two sides drew vastly different inferences from the Kargil conflict of 1999. The proponents of nuclear deterrence argue that the looming presence of nuclear weapons prevented the horizontal escalation of the conflict. Their critics, however, contend that Pakistan felt emboldened to make an intrusion into Kargil because of its acquisition of a nuclear weapons capability.

The Kargil war and after

In 1999, India and Pakistan became involved in the third war over Kashmir. Pakistan initiated this conflict. The precise origins of the war remain controversial, but there is little question that it stemmed from the successful infiltration of Pakistani forces across the Line of Control in the Kargil region in the spring of 1999 (for various discussions of the Kargil conflict, see Bajpai et al. 2001; Chari and Mehta 2001; Malik 2006; Singh 2001; Swami 1999).

What prompted Pakistan to undertake this 'limited probe'?[3] There is no clear-cut answer to this question. However, it appears that the Pakistani military leadership was keen on jump-starting the insurgency in Kashmir, which had started to flag thanks to the success of India's sustained counter-insurgency campaign. To that end, Pakistani military planners undertook a probing action designed to test the extent of India's commitment. At another level, they were no doubt aware that if they succeeded in breaching the Indian defences in the region, they would be able to interdict India's principal link from the Kashmir Valley to the northern region of Kashmir, Ladakh. The initial Pakistani intrusion into this sector was extremely successful for a number of reasons. The most notable of these was the Indian conviction that in the aftermath of the peace process that had been initiated in February 1999, any offensive Pakistani operations in Kashmir were unlikely. As a consequence, both Indian civil and military intelligence organizations had lowered the level of vigilance along the Kashmir border (Kargil Committee Report 2000).

Despite the initial failure to detect the Pakistani intrusions, the Indian military acted with alacrity and vigour to stem them. To that end, India brought considerable firepower to bear in a concentrated fashion. It also utilized its air force, but placed significant constraints on the use of air power. Specifically, the air force was explicitly forbidden from crossing the Line of Control for fear of provoking a wider war. The reasons for Indian restraint were straightforward. This was the first Indo-Pakistani conflict since the two countries had acquired nuclear weapons. Indian decision-makers were acutely aware of the dangers of nuclear escalation (Ganguly 2008; for an alternative view, see Kapur 2008).

Shortly after the Kargil war, Indian defence planners sought to formulate a military doctrine and strategy that would enable them to respond to Pakistani probing actions without risking full-scale war. To that end, various Indian military officials – most notably General Ved Prakash Malik, a former chief of staff of the Indian Army – called for a doctrine of 'limited war under the nuclear umbrella' (Malik 2006). Details about this strategy, however, are mostly lacking in the public domain. Most of the discussions and criticisms of the strategy have focused on its feasibility and the dangers of escalation (Raghavan 2001). These concerns were further reinforced due to the lack of any militarily viable options when India faced another crisis with Pakistan in the wake of a terrorist attack on the Indian parliament on 13 December 2001. In an attempt to induce a change in Pakistani behaviour, India mobilized its substantial conventional forces and embarked upon a massive and prolonged exercise of coercive diplomacy, but to little effect (Ganguly and Kraig 2005).

In the aftermath of these two episodes, Indian military planners focused on developing a doctrine of swift mobilization and calibrated response to limited Pakistani-sponsored terrorist attacks. This doctrine, dubbed 'Cold Start', envisages responding with speed and vigour against a future Pakistani terrorist provocation. However, some scholars who have examined the premises of the doctrine and India's capabilities question its strategic assumptions and operational features (Ladwig 2007).

Coping with internal conflicts

In addition to the two major external security threats from Pakistan and the PRC, the Indian state's security policies have also included a series of domestic counter-insurgency operations (Chadha 2005). The vast majority of these insurgencies are due to Indian domestic politics. Several of them stem from ethnic and religious tensions, although one particular insurgency, the Naxalite Rebellion, is due to class conflict (Chakravarti 2008). However, external involvement in these insurgencies has expanded their scope, increased their intensity, and prolonged their duration. In a number of cases, Pakistan and the PRC played vital roles in sustaining these insurgencies.

Apart from this class-based insurgency India still faces a series of simmering conflicts in its north-east. The origins of most of these insurgencies are indigenous and have deep historical roots. However, both Pakistani and Chinese involvement in those insurrections has kept them alive and has expanded their scope. To compound matters the presence of sanctuaries in Bangladesh and Burma (Myanmar) has hobbled India's ability to suppress them (Lintner 2015).

The Indian state has successfully, albeit at considerable cost, defeated every insurgency barring one. The Kashmir insurgency, which erupted in 1989, has been contained but has yet to be suppressed (Ganguly 1997). There are compelling reasons for India's failure to end the Kashmir insurgency. Kashmir, unlike the other cases, involves a significant territorial dispute. Also, since Kashmir is contiguous to Pakistan, the Pakistani state has been able to provide the Kashmiri insurgents with weaponry, training, logistics, and above all, sanctuaries. It has also organized, trained, and directed a series of insurgent groups to enter and wreak havoc in Indian-controlled Kashmir (Byman 2005; Swami 2007). Apart from Pakistani support, unlike the vast majority of the other insurgencies where disaffection with the Indian state was limited, the Kashmir conflict is fuelled by alienation from India on the part of many Kashmiris. Consequently, the Indian state has had considerable difficulty in interdicting this significant insurgency.

Apart from these insurgencies that have wracked the country, India has faced a renewed spate of ethno-religious violence in recent years. The sources of this discord are complex, but have much to do with growing levels of political mobilization, the decline of political institutions, and the exploitation of internal grievances by external actors (Ganguly 2008).

A recent episode underscored the seriousness of the threat from Pakistan. On 26 November 2008, a group of ten terrorists attacked two prominent hotels, a major railway station, and several other crowded venues in the city of Bombay (Mumbai). Over the next two days they battled local police and national commandos. After a two-day siege they were finally overpowered but after considerable loss of life. Based upon electronic intelligence intercepts, Indian officials asserted that the terrorists belonged to a notionally banned Pakistani terrorist group, the Lashkar-e-Taiba. Despite widespread public anger the government of India chose to exert concerted diplomatic pressure on Pakistan to end its involvement with terrorist organizations and chose not to use military force. Whether or not this strategy will yield the desired results remains an open question.

Current and future directions

All three branches of the Indian armed forces are now in the midst of a major modernization drive. Thanks to a growing economy, India is able to devote a greater share of its resources to defence spending and military modernization. Expanded defence spending is determined by a number of factors. First of all, the shelf-life of various weapons systems that the Indian armed forces had acquired in the 1980s and earlier is now expiring. Consequently, a new generation of weapons systems is required. The replacement of major weapons systems is most urgent in the Indian Air Force, which still relies on the obsolescent MiG-21 fighter. Attempts to acquire a new, Medium Multi-Range Combat Aircraft (MMRCA) have long stalled (Tellis 2011). Even after protracted negotiations with France to purchase 126 Rafale fighters the deal was not finally consummated. However, on a state visit to the country in April 2015, Prime Minister Modi chose to acquire 36 Rafale aircraft in a government-to-government agreement (Bagchi 2015).

In the meantime, despite significant cost overruns and an abject failure to develop an indigenous engine, the first version of India's domestically produced Light Combat Aircraft (LCA), Tejas, was handed over to the Indian Air Force (IAF). However, it will be at least another two to three years before the aircraft receives it final operational clearance and a full squadron is inducted into the IAF (Kumar 2015). Second, despite cosmetic improvements, the Indo-Pakistani relationship remains fraught despite some limited and fitful progress in the waning days of the Musharraf presidency. More to the point, as argued earlier, since the 2001–2 crisis, India has been seeking a new military doctrine designed to deal with Pakistani provocations short of provoking a full-scale war. Third, Indian military planners are still faced with growing and improved

Chinese military capabilities. In the absence of a settlement of the border dispute, the military considers it prudent to invest in the maintenance of an effective conventional deterrent force along the Himalayan border. Fourth and finally, India's defence modernization is also a product of its desire to protect its littoral regions and especially sea-lanes leading to the Persian Gulf. The protection of these sea-lanes is of critical importance to India because 70 per cent of India's oil is imported from the Persian Gulf region (Ganguly and Pardesi 2008).

Conclusion

Indian security policy is driven by certain constant factors, including the stand-off with Pakistan over Kashmir and the disputed border with the PRC. Beyond these factors, however, India is now also involved in a wider competitive relationship with the PRC. Indian policy-makers, fearful of provoking the PRC, are usually loath to admit publicly to the existence of such a competition. Nevertheless, India's force acquisitions clearly suggest that a revanchist PRC remains the country's principal long-term security concern. Such concerns have been exacerbated with increased Chinese naval activity in the Indian Ocean littoral and its growing presence in Myanmar (Burma) (for a discussion of Indian concerns about Chinese naval activity in the Indian Ocean, see International Institute of Strategic Studies, Strategic Survey, 2008). Unfortunately, past naval acquisitions continue to hobble India's naval ambitions. The former Soviet-era *Admiral Gorshkov*, acquired at considerable cost and after significant delays, was finally inducted into the Indian fleet in early 2015. However, shortly thereafter, the vessel, re-named the I. N. S. *Vikramaditya*, ran into operational problems thereby limiting its range (Anandan 2015).

Apart from these bilateral security concerns, given India's recent spurt in economic growth, its policy-makers now visualize a larger role for India in Asia (on India's economic prospects, see Panagariya 2008). India demonstrated its capability as a regional actor when its naval forces acted in concert with those of the US, Japan, Singapore, and Australia to provide relief to Sri Lanka, Thailand, and Indonesia after the tsunami in December 2004.

In the nuclear arena, India will continue to make modest investments in its incipient nuclear capabilities to pursue a secure but robust nuclear deterrent (Basrur 2006). Despite bureaucratic and scientific pressures, it is unlikely that Indian policy-makers will pursue a substantial nuclear arsenal. Such an arsenal would provoke regional adversaries and also place an undue burden on the Indian exchequer. This argument can be asserted with some authority, based upon India's propensity for fiscal prudence in matters of defence spending and its orientation towards incremental decision-making.

What is more disturbing, however, is the bureaucratic-scientific-technological momentum that seems to be driving India's quest for ballistic missile defence (BMD). India's policy-makers, in turn, appear to have seen the pursuit of BMD as a technological panacea to the strategic conundrum that Pakistan's reliance on asymmetric forces poses to its national security. With a deployed BMD capability, they believe that India can call Pakistan's bluff if it threatens to resort to nuclear weapons when faced with an Indian conventional response in the wake of a Pakistan-sponsored terrorist attack.

Unfortunately, given the high level of mistrust that pervades Indo-Pakistani relations, Pakistan's security establishment has construed India's quest for BMD as an attempt to establish escalation dominance. Not surprisingly, Pakistan has sought to diversify its nuclear arsenal and has started to invest in tactical nuclear weapons, thereby lowering the nuclear threshold. These developments, if not checked in tandem, could help undermine strategic stability in the region (O'Donnell and Joshi 2013).

Notes

1 E.g. Sagan (1996) traces the origins of the nuclear programme to what he terms the 'domestic politics model'.
2 For a detailed discussion, see Ganguly (1999).
3 On the concept of a 'limited probe', see George and Smoke (1974).

References

Anandan, S. (2015) 'INS Vikramaditya's Operation Crippled', *The Hindu*, 21 February.
Bagchi, I. (2015) 'How Narendra Modi Reworked Rafale Deal, and Why It's a Winner', *The Times of India*, April 12.
Bajpai, K., Karim, A., and Mattoo, A. (2001) *Kargil and after*, New Delhi: Har-Anand.
Basrur, R. (2006) *Minimum Deterrence and India's Nuclear Security*, Stanford, CA: Stanford University Press.
Brines, R. (1968) *The Indo-Pakistani Conflict*, New York: Pall Mall.
Byman, D. (2005) *Deadly Connections: States that Sponsor Terrorism*, Cambridge: Cambridge University Press.
Chadha, V. (2005) *Low Intensity Conflicts in India: An Analysis*, New Delhi: Sage.
Chakravarti, S. (2008) *Red Sun: Travels in Naxalite Country*, New Delhi: Penguin.
Chari, P. R. and Mehta, A. K. (2001) *Kargil: The Tables Turned*, New Delhi: Manohar.
Cohen, S. P. (1971) *The Indian Army: Its Contribution to the Development of a Nation*, Berkeley: University of California Press.
Cohen, S. P. and Dasgupta, S. (2012) *Arming without Aim: India's Military Modernization*, Washington, DC: The Brookings Institution.
Ganguly, S. (1983) 'Why India Joined the Nuclear Club', *Bulletin of the Atomic Scientists* 39(4): 30–3.
Ganguly, S. (1989) 'Deterrence Failure Revisited: The India–Pakistani War of 1965', *Journal of Strategic Studies* 13(4): 77–93.
Ganguly, S. (1991) 'From Aid to the Civil to the Defense of the Nation: The Army in Contemporary India', *Journal of Asian and African Affairs* 26(1): 1–12.
Ganguly, S. (1997) *The Crisis in Kashmir: Portents of War, Hopes of Peace*, Cambridge: Cambridge University Press.
Ganguly, S. (1999) 'India's Pathway to Pokhran II: The Prospects and Sources of New Delhi's Nuclear Weapons Program', *International Security* 23(4): 174.
Ganguly, S. (2001) *Conflict Unending: India–Pakistan Tensions since 1947*, New York: Columbia University Press.
Ganguly, S. (2007) 'India's Foreign Policy Grows Up', *World Policy Journal* 20(4): 41–7.
Ganguly, S. (2008) 'India Held Back?', *Current History* 107(712): 369–74.
Ganguly, S. (2008) 'Nuclear Stability in South Asia', *International Security* 33(2): 45–70.
Ganguly, S. and Hagerty, D. (2005) *Fearful Symmetry: India and Pakistan in the Shadow of Nuclear Weapons*, Seattle: University of Washington Press.
Ganguly, S. and Kraig, M. (2005) 'The 2001–2 Indo-Pakistani Crisis: Exposing the Limits of Coercive Diplomacy', *Security Studies* 14(2): 290–324.
Ganguly, S. and Mistry, D. (2006) 'The Case for the US–India Nuclear Agreement', *World Policy Journal* 23(2): 11–20.
Ganguly, S. and Pardesi, M. (2008) 'India and Energy Security: A Foreign Policy Priority', in H. V. Pant (ed.) *Indian Foreign Policy in a Unipolar World*, London: Routledge, 99–127.
George, A. and Smoke, R. (1974) *Deterrence in American Foreign Policy*, New York: Columbia University Press.
Gordon, S. (1995) *India's Rise to Power in the Twentieth Century and beyond*, New York: St. Martin's Press.
Gupta, S. (1966) *Kashmir: A Study in India–Pakistan Relations*, Bombay: Asia Publishing House.
Hodson, H. V. (1969) *The Great Divide: Britain, India, Pakistan*, London: Hutchinson.
Hoffmann, S. (1990) *India and the China Crisis*, Berkeley: University of California Press.
Horn, R. (1982) *Soviet–Indian Relations: Issues and Influence*, New York: Praeger.
International Institute of Strategic Studies (2008) *Strategic Survey*, New York: Routledge.
Jackson, R. (1975) *South Asian Crisis: India, Pakistan, Bangla Desh*, London: Chatto and Windus for the International Institute for Strategic Studies.
Jacob, J. F. R. (1997) *Surrender at Dhaka: Birth of a Nation*, New Delhi: Manohar.
Jahan, R. (1972) *Pakistan: Failure in National Integration*, New York: Columbia University Press.
Jervis, R. (1989) *The Meaning of the Nuclear Revolution: Statecraft and the Prospects of Armageddon*, Ithaca, NY: Cornell University Press.

Kapur, A. (1976) *India's Nuclear Option: Atomic Diplomacy and Decision Making*, New York: Praeger.

Kapur, S. P. (2007) *Dangerous Deterrent: Nuclear Weapons Proliferation and Conflict in South Asia*, Stanford, CA: Stanford University Press.

Kapur, S. P. (2008) 'Ten Years of Instability in a Nuclear South Asia', *International Security* 33(2): 71–94.

Kargil Committee Report: From Surprise to Reckoning (2000). Online. Available HTTP: <http://www.fas. org/news/india/2000/25indi1.htm> (accessed 13 October 2008).

Kavic, L. J. (1967) *India's Quest for Security: Defense Policies, 1947–1965*, Berkeley: University of California Press.

Khan, A. (1975) *Raiders in Kashmir*, Islamabad: National Book Foundation.

Kumar, C. (2015) '32 Years on, HAL Finally Hands over Tejas to IAF; Induction Still Far Away', *The Times of India*, January 18.

Ladwig, W. (2007) 'A Cold Start for Hot Wars? The Indian Army's New Limited War Doctrine', *International Security* 23(3): 158–90.

Lintner, B. (2015) *Great Game East: India, China, and the Struggle for Asia's Most Volatile Frontier*, New Haven, CT: Yale University Press.

Malik, V. P. (2006) *Kargil: From Surprise to Victory*, New Delhi: Harper Colllins.

Mearsheimer, J. (1983) *Conventional Deterrence*, Ithaca, NY: Cornell University Press.

Mirchandani, G. G. (1968) *India's Nuclear Dilemma*, New Delhi: Popular Book Services.

Mistry, D. (2014) *The US–India Nuclear Agreement: Diplomacy and Domestic Politics*, New York: Cambridge University Press.

Noorani, A. G. (1967) 'India's Quest for a Nuclear Guarantee', *Asian Survey* 7(7): 490–502.

Nuclear Threat Initiative (2008) *China's Missile Exports and Assistance to Pakistan*. Online. Available HTTP: <http://www.nti.org/db/China/mpakpos.htm> (accessed 8 October 2008).

O'Donnell, F. and Joshi, Y. (2013) 'India's Missile Defense: Is the Game Worth the Candle?', *The Diplomat*, August 2. Online. Available HTTP: <http://thediplomat.com/2013/08/indias-missile-defense-is-the-game-worth-the-candle/> (accessed 13 June 2015).

Panagariya, A. (2008) *India: Emerging Giant*, Oxford: Oxford University Press.

Racioppi, L. (1994) *Soviet Policy towards South Asia since 1970*, Cambridge: Cambridge University Press.

Raghavan, V. R. (2001) 'Limited War and Nuclear Escalation in South Asia', *Nonproliferation Review* 8(3): 82–98.

Sagan, S. D. (1996) 'Why Do States Build Nuclear Weapons? Three Models in Search of a Bomb', *International Security* 21(3): 54–86.

Sen, C. (1960) *Tibet Disappears: A Documentary History of Tibet's International Status, the Great Rebellion and Its Aftermath*, London: Asia Publishing House.

Singh, A. (2001) *A Ridge Too Far: War in the Kargil Heights, 1999*, Patiala: Motibagh Palace.

Swami, P. (1999) *The Kargil War*, New Delhi: LeftWord.

Swami, P. (2007) *India, Pakistan and the Secret Jihad: the Covert War in Kashmir, 1947–2004*, London: Routledge.

Talbott, S. (2004) *Engaging India: Diplomacy, Democracy and the Bomb*, Washington, DC: The Brookings Institution.

Tellis, A. (2000) *India's Emerging Nuclear Posture: Between Recessed Deterrence and Ready Arsenal*, Santa Monica: The Rand Corporation.

Tellis, A. (2011) *Dogfight! India's Medium Multi-Role Combat Aircraft Decision*, Washington, DC: Carnegie Endowment for International Peace.

Thomas, R. G. C. (1978) *The Defense of India: A Budgetary Perspective of Strategy and Politics*, Delhi: MacMillan.

Thomas, R. G. C. (1986) *Indian Security Policy*, Princeton, NJ: Princeton University Press.

Zaheer, H. (1994) *The Separation of East Pakistan: The Rise and Realization of Bengali Muslim Nationalism*, New York: Oxford University Press.

24

AFGHANISTAN: A STATE IN LIMBO

Amin Saikal

Afghanistan has historically been characterized by weak state power in dynamic tension with a strong (but fragmented) society. Its population is composed of various ethnic, tribal, linguistic, cultural, and religious groups forming distinct micro-societies, with most of them having extensive cross-border ties with Afghanistan's neighbours. These social and cultural divisions have traditionally played a critical role in attempts to create national unity and institutionalized processes of statebuilding in the country. Although the turbulence of the past thirty-seven years has profoundly affected Afghanistan, the country's micro-societies have remained salient in shaping Afghan politics and society.

However, since the attacks in the US on 11 September 2001 and Washington's immediate response to them, three additional factors, partly grounded in these social divisions, have come to undermine quite seriously the process of stabilization and reconstruction of Afghanistan: the fragmentation and corruption of the governing elite, the flawed strategy of the US and its NATO allies in dealing with Afghanistan's problems, and the strengthening of counter-systemic actors. However, as a result of the May 2014 election and its run-off, Afghanistan has a new political leadership now, with a promise of improvement in all sectors.

This chapter has five parts, corresponding to the factors outlined above. The first provides historical background information on Afghanistan and its place in world politics. The second addresses elite fragmentation, identifying it as a key problem for Afghanistan's transition. The third part looks at the negative consequences of the US and NATO strategy in dealing with Afghanistan. The fourth looks at 'counter-systemic actors', such as the Taliban. The fifth focuses on the aftermath of the 2014 presidential elections and will identify issues and prospects for positive change under the new leadership.

Background

Afghanistan has been a seriously disrupted country ever since the pro-Soviet communist coup of 27 April 1978, which brought to power a cluster of Marxist-Leninists within the People's Democratic Party of Afghanistan (PDPA). This cluster had no internal cohesion, historical legitimacy, administrative experience, or popular base of support to achieve its publicly professed goal of transforming Afghanistan – a traditional, multifaceted Muslim country – into a modern

Socialist state. As the PDPA disintegrated into factionalism and faced growing popular resistance from religious groups (see Arnold 1983), the Soviet Union finally invaded Afghanistan in late December 1979 to save the rule of the PDPA and to protect its own long-standing political, economic, and military investment in Afghanistan, where it had been engaged in the context of the Cold War from the mid-1950s.

However, three factors prevented the Soviets from accomplishing their mission. First, they could not unite the PDPA's rival factions to create an effective government in Kabul. Second, they could not convince either the Afghan people or the international community that the invasion was justified. Third, the US and its allies found a unique opportunity to inflict a mortal blow on the USSR by backing various Afghan Muslim resistance groups (the mujahideen) to mount a *jihad* ('holy war') against the Soviet occupation. In the process, they helped mobilize a large number of volunteers from the Muslim world, especially from Arab countries, to assist the mujahideen, and used the neighbouring Muslim country of Pakistan as the main conduit for financial, logistical, and military support (see Saikal 2012: Chapter 9).

The Soviet defeat and withdrawal from Afghanistan by May 1989 opened the way for the mujahideen to institute a conservative religious government for the first time in Afghan history (for details of the Soviet withdrawal, see Kalinovsky 2011). Meanwhile, the US dramatically scaled down its involvement in Afghanistan, leaving the post-conflict management of the country to predatory and rival neighbours, especially Pakistan. The mujahideen consisted of a number of disparate groups divided along ethnic, tribal, linguistic, sectarian, and personality lines, reflecting the socially divided nature of Afghan society. As they turned their guns on one another, Afghanistan was plunged into internecine conflict.

To advance its regional interests, which largely coincided with those of the US and several pro-Western conservative Arab states (led by Saudi Arabia), especially against the Iranian Islamic regime, Pakistan, or more specifically its powerful Inter-Services Intelligence (ISI), found it expedient to raise a new extremist Islamic force – the Taliban – to take power in Afghanistan. The Taliban took over Kabul in September 1996, and within two years were in control of 80 per cent of Afghanistan. Commander Ahmed Shah Massoud, who had previously served as the defence minister in the government of mujahideen leader Burhanuddin Rabbani, retreated to north-eastern Afghanistan, now to fight what was widely perceived as Pakistan's 'creeping invasion'. At the same time, a prominent Saudi veteran of the Afghan jihad, Osama bin Laden, accompanied by many of his al-Qaida operatives, returned (via Pakistan) to Afghanistan to help the Taliban in return for safe sanctuaries. In 1997, bin Laden was joined by the leader of the Egyptian Islamic jihad, Ayman al-Zawahiri, and many of his supporters, strengthening the al-Qaida network (see Saikal, 2012: Chapter 9).

It was from Afghanistan that the al-Qaida leadership masterminded a number of terrorist operations against US targets. The most significant of these were the 11 September 2001 attacks on New York and Washington, which prompted the US to retaliate with military operations against the Taliban and al-Qaida in Afghanistan, as well as a broader so-called 'global war on terrorism'. By November 2001, the Taliban government had been toppled. A month later, the internationally backed government of Hamid Karzai (December 2001–October 2014) was installed to transform Afghanistan into a secure, viable, and democratic state (Bird and Marshall 2011: Chapter 2). However, neither the Karzai government nor its international backers, especially the US, were able to achieve their objectives over the next twelve years until the end of Karzai's terms of office and the withdrawal from Afghanistan of most of the US forces and those of its NATO and non-NATO allies. The reasons for this failure are shown in the following section.

Elite fragmentation

The fragmentation of the governing elite has proved to be highly damaging to Afghanistan's transition. Although all elite elements have expressed public allegiance to Islam as the common thread running through Afghan micro-societies, following the US-led toppling of the Taliban regime, they were divided into two informal clusters. One was made up of those who initially took over the reins of power primarily on the basis of an alliance with the US, and signed up to American-induced processes of secular change, democratization, and the so-called 'war on terrorism'. The other was composed of those who originally entered a nominal partnership with the first cluster, but remained sceptical of the US approach and agenda.

The first cluster was essentially led by the US-backed President Karzai, notwithstanding his subsequent disillusionment with Washington, especially after his re-election in 2009 on a fraudulent basis and America's objection to it. It included many figures who came from the ranks of the Afghan diaspora, primarily from the US and Europe, and who occupied most of the important cabinet posts, specifically the ministries of Defence, Finance, the Interior, the Economy, and Foreign Affairs. Lacking popular constituencies of their own in Afghanistan, they generally grew dependent on the US, and were therefore vulnerable to the ideological and policy preferences of the administration of President George W. Bush (2001–9). Initially, the overall goal was not only to marginalize defiant anti-US radical forces of political Islam, most importantly al-Qaida and its supporters, but also to cement the position of the US as the only superpower in the twenty-first century.

Zalmay Khalilzad, an Afghan-born American neoconservative and US presidential envoy to Afghanistan from late 2001 to late 2003, and then ambassador to the country from 2003 to 2005, played a determining part in managing Afghanistan's transition according to the new US foreign-policy agenda. He acted so vigorously that he gained a reputation as being the real ruler of Afghanistan. Despite serving as US ambassador to Iraq (2005–7) and then to the UN (2007–9), he continued an intimate involvement in the conduct of US Afghanistan policy, especially through a close relationship with Karzai and some of the high-ranking members of his entourage, in the appointment of whom he had a critical hand.

From the start, President Karzai and many of his supporters actively worked towards a strong presidential system of government, which was enshrined in a new constitution adopted by a Loya Jirga (the traditional Afghan assembly) in January 2004. In the process, they ignored warnings that such a system was unlikely to work in a war-torn country like Afghanistan with its myriad tribal, ethnic, linguistic, and sectarian divisions, and that it would typically produce one winner and many disgruntled but powerful losers, with the capability to challenge or undermine the victor. A more suitable alternative proposal was to create a parliamentary system of government, with the executive power resting with a prime minister and his or her cabinet, to be drawn from the parliament (see Saikal 2014: 35–44).

There were two important reasons for this: first, it would provide for a range of actors to be locked in a framework of national obligations and responsibilities, giving them involvement in national affairs. On the one hand, it would give micro-societies the necessary degree of autonomy in the exercise of their local affairs, while on the other hand it would embed them in the overall political system through their local representative bodies and the national parliament. Second, it would not place too much burden on one individual, who could easily become the focus of public discontent if things went wrong. In the meantime, it would prevent the winner from using the powers of his office to build up a system of patronage, and from acting as a delegative leader between elections, especially in the absence of a firm separation of powers, of the rule of law, of established systems of checks and balances, and of effective mechanisms of public scrutiny.

Under the 2004 constitution, Afghanistan also elected a two-chamber parliament, with the first one in 2005 and the second in 2010. Only individuals were allowed to stand for election, while political parties were banned under electoral legislation. These parliaments were far from perfect: they were fragmented bodies, reflecting partly the divided nature of Afghan society and partly Karzai's original opposition to party politics. Their members operated within informal groupings and ad-hoc alliances, based mostly on tribal, religious, factional, and ethnic allegiances. They included many strong local power holders or warlords, a number of whom had records of human rights violations and were determined to do whatever it took to protect themselves against any public scrutiny and prosecution. In many ways, these assemblies were reminiscent of the highly fragmented and ineffective parliaments that existed under the monarchy of King Mohammad Zahir during the period of 'New Democracy' (1964–73), when governments often had to resort to bribery, nepotism, and temporary alliances and counter-alliances to ensure the passage of their bills or to secure a vote of confidence for ministers (for a detailed discussion, see Saikal 2012: Chapter 6).

Even so, they proved to be far more representative than any before them. They were elected on the basis of universal suffrage, through a process endorsed by a number of credible international observers as quite fair and free. They provided a venue for a range of voices to be heard, with the potential to act more effectively in fulfilling their constitutional duties. However, Karzai's executive branch vigorously sought to marginalize the role of parliament in the processes of governance.

The growing lack of trust between the executive and legislative branches throughout the Karzai period seriously undermined the processes of building inter-institutional cooperation and institutionalized rather than personalized politics in Afghanistan. One of Afghanistan's deep-seated problems has historically been that power and political culture in the country have revolved around political personalities rather than political institutions as the foundation for stability and continuity. Political institutions have risen and fallen with personalities, rather than the former governing and regulating the behaviour of the latter. When the Taliban were ousted, Karzai, who enjoyed more international support than any of his predecessors, had a unique opportunity to turn a new page in Afghan history in this respect. However, his actions came to perpetuate dysfunctional Afghan political traditions.

Despite his initial promise to downplay the role of ethnicity in the interest of national unity, Karzai increasingly found it expedient to pander to his own ethnic group, the Pashtuns. Indeed, Karzai behaved more or less like any other Pashtun *khan* or tribal leader. He used his powers and international support to fill important governmental positions largely on the basis of family, tribal, ethnic, and factional connections, and to build patronage networks based on a system of favour and disfavour (Risen 2008). While Karzai was mostly bottled up in the presidential palace, some of his ministers turned various ministries into disconnected fiefdoms, often operating independently of the president. There was little effort to institute reforms and to create a unified, viable administration equipped with a well-trained and effective bureaucracy.

Populating mainly southern and eastern Afghanistan along the border with Pakistan, the Pashtuns have historically been made up of rival tribes (most importantly the Durranis, to which Karzai and most of his cohorts belonged, and Ghilzais, who make up the bulk of the Taliban and their supporters). The Pashtuns have traditionally formed the single largest cluster, but not the majority of the Afghan population. By leaning towards the Pashtuns, Karzai in effect promoted a policy of ethnic imbalance, which caused growing concern among the non-Pashtun segments of the population, which was borne out by the dispute over the results of the May 2014 presidential election and which will be discussed later. It is worth noting that the non-Pashtun segments suffered enormously under the highly discriminatory theocratic rule of the Taliban (1996–2001) and waged an armed opposition to it (for details, see Rashid 2000).

The second cluster within the governing elite was generally composed of those who grew increasingly uncomfortable with Afghanistan's pro-Western transformation and Washington's decisive role in the process. They advocated a more indigenously based, pro-Islamic mode of change, ostensibly more in tune with the social and cultural milieu of Afghanistan, and a more independent foreign policy posture. This cluster included many Afghans who remained in Afghanistan during the long years of turmoil preceding the US-led intervention, have had their own power bases in Afghanistan, and came from a strong traditional religious background, but found it expedient to join the governing elite as the best way to advance their personal ambitions and protect the interests of their constituencies. They included many former mujahideen leaders and local strongmen who have emerged since the fall of the Taliban. A number of them held formal government positions.

Although these two clusters were not cohesive and involved a degree of inter-cluster fluidity, some elements within the second cluster came to act from time to time as a counter-elite. They have sought, either through string-pulling within the government or through direct civil society activities, to influence government policies according to their preferences. In this, they have resorted to various civilian and military organs of the state (most importantly the cabinet and parliament), private print and electronic media outlets, and even peaceful public agitation, as well as pandering to the armed opposition whenever appropriate, to maximize pressure on the first cluster.

During Karzai's period, such elite fragmentation (Saikal 2012) resulted not only in highly damaging political intrigues and rivalries, but also in a lack of clear ideological direction within the government. From the start, the government was unclear on what it precisely stood for: was it a pro-Western secular democracy, with a pro-capitalist mode of development, but with which a majority of the Afghan people were not able to traditionally identify? Or was it a blend of Western and Afghan values and practices, amalgamated with traditions of religious authoritarianism, that proved to be very confusing to most Afghans?

The problems at the elite level were echoed within the population at large, particularly in the major urban centres. The years since the pro-Soviet communist coup of April 1978 have been marked by turbulence, bloodshed, uncertainty, and unpredictability. During this time, at least four different ideological groups have seized power in Afghanistan. Many ordinary citizens have had to deal with deceitful and corrupt practices in order to survive.

At the same time, external involvement of too many state and non-state actors in Afghanistan's transition has created a culture of dependency and complacency. As many of these actors have not been driven by altruistic aims, their activities have enhanced rather than diminished the culture of corruption and bribery among the Afghans. Society at large has become in some ways as dysfunctional and corrupt as the state bureaucracy.

US and NATO strategy

From the inception, the US as the driving power in Afghanistan failed to map out a strategy to integrate Afghanistan's security building with the country's political and economic reconstruction (for a detailed discussion, see Bird and Marshall 2011). The US initially deployed only 10,000 troops, toppling – but not defeating – the Taliban and their al-Qaida supporters. Other NATO countries contributed 5,000 troops to the International Security Assistance Force (ISAF) in Kabul. ISAF came under a separate command from the US forces, and there was little coordination between the two contingents. Whereas ISAF was initially only tasked with securing Kabul in support of the Karzai government, the US troops, who formed the bulk of the international military presence as part of 'Operation Enduring Freedom', were focused on hunting down al-Qaida and Taliban leaders. This level of troop deployment soon proved to be inadequate in a country that had been seriously disrupted by twenty-four years of warfare and bloodshed. It left the field wide open for the Taliban, their supporters, and a range of other sub-national actors – from local warlords and poppy farmers to drug traffickers and criminal gangs – to regroup and start making a comeback within a year of the US-led intervention (for failures of US and NATO strategy, see Jones 2006; Rubin and Rashid 2008; Saikal 2014).

Although it became clear as early as mid-2003 that more troops and resources were needed to expand the operations of ISAF and other foreign troops, neither the US nor its allies were willing to meet this requirement, especially because the US focus had already shifted away from Afghanistan to Iraq. On the other hand, for many NATO members, involvement in security building and reconstruction in Afghanistan was from the start a short-term commitment, undertaken largely as a way of avoiding sending troops to Iraq, for which there was little domestic support.

Even so, when the US and its partners finally found it necessary in 2004 to boost their troop deployment and expand their operations, they opted for a safe and incremental troop build-up. By the end of 2008, there were 40,000 ISAF troops (including 10,000 US soldiers) operating under NATO's command, and 20,000 under US command. But several European members of NATO still remained unwilling to deploy their troops in danger zones in the south. Finally, after repeated NATO requests for additional troops and better strategic coordination, the US and its allies boosted their troop numbers to close to 150,000 by 2011/2012. However, after a major review of America's Afghanistan strategy, Bush's Democrat successor, Barack Obama, modified the strategy from 'counterterrorism' to 'counter-insurgency', with an emphasis on greater linkage between reconstruction and security building, as well as exertion of greater pressure on Pakistan to curb its support for the Taliban and their affiliates. Obama, in late 2009, announced that most of the foreign forces would be withdrawn from Afghanistan by the end of 2014.

As the US allies followed suit, the revised strategy stressed the need for building the Afghan National Army (ANA), police force, border guard, and local police formations to take over security operations from the coalition forces and to work towards a political settlement with the Taliban as the best way to stabilize Afghanistan. Today, the Afghan security forces number about 350,000. Although the ANA has acquired a capacity to participate in many operations, many seasoned analysts believe that it is still short of capability to take on major military engagement without the support of foreign forces, the American air force in particular (Bumiller 2012). Its execution of increased operations has resulted in an unsustainable level of casualties. This is expected to remain the case for some years to come. As for the police force and border guard, the first is reportedly quite corrupt and unreliable, and the second remains underdeveloped and poorly equipped to make any meaningful contribution towards securing Afghanistan's borders, especially along the long and treacherous frontier with Pakistan (see Rashid 2008: Chapter 10; Saikal 2008). The same applies to the local police forces. The only security apparatus that has performed with any degree of effectiveness is the intelligence agency, the National Directorate for Security. But even this agency, like other branches of state power and the government as a whole, is suspected of being penetrated extensively by opposition forces (for an example, see Saikal 2014: 26–8; Schmitt 2008).

The US and many of its allies have failed to focus on the significant linkage between military security and human development. US policy-makers in particular have demonstrated a poor understanding of Afghanistan's history and its social, cultural, and regional complexity (see Gates 2014: 33). Washington initially shunned the idea of a 'Marshall Plan for Afghanistan' because, in its view, a small amount of money could go a long way in the country. According to a major report by the Agency Coordinating Body for Afghan Relief (ACBAR), of the more than US$20 billion promised by the international donors between January 2002 and January 2008, some US$9 billion was still outstanding. Of the amount distributed, 40 per cent went back to the donor countries in consultant fees and expatriates' pay, with most of the remaining funds being spent on the operations of the UN and non-governmental organizations as well as foreign contractors and sub-contractors.

The same report makes it clear that 'while the US military spends $100 million a day, the average amount of aid spent by all donors combined has been just $7 million a day since 2001' (Leithead BBC News 2008). The result has been far less investment in the reconstruction of Afghanistan per head of the population than has been the case with three concurrently disrupted states: Bosnia, Kosovo, and East Timor. This has meant that a majority of the Afghans have not benefited from the post-Taliban reconstruction and have not experienced a positive change in their living conditions. They have therefore had little reason to remain supportive of the Karzai government, its succesor, and their foreign backers.

From the start, the US regarded Afghanistan's transformation as being conditional on the success of the 'war on terror' and Pakistan's partnership in achieving this success. However, concerned about possible developments that could result in the isolation of nuclear-armed Pakistan, Washington did not insist upon structural adjustment in Islamabad's approach to Afghanistan. The regime of General Pervez Musharraf, who was forced out of office on 18 August 2008 after nine years of military dictatorship, made the most of Washington's approach to help in promoting his regime's interests rather than those of the US in the region (Hussain 2005: Chapter 6). While he received massive US economic and military assistance, amounting to more than US$10 billion by 2007, Musharraf neither denied the Taliban sanctuaries in Pakistan nor withheld logistic support.

Musharraf's policies contributed to the 'Talibanization' of Pakistan's border areas with Afghanistan, undermining the US and NATO stabilization efforts in Afghanistan on the one hand, and generating a serious threat to Pakistan's stability and security on the other. Musharraf's successor, Asif Ali Zardari (2008–13), a highly controversial, polarizing, and unpopular figure, had little influence with Pakistan's powerful military and intelligence agency (ISI), which has acted as the driving force not only in Pakistan's domestic politics, but also in its Afghanistan and Kashmir policies for a long time. The same has proved to be the case with Zardari's successor, Prime Minister Nawaz Sharif, whose Muslim League (N) party won Pakistan's 2013 elections. Despite his overtures for improved relations with Afghanistan and India, he too cannot be expected either to halt Pakistan's support for the Afghan Taliban or to resolve the Kashmir problem for as long as the Pakistan military, and more specifically the ISI, remains the main actor on these fronts.

Meanwhile, for all practical purposes, Afghanistan has become a narco-state, which will continue to be the case even if the Taliban are eliminated. Once again, its opium poppy cultivation hit an all-time high in 2013/14, making it one of the largest producers in the world, despite years of counter-narcotic efforts on the part of the US and its allies (see *The Guardian* 2014; Rubin and Sherman 2008). Proceeds from the drug trade have become a main source not only for funding the operations of the Taliban and other private militias, but also for enriching many government officials who have been heavily involved in the industry. The Afghan government and outside actors have not come up with a common approach to tackle the problem.

Counter-systemic actors

The factors of elite fragmentation, poor and corrupt governance, societal decline, and a flawed approach by external actors (mainly the US) to Afghanistan's transformation have interacted to generate space and opportunities for a number of counter-systemic actors. Chief among these are the Taliban, with one ISI-linked Taliban-affiliated group, the *Haqqani* network, and two noted spoilers on their tail: the *Hizb-e Islami* (Islamic Party) of former mujahideen leader Gulbuddin Hekmatyar, and al-Qaida. The Taliban are not the best trained, equipped, or led force. The movement is largely made up of poorly trained, fed, and clothed fighting clusters, who have lacked support from external global powers, unlike the mujahideen in the 1980s, who were backed by the US. It has become formidable largely because of the political and security vacuum that the failures of the Karzai government and its foreign allies generated – a vacuum that Karzai's successors have not been able to address. The Taliban have skilfully drawn on these failures at both the strategic and the operational levels to mount a serious challenge from outside the system. The Taliban's projection of themselves as defenders of the faith, country, and honour, as well as providers of better security and living conditions have resonated historically and culturally among some of the Afghan people. This has been nowhere more evident than among the ethnic Pashtuns.

The 2014 presidential election

In the midst of all this, Afghanistan had a crucial presidential election in April 2014. President Karzai's two terms came to an end on 22 May of that year, and he was constitutionally required to transfer power to an elected successor. He had pledged to oversee a clean and fair election under pressure from the US and its allies. However, the results of the second round or run-off in June between the two leading candidates, Abdullah Abdullah and Ashraf Ghani, both of whom had served in Karzai's cabinet in the past as foreign and finance minister respectively, turned out to be very messy. Karzai's handpicked members of the Independent Election Commission and the Independent Electoral Complaints Commission worked hard along ethnic lines to eschew the results in favour of Ghani as a Pashtun frontrunner, involving a claim of extensive fraud against Abdullah, who is from a mixed Pashtun and Tajik background. As Abdullah sought to boycott the results, which extensively reversed his win of 45 per cent of the votes against Ghani's 31.5 per cent in the first round (BBC News 2014) and to declare a government of his own, a dangerous electoral impasse transpired.

An alarmed US Secretary of State, John Kerry, intervened in order to avert a looming crisis. He succeeded in persuading the two candidates to agree to a full audit of all the ballot boxes under international scrutiny and to the creation of a 'government of national unity' irrespective of who won the election. However, in a socially and politically divided and volatile country like Afghanistan, where personalization rather than institutionalization of politics, and a lack of viable electoral processes of political legitimation and appropriate political culture have historically dominated the landscape, Kerry's mediation and President Barack Obama's telephone calls urging the two Afghan political rivals to cooperate for the sake of national unity and stability showed once again the fragility of the Afghan situation. It once more underlined the fact that the future Afghan leaders, like most of their predecessors, could only assume the mantle of leadership with the backing of an outside power.

Finally, after four months of electoral wrangling and mounting pressure from US, European Union, and UN representatives, Ghani and Abdullah signed an agreement on 21 September to form a government of national unity on a 50–50 per cent basis. Accordingly, Ghani was declared president and Abdullah was allocated the newly created post of Chief Executive of the government (equivalent to prime minister), with a proviso to change the Afghan Constitution to formalize the position of prime minister in two years' time (for the full text of the agreement, see Trofimov 2014). The agreement provided for a very complex power-sharing structure and did not reflect what was widely believed to be a rigged election. Ghani hailed the election as a 'success', but this was widely disputed (see Keating 2014; Shahrani 2014)

However, the question of how a government of national unity in a politically and socially fragmented and war-torn country like Afghanistan could work remains daunting. Many seasoned analysts of Afghan politics and society could not remain very optimistic about its success in meeting the enormous challenges facing Afghanistan, although the two sides made a promising start during the first month in office. One of President Ghani's first major acts was to sign the Bilateral Security Agreement (BSA) with the United States to regularize the force status of the 10,000 troops that the US had decided to leave in Afghanistan beyond 2014, primarily on an advise-and-assist mission and for counterterrorism operations, on 30 September 2014. The BSA had been prepared during the last two years of President Karzai's term and had been ratified by a traditional Afghan grand assembly (Loya Jirga), but the president had refused to sign it on the grounds of serious personal discord with Washington.

Conclusion and outlook

The Afghans are now caught between three – each internally diverse – forces. One seeks to lead them down a path of secular political change, which is very much the province of President Ghani and is in conformity with outside interests, especially those of the United States. Another would like to see them move down the lane of an indigenously based moderate Islamic and democratic transformation, to which the Chief Executive Abdullah Abdullah and many of his supporters subscribe. The third wants them to embrace radical political Islam as the only viable ideology of salvation, which is advocated by the Taliban and their affiliates. The latter of these groups has grown convinced that despite their public rhetoric, the US and its allies will not and cannot afford to endure the burdens of Afghanistan indefinitely, and therefore that time is on their side. This is despite the fact that their non-participation in the presidential election marginalized their role in Afghan politics and society.

The major challenge now is how to build and maintain unity between the first two forces, co-opt the third one, and generate the right conditions for stability, security, and viability in Afghanistan. President Ghani's conciliatory moves towards Pakistan in order to reach a political settlement with the Taliban-led insurgents have not paid off so far. The announcement in July 2015 of the death of the Taliban leader, Mullah Mohammad Omar, who had reportedly died in a hospital in Karachi in April 2013, brought fresh complications. A power struggle within the Taliban over the announcement of Mullah Mohammad Mansour as Omar's successor resulted in a hardening of the Taliban's attitude and a spate of bombings in Kabul in early August. This prompted the Afghan Unity Government leaders to once again criticize the Pakistan government for not living up to its promise of curbing the Taliban's activities (*The Dawn* 2015). There is a need for a new approach, a new strategy, and possibly a new compact between Afghanistan and the international community. It is towards this goal that President Ghani and Chief Executive Abdullah now need to work, if they are to meet the enormous challenges that face Afghanistan both on internal and external fronts.

References

Arnold, A. (1983) *Afghanistan's Two-Party Communism: Parcham and Khalq*, Stanford, CA: Hoover Institution Press.

BBC News (2014) 'Afghan Elections: What Is at Stake in Presidential Vote', 7 July. Online. Available HTTP: <www.bbc.com/news/world-south-asia-26747496> (accessed 7 November 2015).

Bird, T. and Marshall, A. (2011) *Afghanistan: How the West Lost Its Way*, New Haven, CT: Yale University Press.

Bumiller, E. (2012) 'Pentagon Says Afghan Forces Still Need Assistance', *The New York Times*, 10 December. Online. Available HTTP: <http://www.nytimes.com/2012/12/11/world/asia/afghan-army-weak-as-transition-nears-pentagon-says.html?_r=0> (accessed 7 November 2015).

The Dawn (2015) 'Abdullah Abdullah Accuses Pakistan of Helping Afghanistan's Enemies', 11 August. Online. Available HTTP: <http://www.dawn.com/news/1199837> (accessed 7 November 2015).

Gates, R. M. (2014) *Duty: Memoirs of a Secretary at War*, New York: Alfred A. Knopf.

The Guardian (2014) 'Afghan Opium Poppy Cultivation Hits All-Time High', 21 October.

Hussain, R. (2005) *Pakistan and the Emergence of the Islamic Militancy in Afghanistan*, Farnham: Ashgate.

Jones, S. G. (2006) 'Averting Failure in Afghanistan', *Survival* 48(1): 111–27.

Kalinovsky, A. M. (2011) *A Long Goodbye: The Soviet Withdrawal from Afghanistan*, Cambridge, MA: Harvard University Press.

Keating, Michael (2014) 'The New Era for Afghanistan Has Come at a Cost', *The Guardian*, 25 September. Online. Available HTTP: <http://www.theguardian.com/commentisfree/2014/sep/25/afghanistan-new-era-come-cost-power-sharing-deal> (accessed 7 November 2015).

Leithead, A. (2008) 'Donors Accused of Failing Afghans', BBC News, 25 March. Online. Available HTTP: <news.bbc.co.uk/2/hi/south_asia/7311972.stm> (accessed 7 November 2015).

Rashid, A. (2000) *Taliban, Militant Islam, Oil and Fundamentalism in Central Asia*, New Haven, CT: Yale University Press.

Rashid, A. (2008) *Descent into Chaos: The United States and the Failure of Nation Building in Pakistan, Afghanistan, and Central Asia*, New York: Viking.

Risen, J. (2008) 'Reports Link Karzai's Brother to Heroin Trade', *The New York Times*, 4 October. Online. Available HTTP: <http://www.nytimes.com/2008/10/05/world/asia/05afghan.html?pagewanted=all> (accessed 7 November 2015).

Rubin, B. R. and Rashid, A. (2008) 'From the Great Game to Grand Bargain', *Foreign Affairs* 87(6): 30–44.

Rubin, B. R. and Sherman, J. (2008) *Counter-Narcotics to Stabilise Afghanistan: The False Promise of Crop Eradication*, New York: Center on International Cooperation, New York University.

Saikal, A. (2008) 'Securing Afghanistan's Border', *Survival* 48(2): 129–41.

Saikal, A. (2012) *Modern Afghanistan: A History of Struggle and Survival*, London: I. B. Tauris.

Saikal, A. (2014) *Zone of Crisis: Afghanistan, Pakistan, Iran and Iraq*, London: I. B. Tauris.

Schmitt, E. (2008) 'Afghan Officials Aided an Attack on US Soldiers', *The New York Times*, 3 November. Online. Available HTTP: <http://www.nytimes.com/2008/11/04/world/asia/04military.html?pagewanted=all> (accessed 7 November 2015).

Shahrani, N. M. (2014) 'Afghanistan at the Brink Again', *Los Angeles Review of Books*, 21 September. Online. Available HTTP: <https://lareviewofbooks.org/essay/afghanistan-brink-long-term-solution-growing-crisis/> (accessed 7 November 2015).

Trofimov, Y. (2014) 'Afghanistan Presidential Rivals Sign Power-Sharing Deal', *Wall Street Journal*, 21 September. Online. Available HTTP: <http://www.wsj.com/articles/afghanistan-presidential-rivals-sign-power-sharing-deal-1411287148> (accessed 7 November 2015).

25

IRAN

Rouzbeh Parsi

The primary reason for Iran's prominent role in the news and world politics in the last decade has been its nuclear programme. This does not mean that there are no other salient reasons for taking Iran into account when analysing Middle East affairs, but in terms of public perception and eventually actual politics, the nuclear issue became the one and only issue from the early 2000s onwards. In this chapter, I want to embed this current discussion in an account that is sensitive to the historical path dependencies (Amanat 1997; Atabaki and Zürcher 2003). I will look at Iran's political history (first section), the economy (second section), and then the foreign policy/security discussions (third section).

While research on Iranian nationalism and facets of identity and state policy has increased and improved in the past decade, decision-making in the Islamic Republic and various aspects of state–society relations remain woefully under-researched. The last major publications remain Buchta 2002 and Moslem 2002, which are in many ways outdated. Similarly Iranian military posture, defence policy, and foreign policy discourse have not been studied at length in a satisfactory manner (Golkar 2015; Ostovar 2016).

Iran's political history

The fear of outside meddling in domestic Iranian affairs, territorial loss, or fomenting of unrest among ethnic/religious minorities is deeply ingrained in the national consciousness, based on its history (Kashani-Sabet 1999). This means that Tehran will always attempt to confront enemies in foreign theatres rather than at home, and that its military doctrine is primarily defensive (Connell n.d.).

The long twentieth century

Throughout the nineteenth century Iran lost territory to both Russia and Great Britain. The treaties of Gulistan (1813) and Turchomanchai (1828) ratified the Russian conquests and remain to this day important chapters in most Iranian national historical narratives. They are concrete instances of denigration and echo the fear of the territorial dismemberment of the country into the present. While Iran was never formally colonized, it was in many ways in the grip of the two great powers present in this part of West Asia: Britain and Russia; in the St Petersburg agreement of 1907 the two countries decided to split Iran into spheres of interest – without informing the Iranian government.

The outward failure to preserve the state has also had its domestic equivalent, reinforcing a narrative of impotence and loss of sovereignty. These included giving the rival imperial powers (Russia and Great Britain) concessions, i.e. monopolies and reduced custom tariffs, or capitulatory rights, i.e. exempting citizens of empires from national law in legal disputes (Zirinsky 2007). These infractions of national sovereignty became increasingly controversial within the body politic of Iran as nationalist sentiment grew in the twentieth century (cf. Aghaie and Marashi 2015; Ansari 2012; Katouzian 1998).

The twentieth century has in many ways been a very eventful century for Iran. Within a span of a century, the country has experienced two revolutions, the first one, the Constitutional revolution of 1906 symbolically inaugurated the century (Afary 1996; Martin 2013), while the second, the Islamic revolution of 1978–9, in many ways brought all the trajectories of change, intentional or otherwise, to their logical meeting point (Abrahamian 2008; Kurzman 2005). Through the century the Iranian state initiated reforms to remake Iran in line with what it perceived as modernity – the perpetually changing condition embodied in a geographical entity, Europe. Europe was understood as modern, and its attributes, ranging from attire to behavioural patterns and institutions, to be imitated and internalized, thus transforming the Iranian state and society into members of the modern world. These various reforms, and the understanding of modernity that underpinned them, in the end represent different understandings and perceptions of the varieties of modernities (plural) that Iran has been exposed to, internalized, and grappled with. The Iranian state Westernized its laws, streamlined the judiciary, universalized education, and implemented uniform military service for all males. The creation of a functioning army (external security) and a national gendarmerie and police force (domestic security) combined with the creation of an expanding bureaucracy and education system constitutes the basic core of state modernization.

The Islamic revolution of 1978–9

The revolution in 1978–9 was built on an alliance of sorts between Islamists and leftists. The former borrowed a lot from the vocabulary and methods of the latter. This made the leftists overestimate their own importance and underestimate the reach and strength of the groups motivated by Ayatollah Khomeini (Abrahamian 1993; Arjomand 1988).

In 1905 the Constitutional revolution had started as a protest movement escalating into a much more fundamental change than anticipated (Bayat 1991). In contrast, the 1978 revolutionaries had a much more explicitly radical goal in mind from the very outset. Whether Islamist or leftist, the ambition was to overthrow the monarch, an outcome which at that point seemed far-fetched, as the Shah had one of the strongest military and security apparatuses in the region and was in no shortage of powerful allies and money. Yet the combination of cyclical perseverance (religious calendar of mourning for those killed by the state) and the clumsy missteps of a repressive state in disarray tested the mettle of the Pahlavi political and security establishment. The Shah (undoubtedly affected by the brain cancer he had been diagnosed with but kept secret) decided not to use overwhelming force against the demonstrators, and all his belated attempts at placating the protestors were rebuffed by the intransigent Khomeini. Very much as during the oil nationalization crisis with Prime Minister Mohammad Mossadeq in 1953, he left the country and allies to fend for themselves. This allowed Khomeini to return and, as the paramount leader of the revolution, take the reins of power.

The Islamic Republic

The Islamic Republic ate its own proverbial children. The Islamists first eliminated the Mojahedin-e Khalq (a sect like an amalgam of Marxism and Islamism, now an opposition movement, cf. Abrahamian 1989) who fought with them for control over the new state. Then the purge of all the variations of communists and socialists followed. The previously so strong Iranian communist party, Tudeh, was already a faint echo of itself in terms of organizational capacity and was more or less wholly eradicated by its previous revolutionary allies (Behrooz 1999).

What remained then were different versions of Islamism which fairly soon developed their own ideological spectrum; depending on the issue, we could recognize these as leftist or rightist positions. The reason for this development lies in the very nature of revolutions and the attempt to maintain political control (theocracy) and engender popular support (republic).

In short, revolutions seldom resolve the societal fissures that gave rise to them. On the contrary they quite often make things worse, exacerbating the social conflicts in society. The structural problems of the Islamic Republic: lack of social justice and economic development, and constantly circumscribed political anticipation for the populace, forces all circles within the power elite to constantly come up with answers and justifications. This need to produce such supposed remedies, short- as well as long-term attempts of all kinds, remains a constant feature of a system whose tolerance of ideological diversity has varied considerably over the years. Just like a parallel natural structure (fractal), e.g. a broccoli, the political discourse in Iran varies in breadth, but no matter how narrow this spectrum may be it will still produce a variety of answers in response to a fundamental set of re-occurring questions. Thus, regardless of how skewed the system may be towards the more conservative end of the spectrum, those conservatives allowed to stand for election will recreate a left–right span within their own group when addressing and identifying a plethora of political and social issues. Thus, one way or another, the functional equivalent of left/right or reformist/conservative positions and representatives will emerge (Parsi 2014).

The religious dimension

One of the salient but often misunderstood dimensions in modern Iranian history and politics is religion. Religion has played an important part in Iranian politics, both as an ideology and, more importantly, because of the status and influence of the *ulama*, the jurisprudents whose profession it is to interpret religious law. Obviously the role of religion and this 'clergy' has also increased with the creation of the Islamic Republic (Akhavi 1996, 2008; Mottahedeh 2000). Yet it is important to remember that religion is many different things that are not necessarily logically or practically entwined. It can be a component of a state ideology; be integral to a commonly held culture in society; be a practised belief among the population. But what it is not is a 'thing' that simply exists and sways minds and influences decisions. A reified concept of religion leads to residual explanations. In short whatever is left after accounting for more 'conventionally' nuanced phenomena (economy; politics) can be stuffed into the box of religion and tradition (Asad 1993, 2003; Shakman Hurd 2008).

Thus the republican element of this theocracy should not be neglected or underestimated. This system is a bewildering amalgam of religiously defined elements cohabiting with republican elements. Sovereignty rests, uneasily, with both those traditionally seen as the interpreters of the word of God (jurisprudents), and the people. The former follows (with variations and innovations) an age old system of theology and religious law, hierarchies that have resisted institutionalization and therefore remained quite dynamic. The latter bestows the right to participatory politics to all citizens, who get to choose president and parliament. Yet the right to vote is circumscribed through mechanisms that allow institutions appointed by the supreme leader to vet candidates for elected institutions – and also overturn decisions by those elected representatives (Arjomand 2009; Parsi 2012).

The Iranian economy

Oil was discovered in Iran in 1908 and when the British First Lord of the Admiralty Winston Churchill completed the switch of the Royal Navy from coal to oil in the 1910s the United Kingdom acquired a majority share in the newly founded Anglo-Persian Oil Company (later Anglo-Iranian Oil Company, presently British Petroleum (BP)). Since then, access to oil has been central to economic growth and military capability for countries across the globe. Just in the last thirty-odd years the Persian Gulf countries have exported 25–30 per cent of the oil available on the world market (see US Energy Information Agency 2015).

Nationalization of oil

Oil has been the single most important transformative element of the Iranian economy in the twentieth century. It provided the struggling Iranian state with income that over time made it rather independent of other forms of domestic revenue (the rentier state argument). This steady income, which grew rapidly with the oil crisis (in general the price of oil is very cyclical and neither boom nor bust has proved to be stable), allowed the state to grow as an institution, i.e. modernize itself and society, at a pace that other means of revenue (e.g. taxation) would never have supported.

The modernizing state was becoming increasingly self-aware, and the new generations of citizens its institutions educated were in turn fostered in a state nationalist ideology. Thus by the late 1940s the political rallying cry to nationalize Iran's oil assets brought cohesion to a very motley group of political and societal forces, and challenged both the British control of Iran's most important natural resource and the Shah, who defended the status quo. Similar sentiments and attempts were evident in other oil-producing countries like Venezuela and Saudi Arabia.

As a countermove to Iran's nationalization of its oil assets in early 1951, Great Britain instigated an oil embargo against Iran (with echoes into the present, when the EU implemented far reaching sanctions against the country) which broke the back of the Iranian economy and exacerbated already existing fissures in Mossadeq's coalition. In August 1953, British and American intelligence services organized a coup which solidified and steadily hardened the Shah's autocratic grip on Iranian society (Kinzer 2003). While the CIA was instrumental, it could not have succeeded without the active support of royalist elements in the Iranian Army and members of the clergy. This 'success' came into a different light with the unexpected and unlikely (as most revolutions are) revolution in 1979 that ended 2,500 years of monarchy in Iran and engendered the first modern theocratic republic in modern times (Kurzman 2005). The coup that allowed the Shah to continue modernizing the country but also left his increasing autocracy unchecked eventually generated a much larger earthquake, a revolution that upset both the regional balance and lost the US a vital ally – in CIA parlance, 'blowback' (Johnson 2004).

Beyond oil

While oil has been very much at the centre of the development of the Iranian state and society, it is important to remember that the Iranian economy has developed beyond oil in several crucial ways. The non-oil sector, covering both manufacturing and service, has grown, especially with lower oil prices and international economic isolation due to sanctions from the mid-2000s. These developments have a long trajectory but have also been accelerated by the isolation of the Islamic Republic. For better or worse, intentionally or not, substitutes have had to be found for goods and services that Iran has been deprived of due to sanctions and boycott. Combined with the baby boom of the 1980s, Iran now has a young and highly educated work force with a high potential both as a consumer market and a regional powerhouse of production of goods (Alizadeh and Hakimian 2014; Pesaran 2011).

The economy is in general badly managed and also hampered by bureaucracy and corruption. The structural problems of the economy, however, have also been exacerbated by isolation and sanctions. The US has sanctioned Iran for various issues (human rights violations; terrorism) since the hostage crisis in 1979–81, both by executive order (president) and acts of congress. The Iran Libya Sanctions Act (ILSA) of 1996 (renewed in 2006 as the Iran Sanctions Act) epitomizes the attempt to box Iran in after the end of the Iran–Iraq war in 1988. By targeting third parties, Washington was trying to isolate and undermine the Islamic Republic. These sanctions increase the cost for those who do business with Iran while limiting Tehran's choice. The real pain inflicted by sanction came, however, with the sanctions implemented by the European Union (based on UN Security Council resolutions, especially no. 1929 of June 2010, and in cooperation with the US) which eventually shut Iran out of the SWIFT global banking system and barred EU member states from purchasing Iranian oil (International Crisis Group 2013).

The state subsidies are a prime example of the difficult intersection of political and economic priorities. They were introduced during the war against Iraq in 1980–8, in order to support the poor and the wobbly middle class, and it has been clear for many years that they need to be dismantled. This is understood by all political factions as a necessary and unavoidable undertaking, yet the process has been avoided because it is politically difficult and socially dangerous. When the Ahmadinejad administration initiated the reform, it botched it, and it remains to be seen how exactly the subsidies are going to shrink without creating socio-economic havoc (Harris 2013, 2015).

Tehran has for some years now worked on becoming a regional energy hub (Central Asia; Pakistan; India) and also exports industrial products to neighbours. Iran's ability to attract and convince its neighbours to participate in such schemes is much better now, as sanctions and banking restrictions will be lifted as part of the nuclear agreement, the Joint Comprehensive Plan of Action (JCPOA) that was signed in July 2015.

Iran and international security

The Islamic Republic has ever since its inception been considered a spoiler and singularly intent on upsetting any regional modus vivendi or balance. In the early hot years of the revolution this was in many respects an accurate description and one the revolutionaries in Tehran would have enthusiastically subscribed to. With the end of the war against Iraq and the inevitable transition of Iranian society into a post-revolutionary phase, the discrepancy between fiery rhetoric and actual capability and willingness to change the regional order has grown. Today Iran is in many ways a status quo power that prefers a predictable environment to one in turmoil.

The nuclear issue

Iran's nuclear activities date back to cooperation with the US in the 1960s. The Shah wanted nuclear reactors for generating electricity and for their status value: in essence, nuclear power was a component in the transformation of Iran from a Third World state into a First World power (Patrikarakos 2012). This ambition yielded the Tehran Research Reactor in 1967, but did not get much further after the revolution, due to the war and lack of interest of the Islamic Republic. In the war against Iraq, Iranian troops were subjected to chemical gas attacks by Iraq, and this reinforced the sentiment that weapons of mass destruction were immoral – thus both Ayatollah Khomeini, the first supreme leader and his successor, Ayatollah Khamenei, have publicly stated their rejection of weapons of mass destruction (Porter 2014).[1] The weight of these statements vis-à-vis actual policy is obviously a matter of debate.

Iran began investigating the means for uranium enrichment in the late 1980s, but it was only after the nuclear-related construction work at Arak and Natanz was 'exposed' in 2002 that the issue became headline news. Most likely some aspects of this work were already known to Western intelligence agencies.

This then became an issue between the International Atomic Energy Agency (IAEA) and Iran, where the former demanded a suspension of all nuclear enrichment-related activities. Iran refused, and what followed were tense negotiations where the EU (eventually known as the E3, i.e. Great Britain, France and Germany) became Iran's counterpart in trying to resolve the issue. The Bush administration refused to negotiate with Iran, since it neither recognized the legitimacy of the polity of the Islamic Republic nor believed, as a principle, in the need to negotiate with 'rogue states'. The high representative of the EU, Javier Solana, and the foreign ministers of the E3 negotiated with Iran from 2003 onwards, trying to enforce the idea of zero enrichment, i.e. no enrichment of uranium on Iranian soil. Solana's successor Catherine Ashton continued this role but in a more formalized manner, as the Lisbon Treaty gave her the role of both vice president of the Commission and high representative with a foreign policy service (the European External Action Service). In effect the high representative became the coordinator of the P5+1 (the five permanent members of the UN Security Council plus Germany) efforts to solve this issue.

The problem with the negotiations was that the Bush administration was absent but yet very present. It was beating the drums of war against Iraq and implicitly putting Iran as next in line for similar treatment (Dunn 2007). The potential goodwill from cooperating with Tehran on defeating the Taliban was destroyed through the infamous State of the Union speech in January 2003 which depicted Iran, Iraq, and North Korea as an 'Axis of Evil'. The Iranians were acutely aware of the Bush administration's bellicosity and so probably the only relevant security-related bargaining chip the E3 could have used would have been an American guarantee of not pursuing 'regime change' in Iran. The E3 effected a freeze on Iranian enrichment activities while negotiations were conducted but this became, to all intents and purposes, a stalling operation, since Washington refused to cooperate. In Iran things turned for the worse as well, as the Khatami administration, humiliated by all the rebuffed attempts at some understanding with the US and EU, was succeeded by hard-right-wing President Ahmadinejad. The new president had made a tougher line against the West, and standing firm on the nuclear issue, a central part of his election platform.

Lacking support from Washington, and unable to get the Iranians to abandon their insistence on enrichment (no matter how symbolic), the negotiation effort collapsed in 2005. What followed was a continuous escalation and hardening of the positions of all sides involved. By the time the Bush administration came around to the idea of a negotiated settlement in 2008, the situation in Iraq had deteriorated (obviously related) and the Iranian government was increasingly attached to nuclear enrichment as a prestige project. In short, all sides had in different ways backed themselves into corners where they were far too comfortable to feel compelled to extract themselves.

The IAEA could not force Iran to comply with its demands and Ahmadinejad's confrontational style made things even worse. In 2006 the IAEA took the unprecedented step of referring Iran to the UN Security Council, which exacerbated and highlighted the extremely complicated political dimension of the matter. From this moment onwards, the UN, the EU, and the US increasingly sanctioned Iran in the hope of forcing it to comply with the zero enrichment demand, while Iran increased its enrichment capacity (centrifuges; stockpiles) in order to signal its refusal to give up enrichment or be cowed by the sanctions inflicted upon it.

Most international state actors, including those inclined to give Iran a fair hearing, became increasingly exasperated with the negotiation stance and style of the Ahmadinejad administration. The president went out of his way to raise the hackles of Western powers with inflammatory comments. These comments played well with more ardent revolution-nostalgic constituents in Iran, but spelled disaster for Iran's ability to sway international opinion in general and that of other state actors in particular. Russia and China had their own reasons for being reticent about stringent UN sanctions on Iran. These reasons ranged from principles of national sovereignty and an unwillingness to sign up to open-ended sanctions regimes reminiscent of those imposed on Iraq after 1991, to trade ties. These caveats notwithstanding, they did agree on UN Security Council resolutions imposing a series of sanctions and restrictions on Iran due to its refusal to cooperate to solve the issue.

The Obama administration was also in the beginning very much on the sanctions and zero enrichment line. In fact by 2009 sanctions had become the only game in town, both in Brussels and Washington (Parsi 2013). At times it was not clear to what end, nor was there much discussion about the actual impact of sanctions. This is an important question both for the research community and the policy world: to what extent can we ascertain the effect of sanctions (impact on target) and whether they are effective (force target to change behaviour or comply with demands)? (See the chapter on sanctions in this volume.) This discussion was rather subdued, if not wholly absent. Simply put, the US/EU could not stomach a frank review of how far sanctions could get them in changing Iran's stand on the nuclear issue. The sanctions policy had taken on a life of its own, substituting for a more comprehensive policy; the instrument had become a goal in itself.

The status dimension of the issue, of being in charge of this dossier, became evident when two emerging regional powers, Turkey and Brazil, pursued a negotiation track of their own with Iran. They initially had the blessing of the Obama administration to do this, but when they actually managed to reach an agreement with Iran, Washington immediately rejected the results. While the deal would not have resolved all the outstanding issues, it would have significantly diminished Iran's stockpile of enriched uranium, while acknowledging Iran's right to enrich. This deal came about just as Washington had managed to get Russia and China on board for a new Security Council resolution (1929) that significantly increased sanctions on Iran. In a classic case of process triumphing over substance, the Obama administration opted for more sanctions rather than a partial solution to the actual problem. Similarly to the out-of-hand rejection of a regional contact group for Syria which would include Iran in 2012, Secretary of State Hillary Clinton dismissed the Turkey/Brazil proposal (Parsi 2010).

Towards the nuclear deal

The ensuing impasse with its escalatory dynamics (more sanctions, more centrifuges) continued until a variable on each side of the equation changed: the Obama administration realized that enrichment on Iranian soil was a reality that could not be sanctioned away, and President Ahmadinejad's second term came to an end. Already, before the end of his tenure, he had in many ways become a lame duck, and secret talks between Iranian and US officials took place in Oman in late 2012/early 2013. In the Iranian presidential elections in 2013 the centrist candidate Hassan Rouhani won, receiving the votes of the reformist candidate, who bowed out. Rouhani is a well-connected national security operator and was the chief nuclear negotiator during the rule of President Khatami. In this regard he was exactly the right person to rekindle the talks on the Iranian side, having the confidence of the supreme leader as well as credibility as a negotiator in the eyes of the US and the EU.

The new Iranian president and his foreign minister, the veteran diplomat Javad Zarif, embarked on a 'charm offensive' to restore the relationship with European countries that Ahmadinejad and sanctions had wrecked. New negotiations began in earnest, and in November 2013 a Joint Plan of Action was agreed upon.[2] This interim agreement slowed the pace of enrichment in Iran and removed parts of the existing stockpile, thus distancing Iran from the amount set as a red line by several parties, including Israel. The break-out time that is often referred to is the time it takes Iran to produce enough 20 per cent enriched uranium that, if enriched to weapons grade, i.e. 90 per cent, would be sufficient for one nuclear explosive device (Thielmann 2014; Vaez 2015). In return, Iran would receive some of the money that had been frozen in accounts all over the world due to the banking sanctions.

This was a breakthrough, as it ended the negative cycle of grandstanding on both sides. The process was immediately set upon by groups and forces on both sides of the barricades, as it were, who have in many ways gotten used to, are comfortable with, and bank on the institutional enmity between Iran and the US. Iranian hardliners, American right-wing politicians, lobby groups like the American Israel Public Affairs Committee (AIPAC), and the Israeli Prime Minister Binyamin Netanyahu opposed the idea of any kind of diplomatic solution to the problem and often employed similar arguments to depict any negotiated settlement as treasonous, dangerous, and capitulation to the rogues on the other side of the conflict.

The extent to which all actors, in their domestic politics, were wedded to the status quo and often had internal opposition and foes more formidable than the counterparts they were engaged in negotiating with, became increasingly clear as the negotiations progressed. The negotiations had a rhythm that stalled in 2014, since they were primarily conducted in intense bursts that indicated that the matter was solvable but also made the gaps between the negotiating positions clear. These high-level meetings did yield results (and surprises) but were, as individual episodes, too short to bring the matter to a close.

In the last round in 2014 the negotiating parties gave themselves two deadlines: 1 April 2015 for reaching a framework agreement encompassing all the basic conditions that needed to be met in a final settlement of the issue. Its content was, in a sense, not particularly surprising, since the fundamental contours had been clear for some time; what had been lacking previously was the political will to accept painful concessions and the risk entailed in making peace with the enemy. The second deadline for the final settlement was 1 July. Thus, instead of continuing with intense bursts of negotiations, the whole spring, especially April–July, became one long negotiation marathon. This allowed the parties to really delve into the knots and resolve them one by one. Even then the negotiations went into overtime, with Secretary of State John Kerry and Foreign Minister Javad Zarif spending an unprecedented amount of time together to iron out all the remaining questions.

On 14 July the deal was sealed by the Iranian foreign minister and the P5+1 representatives led by the EU High Representative Frederica Mogherini. The JCPOA is an incredibly detailed text setting out not only Iran's obligations under the NPT and Additional Protocol, but even more stringent controls and constraints on its nuclear enrichment programme. It also sets out how the sanctions on Iran are going to be removed, in the intricate legal web of UN, US, and EU regulations (International Crisis Group 2013).

Foreign policy

Iran's geopolitical outlook is now one of preserving the regional status quo while insisting on foreign troops (i.e. non-regional – in short American) leaving the theatre. This both plays to

Iran's strength (one of the larger countries of the region) and stays true to the revolutionary ethos of anti-imperialist anti-Americanism. The prospect of this being more than wishful thinking has increased in the last ten years due to the American invasion of Iraq. The invasion removed Saddam Hussein as a threat against Iran, while the disastrous aftermath of the American invasion in turn created opportunities for Iran-friendly Iraqi dissident groups to gain ground, and compelled the US to rethink its presence and commitments in the Middle East (Parsi and Rydqvist 2011; Ramazani 2013)

The nuclear agreement and the concomitant opening of a continuous dialogue and exchange between Washington and Tehran will therefore have repercussions on the strategic balance in the region. Major American allies like Saudi Arabia and Israel, the former more than the latter, will have to adjust accordingly – they can no longer assume that the US will keep Iran boxed in. In fact Tehran and Washington have not only conflicting interests (conventional wisdom all sides are comfortable with highlighting) but also overlapping interests which cannot be ignored by returning to the instinctive mutual condemnation of the past thirty-odd years.

Iran and Turkey have had a long-standing historic rivalry, but this is now subsumed in a very mutually beneficial economic relationship that transcends sectarian rhetoric and proxy wars such as the one in Syria. In this regard Turkey is not a threat to Iran. Similarly Saudi Arabia, for all its belligerent and passive aggressive manoeuvring, does not constitute a conventional military threat. The only country that has actually invaded Iran in modern times is Iraq, and this country constitutes a strategic ally that Tehran can ill afford to turn against it. This, together with the proliferation of *takfiri* jihadists in Iraq and Syria and also now in Afghanistan, are the most pressing military threats against Iran (cf. Esfandiary and Tabatabai 2015).[3] Iran's involvement in Syria is, in this sense, more optional than the engagement in Iraq. In Syria, Iran has two objectives: securing a land route to its ally Hezbollah in Lebanon (its outer defence against Israel), and denying control of Syria to *salafi* jihadist groups ideologically and/or politically aligned with Saudi Arabia. Thus Tehran's support is not predicated on Bashar al-Assad as a person and, considering the cost (money as well as troops), will not be open-ended (Goodarzi 2009).

Conclusion

Iran is torn between its revolutionary past and a need for normalization of its relations with the outside world. The defiant and confrontational version of the revolutionary heritage is propagated by a politically conservative section within the political elite and their supporters, while society at large is more inclined towards normalization and accommodation with the outside world. Iran is in many ways a post-revolutionary society (the majority of the population was born after the 1978 revolution) governed by a political elite that has yet to come to terms with this reality. Thus Iran, as a supposedly revolutionary state, generates at times very contradictory policies and positions, both domestically and in its foreign and security policy.

The security services and armed forces are guardians both of the country and the state, and a specific, quite hard-line, interpretation of what the revolutionary ethos requires of Iran as a state actor on the international scene. This is in general a rather bleak perspective which tends to securitize (Buzan et al. 1998) all kinds of issues, domestic and foreign. Yet, the resolution of the nuclear issue does yield lessons not only on common mistakes but also on ways out of these security dilemma impasses. They furthermore point to some of the grave mistakes made in the Syrian conflict and indicate that while the success of the nuclear negotiations may be replicable to some degree, the lessons of that issue have not yet been fully digested.

First, it is important to underline that the negotiating partners were for a long time locked in their own policy, which was not primarily dictated by the characteristics of the issue at hand, but rather by what was acceptable and feasible in their own domestic political environment. In short, foreign policy is dictated by domestic concerns, and is not necessarily geared toward solving a problem on the international scene. In the political context of Western capitals, sanctions went from being a means, to becoming the least common denominator and thus all too seldom questioned or challenged with regard to whether they would achieve the stated aim of their implementation. In Tehran, in turn, nuclear enrichment and production of centrifuges became an unquestionable policy fixture whose costs and negative political fallout were for a long time left unmentioned.

Second, for quite some time both sides insisted on preconditions for negotiations that preempted the whole point of negotiating (compared with the endless posturing about how to negotiate the Syrian ordeal). Third, when serious negotiations were eventually undertaken, both sides overestimated their own strength and underestimated that of their adversary. Both sides believed that they entered the negotiations from a position of strength, while their adversary had been forced to the table due to its relative weakness. Thus the expectations on what the other side would give up were exaggerated, while the concessions each side imagined it would have to make were too modest.

These three mistakes were made and hence prolonged the impasse and aggravated the problem, and also its implications for resolving other issues in the region such as Iraq and Syria (the US insisting on excluding Iran from political deliberations). Yet, the formula of win–win, i.e. that a negotiated solution is not framed and constrained by a zero-sum game approach, allowed the negotiators to eventually reach a mutually acceptable agreement.

Notes

1 'Imam Opposed Weapons of Mass Destruction (W.M.D)', 2013-09-22, http://en.imam-khomeini.ir/en/n6140/News/Imam_Opposed_Weapons_of_Mass_Destruction_W_M_D_; 'Iran Nuke Program 2 ABCs from Khamenei', 2014-11-18, http://iranprimer.usip.org/blog/2014/nov/18/iran-nuke-program-3-abcs-khamenei

2 Joint Plan of Action, 24 November 2013, http://eeas.europa.eu/statements/docs/2013/131124_03_en.pdf

3 For a collection of reactions by top Iranian officials to the success of Da'esh see 'Why must we tackle Qasem Soleimani's warning about Da'esh attacking Iran seriously?', Mashregh News, 2015-05-30, http://www.mashreghnews.ir/fa/news/422659/چرا-باید-هشدار-قاسم-سلیمانی-درباره-حمله-داعش-به-ایران-را-جدی-بگیریم

References

Abrahamian, E. (1989) *Radical Islam: The Iranian Mojahedin*, London: I. B. Tauris.

Abrahamian, E. (1993) *Khomeinism: Essays on the Islamic Republic*, Berkeley: University of California Press.

Abrahamian, E. (2008) *A History of Modern Iran*, Cambridge: Cambridge University Press.

Afary, J. (1996) *The Iranian Constitutional Revolution, 1906–1911: Grassroots Democracy, Social Democracy, and the Origins of Feminism*, New York: Columbia University Press.

Aghaie, K. S. and Marashi, A. (eds.) (2015) *Rethinking Iranian Nationalism and Modernity*, Austin: University of Texas Press.

Akhavi, S. (1996) 'Contending Discourses in Shici Law on the Doctrine of Wilayat Al-faqih', *Iranian Studies* 29(3): 229–68.

Akhavi, S. (2008) 'The Thought and Role of Ayatollah Hossein'ali Montazeri in the Politics of Post-1979 Iran', *Iranian Studies* 41(5): 645–66.

Alizadeh, P. and Hakimian, H. (eds.) (2014) *Iran and the Global Economy: Petro Populism, Islam and Economic Sanctions*, London: Routledge.

Amanat, A. (1997) *Pivot of the Universe: Nasir al-Din Shah Qajar and the Iranian Monarchy, 1831–1896*, Berkeley: University of California Press.

Ansari, A. M. (2012) *The Politics of Nationalism in Modern Iran*, New York: Cambridge University Press.

Arjomand, S. A. (1988) *The Turban for the Crown: the Islamic Revolution in Iran*, Oxford: Oxford University Press.

Arjomand, S. A. (2009) *After Khomeini: Iran under His Successors*, Oxford: Oxford University Press.

Asad, T. (1993) *Genealogies of Religion: Discipline and Reasons of Power in Christianity and Islam*, Baltimore, MD: Johns Hopkins University Press.

Asad, T. (2003) *Formations of the Secular: Christianity, Islam, Modernity*, Stanford, CA: Stanford University Press.

Atabaki, T. and Zürcher, E. J. (eds.) (2003) *Men of Order: Authoritarian Modernization under Ataturk and Reza Shah*, London: I. B. Tauris.

Bayat, M. (1991) *Iran's First Revolution: Shi'ism and the Constitutional Revolution of 1905–1909*, New York: Oxford University Press.

Behrooz, M. (1999) *Rebels with a Cause: The Failure of the Left in Iran*, London: I. B. Tauris.

Buchta, W. (2002) *Who Rules Iran? The Structure of Power in the Islamic Republic*, Washington, DC: Washington Institute for Near East Policy.

Buzan, B., Wæver, O., and de Wilde, J. (1998) *Security: A New Framework for Analysis*, Boulder, CO: Lynne Rienner.

Connell, M. (n.d.) 'Iran's Military Doctrine', *The Iran Primer*. Online. Available HTTP: <http://iranprimer.usip.org/resource/irans-military-doctrine> (accessed 26 November 2015).

Dunn, D. H. (2007) '"Real Men Want to Go to Tehran": Bush, Pre-Emption and the Iranian Nuclear Challenge', *International Affairs* 83(1): 19–38.

Esfandiary, D. and Tabatabai, A. (2015) 'Iran's ISIS policy', *International Affairs* 91(1): 1–15.

Golkar, S. (2015) *Captive Society: The Basij Militia and Social Control in Iran*, New York: Columbia University Press.

Goodarzi, J. M. (2009) *Syria and Iran: Diplomatic Alliance and Power Politics in the Middle East*, London: I. B. Tauris.

Harris, K. (2013) 'The Rise of the Subcontractor State: Politics of Pseudo-Privatization in the Islamic Republic of Iran', *International Journal of Middle East Studies* 45(1): 45–70.

Harris, K. (2015) 'The Breakaway Boss: Semiperipheral Innovations and the Rise of Mahmoud Ahmadinejhad', *Journal of World-Systems Research* 21(2): 417–47.

International Crisis Group (2013) *Spider Web: The Making and Unmaking of Iran Sanctions*, Middle East Report No. 138, 25 February. Online. Available HTTP: <http://www.crisisgroup.org/~/media/Files/Middle%20East%20North%20Africa/Iran%20Gulf/Iran/138-spider-web-the-making-and-unmaking-of-iran-sanctions.pdf> (accessed 26 November 2015).

Johnson, C. (2004) *Blowback: The Costs and Consequences of American Empire*, New York: Henry Holt.

Kashani-Sabet, F. (1999) *Frontier Fictions: Shaping the Iranian Nation, 1804–1946*, Princeton, NJ: Princeton University Press.

Katouzian, H. (1998) 'The Campaign against the Anglo-Iranian Agreement of 1919', *British Journal of Middle Eastern Studies* 25(1): 5–46.

Kinzer, S. (2003) *All the Shah's Men: An American Coup and the Roots of Middle East Terror*, New York: Wiley.

Kurzman, C. (2005) *The Unthinkable Revolution in Iran*, Cambridge, MA: Harvard University Press.

Martin, V. (2013) *Iran between Islamic Nationalism and Secularism: The Constitutional Revolution of 1906*, London: I. B. Tauris.

Moslem, M. (2002) *Factional Politics in post-Khomeini Iran*, Syracuse, NY: Syracuse University Press.

Mottahedeh, R. (2000) *Mantle of the Prophet: Religion and Politics in Iran*, Oxford: OneWorld Publications.

Ostovar, A. (2016) *Vanguard of the Imam: Religion, Politics, and Iran's Revolutionary Guards*, Oxford: Oxford University Press.

Parsi, R. (2010) 'The Trilateral Iranian Nuclear Agreement: Shell Games, International Style', *EU ISS Analysis*, May. Online. Available HTTP: <http://www.iss.europa.eu/uploads/media/RP-IranTurkeyBrazilpdf.pdf> (accessed 26 November 2011).

Parsi, R. (2012) 'Introduction: Iran at a Critical Juncture', in R. Parsi (ed.) *Iran: A Revolutionary Republic in Transition*, Paris: EU ISS Chaillot No. 128, 9–22.

Parsi, R. (2014) *Astute Gamesmanship and Realistic Ambitions: The Potential Success of the Rouhani Presidency*, International Policy Analysis, Friedrich Ebert Stiftung, November. Online. Available HTTP: <http://library.fes.de/pdf-files/iez/11031.pdf> (accessed 20 June 2015).

Parsi, R. and Rydqvist, J. (eds.) (2011) *Iran and the West: Regional Interests and Global Controversies*, Stockholm: FOI.

Parsi, T. (2013) *A Single Roll of the Dice: Obama's Diplomacy with Iran*, New Haven, CT: Yale University Press.

Patrikarakos, D. (2012) *Nuclear Iran: The Birth of an Atomic State*, New York: I. B. Tauris.

Pesaran, E. (2011) *Iran's Struggle for Economic Independence: Reform and Counter-Reform in the Post-Revolutionary Era*, London: Routledge.

Porter, G. (2014) 'When the Ayatollah Said No to Nukes', *Foreign Policy*, 16 October. Online. Available HTTP: <http://foreignpolicy.com/2014/10/16/when-the-ayatollah-said-no-to-nukes/> (accessed 26 November 2015).

Ramazani, R. K. (2013) *Independence without Freedom. Iran's Foreign Policy*, Charlottesville: University of Virginia Press.

Shakman Hurd, E. (2008) *The Politics of Secularism in International Relations*, Princeton, NJ: Princeton University Press.

Thielmann, G. (2014) 'Breaking Down Iran's Breakout Capacity', Arms Control Association, 24 September. Online. Available HTTP: <https://www.armscontrol.org/system/files/Iran_Brief_Breaking_Down_Irans_Breakout_Capacity.pdf> (accessed 26 November 2015).

US Energy Information Agency (2015). Online. Available HTTP: <www.eia.gov> (accessed 26 November 2015).

Vaez, A. (2015) 'Missing the Point on Iran's Nuclear Breakout Time. Five Common Misperceptions on the Metric That Has Dominated Debate over a Nuclear Deal with Tehran', *Al Jazeera,* 2 March. Online. Available HTTP: <http://america.aljazeera.com/articles/2015/3/2/five-misconceptions-about-iran-nuclear-talks.html> (accessed 26 November 2015).

Zirinsky, M. (2007) 'Riza Shah's Arrogation of Capitulations 1927–1928', in S. Cronin (ed.) *The Making of Modern Iran: State and Society under Riza Shah, 1921–1941*, London: Routledge, 81–98.

26

INTERVENTION IN IRAQ: FROM REGIME CHANGE TO DE FACTO PARTITION

Gareth Stansfield

Thirteen years after the US-led invasion, the situation in Iraq is unstable, dangerous, and transformative. From a relatively easy invasion followed by an early 'honeymoon' period, the US and its allies were confronted by the complexities of Iraqi political life as different sectarian and ethnic agendas came to the fore in the state-building negotiations that led to the passing of the Constitution of 2005. The failure to successfully accommodate Sunni voices into the negotiations led to the beginnings of a violent insurgency from Sunnis against US forces, and against the institutions of the new Iraqi government. Among the many nationalist and jihadist groups operating against the US and Iraqi government from 2004 onwards were a range of former Ba'th regime elements, and jihadists operating under the banner of al-Qaida Iraq led by Abu Musab al-Zarqawi. Later, these groups would reform as the Islamic State of Iraq and al-Sham (ISIS) under the leadership of Abu Bakr al-Baghdadi, who would proclaim himself the Caliph of the Islamic State following the conquest of Mosul in June 2014 (see McCants 2015; Weiss and Hassan 2015).

From 2014 onwards, following the fall of Mosul and the rise of the Islamic State, Iraq has in effect become divided into three separate entities – a Kurdistan Region in the north, a 'recognized' Iraqi state governed from Baghdad in the centre and south, and an Islamic State centred on Mosul between them. From this perspective, the US-led intervention in Iraq has been profoundly transformative. The unitary state no longer exists, and neither does the country enjoy territorial integrity. Sovereignty is no longer contested between different groups; it has been effectively divided between Kurds in Erbil, Sunni Arabs in Mosul, and Shi'is in Baghdad. And regional and international powers no longer deal with Iraq as an integrated whole. Instead, Iraq is dealt with, in foreign policy terms, as three entities. Whether this de facto reality becomes a *de jure* reality in the future remains to be seen.

This chapter has three parts. The first discusses the deteriorating security situation in Iraq after 2005, focusing on the long-term consequences of short-term actions pursued by the US in order to bring an end to the threat posed by AQI, but which ultimately led to the rise of the far more dangerous Islamic State. The second looks at drivers of (in)security on three interlinked levels: the domestic, the regional, and the international. The third focuses particularly on the regional repercussions of a weakened Iraq.

Detoriating security (2005–2014)

In the aftermath of the al-Qaida attacks of 11 September 2001, US policy-makers promoted the idea of regime change and the reconstruction of the Iraqi state as a 'beacon' of neoliberal democracy at the heart of the Middle East (Anderson and Stansfield, 2009). But the US plan failed. Iraq lurched from crisis to crisis, its social fabric unravelled, and power devolved away from the central state and became concentrated in the hands of those actors best placed to use it. Thus, even before the rise of the Islamic State in 2014, Iraq's cohesion had come unstuck and the plans of US policy-makers in 2003 were already consigned to history. But what other options than the one chosen would have been available to US policy-makers? This is addressed in the first subsection. In the second, US responses to the detoriating security situation are discussed. The third looks at the implications of the resurgence of ISIS from 2013 onwards.

The paucity of options

For some analysts, the fault for the deteriorating security situation lies with US policy planners whose conceptualization of Iraq was wrong. Believing Iraqi identity to be fractured, it is argued, the US based its plans on a 'historically illiterate' model (Visser 2008b). This model – which identified communal identities as the principle organizing blocks of Iraqi politics – then determined how the US reconstructed the state.

It is easy to attack the US for doing this, particularly if one considers the scale of the problems that now afflict Iraq. However, how fair is it to do this, and how logically coherent are arguments that contend that a different approach would have been better? While it might have theoretically been advantageous to build a political system in Iraq upon notions of civic nationalism and individual rights, the fact remained that Iraqi actors themselves had become organized into communal blocks. Just as imposing a communal view of Iraqi political life upon the country can be seen as simplistic, to impose a political system that ignored these blocks would have been unrealistic.

While the US has been complicit in building a political structure that is at best cumbersome, at worst unworkable, the critics of US actions did not propose suggestions that were any more workable. The accepted view of Iraqi political mobilization was that a cohesive nationalist project existed that would ultimately harden either in support of the US, or against it. These analysts largely were wrong. Instead, it is more persuasive theoretically and empirically to argue that the endemic insecurity had Iraqi origins.[1]

A more nuanced argument is that US decisions acted as a catalyst in allowing inherent communally based divisions to emerge and deepen in a political environment freed from the strictures of dictatorship. But, rather than a singular nationalist project emerging, multiple Iraqi nationalisms appeared. By 2005, the empowerment of political parties organized along lines of communal identity was complete, and in areas dominated by a particular community, security was provided by the most powerful. In the north, security was managed by the Kurdish 'peshmerga' fighters. In the south, the militias of a range of Shi'i parties organized security.[2] In the Sunni west and north, vast swathes of territory fell under the changeable control of Sunni tribes, remnant Ba'athist organizations, or prominent groupings linked to al-Qaida (Stansfield 2007b; Long 2008).[3]

The situation was such that the smallest spark would have the potential to ignite intercommunal conflict. With sectarian tensions increasing from 2005, Sunni–Shi'ite violence spread across central and south Iraq. This violence erupted in February 2006 with the destruction of the Shi'ite Askariyya shrine in Samarra. The sectarian war that followed resulted in ethnic cleansing of mixed towns and the effective partitioning of Baghdad, with the city effectively being taken over by Shi'ites by the end of 2007. A further, ethnic fault-line opened up from late 2007. Kurdish aspirations to maintain the autonomy within Iraq that they had enjoyed since 1991 and to expand their control to other disputed territories (and particularly the province of Kirkuk) brought them into direct confrontation with both Sunni and Shi'ite Arabs, Turkmens, and Christians (Anderson and Stansfield 2009; Gunter 2007; ICG 2008; Romano 2007; Stansfield 2003).

US responses – the 'surge' and the localization of security

For the embattled US government, which was desperate to show that Iraq was stabilizing, the collapse into civil war was problematic. The US responded with a multifaceted approach based upon increasing the military presence in Baghdad (the 'surge'), and also by seeking to bring into the security structure Sunni Arabs previously attracted to the neo-Ba'athists and AQI. The strategy was built upon the notion of 'local solutions for local problems'. Numbers of fatal attacks in Baghdad dropped spectacularly, as did the targeting of multi-national forces (see Dodge 2012).

Two questions suggest themselves when considering this development. The first is whether the surge was responsible for the decline in violence, or whether other factors, including the ceasefire called by Muqtada al-Sadr, a religious and militia leader, were decisive (Krohley 2015). Did the surge prevent violence, or was the impetus behind sectarian conflict, particularly in Baghdad, diluted because the communities had largely separated themselves into distinct areas by 2007? The second question focuses more on the implications of the 'surge'. Put simply, while the increase of US forces and the participation of Sunnis in the security system may have been successful, do these short-term gains have long-term consequences? Did the localization and communalization of security come at the price of the building of a cross-communal Iraqi identity?

In the north, the peshmerga were re-badged as the Kurdish contingent of the Iraqi Security Forces (ISF). A similar strategy was followed with regard to the militia of the SIIC – the Badr Army. Recruited en masse into the ISF, the intelligence service and the police force, the prominence of Badr members in the ISF led to accusations that the institutions of state security were infiltrated by Shi'ite militias. In Sunni areas, the US set about promoting local 'councils' or groups to take security matters into their own hands. Often referred to as the 'Awakening' movement, this strategy succeeded in empowering tribes and local neighbourhoods against groups claiming association with al-Qaida, yet they remained opposed to the dominance of the state by Shi'ites and Kurds. The animosity was shared by those in government, particularly as the US expected the Iraqi government to incorporate the 'Awakening' groups into the formal security services from mid-2008 onwards. There was little enthusiasm within a Shi'a-dominated Iraqi government at the prospect of not only accepting, but funding what was seen as an extralegal Sunni militia diametrically opposed to those in power.[4]

The Iraqi government of Nouri al-Maliki did not merely fail to honour the promises made by the US to those Sunni Arabs that had taken up arms against AQI. They also used the information they had about these groups to then target prominent Sunni tribal and militia leaders and embarked upon an extensive programme of political suppression. The scene was therefore set for a resurgence of violence in the north of Iraq, though few could foresee the scale and nature of the movement that was set to sweep into Anbar and Nineveh provinces in 2013 and 2014.

ISIS resurgence

Form the end of 2013, ISIS had begun to show a resurgence in its operations in Iraq, including the successful occupying of Fallujah at the end of 2013 and the beginning of 2014 (Weiss and Hassan 2015). Even then, few recognized the threat posed by ISIS, believing that it would be relatively easy to remove them. Indeed, at this time, the bigger domestic security story in Iraq was that of the brinkmanship between the Iraqi Prime Minister Nouri al-Maliki and KRI President Massoud Barzani.

By the spring of 2014 the situation in Mosul had become extremely dangerous, with ISIS elements having infiltrated the city and operating their black-market operations with relative impunity. But this was not enough. Following a series of feint attacks in Samarra and other towns, a small force of some 2000 ISIS fighters entered Mosul. Sleeper cells within the city were activated, and a series of suicide car bombs were used against specific targets across the city. The leadership of the ISF – largely commanders appointed directly by Maliki – evacuated themselves to the safety of the KRI, leaving their largely Shi'a conscripts to the mercy of marauding ISIS attackers. On 9 June, ISF forces numbering some 30,000 men fled the city, leaving behind vast stocks of military material, including M1A1 Abrams tanks, up-armoured HUMVEEs, and transport helicopters.

Meanwhile, the Kurdish leadership moved to occupy those lands to the south of the extant KRI that had been vacated by the ISF. By 12 July, some 90 per cent of the lands claimed by the Kurdistan Regional Government (KRG) had now fallen into the hands of Kurdish peshmerga forces, including the oil city of Kirkuk itself.

The summer months saw ISIS expand the territory, taking control of vast areas between Mosul and Baghdad, including the Baiji oil refinery, and Saddam's birthplace of Tikrit. Moving to legitimize this new territorial entity, and the mission of ISIS, Abu Bakr al-Baghdadi made a surprise appearance at Grand Mosque in Mosul on 29 June, when he announced the formation of the Caliphate, covering the entire global Muslim population. Since then, the Islamic State has become the focal point of international attention to remove its presence, but its existence as a social movement for disaffected Sunni Arabs in Syria, Iraq, and other places, as well as being a military and terrorist organization, will make it extremely difficult to remove from the geographical map or the ideological mind-set of the region.

Drivers for (in)security in three layers

This chapter focuses on security dynamics in three layers – the domestic, the regional, and the international one. Of course, it is somewhat artificial to separate out security dynamics between different layers, but this analytical approach retains some utility, particularly by illustrating that many security-related developments in Iraq have strong domestic drivers. While it is tempting to say that outside powers manipulate local actors in pursuance of their national interests, it is also necessary to show that many of the dynamics inside Iraq are 'made in Iraq'.

The domestic layer

In the years immediately following regime change, the debate among academics was focused heavily upon the nature of Iraqi society and US strategies for reconfiguring the state (Herring and Rangwala 2006; Stansfield, 2007a; Visser 2008a). Most commonly, this literature focused upon the construct of Iraqi state and society. Scholars who presented a vision of Iraqi society as being largely secular and imbued with notions of civic nationalism were countered by those who suggested that communal identities of ethnicity and religion were dynamics that could not be easily dismissed.

The brutality meted out between Iraqis of differing ethnicities and sects during the civil war of 2006–7 served notice that, irrespective of whether Iraqi society had been cohesive, cosmopolitan, and possibly even largely secular, the reality of the present illustrated that this was now far from the case. The devastating fighting of this period saw sectarianism, or more accurately communalism, consolidated as the modus operandi of the Iraqi state, with it now being over-whelmingly important whether an individual was identified as Sunni or Shi'a, Kurd or Arab, Christian or Muslim.

These divisions, and the way in which they were then sharpened by government policies (of marginalizing Sunnis), regional interventions (of Turkey and Arab Gulf states supporting Sunnis, and Iran supporting Shi'as), and Western double standards (of choosing not to recognize the results of the elections of 2010 that saw a marginal victory for the largely Sunni-facing *Iraqiyya* block) would quickly lead to a new, more militant, version of Sunni opposition against the government of Iraq – in the form of ISIS – that would then serve to further the Kurds' secession-ist tendencies, and even bring the Shi'a to the conclusion that their own interests might be better served by consolidating their position in Baghdad and the south, and forgetting the problems posed in Sunni areas and by the Kurds in the north.

The regional sphere

Local security considerations linked into wider regional perspectives. The implementation of a regime-change strategy in Iraq in 2003 prompted many Western, and Arab, observers to turn their attention to the rise of Shi'ite Islam in the Middle East. Notions of a 'Shi'a crescent' spread-ing from Iran through the Gulf States and Iraq and culminating in Lebanon received widespread attention (Nakash 2006; Nasr 2004; Nasr 2006; Pelham 2008), with the threat that this devel-opment would pose to Western interests, and to the survival of Arab Gulf monarchies and the security of the state of Israel being particular causes for concern.

To the north, the consolidation of the KRI prompted Turkey's military establishment to move forcefully to counter any possible threat posed to the territorial integrity of Turkey from groups such as the Kurdistan Workers' Party (PKK) (Gunter and Yavuz 2005; Lundgren 2007). Across the rest of the region, the deterioration of security in Iraq was viewed with alarm, par-ticularly as it became clear that al-Qaida elements led by Abu Musab al-Zarqawi were attempting to establish themselves in what appeared to be a heavily weakened state.

In essence, these fears did not come to pass in the period between regime change in 2003 and the end of the civil war of 2006–7. True, the government of Iraq did become dominated by Shi'ite parties, many of which had strong links to Iran, but they maintained a largely 'Iraqi' position with regard to their actions. The Kurds remained as awkward neighbours for Turkey. Even though Turkey did not view the existence of the KRI as positive, it came to realize that it had at least to be accepted. But the relationship between Ankara and the Kurds' capital of Erbil remained distinctly cool until 2007. And, in Sunni areas, while Zarqawi and his AQI were indeed a serious and worrying threat, they existed alongside many other insurgent groups of a variety of ideological hues – from religious to secular, jihadist to nationalist – each of them having links into the Arab world in different ways.

The regional security environment and its interaction with actors in Iraq changed in various ways, particularly from 2006 onwards. With the rapid heightening of sectarian tensions follow-ing the passing of the constitution in 2005 and the destruction of the Shi'a *Askariyya* mosque in Samarra in 2006 by Zarqawi's AQI, the scene was set not only for the rapid descent into terrible conflict between Sunnis and Shi'as across Iraq, but for the engagement of these domestic actors by regional powers – namely Iran with the Shi'a, and Arab, and principally Gulf, states with the Sunnis.

Meanwhile, in the north, the Turkish government had failed in its attempts to build bridges with the increasingly sectarian government of Iraq, which had also ignored requests to control the ongoing autonomous developments in the KRI. Recognizing that it would be more con-structive, from Turkey's perspective, to control the KRI through benevolent partnerships rather than antagonistic posturing, Erbil and Ankara embarked upon a series of agreements – in construction, general contracting, consumable supplies, and, most importantly, the development of the oil and gas sector – that would see Ankara not only work with the KRI, but become, in the space of relatively few years, its most significant ally.

These dynamics continued through the period of 2008–14, but with few observers realizing that those Sunnis opposed to what they saw as a *safavi*, or Persian, government, far from being subdued by the security services of the Iraqi state, had in fact begun to regroup in war-torn Syria from 2011 onwards. What had become the Islamic State of Iraq (ISI), following Zarqawi's death some years before, became the nucleus not only of jihadist fighters but of those disaffected fighters that had broken with AQI and formed 'Awakening' groups, of former regime elements still desperate to resecure their hold on the state, and increasingly of the vast swathes of disaffected people that had become politicized through the suppressive policies of the Iraqi state.

The international sphere

It is possible to build a convincing analysis of the reasons underpinning Iraq's security problems by referring to domestic and regional dynamics, and the interplay between the two. But the wider international environment cannot be ignored. Indeed, the myriad security problems that have afflicted Iraq since 2003 have three interrelated origins driven largely by complexes of decisions made at the international level. The first of these complexes was the failure of US policy-makers to understand the nature of the Iraqi state in the years prior to 2003. The second of these dynamics was driven by the policies taken to reconstruct Iraq, and these mistakes then created a third dynamic of new realities that needed to be addressed five years later.

With so much political, financial, and human capital invested in the Iraq project, failure in Iraq would have a profound impact on future perceptions of the US in the Middle East (Kahl et al. 2008).[5] Military defeat or the failure of the state-building project, or both, would embolden those opposed to the US in general, but also undermine US domestic support for such actions in the future (Korb et al. 2008). The Iraq experience was not only deeply transformative for the US. It also suggested to other actors that a unipolar world dominated by the US might be more fiction than fact.

Developing security concerns

The current weakened state of Iraq is particularly worrisome to many observers because it has enhanced the influence of neighbouring powers, and particularly that of Iran. However, just as Iraq has a pivotal role in the regional security complex of the Middle East due to the internal characteristics of the country and the domestic conditions of neighbours, so too do these countries have influence inside Iraq.

The threat of Shi'a Islam

The first of these characteristics concerns the nature of Iraq as home to the sacred sites of veneration for Shi'ites, and home to a majority Shi'ite population. Worries about the potential of Shi'a Islam to destabilize the Gulf can largely be reduced to two issues. The first is concern about the potential 'rise of the Shi'a crescent' starting in Iran and ending in Lebanon, and the possibility that Shi'ite communities in Gulf states could regard the rise of their co-religionists in Iraq as a model to emulate. Their behaviour can be influenced by Iran to a considerable degree, and this sword of Damocles hanging over the Gulf States has served to focus minds about the intentions of Tehran.

Considerable attention has been paid to what some analysts have described as the Shi'ites' 'reaching for power' (Nakash 2006; Nasr 2006). For these observers, the terrible events in Iraq cannot be considered in isolation, but are part of a wider regional context. Vali Nasr noted that 'Iraq's sectarian pains are all the more complex because reverberations of Shi'a empowerment will inevitably extend beyond Iraq's borders, involving the broader region from Lebanon to Pakistan' (Nasr 2004).

The second issue is that of proxy war against the US being fought in Iraq that could spill over into a wider confrontation between the US and Iran. Tehran has no chance of defeating the US military in a conventional conflict. But Iran has managed to successfully 'fight' the US inside Iraq, through supporting Shi'ite proxies in particular, in a manner that undoubtedly influenced US decisions as to whether it could attack Iran more openly over Tehran's WMD programme. Any plans for an attack against Iran must factor into the military equation the certainty that Iran can exact a terrible revenge upon the US in Iraq. It can also further destabilize Lebanon, heighten the problems faced by NATO in Afghanistan, and even influence events in Palestine. A proxy war against the US in the Middle East is a struggle that Iran can carry out, and perhaps even win.

However, the rise of IS since 2014 has altered views of the threat posed by Shi'a Islam and Iran, not least because it is Iran that has become the leading regional power in the fight against IS – placing it in a de facto sense as an ally of the US. It is interesting to consider how the defence of Baghdad was organized in 2007, against the ISI organization. Then, it was US generals taking the lead, and US military forces providing the support for ISF units to take the fight to the insurgents. Today, in 2015, the generals are Iranian and the military comes from the Iranian Revolutionary Guards' Corp (IRGC) of Qassem Suleimani. While it may be too early to talk of a Shi'ite crescent in the Middle East, it is certainly the case that Iranian influence in Iraq is now dominant – and particularly in Baghdad and the south.

The rise of the Kurds

The second of these internal characteristics relates to ethnicity. Since its inception, Iraq has been seen as a bulwark of Arab nationalism, and successive regimes sought to position Iraq as the leading power among Arab nations (see Dodge 2003; Stansfield 2007a). While the regional competition created problems with Arab neighbours, the appeal to Arab nationalism also created internal problems with those Iraqis who are not ethnic Arabs. Since their incorporation into Iraq in 1926, the Kurds remained discontented subjects under the monarchy. However, even the Kurds were able to accept an Iraq where Iraqi nationalism was the basis of the state's historical memory and narrative. They could not, however, accept a state whose *raison d'être* was based on Arab nationalism. Faced with an increasingly Arab nationalist regime in the form of the Ba'ath Party, the Kurds engaged in a violent rebellion against Iraqi government forces, with the Ba'ath regime committing ever more grievous atrocities to quell them, culminating in the use of chemical weapons in the now infamous Anfal Campaign of the 1980s.

Nevertheless, the Kurdish insurgency survived and, taking advantage of Hussein's tactical miscalculations that led him into defeat in 1991, carved out an autonomous region in the north of Iraq. Neighbouring countries that also had a significant Kurdish population – especially Turkey and Iran, and to a lesser extent Syria – regarded this development as a threat to their national security. Keen to ensure that the Kurds of Iraq would neither be independent and thereby threaten their own integrity through irredentist demands, nor act as an example to the often fractious Kurds in their own countries, Turkey and Iran have sought through a variety of means to manipulate the situation in the north of Iraq, usually by coercion, but increasingly also by other less obvious means – including economic investment and political negotiations. However, especially in the post-2003 environment, the new-found status of the Kurds of Iraq, now with a constitutionally recognized KRG and significant financial resources, remains a key security concern for all neighbouring states and the US.[6]

But, again, the rise of IS has changed matters markedly. From being seen as 'difficult' actors in Iraq, forever plotting to gain economic sovereignty by exporting oil independently of Baghdad, as a means to then secure 'full' sovereignty as an independent state, the Kurds have now become a most important ally of the West in the fight against IS. Indeed, the Kurds have perhaps secured the biggest successes against IS since their near-defeat in August 2014, when IS very nearly captured the Kurdish capital of Erbil. Now, the Kurdish leadership engages directly with Western military organizations, without the contact being mediated by Baghdad, and complaints about Kurdish oil exports have lessened as they need to generate income to fund their fight. But what is interesting, and potentially unsettling, for the Kurds is that their current position of strength is built not upon the defeat of ISIS, but upon the conflict with ISIS. While ISIS exists, and the Kurds are engaged in a struggle with it, then they will be popular, supported, and successful. But, if IS is defeated, then it is very possible indeed that the regional and international system would return to viewing the Kurds as being 'difficult' actors within the framework of the Iraqi state.

Conclusion: the past as prologue

The invasion of Iraq in 2003 was a watershed in the history of the country. By removing the Ba'ath regime from power, the US-led coalition effectively brought to an end political dominance by Arab Sunnis, which had lasted nearly a century. The period since 2003 has been a time of exceptionally complex political dynamics, with reactions against an occupying force, the emergence of vigorous communal politics, and the extensive involvement of external powers in Iraq's affairs. At the core of this complexity was a change in the domestic political rules of the game. In this respect, the US intervention was of formative political importance.

By invading Iraq, crushing the military, and finally capturing the most important regime personalities, the US not only achieved its first goal of regime change (the second being regime replacement). It also fundamentally altered the nature of politics in Iraq by removing the structures of the authoritarian Ba'athist state and destroying the psychological hold of dictatorship. Following this, it was all but impossible to restore the Iraqi state to its former condition by undertaking some sort of 'lightweight' regime replacement, as was initially intended. Instead, new leaders from previously suppressed communities came forward, while new ideas emerged concerning the future governance of the country, both of which dynamics have had profound implications for Iraq since 2003. Not only did new leaders emerge, but the very idea of Iraq became subject to reinterpretation. The state was no longer legitimized by notions of secularism, Arabism, or notions of unspoken Sunni dominance. Instead, the victors in the new Iraq imposed their own notions of Iraqi identity on the state. The Shi'ites and Kurds, in particular, were well placed to pursue their own agendas without fear of retribution, while Iraqi nationalism is fed by understandable negative sentiments brought about by the US occupation.

Whatever the starting point of the deterioration of security in Iraq, however, two facts can be highlighted. The first is that, by 2008, identity politics had largely taken hold of Iraq. It was no longer possible to understand Iraqi politics without referring to 'Shi'ite', 'Kurdish', or 'Sunni/ Arab' parties. This reality is now manifest in the arrangement that Iraq found itself in in 2015 – of being a country with three distinct states. It is no longer possible to talk of one Iraq, rather there is the Baghdad-Basra region governed from Baghdad, there is the Kurdistan Region governed from Erbil, and there is the Islamic State centred on Mosul. Iraq's future as a unified state – whether federal or unitary – remains deeply questionable. In the coming years, important and indeed existential decisions will be required that go to the very core of the debate over Iraq's identity and the future structure of the state.

These decisions have, to a large extent, been glossed over in previous years but have been brought to the fore by the events that led to the rise of IS in 2014, and its subsequent consolidation. If Iraq is to survive, there first needs to be a strategy not only to remove IS as a military force, but also to remove the reasons why IS managed to grow such deep roots in Sunni society. This will not be easy, if even possible, to achieve. Beyond this, consideration then needs to be given to processes of truth and reconciliation between communities, and mechanisms by which Iraqis of different religious association and ethnic identity can indeed live under one banner. Federal structures would certainly be needed, but these will prove problematic to negotiate in an environment riven with deep-rooted suspicion and mistrusts.

Notes

1 Both sets of analyses tended to use the same source materials, but in very different ways. Hanna Batatu's very detailed book was frequently referred to and used to illustrate not only the development of civic Iraqi nationalism, but also the existence of a society highly variegated by ethnicity, religion, and class. Other works by Iraqis, including Ali Wardi, were often cited in order to illustrate the complexity of Iraqi society and Western analysts' inadequate understanding of it (cf. Batatu 1978 and Wardi 1991).
2 See Jabar 2003 for an overview of Shi'ite parties in Iraq.
3 To make matters even more complicated, in the Sunni areas of Iraq, groups often changed their allegiance. For example, some tribes that had been members of insurgent or religious militias when it proved to be in their interests later took part in the US-sponsored *sahwa* (Awakening) movement when it was deemed beneficial to change sides.
4 Problems between the *sahwa* leaders and the Iraqi government became apparent almost as soon as the US stopped funding them directly from October 2008. Though the militias had previously been paid US$300 per person by the US military, the Iraqi government immediately announced that it would only guarantee reduced salaries of US$250 for 20,000 soldiers out of the 100,000-strong force. The response of *sahwa* leaders was to warn that their people could rejoin insurgent groups or criminal gangs. See Liz Sly, 'Iraq plans to cut Sunni fighters' salaries', *Chicago Tribune*, 2 November 2008.
5 In economic terms alone, Joseph Stiglitz (a Nobel Prize-winning economist) estimated that the Iraq War would cost the US taxpayer some US$3 trillion. With macroeconomic costs and interest included, the sum rose by another 50 per cent (Stiglitz 2008).
6 At the top of the list of concerns is the status of territories disputed by the KRG and the Iraqi government, and especially the oil-rich province of Kirkuk. See ICG 2008; Anderson and Stansfield 2009 for analyses of the problem of disputed territories.

References

Anderson, L. and Stansfield, G. (2009) *Crisis in Kirkuk: The Ethnopolitics of Conflict and Compromise*, Philadelphia: University of Pennsylvania Press.
Batatu, H. (1978) *The Old Social Classes and Revolutionary Movements of Iraq: A Study of Iraq's Old Landed and Commercial Classes and of its Communists, Ba'thists and Free Officers*, Princeton, NJ: Princeton University Press.
Dodge, T. (2003) *Inventing Iraq: The Failure of Nation-Building and a History Denied*, London: Hurst.
Dodge, T. (2012) *Iraq: From War to a New Authoritarianism*, London: Routledge.
Gunter, M. (2007) *The Kurds Ascending: The Evolving Solution to the Kurdish Problem in Iraq and Turkey*, New York: Palgrave Macmillan.
Gunter, M. and Yavuz, H. (2005) 'The Continuing Crisis in Iraqi Kurdistan', *Middle East Policy* 12(1): 122–33.
Herring, E. and Rangwala, G. (2006) *Iraq in Fragments: The Occupation and Its Legacy*, London: Hurst.
ICG (International Crisis Group) (2008) *Oil for Soil: Toward a Grand Bargain on Iraq and the Kurds*, Middle East Report No. 80 (28 October), Washington: International Crisis Group.
Jabar, F. A. (2003) *The Shi'ite Movement in Iraq*, London: Saqi Books.
Kahl, C., Flournoy, M., and Brimley, S. (2008) *Shaping the Iraq Inheritance*, Washington: Center for a New American Security.

Korb, L., Katulis, B., Duggan, S., and Juul, P. (2008) *How Does This End? Strategic Failures Overshadow Tactical Gains in Iraq*, Washington: Center for American Progress.

Krohley, N. (2015) *The Death of the Mehdi Army: The Rise, Fall, and Revival of Iraq's Most Powerful Militia*, London: Hurst.

Long, A. (2008) 'The Anbar Awakening', *Survival* 50(2): 67–94.

Lundgren, Å. (2007) *The Unwelcome Neighbour: Turkey's Kurdish Policy*, London: I. B. Tauris.

McCants, W. (2015) *The ISIS Apocalypse: The History, Strategy, and Doomsday Vision of the Islamic State*, New York: St. Martin's Press.

Nakash, Y. (2006) *Reaching for Power: The Shi'a in the Modern Arab World*, Princeton, NJ: Princeton University Press.

Nasr, V. (2004) 'Regional Implications of Shi'a Revival in Iraq', *The Washington Quarterly* 27(3): 7–24.

Nasr, V. (2006) *The Shi'a Revival: How Conflicts within Islam will Shape the Future*, New York: Norton.

Pelham, N. (2008) *A New Muslim Order: The Shi'a and the Middle East Sectarian Crisis*, London: I. B. Tauris.

Romano, D. (2007) 'The Future of Kirkuk', *Ethnopolitics* 6(2): 265–83.

Stansfield, G. (2003) *Iraqi Kurdistan: Political Development and Emergent Democracy*, London: Routledge.

Stansfield, G. (2007a) *Iraq: People, History, Politics*, Cambridge: Polity Press.

Stansfield, G. (2007b) *Accepting Realities in Iraq*, London: Chatham House.

Stiglitz, J. (2008) *The Three Trillion Dollar War: The True Cost of the Iraq Conflict*, New York: Norton.

Visser, R. (2008a) 'The United States and Iraq: Still Getting It Wrong', *OpenDemocracy*, 3 October.

Visser, R. (2008b) 'Historical Myths of a Divided Iraq', *Survival* 50(2): 95–106.

Wardi, A. (1991–2) *Lamahat Ijtima'iyah min Ta'rikh al-'Iraq al-Hadith*, London: Kufaan Publishing.

Weiss, M. and Hassan, H. (2015) *ISIS: Inside the Army of Terror*, New York: Regan Arts.

27

THE SYRIAN CRISIS AND INTERNATIONAL SECURITY

Raymond Hinnebusch

The crisis in Syria has been widely recognized as constituting a multi-dimensional threat to international security. It is seen as a humanitarian crisis, a breeding ground of transnational terrorism, a site of the use of WMDs and a failed state. Some see it as a turning point in which the 'Responsibility to Protect' (R2P) civilians was abdicated by the international community. It can also be seen as a new site to understand the conduct of 'new wars,' and of insurgency and counter-insurgency, as this chapter proposes. The intractability of the conflict is a challenge to our thinking on conflict resolution and the conduct of diplomacy to address internal wars. The conflict has been a site of vociferous debates among theorists and practitioners over how the international community should respond (Falk 2014; Kaldor 2013).

This chapter has five parts. In the first, the context and roots of the conflict are introduced. It explains why the non-violent resistance paradigm failed to predict the dynamics of the Syrian uprising and shows that in the Syrian case, the conflict was first about (economic) class grievances and only then turned into a sectarianized conflict. In the second, the Syrian conflict is looked at through theories of 'new wars' (Kaldor 1999) and insurgency and counter-insurgency. In the third, the dynamics of violence are described, first by looking at human security vs. state security, and then by focusing on the R2P norm and its influence on the conflict. The fourth section of the chapter looks at the obstacles to a diplomatic resolution of the conflict. The conclusion considers the implications of the Syria conflict for security theory and practice.

Context and roots of the conflict

Statebuilding dilemmas

The Syrian crisis is ultimately rooted in what Ayoob (1995) called the 'Third World security predicament'. This signifies the challenge of twentieth-century state developers who undertake primitive power accumulation in a world in which populations have much greater demands for participation and welfare in comparison to earlier times, and also when the violent methods of earlier state builders (e.g. see Tilly 1985), are no longer seen as legitimate. This Third World security predicament is exacerbated in the case of Syria and its statebuilding dilemmas.

The starting point for the current crisis can be traced back to the post-First World War imposition of a system of states in the region in what David Fromkin (1989) called a 'peace to end all peace'. The Levant states, artificially created by Western imperialism in violation of the dominant identities of the region's peoples, had to compete with powerful sub- and supra-state forces for the loyalties of their populations, and hence suffered built-in legitimacy deficits, which made them more likely to fail. In these circumstances, Arab statebuilders gravitated toward *neo-patrimonial* practices that combined time-honoured indigenous statebuilding formulas – Ibn Khaldun's *assabiya* or elite solidarity built on primordial ties – with modern bureaucratic and security machinery, coupled with surveillance technology. This formula was empowered, beyond its 'shelf life', by the exceptional availability of hydrocarbon and geopolitical rent in the region. It enabled the lubrication of clientele networks supportive of neo-patrimonial rule, and for a period enabled a populist 'social contract' with the masses.

Ba'thist populist authoritarianism in Syria was no exception: Hafiz al-Asad established a regime that combined reliance on the *assabiya* of his Alawi followers – whom he appointed to strategic commands of the military-security apparatus – with rent-fuelled clientelist co-optation of a cross-sectarian coalition of Ba'thi politicos and Sunni business elements; and mass incorporation through the Ba'th party of the state-employed middle class, trade unionists and big segments of the peasantry (via land reform). This regime was legitimized by Arab nationalist ideology and defended by the repression of persistent (mostly Islamic) opposition.

Yet each ingredient of this statebuilding recipe had its costs: sectarian *assabiya* alienated out-groups; rent was finite and its decline enervated co-optative capability; repression left many politically unincorporated; and legitimation from Arab nationalism embroiled Syria in costly regional conflicts and generated Western hostility, which became particularly dangerous once Asad lost his Cold War era Soviet patron. Furthermore, relying on sub-state (Alawi) and supra-state (Arabism) loyalties deterred consolidation of identifications with the Syrian state itself (Hinnebusch 2001).

Across the region, a combination of rent decline and population boom created economic crises that put extreme pressures on the authoritarian republics to move toward what might be called 'post-populism'. In post-populism, the state withdraws from welfare provision and favours investors, thereby creating a new crony capitalism and exacerbating social inequality. Twin global forces exacerbated the situation: neoliberal globalization, as manifested in the International Monetary Fund (IMF)'s 'structural adjustment' campaigns, reduced the capacity of the oil-poor authoritarian republics to materially satisfy mass constituencies. In parallel, the global diffusion of Internet technology – and with it, West-centric democratization discourses – helped to delegitimize authoritarian post-populist ruling formulas (Hinnebusch 2012). In Syria, the younger Asad's post-populism sowed the seeds of the Syrian uprising and the subsequent protracted conflict.

From non-violent protest to the domestic security dilemma

According to the mass non-violent protest paradigm (Stephan and Chenoweth 2008), mass protest can rapidly and effectively destabilize authoritarian regimes, *even if* the regime refuses protestors' demands and uses violence against them. The literature predicts that use of violence is likely to *backfire*, since it stimulates wider anti-regime mobilization, triggers international sanctions and support for the opposition, and most importantly, causes defections in the security forces, which will be reluctant to use violence against fellow citizens who are not, themselves, using violence. This scenario could have been part of the calculations of the Syrian protestors who, in large numbers, took on the regime after March 2011. The outcome, however, was neither democratic transition, revolution nor effective repression, but stalemated semi-sectarian civil war. It was not inevitable that the Syrian uprising would descend into sectarian civil war; so what went wrong?

Security Studies has increasingly focused on the causes of internal wars like Syria's. Studies of communal (ethnic and religious) conflict are differentiated between 'essentialists' who see ancient hatreds as rooted in history, and 'instrumentalists' who see these hatreds stirred up by leaders or their opponents (Kaufman 2008: 203–4). Syria comes much closer to the latter model. As a fragmented state composed of many religious and ethnic minorities, artificially constructed by Western imperialism and with a fragile sense of shared identity, Syria had built-in vulnerabilities. The regime's use of sectarian solidarity *assabiyya* had also created resentments among the majority Sunni population, while the minority but politically-dominant Alawis had a strong sense of insecurity rooted in the previous Islamic fundamentalist insurgency of the 1980s that played on sectarian differences (Goldsmith 2011).

Still, Syria's sects did not hate each other. In fact, considerable intermarriage and inter-sectarian business alliances were evident in the 2000s. The Alawi-led ruling coalition had long included many of the Sunni majority (and still does) and had built an alliance with the Sunni-dominated business class. Rather than being chiefly an issue of sectarian politics, the conditions for the revolt were prepared by the regime's turn to neoliberal policies, marginalizing its former rural constituency and promoting the unequal enrichment of urban-based crony capitalists. The main grievances were economic initially: the conflict was about class and urban–rural cleavages. The discourse of the protestors was secular, inclusive, and cross-sectarian, although a perception of favouritism in access to opportunity gave a sectarian edge to socio-economic grievances.

Once the opposition was able to flood the streets with interminable protests, the regime found itself on the defensive – as in the non-violent protest paradigm. But why did this not create the conditions for a democratic transition? While the mass non-violent protest paradigm gives little attention to the dynamics of such a transition, democratization studies suggest (O'Donnell and Schmitter 1986) that non-violent protest is only likely to lead to a peaceful transition if a coalition between soft-liners in the regime and in the opposition manages to marginalize the hardliners (as happened, in some respects, in Tunisia and Egypt). In the Syrian case, however, the soft-liners were marginalized on both sides.

Asad's choice to respond to the demonstrations with a 'security solution' rather than democratic reforms was decisive: in standing with regime hardliners, he empowered the hardliners in the opposition as well. In resorting to a sectarian discourse against 'terrorism' and increasing state violence against opponents, Asad helped turn peaceful protests into violent sectarian conflict. Equally important were the maximalist demands of the opposition: the removal of the regime. Arguably, the mistake of the Syrian protest movement was its 'rush to confrontation' with the regime while the latter still retained significant support (cf. Mandour 2013). With the hardline opposition insisting on the fall of the regime and resorting to periodic violence, the soft-liners in the regime were unlikely to marginalize the hardliners. Senior soft-liners, who spoke the language of reconciliation, seemed too far from the immediate levers of repression, which were in the hands of hardliners such as Maher al-Asad (Harling 2011). Similarly, internal third parties who tried to mediate were squeezed out, notably the traditional opposition organized in the National Coordination Committee (NCC), whose members were much more experienced than the younger demonstrators. At the famous Samiramis conference in June 2011 they put forth a compromise proposal – but both regime and opposition rejected it.

Even though the regime conceded many reforms that the opposition had been demanding for decades, and proposed dialogue, those committed to its removal dismissed these initiatives as inadequate and insincere. Besides the moral outrage at the killings perpetuated by the government, opposition activists believed that they could only be safe if the regime was totally destroyed, since it would be certain to seek retribution if it survived. The fragmented and localized opposition also lacked credible leaders who could deliver its consent to a negotiated settlement should that have appeared in its interest. With regime concessions being 'too little too late', the opposition escalated its resistance via ever larger mass demonstrations, which in turn provoked violent and repressive counter-escalation by the regime.

But why did mass protest not lead to forced presidential departure, as in Egypt and Tunisia, or, if not that, then regime collapse amidst revolution from below? The president's political and clientele ties reached too deeply into the security apparatus to separate it from him as had happened in Egypt and Tunisia – and many of the elites around him, seeing the regime and their interests in jeopardy, were prepared to use violence against protestors. While the Asad regime's increasing use of lethal force against non-violent protestors *did* alienate wide swathes of the public (as the non-violent resistance paradigm expects), the opposition could be constructed, among the regime's constituency as a jihadist 'other', because society rapidly became communally polarized.

As for the many Syrians caught in the middle, especially the upper and middle classes, the regime's claim to defend order against the disruption unleashed by the uprising caused a significant portion of them to see it as the lesser of two evils. This was all the more the case once radical Islamists, and especially al-Qaida-linked jihadists, assumed a high profile within the opposition, and as the opposition itself fragmented into warring camps. Unable to quickly separate the regime from its backers, the opposition sought to destabilize the regime through interminable mass civil unrest, in order to provoke defections from the security forces, undermine the economy, and break the regime alliance with business. For this strategy to succeed, it was necessary that external constraints deter full-scale regime repression, or else that such repression would provoke outside intervention. The regime, however, was not deterred by fear of intervention from resorting to a 'military solution' that did not spare civilians. This hastened Sunni defections from the army – specifically to the anti-regime 'Free Syrian Army' – and later encouraged the rise of jihadists, leading to the militarization of the uprising. By infiltrating and seizing half of Aleppo in 2012, the opposition gave reason for the regime to resort to air and artillery attacks on urban built-up areas.

In parallel, it was the instrumentalization of sub- and trans-state identities by political entrepreneurs that turned what was initially a largely urban–rural and class conflict into a sectarian one: it was the Asad regime's securitization of peaceful protest by depicting it as Sunni Islamist terrorism that rallied the Alawi community and other minorities to the regime and led to the opposition's later turn, in response, to Sunni Islamist jihadism. As order broke down, the 'security dilemma' kicked in and each side resorted to defensive tactics that made both feel more insecure (Posen 1993). Extremists who advocated pre-emptive violence against other communities were empowered and people began to be treated according to their communal identity. In fact, something approaching ethnic cleansing took place in certain mixed areas, although it was not widespread and elsewhere heterogeneity increased – with, e.g., an influx of Sunni refugees to the Alawi heartland in the west. Hatred and fear of the 'other' spread the conviction on both sides that no political solution was possible, even when it became clear that neither could defeat the other. Overall, the Syrian case validates the instrumentalist view of communal internal wars – that it is political entrepreneurs, not ancient hatreds, that make for conflict. In the Syrian case it was the regime, but also the opposition and external powers later, that sectarianized a conflict that was initially about class grievances.

This outcome is quite at odds with the non-violent resistance paradigm in which an authoritarian regime's violence progressively isolates itself from the vast majority of the population, precipitating its collapse. This distinguishes Syria from Tunisia and Egypt, where the incumbent presidents proved unable to get the army to repress mass protest, thereby enabling a potential democratic transition. This points to the fact, ignored by the resistance paradigm, that differences in the social composition of authoritarian regimes make for important variations in their vulnerability to revolt against them. In more homogeneous societies such as Egypt and Tunisia, mass anti-regime mobilization is likely to be much more thorough and decisive than in communally divided ones like Syria; and where the presidency's ties to the military are stronger and the army's institutional autonomy weaker, the military is far less likely to jettison a president to save itself. What the non-violent protest paradigm also fails to anticipate is the consequences of mass pro-tests that destabilize the state but fail to lead to democratic transition. The outcome may well be a failed state, a Hobbesian world in which life becomes 'nasty, brutish, and short', and which may be very difficult to reverse. This happened in Syria.

'New wars', counter-insurgency, failed states and terrorism

The intractability of the Syrian conflict betrays symptoms of Mary Kaldor's (1999) 'new wars'. In her scenario, state weakening empowers transnational non-state actors engaged in identity wars and ethnic cleansing, in which the distinction between combatants and non-combatants breaks down. All the symptoms she describes are present in the Syrian case: as the normal economy col-lapsed, a 'war economy', in which people deprived of a normal life and income sought survival through spoils and flocked to militant groups with access to largely external funding, gave extra life to the conflict despite the damage it was already inflicting on all sides. Warlordism filled the security gap as rival factions arose across opposition-controlled areas. Trans-state refugee flows, funding by diasporas and identity groups crossing borders, and transnational arms trafficking embedded the conflict in wider regional struggles that made it all the harder to resolve.

Such wars spill over to the neighbours, where insurgents may enjoy safe havens. In the case of Syria, this happened with Turkey, which harboured and encouraged anti-regime rebels (Schanzer and Tahiroglu 2014). Large parts of the Syrian population, caught between the warring sides, were displaced internally or fled to neighbouring countries and beyond. The spill-over of the conflict impacted negatively on the security of Syria's neighbours (Turkey, Lebanon and Jordan), with multi-sectarian Lebanon particularly at risk of being drawn into it, especially after the Lebanese Hezbollah intervened in Syria on the regime side, thereby inflaming anti-Shia sen-timent among Lebanese Sunnis. These states also carried a heavy budget burden for refugee support, creating resentment among their populations against Syrian refugees. Furthermore, the negative impact of protracted conflicts on economic development in border states is well docu-mented (Lambach and Debiel 2010: 164).

The Syrian case throws light on theories of insurgency and counter-insurgency as well. As Speers indicates (2008), insurgents traditionally seek to be the fish in the water of the population, living off their support. This has been the case in rebel-dominated areas of Syria, but, increasingly, the insurgents also live on outside funding that enables them to co-opt elements of the population. Their embedding in the population gave them such wide support that it was impossible for the Syrian regime to crush them. This and outside arming by rival regional and global powers enabled them to wrest large parts of the country from government control. Their main weakness, however, was their extreme fragmentation and extensive intra-opposition fighting, which put an end to the momentum that seemed to be on their side in 2012 and somewhat re-tilted the balance toward the regime in 2013.

The regime's counter-insurgency methods are recognized as 'traditional tactics' (Speers 2008), which includes securing base areas first. It managed to consolidate relative control over its heart-land, running from Damascus northward via Homs and Hama to the coastal provinces where the Alawi community is located. In doing this, the regime resorted to starving out insurgents by food control and blockading villages. Theorists claim (Speers 2008) that counter-insurgency is most successful if it is made up of 80 per cent political and 20 per cent military methods, with a discriminating and well-targeted use of force, since the government needs to win over the less committed insurgents in order to isolate the hard-core opposition. However, in cases where the priority is put on protection of counter-insurgency forces instead of protection of the population, then firepower and airpower will be maximized regardless of collateral damage and political costs. Such firepower is particularly unsuited to urban warfare where recent insurgencies, including Syria's, have been fought. In Syria, the demographic disadvantage of the regime meant it lacked the military manpower to avoid indiscriminate collateral damage and use of heavy weapons against urban neighbourhoods. Indeed, the regime may have deliberately used such violence to create refugees, a kind of ethnic cleansing meant to change the unfavourable demographic balance.

However, mass punishment of populations is likely to be counterproductive and this was certainly the case in Syria, where it provoked the militarization of the opposition. This is especially so in the case of modern media wars, in which use of violence can be easily recorded with smartphones and held against the perpetrator. In the Syrian case, protestors uploaded smartphone images of regime violence to spread disaffection in Syria and invite foreign intervention. Indeed, from the beginning, the Syrian war was a propaganda war waged by disinformation on both sides (Joya 2012).

Three years after the uprising began, the country had become divided between regime-and opposition-controlled regions, an egregious example of a failed state. Failed states are seen as a threat to international security, with at least one involved in 77 per cent of international crises between 1990 and 2005 (Lamback and Debiel 2010: 161). The US/EU saw failed states as potential havens for terrorist groups and Piazza found instability in nineteen Middle East and North Africa (MENA) states correlated with terrorist activity (Lambach and Diebel 2010). Indeed, the Syria conflict was widely seen as a breeding ground of terrorism. The vacuum of governance it created gave al-Qaida the opportunity to recover its declining fortunes and establish a major armed presence, with two al-Qaida franchises, Jahhat al-Nusra and Islamic State of Iraq and the Levant, rising in eastern Syria. They combined ideological motivation, the best fighters, access to natural resources (oil) and generous funding from patrons in the Gulf. One result was the emergence of a proto-state, the Islamic Caliphate, bridging Syria and Iraq. This was constructed as a threat in the West where governments feared that recruits to such jihadist groups from their own citizens would be radicalized and pose a threat when they returned home.

Securitization, human security crisis and humanitarian intervention

Security referents: human security vs. state security

The Syrian case carries relevance for debates in Security Studies over the referents of securitization. In the Syrian case, the human security view that the state can be a threat to its citizens' security is very well exemplified. The regime resorted to use of live fire against demonstrators, and when this stimulated rather than discouraged further protests, it escalated the use of violence. This escalation included the use of artillery and aerial bombing against urban populations, a selective blockade, and starvation of rebel areas, and possibly the use of poison gas against opposition neighbourhoods.

Nevertheless, from the point of view of the regime and its supporters, the opposition were agents of foreign powers seeking to destabilize Syria. There is enough empirical evidence to give this view a modicum of credibility: the role played by external exiles and Internet activists abroad, often Western funded, in provoking or escalating the Uprising was congruent with the regime's perceptions of conspiracy. It tarnished the indigenous opposition with the suspicion of treasonous dealings with foreign enemies, justifying the resort to repressive violence. Qatar's al-Jazeera deliberately encouraged revolt, and Gulf funders provided copious amounts of arms and money to militarize the insurgency (Dickinson 2014). Syria became the battleground in a regional power struggle between rival states, with Turkey and the Gulf Cooperation Council (GCC) on one side and Iran on the other, each of which perceived the regional power balance and their own security to be at stake. Western and Gulf funding and arming of the opposition, and the safe haven provided by Turkey for insurgents, contributed to the militarization of the conflict as well. What was initially a human security issue became also an interstate one.

Intervention and R2P

The prospect of external intervention has loomed over the Syrian conflict from the start. Under the R2P doctrine, sovereignty is contingent on states providing security for their populations, and is forfeited when they become threats to it. Kerr (2010) argues that global intervention followed by peacebuilding has contributed to a reduction in political violence. The Syrian case is widely seen by liberals and Syrian oppositionists as a failure of the R2P doctrine (Adams 2015). However, paradoxically, this very doctrine played a role in actually encouraging and increasing violent conflict in Syria.

From the outset, the possibility of external military intervention shaped both opposition and regime strategies. Anti-regime activists, including Syrian expatriates who were instrumental in initiating and internationalizing the uprising, understood that they could not prevail against the regime without effective external constraints on its repressive options, and some actively courted Western intervention. External activists told those on the ground, pointing to the Libya no-fly zone, that 'the international community won't sit and watch you be killed'. They claimed that another Hama massacre (referring to the violent repression of a 1982 uprising) was not possible because 'Everything is being filmed on YouTube and there's a lot of international attention on the Middle East' (Seeyle 2011). There were reports that the opposition, particularly external Internet activists, systematically exaggerated bloodshed and found willing partners in the Western and Gulf-owned press (Joya 2012).

The previous intervention in Libya played a major role in encouraging protestors to escalate their confrontation with the regime on the expectation that Asad would need to restrain repression to avoid a similar intervention. Indeed, the regime tried to calibrate its violence within limits that would not trigger an international intervention, although over time this bar was steadily eroded. In mid-2011, it felt the need to quickly smash resistance so as not to lose control of territory that could be used to stage intervention, as had happened in Libya. As it became evident that the West had no appetite for intervention, the Syrian regime, not dependent on the West as were the Egyptian and Tunisian regimes, had little need to restrain its use of violence against opponents.

The West did move to diplomatically isolate and demonize the regime, withdrawing its ambassadors, and thereby forfeiting any potential for mediation in the conflict. It slapped sanctions on the regime, meant to deprive it of oil revenue, which was indeed a key step in the debilitation of the Syrian *state* and of its capacity to provide basic services to the population, *but not of the regime*, which found alternative informal sources of revenue. This was yet another example of how blunt an instrument such sanctions can be (Bahrami and Parsi 2012). With Western politicians clamouring for military intervention and raising the spectre of the International Criminal Court (ICC), the regime inner core realized that there was no way back for them and that they had to stick together and do whatever was necessary to survive, including escalating from the 'security to a military solution'. Yet the threats against the regime by the West, while encouraging protestors, proved to be hollow, and hence contributed to making a bad situation even worse.

Conflict resolution and diplomacy

There is considerable research on the conditions for political settlements in Security Studies, notably on negotiations (Zartman 1995) and on techniques (Track II diplomacy) to find common ground between the sides. One of the main propositions is that a 'hurting stalemate' provides a key condition for a political compromise (Zartman 2000).

In the Syrian case, efforts were made from the beginning to mediate a compromise resolution, notably by a moderate opposition group, by the Arab League and by UN special envoys. This was rejected by both sides, however. According to participants in a workshop on prospects for a settlement, Syria has among the worst possible configurations for reaching a negotiated solution (Lynch 2013). To be sure, a hurting stalemate appeared to have been reached by at least the third year of the conflict as it became apparent that neither side could defeat the other (see, e.g., United Nations, 2012). However, as more and more blood was shed, powerful animosities were generated, and neither side could imagine continued coexistence. The so-called 'commitment problem' is exaggerated in such scenarios: an opposition must insist on regime change rather than reform because it believes that the regime will renege on commitments as soon as the threat to its survival has passed (Fearon 2013). On the other hand, the regime could not make too many concessions under threat without looking weak and leading to defections and greater mobilization against it.

Each side continued to hope to win by *further escalating* the level of violence. To the extent that victory seemed unrealistic, each wanted to first acquire the upper hand before going into negotiations. The highly fragmented opposition lacked leadership that could deliver the agreement of the whole opposition, particular the fighters on the ground, in the event that a compromise was reached. There were an excessive number of 'veto players' and 'spoilers' who had no interest in a settlement, such as the jihadists and warlords thriving on the war economy. Each side was encouraged by external backers, but while these continued to provide their clients with enough support to keep fighting, it was not enough to defeat their opponent. A de facto partition soon emerged, with the front lines fairly stabilized. But partition was no solution in Syria, since communal groups are too intermingled, and, except among some Kurds, permanent division enjoyed little support as a solution.

At the time of writing, one side or the other might still collapse, notably if their external supporters withdraw the resources needed to continue. However, external players appear to be too invested in the outcome to accept defeat of their client. Even though 60–70 per cent of recent civil wars resulted in either victory by one side or in partition (Walters 2013), in the Syrian case both sides would probably enjoy too little legitimacy to establish uncontested dominance, with the conflict likely to revive at a later point.

International diplomacy, according to Kerr (2008), is increasingly focusing on problems of violence in other societies. The UN Security Council is interpreting threats to international peace more broadly, to encompass internal wars. Third-party diplomacy is crucial in reaching negotiated settlements and the commitment obstacle can potentially be overcome through an external guarantee of a ceasefire. In the Syrian case, a precedent for international diplomatic cooperation seemed to be set by the agreement of the regime to give up its weapons of mass destruction, which it was accused of having used against its population. Russia's ability to deliver Asad into the agreement stopped the air strikes that the US was preparing, which would have had incalculable consequences. In spite of this incipient great power diplomatic cooperation, the failure of the Geneva II conference held in January 2014 to reach a negotiated political settlement to the Syrian crisis is a case study in the limits of diplomacy.

The two great powers, the US and Russia, which were patrons of the two warring sides, sponsored negotiations between delegations from the regime and the opposition in exile. However, the parties to the conflict had to be pressured by their sponsors to attend and did so only to try to demonstrate the intransigence of the other side. The regime insisted on demonizing the opposition as terrorists; the opposition refused to countenance any solution that included a role for the incumbent president; had the opposition settled for less it would have been isolated from its constituency on the ground in Syria (Soukkary 2014).

To make it work, the regional backers of the two sides would have had to be brought into the process and pressured to stop their support for the conflict, but Iran was actually excluded from the conference and Saudi Arabia had no faith in it. Even though a settlement would have served the apparent shared interest of the two great powers in international stability, neither was willing to sufficiently lean on its client to force them to compromise. The US administration was unwilling to invest political capital, especially since the conflict, despite its risks to regional stability, had become an arena in which US enemies (Hezbollah, al-Qaida) were bloodying each other. Russia saw defence of the Asad regime as a bulwark against what it saw as the hegemonic expansive tendencies of the West (demonstrated, in its view, by the West's use of a Russian-allowed UN humanitarian intervention resolution to engineer regime change in Libya).

Conclusion

Liberals and realists frequently divide over the wisdom of Western policies toward security crises in MENA. The Syrian crisis is no exception, where the debate over intervention has pitted the 'realist' advocates of caution, such as Stephen Walt (2014), against both the aggressive 'liberal imperialism' of the US neo-cons (Parmar 2009), and, since the start of the Syrian uprising, the advocates of humanitarian intervention, inside and outside the Obama administration.

The hesitancy of the Obama administration to intervene in Syria must in part be owing to an appreciation that regional security threats have often been the consequences of previous US interventions in the region. Thus, the threat from ISIS that became so salient in mid-2014 was in many ways a 'blowback' of Western policy. ISIS is a descendant of al-Qaida whose roots go back to Western support of Islamist radicals against the Soviet Union in Afghanistan, but which has risen most directly out of Islamist outrage at US use of Saudi bases to attack Iraq in the 1991 Gulf war (Atwan 2006). The US destruction of the Iraqi state in America's 2003 invasion made the country a magnet for al-Qaida, created a vacuum where it could operate, and also unleashed the Sunni–Shia sectarianization of the region on which jihadism has thrived and found further fertile ground in Syria.

The Syrian uprising can itself be seen as an outcome of Western policies, at least in part. Western democracy promotion and the advocacy of the non-violent resistance paradigm showed itself, in MENA at least, to have a far greater potential to destabilize states than to promote democracy; it ignored both the conditions under which protest could be translated into democratic transition and the high costs, especially in fragmented societies, when it fails. Nor has Western liberalism appreciated how mechanisms such as R2P and the ICC may actually worsen human security because they encourage rebels, expecting external assistance, to uncompromisingly challenge regimes – and because regimes, once they start the use of violence, have no way back. The international normative climate paradoxically incentivized both sides to keep fighting in Syria, when a political solution might have had a better chance had they been left to their own devices or external powers sought to mediate rather than take sides in the conflict. Seeming to promise intervention and then failing to intervene in the Syrian case created the worst of all scenarios.

Finally, framing political struggles in terms of good and bad tends to debilitate the international diplomacy needed to cope with them. Thus, the refusal of the West to engage with *both* regime *and* opposition and invest political capital in diplomatic brokerage of a power-sharing settlement in Syria, manifest in the failure at Geneva II, opened the door to the Islamic State scenario, which drew the West into a conflict with much higher costs that might have been avoided under a different policy. By comparison to the dismal recent harvest of Western liberalism in MENA, 'defensive realism' of the type promoted by Stephen Walt (2014), with its advocacy of caution and limited objectives, respect for sovereignty and priority for diplomacy over military intervention, has garnered increased credibility.

References

Adams, S. (2015) 'Failure to Protect: Syria and the UN Security Council', Global Centre for the Responsibility to Protect, Occasional Papers Series No. 5, March. Online. Available HTTP: <http://www.globalr2p.org/media/files/syriapaper_final.pdf> (accessed 12 November 2015).

Atwan, A. B. (2006) *The Secret History of al Qaeda,* Berkeley: University of California Press.

Ayoob, A. (1995) *The Third World Security Predicament: State Making, Regional Conflict and the International System*, Boulder, CO: Lynne Rienner.

Bahrami, N. and Parsi, T. (2012) 'Blunt Instrument: Sanctions Don't Promote Democratic Change', *Boston Review*, February 6. Online. Available HTTP: <http://bostonreview.net/natash-bahrami-trita-parsi-iran-sanctions> (accessed 12 November 2015).

Chenoweth, E. and Stephan, M. J. (2008) 'Why Civil Resistance Works: The Strategic Logic of Nonviolent Conflict', *International Security* 33(1): 7–44.

Dickinson, E. (2014) 'The Case against Qatar,' *Foreignpolicy.com*, 30 September. Online. Available HTTP: <http://www.foreignpolicy.com/articles/2014/09/30/the_case_against_qatar_funding_extremists_salafi_syria_uae_jihad_muslim_brotherhood_taliban> (accessed 12 November 2015).

Falk, R. (2014) 'Syria: What To Do Now', *Global Justice in the 21st Century*. Online. Available HTTP: <https://richardfalk.wordpress.com/2014/02/26/syria-what-to-do-now/> (accessed 12 November 2015).

Fearon, J. (2013) 'Syria's Civil War,' in M. Lynch (ed.) *The Political Science of Syria's War,* Project on Middle East Political Science, POMEPS Studies No. 5, 13–18.

Fromkin, D. (1989) *A Peace to End All Peace: Creating the Modern Middle East: 1914–1922*, London and New York: Penguin.

Goldsmith, L. (2011) 'Syria's Alawites and the Politics of Sectarian Insecurity: A Khaldounian Perspective', *Ortadoğu Etütleri* 3(1): 46–9.

Harling, P. (2011) 'Syria's Race against the Clock', *Foreign Policy*, 11 April. Online. Available HTTP: <http://foreignpolicy.com/2011/04/11/syrias-race-against-the-clock/> (accessed 12 November 2015).

Hinnebusch, R. (2001) *Syria: Revolution from Above*, London: Routledge.

Hinnebusch, R. (2012) 'Syria: from Authoritarian Upgrading to Revolution?', *International Affairs* 88(1): 95–113.

Joya, A. (2012) 'Syria and the Arab Spring: The Evolution of the Conflict and the Role of Domestic External and Factors', *Ortadoğu Etütleri* 4(1): 40–3.

Kaldor, M. (1999) *New and Old Wars: Organized Violence in a Global Era*, Cambridge: Polity Press.

Kaldor, M. (2013) 'What to Do in Syria?', *OpenDemocracy*, 10 September. Online. Available HTTP: <https://www.opendemocracy.net/mary-kaldor/what-to-do-in-syria> (accessed 12 November 2015).

Kaufman, S. (2008) 'Ethnic Conflict', in P. Williams (ed.) *Security Studies: An Introduction*, London and New York: Routledge, 201–15.

Kerr, P. (2010) 'Human Security and Diplomacy,' in M. Dunn Cavelty and V. Mauer (eds.) *The Routledge Handbook of Security Studies*, London and New York: Routledge, 115–26.

Lambach, D. and Debiel, T. (2010) 'State Failure and State Building,' in M. Dunn Cavelty and V. Mauer (eds.) *The Routledge Handbook of Security Studies*, London and New York: Routledge, 159–68.

Lynch, M. (2103) *The Political Science of Syria's War, POMPES Briefing*, Washington, DC: George Washington University.

Mandour, M. (2013) 'Beyond Civil Resistance: The Case of Syria', *OpenDemocracy*, 26 October. Online. Available HTTP: <https://www.opendemocracy.net/arab-awakening/maged-mandour/beyond-civil-resistance-case-of-syria> (accessed 12 November 2015).

O'Donnell, G. and Schmitter, P. (1986) *Transitions from Authoritarian Rule: Tentative Conclusions about Uncertain Democracies, Part 4*, Baltimore, MD: Johns Hopkins University Press.

Parmar, I. (2009) 'Foreign Policy Fusion: Liberal Interventionists, Conservative Nationalists and Neoconservatives', *International Politics* 46: 177–209.

Posen, B. (1993) 'The Security Dilemma and Ethnic Conflict', *Survival* 35(1): 27–47.

Schanzer, J. and Tahiroglu, M. (2014) *Bordering on Terrorism: Turkey's Syria Policy and the Rise of the Islamic State*, Washington: Foundation for Defense of Democracies.

Seelye, K. (2011) 'Syria Unrest "Cannot Be Contained"', *The Daily Beast,* 28 March. Online. Available HTTP: <www.thedailybeast.com/articles/2011/03/28/syria-unrest-cannot-be-contained-dissidents-say.html> (accessed 12 November 2015).

Spears, J. (2008) 'Insurgency and Counterinsurgency', in P. Williams (ed.) *Security Studies: An Introduction*, London and New York: Routledge, 389–405.

Tilly, C. (1985) 'War Making and State Making as Organized Crime', in P. J. Evans, D. Rueschemeyer, and T. Skocpol (eds.) *Bringing the State Back In*, Cambridge: Cambridge University Press.

United Nations (2012) 'Final Communiqué of the Action Group for Syria', Geneva, 30 June 2012. Online. Available HTTP: <http://www.un.org/News/dh/infocus/Syria/FinalCommuniqueAction GroupforSyria.pdf> (accessed 12 November 2015).

Walt, S. (2014) 'Democracy, Freedom, and Apple Pie Aren't a Foreign Policy', *Foreign Policy.com*, 1 July. Online. Available HTTP: <http://www.foreignpolicy.com/articles/2014/07/01/american_values_are_ to_blame_for_the_worlds_chaos_democracy_human_rights_ukraine_iraq> (accessed 12 November 2015).

Walter, B. (2013) 'The Four Things We Know about How Civil Wars End (and What It Tells Us about Syria)', in M. Lynch (ed.) *The Political Science of Syria's War*, Project on Middle East Political Science (POMEPS Studies No. 5).

Zartman, I. W. (1995) *Elusive Peace: Negotiating an End to Civil Wars*, Washington, DC: Brookings Institution.

Zartman, I. W. (2000) 'Ripeness: The Hurting Stalemate and Beyond,' in Committee on International Conflict Resolution (eds.) *International Conflict Resolution after the Cold War*, Washington, DC: National Academies Press, 225–50.

28

ISRAEL–PALESTINE: AN ARCHIPELAGO OF (IN)SECURITY

Nada Ghandour-Demiri

The Israeli–Palestinian conflict is one of the most central ones in the Middle East. This enduring and seemingly insolvable conflict has had dreadful effects on the lives of Palestinians and Israelis, and on the security of the whole region, for over six decades now. In addition to the competing claims for sovereignty over the land by Jews and Palestinians, there are also several strategic, political, economic, and religious interests that hinder the resolution of the conflict.

The dominant security modality in the Occupied Palestinian Territories (OPT) nowadays is the coexistence of an archipelago and enclaves. In the archipelago, people and goods move relatively freely and smoothly. The enclaves, however, are spaces of exception where the rule of law and the emergency procedure merge into indistinction (Agamben 2005). The archipelago/enclaves typology is helpful to understand the complexity of the Israeli–Palestinian conflict, and it is one of main reasons the conflict remains unresolved. The architect Alessandro Petti explains:

> [on] the one hand, we have an elite that is managing the space of flows, living in an archipelago-type world which it perceives as the only world, with no exterior to it; while on the other, the suspension of the rules of the archipelago creates legal and economic vacuums that make the enclave system a black hole, a shadowy area.
>
> *(2008: 11)*

This conceptualization of this particular urban and political reality is characteristic of the situation in the West Bank: settlements and Israeli bypass roads belong to an archipelago in which circulation is smooth and uninterrupted, while Palestinian villages and towns are enclaves characterized by containment, policing, and minimal circulation (if not immobility).

The coexistence of these two different forms of circulation is well depicted on the imaginary map *L'archipel de Palestine orientale* (The Archipelago of Eastern Palestine) created by the French cartographer Julien Boussac (2009) where the area controlled by Israel (area C) is depicted as a blue sea and in it there are many islands illustrating either Palestinian enclaves or Jewish settlements and military bases. The resulting fictional archipelago connects certain islands (i.e. Jewish settlements and Israeli military bases), while it disconnects others (i.e. Palestinian enclaves). Thus, graduated forms of circulation are governing the fragmentation of space. In addition, space is fragmented according to what needs to be secured (i.e. protected and included) and what needs to be confined (i.e. contained and excluded). The territorial fragmentation based on the archipelago/enclaves typology is maintained by a number of (in)security mechanisms, two of which will be discussed in this chapter (i.e. the Wall and the blockade on Gaza). I use the term '(in)security' in reference to these mechanisms because, as it will be demonstrated below, they are meant to provide security for a certain group of people, while at the same time they create insecurity for others.

The chapter will explain the current situation of an archipelago of (in)security in the OPT. It will first provide a brief historical overview of the conflict. Then, the chapter will focus on two Israeli security mechanisms that have played a key role in maintaining the coexistence of an archipelago and enclaves: the Wall and its associated closure regime, and the blockade on the Gaza Strip. In analysing each of these mechanisms, the typology of archipelago and enclaves will be clarified, and the ways in which these mechanisms contribute to the insecurity of Palestinians will be demonstrated. Finally, the chapter will conclude by considering the implication of this security typology for the unsolvability of the conflict and for its proliferation in other parts of the world as well.

Historical background

The origins of the conflict

The conflict between Palestinian Arabs and Jews dates from the late nineteenth century. Although these two groups have different religions, religious differences are not the major cause of the conflict. Rather, the problem lies in the ownership of the land. On the one hand, the Jews claim that this land has been promised to them since biblical times, and due to an increase in anti-Semitism around the world, they have the right to return to 'Eretz Israel' (the Hebrew name for the biblical land of Israel, Zion). On the other hand, the Palestinian Arabs' claims are mostly based on their continuous residence on the land for hundreds of years and, hence, their right to remain in their homeland.

At the turn of the twentieth century, Zionism, the Jewish nationalist movement, emerged due to increased discrimination and persecution of the Jews in Europe. Zionists supported the self-determination of the Jewish people and the establishment of a Jewish state in Palestine (Avineri 1981). With the establishment of the World Zionist Organization in 1897 by Theodore Herzl, this vision started to become increasingly popular. The realization of this project was becoming evident by the rising number of Jewish people immigrating to Palestine. The large immigration waves increased tensions in the region.

European geopolitics in the Middle East at that time contributed to the instability of the region. In 1915, Britain promised Sharif Hussein of Mecca that it would support the establishment of an Arab state, in return for an Arab revolt against the Ottoman Empire. The following year, Britain reached a secret agreement, known as the Sykes-Picot agreement, with France to divide the Middle East into spheres of influence. According to this agreement, Palestine was to be placed under international control. Furthermore, in 1917, the British foreign minister at that time, Lord Arthur Balfour, issued a declaration (known as the Balfour Declaration) announcing the support of its government for the establishment of a Jewish homeland in Palestine. Therefore, Palestine was promised several times during that period, and behind all three texts was an underlying sense of double-dealing and betrayal (Shlaim 2005). This lack of trust towards the British (from both Arabs and Jews) did not vanish during the British Mandate of Palestine (1922–48).

Palestinian resistance to British control and Zionist settlement climaxed with the Arab revolt of 1936–9, which Britain suppressed with the help of Zionist militias. During the Second World War, Jewish immigration to Palestine increased dramatically, leading to a rise in the number of Jewish settlements. After the Second World War, clashes between Arabs and Jews and between the

Zionist militias and the British army forced Britain to relinquish its mandate over Palestine. As a result, the future of Palestine was in the hands of the United Nations.

The creation of the state of Israel and the beginning of the conflict

The United Nations partition plan (1947) divided the country in two states, one Arab and the other Jewish, and the city of Jerusalem became an international zone. The Jewish minority received the majority of the land. Consequently, this partition led to the escalation of hostilities between the two parties. All these events led to the establishment of the state of Israel, the Palestinian *Nakba* (Arabic for 'catastrophe'), and the first Arab–Israeli war, in 1948. Israel came out successful from this war. It became an important power in the region, after defeating most Arab armies and occupying even more land from the Palestinians. The country was divided into three: Israel included 77 per cent of what was once known as Palestine, Egypt controlled the Gaza Strip, and Jordan occupied East Jerusalem and the West Bank (Beinin et al. 2000: 5). Therefore, the UN partition planned was never implemented. Another important consequence of this war was the displacement of many Palestinians and the creation of the refugee problem. Hundreds of thousands of Palestinians were obliged to flee their houses and become refugees throughout the Middle East and around the rest of the world.

As the crisis in the region continued, in June 1967 Israel pre-emptively attacked Egypt, Syria, and Jordan. This war lasted only six days and was an unprecedented success for Israel and a humiliating defeat for the Arab states. Israel acquired key lands: the Gaza Strip and the Sinai Peninsula from Egypt, the West Bank, and East Jerusalem from Jordan, and the Golan Heights from Syria. As a result, Israel became the dominant military power in the Middle East.

Meanwhile, the Palestine Liberation Organization (PLO) had been established in 1964 to organize Palestinian nationalism. The PLO was composed of various political and military groups holding different ideological beliefs. After the six-day war Yasser Arafat (the leader of Fatah – the largest political group) became chairman of the organization. With time, the organization became recognized by the Arab states and the UN as the representative of the Palestinians.

The first intifada and the 1993 Oslo Agreement

In 1987, a mass uprising against the Israeli occupation started in the West Bank and Gaza. This uprising, or *intifada* (meaning 'shaking off' in Arabic), was a popular mobilization that drew on the civil society organizations that had developed under occupation. The intifada involved hundreds of thousands of people, including children and women, and it was based primarily on acts of civil disobedience, such as demonstrations, general strikes and boycotts of Israeli products (King 2007; Smith 2007: 419).

The intifada lasted until 1993, but it drew unprecedented international attention to the Palestinian–Israeli conflict. Due to international and internal pressure, the Israeli Prime Minister Yitzhak Rabin and his cabinet were forced to change their political agenda and start negotiations with Arafat and the PLO. These negotiations led to the Oslo Agreement that was signed in 1993 between the two parties. According to the Oslo Agreement, Israel would withdraw from the Gaza Strip and Jericho, and then from further unspecified areas of the West Bank during a five-year interim period. During this period, the PLO would form a Palestinian Authority (PA) with 'self-governing' (i.e. municipal) powers in the areas from which Israeli forces were redeployed (Beinin et al. 2000: 12).

The most important consequence of the Oslo Accords was the division of the West Bank into three non-contiguous areas A, B, and C. In area A (17.2 per cent of the West Bank), the

PA has (theoretically) civil jurisdiction and security control, while Israel controls movement in and out of the area. In area B (23.8 per cent of the West Bank), the PA has civil authority and responsibility for public order, whereas Israel maintains security presence and superseding security responsibility. Area C (59 per cent of the West Bank) is under full civil and military Israeli control (*Le Monde Diplomatique* n.d.). However, apart from the division and diversified allocation of power, each area lacks territorial contiguity. For example, area A, rather than being a contiguous territory, is further divided into small 'islands'. As a result, in order to pass from one 'island' of Area A to the other, Israeli permission is necessary. Therefore, practically, the PA has no real control over any territory and the West Bank has been turned into an archipelago of enclaves, each one with different levels of security.

The Oslo Agreement has been very controversial. It has been criticized by both sides. By many Palestinians, it was considered as a one-sided accord that benefited only Israel, since it gave Israel control of most of the land, water, roads, and other resources. For the rightist Jews, a withdrawal from parts of the West Bank would deny them their biblical heritage. In addition to these disagreements, many of the provisions of the agreement were not carried out by either side. All these controversies and the inability to find a workable solution led to an increase in violence, and finally the eruption of the second intifada.

From the second intifada until today

The difficulties and humiliations experienced by Palestinians in their daily lives due to the occupation, as well as the corruption within the PA, were the main reasons that led to the second intifada in September 2000. This uprising was more violent than the first one. Israel used severe repression from the very beginning to avoid a prolonged civil uprising. During that period, Palestinian armed operations and suicide bombings increased.

In the meantime, Israel started implementing plans for a more concrete and radical separation. The main justification for these separation measures was the protection of Israeli civilians from security threats (e.g. suicide bombings targeting Israeli civilians). One of the clearest examples of this separation policy was the construction of the Wall in the West Bank that began in 2002 and is still ongoing. This security mechanism and its associated closure regime will be analysed in the next section of this chapter.

In 2003, the Israeli Prime Minister Ariel Sharon announced the 'disengagement plan' from the Gaza Strip. This plan was portrayed as a bold Israeli move towards peace and a way to increase Israeli citizens' security. The Israeli withdrawal from the Strip was implemented in 2005. However, this move was done unilaterally and it meant an increase in settlement construction in the West Bank. Moreover, while the Strip was evacuated by settlers and soldiers, it did not become free of Israeli control; in fact, Israel tightened the control and surveillance of the Palestinians living in the Gaza Strip.

After Arafat's death in 2004 and Mahmood Abbas' ascent to the leadership of the PLO, Palestinian internal political divisions worsened. In 2006, the Islamist party of Hamas won the elections, leading to a setback in all negotiations, since it was viewed by Israel and many other countries as a terrorist organization. Since these elections, the PA has been experiencing an internal conflict that has fragmented Palestinian society and, as a result, has hindered the peace negotiations with Israel. As a punitive response to Hamas's victory, Israel imposed a blockade on the Gaza Strip – that is still ongoing.

Meanwhile, the Israeli occupation has grown more sophisticated, using advanced military techniques, weapons, and a more complex occupation policy that not only maintains the occupation of the Palestinian Territories, but also makes a two-state solution impossible to implement on the ground (due to the increased number of settlements and the fragmentation of the OPT). Apart from these important factors, in the last nine years Israel has also launched a series of deadly military incursions on the Gaza Strip that have stalled peace efforts.

Israeli (in)security mechanisms

The wall

'Good fences make good neighbours'. The former Israeli Prime Minister Ehud Barak was very much in favour of this proverb. It influenced his 1999 election campaign motto: 'Peace through Separation: we are here, they are there'. The slogan brought back the idea of a physical blockade between Israel and the West Bank. This idea started being materialized in 2002 by Ariel Sharon.

The official Israeli position for the erection of a physical barrier separating Israel from the West Bank is the prevention of terrorist attacks against Israeli civilians. The Israeli government labels its fortified fence as the 'anti-terrorist fence' or 'security fence' (Israel Ministry of Foreign Affairs 2004). In contrast, Palestinians and critics of the fence call it 'apartheid wall', 'wall of shame', or 'separation barrier' (see HSRC 2009; Lentin 2008; Shihab-Eldin 2009).

While Israel is claiming that the Wall is being built to protect Israeli citizens, there are other subtler, but more important, reasons for its construction. One of the main purposes of the Wall is the connection of settlements to Israel, and their dissociation from the Palestinians (B'Tselem et al. 2005; Weizman 2007: 168). In fact, the Wall encircles seventy-one settlements (comprising 85 per cent of the settlers), and connects them physically to Israel (OCHA 2013b). Another reason, often mentioned by the critics of the Wall, is the appropriation of more Palestinian land in order to expand the state of Israel (or minimize even more the OPT) (see B'Tselem et al. 2005: 6; Gordon 2003; Koury 2005: 49; OCHA 2007). While the Wall was supposed to be built on the Green Line (the 1949 armistice lines), it started 'invading' more and more of the West Bank. That is, nearly three-quarters of the total projected fence route runs inside the West Bank, and not along the Green Line (B'Tselem 2011; OCHA 2010). This means that it is not a single continuous line but it is curling around areas of interest, such as settlements. In other words, it represents de facto annexation. Moreover, the Wall has proved to be (together with other mechanisms, such as settlements, road networks, checkpoints, etc.) an essential spatial mechanism contributing to the fragmentation of the West Bank, reinforcing the creation of an archipelago of enclaves (Petti 2008: 9; Sorkin 2005: xix; Weizman 2007: 178).

The Wall is approximately 712 kilometres long (OCHA 2013b). Its majority is fence-like, made up of a series of electronic fences, patrol roads, ditches, and razor wire up to 70 metres wide (Müller 2006: 18). The main element of the Wall is 'a touch-sensitive, "smart", three-meter-high electronic fence, placed on a 150-centimetre-deep concrete foundation (to prevent digging under it) and topped with barbed wire (to prevent climbing over it)' (Weizman 2007: 292). It is also equipped with day/night vision video cameras and small radars. In some places, especially within and around Palestinian urban areas, the electronic fence is replaced by an enormous concrete wall up to 8 metres high (Müller 2006: 18). In addition, along the Wall there are watchtowers for Israeli soldiers to keep an eye on the Palestinians.

The Wall and its bureaucratic apparatus (e.g. checkpoints) create different population groups. On the one hand, there are Israeli citizens and West Bank settlers, and on the other, diverse categories of Palestinians (see Tawil-Souri 2011). The aim of the mechanisms of the occupation is to prevent any contact between these different population groups. In addition, the Wall creates its own cartographic reality, investing in its own spatial partitioning by dividing the West Bank into different areas. The Wall has created two types of space: on the one hand, there is a continuous and fluid Israeli space that is full of certainty and predictability, where Israelis (including settlers) can move quickly and easily (i.e. archipelago). On the other hand, there is a fragmented Palestinian space full of obstacles that generate unpredictability and uncertainty, which severely impede Palestinians' movement (i.e. enclaves) (Parizot 2009: 3).

This management of population flow and fluidity of space is further maintained by a discriminatory roads regime. Israel has imposed on Palestinians what B'Tselem calls a 'Forbidden Roads Regime' (2015). Since 1967, Israel has built a large network of roads within the West Bank which is intended almost completely to serve and perpetuate the Jewish settlements. These roads link the settlements and connect them to Israel proper, while they separate Palestinians. In the late 1970s, during the settlement push, the notion of bypass roads was developed: bypassing Arab villages and towns. With the Oslo Agreement the idea of bypass roads and the forbidden roads regime gained momentum. Since then, Israel totally prevents Palestinians accessing certain roads, also known as 'sterile routes' (B'Tselem 2004: 44). There are roads partially open for Palestinians, while others are mainly for Palestinians, since Israeli civilians are prevented from accessing those. The main mindset behind this regime is that Palestinians are perceived as threats to the security of Israeli civilians, and hence any contact with them needs to be minimal or absent. Yet, there is no law or official documentation explaining this policy, apart from Route 443, and the prohibitions on Palestinian travel are based on 'verbal orders' given by Israeli soldiers along the roads or at checkpoints (B'Tselem 2015; Groag 2006).

The Wall and its associated gate and permit regime violates international law according to the International Court of Justice (ICJ) (Gross 2006; ICJ 2004; OCHA 2007: 46). More specifically, the Wall violates Palestinian access to health care, education, work, agricultural land, and family life (ICJ 2004). Nevertheless, and despite its illegality, Israel continues its construction.

The Gaza Strip blockade

The Gaza Strip has been subject to an ongoing blockade for almost nine years now. Israel has gradually tightened its control of the area following its disengagement and the subsequent institutionalization of Hamas rule. In September 2005, Israel completed the so-called 'disengagement plan', which entailed the dismantling of all Israeli settlements in the Gaza Strip, the evacuation of their residents to Israeli territory, and the withdrawal of all Israeli army forces from the area. There is a wide literature on the disengagement written both by its supporters and its opponents. Those in favour tend to perceive (or to portray) the redeployment as an opportunity to bring a certain kind of peace to the political impasse between Palestinians and Israelis (Caplen 2006; Roy 2005: 65). Moreover, Israel is depicted as a civilized state that is willing to make great sacrifices (especially regarding the suffering of Jewish settlers removed from the Strip) for peace (Falah 2005: 1348; King and Kahan 2006). Embedded in the early debates was also the assumption that after the disengagement Palestinians would be free to build their own democratic state in the Strip and that if they failed the responsibility would be theirs and theirs alone (Caplen 2006: 715–16; Roy 2005: 65).

Yet many are critical of this Israeli withdrawal from the Strip, and especially of what this move really meant (see Li 2006; Mari 2005; Scobbie 2006; Yiftachel 2005). The disengagement plan was a *unilateral* plan decided and executed by Israel alone, rather than an *agreement* between Israel and other parties. Furthermore, it is not to be taken in the literal sense of the term: while Israel did indeed remove its settlements and military bases from the Gaza Strip, it did not give away its control over it.

Israel's control over Gaza was tightened further when Hamas took power. In January 2006 Hamas secured a majority of seats in the Palestinian legislative elections – a result that was not accepted by the United States, the European Union, or Israel, despite the democratic and transparent character of the elections (Goerzig 2010: 17). The rise in support for Hamas has been attributed to the organization's civil service provisions and firm political and military leadership in a context of continuous fragmentation in Palestinian politics (especially since the second Intifada) and widespread Palestinian disillusionment after years of Fatah's corruption and misrule of the Palestinian Authority (Bhungalia 2010; Tamimi 2007; Usher 2006: 21). After the elections, internal clashes erupted between Fatah and Hamas, leading to Fatah's military defeat and Hamas taking control over Gaza in June 2007. Since then, Qassam rockets have been intermittently launched from Gaza into southern Israeli territory. Citing these attacks as motive, Israel's security cabinet declared Gaza a 'hostile territory' in September 2007 and intensified the sanctions policy to an unprecedented degree (Israel Ministry of Foreign Affairs 2007). From then on, Israel has maintained a three-dimensional blockade on Gaza by controlling its territorial borders, as well as its air and sea space. For example, Gazans are not allowed to exit or enter the Strip except in rare cases (usually deemed humanitarian) and the movement of goods into and out of the Strip is strictly controlled (Bhungalia 2010; Israel Ministry of Foreign Affairs 2007).

The sanctions policy was complimented by a series of military incursions, such as: Operation Summer Rains (started in June 2006); Operation Cast Lead (27 December 2008 – 18 January 2009); Operation Pillar of Defense (14–21 November 2012); and Operation Protective Edge in 2014. Indicatively, during Operation Cast Lead, 1,385 Palestinians were killed, 762 of whom did not take part in the hostilities (including 318 children), and more than 5,300 Palestinians were wounded (B'Tselem 2009). Apart from the high death toll, these operations are characterized by the bombing of civilian infrastructure and incursions into crowded population areas – cities in particular.

According to an OCHA report, in January 2011 it was estimated that approximately 200–300 tunnels were operating on a regular basis, about half the number of that operated the year before (OCHA 2011a: 7). In 2009, approximately 90 per cent of Gaza's economic activity was devoted to smuggling (Roy 2009: 1). The tunnels have become the main lifeline for Gaza's population: essential food and medicine, construction material, animals, and even weapons, are smuggled into Gaza from Egypt. For Palestinians, tunnels have become an instrument of resilience, through which they can avoid extinction. For Israel, they are an informal regulatory mechanism to maintain the humanitarian situation in the Strip at the level of crisis rather than absolute catastrophe. This is the main reason Israel tolerates the tunnels between Gaza and Egypt (when it does not bomb them under the excuse of weapon smuggling).

In addition to the tunnels, Gazans mainly receive their basic needs for survival through humanitarian agencies. In fact, humanitarian aid is the main way through which Palestinians in Gaza are kept alive. In 2013, 80 per cent of the Palestinian population in the Gaza Strip was aid-dependent and 57 per cent was food-insecure (OCHA 2013a). Therefore, in Michel Agier's words, an entire population is kept artificially alive through an international 'transfusion' provided by international organizations (2008: 47). Despite this obvious aid dependency of an entire population, Israel's policy-makers continue to deny that there is a humanitarian crisis (see Government of Israel 2011; Israel Ministry of Foreign Affairs 2010; Ravid 2009). At the same time, however, Israel is imposing a strict policy of caloric determination to prevent a humanitarian disaster (i.e. the death of thousands of Palestinians) by barely keeping them alive (Bhungalia 2012). According to Gisha (the Israeli Legal Centre for Freedom of Movement), this policy has been 'articulated informally by Israeli officials as one of 'no development, no prosperity, no humanitarian crisis' – allowing the minimum needed for survival, but no more' (2010: 4). This imposed policy of bare survival severely inhibits Gazans' capacity to conduct a full or normal life. All this attests to the significant role humanitarian considerations have come to play as an integral part of the machinery of the occupying power.

In addition to the denial of a normal life, Israel is denying Palestinians the right to development. The Israeli siege has resulted in what Sara Roy has termed 'de-development' of the Gaza Strip. De-development refers to 'the deliberate, systematic, and progressive dismemberment of an indigenous economy by a dominant one – and by extension, societal potential is not only distorted but denied' (Roy 2007). It is shaped and advanced by policies reflecting the ideological imperatives of Zionism: expropriation and dispossession, integration and externalization, and de-institutionalization. According to Roy, these policies are essential to the process of de-development in that they dispossess Palestinians of critical economic resources or factors of production needed to create and sustain productive capacity, create extreme dependency on employment in Israel as a source of GNP growth, and restrict the kind of indigenous institutional development that could lead to structural reform that is economic, social, and political. Hence, unlike underdevelopment, which allows some form of development, de-development's main aim is the prevention and denial of development.

The Gaza Strip has therefore turned into an enclave where its 1.8 million population live in a constant state of insecurity. The three-dimensional blockade forbidding the free movement of people and goods, the violent military incursions, and policies such as de-development, deny Gazans a secure life. The Gaza Strip has been turned into the biggest 'exemplary' enclave, where the rule of law is suspended and the state of exception has become the norm.

Conclusion

The coexistence of an archipelago and enclaves is currently the dominant security modality in the OPT. The aim of this chapter was to explain the archipelago and enclaves typology, and argue that it does not provide security in the long term as it creates further insecurity for the occupied and makes the creation of a viable Palestinian state impossible.

Because of its policies, Israel has recently emerged as a unique global exemplar of urban militarism and securitization (Graham 2011: 143). Apart from the sophistication of the military and surveillance equipment that Israel is exporting, it is using the 'combat-proven' status of its security systems and warfare machinery to its advantage. Gaza and the West Bank are used as laboratories of urban warfare and surveillance to test in real-time technologies and weapons (Gordon 2011: 162; Graham 2011: 138).

Hence, Gaza and the West Bank are 'exemplary [fields] in the experimentation of new architectures, geographies and technologies of control-at-distance, which are becoming widely imitated and exemplified elsewhere' (Graham 2011: 142). The architecture of occupation found in Israel is now common across the world (Zureik et al. 2011: xviii). By being exported globally, 'these Israeli practices and technologies have connected the uniqueness of the conflict with worldwide predilections to address security anxieties through "circulation management"' (Weizman 2007: 154).

The archipelago and enclaves paradigm created in the West Bank by Israel is found in many places around the globe (e.g. gated communities, prisons, camps, ghettos, quarantined zones, etc.): not only in the global South or in colonial and occupation regimes, but, in fact, also in the global North, including metropolises such as New York, London, and Paris. Mark Duffield's idea of bunkers and camps is particularly insightful in this respect: while contemporary bunkers take many forms, they all share a basic characteristic in that they are 'defended spaces that can be hermetically sealed against a threatening and unknown environment' (2011: 764).

The politics of inclusion, protection, and fortification characterizing the Jewish settlements and Israeli military bases are reflected in the idea (and reality) of bunkers, and the exclusion and abandonment of the Palestinian enclaves are found in today's camps across the world. Gated communities (e.g. Jewish settlements, elite residential compounds, and UN and other humanitarian agencies' compounds in the developing world) are a typical example of bunkers. The side-by-side coexistence of over-protected (almost sterilized) gated communities (or bunkers) and camps of undesirables is now becoming a globalizing phenomenon. Israel's role in the globalization of this phenomenon is crucial in the sense that it is a microcosm of bunkers and camps and the technologies that sustain them.

References

Agamben, G. (2005) *State of Exception*, London: University of Chicago Press.

Avineri, S. (1981) *The Making of Modern Zionism: The Intellectual Origins of the Jewish State*, New York: Basic Books.

B'Tselem (2004) 'The Forbidden Roads Regime: The Discriminatory West Bank Roads Regime.' Report. Online. Available HTTP: <http://www.btselem.org/download/200408_forbidden_roads_eng.doc> (accessed 30 June 2014).

B'Tselem (2009) 'One and a Half Million People Imprisoned', *B'Tselem*, 27 December. Online. Available HTTP: <http://www.btselem.org/gaza_strip/20091227_a_year_to_castlead_operation> (accessed 8 August 2014).

B'Tselem (2011) 'Separation Barrier', *B'Tselem*, 1 January. Online. Available HTTP: <http://www.btselem.org/english/Separation_Barrier/> (accessed 8 August 2014).

B'Tselem (2015) 'Restrictions on Movement: Checkpoints, Physical Obstructions, and Forbidden Roads', *B'Tselem*, 20 May. Online. Available HTTP: <http://www.btselem.org/english/Freedom_of_Movement/Checkpoints_and_Forbidden_Roads.asp> (accessed 7 September 2015).

B'Tselem and Bimkom (2005) 'Under the Guise of Security: Routing the Separation Barrier to Enable Israeli Settlements Expansion in the West Bank', *B'Tselem*, December. Online. Available HTTP: <http://www.btselem.org/Download/200512_Under_the_Guise_of_Security_eng.pdf> (accessed 8 August 2014).

Beinin, J. and Hajjar, L. (2000) 'Palestine, Israel and the Arab-Israeli Conflict: A Primer', *Middle East Research & Information Project* (MERIP). Online. Available HTTP: <http://www.merip.org/palestine-israel_primer/Palestine-Israel_Primer_MERIP.pdf> (accessed 7 August 2014).

Bhungalia, L. (2010) 'A Liminal Territory: Gaza, Executive Discretion, and Sanctions Turned Humanitarian', *GeoJournal* 75: 347–57.

Bhungalia, L. (2012) 'Im/Mobilities in a "Hostile Territory": Managing the Red Line', *Geopolitics* 17(2): 256–75.

Boussac, J. (2009) 'L'archipel de Palestine orientale', *Le Monde Diplomatique*. Hors-série. L'Atlas: Un monde à l'envers, 129.

Caplen, R. (2006) 'Rules of Disengagement: Relating the Establishment of Palestinian Gaza to Israel's Right to Exercise Self-Defense as Interpreted by the International Court of Justice at the Hague', *Florida Journal of International Law* 18(2): 679–716.

Duffield, M. (2011) 'Total War as Environmental Terror: Linking Liberalism, Resilience and the Bunker', *South Atlantic Quarterly* 110(3): 757–69.

Falah, G. (2005) 'The Geopolitics of "Enclavisation" and the Demise of a Two-State Solution to the Israeli–Palestinian Conflict,' *Third World Quarterly* 26 (8): 1341–72.

Gisha (Legal Centre for Freedom of Movement) (2010) 'Restrictions on the Transfer of Goods to Gaza: Obstruction and Obfuscation', January. Online. Available HTTP: <http://www.gisha.org/UserFiles/File/publications/Obstruction_and_obfuscation.doc> (accessed 12 November 2015).

Goerzig, C. (2010) *Transforming the Quartet Principles: Hamas and the Peace Process*, The Institute for Security Studies, Occasional Papers Series, 85 (September).

Gordon, N. (2003) 'Can Bad Fences Make Good Neighbours?: Israel's Separation Wall is Being Used to Annexe Territory', *The Guardian*, 29 May.

Gordon, N. (2011) 'Israel's Emergence as a Homeland Security Capital', in E. Zureik, D. Lyon, and Y. Abu-Laban (eds.) *Surveillance and Control in Israel/Palestine: Population, Territory, and Power*, London: Routledge, 153–70.

Government of Israel (2011) 'Measures Taken by Israel in Support of Developing the Palestinian Economy and Socio-Economic Structure', Report to the Ad Hoc Liaison Committee, 13 April, Brussels. Online. Available HTTP: <http://www.mfa.gov.il/NR/rdonlyres/3F532B57-F377-4FEF-99C8-68A810CA7AAC/0/IsraelReportAHLCApril2011.pdf> (accessed 10 February 2012).

Graham, S. (2011) 'Laboratories of War: Surveillance and US–Israeli Collaboration in War and Security', in E. Zureik, D. Lyon, and Y. Abu-Laban (eds.) *Surveillance and Control in Israel/Palestine: Population, Territory, and Power*, London: Routledge, 133–52.

Groag, S. (2006) 'The Politics of Roads in Jerusalem', in Z. Efrat, R. Khamaisi, and R. Nasrallah (eds.) *City of Collision: Jerusalem and the Principles of Conflict Urbanism*, Basel: Birkhäuser – Publishers for Architecture, 176–84.

Gross, A. M. (2006) 'The Construction of a Wall between the Hague and Jerusalem: The Enforcement and Limits of Humanitarian Law and the Structure of Occupation', *Leiden Journal of International Law* 19: 393–440.

Human Sciences Research Council (HSRC) (2009) 'Occupation, Colonialism, Apartheid? A Re-assessment of Israel's Practices in the Occupied Palestinian Territories under International Law', May. Online. Available HTTP: <http://www.hsrc.ac.za/Document-3202.phtml> (accessed 20 January 2011).

Israel Ministry of Foreign Affairs (2004) 'Saving Lives: Israel's Anti-Terrorist Fence'. Online. Available HTTP: <http://www.mfa.gov.il/mfa/foreignpolicy/terrorism/palestinian/pages/saving%20lives-%20israel-s%20anti-terrorist%20fence%20-%20answ.aspx> (accessed 7 September 2015).

Israel Ministry of Foreign Affairs (2007) 'Security Cabinet Declares Gaza Hostile Territory', 19 September. Online. Available HTTP: <http://www.mfa.gov.il/MFA/Government/Communiques/2007/Security+Cabinet+declares+Gaza+hostile+territory+19-Sep-2007.htm> (accessed 7 September 2015).

Israel Ministry of Foreign Affairs (2010) 'Prime Minister's Office Statement following the Israeli Security Cabinet Meeting', 20 June. Online. Available HTTP: <http://www.mfa.gov.il/MFA/Government/Communiques/2010/Prime_Minister_Office_statement_20-Jun-2010.htm> (accessed 7 September 2015).

King, M. E. (2007) *A Quiet Revolution: The First Palestinian Intifada and Nonviolent Resistance*, New York: Nation Books.

King, W. and Kahan, E. (2006) *Disengagement Through the Lens: A Glimpse at Gush Katif Before and After*, Jerusalem: Images of Israel.

Koury, S. (2005) 'Why This Wall?', in M. Sorkin (ed.) *Against the Wall: Israel's Barrier to Peace*, New York: The New Press, 48–65.

Le Monde Diplomatique (n.d.) 'The Oslo Process'. Online. Available HTTP: <http://mondediplo.com/focus/mideast,1279/> (accessed 8 September 2015).

Lentin, R. (ed.) (2008) *Thinking Palestine*, London: Zed Books.

Li, D. (2006) 'The Gaza Strip as Laboratory: Notes in the Wake of Disengagement', *Journal of Palestine Studies* 35(2): 38–55.

Mari, M. (2005) 'The Israeli Disengagement from the Gaza Strip: an End of the Occupation?', *Yearbook of International Humanitarian Law* 8: 356–68.

Müller, A. (2006) *A Wall on the Green Line? Israel's Wall Project under Scrutiny*, Jerusalem: Alternative Information Centre.

OCHA (UN Office for the Coordination of Humanitarian Affairs) (2007) 'The Humanitarian Impact on Palestinians of Israeli Settlements and other Infrastructure in the West Bank', July. Online. Available HTTP: <https://www.ochaopt.org/documents/thehumanitarianimpactofisraeliinfrastructurethewestbank_intro.pdf> (accessed 12 November 2015).

OCHA (UN Office for the Coordination of Humanitarian Affairs) (2010) 'Six Years After the International Court of Justice Advisory Opinion on the Barrier: The Impact of the Barrier on Health', *OCHA Special Focus*.

OCHA (UN Office for the Coordination of Humanitarian Affairs) (2011a) 'Easing the Blockade: Assessing the Humanitarian Impact on the Population of the Gaza Strip', *OCHA Special Focus*, March.

OCHA (UN Office for the Coordination of Humanitarian Affairs) (2011b) 'Occupied Palestinian Territory: Overview Map', December.

OCHA (UN Office for the Coordination of Humanitarian Affairs) (2011c) 'The Barrier Route in the West Bank', July.

OCHA (UN Office for the Coordination of Humanitarian Affairs) (2013a) 'The Gaza Strip: the Humanitarian Impact of the Movement Restrictions on People and Goods', *Fact Sheet*, July.

OCHA (UN Office for the Coordination of Humanitarian Affairs) (2013b) 'The Humanitarian Impact of the Barrier', *Fact Sheet*, July.

Parizot, C. (2009) 'Temporalities and Perceptions of the Separation between Israelis and Palestinians', *Bulletin du Centre de recherche français de Jérusalem*, issue 2.

Petti, A. (2008) 'Archipelagos and Enclaves: Dubai, Jerusalem, Baghdad and Other States of Exception', Paper Presented at the International Workshop 'Power, Governmentality, Resistance and State of Exception in the Arab World', American University of Beirut, Lebanon, August 29–30.

Ravid, B. (2009) 'Livni: Cease-Fire in Gaza Would Grant Hamas Legitimacy', *Haaretz*, 1 January. Online. Available HTTP: <http://www.haaretz.com/news/livni-cease-fire-in-gaza-would-grant-hamas-legitimacy-1.267233>(accessed 12 November 2015).

Roy, S. (2005) 'Praying with Their Eyes Closed: Reflections on the Disengagement from Gaza', *Journal of Palestine Studies* 34(4): 64–74.

Roy, S. (2007) *Failing Peace: Gaza and the Palestinian–Israeli Conflict*, London: Pluto Press.

Roy, S. (2009) 'The Peril of Forgetting Gaza', *The Harvard Crimson*, 2 June. Online. Available HTTP: <http://www.thecrimson.com/article/2009/6/2/the-peril-of-forgetting-gaza-the/> (accessed 12 November 2015).

Scobbie, I. (2006) 'Is Gaza Still Occupied Territory?', *Forced Migration Review* 26: 18.

Shihab-Eldin, A. (2009) 'Celebrating Berlin While Enabling Israel's Apartheid Wall', *Huffington Post*, November 11.

Shlaim, A. (2005) 'The Balfour Declaration and Its Consequences,' in William R. Louis, (ed.) *Yet More Adventures with Britannia: Personalities, Politics and Culture in Britain*, London: I. B. Tauris, 251–70.

Smith, C. D. (2007) *Palestine and the Arab–Israeli Conflict: A History with Documents*, London: Palgrave Macmillan.

Sorkin, M. (ed.) (2005) *Against the Wall: Israel's Barrier to Peace*, New York: The New Press.

Tamimi, A. (2007) *Hamas: Unwritten Chapters*, London: Hurst.

Tawil-Souri, H. (2011) 'Orange, Green and Blue: Color-Coded Paperwork for Palestinian Population Control', in E. Zureik, D. Lyon, and Y. Abu-Laban (eds.) *Surveillance and Control in Israel/Palestine: Population, Territory, and Power*, London: Routledge, 219–38.

Usher, G. (2006) 'Hamas Risen', *Middle East Report*, 238: 2–11.

Weizman, E. (2007) *Hollow Land: Israel's Architecture of Occupation*, London: Verso.

Yiftachel, O. (2005) 'Neither Two States Nor One: The Disengagement and "Creeping Apartheid" in Israel/Palestine', *The Arab World Geographer* 8(3): 125–9.

Zureik, E., Lyon, D. and Abu-Laban, Y. (eds.) (2011) *Surveillance and Control in Israel/Palestine: Population, Territory, and Power*, London: Routledge.

29

ANALYSING DRUG VIOLENCE IN MEXICO

Kimberly Heinle, Octavio Rodríguez Ferreira, and David A. Shirk

In the mid-2000s, Mexico began to experience an increase in violent acts perpetrated by organized crime groups (OCGs) involved in drug trafficking, even as overall levels of societal violence continued a decades-long decline. By 2007, when Mexico's homicide rate reached the all-time low of 8.1 per 100,000 inhabitants, the number of homicides attributed to organized crime groups involved in drug trafficking had more than doubled from about 1,000 such killings in 2001. Yet, this was only the beginning. Over the next five years, Mexico's homicide rate nearly tripled as a result of a dramatic increase in the number of so-called drug-related killings – or 'drug violence' – that accompanied an all-out shooting war among OCGs.

Amid this dramatic increase in violence, the authors coordinated a research initiative to track and analyse the patterns of homicide associated with OCGs involved in drug trafficking through a series of policy reports (Heinle et al. 2014; Heinle et al. 2015; Molzahn et al. 2012; Molzahn et al. 2013). This chapter draws on these efforts and the dataset collected by the authors to examine the patterns of violence associated with Mexican OCGs, and offers several observations about the nature and implications of this violence.

The chapter has three parts. In the first, we look at patterns of violence in Mexico, using data on homicides, looking specifically at the role of organized-crime-style violence. In the second, we present data on specificities of the violence, including local distribution, changing modes of violence, and victim characteristics. In the third, we analyse the data and link it to the broader context of politics and security in Mexico.

Understanding Mexico's recent violence

It is important to note that how one measures violence is contingent on many, often highly subjective factors. By some measures, the level of violence in Mexico is 'modest', particularly within the Western Hemisphere. Even when Mexico's organized-crime-related violence was arguably at its worst, the national homicide rate – one of the most commonly used indicators for comparing levels of violence – was much lower than in other countries in the Americas (UNODC 2014). However, other factors make it appear far less modest. This is the focus of the first sub-chapter. In addition to understanding the scale and rate of crime and violence in Mexico in recent years, it is also necessary to underscore its sources. In the second sub-chapter, we turn to the role of OCGs in the recent increase of violence, particularly those involved in drug trafficking.

Mexico's homicide rate in comparison

Despite valid concerns about the problems of crime and violence in Mexico, the country's homicide rate was about average for the Western Hemisphere, even amid the dramatic increase in violence in the first ten to fifteen years of the century. However, while Mexico's violence is about average when it comes to the rate of homicides per capita in Latin America, its security challenges are arguably of significant concern for a number of reasons. First, the rate of homicides in Mexico escalated quite dramatically in recent years, reversing a multi-decade downward trend (see Figure 29.1). Historical data suggest that homicide in Mexico generally declined from the 1930s into the mid-2000s.[1] However, Mexico's rate climbed sharply from 2007 to 2011, increasing threefold from roughly 8.1 to 23.5 homicides per 100,000, according to figures from Mexico's National Institute of Statistics, Geography, and Information (INEGI) (INEGI 2014).[2] By World Health Organization standards, a homicide rate over 10 per 100,000 is considered to be at 'epidemic' levels (UNDP 2013). While recent data suggest that the homicide rate has now fallen below this threshold, both domestic and international concerns about the problem of violence in Mexico persist because the problem of violence is also accompanied by rampant impunity (Heinle et al. 2015). As a result, the vast majority of murders are not investigated and, as a result, perpetrators go unpunished under the law.

A second reason why Mexico's violence has provoked such enormous concern has to do with the sheer number of murders in the country that resulted from these increases. Because Mexico had an estimated population of nearly 120 million people in 2014 – the third largest population among all countries in the Americas, after the United States and Brazil – even a modest increase in Mexico's homicide rate translates into the loss of thousands of lives. Indeed, during the four-year rise in violence from 2007 to 2011, the number of murders increased from 8,867 to 27,199. While Mexico might *appear* to be 'average' for the region, no other country in the Western

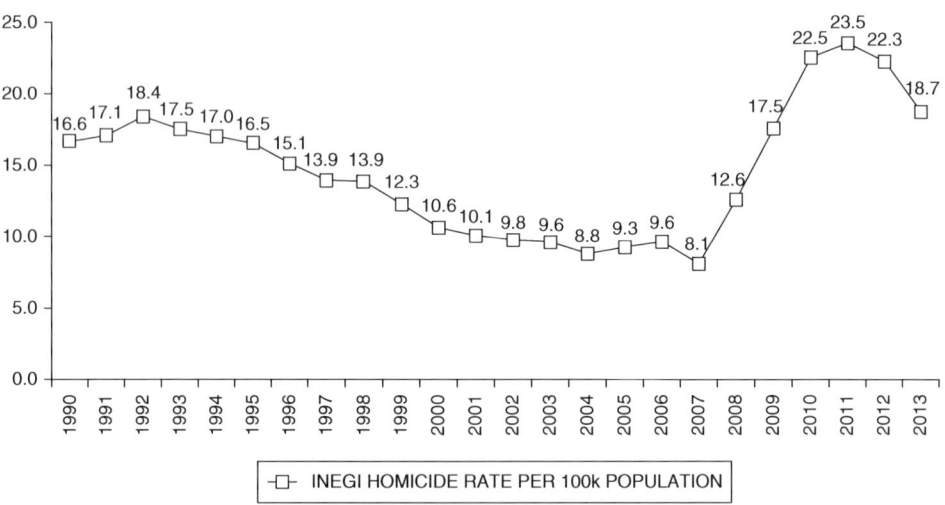

Figure 29.1 Homicide rate in Mexico, 1990–2013

Source of data: INEGI (2014). Authors' calculations based on INEGI homicide data and Consejo Nacional de Población's (CONAPO) population estimates for all years. Results vary when revised CONAPO population estimates from later years are applied (CONAPO 2014).

Hemisphere saw such a large increase either in the homicide rate or in the absolute number of homicides over the last two decades.[3]

What is particularly concerning about Mexico's sudden increases in homicides in recent years is that much or most of this violence is attributable to OCGs, commonly defined as groups of individuals acting in concert over a sustained period of time with the objective of deliberately violating established law, often with transnational organizational capabilities and influences. Still, as scholars of organized crime have demonstrated, violence is not necessarily the norm even in the underworld (Andreas and Wallman 2009). Thus, Mexico's recent surge in violence requires some understanding of recent dynamics among Mexican OCGs, particularly those involved in drug trafficking.

The role of drug trafficking and organized crime in Mexico

Mexico's increases in violence have been closely connected to the problem of organized crime, and especially drug trafficking and related activities. Mexico's contemporary OCGs have their roots in the advent of alcohol and drug prohibition in the 1920s and 1930s. While alcohol smuggling from Mexico faded away almost immediately after prohibition was repealed in the United States in 1933, the smuggling of heroin and marijuana – both produced in Mexico – has continued into the present (Astorga and Shirk 2010).

Drug trafficking became dramatically more profitable and well consolidated in Mexico when it became a major transit point for cocaine trafficking from Colombia to the United States in the 1970s and 1980s (cf. Astorga and Shirk 2013; Shannon 1988). With the decline of Colombia's major drug-trafficking organizations, Mexican criminal organizations came to dominate the business by the late 1980s. As they did, Mexican traffickers also became involved in producing and trafficking synthetic drugs, like methamphetamines and MDMA (Ecstasy). Like the Colombians that they superseded, Mexican traffickers were commonly described as 'cartels' because they employed some of the same practices as business organizations that seek to generally reduce market competition (e.g., explicitly or implicitly negotiating territories for operation and distribution). Indeed, the lack of market competition was key to the success of Mexican drug traffickers, who are believed by many experts to have been directly involved in protecting and regulating the illicit drug trade (cf. Astorga 2000; Flores 2009).

This relatively harmonious arrangement changed in the aftermath of the 1985 murder of US Drug Enforcement Agency (DEA) agent Enrique 'Kiki' Camarena, which led to intense US pressure on the Mexican authorities to arrest the three main leaders of the so-called Guadalajara Cartel. The splitting of the Guadalajara Cartel into rival, regionally based factions in around 1989 set in motion a competitive struggle for supply routes that has continued into the present. Starting in the early 2000s, that competition grew significantly more intense and more violent due to a series of government crackdowns, internal power struggles, and splits among Mexico's OCGs (Astorga and Shirk 2010).

Over the last several years, the accumulated toll of this violence has been the loss of tens of thousands of lives, and the problem has become a central preoccupation for both government officials and ordinary citizens. Moreover, as the level of violence in Mexico grew, it also became more diffuse in a number of ways. While there is now considerable evidence that the number of homicides in Mexico has begun to subside over the past few years, violence remains relatively high and the security situation remains highly problematic in certain parts of the country. Thus careful monitoring and study are still needed to understand the manifestations, root causes, and possible solutions to the problem of violence in Mexico.

Drug violence in Mexico: data and findings

This section examines Mexico's drug-related and organized-crime-style violence in substantial detail, drawing on several years of data gathering and research, as well as the latest available data from a variety of sources.[4] This section has three sub-sections. The first looks at organized-crime-style violence in relation to other types of violence; the second at its local distribution and geographic dispersion. The third notices a change in modes of violence and looks particularly at the type of victims this violence is causing.

Organized-crime-style violence

A review of data generated by various independent sources shows that a large proportion of homicides in recent years bears characteristics typically associated with organized-crime-style violence: gun battles, group executions, torture, dismemberment, high-powered weaponry, beheadings, narco-messages, mass graves, and other methods used by drug trafficking groups and OCGs. About a third – and as many as half – of all homicides identified in 2014 bore such characteristics (Heinle et al. 2015). The solid lines in Figure 29.2 plot the available data on organized-crime-style homicides from National Public Security System (SNSP) (2007–11), and national media outlets *Reforma* (2006–12 and 2013–14) and *Milenio* (2007–14), while the dotted lines show the authors' projections for SNSP (2012–13) and also *Reforma* (2013).[5] All available figures and projections on organized-crime-style homicides are plotted as lines against the bars that show the official tallies of intentional homicides reported by both INEGI and SNSP.

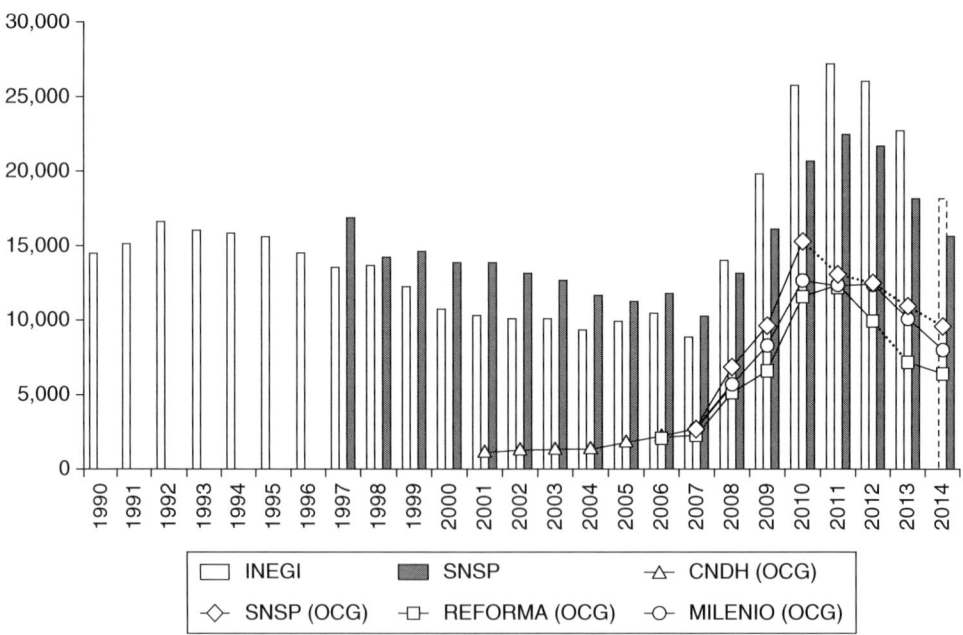

Figure 29.2 Comparison of homicide and organized crime homicide data for various sources, 1990–2014

Sources of data: INEGI (2014), SNSP (2014), *Reforma, Milenio*.

The last complete annual dataset from the Mexican government on organized-crime-style homicides was released in 2010, so there have been no publicly available official annual figures on such killings since then. However, based on the trajectory of figures released in recent years, the authors estimate that the government's official tally for organized-crime-style homicides came to roughly 8,000 deaths in 2014. *Milenio*, which produced its figures throughout the year, reported 7,993 organized-crime-style homicides for the same year. Meanwhile, in 2014, *Reforma* put the figure for organized-crime-style homicides at 6,400, the lowest number reported by that newspaper since 2008. However, it is notable that *Reforma*'s tallies appeared to be less complete and less consistent in 2014 than in previous years.

Determining the approximate proportion of homicides resulting from organized-crime-style violence depends upon which sources are used to calculate each figure (see Table 29.1). Based on the estimated number of INEGI homicides provided above, in 2014 organized-crime-style homicides represented approximately 30–40 per cent of the total number of all homicides, according to figures from *Milenio* (38.7 per cent), *Reforma* (31.0 per cent), and the consulting firm Lantia (36.3 per cent).[6] Because SNSP intentional homicide figures are typically lower than those produced by INEGI, tallies of organized-crime-style homicides represent a significantly larger proportion – 40–50 per cent – of all homicides when SNSP data are referenced using these same tallies and estimates: *Milenio*, 51.1 per cent; *Reforma*, 40.9 per cent; and Lantia, 48.0 per cent. In short, whether organized-crime-style homicides represent just one-in-three or as many as half of all homicides, they constitute a major form of murder in Mexico.

Here the authors observe two additional patterns associated with Mexico's recent increase in violence, and especially the pattern of violence commonly associated with drug trafficking. First, while there is a general perception that Mexico's violence is pervasive and persistent throughout the country, the reality is that violence has been highly localized, has been sporadic, and has frequently shifted from one geographic area to another in recent years. However, as the authors note below, the pattern of violence is spreading even as levels of violence have diminished. Second, the characteristics of victims of homicide in Mexico fit with some of the general

Table 29.1 Percentage of INEGI and SNSP homicides attributed to organized-crime-style homicide in *Reforma, Milenio,* and Lantia tallies, 2006–2014

YEAR	Milenio OCG (as % INEGI)	Milenio OCG (as % SNSP)	Reforma OCG (as % INEGI)	Reforma OCG (as % SNSP)	Lantia OCG (as % INEGI)	Lantia OCG (as % SNSP)
2006	n.a.	n.a.	20.3	18.0	n.a.	n.a.
2007	31.3	27.0	25.6	22.1	n.a.	n.a.
2008	40.5	43.2	36.6	39.0	n.a.	n.a.
2009	41.8	51.4	33.3	40.9	n.a.	n.a.
2010	49.1	61.2	45.0	56.0	n.a.	n.a.
2011	45.2	54.6	45.5	55.0	n.a.	n.a.
2012	47.7	57.2	38.1	45.7	n.a.	n.a.
2013	44.4	55.6	31.5	39.5	49.6	62.1
2014	38.7	51.1	31.0	40.9	36.3	48.0
Average	**42.3**	**50.2**	**34.1**	**39.7**	**43.0**	**55.0**

Sources of data: INEGI, SNSP, *Reforma, Milenio,* and Lantia for all available years and projections.

Note: This table shows the proportion of organized-crime-style homicides relative to all homicides, as reported by each source (relative to the two official sources of data on homicide: INEGI and SNSP).

patterns of homicides around the world. Homicides are committed primarily by men and against men. Firearms, especially high-calibre weapons, are an important modus operandi for intentional homicide. However, there are some aspects of homicide, and especially organized-crime-style homicides, that stand out, particularly the extreme nature of the violence employed, the extent to which public officials and journalists are often targeted, and the extent to which the military and especially the police have been targeted (Heinle et al. 2015).

Local distribution and geographic dispersion

In 2007, the historic low point in homicide rates in Mexico, INEGI figures reported that approximately 1,073 of Mexico's roughly 2,450 municipalities had zero homicides.[7] Indeed, for the entire term of President Vicente Fox (2000–6) and the first year of the Calderón administration (2006–12), there was a historically unprecedented period in which over 40 per cent of Mexican municipalities saw not a single murder. Thereafter, Mexico experienced a fairly steady decline in the number of 'murder-free' municipalities each year, reaching a low of 727 municipalities in 2012. Meanwhile, during the same time period, there was a steady increase in the number of municipalities with more than 25 homicides, growing from 62 in 2007 to 178 in 2012. However, in 2013, the geographical dispersion of homicide reversed for the first time since 2007. That is, from 2012 to 2013, the number of municipalities with more than 25 homicides declined from 178 to 171, and the number with zero homicides grew from 727 to 776 (see Figure 29.3).

Taken together, the data show the increase and geographic dispersion of homicides from 2007 to 2012 (especially after 2009), as well as the relative increase of such homicides per capita during that period. We also see that violence receded significantly from 2012 onward, according to the available data from both INEGI and SNSP. There were also some important changes that became especially noticeable in 2014. For example, from 2010 to 2013, at least 35 municipalities have had more than 100 murders per 100,000 people, regardless of whether the rate is calculated using available INEGI or SNSP figures. However, in 2014, SNSP's data (though incomplete) suggest that the number of municipalities with more than 100 homicides per capita dropped to just 21.

Furthermore, the data also shows that homicides have been regionally concentrated in the major drug-trafficking zones in the north-west, the north-east, and the Pacific coast. The states that were hardest hit by violence after 2008 include the six Mexican border states – Baja California, Sonora, Chihuahua, Coahuila, Nuevo León, and Tamaulipas – as well as the Pacific states of Sinaloa, Nayarit, Michoacán, and Guerrero. However, violence began to diminish in certain areas in 2011 and 2012, particularly as the number of homicides fell in key states in northern Mexico, including Baja California, Sonora, and Chihuahua.

In 2014, using the data available from SNSP on homicides, we see that the states with the largest number of intentional homicides were in the State of México (1,994), Guerrero (1,514), Chihuahua (1,086), Sinaloa (986), Michoacán (904), and Jalisco (900). Nearly all of these states (that is, all except México) saw a decrease in the number of murders compared to the previous year.[8] This is notable not only because the State of México is now thrust into the position of having the most homicides in the country, but also because the other states that saw declines are widely considered to have far more serious problems with crime and violence. Indeed, in 2014, Michoacán and Guerrero were easily the two states that attracted the most attention for their security challenges. The growth of organized-crime-style violence in the State of México also has political salience, given that President Enrique Peña Nieto (2012–18) was formerly its governor. Nationwide, the largest decreases in the number of homicides in 2014 were found in the states of Guerrero (−27.5 per cent), Chihuahua (−24.7 per cent), Coahuila (−39.5 per cent), Nuevo León (−31.8 per cent), and Sinaloa (−18.4 per cent). Meanwhile, the five Mexican states

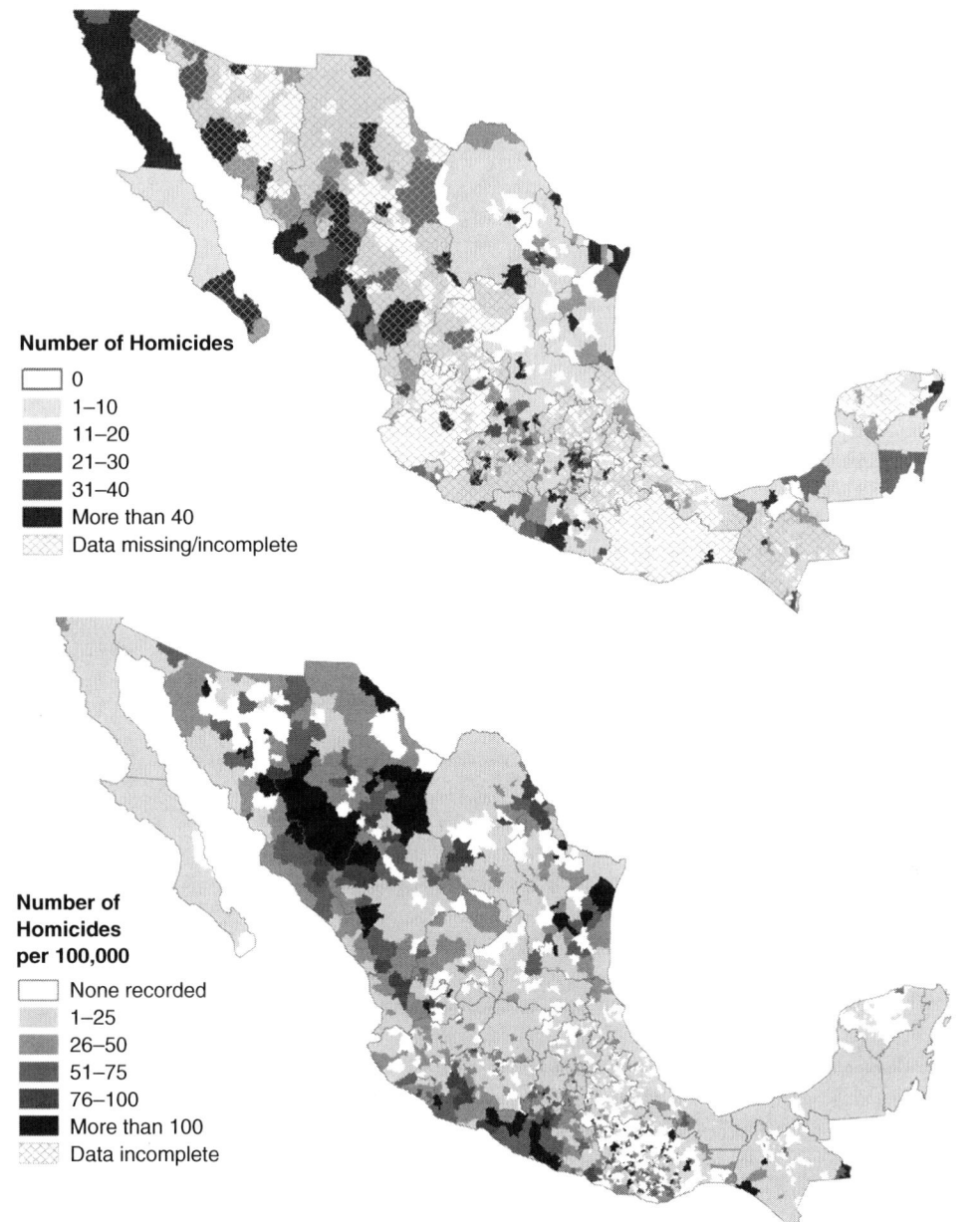

Figure 29.3 Geographic distribution of homicides by total number and homicide rate at the municipal
    level in 2014

Source of data: SNSP and CONAPO. Maps generated by Theresa Firestine.

exhibiting the largest numerical increases in homicide in 2014 were Oaxaca (19.4 per cent),
Tamaulipas (13.2 per cent), Guanajuato (10.6 per cent), México (3.2 per cent), and Tabasco
(20.9 per cent), according to SNSP.

The decrease in violence in 2014 was also apparent in the data for the ten municipalities that registered the highest number of homicides. From 2008 through 2011, as measured by the number of homicides, the largest share of homicides was concentrated in the border metropolis of Ciudad Juárez, Chihuahua, but thereafter the number of homicides in that city declined significantly. In 2014, SNSP statistics still placed Ciudad Juárez as the municipality with the fourth highest number of homicides, though this number continued to decline by perhaps as much as 14 per cent from the previous year (with the caveat that Ciudad Juárez was one of many cases for which data were incomplete). Meanwhile, the number of homicides also declined again in Acapulco, Guerrero, the city that has registered the most homicides since 2012, from 883 to 590 homicides, a decrease of more than a third.

It is also notable that nearly all of the ten most violent cities in Mexico in 2014 experienced a decrease in the number of homicides, with the only exception being Ecatepec de Morelos in the State of México. Also, none of the top ten most violent municipalities came close to 1,000 homicides or had a homicide rate greater than 100 murders per 100,000 inhabitants, which is a significant and positive change from previous years. Amid these declining rates, three cities – Torreón, Coahuila; Monterrey, Nuevo León; and Zapopan, Jalisco – moved off the 'top ten' list entirely in 2014. Again, unless they have been significantly under-reported by SNSP, these figures show a significant shift in the number and rate of homicides in Mexico.

Changing modes of violence and victim characteristics

As the sheer number of organized-crime-style homicides has declined since 2012, the nature of this violence has also appeared to change. As the authors reported in 2014, there appears to be a significant reduction in homicide cases involving the use of torture, narco-messages (*narcomensajes*), and decapitation (Heinle et al. 2015). Unfortunately, in 2014 such details on organized-crime-style homicides were not forthcoming from the Mexican daily newspaper *Reforma*, the primary source that the authors have used to tally such information in previous years. While *Reforma* has a reputation as one of Mexico's most independent newspapers, its detailed monitoring of crime and violence has declined considerably since the start of the Peña Nieto administration, consistent with other news media organizations.

In light of the reduced availability of information from *Reforma* and other sources in recent years, Justice in Mexico has worked with a network of researchers and volunteers to compile the *Memoria* database, which includes more than 5,000 individual cases of organized-crime-style homicides that occurred from 2006 through 2014. The authors analysed a variety of victim characteristics and circumstances surrounding the cases collected, thus the *Memoria* database provides a useful sample of the kind of violence perpetrated by OCGs. Of the available information for all years, for example, firearms were used in over 2,800 cases (56 per cent) and the authors found evidence of torture reported in 739 cases (14.7 per cent). However, as noted above, reporting of such data is irregular and often incomplete, so these are conservative estimates at best.

The most obvious, but under-appreciated observation that can be made about homicide anywhere in the world is that it is a predominantly male problem. This is certainly the case in Mexico. As noted by José Merino and Jessica Zarkin in an article for *Animal Político* in December 2014, in terms of homicide, there are effectively two Mexicos (Merino and Zarkin 2014). Mexican men have a homicide rate of 33.5 per 100,000 people (on a par with South Africa), while Mexican women have a homicide rate of 4.6 per 100,000 people (on a par with the United States). When separated by age, however, the leading cause of death for young men in Mexico hinges on economic status, since wealthy young men are more likely to die in car accidents and those of modest means more likely to be murdered.

With regard to organized-crime-style homicides, using the Justice in Mexico *Memoria* database, the authors have also found that the vast majority of victims – at least 75 per cent – were identified as men, with just 9 per cent of the victims identified as female (the remainder were unidentified). Surprisingly, the average age of victims of organized-crime-style homicides is about 32 years, which appears to contradict widespread assumptions that organized crime violence involves uneducated, unemployed, and disaffected youths. However, the authors also believe that the deaths of older persons – especially those of government personnel – are more likely to be over-reported in the media sources used to build the *Memoria* database, so these figures must be interpreted with consideration of the biases inherent in information gleaned from media reports.

Meanwhile, of the more than 5,000 homicide cases identified in the Justice in Mexico sample, the age of the victim was reported in nearly a third of all cases. There were also over 712 victims (14.2 per cent) whose corpses were accompanied by some kind of message (narco-message). Although not all of the messages' contents were publicly released, many at least mentioned a specific organized crime group: about 10 per cent mentioned the Zetas or its members; about 3 per cent mentioned the La Familia Michoacán Organization, or Knights Templar Organization, or their members; and about 1 per cent referred to the Sinaloa Cartel or its members. Also, based on the time of day that deaths were documented, a large proportion of organized-crime-style homicides (and the discovery of such crimes) occur during daylight hours, especially during the morning, contrary to common assumptions.

Three groups of victims stand out in particular: mayors, journalists, and police and military personnel.

Mayors

Justice in Mexico's *Memoria* database includes seventy-five mayors and former mayors killed from 2006 through 2014, many with the characteristics of organized-crime-style homicides. While the peak of violence in Mexico occurred during 2011, the year with the most killings of mayors was actually 2010, when seventeen cases were reported. Despite the reduction of the total number of homicides in Mexico since 2011, there have been a total of thirty mayors killed. However, the rate of mayoral killings dropped by half in 2014, with six mayors killed, compared to twelve mayors in each of the two previous years. This was the lowest number of mayors killed since 2007.

Journalists

Dozens of reporters and media workers have been killed or have disappeared in Mexico, making it one of the world's most dangerous places for journalists. The various organizations tallying homicides involving reporters in Mexico use different criteria for tallying and classifying this violence, since motives are often difficult to confirm. For example, one of the most respected sources, the Committee to Protect Journalists (CPJ), focuses primarily on cases where a murder was confirmed to have been committed in relation to the journalist's profession (CPJ 2015a). From 1992 through 2014, CPJ reported that there were thirty-two confirmed cases, forty-one unconfirmed cases, and four media-support workers killed in Mexico. Over 80 per cent of those cases involved reporters working the crime beat, a third involved reporters working on issues related to corruption, and a fifth involved reporters working on issues related to politics (CPJ 2015b).

CPJ's criteria for identifying the murders of reporters and media workers are fairly conservative, since they focus only on cases where there is a confirmed motive associated with the journalist's profession. The Justice in Mexico *Memoria* database includes cases of organized-crime-style homicides, and includes cases of journalists who may have been killed for a variety of motives not limited to their reporting. From 2000 to 2014, Justice in Mexico identified 127 journalists and media-support workers who were murdered, with the vast majority of these deaths (98) occurring after 2006. This tally includes journalists and media-support workers employed with a recognized news organization at the time of their deaths, as well as independent, freelance, and former journalists, and media-support workers.

By this tally, 2011 was the worst year on record for murders of reporters and media workers in Mexico. However, the sharp increase in 2014 – the second-worst year on record – goes against the overall trend of reduced violence and substantiates ongoing concerns about protection for journalists in Mexico. For this reason, the organization Artículo 19 claimed that 2013 was the most dangerous on record for journalists in Mexico, taking into consideration other types of violence such as kidnappings, beatings, threats, and other types of aggression (Articulo 19: 2013). According to Justice in Mexico's tally, on average at least eight members of the media were killed each year since 2000, and an average of twelve were killed in each full year of the Calderón administration (counting 2007–12) and in each full year of the Peña Nieto administration (counting 2013 and 2014).

Police and military personnel

Over the last several years, hundreds of police officers and dozens of military personnel have been killed in the line of duty in circumstances that appeared to involve organized crime. In recent years, *Reforma* newspaper has been the only source that consistently tracks and reports these deaths. However, in 2014, *Reforma* stopped reporting these figures. Using the Justice in Mexico *Memoria* database, the authors identified over 550 federal, state, and local law enforcement personnel, and 60 military personnel who have been victims of OCG-style violence since 2006. This database provides only a sample of cases, and details were not available in every case.

Analysis and conclusion

The data available in recent years suggest that the situation in Mexico is improving, particularly as measured by intentional homicides and those related to OCGs. However, there does remain room for further improvement, particularly in areas of the country where the causes of public insecurity are particularly deeply rooted and supported by local populations. For example, the southern Pacific state of Michoacán has presented persistent challenges across both the Calderón and Peña Nieto administrations. In Michoacán, many citizens have so little faith in the federal government authority that they have supported vigilante groups as a means to stave off the influence of organized crime. In early 2014, the federal government officially recognized the so-called self-defence groups (*autodefensas*) that had emerged to counter the criminal activities of the organized crime group known as the Knights Templar Organization. Despite efforts by the federal government to deputize such citizen vigilante groups, this resulted in ongoing problems and concerns, including allegations that some such groups were in league with organized crime, and persistent clashes among rival local defence groups.

Another important lesson from Mexico is that eliminating one OCG may simply create opportunities for another. Meanwhile, as the Mexican government has made headway in some locations, problems have broken out elsewhere. In 2014 and 2015, for example, the Cartel de Jalisco Nueva Generación (CJNG) grew significantly in power and scope in its home state of Jalisco, as well as Colima, Michoacán, Guanajuato, Nayarit, Guerrero, Morelos, Veracruz, and the Federal District (Mosso 2015). The group burst onto the national scene in Mexico in 2010, and was able to capitalize on the weakening of other groups in the region such as the Knights Templar in Michoacán.[9] The group emerged as the predominant force in Jalisco thanks in large part to its ties with the Milenio Cartel, the organization that dominated Michoacán prior to the rise of the La Familia Organization and the Knights Templar, which effectively took over that state in the 1990s and early 2000s. The CJNG struck off on its own and has held a strong presence in neighbouring Michoacán since 2000 (Pérez Caballero 2014). The CJNG directly challenged the state in several attacks in 2015, killing dozens of state and local police mid-year, and causing the federal government to deploy federal police and military personnel throughout the state.

A third lesson from Mexico is that state corruption can lead to serious human rights abuses. Perhaps the most reviled case of official corruption in recent years in Mexico was the 2014 case of local authorities in Iguala, a small inland town in the state of Guerrero. On 26 September 2014, dozens of student protestors and innocent civilians came under fire and were assaulted by police, and dozens were taken into custody. Of these, forty-three students from a rural teachers' college based in the nearby town of Ayotzinapa, who were taken into custody, were never seen again, and quickly became known as the 'Ayotzinapa 43'.

It took the federal government until January 2015 to confirm that the students were actually dead. While authorities searched, they unearthed dozens of other victims whose bodies had been buried in and around Iguala in recent years, suggesting that such disappearances – perhaps with similar government complicity – were a serious problem. The families and the public decried the complicity or ineptitude of government officials at all levels. Marches, public demonstrations, and even acts of violence took place around the country, including an assault on the state capitol in Chilpancingo, which was subsequently set ablaze by Molotov cocktails. Even though the immediate blame for the massacre was placed squarely on Iguala's local authorities, the state's governor stepped down in disgrace within weeks of the incident and, while federal authorities ultimately captured the perpetrators of the massacre, many also severely criticized the Peña Nieto administration for failing to respond quickly and effectively to the crisis. In public protests and social media, some even adopted the more critical view that the Iguala massacre should be considered an act of state ('fue un acto de estado'), and called for the resignation of Peña Nieto himself.

Finally, one consideration that cannot be ignored when evaluating homicides committed in Mexico is the number of disappeared people, underscored by the continued discovery of clandestine graves in a number of states throughout Mexico. 2014 was the year with the highest number of disappearances on record, due partly to increased monitoring by the country's new National Registry for Missing or Disappeared Persons (SNPED). As this chapter went to press in late September 2015, only one of the students from Ayotzinapa had been positively identified among many charred remains found scattered in a riverbed close to where the students disappeared. One possible explanation for an apparent increase in disappearances is that criminal organizations – no longer as extensively involved in open, armed conflict with one another – now tend more towards concealing the remains of their victims, in contrast with the peak of cartel violence in 2011–12 when bodies were regularly displayed in public, often mutilated and displaying narco-messages directed toward rival groups. With increased contact between criminal organizations and the general public, it is plausible that the groups might wish to keep a lower profile, as unsanctioned illicit activities such as extortion might be hindered by increased attention from the authorities.

The general conclusion of this chapter is that Mexico's wave of violence appears to have crested, with significant decreases in recent years. However, the data presently available are incomplete and widely viewed with circumspection because of concerns about possible government manipulation and pressure on media organizations to de-emphasize problems of crime and violence. In other words, the problems related to the availability and credibility of data that can help to monitor and evaluate Mexico's security situation allow for only tentative conclusions when it comes to specifics. The widespread perception that the Mexican authorities have failed to properly report the level of violence seriously detracts from the credibility of government efforts. Indeed, there has been widespread disenchantment with Mexico's public authorities and key institutions in general in recent years. In 2014, over a third of Mexicans expressed little or no confidence in the Mexican army (a considerable decrease compared to previous years), over half expressed little or no confidence in the National Human Rights Commission (CNDH), more than two-thirds expressed little or no confidence in the presidency, and three-quarters expressed little or no confidence in the country's political parties (*Parametría* 2014). These indicators reflect sharp increases in public dissatisfaction, and have been accompanied by the lowest measures of support for democratic governance more generally since the year 2000. Mexico's public security crisis has created a serious political crisis that may take many years to resolve.

Notes

1 Shirk and Ríos Cázares (2007) use data from homicide prosecutions to show the longer term downward trend in homicide cases from the 1930s to the mid-2000s. Escalante Gonzalbo (2009) uses actual homicide data to demonstrate that this trend continued from the 1990s to the late 2000s.

2 It is important to note that these INEGI figures do not differentiate between intentional homicides and unintentional homicides (e.g., car accidents).

3 Information drawn from Heinle et al. 2015.

4 For a full discussion of the data and methodology employed here, see Heinle et al. 2015.

5 Mexican national media outlets *Reforma* and *Milenio* tally homicides presumably related to organized crime in Mexico, and are probably the most-used independent source of such data. One of the limitations of both official and non-governmental tallies of organized-crime-style homicides is that there are significant gaps in reporting by some sources, notably SNSP and Reforma.

6 Lantia is a consulting firm headed by Mexican security expert Eduardo Guerrero. Lantia's data are not publicly available for previous years.

7 These figures are approximate because there is no data for some municipalities. Also, the number of municipalities in Mexico changes from time to time as new ones are created. From 2012 to 2013, for example, it appears that dozens of new municipalities were added to INEGI's homicide dataset.

8 In fact, only nine Mexican states saw an increase in homicides in 2014: Aguascalientes (7.7 per cent), Baja California Sur (25 per cent), Guanajuato (10.6 per cent), Hidalgo (13.7 per cent), México (3.2 per cent), Oaxaca (19.4 per cent), Tabasco (20.9 per cent), Tamaulipas (13.2 per cent), and Yucatán (5.0 per cent).

9 The CJNG, led by Nemesio Osegera Cervantes, 'El Mencho', was formed after the death of Ignacio 'Nacho' Coronel, who had been the leader of the Sinaloa Cartel in Jalisco.

References

Andreas, P. and Wallman, J. (2009) 'Illicit Markets and Violence: What is the Relationship?', *Crime, Law, and Social Change* 52: 225–9.

Artículo 19 (2013) 'Disentir en silencio'. Online. Available HTTP: <http://www.articulo19.org/wp-content/uploads/2014/03/Art19_Informe2013web.pdf > (accessed 26 April 2015).

Astorga, L. (2000) 'Traficantes de drogas, políticos y policías en el siglo XX mexicano', in C. Omnitz (ed.) *Vicios públicos, virtudes privadas: La corrupción en México*, Mexico City: CIESAS, 167–93.

Astorga, L. and Shirk, D. A. (2010) 'Drug Trafficking Organizations and Counter-Drug Strategies in the US–Mexican Context', in E. L. Olson, D. A. Shirk, and A. Seele (eds.) *Shared Responsibility*, Washington DC: Woodrow Wilson International Center for Scholars, 31–61.

Astorga, L. and Shirk, D. A. (2013) 'Drugs, Crime, and Violence', in P. H. Smith and A. Selee (eds.) *Mexico and the United States: The Politics of Partnership*, Boulder, CO: Lynne Rienner, 161–90.

CPJ (Committee to Protect Journalists) (2015a) 'Methodology'. Online. Available HTTP: <https://cpj.org/killed/methodology.php> (accessed 8 October 2015).

CPJ (Committee to Protect Journalists) (2015b) '35 Journalists Killed in Mexico since 1992/Motive Confirmed'. Online. Available HTTP: <https://cpj.org/killed/americas/mexico/> (accessed 8 October 2015).

Escalante Gonzalbo, F. (2009) 'Homicidios 1990–2007', *Nexos*, 1 September. Online. Available HTTP: <http://www.nexos.com.mx/?p=13270> (accessed 8 October 2015).

Flores Pérez, C. (2009) 'Organized Crime and Official Corruption in Mexico', in R. A. Donnelly and D. A. Shirk (eds.) *Police and Public Security in Mexico*, San Diego: Trans-Border Institute, 87–116.

Heinle, K., Molzahn, C., and Shirk, D. (2015) *Drug Violence in Mexico: Data and Analysis through 2014*, San Diego: Justice in Mexico.

Heinle, K., Rodriguez, O. and Shirk, D. (2014) *Drug Violence in Mexico: Data and Analysis through 2013*, San Diego: Justice in Mexico.

INEGI (2014) 'Estadísticas de mortalidad', Instituto Nacional de Geografía y Estadística. Online. Available HTTP: <http://www3.inegi.org.mx/sistemas/temas/default.aspx?s=est&c=17484> (accessed 8 October 2015).

Merino, J. and Zarkin, J. (2014) 'Violencia: los 6 Méxicos (Meade ve 2)', *Animal Político*. Online. Available HTTP: <http://www.animalpolitico.com/blogueros-salir-de-dudas/2015/01/22/violencia-los-6-mexicos-meade-ve-2/> (accessed 8 October 2015).

Molzahn, C., Ríos, V., and Shirk, D. (2012) *Drug Violence in Mexico: Data and Analysis through 2011*, San Diego: Justice in Mexico.

Molzahn, C., Rodriguez, O., and Shirk, D. (2013) *Drug Violence in Mexico: Data and Analysis through 2012*, San Diego: Justice in Mexico.

Mosso, R. (2015) 'Invade cártel de Jalisco ocho estados y el DF', *Milenio*, 20 April.

Parametria, (2014) 'El Ejército mexicano mantiene altos niveles de confianza'. Online. Available HTTP: <http://www.parametria.com.mx/carta_parametrica.php?cp=4622> (accessed 8 October 2015).

Pérez Caballero, J. (2014) 'CJNG: Cómo adaptarse con éxito a la 'guerra al narcotráfico' en México', *Insight Crime*, 14 October.

Shannon, E. (1988) *Desperados: Latin Drug Lords, US Lawmen, and the War America Can't Win*, New York: Viking.

Shirk, D. A. and Ríos Cázares, A. (2007) 'Introduction: Reforming the Administration of Justice in Mexico', in W. A. Cornelius and D. A. Shirk (eds.) *Reforming the Administration of Justice in Mexico*, Notre Dame: La Jolla, 1–47.

SNSP (Secretariado Ejecutivo del Sistema Nacional de Seguridad Pública) (2014) *Incidencia delictiva 2014*. Online. Available HTTP: <http://secretariadoejecutivo.gob.mx/docs/pdfs/estadisticas%20del%20fuero%20comun/Cieisp2014_052015.pdf> (accessed 8 October 2015).

UNDP (United Nations Development Programme) (2013) *Citizen Security with a Human Face: Evidence and Proposals for Latin America*, New York: United Nations.

UNODC (United Nations Office on Drugs and Crime) (2014) *Global Study on Homicide 2013*, Vienna: United Nations.

30

CONFLICT IN THE DEMOCRATIC REPUBLIC OF CONGO

Pierre Englebert

The Democratic Republic of Congo (DRC) has suffered from continuous conflict, at least in parts of its territory, since 1993. Altogether, the (mostly indirect) death toll of this sustained violence was estimated by the International Rescue Committee (2007) to have reached in excess of 5 million. A 2011 study also found that up to 1.8 million Congolese women had been raped, with the greatest likelihood occurring in North Kivu, the epicentre of Congolese political violence (Peterman et al. 2011). And, despite the country being officially post-conflict since 2006, there were still as many as 2.7 million internally displaced Congolese as of November 2014, mostly in the North and South Kivu, Maniema, Katanga and Orientale provinces (OCHA 2014), a greater amount than in 2006.

Whichever way one looks at it, conflict remains thus a fundamental feature of Congolese politics. However, unlike places such as Côte d'Ivoire or Sudan, where the logic of violence, the nature and identity of actors, and their agenda are relatively clear, conflict in Congo is particularly complex, decentralized, and multi-layered. It has equilibrium characteristics, results from mixed motivations, and has proved resistant to resolution: even the largest UN mission in the world, in the country since 2000, has failed to put an end to it.

This chapter offers some elements towards making sense of conflict in Congo. It has three main parts. It begins with a descriptive section on violent political actors and their activities. Second, it singles out the proximate causes of conflict. Finally, it addresses the more fundamental causes of conflict.

Violent actors and their activities

To begin making sense of political violence in eastern Congo (where North and South Kivu, the epicentre of Congolese political violence, are located), one must distinguish between three sets of actors: foreign movements, Congolese insurgencies (some of which are backed by foreign governments), and the Congolese military itself or Forces Armées de la République Démocratique du Congo (FARDC).

Foreign movements

The main foreign movements that have operated in the country since 2006 are Uganda's Allied Democratic Forces (ADF), the Forces Démocratiques de Libération du Rwanda (FDLR), the

Lord's Resistance Army (LRA), and Burundi's Forces Nationales de Libération (FNL). The ADF is an Islamist anti-Museveni Ugandan movement that was established in 1995 with help from then Zairean President Mobutu and the Sudanese government in order to undermine the Museveni regime. They were pushed out of Ugandan territory over the years. They also recruit in the DRC and had a resurgence of activity in 2013. At their peak in 2013, ADF troops numbered some 1,200–1,500. They survive through alliances with local chiefs (who were mostly terrorized into compliance), networks of businesses that give them resources, some gold mining, and exploitation of timber (UN 2014: 23). In 2014, they endured significant military defeats at the hands of joint UN and Congolese troops, and were pushed out of their strongholds in Beni territory. Several hundred were killed, and the remaining ones flushed out into the Virunga National Park. Later in the year, however, they showed some resurgence, and have since remained a thorn in the side of local populations and authorities.

Ever since the end of the Rwandan genocide, the FDLR has been the prominent and most problematic foreign group operating in Congo. As of 2014, however, they had largely become a spent force and numbered a mere 1,500 compared to about 40,000 in 1994. Mostly located in North Kivu, they are a hybrid group, with a significant proportion of Congolese members, who mix with local populations and live with wives and children. Because they are dispersed and scattered in forested areas and blend with the locals, they have been hard to dislodge militarily. Nevertheless, repeated joint operations with Rwanda in 2009 and 2010 (Umoja Wetu, Kimia II, and Amani Leo) were largely responsible for the FDLR's dwindling. A few hundred of their members surrendered in 2014 and were relocated to Orientale province, outside Kisangani. The remaining ones live by looting, gold mining, illegal taxation, and even charcoal production. They have historically collaborated with the FARDC, from whom they buy ammunition (UN 2014). They also receive some funding from the Hutu diaspora. As of late 2014, they officially remained MONUSCO's (the UN Mission for the Stabilization of Congo) number one military target.

The LRA in Congo is also a group whose effective presence is in no proportion to its reputation, having become little more than a small gang of vagrant bandits by 2014. There are fewer than 100 LRA in the DRC and probably another 200 in the Central African Republic (CAR). Joseph Kony, their International Criminal Court (ICC)-indicted leader, probably moved to Sudan in 2013. Nevertheless, the LRA is the target of a Regional Task Force composed of 2,000 troops from Uganda, 500 from South Sudan, 350 from the CAR, and 500 FARDC, with training support from the US (UN 2014: 28).

The other remaining foreign group is the FNL, a largely Hutu insurgency from Burundi active in South Kivu. However, it is not engaged in conflict with local populations and actually collaborates with local militias. With a few hundred members, it too is a weakened threat and clearly bears limited responsibility for the state of violence in the region.

Congolese insurgencies

'Autochthonous' eastern Congolese armed insurgencies and militias are a mixed bag. The most important one among them has had multiple incarnations since the 1990s and is generally seen as representing the interests of Congolese Tutsi or more broadly 'Rwandophone' populations in the Kivus (see Stearns 2012b; Stearns et al. 2013; Vlassenroot 2013; Willame 1997). Its latest manifestation was the Mouvement du 23 mars (M23), a rebellion that began in 2012 and was defeated in 2013. M23 arose in April 2012 as a splinter group from the Congrès National pour la Défense du Peuple (CNDP), which had been established in 2006 by Rwandophone and largely Tutsi former Rassemblement Congolais pour la Démocratie (RCD) officers and troops concerned that the miserable showing of the RCD in the national elections undermined their interests, and worried about losing local leverage if integrating into the FARDC (Stearns 2012a).

The CNDP insurgency was military successful and controlled significant portions of North Kivu until 2009, defeating the FARDC in battle on several occasions. On 23 March 2009, after a rapprochement between Kigali and Kinshasa, the CNDP, then under the leadership of Bosco Ntaganda, agreed to join the FARDC, but under highly unusual conditions (known as *mixage*) which allowed them to retain control of CNDP units within the military and not to deploy outside their areas of interest in Rutshuru, Masisi, and a few other districts in both Kivus. Moreover, Ntaganda was given effective leadership over the Congolese side of operations against the FDLR in the region, largely bypassing the local existing military hierarchy.

After the flawed elections of November 2011, however, donor pressure increased on President Kabila to make some concessions. Ntaganda being the object of an ICC indictment, Kabila found it expeditious to politically abandon him by suggesting in early 2012 that he could be arrested. The M23 was born that same April of the defection of some CNDP troops, under the leadership of Ntaganda and Sultani Makenga, as a result of such pressures (and over alleged grievances that parts of the March 2009 agreement, particularly as regards ranks, administrative positions, and deployment, had not been implemented).

M23 started with some 2,000 troops, out of the roughly 5,500 CNDP who had been integrated into the FARDC in 2009. Additional later recruitment swelled their ranks up to 3,500 (Berghezan 2013). It made quick military progress in part because of Rwandan support (UN 2014) and as a result of the incompetence of the FARDC, leading to the capture of Goma in November 2012, which led to the government agreeing to open negotiations with the rebels in Kampala, Uganda, in December.

M23's successes were short-lived, however. With Ntaganda a marked man, a second wing developed in February 2013 under Sultani Makenga's leadership. Fearful for his personal security, Ntaganda surrendered to the ICC via the US Embassy in Kigali on 18 March 2013 and was transferred to The Hague. Seven hundred and eighty-eight troops defected with him (UN 2014: 5). The remainder of M23 suffered progressive decline thereafter, largely because of more aggressive military operations against them by the FARDC, heavily supported by MONUSCO's new Force Intervention Brigade (FIB), a 3,000-strong contingent authorized by the UN Security Council to use more aggressive force. By November 2013, the rest of M23 had been defeated and about 1,000 of them had crossed into Uganda with Makenga (UN 2014: 9).

Many of the other local groups, mostly known as Mai Mai, derive their existence from their opposition to local Tutsi or Hutu groups. Mai Mai Yakutumba in South Kivu, for example, is largely derived from Bembe antagonisms with Rwandophones. Other anti-Tutsi or anti-Hutu militias include Mai-Mai Sheka which was originally a Nyanga anti-FDLR movement in North Kivu; the Alliance des Patriotes pour un Congo Libre et Souverain (APCLS), a Hunde anti-Tutsi movement from North Kivu; Mai-Mai Raia Mutomboki ('angry citizens'), an anti-FDLR coalition operating throughout the region; and Nyatura, an anti-Tutsi Hutu spin-off from PARECO, a Hutu militia, which was integrated into the FARDC together with the CNDP in the March 2009 agreement. Some of these groups also oppose the FARDC because of its integration of Hutu and Tutsi combatants. Raia Mutomboki, for example, evolved over the years from being a Lega/Tembo-based anti-FDLR group to being simply anti-FARDC (Berghezan 2013: 12). Raia Mukombozi ('saviour citizens'), a spin-off of Mutomboki, formed in 2013, is also opposed to FARDC and to Kabila and calls itself at times a 'politico-military coalition against balkanization and Kabilism' (Berghezan 2013: 16).

In addition to fighting, most of these groups also actively engage in commercial activities. Mai Mai Morgan in Ituri is deeply involved in poaching and the gold trade. Mai Mai Sheka (or Nduma Defence for Congo) is an extension of the diamond business of its founder. And Mai Mai Yakutumba in South Kivu is involved in racketeering, piracy on Lake Tanganyika, and smuggling with Tanzania (Stearns at al. 2013b).

Altogether, the total number of fighters from foreign groups, Mai Mai, and other militias probably amounted to about 10,000 in 2014. In contrast, about half of the FARDC's 140,000 troops were deployed in the east, together with most of MONUSCO's 19,000 personnel. An additional estimated 10,000 presidential guard troops, largely composed of soldiers from Kabila's Katanga province, were deployed mostly elsewhere in the country.

The Congolese military (FARDC)

Given their numerical domination in the region, the FARDC deserve some attention as a local actor of insecurity. Created as part of the transition in 2003, they are a hotchpotch made of multiple layers of other organizations, many of which fought each other at some point. First, they include some of Mobutu's former Forces Armées Zairoises (FAZ), which were known for their military incompetence. Second, they comprise the former Forces Armées du Congo (FAC) of Laurent-Désiré Kabila. The FAC themselves were a mixture of troops from Kabila's Alliance of Democratic Forces for the Liberation of Congo (AFDL), young recruits named *kadogos*, and even former Katanga separatist fighters from the 1960s known as *Tigres*. To these were added troops from the RCD and from Jean-Pierre Bemba's Mouvement de Libération du Congo (MLC) as well as a few Mai Mai groups during the transition. After 2009, CNDP and PARECO (a largely Hutu movement) troops joined, as well as a multitude of additional Mai Mai. The integration of all these groups over time has not been an organizational success.

One of the main – and largely problematic – results of successive rounds of integration has been the domination of the military hierarchy in the east by Tutsi and other Rwandophones, although they are a demographic minority in the region. After 2009, ex-CNDP officers received 36 per cent of command positions in North Kivu as against 48 per cent from previous FARDC officers. However, 'at least 60 per cent of the [previous] government appointees were from the ex-RCD, which was dominated by Hutu and Tutsi' (Baaz and Verweijen 2013: 26). As a result, even after the M23 insurgency, a majority of command positions in the east were in the hands of Rwandophones. This dominance magnifies the sense of Rwandan colonization for other local communities and feeds the narrative of Kabila being a stooge of Rwanda, which underpins the mobilization of many Mai Mai groups. In addition, because many rebel and Mai Mai leaders demand to be integrated into the FARDC at the largely self-appointed ranks they had in their movement, the successive waves of integration have also led to a particularly top-heavy military. Twenty-five per cent of FARDC are officers, 37 per cent petty officers and 38 per cent troops (Berghezan 2014: 15).

The FARDC is also crisscrossed by patronage networks that function in parallel to – and largely against – official channels of hierarchy (Baaz and Verweijen 2013). Many officers are linked to local or Kinshasa politicians via commercial ventures, and some are directly involved in entrepreneurial activities of their own. These characteristics make it not only exceedingly difficult for the FARDC to perform their basic functions, but also very difficult to reform them, which is in part why security sector reform has met with such little success since the formal end of the war in 2003. President Kabila and his entourage control some of these patronage networks but certainly not all of them, particularly in the east. Those he controls he can get access to directly, bypassing his own military hierarchy. Officers in these networks are expected to send resources back to their superiors in order to be allowed to operate their business. This is known in Congo as *rapportage*, a widespread practice in all dimensions of administration and police (see also Baaz and Olson 2011). As a result, officers in the field are often more consumed with revenue generation than with military tactics, resulting in very weak capacity and deep internal competition in the search for revenue (Baaz and Verweijen 2013; Stearns 2013).

There has also been significant and recurring political violence in the west of the country since the official end of the transition in 2006. Most incidents of political violence in that half of the country have been linked to a deep discontent at the government and at living conditions. In 2007 and 2008, the Bundu Dia Kongo (BDK) movement launched insurrections in Bas-Congo which were violently repressed at the cost of several hundred human lives (MONUC 2008). In October 2009, in Equateur province, after several months of rising tensions between two local communities over fishing rights, a group of Enyele insurgents attacked the city of Dongo and killed up to 500 civilians of a different ethnic subgroup. They then launched attacks on the cities of Gemena and Mbandaka, which they briefly captured. They were eventually defeated by FARDC battalions aided by MONUSCO, which pushed them back to their village where some 150 of them were killed. In November 2010, there was an attack against FARDC soldiers and the headquarters of Kabila's party in Kikwit (Bandundu province). Credit for this operation was later claimed by the Armée de Résistance Populaire (ARP) of Faustin Munene, a former general in the FARDC, who then escaped to Congo-Brazzaville (UN 2011: 71).

It is in Katanga, however, that the rise of political violence has become most of a concern. Violent incidents began around 2011. The Lubumbashi airport was seized for a few hours in February by alleged *Tigres* who raised a Katanga flag.[1] In June, a group of *Tigres* attacked and looted an ammunition depot in Lubumbashi. In September, a raid on Lubumbashi's Kasapa prison freed some 967 prisoners, including former Mai Mai rebel Gédéon Kyungu Mutanga (UN 2011: 77). Gédéon and his new troops then put together Kata Katanga ('cut off Katanga') in 2012, an allegedly secessionist insurgency which spread terror through the Manono and Pweto districts of northern Katanga, burning villages where FARDC had stationed, and killing chiefs suspected of government allegiance. In March 2013, some 300 Kata Katanga insurgents entered Lubumbashi and rallied downtown by the statue of secession leader Moise Tshombe before being pushed back by the presidential guard. There were subsequent skirmishes between Kata Katanga and the FARDC outside of Lubumbashi, along the road to Kolwezi (close to some of the main copper mines) and further north into 2014.

Kata Katanga is not a genuine secessionist movement, however. Rather, it appears connected to the increased sense of vulnerability of northern Katanga elites (mostly Balubakat) who have seen their relative position in the regime eroded since the aftermath of the 2011 elections, and may be trying to dissuade Kabila from seeking further autonomy from them or further marginalizing them. The same people were probably behind the alleged coup attempt that took place on 29 December 2013, in Kinshasa, when rebels briefly attacked the headquarters of the Radio-Télévision Nationale Congolaise, Ndjili Airport, and the Colonel Tshatshi army camp. By midday, the Republican Guard had defeated them at a cost of at least 100 deaths. Simultaneous attacks were launched in Lubumbashi and Kindu (*Africa Confidential* 2014).

Proximate causes of conflict

Having started in 1993 and been still ongoing in 2014, conflict in Congo appears resistant to resolution. There are several factors that have contributed to this resilience. The first one is that the Congolese themselves do not control all the cards. Foreign intervention, and particularly Rwanda's propensity since 1996 to displace its own conflict to eastern Congo (but also Uganda to a certain extent, with the ADF and LRA), has been a major impediment to conflict resolution in Congo. Given the Rwandan government's unwillingness to consider any degree of negotiation with *génocidaires* to reach national reconciliation, the roots of its own domestic conflict have persisted. However, the degree to which it will continue to project into the DRC is likely to be limited, because of the effective defeat of the FDLR by repeated military actions since 2009, because of Rwanda's concern about the risk of international isolation if it continues meddling, and because an increasing number of Congolese Rwandophones no longer consider military adventurism with Rwanda a productive solution to their own predicament, as the limited appeal of M23 illustrated.

Second, and more problematic, is the generally very weak capacity (and limited interest) of the Congolese government and military to deal with most public policy or security problems. This lack of capacity and interest derives largely from a widespread understanding of public office as a resource rather than a tool of public policy. According to a recent survey by the US National Democratic Institute, the Congolese believe 'that [. . .] corruption among political leaders is the reason that the country's problems and, specifically, the basic needs of people, remain unaddressed' (Feeley and Choukry 2012: 10).' And, indeed, even by African standards, Congo's corruption is in a league of its own (for telling examples, see APC 2013: 55–8 and 100–6; Baaz and Olson 2011; EITI 2013; Englebert 2014; *Global Witness* 2014; Joyce 2011; ODEP 2013; Tedika 2012). Such corruption makes the state both inefficient and too absorbed in business to deal with conflict, particularly when it takes place far away from Kinshasa and can be instrumentalized by some politicians for profit. Additionally, as the next section returns to, it creates grievances, as it perverts the social fabric of life, undermines the development of social capital, fosters alienation and despair, and ends up both directly and indirectly contributing to crises and violence.

Third, and relatedly, the propensity of the Congolese government to rely on co-optation – or the incorporation of trouble makers into state structures – to resolve conflict has bought it some short-term successes, while paradoxically encouraging the broader reproduction of conflict. Co-optation is at the core of the formation of the FARDC, many of whose officers were once rebels or Mai Mai, as discussed in the previous section. Co-optation is also the life of the political system. The *Majorité Présidentielle* (MP) coalition is built around the purchase of votes and support by the Kabila regime, and the inclusion of six opposition leaders in the government in December 2014 was seen as an attempt by Kabila to buy some support for his likely forthcoming efforts to stay in power past his constitutional term.

While co-optation is a universal element of statebuilding strategies, it is plagued in Congo with problems which undermine its supposed benefits. First, it yields a plethoric and highly ineffective army with little or no centralized command (Berghezan 2014: 15), as well as a government that lacks cohesion and capacity. The FARDC has only one military success on its record – the defeat of M23 – and it came with considerable support of UN troops. Thierry Nlandu's observation about Congo's police, that it is a 'heterogeneous force made up of former officers from various backgrounds' and 'a non-professional atypical police force' equally applies to the FARDC (Nlandu 2012). There is significant competition and jealousy among the different integrated groups, with each one suspecting the others of receiving preferential treatment. Co-opted actors also often fail to renounce their earlier goals or alliances.

Second, co-optation has historically promoted the multiplication of rebel groups seeking to be co-opted (Mehler and Tull 2005). There were at least as many armed groups in the east in 2014 as there were at the beginning of the post-conflict period in 2006, and possibly more than during the war of 1998–2002. Many of the current groups are splinters of previous ones, often composed of individuals who were not satisfied with their terms of integration. Others are new groups that have since arisen to capitalize on opportunities for integration. Thus, solving conflict by co-optation encourages the multiplication of violent actors and reproduces conflict.

Third, whether because of bad faith, limited resources, or incompetence, the government rarely lives up to its co-optation promises, with the result that co-opted elites often subsequently defect, leading to an endless cycle of conflict, and defeating the nation-building potential of co-optation. It was partly such broken promises in terms of promotions, pay, and assignments that led to the defection and insurrection of CNDP troops in April 2012 to form M23. Even though the government defeated M23 in 2013, they still agreed on an amnesty for those rebels who escaped to Uganda and on allowing them to form a political party. Yet, as of the end of 2014, these promises, too, had yet to be fulfilled, and the rebels had refused to return home, representing another potential source of future conflict.[2] However, in some respects, the failure of government to deliver on its co-optation promises might have also deflated the enthusiasm of at least some would-be insurgents. This seems true of the Tutsi populations of the east. It is indeed worth noting the dwindling size of Tutsi-led insurgencies over the years. The RCD–Goma probably had between 20,000 and 30,000 troops; the CNDP around 5,500; and M23 peaked at 3,500 after heavy forced recruitment, but averaged around 2,000 and ended up badly divided. More and more of them might be deciding that they stand to lose more from rebellion than to gain from it.

Fundamental causes of conflict

Beyond these factors that complicate conflict resolution, deeper and more fundamental variables provide the crucible of political violence in the region. To a large extent, the deepest one is to be found in the predicament of local populations (which is true of violence in the west too), which in the east crystallizes around access to land. This predicament is complex, made up of multiple reinforcing layers, of accumulated grievances among communities, and of hardened and polarized identities. It takes place against a background of corrupt governance and high population density (which, in much of the Kivus, is well above 100 inhabitants per square kilometre, or about five times the national average), in a region where agriculture and cattle raising remain essential activities, making access to land the number-one problem. This access is hopelessly intertwined with political, administrative, and identity issues (Autesserre 2010; Stearns 2012b; Vlassenroot 2012).

A 1971 law says that all land belongs to the state, with people only having a residual right to it. While there has since been some development of private markets for land, property rights in land remain tenuous, which people partly compensate for by organizing for the physical defence of their land assets. The formal state ownership of land gives local state representatives excessive power in allocating, selling, or confiscating land. Because these state representatives are chiefs (the local administrative units of *groupements*, *secteurs*, and *chefferies* are all administered by 'traditional' chiefs who are actually appointed by the state, a feature that dates back to the 1910s), controlling chiefdoms became over time a big part of any strategy to get or maintain access to land. Being able to appoint chiefs by seizing control of local political power, as do most rebel and militia groups, is one such means of control. Killing chiefs is another one, popular with those who do not have access to political power, as might be the case of weaker Mai Mai or rebel groups. The fact that chiefdoms tend to partly overlap with the regions that some ethnic groups identify as their homeland and that chiefs are often chosen among dominant ethnic groups, imbues the land issue with a strong ethnic connotation. Thus Rwandophones, who have migrated to the region for about a century, have never had their own chiefdoms and have therefore felt highly vulnerable to local autochthonous groups, a problem compounded by the high demand for land of the cattle herders among them.

In part, land is so important because people are poor. Poverty induces reliance on one's kin and mutual distrust among identity groups. Access to land and to other state-controlled resources is a familiar trigger of conflicts that share the language of autochthony ('sons of the soil' against 'foreigners') as a common denominator. But it is poverty and a general sense of alienation from economic opportunities that are the deep causes of these identity conflicts, which local and national politicians do not hesitate to instrumentalize. In Bas–Congo too, the BDK insurrections partly derived from perceptions of the 'economic exploitation' of the province by the central government and of 'unwarranted economic decline and marginalization' (Tull 2010: 649). In Equateur, the violence of 2009 had its roots in local struggles over fishing ponds, which suggests the precariousness of life and reliance on an economy of subsistence. Access to resources in Congo might be a matter of criminal accumulation for top elites but it is usually little more than a question of survival for everybody else.

The second most important deep cause of conflict is the political economy of war that has characterized eastern Congo for a long time and that revolves in part around its considerable endowment in natural resources. Although it might not be the prime cause of war, the violent resource economy that dominates much of eastern Congo has been an essential reason for its continuation since the 1990s. Much has been done against it, including systematic reporting by the UN and the Extractive Industries Transparency Initiative, the tracing of 'blood' diamonds by the Kimberly Process, and the prohibition of undocumented sourcing of raw material from eastern Congo by the Dodd-Frank Act, and there has been some visible progress (Bafilemba et al. 2014). However, government-affiliated and non-government actors remain embedded in the local violent extraction of resources, which typically takes one of two forms: direct armed control of production (as when rebels or FARDC battalions seize control of a mine), which has diminished according to Bafilemba et al. (2014) or, more frequently, indirect control of extractive activities through 'taxation', smuggling, and even piracy. Most local groups act like the state and tax local populations (while, also like the state, they typically fail to give any service in exchange). M23, for example, financed itself largely through household, business, and transport (roadblocks) taxes (UN 2014: 12). The control of border posts was also a significant source of revenue as the M23, like other groups, made theirs the multiple custom fees that the government typically charges at borders. The UN Group of Experts estimated that M23 made $650,000 per month in such activities (UN 2014: 13). It is hard to conceive of pacification or demobilization programmes that could afford individuals, particularly leaders, similar economic opportunities.

Finally, the political nature of violence must be apprehended at the national level. Congo's east does not operate in a vacuum from the rest of the country. It has historically been the least integrated part of the country (and was already more connected to East Africa before colonization – through the slave trade of Tippo Tip). It took until 1967 to bring the east back under centralized state control after the chaos of the immediate post-independence period (and some small part of South Kivu remained unincorporated into the 1980s), and it was 'lost' again in the 1990s. Hence, the idea of restoring state authority to the east is partly misleading, as the Congolese state has been the dominant mode of political organization there only a minority of the time. A better way to think of eastern Congo is along the notion of 'indirect rule' proposed by Baaz and Verweijen (2012: 32), for whom Kinshasa projects power in the east 'through intermediaries'. Kinshasa intermediaries are only some among the local actors. Others might be intermediaries of foreign powers like Rwanda or relatively autonomous agents.

To some extent, such indirect rule is somewhat reminiscent of feudalism in Europe. In Europe, the medieval period was characterized by a similar multitude of semi-autonomous actors controlling local tools of violence and practising extraction of resources from local populations while entertaining relations of various degrees of autonomy or vassalization with larger kingdoms. Kinshasa exercises partial control in the east through vassals. Hence the violence there might not be so much an indicator of state failure or statelessness as a marker of state formation attempts. Across the world, indirect rule is a common mode of power consolidation (as it was for colonization in Africa too). While such a parallel is no doubt far-fetched, it provides an alternative reading of local Congolese dynamics, less focused on failure and more connected to long-term state formation trends. If one abstracts for a moment from current official borders, eastern Congo clearly constitutes a peripheral zone of influence of both Kinshasa and of the long-established and relatively strong and centralized state of Rwanda. From this perspective, violence in the east is part and parcel of a fairly universal process of state formation, but it is unclear whether the current state of the DR Congo will end up being the one benefiting from it.

Conclusion

Congo has been living with conflict for most of its existence. The reasons for its pervasive political violence are multiple: intrusive neighbours, weak institutions, corrupt governance, poverty, greed, and polarized identities, to name a few. With Kabila showing no sign of being ready to retire, despite the end of his legal term in office approaching in 2016, electoral fraud or constitutional manipulations are likely to add themselves to the future causes of conflict. At any rate, conflict and violence are likely to remain structural features of Congolese politics for the foreseeable future.

Notes

1 Katanga Tigres go back to the Katanga secession of 1960. After the secession, in 1963, many of them escaped to Angola, where they helped the Portuguese government fight the insurgencies. After 1975, they became a loose group of quasi-mercenaries used by the MPLA regime for occasional actions. By the time they joined the AFDL in 1996, they were a very different group of individuals, presumably mostly the children of the original ones. Their integration into the Kabila regime and the Congolese military largely failed and they found themselves on the loose again. It is unclear whether they represent a genuine group or whether individuals launching specific actions in the region merely invoke their name to gain legitimacy.
2 An amnesty law was passed by parliament in early February 2014. It provides amnesty for all acts of insurrection, war, and 'political infractions' from 1 January 2006 to 20 December 2013 (two previous amnesty laws, from 2005 and 2009, covered previous periods). The amnesty is conditioned upon a promise not to recidivate and excludes so many practices (including genocide; crimes against humanity; war crimes; torture; cruel, inhuman and degrading treatment; rape and other sexual violence; recruitment of children; looting and stealing of public funds; and drug trafficking), that most M23 leaders (and many other local violent actors) would seem to remain liable to prosecution.

References

Africa Confidential (2014) 'Coup Bid Raises Alarm', *Africa Confidential* 55(1), 10 January.
APC (Africa Progress Panel) (2013) *Africa Progress Report: Equity in Extractives*, Geneva: Africa Progress Panel.
Autesserre, S. (2010) *The Trouble with the Congo: Local Violence and the Failure of International Peacebuilding*, Cambridge: Cambridge University Press.
Baaz, M. E. and Olson, O. (2011) 'Feeding the Horse: Unofficial Economic Activities within the Police Force in the Democratic Republic of the Congo', *African Security* 4(4): 223–41.
Baaz, M. E. and Verweijen, J. (2013) *Between Integration and Disintegration: The Erratic Trajectory of the Congolese Army*, New York: Social Science Research Council.
Bafilemba, F., Mueller, T., and Lezhnev, S. (2014) 'The Impact of Dodd-Frank and Conflict Minerals Reform on Eastern Congo's Conflict', *The Enough Project*, June. Online. Available HTTP:<http://www.enoughproject.org/reports/impact-dodd-frank-and-conflict-minerals-reforms-eastern-congo%E2%80%99s-war> (accessed 15 December 2014).
Berghezan, G. (2013) *Groupes armés actifs en République Démocratique du Congo: Situation dans le 'Grand Kivu' au 2ème semestre 2013*, Brussels: Groupe de Recherche et d'Information sur la Paix et la Sécurité.
Englebert, P. (2014) *DR Congo: Making the Economy Work for the Congolese People*, Johannesburg: Brenthurst Foundation. Discussion Paper 6/2014.
EITI (Extractive Industries Transparency Initiative) (2013) *Rapport ITIE-RDC 2011: Secteur des Mines*, Kinshasa: ITIE.

Feeley, R. and Choukry, C. (2012) *Reach out to Us: Findings from Focus Groups with Young Men and Women in the Democratic Republic of Congo*, Washington, DC: National Democratic Institute.

Global Witness (2014) 'Congo Fails to Reveal Loss-Making Oil Deal with Controversial Businessman's Offshore Firm', 23 January. Online. Available HTTP: < https://www.globalwitness.org/archive/congo-fails-reveal-loss-making-oil-deal-controversial-businessmans-offshore-firm/ > (accessed 12 November 2015).

International Rescue Committee (2007) 'Mortality in the Democratic Republic of Congo: An Ongoing Crisis'. Online. Available HTTP: <http://www.rescue.org/special-reports/congo-forgotten-crisis> (accessed 15 December 2014).

Joyce, E. (2011) 'Congo Shell Companies Reported to Serious Fraud Office'. Online. Available HTTP: <http://ericjoyce.co.uk/2011/11/congo-fire-sale-4/> (accessed 15 December 2014).

Mehler, A., and Tull, D. (2005) 'The Hidden Costs of Power-Sharing: Reproducing Insurgent Violence in Africa', *African Affairs* 104(416): 375–98.

Nlandu, T. M. (2012) *Mapping Police Services in the Democratic Republic of Congo: Institutional Interactions at Central, Provincial and Local Levels*, Brighton: IDS. Research Report 71, January.

OCHA (UN Office for Coordination of Humanitarian Affairs) (2014) 'RD Congo: Aperçu Humanitaire (Novembre 2014)'. Online. Available HTTP: <http://www.humanitarianresponse.info/fr/operations/democratic-republic-congo/infographic/carte-rd-congo-aper%C3%A7u-humanitaire-novembre-2014> (accessed 15 December 2014).

ODEP (Observatoire de la Dépense Publique) (2013) *Rapport de l'enquête sur l'évaluation participative de la transparence dans la collecte et l'utilisation des taxes pour l'amélioration du marché central de Kinshasa*, Kinshasa: ODEP.

Peterman, A., Palermo, T., and Bredenkamp, C. (2011) 'Estimates and Determinants of Sexual Violence Against Women in the Democratic Republic of Congo', *American Journal of Public Health* 101(6):1060–7.

Stearns, J. (2012a) *Du CNDP au M23: Evolution d'un mouvement armé dans l'est du Congo*, London: Institut de la Vallée du Rift.

Stearns, J. (2012b) *North Kivu: The Background to Conflict in North Kivu Province of Eastern Congo*, London: Rift Valley Institute, Usalama Project.

Stearns, J. and Anonymous (2013) *Banyamulenge: Insurgency and Exclusion in the Mountains of South Kivu*, London: Rift Valley Institute, Usalama Project.

Tedika Kodila, O. (2012) 'Corruption en République Démocratique du Congo : Tyrannie des nombres', *Congo-Afrique* 51(464), April.

Tull, D. (2010) 'Troubled State-Building in the DR Congo: The Challenge from the Margins', *Journal of Modern African Studies* 48(4): 643–61.

United Nations (2011) *Final Report of the Group of Experts on the Democratic Republic of the Congo*, UN Security Council, S/2011/738, 2 December.

United Nations (2014) *Final Report of the Group of Experts on the Democratic Republic of the Congo*, UN Security Council, S/2014/42, 23 January.

Vlassenroot, K. (2012) *Dealing with Land Issues and Conflict in Eastern Congo: Towards an Integrated and Participatory Approach*, Report on the Conflict Research Group Seminar held in Brussels on September 21–2.

Vlassenroot, K. (2013) *Sud Kivu: Identité, territoire et pouvoir dans l'Est du Congo*, London: Rift Valley Institute, Usalama Project.

Willame, J-C. (1997) *Banyarwanda et Banyamulenge: Violences ethniques et gestion de l'identitaire au Kivu*, Paris: L'Harmattan.

31

RUSSIA'S REVIVAL

Jeffrey Mankoff

Russia's February 2014 annexation of Ukraine's Crimean Peninsula and subsequent intervention in support of eastern Ukrainian separatists marked a watershed for Russian foreign policy. This forceful revision of borders confirmed Russia's mounting tendency to view the West as a strategic rival, while highlighting the wide range of diplomatic, economic, and military tools Moscow was willing to employ to secure its interests in its immediate neighbourhood. The crisis over Ukraine was also symptomatic of an estrangement between Moscow and the West that had been mounting for several years. Indeed, Russia has constructed an ideological and historical narrative emphasizing its non-Western identity and supporting the Kremlin's aspiration to become an independent pole in an increasingly multipolar global order. In so doing, Vladimir Putin's Russia has precipitated what is likely to be a long-running stand-off with the West that deepens Russian dependence on China and creates increased political uncertainty within Russia itself.

When the Cold War ended, elites in both Russia and the West largely assumed that Russia, like its post-Communist neighbours, would follow a natural progression to democracy and inclusion in Western liberal institutions (Carothers 2002; Stent 2015: 35–48). Rather than converging with the West though, by the mid-1990s Russia increasingly began portraying the West as an 'other', despite cooperation in the context of the war in Afghanistan and the West's broader efforts to combat Islamic extremism, not to mention the old standby of strategic arms control.

At the same time, Moscow increasingly objected to its exclusion from the NATO-centric European security order, as well as to Washington's willingness to use force in pursuit of its own interests – whether in Yugoslavia, Iraq, or elsewhere – without regard for international law or the concerns of other major powers. The inability to constrain US military action reflected Russia's diminished stature, and would become an important theme in subsequent discussions about the need to restore Russian greatness.

These twin challenges converged in the post-Soviet states of Eastern Europe, the South Caucasus, and (to a lesser degree) Central Asia, a region Moscow continues to view as a zone of Russian special interest. Political transitions in these states have tended to correlate with efforts to move closer to the West through institutional ties, or even membership, in the European Union (EU) and NATO. The post-Soviet region has consequently been the site of the most serious crises in relations between Russia and the West, including the 2008 war in Georgia as well as the more recent Ukraine conflict.

Accelerating Russia's estrangement from the West has been the failure of Russia's own democratic experiment, which has left Moscow wary of the West as a values-driven collective intent on spreading its own norms abroad, often at the expense of stability. Meanwhile, high oil prices and Russia's recovery from the economic and political chaos of the 1990s fed a renewed sense of confidence. Economic and political difficulties within the West, most notably following the 2008 financial crisis, reinforced Russian elites' belief about the limitations of the Western liberal democratic model, while increasing the attractiveness of Chinese-style authoritarian capitalism.

The emergence of an increasingly dissatisfied middle class within Russia, which took to the streets in large numbers to protest against rigged parliamentary and presidential elections in 2011–12, accelerated the Kremlin's embrace of nationalist, anti-Western ideology as a means of reinforcing its own legitimacy. Putin now faces a dilemma largely of his own making: his domestic legitimacy increasingly requires a confrontational approach to Western influence in the post-Soviet region, but escalating confrontation risks an expansion of Western economic, political, and military countermeasures that Russia has limited capacity to endure.

This chapter starts with an overview of Russia's stark political and economic decline after the end of the Cold War. It continues with an analysis of the restoration of political stability in the following decade under Putin, which led to an increasingly assertive, self-confident Russian foreign policy, and goes on to describe the unfolding confrontation between Russia and the West, centred on Ukraine. It argues that the main challenges for the West in dealing with Moscow lie in halting Russian efforts to upend the post-Cold War liberal international order while keeping the door open to re-engagement once the immediate crisis has passed.

Decline: the 1990s

Russia's political and economic decline after the fall of the Soviet Union was stark. The Soviet command economy was dismantled almost immediately. Former officials, especially from the security services, manoeuvred to seize control of many of the most lucrative assets for themselves, creating a new class of oligarchs whose reach extended from business into politics (Dawisha 2015: 13–36). Oligarchic capitalism entailed corruption on a massive scale, which, along with mounting unemployment, high inflation, and pervasive gangland violence, led many Russians to look back nostalgically to the stability of the Soviet Union. This chaos and corruption undermined the legitimacy of President Boris Yeltsin's government, as well as for many Russians the very concept of liberal democracy.

During the early 1990s, inflation reached over 2,400 per cent per year. Another bout of high inflation following the 1998 financial crisis then crippled the nascent middle class that had begun to emerge from the wreckage. According to the State Statistics Committee (*Goskomstat*), unemployment during Yeltsin's final year in power was 13.3 per cent, though the real figure may have been nearly twice as high (Rosenfielde 2000: 1437–8). Meanwhile, the incomplete privatization of many large firms (which remained a drain on the state budget), coupled with the drying up of markets for Russia's uncompetitive exports, left the country badly indebted to foreign creditors (O'Donnell 2006).

The impression of decline that such economic difficulties conveyed was exacerbated by Russia's geopolitical retreat. With the end of the Cold War, Russia lost the empire it had controlled within the Soviet Union, as well as the extended empire of the Warsaw Pact and the international Communist bloc. The Soviet Union itself fragmented into fifteen independent states. Russia was reduced to its smallest territorial extent since the early modern period. The Warsaw Pact states, which had served the USSR as a strategic glacis against the West, threw off their Communist leadership and clamoured, many successfully, for admission to NATO and the European Union. Moscow's most important satellite – East Germany – vanished from the map entirely, swallowed up by capitalist West Germany. Soviet proxies around the globe either vanished (South Yemen) or made their peace with the triumph of capitalism (Vietnam).

Even the integrity of the Russian Federation was threatened during the 1990s. The two wars in Chechnya (1994–6 and 1999–2006) exposed not only the Russian military's decline, but also the strong centrifugal tendencies at work in a country with a weak central government and a wide range of ethnic groups inhabiting its territory. While Chechnya represented the most extreme manifestation of Russia's fragmentation, other regional governments also asserted extensive autonomy from the Kremlin (Erlanger 1992; Teague 1994).

Powerful economic actors, including state-owned companies like gas monopoly Gazprom, also operated largely independently of Kremlin control. Gazprom placed its own people in important positions in the upper reaches of the Russian government and controlled access to Russia's network of gas export pipelines, while blocking Kremlin attempts to impose restructuring on the company, despite the fact that the state remained its largest shareholder (Stulberg 2007: 68–9). Other oligarchs, including the notorious Boris Berezovsky, who served as deputy head of the Russian Security Council, used their connections to Yeltsin and their domination of the media to promote their own economic interests.

Revival: the 2000s

The beginning of Russia's global resurgence largely coincided with the start of Vladimir Putin's first term in the Kremlin. If the 1990s in Russia were a time of upheaval and decline, the subsequent decade saw the restoration of political stability and an increasingly assertive, self-confident foreign policy. Aided by rising oil prices, Putin presented a stark contrast to the erratic and often seriously ill Yeltsin. By re-establishing Kremlin control over the bureaucracy, the Duma, the media, local elites, and big business, Putin reversed much of Russia's Yeltsin-era fragmentation. This consolidation of power allowed the Kremlin to pursue a more ambitious role on the world stage.

One of Putin's major initiatives was to reassert Kremlin authority over both regional elites and powerful economic actors. This process, which Putin termed 'restoring the power vertical', led to the appointment of powerful presidential envoys to seven newly created 'super-regions' as early as 2000. Agreements between Moscow and the regions were renegotiated, limiting the ability of local officials to conduct their own foreign policy (*Izvestiya*, 2005). Apart from the centralization of power, Russia's revival in the first decade of the twenty-first century had much to do with events beyond the Kremlin's control. The most obvious reason was the dramatic increase in world energy prices in the years up to 2008. When Putin came to power at the beginning of 2000, oil prices hovered around US$10 per barrel. Eight years later, when Dmitry Medvedev became president, oil was trading at over US$120 per barrel. Thanks to the resulting influx of wealth, Moscow had paid off its foreign debts by 2003, and amassed the third-largest foreign currency reserves in the world (a total of US$476 billion) by 2008.

Not only do oil and gas help to fill the Russian treasury, but Moscow's control of the infrastructure to move energy from Russia and Central Asia to Europe and, in the future, East Asia gives it significant leverage over both producers and consumers through its ability to manipulate prices and supplies. Control of energy transit has been a key piece of Russian influence in Ukraine. In both 2006 and 2009, payment disputes, underpinned by Ukraine's efforts to move closer to the West, led Moscow to cut deliveries through gas pipelines across Ukrainian territory, prompting shortages both within Ukraine and in Europe. Following Ukraine's 2013 Maidan revolution, Moscow sought to end gas transit through Ukraine entirely by constructing a new bypass pipeline, dubbed South Stream, and when that project collapsed, Turkish Stream, beneath the Black Sea to Turkey (Farchy and Dombey 2015; Gazprom 2015).

Unfortunately for Russia, the limits of this growth model were already becoming clear even before the onset of the crisis in Ukraine and the resulting Western sanctions. Russia's economic performance is more dependent on fluctuations in the oil price than even most other petro-states (Hanson 2015: 17), and the decline of oil prices from more than $110 per barrel in mid-2014 to around $60 per barrel a year later badly dented Russian growth projections (Central Bank of Russia 2015).

Higher oil prices allowed Russia to avoid addressing the deeper systemic problems that have long handicapped its economic performance. These include contingent property rights, weak rule of law, corruption, and the overweening role of the state (and well-connected oligarchs) across the leading sectors of the Russian economy. Despite still-significant foreign currency reserves, under-investment, capital flight, and high levels of corporate debt continue to weigh down prospects for sustainable growth. The sanctions imposed following Moscow's annexation of Crimea have added to the difficulties and provided the Kremlin a scapegoat for the downturn, but also serve to obscure the deeper structural problems Russia faces.

The 2010s: Russia in a multipolar world

The Soviet collapse had left the US as the world's sole superpower. Over the course of the ensuing two decades, the emergence of new power centres, particularly in East Asia, coupled with the US' own economic and political difficulties, contributed to the replacement of unipolarity by a more complex international system. Despite the diffusion of power in the twenty-first century and the alleged passing of Western hegemony, Putin accuses Washington of still 'trying to establish a unipolar world' that leaves no space for other great powers (Putin 2015). Carving out space for Russia to act as an independent great power, especially in its own neighbourhood, has been the primary goal of Russian foreign policy under Putin.

The belief that the West's era of global dominance is over facilitates the more independent foreign policy course Putin's Russia has pursued. This course mixes bandwagoning with balancing, emphasizes non-Western multilateral blocs like the Brazil, Russia, India, China, and South Africa (BRICS) forum and the Shanghai Cooperation Organization (SCO), and often treats Asia as at least a potential counterweight to the liberal powers of the US and Europe. Russian elites have long sought such an autonomous foreign policy for their country, but the West's difficulties in the years since the financial crisis, coupled with the Kremlin's comparative success in ensuring political and economic stability while bolstering its hard and soft power tools have allowed it increasingly to act on those preferences.

Russia's vision of the global order emphasizes the interaction of sovereign states as the basis for international relations. Yet, as its interventions in Georgia, Ukraine, and elsewhere demonstrate, it does not regard all states as equally sovereign. Rather, Moscow's approach to foreign policy focuses on the role of a handful of great powers, particularly Russia, the United States, and China, which collectively shape the international system. While Russian strategy documents give passing reference to transnational challenges such as stateless terrorist groups, criminal networks, and global economic imbalances, their focus remains heavily state-centric (Russian Ministry of Foreign Affairs 2014).

Moscow points to the UN Security Council, where it continues to hold a veto, as the principal arbiter of international law, and frequently criticizes the US for actions affecting international peace and security taken without Security Council approval, such as the bombing of Yugoslavia or the invasion of Iraq. Putin and other Russian officials charge that Washington's unwillingness to respect the interests of other powers is among the major sources of global instability

(Putin 2007). At the same time, Moscow points to Western actions as justifications for its own violations of international law: the West used military force to secure Kosovo's independence, ergo Russia is justified in using force to secure the 'independence' of South Ossetia and Abkhazia or the annexation of Crimea (Putin 2014).

During the early post-Soviet period, Russian and foreign elites largely assumed Russia would follow the same path of liberalization and democratization pursued by its onetime Eastern European satellites, with Moscow ultimately assimilating into the liberal-democratic West. Always a questionable proposition given Russia's vastly different historical experience and failure to fully reckon with its Soviet past, the notion of Russia 'joining' the West has become increasingly improbable during the Putin years. Rather, the emphasis on Russia's role as an independent great power, at the head of a distinct Eurasian bloc, has gained traction. The conflict in Ukraine, which began over Kyiv's efforts to deepen political and economic ties with the European Union, at once reflected this view of the West and Russia/Eurasia as separate, incompatible blocs, and reinforced the division between them by unleashing the most serious European security crisis since the end of the Cold War.

To give this emphasis on Russia as an independent pole in a multipolar global order an intellectual foundation, the Kremlin has actively appropriated the ideas and rhetoric of Eurasianism, a doctrine originating among the White Russian émigrés who fled the early Soviet Union. According to Eurasianist ideologues like Moscow State University professor Aleksandr Dugin, Russia is destined by its historical, cultural, and possibly even biological legacy to remain apart from the liberal West (Barbashin and Thoburn 2014; Laruelle 2012). The implication of Eurasianism is that Russia constitutes the centre of a separate Eurasian civilization that encompasses, at a minimum, the rest of the former Soviet Union, and should behave as an equal analogue to the US-dominated West and what is likely to be an increasingly Sino-centric Asia. Putin and other Russian officials emphasize a growing ideological and cultural rift with the West (with LGBT rights as an important proxy) to provide legitimacy for this project of establishing a separate Eurasian political-economic bloc (Putin 2013).

The most visible embodiment of this Eurasian ideal is the Eurasian Economic Union (EEU), a centrepiece of Putin's campaign to return to the Kremlin in 2012. According to Putin's pre-election essay on the subject, the EEU would be 'a powerful supranational association capable of becoming one of the poles in the modern world and serving as an efficient bridge between Europe and the dynamic Asia-Pacific region' (Putin 2011). Starting with a customs union among Russia, Belarus, and Kazakhstan, the EEU was designed to gradually take on additional supranational powers, which were to be vested in a Eurasian Economic Commission that Moscow dominated. In addition to deepening the EEU, Moscow also sought to broaden it by bringing in new members from the former Soviet Union.

With Brussels strengthening its own engagement with Eastern Europe and the South Caucasus through its European Neighbourhood Policy and Eastern Partnership (EaP) Programme, Moscow used its political and economic leverage to press these states to eschew Europe in favour of this new Eurasia. Such strong-arming compelled Armenian President Serzh Sargsyan to abruptly revoke his commitment to sign an association agreement with the EU in favour of joining the EEU in late 2013. Similar efforts with Ukraine backfired spectacularly, as then-Ukrainian President Viktor Yanukovych's decision to back out of an already negotiated EU association agreement spawned the protests that eventually led to his being ousted and Russian military intervention. Moscow had marginally more success in Central Asia, convincing Kyrgyzstan to join the EEU in mid-2015 and getting Tajikistan to indicate that it would likely join in the future (Michel 2015; Schottenfeld 2015).

Whatever the EEU's ultimate impact on trade and investment, Moscow's support for Eurasian integration owes more to geopolitics than to economic efficiency. As Putin noted in his pre-election essay, Moscow sees the Union as both a pole and a bridge. Russian elites are largely united in their conviction that the unipolar moment in modern history is over, its demise accelerated by the global financial crisis that struck Europe and the United States in 2008–09. In the ensuing multipolar world, Russia must take steps to ensure that it remains a pillar of the new global order. Integration in this sense is about establishing Eurasia, with Russia at its centre, as one pole of an international system dominated by a concert of major powers, while ensuring that former Russian dependencies in Eastern Europe, the South Caucasus, and Central Asia do not enter the orbit of competing powers.

Between West and East

Even before the creation of the EEU, the post-Soviet region had become the biggest flashpoint in relations between Russia and the West. Moscow continues to assert that it maintains 'privileged interests' across the former Soviet Union (Medvedev 2008). While Moscow never fully renounced its claim to supremacy in the 'Near Abroad', Russian attention to the region increased dramatically as a result of political upheaval in several post-Soviet states, above all the 2004 Orange Revolution in Ukraine. The Orange Revolution, along with similar 'coloured revolutions' in Georgia and Kyrgyzstan, and serious unrest that shook the government in Uzbekistan, demonstrated that the rule of post-Soviet strongmen faced a crisis of legitimacy, and Russian elites feared that similar discontent could threaten their own rule.

They also saw Russia's influence over its former empire slipping away, since the new regimes in Tbilisi and Kyiv were strongly pro-Western and supported membership in NATO (Trenin 2005). The Kremlin thus came to see pro-democracy movements as a kind of stalking horse for the expansion of Western influence. Consequently, Russian foreign policy in the former Soviet bloc increasingly came to focus on preserving the post-Soviet status quo, where corrupt, secular, largely Russian-speaking elites continue to dominate business and politics – as well as stopping or slowing the drift of former Soviet republics into Western-dominated institutions like NATO.

In part, this strategy has entailed supporting pro-Russian politicians, as well as separatist movements in places like Abkhazia, South Ossetia, Transnistria, and Crimea – regardless of the fact that doing so violates the principle of state sovereignty that the Kremlin defends elsewhere. The push for Eurasian integration is another element in this strategy for consolidating Russian influence across the post-Soviet region. Of course, Russia has also turned to direct military intervention, both in Georgia and Ukraine, as a means of maintaining Russian influence and limiting the drift of these post-Soviet states into the West (Mankoff 2014).

In resisting the West's perceived attempts to dictate the functioning of the post-Cold War world unilaterally, Russia has also increasingly sought backing from China, both bilaterally and through institutions like the SCO. China is in many ways a natural economic partner for Russia given its large, rapidly growing, and resource-hungry economy. During Putin's time in power, China has emerged as Russia's largest individual trading partner. An authoritarian state increasingly hostile to both Western-style liberalism and US power, China has also come to back Russia on a range of contentious international issues, from the war in Iraq to opposing US democracy promotion efforts.

China's salience has further increased as Russia's relations with the West have deteriorated over the past few years. Moscow promotes its 'comprehensive strategic partnership' with Beijing in part as a means of demonstrating to Western audiences that it has other alternatives, especially in the aftermath of the Ukraine crisis and the West's active efforts to isolate Russia through sanctions. Fearing the impact of sanctions, Moscow has turned to Beijing as an outlet for its energy. Moscow and Beijing have also increased their military cooperation in the form of Russian weapons sales, as well as joint exercises. Russia has also worked with China to establish new international institutions like the BRICS forum (and its in-house development bank) that can act as a counterweight to Western-dominated bodies such as the World Bank and IMF.

Yet using China as a counterweight to the West remains problematic. China's economy is much more dynamic than Russia's, and many Russians fear being relegated to the status of junior partner. More immediately, Russia's isolation from the West has raised the cost of Chinese cooperation. A major Sino-Russian gas deal, which had been under negotiation for more than a decade, was finally signed in May 2014 after the West had imposed sanctions on the Russian energy industry. Yet the agreement was reported to tilt heavily in China's favour, as Russia found itself with little choice other than to accept Chinese terms (Johnson 2015). Similarly, Russia appears to have swallowed its longstanding concerns about China's growing military power and resumed large-scale arms sales (Schwartz 2015).

Nor can partnership with China aid Russia's quest to be accepted as a responsible global player or member in key international organizations. At best, Russia and China can work to set up alternative international institutions, such as the BRICS forum or the SCO, which are defined primarily by their aspirations to rebalance the international system for the benefit of their members, rather than their ability to solve major international challenges.

The challenge for the West: conclusion and outlook

Russia's leaders have long seen the world order forged at the end of the Cold War as one that excludes them from any meaningful role (Simes 2007; Trenin 2006). Western policy for most of the twenty-first century has focused on seeking Russia's ultimate reconciliation with that order. With Moscow's offensive in Ukraine, coupled with the Eurasianist challenge to Western liberal values, and growing authoritarianism within Russia itself, the project of reconciliation may have to take a back seat to efforts aimed at checking Russian efforts to overturn the status quo by force.

It remains tempting to invoke the containment strategy that facilitated the West's Cold War victory, but the effort needed this time will be different, on a smaller scale and only one priority among many in an increasingly complex world. While checking Russia's revisionist ambitions is a necessary step in the short run, it should not preclude longer-term efforts to anchor a more liberal, modernized Russia into the existing global order (Brzezinski 2012), nor prevent the West from focusing on other pressing challenges.

Notwithstanding economic weakness at home and increasing isolation abroad, Russia remains a revisionist power, at least in Europe and the post-Soviet region. Ukraine lies on the front line of the confrontation, but Russian ambitions are not confined to keeping Ukraine out of the hand of the West. Other post-Soviet states including Armenia, Azerbaijan, Georgia, and Moldova also face varying amounts of Russian pressure to limit their drift towards the West.

Even the Baltic States, which have been members of the European Union and NATO for over a decade now, face increased political and economic pressure from Moscow, including efforts to leverage Russian minorities and to call into question the efficacy of NATO security guarantees (Kara-Murza 2015). Russian-style soft power, which encompasses support for political parties and quasi-NGOs promoting Kremlin-friendly policies as well as manipulation of the media (including social media) extends into the heart of Europe as well. Motivating the deployment of these tools are a set of objectives that hearken back to the Soviet past: undermining Western cohesion and transatlantic unity, obtaining recognition of a sphere of influence along Russian borders, and weakening US global leadership (Pomerantsev 2015; Snyder 2014).

In contrast to the Cold War, the West's confrontation with Russia is regional more than global. Indeed, Russia remains open to some degree of collaboration with Washington and Brussels, mainly on issues outside the European and Eurasian space. The Obama Administration's push for a nuclear deal with Iran, as well as its attempts to manage the fallout of the conflict in Syria, have involved efforts to cultivate Russian assistance. Not only does Russia have at least some interests in common with the West in places like Iran and Syria; this openness to collaboration is a useful bargaining chip: the value of Russian assistance elsewhere helps limit the Western appetite for confrontation in Ukraine or elsewhere in the region. The challenge for Western policy is thus to check Russian efforts at overturning the post-1991 status quo in Europe and Eurasia, but in a way that minimizes the spillover effects on other priorities, and that leaves open the door to reconciliation with a post-Putin Russia that embraces its role as a responsible global stakeholder.

Ukraine, of course, is the immediate priority. Helping Ukraine succeed – in the sense of avoiding economic and political collapse, supporting its territorial integrity (likely without Crimea at least for now) while preserving its ability to choose its own international engagements – should be the top priority for US and European policy in the short term. The challenge, of course, is enormous given the scale of Ukraine's debts and the governance failures of the past two-plus decades, not to mention Russia's active campaign to undermine Ukrainian statehood.

Unfortunately, having Ukraine as a festering sore on the edge of Europe is a recipe for not only continued suffering, but also for continuing confrontation between Russia and the West. Russian success on the Ukrainian front will only encourage an increasingly isolated, paranoid Kremlin to seek other victories, not just out of a sense of grievance at the West, but also as a means of mobilizing domestic support as the Russian economy faces long-term stagnation (Rogov 2015). Limiting prospects for the confrontation with Russia to spread requires greater Western efforts, and greater Western resources, in Ukraine.

At the same time, the West needs to do more to insulate itself politically, economically, militarily, and ideologically, from Russian efforts to manipulate information and sow dissension. After a decade-plus of focusing on out-of-area operations in places like Afghanistan, NATO is again starting to take its mission of European security seriously. The West has been slow however to target Russian corruption in a systematic way, despite the role that corruption plays both in sustaining Putin's rule at home and as a transmission belt for Russian influence abroad. Despite much discussion about the Kremlin's weaponization of information, Europe and the US have taken few steps to push back against Russian-sponsored disinformation campaigns. One area where progress has been made is energy. European efforts to weaken Gazprom's monopoly power through legal and regulatory manoeuvres is bearing fruit, though the now suspended push to build the Turkish Stream pipeline and cut out Ukraine as a transit state show that Moscow continues looking for ways to maximize its energy leverage.

While seeking to reinforce Ukraine and deter Russian revisionism elsewhere, the West needs to be careful not to fall too far into a Cold War-style mindset. Quarantining Russia behind a new Iron Curtain will not work in the long run; nor does the West have the resources to carry out a full-bore containment policy without sacrificing other, higher priorities, such as stabilizing the Middle East in the wake of the Arab Spring and carrying out the United States' 'pivot' to Asia. It also risks becoming a self-fulfilling prophecy, reinforcing the Kremlin's autarkic tendencies and reducing its incentive to search for a modus vivendi with the West. Already, many Russian officials view the West's sanctions as a means of promoting regime change, and believe the West will not stop until Putin is ousted (TASS 2015).

Putin's intervention in Ukraine and the growing confrontation with the West has exacerbated uncertainty within Russia itself as well. Without durable institutions or alternative centres of power, Russia's near-term future depends more and more on a single individual. Facing mounting economic challenges and a confrontation that, over the longer term, it lacks the resources to pursue, Putin's Russia is trapped. Without political change, it appears condemned to decline both economically and geopolitically despite Russia's increasing active foreign policy in Ukraine as well as Syria.

In this Russia, political change is unlikely to come smoothly, but it will come – and perhaps sooner than is commonly recognized. When it does, many Russians from outside the current elite, including those who seek a more hopeful, more democratic future for their country, will have a new opportunity to shape Russian politics and foreign policy. The West needs to be careful not to alienate them, and to continue reaching out to Russian society even as it seeks to isolate the Kremlin and its cronies.

References

Barbashin, A. and Thoburn, H. (2014) 'Putin's Brain: Alexander Dugin and the Philosophy behind Putin's Invasion of Crimea', *Foreign Affairs*, 31 March. Online. Available HTTP: <https://www.foreignaffairs.com/articles/russia-fsu/2014-03-31/putins-brain> (accessed 24 June 2015).

Brzezinski, Z. (2012) *Strategic Vision: America and the Crisis of Global Power*, New York: Basic Books

ank of Russia (2015) 'On Bank of Russia Key Rate'. Online. Available HTTP: <http://www.cbr.ru/Eng/press/pr.aspx?file=15062015_133026eng_keyrate2015-06-15T13_26_45.htm> (accessed 6 July 2015).

Dawisha, K. (2015) *Putin's Kleptocracy: Who Owns Russia?*, New York: Simon & Schuster.

Erlanger, S. (1992) 'Most Pieces of Russia Agree to Coalesce, for Now', *The New York Times*, 1 April. Online. Available HTTP: <http://www.nytimes.com/1992/04/01/world/most-pieces-of-russia-agree-to-coalesce-for-now.html> (accessed 12 November 2015).

Farchey, J. and Dombey, D. (2015) 'Gazprom Announces Deal with Ankara to Build Black Sea Pipeline', *Financial Times*, 7 May. Online. Available HTTP: <http://www.ft.com/cms/s/0/b377fc9a-f4d0-11e4-8a42-00144feab7de.html#axzz3rH6658sh> (accessed 12 November 2015).

Gazprom (2015) 'Turkish Stream', Online. Available HTTP: <http://www.gazpromexport.ru/en/projects/6/> (accessed 24 June 2015).

Hanson, P. (2015) 'An Enfeebled Economy', in K. Geils et al. (eds.) *The Russian Challenge*, London: Chatham House.

Izvestiya (2005) 'Tatarstan vzial stol'ko suvereniteta, skol'ko pozvolila Moskva', *Izvestiya*, 31 October.

Johnson, K. (2015) 'Russia's Stumbling Pivot to Asia', *Foreign Policy*, 8 May. Online. Available HTTP: <http://foreignpolicy.com/2015/05/08/russias-stumbling-pivot-to-asia-putin-xi-natural-gas-gazprom-altai/> (accessed 12 November 2015).

Kara-Murza, V. (2015) 'Russia and the Baltics: Once Friend, Now Foe', *World Affairs Journal*, Jan/Feb.

Laruelle, M. (2012) *Russian Eurasianism: An Ideology of Empire*, Baltimore, MD: Johns Hopkins University Press.

Mankoff, J. (2014) 'Russia's Latest Land Grab: How Putin Won Crimea and Lost Ukraine', *Foreign Affairs* 93(3): 60–8.

Medvedev, D. (2008) 'Interview Given by Dmitry Medvedev to Television Channel One, Rossiya, NTV',The Kremlin, 1 September. Online. Available HTTP: <http://en.kremlin.ru/events/president/transcripts/48301> (accessed 4 July 2015).

Michel, C. (2015) 'The Sputtering Eurasian Economic Union', *The Diplomat*, 1 May. Online. Available HTTP: <http://thediplomat.com/2015/05/the-sputtering-eurasian-economic-union> (accessed 5 July 2015).

O'Donnell, S. (2006) 'S&P raises Russia Currency Debt Ratings: Balance Sheet Seen as Strengthening', *The International Herald Tribune*, 5 September.

Pomerantsev, P. (2015) 'The Big Chill: The Battle for Central Europe', *World Affairs Journal*, Jan/Feb.

Putin, V. (2007) 'Putin's Prepared Remarks at 43rd Munich Conference on Security Policy', *Washington Post,* 12 February. Online. Available HTTP: <http://www.washingtonpost.com/wp-dyn/content/article/2007/02/12/AR2007021200555.html> (accessed 22 November 2015).

Putin, V. (2011) 'Novyi integratsionnyi proekt dlya Yevrazii–budushchee, kotoroe rozhdaetsya segodnya', *Izvestiya*, 3 October.

Putin, V. (2013) 'Vladimir Putin Meets with Members of the Valdai International Discussion Club', 20 September. Online. Available HTTP: <http://valdaiclub.com/politics/62880.html> (accessed 24 June 2015).

Putin, V. (2014) 'Address by the President of the Russian Federation', The Kremlin, 9 March. Online. Available HTTP: <http://en.kremlin.ru/events/president/news/20603> (accessed 2 July 2015).

Putin, V. (2015) 'We Pay Tribute to All Those Who Fought to the Bitter End for Every Street, Every House and Every Frontier of Our Motherland', The Kremlin, 9 May. Online. Available HTTP: <http://en.kremlin.ru/events/president/transcripts/49438> (accessed 4 July 2015).

Rogov, K. (2015) 'Can Putinomics Survive?', European Council on Foreign Relations Policy Memo, 5 June. Online. Available HTTP: <http://www.ecfr.eu/publications/summary/can_putinomics_survive3049> (accessed 3 July 2015).

Rosenfielde, S. (2000) 'The Civilian Labor Force and Unemployment in the Russian Federation,' *Europe-Asia Studies* 52: 1433–57.

Russian Ministry of Foreign Affairs (2014) 'Vneshnopoliticheskaya i diplomaticheskaya deyatel'nost' Rossiiskoi federatsii v 2013 godu: Obzor vneshnei politiki Rossiiskoi Federatsii'. Online. Available HTTP: <http://www.mid.ru/bdomp/brp_4.nsf/2a660d5e4f620f40c32576b20036eb06/a00d1cfa235 1f2b144257caf004719a6!OpenDocument> (accessed 2 July 2015).

Schottenfeld, J. (2015) 'Tajikistan's Russian Dream', *Foreign Affairs*, 11 May. Online. Available HTTP: <https://www.foreignaffairs.com/articles/tajikistan/2015-05-11/tajikistans-russian-dream> (accessed 5 July 2015).

Schwartz, P. (2015) 'Russia's Contribution to China's Surface Warfare Capabilities: Feeding the Dragon', Center for Strategic and International Studies, 28 August. Online. Available HTTP: <http://csis.org/publication/russias-contribution-chinas-surface-warfare-capabilities> (accessed 14 February 2016).

Simes, D. K. (2007) 'Losing Russia', *Foreign Affairs* 86: 36–52.

Snyder, T. (2014) 'Fascism, Russia, and Ukraine,' *New York Review of Books*, 12 March. Online. Available HTTP: <http://www.nybooks.com/articles/archives/2014/mar/20/fascism-russia-and-ukraine> (accessed 3 July 2015).

Stent, A. (2015) *The Limits of Partnership: US–Russian Relations in the Twenty-First Century*, Princeton, NJ: Princeton University Press.

Stulberg, A. N. (2007) *Well-Oiled Diplomacy: Strategic Manipulation and Energy Statecraft in Eurasia*, Albany: SUNY Press.

TASS (2015) 'Patrushev: Tsel' zapadnykh sanktsii – smena rukovodstva Rossii', 3 July.Online. Available HTTP: <http://tass.ru/politika/2092914> (accessed 6 July 2015).

Teague, E. (1994) 'Russia and Tatarstan Sign Power-Sharing Treaty', RFE/RL Research Report, 8 April.

Trenin, D. (2005) 'Vneshnee vmeshatel'stvo v sobytiia na Ukraine i rossiisko-zapadnye otnosheniia', Carnegie Moscow Center Briefing Paper.

Trenin, D. (2006) 'Russia Leaves the West', *Foreign Affairs* 85(4): 87–96.

PART IV

Security governance

32

ALLIANCES

Carlo Masala and Alessandro Scheffler Corvaja

Alliances have been an important element of security policy since long before the rise of the modern nation-state. Therefore, the history of alliances is as long as the history of relations between cohesive units of human coexistence; in other words, 'alliances are [. . .] a universal component of relations between political units, irrespective of time and place' (Holsti et al. 1973: 2). Following Stephen Walt (1987: 1), we define alliances as a 'formal or informal relationship of security cooperation between at least two sovereign states' in this chapter.

Alliances can take the shape of either formal or informal international institutions (Duffield 2007). Furthermore, their structure can correspond to one of two ideal types: hierarchical or egalitarian.[1] The former type is characterized by significant imbalances of capabilities between alliance members, whilst in the latter type, power is distributed more or less evenly among most members. Hierarchically structured alliances can be further differentiated into hegemonic and imperial alliances. If the strong state leads with the consent of the smaller powers, their relationship is considered to be a hegemonic one (cf. Triepel 1938). Arrangements under which the relationship between the strongest state and the other alliance members is based on coercion (as was the case, e.g., in the Warsaw Pact) are considered imperial alliances.

However, although alliances are a core element in the history of international relations and the concept itself is a 'key term' (Modelski 1962: 773) in academic discourse, alliances are at the same time 'understudied' (Snyder 1995: 1). There have been only three attempts to create anything close to a comprehensive theory of alliances. The first attempt was George Liska's (1962) *Nations in Alliance*, followed twenty-five years later by the seminal work of Stephen Walt (1987) on *The Origins of Alliances* and, another decade later, Glenn Snyder's (1997) work on *Alliance Politics*. All three studies have their limitations, however. Liska's work gives some useful insights on the creation of alliances and patterns of cooperation amongst their members, but it suffers from its anecdotal character. Walt's work is limited, as the title indicates, to the origins of alliances, and Snyder's book on alliances in multipolar systems focuses only on the management of member relations.

More precisely, while there are plenty of studies on alliance management, research is lacking on why alliances are formed and when they dissolve. A possible reason for this is that the issue of alliances is difficult to separate from other fields in the discipline of International Relations (IR). It is impossible to discuss alliances without making reference to more general theories of IR (realism, neorealism, neoliberal institutionalism, and constructivism), or without touching upon so-called 'substantive issues' (Carlsnaes et al. 2002: iv), e.g. conflict theory or deterrence.

And because the topic of alliances is inextricably intertwined with other fields of the discipline, theorists have either focused on a particular alliance (mostly on NATO) or have developed partial theories focusing on particular aspects of alliances.

This chapter attempts to provide a more comprehensive overview. We propose that four issues are fundamental for the understanding of alliance politics and present them in four parts. First, we look at the origins of alliances. Second, we look at alliance management issues and how they function. Third, we focus on alliances in practice, looking at how they behave in wartime. Fourth, we are interested in the conditions that favour alliance dissolution or survival.

The origins of alliances

There is a widespread agreement among the neorealist, neoliberal institutionalist, liberal, and constructivist schools of thought that states do act and interact in the absence of a centralized authority capable of providing protection and the 'redress of grievances' (Grieco 2002: 65). Each of these approaches to understanding alliance formation is discussed below.

Balancing and bandwagoning (neorealism)

For neorealists, alliances are tools for balancing where states are unable to establish equilibrium by relying on their own means.[2] Therefore, states use alliances as an instrument to maintain or improve their relative power position globally or regionally. Neorealists believe that states decide to form or to join alliances based on exogenous, not endogenous motivations, because '[a]lliances are against, and only derivatively for, someone or something' (Liska 1962: 12). Alliances therefore can be regarded as a particular outcome of a conflict. By building alliances, states try to maximize their capabilities in order to counterbalance the overwhelming power of another individual state or group of states.

Stephen Walt (1987) has somewhat modified this neorealist account of alliance formation. By including perceptual and behavioural variables in the body of neorealist theory, he argues that states do not aim to counterbalance power per se, but the power of actors they perceive as threatening (1987: 21–8). However, seeking to establish equilibrium is only one option available to states. If states that feel threatened are unable to pursue a balance-of-power strategy on the strength of their own capabilities and have no potential allies, they may be forced to 'accommodate the most imminent threat' (Walt 1987: 30) to their security. From this point of view, bandwagoning is a strategy to avoid becoming the victim of a threatening state or to enjoy the anticipated spoils of victory. But, in general, Walt concludes (1987: 33), states are inclined to balance rather than to bandwagon, since bandwagoning always involves an unequal exchange where one state (the weaker one) accepts a subordinate role.

While Walt considers bandwagoning to be a kind of anomaly within the neorealist research framework on alliances, Randall Schweller (1994) regards it as being compatible with realist assumptions about state behaviour, if the motivation of a state that joins the stronger rather than the weaker side is revisionist, meaning that the state in question is primarily concerned with destroying the current order and securing additional gains. 'Many, therefore, choose to bandwagon with revisionist great powers bent on constructing a new international system; they are "power-maximizing states"' (Zongyou 2006: 196).

Recent scholarship has taken the idea of bandwagoning further and proposed more reasons for allying with an adversary: through hedging and tethering (Weitsman 2004). The term hedging describes low-level commitments designed to both improve relations and foreclose opportunities for a rival's expansion. Tethering on the other hand refers to alliances whose members pose a moderate level-of-threat to each other. These countries will ally in order to manage their conflicts of interest, and will profit from the increased transparency in their relationship to their rival. For Patricia Weitsman, hedging, tethering, balancing, and bandwagoning present a continuum of responses at different levels of threat: with a growing threat, countries will first move from hedging to tethering, then start balancing, and finally bandwagon with a threat once they cannot balance it.

From a neorealist perspective, alliances are a form of 'regression' (which refers to an elimination of tensions through reduction of complexity in the relations between alliance members and the threatening power[s]) in conflict regulation behaviour (Singer 1949). Such regression amongst conflict parties goes hand in hand with integration, or strengthening of the alliance's overall fabric as a result of intensified relations among its members. Therefore, members of an alliance face an additional constraining effect on their action and interaction, because, from a neorealist perspective, an alliance does not abolish the constraining effects emanating from the anarchical structure of the international system on state behaviour, but merely modifies them.

Cooperation as reward (neoliberal institutionalism)

While neoliberal institutionalists do not deny that states are acting and interacting under conditions of system-wide anarchy, they do not attribute the same effects of anarchy to state behaviour that realists/neorealists do (Keohane 1984; Masala 2005: 92). Anarchy, therefore, is not an obstacle to lasting cooperation amongst states. States engage in alliances because, as self-interested actors, they anticipate a mutually rewarding exchange among the members of an alliance (Stein 1990: 7). But what exactly are those rewards that states expect to reap?

First, states create alliances in the expectation that their members can achieve a certain degree of cooperation. As long as the costs for the creation of alliances do not outweigh the perceived benefits from cooperation, states are eager to cooperate (Wallander 2000: 706). From this point of view, an external threat can trigger alliance formation, but there are further advantages beyond the mere engagement in a counterbalancing effort that make alliance membership an attractive proposition for states. From a neoliberal institutionalist viewpoint, alliances provide reciprocity, make members accountable for their actions, and contribute to the creation and maintenance of cooperative security strategies. They also reduce uncertainty by providing credible information on the behaviour of member states and make state behaviour amongst members of the alliance more predictable by developing norms and rules that regulate it (Haftendorn et al. 1999: 3–4).

Although there is a price to pay for joining such institutions, as they impose constraints upon state strategies and have an influence on state preferences, it is a price that states may consider commensurate with the expected benefits. In fact, it is precisely because institutions and actions undertaken by them are costly (politically and economically) that they are credible and therefore can be valuable to self-interested states (Wallander and Keohane 1999: 30). To sum up: from an institutionalist perspective, alliances offer their member states many advantages, which guarantee that alliances persist beyond the conditions in which they were created.

The domestic factor (liberal school)

A third and relatively new account of how and why alliances are created is offered by the liberal school. Liberalism in general 'seeks the roots and causes of external behaviour in domestic structure and process' (Müller 2002: 376). Liberals share the belief that states engage in alliances when there is a convergence of national preferences created by domestic coalitions (Moravcsik 1998; Risse-Kappen 1991). Risse-Kappen believes that the creation of NATO was not dependent on a real or perceived threat, or even a constructed one. However, Risse-Kappen and Moravcsik both focus on democracies only, leaving aside the possibility of preference conversion amongst non-democratic states. Thus, liberals are able to explain why NATO was created, but have difficulties explaining the foundation of the Warsaw Pact Organization, which was formed under Soviet leadership amongst Socialist or Communist countries.

Common identity and ideas, values, and norms (constructivism)

So far, there has not been much work by constructivists on alliances. The most elaborate and sophisticated constructivist-inspired analysis on the question of why alliances (specifically NATO) are created is offered by Thomas Risse-Kappen (1996).

According to him, NATO was not created as an effort to counterbalance the Soviet threat. Rather, NATO represents the institutionalized form of common ideas and worldviews about the coming international order after World War II shared by the founding states of the alliance (Risse-Kappen 1996: 387). Those with similar worldviews and fundamental beliefs founded an alliance whose guiding principles were consistent with their values and norms. In this respect, NATO is an alliance of identity that is not threat-based, but reflects a relationship between states based on a common understanding of their shared traits.

With his emphasis on shared beliefs, Risse-Kappen paved the way for others to apply the same concept to other alliances. Michael Barnett (2002) in his article on alliance formation in the Middle East directly challenges Stephen Walt's assertion that ideologies have played an 'important but ultimately limited role' (1987: 203). Barnett argues instead that identity, and thus ideology, is a key element to social and political interactions that has to be examined closely to understand why states do form an alliance.

Alliance management – how do alliances work?

In comparison to studies about why and how alliances are created, the literature on the management of relations amongst alliance members is abundant. There are a number of partial theories focusing on different aspects of alliance management. Depending on their internal structure, alliances may face different management challenges. This chapter touches on three central aspects of alliance management: hegemonic stability; the alliance internal security dilemma; and alliance cohesion. While the latter two aspects are important for understanding alliance management within hegemonic/imperial as well as egalitarian alliances, the first occurs only in hegemonic alliances.

Hegemonic stability

In a hegemonic alliance, smaller states are only willing to subordinate themselves to the leadership of a bigger state, thereby constraining their sovereignty, if the hegemon provides a public good that the smaller states are unable to produce sufficiently by themselves. This is the core of the hegemonic stability theory (Kindleberger 1986). The hegemonic power provides the public good and lets others participate because it is in the interest of all member states of an alliance (Keohane 1984). There are, however, differences in explaining why hegemons provide public goods: neorealists highlight the fact that the hegemon gains a political advantage from the provision of a public good and only provides this good for as long as it is in the interest of the leading power. In other words, public goods are provided because the hegemon is interested in relative gains. Neoliberals on the other hand argue that the hegemon is interested in absolute gains and will therefore refrain from exploiting the fact that its relations with the other alliance members are asymmetric in nature.

Both schools of thought would agree, however, that the type of relationship between the hegemon and its followers as outlined above entails the risk of free riding. If the hegemon provides a collective good, smaller states do not see the need to increase their efforts to contribute to the production of this public good. Over the long run, this creates tension within the alliances. The difference between the schools of thought is, however, that realists argue that tensions only occur in the absence of a commonly faced threat, while neoliberal institutionalists see tensions as a permanent feature of relations between alliance members.

The internal security dilemma

A feature that is common to both the hegemonic and the egalitarian alliance is what Glenn Snyder has described as the alliance internal security dilemma (1997: 180–3). In an alliance, as in the international system in general, the absence of a supranational authority leads to a situation where many of the steps pursued by states to bolster their security have the effect – often unintended – of making other states less secure. Since alliance members can never be certain of other alliance members' future or present intentions, they embark on policies vis-à-vis their alliance partners aimed at enhancing security.

Snyder's starting assumption is that the interests of allies never fully converge. Since they have committed themselves in a more or less binding way to certain goals, each alliance member faces two potential dilemmas. The first is the risk of entrapment (Snyder 1995: 181). Entrapment refers to a situation where an ally (A) faces the choice of supporting another ally (B) as a result of treaty obligations, although A has no particular interest in supporting B, or staying out of a conflict. Country A fears involvement in a conflict that does not involve its vital interests. On the other hand, if A, despite its commitments, stays out of the conflict, it may risk defection by its ally. The second risk Snyder describes is the fear of abandonment. Abandonment characterizes a situation from the perception of state A, which has a particular interest in a conflict with a non-alliance member, but cannot be sure of the active support of other allies.

To attenuate both dilemmas by avoiding entrapment as well as abandonment is one of the biggest tasks in the management of an alliance. Both the management of the alliance internal security dilemma and the structural problems inherent in hegemonic stability theory point to a much larger problem alliance members do face in the management of their relations, namely how to ensure alliance cohesion.

Alliance cohesion

From the neorealist point of view, alliance cohesion, both in hegemonic and egalitarian alliances, depends on the degree of the external challenge. The bigger the threat that alliance members face (or perceive), the greater alliance cohesion will be (Mearsheimer 1990). There is disagreement, however, as to the role that the hegemon plays in maintaining alliance cohesion. While some authors regard it as crucial (Gowa 1999), others are sceptical, especially concerning the phase when the commonly perceived threat decreases (Masala 2003). When the threat decreases, smaller allies are less and less willing to subordinate themselves to a hegemon. The simple causality of neorealist reasoning is as follows: high levels of threat perception lead to high alliance cohesion, while conversely, low threat perception levels result in low alliance cohesion.

From a (liberal) institutional perspective, alliance cohesion is guaranteed by the multiple advantages alliances do provide for their member states. The reduction of transaction costs through established procedures; the ability to control other alliance members; the access to information about the intentions and behaviour of alliance partners; and the iterated games that are played within the cooperative framework of an alliance – all of these advantages out-weigh the potential costs and frictions emanating from different national preferences (Keohane and Nye 1993).

Constructivists (similarly to neoliberal institutionalists) argue that alliances among liberal democracies have cohesion because of the 'republican liberalism linking domestic polities sys-tematically to the foreign policy of states' (Risse-Kappen 1996: 358). Among liberal democracies, coherence is guaranteed because liberal democracies are more inclined to cooperate closely with other liberal democracies. This is because liberal democracies do not regard other liberal democ-racies as a potential threat. Among liberal democracies, there is no fear that cooperation will be exploited by allies in the future; therefore, the problem of relative gain distribution (Grieco 1990) does not exist. Additionally, constructivists point to the fact that democracies are charac-terized by transparency; high audience costs; consistent policy behaviour; civilian control of the armed forces (which is important for military alliances between democracies); and the capacity to make enduring commitments (Lai and Reiter 2000) – all of which are factors that facilitate closer cooperation between such regimes. To sum up: the more similar the regimes are that cooperate, and the more their values converge, the more cohesive the alliance they form will be.

The military aspect: alliances in practice

Few theories exist on how the advent of a conflict changes the calculus of allies, and particularly on how and why countries partner in conflicts that are not existential. This lack of literature is puzzling when considering that operating through an alliance or coalition has increasingly become the norm rather than the exception, and is often considered a key component of the *American Way of War* (Tierney 2010).

Explanations of the increasing multilateralism in warfare are both strategic and ideational (Weitsman 2014): while some have argued on liberal grounds that countries follow a 'normative pull' to multilateral warfare out of a logic of appropriateness (Finnemore 2003), others have tried to reconcile this trend with traditional realist arguments and asserted that military multilateral-ism is a power-preserving strategy that allows partners to reassure allies, spread burdens, and reap legitimacy benefits – both abroad and at home. Accordingly, states only opt for a unilateral operation if the imminence of the threat does not afford them the time to build a coalition, or if the burden is supposed to be low (Kreps 2011). But while modern states are thus natural mul-tilateralists, this doesn´t mean that their cooperation is easy. This section looks at burden-sharing and other common problems in multinational operations.

Burden-sharing in wartime

Burden-sharing is a particularly sensitive subject in multinational operations – as demonstrated by the contentious issue of operational caveats in recent campaigns. The wide variation in the size and quality of contributions across countries – but also across cases – in the last two decades has spurred significant research on what determines countries' commitments to multinational campaigns.

The two most prominent assessments, Bennett et al. (1997) and Auerswald (2004), have demonstrated that burden-sharing could best be explained by a model that considered both systemic – that is, international – and domestic factors. Von Hlatky (2013) has reaffirmed this for recent campaigns, and argues that a country's contribution to multilateral campaigns will be determined by alliance expectations, while its form will be determined by government cohe-sion and its military capabilities. Baltrusaitis (2008) and Auerswald and Saideman (2014) make a similar case and emphasize the importance of domestic political factors on the national control of armed forces. In their view, a country´s desire for control is a function of its political system: strong executives tend to surrender the control of their forces much more easily than strong parliaments and place much fewer caveats on them.

The problematic nature of multinational operations

The divisive issue of burden-sharing has already pointed to the problems associated with multilateral warfare. If there is one point everyone can agree to, it is probably that coalition warfare is a difficult undertaking. When push comes to shove, alliances and coalitions tend to amount to considerably less than the sum of their parts (Silkett 1993). The problems associated with multilateral warfare can be broadly associated with three interrelated factors, which broadly correspond to the three levels of war: political cohesion (strategic), unity of command (operational), and interoperability (tactical).

On the strategic level, the diverging interest of allies will lead to constant 'centrifugal tendencies' (Bensahel 1999) which threaten to draw an alliance apart. These tendencies increase in wartime as the stakes get higher and more expedient: it becomes less feasible to make long-term promises and states are called to fulfil previous commitments (Weitsman 2014). The compromises needed for maintaining cohesion often lead to broad and inconsistent war aims that put the entire campaign at risk. The level of these centrifugal tendencies depends on the theoretical perspective: as in theories of alliance maintenance, realist theories assume that a common, manageable, and non-exclusive external threat will glue allies together (Weitsman 2004), while institutionalist arguments stress the staying power of coalitions (Kreps 2011) and liberal and constructivist theories argue that the regime type defines the level of cohesion (Choi 2012).

Achieving unity of command – and its 'next-best-alternatives' of unity of effort and purpose – is instead believed to present the toughest challenge on the operational level (Rice 1997). This problem is a direct result of differences on the strategic level: because interests diverge on the strategic level, nations will hedge their bets and hesitate to cede control of their armed forces to a different nation. The result is military structures geared towards preserving political cohesion rather than military effectiveness – and therefore a lack of unity of command (Bensahel 1999). By using principal-agent theory, Auerswald and Saideman (2014) have also shown that even where unity of command exists, nations will retain a high level of control over their officers due the variety and importance of domestic channels such as promotion, etc.

Finally, interoperability is the most obvious challenge for multinational operations: militaries are complex organizations, and the same problems that appear between different services within a single armed force must be even more daunting where several countries are involved. The relevant literature – often focusing on problems experienced in specific campaigns – therefore emphasizes the importance of technological, doctrinal (Terriff et al. 2010), and cultural factors (Luft 2009).

Why do alliances end, why do they survive, and how?

The issue of how alliances survive and why they end was hotly debated among scholars of IR during the first half of the 1990s. It should not come as a surprise that the results were, at best, mixed. The linchpin for this debate was the question of whether NATO would survive the end of the Cold War. Unsurprisingly, neorealists were very sceptical concerning the future of alliances after the disappearance of the cohesive force that holds them together; namely, the commonly perceived threat.

Scholars like Waltz or Mearsheimer were quite outspoken about the future of alliances, especially of NATO, after the collapse of the Soviet Union. They believed NATO had become an anachronism (Mearsheimer 1990; Waltz 1990: 21, 2000: 18). Waltz believed that the reason why NATO still existed, even ten years after the fall of the Berlin Wall, was the fact that the US had an interest in maintaining its 'grip' (Waltz 2000: 19) on developments in Europe. Stephen Walt joined this rationale by pointing out that US hegemony could well explain why NATO remained one of the main relevant political institutions in transatlantic affairs (Walt 1997: 171). But even the continuation of US hegemonic policy, according to Waltz, would not prevent NATO from becoming an irrelevant institution, because other alliance members would be less and less willing to accept US supremacy within the institution.

In contrast, neoliberal institutionalists have been extremely optimistic with regard to the possibility of cooperation within alliances even without an external threat or a hegemon (Haftendorn et al. 1999). Besides the already mentioned positive effects that alliance members enjoy by virtue of their alliance membership, institutional inertia contributes to the durability of an alliance.[3] Furthermore, as long as alliance members do have an interest in keeping their cooperation alive (Keohane 1984: 31), the chance that alliances may survive and even adapt to a new environment – even in the absence of an overwhelming threat – are quite high.

An argument as to why NATO survived the end of the East–West conflict that is fully in line with the basic tenets of neoliberal institutionalism has been developed by Celeste Wallander (2000). Institutions with general assets,[4] she argues, will be adaptable to new problems. Because the assets are not specific to a given relationship, location, or purpose, using them for new purposes will be low-cost and broadly effective (Wallander 2000: 709). NATO, she concludes in her empirical analysis, has been successful in adapting its assets to a new security environment (Wallander 2000: 732) that is not characterized by a unifying threat.

According to the constructivist point of view, the survival of an alliance depends on the continuation of the underlying reason for the alliance's existence, which, as discussed above, is not a common threat, but the perception of having a common destiny. Therefore, alliances can survive major changes in their environment if their members still feel that they belong together and share the same norms and values. Thus, the end of the East–West conflict does not mark the end of NATO, since it did not terminate the community of values. Frank Schimmelfennig (1999) argued that after the fall of the Berlin Wall, the Western value community extended into the newly democratic countries of Eastern Europe, and NATO played (and still plays, according to this view) a crucial role in socializing these states. As long as alliance members build a security community (Deutsch et al. 1957) and have a sense of belonging to it, security cooperation will continue.

Conclusion and outlook

This chapter looked at literature on alliance in four major categories: alliance formation, alliance maintenance, alliances in practice, and finally alliance continuity or dissolution. We are left with the insight that, although alliances are important in structuring relations between states, we still do not know much about them. This has policy implications. One important question concerns the purpose of alliances (from an alliance member perspective). Do they serve as an instrument for (counter-)balancing real or perceived threats and risks? Are they instruments for the management of relations between member states? Or are the ties that bind members of an alliance together based on the notion that the states in question belong to a community of a shared identity?

The answer is that each of the competing perspectives sketched above captures important aspects of alliances, and it would be misleading if policy-makers confined their thinking to only one perspective. Heads of state and diplomats should be aware of the role that neorealists allocate to power, but also take into account the domestic and institutional aspects, as well as the ideational foundations, that scholars from the neoliberal institutionalist, liberal, and constructivist camps assign to alliances. A syncretistic conception of alliances might result in a better understanding of the 'real-world developments' of alliances than the one resulting from a continuous battle for supremacy between various schools of thought. Furthermore, all three major schools of IR theory focus on the question of whether or not alliances ultimately wither away. As far as this issue is concerned, neorealism, neoliberal institutionalism, and constructivism offer relatively static explanations. What is lacking is a dynamic approach focusing not on the question of why NATO still exists, but on how NATO is developing.

In the process of institutional readaptation, the internal security dilemma poses a major challenge to alliance members. At the theoretical level, there are two ways of attenuating this dilemma: either through a higher degree of institutionalization or through a weakening of institutional ties amongst member states. The first option, which entails the strengthening of commitments among alliance member states, can be successful in the case of an increase in threat perception. If the new alliance environment is characterized by a commonly perceived threat, an integrative strategy (reinforcing institutional ties) might be an appropriate way to ensure that fears of entrapment or abandonment are assuaged.

The second strategy seems to be adequate if member states cooperate in an environment that is characterized by 'risk-diffusion' (Masala 2003: 13) and an interest on the part of member states in maintaining institutionalized cooperative relations. In such a situation, a lessening of institutional constraints might give member states a higher degree of freedom of action while at the same time minimizing any fears of abandonment or entrapment that might exist. Such a flexible alliance (Masala 2003: 32–6) could – from a member-state perspective – constitute an appropriate response to the changed environment and thereby guarantee the continuation of institutionalized security cooperation in the form of alliances even in the future.

This approach to studying changes in alliances has two distinct advantages: first, it borrows important insights from most of the theories dealing with alliances and tries to combine them into a line of inquiry that is not only relevant from a political-science point of view, but also from a political point of view. Second, it leaves open the question of whether an alliance will survive or not. Both trajectories are possible, and the answer depends on real-world developments within alliances and among their members.

Notes

1 Holsti et al. distinguish between monolithic and pluralistic alliances (1973: 166).
2 On the distinction between internal and external balancing, see Waltz (1979: 116–28).
3 For an elaborate argument that NATO's continued existence after the end of the East–West conflict can be explained by institutional inertia, see McCalla 1996.
4 Wallander (2000: 731) distinguishes between general assets (e.g. transparency, procedures, interoperability, etc.) and specific assets (e.g. Article 5 of the North Atlantic Treaty).

References

Auerswald, D. P. (2004) 'Explaining Wars of Choice: An Integrated Decision Model of NATO Policy in Kosovo', *International Studies Quarterly* 48(3): 631–62.
Auerswald, D. P. and Saideman, S. M. (2014) *NATO in Afghanistan: Fighting Together, Fighting Alone,* Princeton, NJ: Princeton University Press.
Baltrusaitis, D. F. (2008) 'Friends indeed? Coalition Burden Sharing and the War in Iraq', Ph.D. thesis, Georgetown University. Online. Available HTTP: <http://hdl.handle.net/10822/553069> (accessed 27 September 2013).

Barnett, M. (2002) 'Alliances, Balances of Threats, and Neo-Realism: The Accidental Coup', in C. Elman and J. Vasquez (eds.) *Realism and the Balancing of Power: A New Debate?*, New York: St. Martin's Press, 222–49.

Bennett, A., Lepgold, J., and Unger, D. (eds.) (1997) *Friends in Need: Burden Sharing in the Persian Gulf War*, New York: St. Martin's Press.

Bensahel, N. (1999) *The Coalition Paradox: The Politics of Military Cooperation*, Stanford, CA: Stanford University Press.

Carlsnaes, W., Risse, T., and Simmons, B. (eds.) (2002) *Handbook of International Relations*, London: Sage.

Choi, A. (2012) 'Fighting to the Finish: Democracy and Commitment in Coalition War', *Security Studies* 21(4): 663–82.

Deutsch, K. W., Burrell, S. A., Kann R. A., and Lee, M. Jr (1957) *Political Community and the North Atlantic Area : International Organization in the Light of Historical Experience*, Princeton, NJ: Princeton University Press.

Duffield, J. (2007) 'What are International Institutions?', *International Studies Review* 9(1): 1–22.

Finnemore, M. (2003) *The Purpose of Intervention*, Ithaca, NY: Cornell University Press.

Gowa, J. (1999) *Ballots and Bullets: The Elusive Democratic Peace*, Princeton, NJ: Princeton University Press.

Grieco, J. M. (1990) *Cooperation among Nations: Europe, America and Non-Tariff Barriers to Trade*, Ithaca, NY: Cornell University Press.

Grieco, J. M. (2002) 'Modern Realist Theory and the Study of International Politics in the 21st Century', in M. Brecher and F. P. Harvey (eds.) *Millennial Reflections on International Studies*, Ann Arbor: University of Michigan Press, 65–78.

Haftendorn, H., Keohane, R. O., and Wallander, C. A. (eds.) (1999) *Imperfect Unions: Security Institutions over Time and Space*, Oxford: Oxford University Press.

Holsti, O. R., Hopmann, P. T., and Sullivan, J. D. (1973) *Unity and Disintegration in International Alliances*, New York: Wiley.

Keohane, R. O. (1984) *After Hegemony*, Princeton, NJ: Princeton University Press.

Keohane, R. O. and Nye, J. (1993) 'Introduction: The End of the Cold War in Europe', in R. O. Keohane, J. S. Nye, and S. Hoffmann (eds.) *After the Cold War. International Institutions and State Strategies in Europe 1989–1991*, Cambridge, MA: Harvard University Press, 1–19.

Kindleberger, C. (1986) *The World in Depression 1929–1938*, Berkeley: University of California Press.

Kreps, S. (2011) *Coalitions of Convenience*, New York: Oxford University Press.

Lai, B. and Reiter, D. (2000) 'Democracy, Political Similarity, and International Alliances 1816–1992', *Journal of Conflict Resolution* 44(2): 203–27.

Liska, G. (1962) *Nations in Alliance*, Baltimore, MD: Johns Hopkins University Press.

Luft, G. (2009) *Beer, Bacon, Bullets*, Lexington, KY: BookSurge.

Masala, C. (2003) *Den Blick nach Süden? Die NATO im Mittelmeerraum (1990–2003). Fallstudie zur Anpassung militärischer Allianzen an neue sicherheitspolitische Rahmenbedingungen*, Baden-Baden: Nomos.

Masala, C. (2005) *Kenneth N. Waltz*, Baden-Baden: Nomos.

McCalla, R. B. (1996) 'NATO's Persistence after the Cold War', *International Organization* 50(3): 445–75.

Mearsheimer, J. J. (1990) 'Back to the Future: Instability in Europe after the Cold War', *International Security* 15(4): 5–56.

Modelski, G. (1962) *A Theory of Foreign Policy*, New York: Praeger.

Moravcsik, A. (1998) *The Choice for Europe*, Ithaca, NY: Cornell University Press.

Müller, H. (2002) 'Security Cooperation', in W. Carlsnaes, T, Risse, and B. Simmons (eds.) *Handbook of International Relations*, London: Sage, 369–92.

Rice, A. J. (1997) 'Command and Control: The Essence of Coalition Warfare', *Parameters* 27(1): 152–67.

Risse-Kappen, T. (1991) 'Public Opinion, Domestic Structure, and Foreign Policy in Liberal Democracies', *World Politics* 43(4): 479–512.

Risse-Kappen, T. (1996) 'Collective Identity in a Democratic Community: The Case of NATO', in P. Katzenstein (ed.) *The Culture of National Security. Norms and Identity in World Politics*, New York: Columbia University Press, 357–99.

Schimmelfennig, F. (1999) 'NATO's Enlargement: A Constructivist Explanation', *Security Studies* 8(2–3): 198–234.

Schweller, R. L. (1994) 'Bandwagoning for Profit: Bringing the Revisionist State Back In', *International Security* 19(1): 72–107.

Silkett, W. A. (1993) 'Alliance and Coalition Warfare', *Parameters* 23(2): 74–85.

Singer, K. (1949) *The Idea of Conflict*, Melbourne: Melbourne University Press.

Snyder, G. H. (1997) *Alliance Politics*, Ithaca, NY: Cornell University Press.

Terriff, T., Osinga, F., and Farrell, T. (eds.) (2010) *A Transformation Gap? American Innovations and European Military Change*, Stanford, CA: Stanford University Press.

Tierney, D. (2010) *How We Fight: Crusades, Quagmires, and the American Way of War*, New York: Little Brown.

Triepel, H. (1938) *Die Hegemonie. Ein Buch von führenden Staaten*, Stuttgart: Kohlhammer.

von Hlatki, S. (2013) *American Allies in Times of War: The Great Assymmetry*, London: Oxford University Press.

Wallander, C. A. (2000) 'Institutional Assets and Adaptability: NATO after the Cold War', *International Organization* 54(4): 705–36.

Wallander, C. A. and Keohane, R. O. (1999) 'Risk, Threat and Security Institutions', in H. Haftendorn, C. A. Wallander, and R. O. Keohane (eds.) (1999) *Imperfect Unions: Security Institutions over Time and Space*, Oxford: Oxford University Press, 21–47.

Walt, S. (1987) *The Origins of Alliances*, Ithaca, NY: Cornell University Press.

Walt, S. (1997) 'Why Alliances Endure or Collapse', *Survival* 39(1): 156–79.

Waltz, K. N. (1979) *Theory of International Politics*, Reading: Addison-Wesley.

Waltz, K. N. (1990) 'Realist Thought and Neorealist Theory', *Journal of International Affairs* 44(5): 21–37.

Waltz, K. N. (2000) 'Structural Realism after the Cold War', *International Security* 25(1): 5–41.

Weitsman, P. (2004) *Dangerous Alliances. Proponents of Peace, Weapons of War*, Stanford, CA: Stanford University Press.

Weitsman, P. (2014) *Waging War: Alliances, Coalitions, and Institutions of Interstate Violence*, Stanford, CA: Stanford University Press.

Zongyou, W. (2006) 'In the Shadow of Hegemony: Strategic Choices', *Chinese Journal of International Politics* 1(1): 195–229.

33

INTERNATIONAL SANCTIONS

Olivier Schmitt

International sanctions have become a commonly used tool of statecraft on the international stage. The most comprehensive database compiling sanctions 'episodes' since 1914 notes that their number has nearly doubled in two decades, from 103 in 1985 to 204 in 2007 (Hufbauer et al. 2008). The growing importance of sanctions has generated a number of debates in scholarly and policy circles, the most famous asking whether economic sanctions 'work' or not. Other sub-debates have emerged over time, including the effectiveness of multilaterally imposed sanction regimes compared with unilateral sanctions, the right mixture of comprehensiveness and accuracy in selecting the targets of the sanction episode, or the unintended (and potentially counterproductive) effects of sanctions (Andreas 2005).

While it is clear that the academic literature on sanctions has made very important progresses, using the methods of social sciences to the best of their possibilities by generating original databases and important quantitative and qualitative analysis, it has sometimes fallen into the trap of being caught within the poorly conceptualized vocabulary and issues defined by policy-making debates in an effort to influence decision-makers. This chapter takes stock of this literature, illustrating how international sanctions are now an integral and important part of the international security agenda. It has four parts. The first looks at different types and definitions of sanctions as a basis for their analysis. The second focuses on one core debate in the literature: whether sanctions work or not and how academic knowledge about this fact does not travel to policy-makers well. The third section shifts the debate to a broader understanding of sanctions, away from their utility, towards the question of whether they are the best tool available for policy-makers in specific contexts. The fourth discusses newer types of literature that study how and why sanctions are actually employed, rather than focusing on their level of success.

What are international sanctions?

In very broad terms, sanctions can be defined as the imposition, by a sender, of measures designed to impose a cost on a receiver, short of the use of military force. As such, there is a wide variety of sanction types, which target different areas of interactions between states; and several different functions. Furthermore, there are different rules for, and ways of, implementation.

Types

Cultural and sportive sanctions are usually symbolic, but are a means for the international community, or a group of countries, to express their disagreement towards the target's specific policy, without imposing further costs. For example, during the apartheid era, South African teams were banned from a number of sports competitions.

Diplomatic sanctions target state representatives and key individuals. Diplomats, politicians, or important personalities from the targeted state can have their visa denied, or be excluded from international organizations. In the wake of the Ukraine crisis in 2014, the European Union, the United States, and other countries adopted a list of Russian individuals who would be denied entry visas to those countries. Russia retaliated a few days later by publishing a list of its own, targeting a number of Western officials.

Military sanctions target specific forms of military cooperation. Training programmes, arms deals, or joint exercises can be suspended or cancelled. For example, France cancelled the selling of two warships of the *Mistral* class to Russia, after Moscow invaded Crimea and continued to support an armed rebellion in Ukraine.

Economic sanctions are of two kinds: trade sanctions and financial sanctions. Trade sanctions are usually comprehensive, such as the embargo the US imposed on Cuba for several decades. Financial sanctions are more targeted, and usually consist of the freezing of the foreign assets of specific individuals. Economic sanctions are the most commonly used type of sanctions, and have thus received a large attention in the literature, and are the type that is primarily addressed in this chapter.

Functions

Sanctions can have different functions, in particular signalling, coercing, or punishing the receiver.

Signalling is an important aspect of what sanctions are supposed to achieve. By imposing sanctions, the sending state signals its discontent with another state's policy, and leaves open the possibility for further measures. Signalling can also serve to stigmatize states breaking acknowledged international norms. The target audience of the signalling move can also be the sender's own population, for example in order to satisfy a popular demand without jeopardizing further relations with the receiver (Giumelli 2011).

Coercing is the second potential role of sanctions. In this case, the goal is to force the target to change its policies by imposing a cost. The dynamic is similar to those observed in other forms of coercion (in particular military coercion), and there is usually a complementarity, and not a caricatural dichotomy, between sanctions (in particular economic sanctions) and military-based coercion (Schmitt 2015).

Finally, *punishing* is another function of international sanctions, which to a degree overlaps with signalling and coercing, but not entirely. International interactions are never conducted between rational actors maximizing their utility based on a material definition of interests. In fact, passions play an important role in the conduct of statecraft. As such, sanctions can be imposed because a sender feels like doing justice itself, notably of international institutions are perceived as unable to act (Nossal 1989). Punishing can also be understood as a form of constraint, in limiting the target's access to specific commodities, or financial facilities.

Implementation

The imposition of sanctions is legally defined, and must respect the general principles of international law. In order for sanctions to be implemented, the legal requirements of Article 39 of the UN Charter must normally be satisfied; that is, that there is a threat to the peace, a breach of the peace, or an act of aggression, and that the purpose of the sanctions is to maintain or restore international peace and security. Of course, several types of sanctions (for example cultural sanctions mostly fulfilling the signalling function), fall outside this legal scope, which is more appropriate for sanctions with a coercive intent. Sanctions must also respect human rights and the general principle of not aggravating any humanitarian situation: for example, they should not target products necessary to the survival and well-being of the population (Segall 1999).

Sanctions can also be multilateral or unilateral. International organizations such as the United Nations or the European Union can decide to impose sanctions, but so can individual states. It is very common to see several types of sanctions imposed simultaneously on a receiver, for example with multilateral sanctions agreed upon within an international organization and imposed by their members, and individual states deciding to go further than the commonly agreed framework. The sanctions regime imposed on Iran was composed of several layers of UN sanctions, EU sanctions, and sanctions implemented by the United States. While the UN sanctions did not target the Iranian energy and petroleum industry, the EU and the US sanctions did. The US was also the only actor to impose sanctions on foreign firms dealing with Iran.

Finally, sanctions regimes can be comprehensive, or target specific individuals. The idea of imposing economic sanctions came under heavy criticism because of the human rights costs of the comprehensive sanctions regime imposed on Iraq after the Gulf War. Therefore, much thinking was devoted to improving the design of sanctions in order to avoid other humanitarian disasters. This triggered the move from comprehensive sanction regimes towards targeted (or so-called 'smart') sanctions (Brzoska 2003).

Table 33.1 summarizes the different factors to take into account in order to analyse a sanction regime.

The debate about sanctions' effectiveness

The question 'do sanctions work?' has dominated the academic debate about sanctions from its inception to the past decade, when scholars finally developed more sensible approaches taking into account the context in which sanctions are applied, but is still prevalent in the policy debate

Table 33.1 Factors and characteristics of sanctions

Types of sanctions	Objective of sanctions	Legal framework	Number of senders	Scope
Cultural/sportive	Signalling	UN charter	Multilateral	Comprehensive
Diplomatic	Coercing	Respect for	framework	Targeted
Military	Punishing	human rights	Unilateral sender	
Economic				

at every sanction episode. In part, this is due to a normative commitment from policy-makers and scholars alike to find viable alternatives to military force in the strategic interaction between states: if sanctions 'work', they may become a tool for non-violent coercion, and thus reduce the calamities of war. This question was also triggered by the apparent failure of sanctions to change a state's behaviour in a number of historically important cases, such as the sanctioning of Italy for its invasion of Ethiopia (1936), the US embargo against Cuba (1962–2015), or the UN sanctions against Serbia (1992–6). Given the absence of obvious high-profile cases of sanctions' effectiveness, the focus on whether sanctions work or not is justified from a normative perspective, but also from a scientific one: if sanctions do not work, why do states keep using them?

This focus on the utility and effectiveness of sanctions (in particular economic sanctions) has a methodological consequence. The first step of many analyses is to classify cases of sanctions based on their 'success' or 'failure', the degree of success being measured by observing whether the target complied and changed its behaviour according to the desires of the sender. The second step is to conduct a quantitative and/or qualitative analysis in order to identify the variables with which success or failure correlate more strongly, and thus derive policy prescriptions about the conditions under which sanctions 'work' or not (Allen 2005; Cortwright and Lopez 2000, 2002; Hufbauer et al. 2008; Pape 1997). As David Baldwin explains, setting the record straight on success rates is critical in order to identify 'the conditions under which sanctions are likely (or unlikely) to succeed. Knowledge of such conditions is necessary [. . .] for deciding whether sanctions should be employed in a given situation' (Baldwin 1999/2000: 87).

To summarize, the main issue addressed in the literature comes from a desire to advise policy-makers on when and how to employ sanctions effectively, but this ambition has strong methodological and theoretical consequences. First, this effort has downgraded the theorizing about how sanctions are used and how they operate. The main debate in the literature on sanctions, which opposed sanctions optimists (arguing that sanctions can be a useful tool for policy-makers) such as Baldwin and sanctions pessimists (arguing that sanctions are useless) such as Pape, is actually a methodological debate about measuring and classifying the success or failure of sanctions episodes. David Baldwin's important argument about sanctions is that their critics adopt a too narrow definition of success (Baldwin 1985, 1999/2000). Similarly, there was an important debate between Pape, Baldwin, and Elliott at the end of the 1990s, which stemmed from the fact that Robert Pape had classified as 'failures' thirty-five of the forty cases that the comprehensive database compiled by Hufbauer, Schott, and Elliott had identified as 'successes' (Baldwin 1999/2000; Baldwin and Pape 1998; Elliott 1998; Pape 1997, 1998).

Thus, the long-standing debate over whether sanctions work is actually a debate about the proper taxonomy of cases. The problem with this focus on taxonomy is that it generated little progress on the understanding of how economic power works. The reference on this issue remains Baldwin's 1985 book on *Economic Statecraft*, and little progress has been made since then. As Marinov correctly observes: 'after more than two decades of debating the effectiveness of economic pressure, the state of disagreement on whether pressure works remains something of an embarrassment' (Marinov 2005: 565).

Moreover, this literature is at pains to explain why policy-makers keep using economic sanctions while the main conclusion that stems from the comparative analyses is that they are a relatively weak instrument of statecraft when it comes to influencing a target's behaviour. Depending on the authors, and their classification of what passes as 'success', sanctions work from 5 per cent to about 30 per cent of the cases (Hufbauer et al. 2008; Pape 1997): even the most optimistic accounts do not identify a stellar success rate for economic sanctions. Moreover, the successes are usually recorded in cases where the issues at stake were of limited importance. Logically, the literature advises policy-makers to use sanctions sparingly, and not to invest too much hope in their effect. Robert Pape writes that there is 'little empirical evidence that sanctions can achieve ambitious foreign policy goals' (Pape 1998: 76). Yet, despite what the literature suggests, sanctions have been increasingly used by policy-makers over the past twenty years, sometimes for ambitious goals. There are three potential explanations for this disconnect between the policy prescriptions of the literature and the actual practice of policy-makers: policy-makers do not read the academic literature and its results (even disseminated in a more digestible form); policy-makers are stupid; or the academic literature failed to address their needs. While the first two explanations could be perfectly plausible in other contexts, the next section explains why the third is actually more likely when it comes to economic sanctions.

Do sanctions have to 'work'?

As noted above, the main debate about sanctions has generated little progress on the interactions between economic power and statecraft, most notably because it is stuck with a taxonomic effort of classifying sanctions as either success or failures.

Success is usually defined as the capability for sanctions to achieve the goals for which policy makers use them. However, Baldwin acknowledged early on that this classification based on an *ex post* assessment of policy makers' intentions is problematic (Baldwin 1985). First, it is very difficult to know what it is that policy-makers wanted to achieve in the first place: the declared objectives (on which an assessment is usually made) can be very different from the actual motivations to use the sanctions tool. It is naive to base an assessment of sanctions' effectiveness on the declared objectives of policy-makers, as these are not the most credible sources to evaluate the actual intention. Moreover, it is quite rare that the imposition of sanctions has a single objective. In fact, coercion, signalling, and punishing can be simultaneous objectives, aiming at different audiences. The problem of classifying sanctions episodes as 'success' or 'failure' is then obvious: not only is the attempt riddled with a difficulty to actually know what the objective really was; it also reduces the utility of sanctions to an 'either/or' dichotomy which obscures the fact that sanctions serve several purposes simultaneously. A fair assessment of the success rate of sanctions should take into account their multiple objectives, and the multiple levels on which they operate.

Thus it is much more productive to envision the utility of sanctions in the context of the coercive toolbox at the policy-makers' disposal. In that regard, usefulness is more important than effectiveness: the debate is not so much about whether sanctions 'work' or not as whether they are the best tool available for policy-makers. Let us take the example of a state willing to coerce another state. The available tools range from diplomatic measures (such as an initiative in a multilateral framework) to military force, and include economic sanctions. Depending on the situation, the use of military force is just unthinkable, and diplomatic measures would be considered insufficient. In such a case, economic sanctions would be the best available option, because it is the most tailored one. For example, during the 1956 Suez crisis, the United States wanted to coerce France and the United Kingdom to stop their aggression against Egypt. Of course, the United States never envisioned the use of military force against its NATO allies. Yet, the stakes were deemed high enough for President Eisenhower to prevent the International Monetary Fund from granting a loan to the United Kingdom, which badly needed it. This sanction weighed heavily in London's strategic calculation and in the unfolding of the crisis.

Therefore, sanctions should not be approached through the question of 'effectiveness', i.e. whether they 'work' or not. They should be understood as part of a broader spectrum of policy tools, and assessment should be based on a comparison with other available options. Had the dominating literature focused on this aspect, our understanding of the dynamics of economic power would have been significantly better, and the literature more policy-relevant.

What's next for the study of international sanctions

As discussed, the debate over whether sanctions 'work' or not, even though it is often referred to in international media, is actually a theoretical dead end. Fortunately, the literature on sanctions has moved towards new areas of research that appear much more promising, both in theoretical and empirical terms. These areas share an interest in studying how and why sanctions are actually employed, instead of focusing on their results.

Sanctions and international organizations

An interesting development is the systematic analysis of the conception and implementation of the United Nations' targeted sanctions between 1991 and 2013 (Bianchi 2007; Graham-Brown 1999; Noland 2009; Thielman 2010). A project compiling data on such sanctions episodes, involving a consortium of international researchers and hosted at the Graduate Institute of International and Development Studies (Geneva), is currently ongoing. A quantitative database is expected for 2016, and preliminary results have already been disseminated. The analysis of twenty-two UN targeted sanctions regimes leads to several interesting insights. First, it seems that sanctions are more effective in signalling or constraining a target than they are in coercing a change of behaviour. However, sanctions regimes are unique and complex, and reflect different contexts, previous experiences being hardly predictive of future outcomes. This sensitivity to context is a welcome development compared to the previous literature on sanctions effectiveness. Moreover, UN sanctions regimes are never applied in isolation, and must be evaluated within the context of an overall approach to security challenges. In that regard, UN sanctions are usually complemented by regional sanctions (which often even precede the UN regime).

Other findings are also important. For example, although arms embargos are the most frequently imposed types of sanctions, they are the least effective ones when they are not complemented with sanctions targeting individuals or commodities. In contrast, commodity sanctions (diamond-trade sanctions for example) seem to be highly effective. Targeting also matters greatly: the list of targets must be carefully elaborated in order to reflect the purposes of sanctions, as a wrong targeting undermines the credibility of the regime. Moreover, it seems that a great deal of institutional learning has occurred within the United Nations over time. In particular, systems such as the use of panel experts, greater precision in making individual designations, and internal review procedures have developed and are now common practice. However, the UN institutional machinery is difficult to operate within, and coordination problems within the UN system still occur. It takes the UN Security Council six months between the time that it first takes note of a security situation and the imposition of a sanctions regime in the case of proliferation. However, it is an average of seventeen months in case of conflict, which reflects the political priorities and divergences within the UNSC (Biersteker et al. 2013).

Another area of research has been the use of international sanctions as a tool of foreign policy for the European Union (EU). In fact, the EU has been imposing sanctions without a UNSC mandate since the early 1980s and, since the mid-1990s, the EU has adopted a practice of imposing targeted sanctions rather than comprehensive embargoes (Giumelli 2011; Hufbauer and Oegg 2003; Kryvoi 2008). The EU adopts sanctions in a variety of frameworks. First, sanctions adopted in the intergovernmental framework of the Common Foreign and Security Policy (CFSP) are reflected in a Common Position. Measures imposed in this framework constitute the only 'sanctions' according to the EU's own understanding. Second, informal sanctions are sanctions decided by the Council or the European Council outside the formal framework of the CFSP. They are reflected in council conclusions or presidential statements rather than in legally binding documents. Finally, there are also Article 96 sanctions suspending the application of the partnership agreement between the EU and African, Caribbean, and Pacific (ACP) states – routinely called the Cotonou Agreement – on parties in breach of human rights and democratic principles. This entails the suspension of trade preferences and the freezing or redirection of development cooperation.

What is most surprising is that Article 96 suspensions record the highest incidence of positive outcomes. By contrast, the CFSP sanctions display mostly failures, and informal sanctions have an even lower success rate. The concentration of most positive outcomes in the Article 96 groups seems to illustrate that even in the era of targeted measures, sanctions continue to prove more effective if they entail economic disutility for the target, which is normally the case with Article 96 sanctions, given that they consist of the partial suspension or the redirection of aid. Yet, the number of episodes in which Article 96 sanctions did not lead to success remains high enough to invalidate any assumption of automaticity between their presence and a positive outcome.

A detailed examination of how EU sanctions are implemented also reveals interesting dynamics. First, in those cases in which the crises were resolved, the lifting of the measures came about after the sender had conducted an intensive diplomatic campaign in which a deal was struck between the sender and the target. Such a deal often emerged from a direct negotiation between both actors and consisted in an exchange in which both sides conceded to some extent, resulting in a watered-down version of the original demands. In other words, the EU managed to obtain some key concessions from the target, but it settled for outcomes notably inferior to the original aspiration. Secondly, the assumption that the pain inflicted by sanctions compels the target to seek accommodation with the sender is disconfirmed by the examination. Targets' motivation to seek accommodation with the EU is due less to a desire to be freed from the effects of CFSP sanctions than to the targets seeing their ambitions of economic growth frustrated by the presence of sanctions. From the targets' vantage point, the removal of sanctions opens up the possibility of enhanced investment and trade with the EU, along with the benefits they entail, which are unavailable elsewhere (Portela 2009).

This area of research, focusing on the multilateral nature of the sender, illustrates interesting dynamics, in particular in terms of how sanctions are designed, and to what extent they may be applied effectively. A promising development would be to keep exploring in detail the ways sanctions regimes imposed by different international organizations interact, or how they may inspire each other in their design and implementation.

Bridging the gap with the literature in Strategic Studies

For researchers familiar with the literature on Strategic Studies, observing the debates happening in the field of sanctions seems familiar, as many concerns are shared by authors on both sides.

Going through the academic literature about sanctions, it is striking to observe two phenomena. First, authors may use concepts developed by Strategic Studies without a complete recognition of their full implications or, second, they can describe a concept without identifying and defining it correctly. The assumed deterrent effect of sanctions perfectly exemplifies this phenomenon.

Several authors emphasize the fact that sanctions may have a deterrent effect, or try to identify the conditions for the deterrence effect to be effective. Building on Margaret Doxey's initial thoughts about the deterrent effect of sanctions (Doxey 1972), many authors acknowledge that 'the threat of sanctions is often more powerful than sanctions themselves' (Cortwright and Lopez 2002: 13). Such statements are based on a counting of case studies where deterrence is supposed to have been efficient. However, looking closely at these assumptions reveals that they rely heavily on a basic rational-actor model and do not take into account how sophisticated deterrence theories have become. The conditions described by Hovi et al. for successful sanctions are based on such a simplistic understanding of deterrence:

> Assuming that both sender and target behave rationally, there are three main possibilities. First, a threat of sanctions could fail because it is not deemed credible by the target. Second, the threat might fail because it is not sufficiently potent, meaning that the target considers sanctions, however regrettable their consequences, to be a lesser evil than yielding to the sender's demands. Finally, a threat of sanctions might fail because the target expects sanctions to be imposed regardless of whether it yields to the sender's demands.
>
> *(Hovi et al. 2005: 484–5)*

Basing the model on the assumption of both actors being rational is problematic and needs further conceptualization. Deterrence theories, as they have been developed in the field of Strategic Studies and have moved away from the assumptions of rationality, may provide such concepts for the analysis of sanctions.

But the opposite phenomenon also appears: describing a strategic concept without naming it correctly. For example, Galtung's statement that 'the central concept here is vulnerability' (Galtung 1967, 385) is very close the Clausewitzian concept of 'centre of gravity'. Clausewitz describes centres of gravity as:

> particular factors [that] can often be decisive . . . One must keep the dominant characteristics of both belligerents in mind. Out of these characteristics a certain centre of gravity develops, the hub of all power and movement, on which everything depends. That is the point against which all our energies should be directed.
>
> *(Clausewitz 1984 (1832): 595–6)*

But we should keep in mind that there may be several centres of gravity at all levels of strategy. At the tactical and operational levels, candidate centres of gravity may include certain military formations, fortifications, or strategic communication lines. But at the strategic level, a political leader can be the centre of gravity, for instance. This notion is a very powerful analytical tool but raises a series of questions concerning its implementation: 'does the enemy actually have a centre of gravity? Can the enemy's centre of gravity be identified? [. . .] Even if a centre of gravity has been correctly identified, is it always possible to put it under sufficient pressure?' (Lonsdale 2008: 45).

Those questions underline the necessity of reliable intelligence information and the specificities of each case. There may be no 'toolkit for military action' listing the enemy's centres of gravity, as the list of such centres depends on each case. In line with Galtung's observation, Crawford and Klotz identify four 'sites for potential consequences of sanctions' inside a political system: elite decision-makers, government structures, economy, and civil society (Crawford and Klotz 1999: 31). It is also the logic underpinning smart sanctions: by targeting heads of state, high-ranking officials, and some institutions (banks, for instance), the targeted state should comply more easily. However, what Strategic Studies teach us is that centres of gravity can be multiple and, more importantly, that the pressure must be applied upon the 'crucial vulnerability'. It is outside the scope of this chapter to engage in a systematic review of sanctions mechanisms in order to determine whether or not they are designed in order to put pressure effectively on the 'crucial vulnerability', but we can argue that strategic thinking during the phase of sanction design would likely increase their efficiency; it would be required during decision-making (resolution taken by the Security Council) and that of implementation by the Sanctions Committee.

The issue of senders could also benefit from a thorough analysis. By applying sanctions, sender states face a dilemma: if they send sanctions alone, how can they be sure that other states will do the same, and if they send sanctions collectively, how can they be sure that their partners will adopt an attitude as strict as theirs? The best historical example of this dilemma is given by Napoleon's attempt to make Russia comply with the 'continental blockade' he was trying to impose on Great Britain. Napoleon attacked Russia, which led to a disaster, and eventually to his loss of power a few months later. As Colin Gray emphasizes, 'allies are both a curse and a blessing' (Gray 1999: 169). Alliance theorists have for a long time identified the difficulties of being part of an alliance:

> Rigidity of organization, superpower domination, lack of consultation, domestic instability among the partners, suspicion between allies, uncertainty about the status of one's allies, doubt about the exact nature of the commitments one has entered into, the existence of acrimonious sub-groups within an alliance, disagreements about issues not concerned with the alliance, and differences about the appropriate share of burdens, influence and rewards.
>
> *(Booth 1987: 269)*

To address those problems, the answer is invariably the same: the need of mutual trust and cohesion between allies (see the chapter on alliances in this volume). Similar problems in the field of sanctions are demonstrated by the phenomenon of 'sanctions busters' (states refusing to apply sanctions to another state) which undermine the effectiveness of sanctions regimes (Early 2015).

Other issues could be covered, for example including exploiting sanctions into thinking about coercion, or drawing useful parallels between limited and total wars on the one side and targeted and comprehensive sanctions on the other (Schmitt 2012).

It is also useful to envision sanctions within the larger framework of grand strategies and the multiple objectives they can fulfil for great powers, for example as a bargaining tool: 'while great-power policy-makers will typically invoke sanctions with the stated aim of coercing a publicly designated 'target' actor, their actual goal is often to influence one another in the context of executing and advancing their respective grand strategies' (Taylor 2010: 15). Also, an interesting area of research looks at the sanctions' impact on nuclear proliferation, a classic concern in Strategic Studies (Solingen, 2012). Connecting the literature in Strategic Studies with the literature on sanctions could be an interesting theoretical development.

Conclusion

The study of international sanctions is a promising venue for understanding international security dynamics. Now that the academic debate is moving away from determining whether sanctions 'work' or not, it is possible to have a theoretically richer debate, exploring different (and more interesting) questions. This renewed approach on sanctions also has the potential to actually fulfil a long-term objective of sanctions research: policy relevance. By investigating how sanctions are actually employed, by obtaining a more nuanced understanding of their potential effects, and by integrating them within a broader range of tools of statecraft, it becomes possible to speak more directly to policy-makers' concerns.

References

Allen, S. H. (2005) 'The Determinants of Economic Sanctions Success and Failure', *International Interactions* 31(2): 117–38.

Andreas, P. (2005) 'Criminalizing Consequences of Sanctions: Embargo Busting and Its Legacy', *International Studies Quarterly* 49(2): 335–60.

Baldwin, D. A. (1985) *Economic Statecraft*, Princeton, NJ: Princeton University Press.

Baldwin, D. A. (1999/2000) 'The Sanctions Debate and the Logic of Choice', *International Security* 24(3): 80–107.

Baldwin, D. A. and Pape, R. A.(1998) 'Correspondence: Evaluating Economic Sanctions', *International Security* 23(2): 189–98.

Bianchi A. (2007) 'Assessing the Effectiveness of the UN Security Council's Anti-Terrorism Measures', *European Journal of International Law* 17(5): 881–919.

Biersteker, T., Eckert, S., Tourinho, M., and Hudáková, Z. (2013) 'The Effectiveness of United Nations Targeted Sanctions. Findings from the Targeted Sanctions Consortium', Graduate Institute of International and Development Studies Working Paper. Online. Available HTTP: <http://graduateinstitute.ch/files/live/sites/iheid/files/sites/internationalgovernance/shared/Effectiveness%20of%20UN%20Targeted%20Sanctions%20-%206.Nov.2013%20.pdf> (accessed 16 November 2015).

Booth, K. (1987) 'Alliances', in J. Baylis, K. Booth, J. Garnett, and P. Williams (eds.) *Contemporary Strategy I: Theories and Concepts*, New York: Holmes and Meier, 258–309.

Brozska, M. (2003) 'From Dumb to Smart? Recent Reforms of UN Sanctions', *Global Governance* 9(4): 519–35.

Clausewitz, C. (1984 [1832]) *On War*, Princeton, NJ: Princeton University Press.

Cortwright, D. and Lopez, D. (2000) *The Sanctions Decade; Assessing UN Strategies in the 1990s*, Boulder, CO: Lynne Rienner.

Cortwright, D. and Lopez, D. (2002) *Sanctions and the Search for Security: Challenges to UN Action*, Boulder, CO: Lynne Rienner.

Crawford, N. and Klotz, A. (eds.) (1999) *How Sanctions Work: Lessons from South Africa*, London: MacMillan.

Doxey, M. (2012) 'International Sanctions: A Framework for Analysis with Special References to the UN and Southern Africa', *International Organization* 26(3): 525–50.

Early, B. R. (1995) *Busted Sanctions: Explaining Why Economic Sanctions Fail*, Palo Alto, CA: Stanford University Press.

Elliott, K. A. (1998) 'The Sanctions Glass: Half Full or Completely Empty?', *International Security* 23(1): 50–65.

Galtung, J. (1967) 'On the Effects of International Economic Sanctions: With Examples from the Case of Rhodesia', *World Politics* 19(3): 378– 416.

Giumelli, F. (2011) *Coercing, Constraining and Signalling. Explaining UN and EU Sanctions After the Cold War*, Colchester: ECPR Press.

Graham-Brown, S. (1999) *Sanctioning Saddam*, New York: I. B. Tauris.

Gray, C. (1999) *Modern Strategy*, Oxford: Oxford University Press.

Hovi, J., Huseby, R., and Sprinz, D. (2005) 'When Do (Imposed) Economic Sanctions Work?', *World Politics* 57(4): 479–99.

Hufbauer, G. and Oegg, B. (2003) 'The European Union as an Emerging Sender of Economic Sanctions', *Aussenwirtschaft* 58(4): 547–71.

Hufbauer, G., Schott, J., and Elliott, K. (2008[1985]) *Economic Sanctions Reconsidered*, Washington, DC: Peterson Institute for International Economics.

Kryvoi, L. (2008) 'Why European Union Trade Sanctions Do Not Work', *Minnesota Journal of International Law* 17(2): 209–46.

Lonsdale, D. J. (2008) 'Strategy', in D. Jordan, J. Kiras, D. Lonsdale, I. Speller, C. Tuck, and C. Walton (eds.) *Understanding Modern Warfare*, Cambridge: Cambridge University Press, 14–63.

Marinov, N. (2005) 'Do Economic Sanctions Destabilize Country Leaders?', *American Journal of Political Science* 49(3): 564–76.

Noland, M. 'The (Non) Impact of UN Sanctions on North Korea', *Asia Policy* 7: 61–88.

Nossal, K. R. (1989) 'International Sanctions as International Punishment', *International Organization* 43(2): 301–22.

Pape, R. (1997) 'Why Economic Sanctions Do Not Work', *International Security* 22(2): 90–136.

Pape, R. (1998) 'Why Economic Sanctions Still Do Not Work', *International Security* 23(1): 66–77.

Portela, C. (2009) *European Union Sanctions and Foreign Policy: When and Why Do They Work?*, Abingdon: Routledge.

Schmitt, O. (2012) 'Thinking Strategically about Sanctions: A Research Agenda', *Paris Papers* 4, IRSEM.

Schmitt, O. (2015) 'La Coercition', in J. Henrotin, O. Schmitt, and S. Taillat (eds.) *Guerre et stratégie. Approches, concepts*, Paris: Presses Universitaires de France, 441–60.

Segall, A. (1999) 'Economic Sanctions: Legal and Policy Constraints', *International Review of the Red Cross*, No. 836.

Solingen, E. (ed.) (2012) *Sanctions, Statecraft and Nuclear Proliferation*, Cambridge: Cambridge University Press.

Taylor, B. (2010) *Sanctions as Grand Strategy*, Abingdon: Routledge.

Thielmann, G. (2010) 'The UN Sanctions' Impact on Iran's Military', *Arms Control Association*, Issue Brief 1(7), 11 June.

34

DETERRENCE

Richard Ned Lebow

Threat-based strategies have always been central to International Relations (IR). Deterrence and compellence represent efforts to conceptualize these strategies to make them more understandable in theory and more effective in practice. These efforts, which have been under way since the end of the Second World War, remain highly controversial. There is no consensus among scholars or policy-makers about the efficacy of these strategies or the conditions in which they are most appropriate.

Deterrence is a theory in IR and a strategy of conflict management. Deterrence can be defined as an attempt to influence other actors' assessment of their interests. It seeks to prevent an undesired behaviour by convincing the party who may be contemplating such an action that its cost will exceed any possible gain (Lebow 1981: 83). Deterrence presupposes decisions made in response to a rational cost-benefit calculus, a calculus that can be successfully manipulated from the outside, by increasing the cost side of the ledger. Compellence, a related strategy, uses the same tactics to attempt to convince another party to carry out some action it otherwise would not.

Deterrence has always been practised, but the advent of nuclear weapons made it imperative for policy-makers to find ways of preventing catastrophically destructive wars while exploiting any strategic nuclear advantage for political gain.

This chapter has four parts. In the first, it describes early theoretical approaches to deterrence; in the second, their application in practice; and in the third, the subsequent critique of them. After introducing the most contemporary literature in part four, the chapter concludes with a discussion of post–Cold War deterrence and recent research.

The golden age of deterrence theory

Theories of deterrence must be distinguished from the strategy of deterrence. The former address the logical postulates of deterrence and the political and psychological assumptions on which they are based; the latter the application of the theory in practice. The theory of deterrence developed as an intended guide for the strategy of deterrence.

Scholars and policy-makers became interested in deterrence following the development of the atom bomb. The first wave of theorists wrote from the late 1940s until the mid-1960s. Early publications on the subject (Brodie 1947) recognize that a war between states armed with atomic weapons could be so destructive as to negate Carl von Clausewitz's (1976: 75–89) classic description of war as a continuation of politics by other means. In 1949, the problem of deterrence gained a new urgency as the Cold War was well under way and the Soviet Union, in defiance of all US expectations, detonated its first nuclear device in October of that year. In the 1950s, often referred to as the Golden Age of deterrence, Bernard William Kaufmann (1954), Henry Kissinger (1957), and Bernard Brodie (1959), among others, developed a general approach to nuclear deterrence that stressed the necessity but difficulty of imparting credibility to threats likely to constitute national suicide. The 1960s witnessed an impressive theoretical treatment by Thomas Schelling (1966) that analysed deterrence in terms of bargaining theory, based on tacit signals.

The early literature (Brodie 1959; Kaufmann 1954; Schelling 1966) began with the assumption of fully rational actors, and was deductive in nature. It stressed the importance of defining commitments, communicating them to adversaries, developing the capability to defend them, and imparting credibility to these commitments. It explored various tactics that leaders could exploit toward this end, concentrating on the problem of credibility. This was recognized as the core problem when deterrence was practised against another nuclear adversary – and the implementation of the threats in question could entail national suicide (Jervis 1979). Thomas Schelling (1966) argued that it was rational for a leader to develop a reputation for being irrational so his threats might be believed. Richard Nixon took this advice to heart in his dealings with both the Soviet Union and North Vietnam (Kimball 1998: 76–86).

The so-called Golden Age literature focuses almost entirely on the tactics of deterrence, as do Kaufmann and Brodie, or, like Kissinger, on the force structures most likely to make deterrence credible. Thomas Schelling fits in the former category, but unlike other students of deterrence in the 1950s and 1960s he attempts to situate his understanding of tactics in a broader theory of bargaining that draws on economics and psychology. His *Strategy of Deterrence* (1960) and *Arms and Influence* (1966) are the only works on deterrence from this era that continue to be cited regularly.

In *Arms and Influence*, Schelling makes a ritual genuflection to material capabilities on the opening page, when he observes that with enough military force, a country may not need to bargain. His narrative soon makes clear that military capability is decisive in only the most asymmetrical relationships, and even then only when the more powerful party has little or nothing to lose from the failure to reach an accommodation. When the power balance is not so lopsided, or when both sides would lose from non-settlement, it is necessary to bargain. Bargaining outcomes do not necessarily reflect a balance of interests or military capabilities. Three other influences are important.

First comes *context*, which for Schelling consists of the stakes, the range of possible outcomes, the salience of those outcomes, and the ability of bargainers to commit to those outcomes. In straightforward commercial bargaining, contextual considerations may not play a decisive role. In bargaining about price, there will be a range of intervals between the opening bids of buyer and seller. If there is no established market price for the commodity, no particular outcome will have special salience. Either side can try to gain an advantage by committing itself to its preferred outcomes. Strategic bargaining between states is frequently characterized by sharp discontinuities in context. There may be a small number of possible outcomes, and the canons of international practice, recognized boundaries, prominent terrain features, or the simplicity of all-or-nothing distinctions can make one solution more salient than others. Salient solutions are easier to communicate and commit to, especially when the bargaining is tacit (Schelling 1966: 6–16).

The second consideration is *skill*. Threats to use force lack credibility if they are costly to carry out. To circumvent this difficulty, clever leaders can feign madness, develop a reputation for heartlessness, or put themselves into a position from which they cannot retreat. Other tactics can be used to discredit adversarial commitments or minimize the cost of backing away from one's own (Schelling 1960).

The third, and arguably most important, determinant of outcome is *willingness to suffer*. Paraphrasing Carl von Clausewitz, Schelling describes war as a contest of wills. Until the mid-twentieth century, force was used to bend or break an adversary's will by defeating his army and holding his population and territory hostage. Air power and nuclear weapons revolutionized warfare by allowing states to treat one another's territory, economic resources, and population as hostages from the outset of any dispute. War is no longer a contest of strength, but a contest of nerve and risk-taking, of pain and endurance. For purposes of bargaining, the ability to absorb pain counts just as much as the capability to inflict it (Clausewitz 1976: book 6, ch. 26).

Schelling does not say so, but it follows from his formulation that the capacity to absorb suffering varies just as much as the capacity to deliver it. Clausewitz recognized this variation. Increases in both capabilities, he argued, made possible the nation in arms and the revolutionary character of the Napoleonic Wars (Clausewitz 1976: 585–94). By convincing peoples that they had a stake in the outcome of the wars, first the French and then their adversaries were able to field large armies, extract the resources necessary to arm and maintain them, and elicit the extraordinary level of personal sacrifice necessary to sustain the struggle.

The Clausewitz emphasis on pain has wider implications for bargaining. The ability to suffer physical, economic, moral, or any other loss is an important source of bargaining power and can sometimes negate an adversary's power to punish. Realist approaches to bargaining tend to neglect this dimension of power and focus instead on the power to hurt and how it can be transformed into credible threats. Schelling also ignores the pain-absorption side of the power–pain equation when analysing compellence in Vietnam, an oversight that led to his misplaced optimism that Hanoi could be coerced into doing what Washington wanted. The power to punish derives only in part from material capabilities. Leaders must also have the will and freedom to use their power. Schelling observes that Genghis Khan was effective because he was not inhibited by the usual mercies. Modern civilization has generated expectations and norms that severely constrain the power to punish. The US bombing campaign in Vietnam, in many people's judgement the very antithesis of civilized behaviour, paradoxically demonstrates this truth.

Deterrence strategy

Deterrence played a central role in the US strategy in Indochina during the Johnson and Nixon administrations. Deployment of forces, the character of the engagements they sought and the level and choice of targets for bombing were never intended to defeat the National Liberation Front of South Vietnam (Viet Cong) or North Vietnam, but to compel them to end the war and accept the independence of South Vietnam. The Indochina intervention ended in disaster and helped to spawn a series of critiques of the theory and strategy of deterrence in the 1970s.

As mentioned, Vietnam paradoxically demonstrates the truth that modern civilization has generated expectations and norms that severely constrain the power to punish. The air and ground war aroused enormous opposition at home, in large part because of its barbarity, and public opinion ultimately compelled a halt to the bombing and withdrawal of US forces from Indochina. The bombing exceeded the Second World War in total tonnage, but was also more restricted. The US refrained from indiscriminate bombing of civilians, and made no effort to destroy North Vietnam's elaborate system of dykes. The use of nuclear weapons was not even considered. Restraint was a response to ethical and domestic political imperatives. Similar constraints limited US firepower in Iraq in the Gulf War of 1990–1, and enabled the Republican Guard and Saddam Hussein to escape destruction.

The ability to absorb punishment derives even less from material capabilities, and may even be inversely related to them. One of the reasons why Vietnam was less vulnerable to bombing than

Schelling and Pentagon planners supposed was its underdeveloped economy. There were fewer high-value targets to destroy or hold hostage. With fewer factories, highways, and railroads, the economy was more difficult to disrupt, and the population was less dependent on existing distribution networks for its sustenance and material support. According to North Vietnamese strategic analyst Colonel Quach Hai Luong: 'The more you bombed, the more the people wanted to fight you' (McNamara et al. 1999: 194). Department of Defense studies confirm that bombing 'strengthened, rather than weakened, the will of the Hanoi government and its people' (McNamara et al. 1999: 191, 341–2). It is apparent in retrospect that the gap between the protagonists in material and military capabilities counted for less than their differential ability to absorb punishment. The US won every battle, but lost the war because its citizens would not pay the moral, economic, and human cost of victory. Washington withdrew from Indochina after losing 58,000 American lives, a fraction of Viet Cong and North Vietnamese deaths even at conservative estimates.

A comparison between South and North Vietnam is even more revealing. The Army of the Republic of South Vietnam (ARVN) was larger and better equipped and trained than the Viet Cong or the North Vietnamese, and had all the advantages of US air power, communications, and logistics. The Republic of South Vietnam crumbled because its forces had no stomach for a fight. The Viet Cong and North Vietnamese sustained horrendous losses whenever they came up against superior US firepower, but maintained their morale and cohesion throughout the long conflict. Unlike ARVN officers and recruits, who regularly melted away under fire, more Viet Cong and North Vietnamese internalized their cause and gave their lives for it. At the most fundamental level, the Communist victory demonstrated the power of ideas and commitment.

Critiques

From the beginning, deterrence theory and strategy has spawned critiques. The most interesting are those that evaluate deterrence strategy in the light of empirical evidence from historical cases. The work of Milburn (1959), Snyder and Diesing (1977), George and Smoke (1974), Lebow (1981), and Jervis, Lebow and Stein (1984) is representative. George and Smoke recognized that challenges short of full-scale attacks – what they called 'probes' – were difficult to deter and might be instituted by adversaries to test a state's resolve. They and Milburn attempted to put deterrence into a broader context and argued that it might be made a more efficacious strategy if threats of punishment were accompanied by promises of rewards for acceptable behaviour.

An important distinction must further be made between general and immediate deterrence (Morgan 1983). *General deterrence* is based on the existing power relationship and attempts to prevent an adversary from seriously considering any kind of military challenge because of its expected adverse consequences. *Immediate deterrence* is specific; it attempts to forestall an anticipated challenge to a well-defined and publicized commitment. Immediate deterrence is practised when general deterrence is thought to be failing. It is almost impossible to know when general deterrence succeeds because non-action by a target state can be the result of many reasons, including any lack of intention to use force. Because cases of immediate deterrence success and failure are somewhat easier to identify, most research has sought to explain their outcomes. Analyses of immediate deterrence that ignore its relationship to general deterrence offer a biased assessment of its success rate and an incomplete picture of the conditions and processes that account for its outcome.

For many years, however, empirical research on deterrence, whether qualitative or quantitative, drew primarily on cases of immediate, conventional deterrence. Empirical studies of immediate deterrence are surrounded by considerable controversy in the absence of compelling evidence about the intentions and calculations of the leaders of target states (Huth and Russett 1984, 1988; Lebow and Stein 1990). Beginning in the late 1980s, evidence on Soviet and

Chinese foreign policy began to become available, and it became possible for the first time to reconstruct critical Soviet–US and Sino-US deterrence encounters and to make some observations about the role of general deterrence in these relationships. It transpired that there had been striking differences among leaders on opposing sides about who was practising deterrence and who was deterred. In many so-called deterrence encounters (Garthoff 1989; Lebow and Stein 1990), both sides considered themselves the deterrer. This is often due to different interpretations of the status quo. In the Cuban missile crisis (Lebow and Stein 1994), Khrushchev understood the secret Soviet missile deployment in Cuba to be part and parcel of his attempt to deter a US invasion of Cuba. Kennedy and his advisors interpreted the deployment as a radical and underhand effort to upset the strategic status quo.

Immediate deterrence

From cases such as these, Janice Gross Stein and Richard Ned Lebow (Jervis, Lebow and Stein 1984; Lebow 1981; Lebow and Stein 1987) developed an extensive critique of immediate deterrence with three interlocking components: political, psychological, and operational. The political component concerns the motivation behind foreign policy challenges. Deterrence is unabashedly a theory of 'opportunity'. Adversaries are assumed to seek opportunities to make gains and pounce when they find them. Case studies of historical conflicts point to an alternative explanation for challenges, including resorts to force, which Lebow and Stein term a theory of 'need'. Strategic vulnerabilities and domestic political needs can push leaders into acting aggressively. Khrushchev's Cuban missile deployment, to cite one instance, was motivated by his perceived need to protect Cuba and offset US strategic superiority, and his anger at Kennedy for deploying missiles in Turkey – making him look weak in the eyes of hardliners (Lebow and Stein 1994: 19–66). When leaders become desperate, they may resort to force even when the military balance is unfavourable and there are no grounds for doubting adversarial resolve. Deterrence may be an inappropriate and provocative strategy in these circumstances.

The psychological component is also related to the motivation behind deterrence challenges. To the extent that policy-makers believe in the necessity of challenging the commitments of their adversaries, they become predisposed to see their objectives as attainable. When this happens, motivated bias can be pronounced and take the form of distorted threat assessments and insensitivity to warnings that the policies to which our leaders are committed are likely to end in disaster. Policy-makers can convince themselves, despite evidence to the contrary, that they can challenge an important adversarial commitment without provoking war. Because they know the extent to which they are powerless to back down, they expect their adversaries to accommodate them by doing so. To continue with our Cuban missile crisis example, Khrushchev brushed aside the advice of top political and diplomatic advisors who warned him that the missiles would be discovered before they were operational and would provoke a serious crisis with the US. He sought refuge instead in promises of marginal military officials with little knowledge of Cuba or US intelligence capabilities (Lebow and Stein 1994: 67–93).

The practical component highlights the distorting effects of cognitive biases and heuristics, political and cultural barriers to empathy, and the differing cognitive contexts that the deterrer and would-be challengers are apt to use to frame and interpret signals. Problems of this kind are not unique to deterrence; they are embedded in the very structure of IR. They nevertheless constitute particularly severe impediments to deterrence because of a deterrer's need to understand the world as it appears to the leaders of a would-be challenger in order to manipulate effectively its cost–benefit calculus. Failure to do this in the desired direction can make the proscribed behaviour more attractive to a challenger. In the case of Cuba, Kennedy's deployment of Jupiter missiles in Turkey and his warnings that under some circumstances the US would not hesitate to strike first, given its strategic nuclear advantage, were intended to moderate Khrushchev, but instead convinced him of the even greater costs to the Soviet Union of remaining passive in the face of these US threats. Kennedy, in turn, had made these threats because of Khrushchev's brow-beating of him at the Vienna summit and threats to the Western position in Berlin (Lebow and Stein 1994: 19–50). The missile crisis was, in effect, the product of a series of escalating threats and actions by both sides, each attempting unsuccessfully to deter the other.

General nuclear deterrence

Research on the Cuban missile crisis, the Soviet–US crisis arising out of the 1973 Middle East War, and the two Taiwan Straits crises of 1954 and 1958 tend to confirm the findings of critics of conventional deterrence. So does research on general nuclear deterrence. Based on the study of Soviet–US relations in the Khrushchev and Brezhnev eras, Lebow and Stein offer the follow-ing conclusions about the role of general nuclear deterrence: (1) Leaders who try to exploit real or imagined nuclear advantages for political gain are not likely to succeed; (2) Credible nuclear threats are very difficult to make; (3) Nuclear threats are fraught with risk; (4) Strategic buildups are more likely to provoke than to restrain adversaries, because of their impact on the domestic balance of political power in the target state; (5) Nuclear deterrence is robust when leaders on both sides fear war and are aware of each other's fears.

We must distinguish between the reality and the strategy of nuclear deterrence. The former, at least in the case of the Cold War, led to self-deterrence, as leaders on both sides were horrified by the prospects of a nuclear conflict. Not knowing of each other's fears, or refusing to acknowl-edge them, both superpowers practised the strategy of deterrence with a vengeance. This entailed arms buildups, forward deployments, and threatening rhetoric, often in combination. Practised this way, the strategy of deterrence was responsible for the series of crises that escalated to the Cuban missile crisis, where both sides stepped down from the brink and sought to reassure their adversary (Lebow and Stein 1994: 348–68).

Zhang (1992) and Lebow and Stein (1994) further find that deterrers do worry about their reputations and the credibility of commitments, but that the targets of deterrence rarely question their adversary's resolve. For this reason, efforts to communicate resolve were often perceived as gratuitously aggressive behaviour and sometimes provoked the kind of challenges they were designed to prevent. In doing so, the strategy of deterrence helped to provoke the Cuban missile and Taiwan Straits crises and to prolong the Soviet–US and Sino-US conflicts.

End of the Cold War

The end of the Cold War, accompanied by the opening of the archives of the participants, brought another wave of reassessment. No consensus has emerged, but the issues have been clarified and enriched by much new evidence. The debate about deterrence has also extended beyond conflict management to conflict resolution. Supporters of former US President Ronald Reagan, and conservatives more generally, credit Reagan's arms buildup and the Strategic Defense Initiative (Star Wars) with ending the Cold War. They are alleged to have brought the Soviet Union to its senses and provided strong incentives for it to seek an accommodation with the US (Matlock 1995). According to this thinking, Gorbachev and his advisors became con-vinced that they could not compete with the US and ought to negotiate the best deal they could before Soviet power declined even further (Davis and Wohlforth 2004). Western liberals, former Soviet policy-makers, and many scholars attribute the end of the Cold War to 'New Thinking' and the political transformation it brought about within the Soviet leadership. Gorbachev, they contend, considered the Cold War dangerous and a waste of resources, and sought to end it to bring the Soviet Union back into Europe, facilitate political reform at home, and free resources for domestic development (Brown 1996; English 2000; Herrmann 2004; Levesque 1997).

These contending interpretations base their respective assertions on very different kinds of arguments. Those who credit the Reagan arms buildup with ending the Cold War build their case entirely on inference. The arms buildup is supposed to have signalled resolve to Moscow, and convinced rational Soviet leaders to make the concessions necessary to end the Cold War. No evidence is offered to indicate that Gorbachev and his advisors were influenced by this logic. Those who assert Gorbachev's eagerness to end the Cold War, and to make some important one-sided concessions toward that end, offer considerable evidence in support of their contentions based on records of discussions among Soviet leaders, including notes of Politburo meetings, interviews with Gorbachev and his principal advisors between 1986 and 1992, and interviews with former Eastern European officials reporting their discussions with the Soviet leadership. In any court, evidence trumps inference, so for the moment at least, the liberal claims that changing ideas were the catalyst for the Cold War's end are more credible than the conservative assertion that it was a growing differential in power between the superpowers.

Contemporary deterrence and compellence

The contemporary debate is far more international than it was during the Cold War, in part because there are more nuclear powers. There are also more targets for deterrence, among them North Korea, Iran, the Arab states for Israel, Israel for Iran, India and Pakistan for each other, and a large and growing number of non-state organizations deemed terrorists by those they struggle against. Most of these states have, or are seeking, nuclear weapons. Deterrence has also been extended beyond the domain of violent warfare to include cyber-attacks. Finally, the literature on deterrence has been enriched with studies by Indian, Pakistani, and Chinese scholars and military think-tanks.

The big question for scholars may not be whether deterrence helped to prevent a Third World War, but why and how officials and academics in both superpowers who convinced themselves that it was necessary confirmed this belief tautologically. Reputable scholars routinely claim that nuclear weapons kept the peace between India and China and promote more peace generally (see Sagan and Waltz 1995 for a debate). As in the Cold War, what theorists and analysts say about deterrence often reveals more about their ideological assumptions and their country's strategic culture than it does about the nature and efficacy of threat-based strategies.

During the Cold War, the theory and practice of deterrence and compellence focused on making credible threats on the assumption that they were necessary to moderate adversaries. Self-deterrence – the unwillingness of actors to assume the risks and costs of using force independently of efforts by others to deter them – received little attention or credence. Subsequent research (Lebow and Stein 1994; Paul 2009) suggests that self-deterrence was more important than deterrent policies of adversaries. It was a product of fear of nuclear war and a growing tradition of non-use that became increasingly costly to violate.

Self-deterrence is more evident in the post-Cold War era. In Somalia, the US withdrew its forces after losing eighteen US Army Rangers. In Rwanda, genocidal Hutus deterred Western intervention by killing ten Belgian soldiers. In Bosnia, compellence clearly failed against Milosevic, who continued his policy of ethnic cleansing of Albanians in Kosovo despite Western threats. Pushed by Western public opinion, NATO finally screwed up its courage to intervene, but then failed to go after known war criminals because of the vulnerability of its lightly armed forces, whose primary mission was the distribution of aid (Freedman 2004: 124–5). Self-deterrence also kept the Western powers from intervening in Syria or taking a harder line against Russia in the Ukraine crisis.

There are important lessons here and they have not been widely examined by theorists of threat-based strategies. One of the most important has to do with the ability to inflict pain versus the willingness to suffer it. As we observed, Schelling and US policy-makers ignored the latter in Indochina, concentrating only on how much damage they could inflict on North Vietnam and the Viet Cong. The US lost the war because its Vietnamese opponents were willing to accept far more suffering than the American people. This phenomenon is equally apparent in Afghanistan and Iraq, where it compelled withdrawal of US and other foreign forces. Emanuel Adler (2009) rightly observes that weaker states draw in more powerful states, whose leaders feel the need to demonstrate resolve and carry out military action toward that end. Their intervention and the collateral damage it causes mobilizes support for the weaker state while generating opposition to the more powerful one. Frost and Lebow (under review) refer to these situations as 'ethical traps', and theorize the conditions under which they are successfully set or self-inflicted.

In the West, deterrence theorists have thoughtfully begun to consider the implications of deterrence in a complex world where there are more nuclear powers, where the rationality assumption may not always be applicable, where many conflicts are chronic rather than acute, and where there are chemical and biological weapons to consider in addition to conventional and nuclear ones (Morgan and Paul 2009; Paul et al. 2009).

On the whole, however, the focus of deterrence has turned away from restraining large state actors with nuclear weapons to smaller, so-called 'rogue' states or non-state actors. Excellent work has been done on why states seek to acquire nuclear weapons and why some have discontinued ongoing nuclear programmes (Hymans 2006; Solingen 2007). The US and its European allies sought to deter Iraq, Iran, and North Korea from developing or testing nuclear weapons – or, alternatively, to compel them to give up their existing programmes. Deterrence may have prevented Iraq from going nuclear, but did not work in North Korea. A principal question now is how to deal with nuclear-armed states that reject the international order (Harvey and James 2009; Paul et al. 2009; Davis and Pfaltzgraff 2013; Tan 2013). There is widespread recognition that deterrence is much more difficult in these cases because outside threats are not adequate in light of domestic and perceived security reasons for proliferation, and that threats might make these weapons more attractive.

Since 11 September 2001, there has been an ongoing debate about the applicability of deterrence to the problem of terrorism. Libya, North Korea, and Iran have been the major targets of US pressure because of their support of terrorism and pursuit or funding of nuclear weapons programmes. Efforts have also been made to deter non-state actors, notably Palestinians, Kurds, and so-called terrorist organizations like al-Qaida (Barr 2012; Cohen 2012; Romano 2012; Wehling 2012). One of the emerging conclusions is that it is impossible to deter terrorists who are willing to give up their lives but that it may be possible to reduce overall terrorism by deterrence that promises other kinds of punishment and is coupled with non-coercive efforts to reduce some of its incentives (Stein 2012).

Conclusion and promising areas of research

Two concluding observations are in order. The first grows out of the record of deterrence and compellence during the Cold War and its aftermath. These conflicts suggest that the political and psychological dynamics governing cost estimates and relative willingness to bear the costs of military action remain the critical consideration for leaders contemplating the use of threat-based strategies and their probability of success or failure. Much important research can be done in this connection, especially in conflicts that pit highly developed industrial powers, with a low tolerance for loss of life, against weaker, less developed, more traditional countries where honour remains important and death in combat or by suicide missions is more acceptable (Paul et al. 2009).

The second concerns the general efficacy of deterrence as a strategy. Its many drawbacks do not mean that it should be discarded. Rather, scholars and statesmen must recognize the limits and inherent unpredictability of deterrence and make greater use of other strategies of conflict prevention and management. Deterrence can sometimes be used more effectively when combined with other strategies that offer rewards for what is regarded as acceptable behaviour and aim to remove some of the grievances that give rise to proliferation or terrorism.

References

Adler, E. (2009) 'Complex Deterrence in the Asymmetric-Warfare Era', in T. V. Paul, P. M. Morgan, and J. Wirtz (eds.) *Complex Deterrence: Strategy in the Global Age*, Chicago: University of Chicago Press, 85–108.

Barr, S. (2012) 'Deterrence of Palestinian Terrorism: The Israeli Experience', in A. Wenger and A. Wilner (eds.) *Deterring Terrorism: Theory and Practice*, Stanford, CA: Stanford University, 205–27.

Brodie, B. (1947) 'The Absolute Weapon: Atomic Power and World Order', *Bulletin of the Atomic Scientists* 3: 150–5.

Brodie, B. (1959) 'The Anatomy of Deterrence', *World Politics* 11(2): 173–92.

Brown, A. (1996) *The Gorbachev Factor*, Oxford: Oxford University Press.

Clausewitz, C. (1976[1832]) *On War*, trans. and ed. by M. Howard and P. Paret, Princeton, NJ: Princeton University Press.

Cohen, M. (2012) 'Mission Impossible? Influencing Iranian and Libyan Sponsorship of Terrorism', in A. Wenger and A. Wilner (eds.) *Deterring Terrorism: Theory and Practice*, Stanford, CA: Stanford University Press, 251–72.

Davis, J. and Pfaltzgraff, R. Jr (2013) *Anticipating a Nuclear Iran: Challenges for US Security*, New York: Columbia University Press.

Davis, J. and Wohlforth, W. (2004) 'German Unification', in R. K. Herrmann and R. N. Lebow (eds) *Ending the Cold War: Interpretations, Causation, and the Study of International Relations*, New York: Palgrave, 131–57.

English, R. D. (2000) *Russia and the Idea of the West: Gorbachev, Intellectuals and the End of the Cold War*, New York: Columbia University Press.

Freedman, L. (2004) *Deterrence*, Cambridge: Polity Press.

Frost, M. and Lebow, R. N. (under review), 'Ethical Traps in International Relations'.

Garthoff, R. (1989[1987]) *Reflections on the Cuban Missile Crisis*, Washington, DC: Brookings Institution.

George, A. L. and Smoke, R. (1974) *Deterrence in American Foreign Policy: Theory and Practice*, New York: Columbia University Press.

Harvey, F. and James, P. (2009) 'Deterrence and Compellence in Iraq, 1991–2003: Lessons for a Complex Paradigm' , in T. V. Paul, P. M. Morgan, and J. Wirtz (eds.) *Complex Deterrence: Strategy in the Global Age*, Chicago: University of Chicago Press, 222–58.

Herrmann, R. K. (2004) 'Learning from the End of the Cold War,' in R. K. Herrmann and R. N. Lebow (eds.) *Ending the Cold War*, New York: Palgrave-Macmillan, 219–38.

Huth, P. and Russett, B. (1984) 'What Makes Deterrence Work? Cases from 1900 to 1980' , *World Politics* 36(4): 496–526.

Huth, P. and Russett, B. (1988) 'Deterrence Failure and Crisis Escalation', *International Studies Quarterly* 32: 29–46.

Hymans, J. E. (2006) *The Psychology of Nuclear Proliferation: Identity, Emotions, and Foreign Policy*, Cambridge: Cambridge University Press.

Jervis, R. (1979) 'Deterrence Theory Revisited,' *World Politics* 31(2): 289–324.

Jervis, R., Lebow, R. N., and Stein, J. G. (1984) *Psychology and Deterrence*, Baltimore, MD: Johns Hopkins University Press.

Kaufmann, W. W. (1954) *The Requirements of Deterrence*, Princeton, NJ: Center of International Studies.

Kimball, J. (1998) *Nixon's Vietnam War*, Lawrence: University Press of Kansas.

Kissinger, H. (1957) *Nuclear Weapons and Foreign Policy*, New York: Harper.

Lebow, R. N. (1981) *Between Peace and War: The Nature of International Crisis*, Baltimore, MD: Johns Hopkins University Press.

Lebow, R. N. and Stein, J. G. (1987) 'Beyond Deterrence', *Journal of Social Issues* 43(4): 5–71.

Lebow, R. N. and Stein, J. G. (1990) 'Deterrence: The Elusive Dependent Variable', *World Politics* 42(3): 336–69.

Lebow, R. N. and Stein, J. G. (1994) *We All Lost the Cold War*, Princeton, NJ: Princeton University Press.

Levesque, J. (1997) *The Enigma of 1989: The USSR and the Liberation of Eastern Europe*, Berkeley: University of California Press.

Matlock, J. (1995) *Autopsy on an Empire: The American Ambassador's Account of the Collapse of the Soviet Union*, New York: Random House.

McNamara, R., Blight, J. G., and Brigham, R. K. (1999) *Argument without End: In Search of Answers to the Vietnam Tragedy*, New York: Public Affairs.

Milburn, T. W. (1959) 'What Constitutes Effective Deterrence?', *Journal of Conflict Resolution* 3: 138–46.

Morgan, P. M. (1983[1977]) *Deterrence: A Conceptual Analysis*, Beverly Hills, CA: Sage Library of Social Science.

Morgan, P. M. and Paul, T. V. (2009) 'Deterrence among the Great Powers in an Era of Globalization', in T. V. Paul, P. M. Morgan, and J. Wirtz (eds.) *Complex Deterrence: Strategy in the Global Age*, Chicago: University of Chicago Press, 259–76.

Paul, T. V. (2009) *The Tradition of Non-Use of Nuclear Weapons*, Stanford, CA: Stanford University Press.

Paul, T. V., Morgan, P. M., and Wirtz, J. (eds.) (2009) *Complex Deterrence: Strategy in the Global Age*, Chicago: University of Chicago Press.

Romano, D. (2012) 'Turkish and Iranian Efforts to Deter Turkish Attacks', in A. Wenger and A. Wilner (eds.) *Deterring Terrorism: Theory and Practice*, Stanford, CA: Stanford University Press, 228–50.

Sagan, S. and Waltz, K. (1995) *The Spread of Nuclear Weapons: A Debate*, New York: W. W. Norton.

Schelling, T. (1960) *The Strategy of Conflict*, Cambridge, MA: Harvard University Press.

Schelling, T. (1966) *Arms and Influence*, New Haven, CT: Yale University Press.

Snyder, G. H. and Diesing, P. (1977) *Conflict among Nations: Bargaining, Decision Making, and System Structure*, Princeton, NJ: Princeton University Press.

Solingen, E. (2007) *Nuclear Logics: Contrasting Paths in East Asia and the Middle East*, Cambridge: Cambridge University Press.

Stein, J. G. (2012) 'Deterring Terrorism, Not Terrorists', in A. Wenger and A. Wilner (eds.) *Deterring Terrorism: Theory and Practice*, Stanford, CA: Stanford University Press, 46–66.

Tan, E. (2013) *The US Versus the North Korean Nuclear Threat: Mitigating the Nuclear Security Dilemma*, New York: Routledge.

Wehling, F. (2012) 'A Toxic Cloud of Mystery: Lessons from Iraq for Deterring CBRN Terrorism', in A. Wenger and A. Wilner (eds.) *Deterring Terrorism: Theory and Practice*, Stanford, CA: Stanford University Press, 273–300.

Wenger, A. and Wilner, A. (eds.) (2012) *Deterring Terrorism: Theory and Practice*, Stanford, CA: Stanford University Press.

Zhang, S. H. (1992) *Deterrence and Strategic Culture: Chinese-American Confrontations, 1949–1958*, Ithaca, NY: Cornell University Press.

35

NUCLEAR
NON-PROLIFERATION

Wilfred Wan

The Nuclear Non-Proliferation Treaty (NPT) has served as the centrepiece for global nuclear governance since opening for signatures in 1968. Regulating an issue that stands at the core of security considerations, the treaty counter-intuitively has become one of the most long-lasting and widely adhered-to cooperative arrangements at the international level. At the same time, the nuclear landscape is rife with challenges, with 'legacies, reiterations, or reincarnations of problems that the regime has failed over many years to tackle effectively' (Johnson 2010: 429). These include twin issues of security and safety, non-compliance sagas in Iran and North Korea (the latter still unresolved), and the lingering status of treaty non-parties. The inability of parties to reach consensus on a final document at the 2015 Treaty Review Conference suggests fundamental discord with the arrangement. How do we reconcile this image of a troubled and long-ineffective non-proliferation campaign with its longevity, and what does it mean for its future?

This chapter examines the NPT regime's place in the global security order. It has four parts. First, it parses the International Relations (IR) literature for varying perspectives on the regime's contributions to preventing proliferation. Second, it synthesizes existing empirical analyses of this security arrangement, with particular attention devoted to how different scholars and analysts measure its successes and failures. Taking stock of past challenges, the chapter then links the evolution of the regime to changes in the character of proliferation itself in a third part. It argues that the proliferation pathways in the post-Cold War era require more drastic action on the part of the international community – some of which has already taken place. In the fourth part, I argue that the character of nuclear governance must evolve if it is to remain effective at combating proliferation, and include instruments that are more flexible, more focused, and more regionalized.

Preventing proliferation in theory

Despite the durability and prominence of the NPT, there remains a spectrum of opinions – and a healthy dose of scepticism – regarding its impact over state nuclear decision-making. For some, the treaty is a massive success, as fears of widespread proliferation and nuclear chain reactions from the 1950s and 1960s have proved unfounded. For others, it is insignificant, a largely hollow document with no direct impact in modifying state behaviour. The absence of a strong empirical foundation linking the regime to nuclear decisions compounds the difficulties of judgement in either direction. This discussion links to a broader theoretical debate in political science regarding the power and limitations of international institutions.

Existing explanations for nuclearization have been grounded in the major approaches in IR. How each school of thought generally perceives international institutions filters down to how they do – and would – define the role of the NPT regime. Realists point to the assurance provided to states, albeit temporary, that their neighbours will refrain from proliferating. Neoliberal institutionalists highlight the rules in place to govern all nuclear programmes. Constructivists underline the normative movement that has seen such weapons defined as unacceptable. Meanwhile, domestic approaches offer explanations as to why particular states might be more or less susceptible to the above influences, while supply-side analyses shed light as to the technical dimension of nuclear policy.

Realism

The conventional explanation for proliferation is informed by realist theory. From this view, states pursued the ultimate weapon in order to secure their survival in a world characterized by competition, uncertainty, and anarchy. With self-help as the guiding principle of state behaviour, stronger states would logically seek to develop their own weapons capabilities, while weaker states – faced with more limited choices – would seek out alliances with nuclear powers, as means of access to extended deterrence. The security-based model of nuclear motivation views the NPT as a tool that can mitigate deterrence strategies among the non-nuclear-weapon states. After all, the arrangement granted each state greater assurances that their neighbours would refrain from weapons capabilities, so long as they did the same (Sagan 1996).[1]

This rationalistic interpretation of the NPT jibed with the expectations of neorealist scholars who focused on the role of external threats in determining state behaviour. Yet the NPT only represents a temporary solution. The underlying assumption of anarchy and the primacy placed on state security imposes inherent limitations on the ability of any arms control agreement to affect long-term state behaviour. The credibility of any commitment must be questioned, as 'at the very core of realism lies the notion that friends today may become enemies tomorrow' (Hymans 2006: 456). From this security-centric approach, proliferation is ultimately not just inevitable, but rational.

The realist school of thought would also call into question the independent standing of the treaty and regime altogether. The two-class system established by the NPT, the general inattention to the issue of nuclear disarmament, and the increasingly stringent safeguards agreements placed upon non-nuclear-weapon states suggest that the arrangement stands as a mere extension of Western power, an instrument with which strong states can perpetuate the status quo. Any impact the NPT has in preventing states from nuclearizing therefore represents not institutional effects but hegemonic ones: coercion by other means. Ultimately, from the realist perspective, security considerations serve as the driving force to nuclear decision-making, with institutions secondary (Hecker 2010; Mearsheimer 1994; Paul 2000).

Neoliberal institutionalism

The import of security arrangements such as the NPT regime figures more prominently in neoliberal institutionalism. Scholars from this school rejected the vision of the world presented by realists, positing that the character of anarchy and the resulting predominance of self-help strategies could be tempered. While strategic considerations remain at the centre of state decision-making, this perspective highlights the role of institutions in preventing conflict 'by facilitating secure and equitable agreements' (Jervis 1999: 50). Central to their impact was the idea that state interactions were not one-offs, with the expectation of repeated and continuous interactions. This iterative element – the 'shadow of the future' – provided incentive for parties to engage in long-term, meaningful cooperation (Axelrod and Keohane 1985).

While again offering a rationalistic perspective, a neoliberal institutionalist approach would note the positive externalities of the NPT regime.[2] Regular review conferences and preparatory committees lower transaction costs for the discussion of nuclear issues, while providing information about policy preferences of state signatories. The safeguards agreements under the International Atomic Energy Agency (IAEA) comprise a critical information system, compliance monitoring, and defection detection mechanisms, while its board of governors and the UN Security Council are tasked to enforce them. The treaty's explicit rules and guidelines offer consistency for member-states, perpetuating shared expectations about non-proliferation, disarmament, and nuclear energy, constraining behaviour as a result (Keohane 1982; Koremenos, Lipson, and Snidal 2001; Lipson 1984).

Yet, for these myriad benefits offered by the NPT regime, the direct impact it has on nuclear policy remains uncertain. Some argue that state decisions to nuclearize (or not) are made independently of the treaty, with membership in and compliance with the regime as symptoms rather than causes of policy. For instance, domestic considerations and hegemonic coercion represent potential determinants of subsequent state decisions vis-à-vis the NPT (Solingen 2007). That systematic empirical evidence to date has been limited to a dichotomous treatment of the regime (defined by treaty membership) has proved especially problematic for neoliberal institutionalism. How the presence of rules and the promise of benefits actually alter incentive structures for and against nuclearization remains severely understudied (Rublee 2008; Sagan 2011).

Constructivism

It was with the constructivist approach that scholars departed altogether from the rationalistic treatment of international institutions. The sociological prism at its heart shifts attention to non-material factors in explaining state decision-making. Institutions such as the NPT regime must not be looked at as state creations, subject to the whims of great powers, nor as standing completely on their own, but as a phenomenon that reflects and perpetuates the shared beliefs and collective identity of member states. These entities also actively produce information: offering classifications, fixing meanings, and diffusing norms – all of which helps to develop and extend their cognitive frameworks further (Barnett and Finnemore 1999; Finnemore and Sikkink 1998; Johnston 2001).

This perspective underscores the role of the NPT regime in the diffusion of 'deeper norms and shared beliefs about what actions are legitimate and appropriate' (Sagan 1996: 73). Current views about nuclear weapons date to the aftermath of Hiroshima and Nagasaki, as a host of anti-nuclear grassroots movements emerged to shape public discourse about the use of nuclear weapons. These views in turn filtered into national security postures and operational policies in the 1950s and 1960s, with the Cuban Missile Crisis a pivotal event in this process. Policy-makers came to regard nuclear weapons as inherently different from other types of weapons, not just unconventional but altogether unethical. The possibility of horizontal proliferation was therefore viewed as highly undesirable. US–Soviet arms controls agreements and test bans in the midst of the Cold War reflected the emerging taboo, eventually leading to the NPT.

The significance of the NPT regime thus centres on the 'internalized belief among its participants that [nuclear weapons are] illegitimate and abhorrent' (Tannenwald 2007: 334). The centrepiece treaty simply prohibits states from moving towards nuclearization. Recent review conferences have specified that non-parties India, Pakistan, and Israel can accede to the treaty *only* as non-nuclear-weapon states, thus protecting the NPT's delegitimization of nuclear weapons. Regime components such as the Nuclear Suppliers Group, the IAEA safeguards agreements, and the Convention on the Physical Protection of Nuclear Material uphold these beliefs by regulating transfers of nuclear-related technologies and equipment even for peaceful usage. It is in the context of this environment that state nuclear decision-making takes place (Rublee 2009).

Domestic considerations

Another thread of the proliferation literature weighs the primacy of domestic political consid-erations in decision-making. Scholars in this tradition look to those actors with, or seeking to retain, political power. They pinpoint bureaucrats within the scientific-military-industrial com-plex, coalitions seeking greater integration into the global political economy, even individual leaders and their unique personalities and psychologies. Notably, these domestic-oriented per-spectives do not discount the impact of external threats, of global norms, or of international institutions. Rather, the domestic political context serves as a critical prism that determines the degree to which the aforementioned variables affect nuclear decisions (Fuhrmann and Li 2008; Hymans 2012; Liberman 2001; Solingen 2007).

The domestic politics approach thus interprets state support for the NPT regime as a corol-lary of those considerations. Yet, the perspective does not preclude a causal role for the regime in nuclear policy. On the contrary, the treaty's long life has created 'a well-placed elite in the foreign and defense ministries with considerable bureaucratic and personal interests in maintaining the regime' (Sagan 1996: 72). The same is true in the technical arena, given the extensive safeguards and export controls systems that comprise the regime's main enforcement mechanism. A move to proliferate for any leader or ruling group jeopardizes political support from these sources. Additionally, the regime's health can itself shape domestic debate, its strength providing additional justification for actors inclined towards internationalizing to forgo the nuclear option.

Supply-side: an additional perspective

All of the works above coalesce around one question: what are the driving forces behind state decisions to nuclearize (or not)? These authors engage in demand-side analyses, parsing the nature of political will. A second set of works in the proliferation literature centres on supply-side considerations, examining the opportunities that state actors have to follow through and obtain such weapons. These works have been primarily quantitative in nature. They offer measurements of technical capability both in terms of domestic capacity and international assistance. Notably, supply-side studies – what Hymans (2014) terms *techno-centric analyses* – do not claim to present the entire picture. As with the domestic approach, the state of affairs on the supply-side may merely increase or decrease actors' receptivity to external factors.

Works informed by the supply-side approach offer a unique reading of the NPT regime. After all, some argue that 'the diffusion of nuclear knowledge and technology eases opportunity barriers to the proliferation of programmes and nuclear weapons' (Jo and Gartzke 2007: 186). Given the 'inalienable right' to pursue nuclear energy outlined by the NPT, that parties are pledged 'to facilitate … the fullest possible exchange of equipment, materials and scientific and technological information' may in fact be enough to foster proliferation as well (*Treaty on the Non-Proliferation of Nuclear Weapons* 1968: Article IV.2). However, not enough evidence exists to confirm this relationship. For some, the link applies only with the provision of sensitive nuclear assistance – the type strictly prohibited by the NPT.[3] Others suggest that even general forms of nuclear aid would suffice. Whether the treaty has facilitated even that, and lived up to its grand bargain, provides another point of contention (Fuhrmann 2009).

Nuclear governance is rarely the focal point of the proliferation literature. But by parsing explanations for state nuclear decision-making, we can see the openings granted to the international community to prevent nuclearization. In the next section, I consider how scholars and analysts interpret the arrangement's place in nuclear governance, and define the successes and failures of the regime aimed to prevent nuclear proliferation.

Preventing proliferation in practice

That the NPT regime has been discussed in the proliferation literature has not translated to a wealth of empirical studies. Reflective of this is the lack of clear delineation even of the regime's boundaries. As mentioned, some scholars implicitly equate membership in the NPT regime to membership in the NPT. Others focus on related treaties and agreements, guiding principles, or themes (e.g. energy, disarmament, regional zones, etc.). The definitional ambiguity has hindered the ability of works to talk to one another. The fact is that the NPT regime encompasses all of these items, its fluidity being a byproduct of the lack of a singular, permanent organizational apparatus. The treaty – in terms of both Article content and underlying normative elements – stands as the consensus core component around which all linkage exists.[4]

Regime successes

While few espouse the NPT regime as an unqualified success, those who herald its achievements do settle on some common themes, covering the range of theoretical approaches discussed above. Focusing on proliferation outcomes, they refer to the general lack of new nuclear states in the past four decades: just Israel, India, Pakistan, and North Korea. This modest increase is significant in light of widespread predictions in the 1950s and 1960s that the number of nuclear-weapon states could reach as high as fifteen to twenty (expressed most famously by John F. Kennedy). Proponents also refer to the number of states that at one point considered the nuclear option but chose to abstain, including Brazil, Japan, and Egypt, among others. The overall proliferation rate is especially impressive given the presence of thirty to forty nuclear latent states in the post-Cold War era.[5]

NPT supporters also highlight its persistence, reach, and structure. The treaty is the most widespread arms control agreement in existence, with no comparable global nuclear convention or treaty, and provides the legal foundation for a vast network of supply restraints and export controls. Only 12 of the 184 non-nuclear-weapon states do not have comprehensive safeguards agreements with the IAEA in force (as required by the NPT), and 7 of those 12 have signed agreements. The NPT's near-universality 'is truly extraordinary' given the nature of the bargain and the unequal status granted to non-nuclear-weapon states (Miller 2007: 50). Supporters refer to the indefinite extension and strengthened review process that emerged in 1995. IAEA growth, the Comprehensive Test Ban Treaty, and nuclear-weapon-free zones further demonstrate the extension of goals and principles outlined in the NPT.

For proponents of the NPT then, the July 2015 conclusion of the Joint Comprehensive Plan of Action (JCPOA) between the permanent five members of the UN Security Council plus Germany (P5 + 1) and Iran reflects the sum of its various contributions, a 'crucial test' that the NPT regime has evidently finally passed (Shaffer 2003). Back in 2002 and 2003, it was a series of IAEA inspections and queries that raised questions about the veracity of

Tehran's past declarations as treaty party. International pressure then led Iran to suspend its uranium and enrichment activities, and to negotiate and implement an Additional Protocol. When Iran ceased cooperation with the IAEA after diplomatic progress stalled in 2005, the Board of Governors adopted a resolution that found Tehran to be in non-compliance with its safeguards agreement. The subsequent referral of the case to the Security Council in 2006 paved the way for the imposition of the expansive sanctions regime credited with eventually bringing Tehran back to the negotiating table under President Hassan Rouhani (Monshipouri and Dorraj 2013). That the JCPOA ultimately reinstates the Additional Protocol underscores the centrality of the NPT's verification, monitoring, and enforcement mechanisms in the resolution of the Iranian case.

Besides such institutional features, proponents of the NPT underscore its normative contributions. The nature of discourse, attitude, and behaviours around nuclear weapons has been irrevocably altered because of the treaty's impact on the costs and benefits of nuclearization. One prominent study explores the psychological mechanisms through which the regime affects state nuclear decision-making; the featured case study underlines how Japanese commitment to the treaty coloured subsequent debate about military strategy even when faced with aggression from nuclear-armed neighbours (Rublee 2009). Quantitative studies have compared state behaviours before and after the non-proliferation norm and suggested a process of 'deproliferation in absolute terms' as states sought to be seen as appropriate, a 'good citizen' (Muller and Schmidt 2010: 147–8). However, whether such normative variables drive policy absent of other security, economic, or political variables remains debatable.

Regime failures

Those who express concern about the NPT regime offer a host of criticisms. To begin, they call into question the causal impact of the arrangement. That four of the five NPT holdouts have nuclear weapons reveals the clear limitations of the regime. Treaty membership also did not prevent Iraq, North Korea, or Libya from developing clandestine nuclear weapons programmes. That Libya ultimately rolled back its programme was a decision entirely unrelated to its long-standing NPT obligations. Similarly, South Africa dismantled its weapons programmes prior to treaty accession. Sceptics would suggest that domestic politics, external threats, and other considerations are better suited than the regime – or even the international social environment for non-proliferation – in explaining the timing of denuclearization.

Non-compliance cases in the post-Cold War era suggest problems in treaty implementation as well. Experts point to the ambiguity and inconsistency that have characterized safeguards cases, with no clear-cut definition or procedure applied even when the IAEA Board of Governors has determined non-compliance (Carlson 2009). The protracted nature of the Iran and North Korea cases highlights difficulties in enforcement. Even the successful conclusion of the JCPOA with Iran must be taken with a grain of salt, as it comes nearly a full decade following the initial non-compliance ruling by the IAEA Board of Governors; furthermore, the collapse of the Agreed Framework with North Korea in the 1990s serves as a cautionary tale about the execution of such complex agreements. Some express concern that those two states could present a model for future would-be proliferators, with NPT signatories achieving 'nuclear breakout' capability under the arrangement. That the Security Council failed to pass a resolution against the clear breach of treaty protocol in the aftermath of North Korea's 2003 withdrawal – it bypassed the required three months' notice – further exposes the loophole.

Fears of latent proliferation tap into more fundamental concerns about the principles undergirding the NPT regime. For some, the 'inalienable right' to peaceful development has run amuck, granting states access to the whole of the fuel cycle and thus placing them on the verge of a weapons programme. This inherent tension between the treaty's non-proliferation and energy provisions has led some to call for greater controls on civilian programmes. Criticism has come from the opposite direction as well, with the nuclear-weapon states accused of falling short in fulfilling their obligations to facilitate energy access or move towards disarmament. The feeling of 'unequal rewards for disproportionate sacrifices' undertaken by the non-nuclear-weapon states has been reinforced by recent benefits offered to non-treaty signatories India and Pakistan, in the form of a Nuclear Suppliers Group exemption for the former, and bilateral nuclear cooperation deals with the US and China, respectively (Tannenwald 2013: 313).

A final line of criticism looks broadly at the current nuclear landscape, identifying the presence of non-state actors, black markets, terrorist threats, and loose fissile materials. While these elements fall outside the jurisdiction of the NPT itself, it is impossible to truly separate them from the global regime tasked with the prevention of nuclear proliferation (Walsh 2005). In the next section, I examine the impact these new pathways have had on the overall non-proliferation campaign, as well as the changes brought about by previous critical events.

The evolution of proliferation

When the NPT opened for signatures in 1968, parties were primarily concerned with a select group of advanced industrial and industrializing states with research and production capabilities. As such, they specified one means of proliferation in the final text: the 'diversion of nuclear energy from peaceful uses to nuclear weapons or other nuclear explosive devices' (*Treaty on the Non-Proliferation of Nuclear Weapons* 1968: Article III.1). The treaty thus established a safeguards system that was aimed almost exclusively at diversion: specifying nuclear materials rather than facilities, stressing the importance of domestic accountability and control, and creating an authenticating, supervisory role for the IAEA. In the decades that have elapsed, however, the character of proliferation has changed – and the NPT regime along with it.

Select shocks

India's 1974 explosion of a nuclear device did not reflect a new pathway of proliferation, but an expanded conception and clear model thereof. Its use of a Canadian research reactor and an American heavy-water supply highlighted the difficulty of filtering peaceful from weaponizable nuclear materials, especially in the long run.[6] That the early 1970s were characterized by a burgeoning nuclear trade reinforced fears about the diversion threat. Exporting states had already expressed concern about the threat stemming from state-to-state transfers, discussing technical issues in an informal series of meetings (as the Zangger Committee) beginning in 1971. India spurred immediate action. The Zangger Committee published a trigger list of equipment and material to be encompassed by safeguards agreements. In 1975, the Nuclear Suppliers Group emerged with self-imposed, stringent controls for supplier states, while the IAEA established the Standing Advisory Group for Safeguards Implementation. The regime was reconceptualized, tightening the application of safeguards, and setting forth common – and detailed – export controls.

While India circumvented the NPT regime as an outsider, Iraq simply defied it. Its concealment of undeclared nuclear material and willing deception – uncovered in 1991 – represented the first such acts by a signatory state. Iraq's clandestine programme thus symbolized a new proliferation pathway, one that extended beyond the concept of diversion targeted by the NPT regime. The 1993 non-compliance finding in North Korea echoed this concealment blueprint. An intensive review followed, aimed to 'facilitate the early detection of undeclared nuclear activities.'[7] The result was a new legal foundation for safeguards, with the Additional Protocol allowing the IAEA a more comprehensive view of a state's nuclear programme via the use of special inspections, increased access to broad-based information, and expansion in other reporting requirements. The shift from a 'correctness' principle to one of 'completeness' was bolstered by activity outside the NPT review process, as the Nuclear Suppliers Group and Zangger Committee published trigger lists for dual-use equipment, materials, and technologies.

An unprecedented wave of safeguards breaches reported by the IAEA Secretariat in 2003 and 2004 provided another proliferation shock for the international community. However, no corresponding system-level changes came to the NPT regime. While this may seem surprising at face value, the cases of Iran, Libya, Egypt, and South Korea ultimately did not represent new pathways of proliferation. As with Iraq and North Korea, they concerned clandestine efforts: with inspectors uncovering the presence of undeclared materials, facilities, and fuel cycle activities. That none of the countries had Additional Protocols in place at the time suggested that the institutional solution to these cases already existed – it just needed to be disseminated among regime members. That each country took decisive, corrective action and cooperated with the IAEA investigation helped to further quell any concern at the time.[8] These were issues of execution, not conceptualization.

Beyond the state

In the past decade, however, proliferation has become reconceptualized in a manner exceeding even the India and Iraq shocks. While nuclear material security had reached the agenda of the international community in the past, it had done so in a limited fashion. For instance, the 1980 Convention on the Physical Protection of Nuclear Materials (CPPNM) impressed upon national governments the obligation to protect materials in use, storage, and transport, but that applied only to materials involved in international shipments – a part of the post-India agenda targeting state-to-state transfers. Meanwhile, the 1992 Cooperative Threat Reduction Programme provided standards for long-term safe and secure storage for fissile materials, but its focus was on dismantling existing stockpiles in the post-Soviet satellites. But the issue of nuclear security came to take on a different, independent tenor in the early stages of the twenty-first century.

Revelations of al-Qaida's nuclear aspirations in the aftermath of the 11th September attacks brought the spectre of nuclear terrorism to the forefront of the global security agenda (the US' 2002 National Strategy to Combat Weapons of Mass Destruction as a primary example). Problematically, existing instrumentation in the NPT regime simply did not encompass non-state actors. The IAEA moved quickly to create the Nuclear Security Fund in 2001, and then the Office of Nuclear Security in 2002 – symbolically removing the latter from its previous confines within the Safeguards Department. These actions constituted a response to the new players in nuclear proliferation. And in contrast to policy changes following previous proliferation shocks, these actions had no connection to the NPT.

The limitations of the existing regime became further manifest with the 2003 uncovering of the A. Q. Khan network. The so-called father of the Pakistani atomic bomb admitted to running a proliferation ring, having sold weapons technology to Iran, North Korea, and Libya beginning in the 1980s. These revelations about the reach and complexity of the nuclear black market thus reaffirmed the significance of non-state actors in proliferation.

Beyond the NPT regime

The beginning of the twenty-first century was marked by the development of a nuclear-security-centric non-proliferation apparatus. A 2002 incident involving a North Korean ship bound for Yemen with ballistic missile parts reflected the strength of the black market, spurring President George W. Bush to establish the Proliferation Security Initiative (PSI) in 2003. Eleven developed countries committed to a series of interdiction principles aimed to dismantle proliferation rings. Following the Khan confession, the US pushed for UN Security Council Resolution 1540 in 2004, imposing legislative obligations for all 193 member states – an unprecedented manoeuvre – on the issue of non-proliferation. Both it and PSI explicitly targeted non-state actors in addition to state actors.

The multifaceted activity on the issue of nuclear security was buttressed by other actions aimed to deter smuggling: the US commenced the Global Threat Reduction Initiative in 2004 to target nuclear material at high-risk civilian sites, the CPPNM was amended in 2005 to include national material transfers, while the Nuclear Security Summit was convened in 2010 to secure political commitments on the part of states regarding nuclear terrorism. Calls for a global system to address the issue of nuclear security have emerged, with the NPT's narrow focus on diversion and state-to-state transfers ill-suited for this purpose. Issues of illicit trafficking and nuclear security were kept off the NPT Review Conference agenda entirely, with no mention of PSI or 1540 in the final declaration, and minimal reference to non-state threats within the proceedings.[9] It seems that states recognize the need to move beyond the NPT regime to address the evolving nature of proliferation.

Conclusion: the future of non-proliferation

Over the course of the past four decades, the non-proliferation regime has evolved into an intricate system of global, regional, and national instruments. The Nuclear Non-Proliferation Treaty stands as its cornerstone: its Article III is the foundation for a reformulated IAEA safeguards system and the Additional Protocol, while trigger lists from the Nuclear Suppliers Group and the Zangger Committee have expanded the parameters around those agreements. Without any amendments to the text, the character of the NPT review process itself has also expanded: the establishment of a third main committee and subsidiary bodies, the adoption of barometers for progress, the overall shift to a more prescriptive approach. The treaty's history is also intertwined with, and responsible for, the spread of nuclear-weapon-free zones, the negotiation of the Comprehensive Test Ban Treaty, and the establishment of the first international fuel banks.

Yet, despite the expansive reach of the NPT regime, the character of its foundational treaty has become somewhat of a detriment in the new global order. With the treaty's two-class system, its far-reaching aim of nuclear disarmament, and its lack of detail on the means of facilitating peaceful development, nuclear non-proliferation has become too often entangled in North–South politics. That the treaty is legally equipped to target only a particular pathway of proliferation underlines its antiquated nature. The regime has previously evolved in sync with the character of proliferation, as demonstrated in the aftermath of India's 1974 test explosion and the 1991 discovery of Iraq's clandestine activity. In the post-Cold War era, the regime has shifted again, in response to emerging concerns over the involvement of non-state actors, as encapsulated by issues of nuclear terrorism and materials security. This time however, the shift has necessarily moved outside the NPT.

The NPT-IAEA safeguards agreements and related export controls systems remain the arbiters in state proliferation. But the segmentation of the non-proliferation regime is a welcome process. The involvement of non-state actors in new proliferation pathways suggests the need to cultivate and maintain the emergent nuclear security structure.[10] Other arenas under the broad jurisdiction of the NPT could use further development as well: the regional nature of security conflicts suggests a greater role for nuclear-weapon-free zones, which have the advantage of localized origins and verification regimes. An accelerated process of institutionalization there could bolster existing non-proliferation instruments, while redressing the security conflicts that underlie consideration of the nuclear option.[11] Meanwhile, long-standing NPT stagnation in disarmament suggests that more varied activity there is merited: perhaps a fourth Special Session on Disarmament, or an ad-hoc committee to discuss the dormant Fissile Material Cut-Off Treaty.

The theoretical promise of the NPT can be achieved only with more specialized, decentralized, and localized components in the non-proliferation regime. Regardless of perspective, there is consensus that the arrangement has little value if signatory states lose faith in its ability to deter states from nuclearization, its ability to provide information and set expectations about nuclear behaviour, and its ability to delegitimize nuclear weapons. Proliferation in any shape or form undermines all of these. The change in the nature of proliferation means that the nature of non-proliferation must too. In the past, the NPT has been sufficient. But the limitations of the treaty have become impediments to its adaptive prowess; meanwhile, its very structure and overarching scope breed stagnation and resentment. In the current and future nuclear landscape, the role of other structures – complementary but separate – is key to delivering on the lofty ambitions set forth by the treaty. A pivot from the NPT will help to preserve it, and maintain the whole of the nuclear non-proliferation regime.

Notes

1 See Lebow's chapter in this volume for more on deterrence strategies.
2 Despite being a seemingly natural fit, the NPT regime has served as the empirical case for few neoliberal institutionalist works.
3 Kroenig (2009) lists weapons design and construction, weapons-grade fissile material transfers, and uranium-enrichment or plutonium-reprocessing facility construction as examples of sensitive nuclear assistance contributing to proliferation (all prohibited by the NPT).
4 I thus distinguish the 'NPT regime' from the broader 'non-proliferation regime', which would include the Missile Technology Control Regime, the START and SALT treaties, and so forth.
5 States with the industrial and scientific capabilities to proliferate.
6 While India was not a NPT member, its interest in a weapons programme was public knowledge; its programme was in fact one that the NPT was established to prevent. That it far outstripped expectations in its development suggests regime failure on some level. Additionally, India's claim of a peaceful nuclear explosion exposed the loophole in the treaty on the topic.
7 Hans Blix, Statement to the 46th Session of the UN General Assembly, 21 October 1991; United States, IAEA General Conference, September 1991, GC(35)/OR.333, para. 128–30.
8 As mentioned in this chapter, Iran's cooperation with the IAEA dissipated, and it was found in non-compliance by the Executive Board in 2005.
9 Prior to the Review Conference, Dunn (2009) argued that a recognition of 1540 would have sent a unifying message, rendering interchangeable non-proliferation norms among state actors and non-state actors. That parties chose not to do so suggests they perceive the arenas as separate.
10 The global nuclear safety regime can serve as a model. Safety is centered on national governments and industry stockholders, but reinforced by multilateral agreements – many of which are incorporated as requirements in the non-proliferation campaign.
11 The convening of the Conference of States Parties and Signatories to Treaties that Establish Nuclear-Weapon-Free Zones is a positive step from this perspective, enabling future assistance and coordination.

References

Axelrod, R. and Keohane, R. O. (1985) 'Achieving Cooperation under Anarchy: Strategies and Institutions', *World Politics* 38(1): 226–54.

Barnett, M. and Finnemore, M. (1999) 'The Politics, Power, and Pathologies of International Organizations', *International Organization* 53(4): 699–732.

Carlson, J. (2009) 'Defining Noncompliance: NPT Safeguards Agreements', *Arms Control Association*, 8 May. Online. Available HTTP: <http://www.armscontrol.org/act/2009_5/Carlson> (accessed 10 August 2015).

Dunn, L. A. (2009) 'The NPT: Assessing the Past, Building the Future', *The Nonproliferation Review* 16(2): 143–72.

Finnemore, M. and Sikkink, K. (1998) 'International Norm Dynamics and Political Change', *International Organization* 52(4): 887–917.

Fuhrmann, M. (2009) 'Spreading Temptation: Proliferation and Peaceful Nuclear Cooperation Agreements', *International Security* 34(1): 7–41.

Fuhrmann, M. and Li, X. (2008) *Legalizing Nuclear Abandonment: The Determinants of Nuclear Weapon Free Zone Treaty Ratification*, Cambridge, MA: Harvard Kennedy School.

Hecker, S. S. (2010) 'Lessons Learned from the North Korean Nuclear Crises', *Daedalus* 139(1): 44–56.

Hymans, J. E. C. (2006) 'Theories of Nuclear Proliferation', *The Nonproliferation Review* 13(3): 455–65.

Hymans, J. E. C. (2012) *Achieving Nuclear Ambitions: Scientists, Politicians, and Proliferation*, New York: Cambridge University Press.

Hymans, J. E. C. (2014) 'No Cause for Panic: Key Lessons from the Political Science Literature on Nuclear Proliferation', *International Journal* 69(1): 85–93.

Jervis, R. (1999) 'Realism, Neoliberalism, and Cooperation: Understanding the Debate', *International Security* 24(1): 42–63.

Jo, D.-J. and Gartzke, E. (2007) 'Determinants of Nuclear Weapons Proliferation', *Journal of Conflict Resolution* 51(1): 167–94.

Johnson, R. (2010) 'Rethinking the NPT's Role in Security: 2010 and Beyond', *International Affairs* 86(2): 429–45.

Johnston, A. I. (2001) 'Treating International Institutions as Social Environments', *International Studies Quarterly* 45(4): 487–515.

Keohane, R. O. (1982) 'The Demand for International Regimes', *International Organization* 36(2): 325–55.

Koremenos, B., Lipson, C., and Snidal, D. (2001) 'The Rational Design of International Institutions', *International Organization* 55(4): 761–99.

Kroenig, M. (2009) 'Importing the Bomb: Sensitive Nuclear Assistance and Nuclear Proliferation', *Journal of Conflict Resolution* 53(2): 161–80.

Liberman, P. (2001) 'The Rise and Fall of the South African Bomb', *International Security* 26(2): 45–86.

Lipson, C. (1984) 'International Cooperation in Economic and Security Affairs', *World Politics* 37(1): 1–23.

Mearsheimer, J. J. (1994) 'The False Promise of International Institutions', *International Security* 19(3): 5–49.

Miller, S. E. (2007) 'Proliferation, Disarmament, and the Future of the Non-Proliferation Treaty', in M. B. Mærli and S. Lodgaard (eds.) *Nuclear Proliferation and International Security*, New York: Routledge, 50–69.

Monshipouri, M. and Dorraj, M. (2013) 'Iran's Foreign Policy: A Shifting Strategic Landscape', *Middle East Policy* 20(4): 133–47.

Muller, H. and Schmidt, A. (2010) 'The Little-Known Story of Deproliferation: Why States Give up Nuclear Weapons Activities', in W. C. Potter and G. Mukhatzhanova (eds.) *Forecasting Nuclear Proliferation in the 21st Century: The Role of Theory*, Stanford, CA: Stanford University Press, 124–58.

Paul, T. V. (2000) *Power versus Prudence: Why Nations Forgo Nuclear Weapons*, Montreal: McGill Queens University Press.

Rublee, M. R. (2008) 'Taking Stock of The Nuclear Nonproliferation Regime: Using Social Psychology to Understand Regime Effectiveness', *International Studies Review* 10(3): 420–50.

Rublee, M. R. (2009) *Nonproliferation Norms: Why States Choose Nuclear Restraint*, Athens: University of Georgia Press.

Sagan, S. D. (1996) 'Why Do States Build Nuclear Weapons? Three Models in Search of a Bomb', *International Security* 21(3): 54–86.

Sagan, S. D. (2011) 'The Causes of Nuclear Weapons Proliferation', *Annual Review of Political Science* 14(1): 225–44.

Shaffer, B. (2003) 'Iran at the Nuclear Threshold', *Arms Control Association*, 1 November. Online. Available HTTP: <http://www.armscontrol.org/act/2003_11/Shaffer> (accessed 11 August 2015).

Solingen, E. (2007) *Nuclear Logics: Contrasting Paths in East Asia and the Middle East*, Princeton, NJ: Princeton University Press.

Tannenwald, N. (2007) *The Nuclear Taboo: The United States and the Non-Use of Nuclear Weapons since 1945*, New York: Cambridge University Press.

Tannenwald, N. (2013) 'Justice and Fairness in the Nuclear Nonproliferation Regime', *Ethics and International Affairs* 27(3): 299–317.

Treaty on the Non-Proliferation of Nuclear Weapons (1968), opened for signatures 1 July 1968, entered into force 5 March 1970.

Walsh, J. (2005) *Learning from Past Success: The NPT and the Future of Non-Proliferation*, Stockholm: Weapons for Mass Destruction Commission.

36

PUBLIC DIPLOMACY IN A NATIONAL SECURITY CONTEXT

Nancy Snow

There is a steep learning curve between government efforts to inform, influence, and engage global publics (public diplomacy) and the need to preserve and protect the interests of the state (national security) and its people. Its key challenge today is how individuals and institutions can strike a balance between growing demands for global communications transparency and accountability, a challenge in the twenty-first century, with strategic communication classification and secrecy, the legacy of the twentieth century. In the age of WikiLeaks, information exchange is neither scarce nor sacred, and diplomacy to publics in service of national security objectives is open to scrutiny from all levels of education and ability. Public diplomacy is everybody's business because the state as primary international actor has lost its lofty spot of credibility. We trust our smart phones and our Facebook friends as much, if not more, than our elected officials, and this reality has led to many non-state actors jumping into the public diplomacy fray.

This chapter has three parts. It is written from the viewpoint of my personal experience as a former USIA official and details both the origins of public diplomacy as we know it and the changes that public diplomacy underwent as a result of 9/11.[1] The first part provides an overall overview of public diplomacy as a field of research and teaching. The second deals with the founding fathers of public diplomacy in the US, showing their influence in shaping the field. The third part shows the influence of 9/11 on public diplomacy, with particular emphasis on the turn to 'total' diplomacy in the Global War on Terror (GWOT) and an overall shift towards the militarization of public diplomacy.

Public diplomacy research

The present state of public diplomacy research and literature is so broad and varied that it suffers from what was once the common refrain of late 1930s America, 'it's all propaganda, anyway' (Sproule 1997: 16). This is a field that consists of scholars, practitioners, and just about anyone who has ever taken at least one course in public diplomacy; many of those practising public diplomacy operate in the realm of non-coercive persuasion and influence, which we know better as soft power (Nye 2004) or 'smart power' (Nye 2009).

Unlike soft power, no one scholar or practitioner has the advantage in explaining just what public diplomacy is. It is at times home in public relations (Fitzpatrick et al. 2013; Golan et al.

2015) post-9/11 national security (Gregory 2008; Wiseman 2015) or modern propaganda studies that covers the post-Second World War years, including the Cold War (Carroll 1948; Green 1988; Snyder 1995). For Wiseman, public diplomacy is dichotomous when confronting enemies: 'The US government has essentially two choices when dealing with adversarial states – isolate them or engage them' (2015: 1); engagement is the realm of public diplomacy. Former Under Secretary of State Karen Hughes (2005) utilized the 'four E's' of public diplomacy (engagement, exchanges, education, empowerment) and former Secretary of State Colin Powell described public diplomacy as nothing short of salesmanship. In explaining his support for advertising maven Charlotte Beers as public diplomacy czar, he explained just days before 9/11:

> I wanted one of the world's greatest advertising experts, because what are we doing? We're selling. We're selling a product. That product we are selling is democracy. It's the free enterprise system, the American value system. It's a product very much in demand. It's a product that is very much needed. It is our job to be salespersons.
>
> *(Hayden 2007: 237)*

Winning friends and repelling enemies has become far murkier territory in the decade-and-a-half since Powell made those remarks. What has been called 'thick globalism' drives today's global competition for attention and influence. Gregory (2008: 2) describes it as a recipe consisting of 'non-state actors, a mix of secular and religious "big ideas", digital technologies, and new forms of communication'. All of these were not as pronounced pre-9/11 as they have become post-9/11.

It was the post-9/11 era when public diplomacy study really took off at the university level.[2] Public relations scholars and practitioners began to embrace it as a natural fit or sub-field to their curriculum and practice, an integration that has met with some scepticism (Snow 2015a, 2015b). Public diplomacy is not historically associated with corporate-driven public relations; moreover, public relations has its own 'identity crisis' problems (Heath 2001: 212) not shared by the more accepted public diplomacy. There are scholars who believe that the best way to win the hearts and minds of global publics is through the stomach, what is known as culinary diplomacy or gastrodiplomacy (Chapple-Sokol, 2013; Rockower 2012). There are scholars who choose to distinguish reputable and credible public diplomacy from propaganda (Gass and Seiter 2009), with the former associated mostly with non-controversial efforts to persuade and the latter with a full spectrum of persuasion tactics, including deception, omission of facts, and/or bias (Taylor 2003).

The origins of public diplomacy

When did diplomacy to global publics as a subset of national security really start to matter? We can trace modern roots to three individuals, one military (Elihu Root), one journalist (Walter Lippmann), and one diplomat (Edmund Gullion), although there are others who contributed historically to wartime propaganda efforts (like Harold Lasswell or Edward Bernays).

Elihu Root served as Secretary of War and Secretary of State for President Theodore Roosevelt, and received the 1912 Nobel Peace Prize for his arbitration efforts. In his own words, Root (1922) explained the rise of what he called 'popular diplomacy' in the premiere issue of *Foreign Affairs*. The piece was so influential that upon his death, the leading journal of international relations reprinted 'A Requisite for the Success of Popular Diplomacy' (Root 1937). He places public opinion and public information at the heart of international negotiation that precedes or follows international conflict: 'We have learned that war is essentially a popular business' (Root 1922: 3). He also bemoans the lack of interest for international relations among the isolationist and world–affairs-ignorant Americans. Root proposed nothing short of a public education overhaul. In that capacity, the former Secretary of War would also become 'founding father' to the nation's leading military education training school, the US Army War College, to train a new generation of information warriors who would help unite the social sciences (communications, psychology in particular) with the business of war.

In that same year of 1922 when Root wrote about popular diplomacy, Walter Lippmann, lifelong adviser to presidents from Wilson to Johnson, and in his time the world's most influential pencil press man, made essentially the same argument as Root. Representative government works best when specialized experts manage information and repackage it for the public, which is prone to irrational or incomplete pictures of persuasion that are largely driven by prejudice, emotion, and stereotypes. An absolute democracy can never exist, in that the world is too complex for a novice follower of public affairs to understand it; the experts must preside (McPherson 1980). In service to the best policy, organized intelligence and media censorship (propaganda) must bookend efforts to manage international affairs (cf. Steel 1980).

Root and Lippmann, whose influence is explicitly tied to intelligence and security affairs, are not regularly cited as formative influencers of the field of public diplomacy, however. That title belongs to Edmund Gullion, who is regularly mentioned as the first to coin the new US term 'public diplomacy' in the 1960s. Gullion was a career foreign service officer who later served as longtime dean of the Fletcher School of Law and Diplomacy at Tufts University in Massachusetts (Schneider 2005: 159). At Fletcher, Dean Gullion established the Edward R. Murrow Center of Public Diplomacy in 1965, to honor the journalist turned government propagandist who served as director of the USIA under JFK before his death in April of that same year.

Public diplomacy as defined by Gullion in the mid-1960s was rather milquetoast in comparison to the total diplomacy profile it has today. Gullion explained its purpose at the dedication ceremony for the Center:

> [Public diplomacy] deals with the influence of public attitudes on the formation and execution of foreign policies ... encompasses dimensions of foreign relations beyond traditional diplomacy, the cultivation by governments of public opinion in other countries; the interaction of private groups and interests in one country with those of another; the reporting of foreign affairs and its impact on policy; communication between those whose job is communication, as between diplomats and foreign correspondents; and the process of intercultural communications. Central to public diplomacy is the transformational flow of information and ideas..
>
> *(Szondi 2008: 8)*

Public diplomacy was chosen over Edmund Gullion's preference for the term propaganda. Gullion viewed public diplomacy as a euphemistic replacement for what many Americans considered then, as now, as a dirty word (Cull 2006). It was a public relations move. The Murrow Center's directive was to build mutual understanding, not only between American diplomats and their global audiences, but also between diplomats and those who cover international relations. Gullion said shortly before his death: 'I always thought journalists and diplomats could learn a great deal from one another' (Saxon 1998). Ironically, Edward R. Murrow himself referred to his work with President John F. Kennedy as that of a government propagandist (Snow 2013).

Edmund Gullion's legacy to public diplomacy has been reduced to mostly an etymological one, which downplays his extraordinary diplomatic career that placed him in the front seat of history from South East Asia to Africa. Gullion's appointment by Kennedy as ambassador to the Democratic Republic of Congo (Zaire) in 1961 shortly after the shocking assassination of its anti-colonial leader, Patrice Lumumba, reveals an ongoing debate in the field of public diplomacy about its natural home. Is it diplomacy, where it is linked to public affairs and public information, or military, where it takes on a tougher sheen of strategic communication (STRATCOM) and psychological operations (PSYOP)?

Gullion, the diplomat, placed priority on mutual understanding and sensitivity to the nationalistic goals of people who had lived under colonial rule. He did not view the world through a strictly bipolar (Communist/Anti-Communist) lens. As J. F. Kennedy's ambassador, Gullion sought more US support for the national revolution in the Congo, not condemnation or intervention. This put Gullion at odds with the CIA and its then director, Allen Dulles, who viewed Third World anti-colonial nationalist movements as Soviet propaganda tools that must be directly challenged and put down (Kinzer 2013).

After the Bay of Pigs debacle, a direct consequence of this policy advocated by Dulles, Edward R. Murrow pleaded with the new Democratic president to have his USIA 'in on the take-offs, not just the crash landings', a proposal that elevated public diplomacy to more of a national security concern (Bennett 2003). Kennedy's political assassination in 1963 and the subsequent buildup of troops in Vietnam set the US on a foreign policy path that would increasingly utilize public diplomacy in a battle of narratives that continued with the systematic integration of full-spectrum dominance surrounding the post-9/11 Global War on Terror (GWOT).

9/11 as tipping point

11 September 2001 was the tipping point in favour of reuniting public diplomacy in the service of national security and counterterrorism. The architectural foundation had already been in place from Truman's Psychological Strategy Board (1951) to Reagan's National Security Decision Directive 77 (1983) to Clinton's Presidential Decision Directive 68 that created an International Public Information to address problems of confusion identified during military missions in Kosovo and Haiti, 'when no US agency was empowered to coordinate US efforts to sell its policies and counteract bad press abroad' (Barber 1999; David 2009: 118).

Towards 'total' diplomacy

Less than a month after 9/11, British magazine of influence, *The Economist*, named the new post-9/11 era 'The propaganda war' (*Economist* 2001). That war preceded the invasion of Afghanistan; it involved how the United States would explain its motives and intentions to the world vis-à-vis invasion of Muslim-majority countries like Afghanistan (2001) and Iraq (2003), while it simultaneously engaged in a GWOT against Islamic terror organization al-Qaida and its host regime, the Taliban. In this propaganda war, all assets of national power and security would be deployed through a STRATCOM campaign that would make the military and Department of Defense take the lead over the Department of State on a global influence scale (Gygax and Snow 2013) that was reminiscent of a new cold war, or what Dean Acheson under Truman once called 'total diplomacy'.

In total diplomacy, as in total war, national goals require sacrifice on the part of the people in giving up peacetime privileges and rights. In return, the democratic state is required to educate the public about foreign relations management. In a total diplomacy milieu, a network of experts leads the public education effort to instruct about the rightness of mission. In the Truman total diplomacy case, Secretary of State Acheson led the cause in forcing countries to choose whose side they were on, what *Time* magazine called 'seeking allies with the grim realism of war':

We are not dealing here with the kind of situation where we can go from one country to another with a piece of litmus paper and see whether everything is true blue. The only question we should ask is whether they are determined to protect their independence against Communist aggression.

(Time 1950)

Half a century later, the US president (Bush 2001) led these public education efforts ('Either you are with us, or you are with the terrorists'), an indoctrination of Manichaean principles that forced the hand of the American people to accept unpopular invasions in order to take the fight to the terrorists and win the GWOT. Just as Acheson and Truman viewed the Soviet Union as a formidable threat to US interests in geopolitical influence, so did Bush, Cheney, Rumsfeld, and Rice view al-Qaida and its offshoots in the same 'us' vs. 'them' light. The total defeat of the enemy required the total spectrum of communication. Admiral Mike Mullen, Chairman of the Joint Chiefs of Staff at the time, put it this way to explain the ratcheting up of communication efforts after 11 September 2001:

If we've learned nothing else these past eight years, it should be that the lines between strategic, operational, and tactical are blurred beyond distinction. This is particularly true in the world of communication, where videos and images plastered on the Web – or even the idea of their being so posted – can and often do drive national security decisionmaking.

(Mullen 2009: 2)

The militarization of public diplomacy

Such an 'all in' philosophy drove public diplomacy campaigns, traditionally an open-sourced diplomacy-to-publics outreach effort, into the arms of military planners inside the Department of Defense. The militarization of public diplomacy raised its internal credibility among intelligence and information specialists, but diluted its power (financially, persuasively) inside the Department of State.

For example, when I was working at the United States Information Agency in the early to mid-1990s, our annual budget was roughly $1 billion or one three-hundredth of the budget of the US military. After 9/11, the budget for public diplomacy stayed roughly the same while the Pentagon budget rose substantively to accommodate two active wars. In a two-year span (2010–11), the US embassy in Kabul, Afghanistan, funded 560 public diplomacy grants at a cost of about US $148 million or just over $100,000 per day. In contrast, the combined costs for the wars in Afghanistan and Iraq are now estimated to be over $4 trillion.

A Stimson report, 'The Pentagon as Pitchman: Perception and Reality of Public Diplomacy' (Rumbaugh and Leatherman 2012) downplayed any rise in the military's public-diplomacy-like activities, but acknowledged that it had no figures for the two highest-budget war zones, since they were classified. Further, the report seemed to disregard what the Pentagon's own brass (e.g., Rumsfeld, Gates, Mullen) was saying about the Pentagon's pitchman role: 9/11 required its expansion.

It was Bush's former Secretary of Defense Donald Rumsfeld who had proposed an Office of Strategic Influence (OSI) in October 2001 to expand PSYOP in the GWOT, not unprecedented for the US, which had done the same in the Cold War and Vietnam War. The office lasted just a week in the wake of a *The New York Times* hit piece reporting the concerns of unidentified Pentagon officials, most likely senior public affairs officials, who forecast a loss of credibility in the wake of massaged information: 'The Pentagon is developing plans to provide news items, possibly even false ones, to foreign media organizations as part of a new effort to influence public sentiment and policy-makers in both friendly and unfriendly countries' (Dao and Schmitt 2002).

The OSI may have gone under, but its legacy was preserved in the form of a counter-insurgency doctrine of post-9/11 that required the new twenty-first century soldier to be a nation-builder as much as a traditional warrior, tracking, capturing, or killing the enemy. The 2008 Army's Field Manual (Caslen 2011: 84) established 'full-spectrum operations – simultaneous offensive, defensive, and stability or civil support operations – as the central concept of Army capabilities' in the Afghanistan and Iraq theaters.

Secretary of Defense Robert Gates, who had served both Republican and Democratic presidents, described the battle of narratives between the Soviet Union and the United States as a mixture of both military and non-military efforts, including the work of the US Agency for International Development and the US Information Agency. 'In all, these non-military efforts – these tools of persuasion and inspiration – were indispensable to the outcome of the defining ideological struggle of the twentieth century. I believe that they are just as indispensable in the twenty-first century – and maybe more so' (Gates 2008). Gates would become the chief architect, along with Secretary of State Hillary Clinton, of what came to be known as 'smart power' – a national defence strategy that combined the military with the civilian, the public with the private, to address the new counterterrorism challenges.

In other words, nations cannot rely strictly on soft-power strategies – using attraction to preference outcomes – or entirely on hard power – using coercion, threat of force, payment – to thwart outcomes. At times, both sources are needed to 'get smart' (Nye 2009) in foreign policy. Consider, for instance, the military and economic power of the United States after Japan's triple disaster (earthquake, tsunami, nuclear power plant breakdown) known as 3/11. The US military relief mission Operation Tomodachi was able to rebuild roads and airstrips and provide victim assistance in the immediate aftermath of the disaster. It generated enormous goodwill for the United States. A June 2011 survey by the Washington, DC-based Pew Center showed that 85 per cent of the Japanese had a favourable opinion towards the United States (Wike 2012), nearly a decade-high percentage in a country that has had mixed feelings about the US military presence in its post-Second World War history.

The position of Under Secretary of State for Public Diplomacy and Public Affairs, first created under President Clinton in 1999, failed to produce memorable occupants, except for the eighteen-month tenure of Charlotte Beers (2001–3) and the two-year tenure of Bush's closest communications confidante, Karen Hughes (2005–7). But neither Beers nor Hughes was memorable for being particularly effective in this position; rather, each woman was remembered for her respective reputation – Beers in advertising and Hughes in public relations and press communications. The around-the-clock persuasive news campaign to 'sell' the GWOT objectives to the American people and an overseas public was placed in the hands of a network of experts that included high-ranking military officials as well as military veterans and military analysts – a military-academic-industrial network that David Barstow (2008) referred to in *The New York Times* as the 'Pentagon's Hidden Hand.'

While the American people were very much on board with Afghanistan when nerves were frayed and anger was raging for military action in the immediate aftermath of 9/11, it was a much harder sell of sacrifice for Iraq, which, to the amateur international relations observer, seemed remotely tied, at best, to the attacks of 9/11. In relation to Afghanistan and Iraq, global publics were never swayed, raising the ever-present question of why propaganda designed exclusively for an overseas audience seemed to have its greatest impact on the domestic audience.

The Council on Foreign Relations' 'Finding America's Voice' report (2003) stated what dozens of similar task forces and white papers concluded – that public diplomacy influence was part of the battle of narratives in the US-led GWOT:

> Washington must realize that defending the homeland, seeking out and destroying terrorists, and using public diplomacy to make it easier for allies to support the United States and to reduce the lure of terrorism are all parts of the same battle.
>
> *(Peterson et al. 2003: 6)*

This report from the most influential elite foreign affairs organization came on the heels of the US invasion of Iraq and President George W. Bush's triumphant 'Mission Accomplished' speech aboard the USS Lincoln, and hereafter secured the Department of Defense as the leading government entity involved in America's total diplomacy approach to the GWOT.

The Department of State would take a back seat to the DoD's efforts to sell a security-led and military-central public diplomacy. The Defense Science Board Task Force (2004) calls its efforts 'strategic communication,' consisting of four core instruments: public diplomacy, public affairs, non-military US international broadcasting services, and open military information operations. Problems arise when public affairs and public diplomacy careerists at the Department of State or in overseas embassies try to do their jobs in an international communications arena that they define as overt and open and not subject to the military intelligence environment tendency to look at the world in terms of bipolar realities (Domino Theory, GWOT, Cold War).

George Washington University scholar Bruce Gregory (2005) explains the problems that are inherent in this. He refers to public diplomacy as an open instrument of statecraft where successful outcomes are driven by perceived believability and trustworthiness. In contrast, military and intelligence instruments of statecraft use both overt and covert forms of influence that rely on deception and black and gray forms of propaganda. Firewalls of protection across the information influence spectrum often break down and impact the ability of public diplomacy professionals to do their jobs:

> Political leaders, ambassadors, military commanders, and public affairs officers know that to persuade others they must be credible. To build consent for strategies, there must be a basis for trust in what they say and do, an inclination by others to believe, and perceptions of their reliability over time. Credibility is diminished when words and actions do not match, when statements directed to multiple audiences are inconsistent, when overt and covert activities are seen to be co-funded and co-located.
>
> *(Gregory 2005: 17)*

The firewalls of protection between information warfare and open statecraft broke down for good when the events of 11 September 2001 took place. The surprise attacks served to spark efforts to incorporate communication technologies into the service of the US national security framework. Security-above-all and a net-centric philosophy in the war on terror targeted radical Muslims particularly and all Muslims generally, who were thought to be susceptible to the grips of those who sought to attack US interests around the world. Senior diplomat, Richard Holbrooke, who had served as President Clinton's US representative to the United Nations and who would later be appointed special representative for the AfPak (Afghanistan-Pakistan) region under President Obama, accurately described this new war from the start as a battle of narratives:

> Call it public diplomacy, or public affairs, or psychological warfare, or – if you really
> want to be blunt – propaganda. But whatever it is called, defining what this war is
> really about in the minds of the 1 billion Muslims in the world will be of decisive and
> historic importance.
>
> *(Holbrooke 2001)*

As the wars in two theaters waged on for years and the war in Afghanistan became the longest
war in US history (2001–14), US military top brass acknowledged their deficit in the perception
game. Admiral Mike Mullen, former chairman of the Joint Chiefs of Staff, projected sensitivity
to a culture-learning perspective that reflects the US military missteps taken in Pakistan and
Afghanistan that favoured the short-term hunting, killing, and capturing of the targeted enemy
over the longer-term relationship-building task of rebuilding a society from a war zone:

> No, our biggest problem isn't caves; it's credibility. Our messages lack credibility
> because we haven't invested enough in building trust and relationships, and we haven't
> always delivered on promises. The most common questions that I get in Pakistan and
> Afghanistan are: 'Will you really stay with us this time?' 'Can we really count on you?' I
> tell them that we will and that they can, but when it comes to real trust in places such
> as these, I don't believe we are even in Year Zero yet. There's a very long way to go.
>
> *(Mullen 2009)*

On the other side of the Potomac River from the Pentagon sat Foggy Bottom, where State
Department leadership downplayed the propaganda/security angle in favour of a public diplomacy emphasis on long-term relationship building. In a speech titled 'Public Diplomacy – A
National Security Imperative', and presented at the Washington, DC think tank, Center for a
New American Security, Under Secretary of State Judith McHale put it succinctly: 'This is not
a propaganda contest – it is a relationship race' (2009). Her prescription for rebuilding America's
loss of credibility generally, but also specific to the two long wars, was to utilize a hybrid model
of traditional engagement and cutting-edge technology:

> Broadly speaking, public diplomacy operates on two levels. First, communication.
> This is the air game, the radio and TV broadcasts, the websites and media outreach
> that all seek to explain and provide context for US policies and action; and second,
> engagement, the ground game of direct people-to-people exchanges, speakers, and
> embassy-sponsored cultural events that build personal relationships.
>
> *(McHale 2009)*

This getting back to basics approach of the Department of State was a continuation of the philosophy of her predecessors, like former Ambassador to Morocco Margaret Tutwiler (2003) who had
said at her confirmation hearing in October of that year that Washington needed 'to do a much
better job of listening. I have served in two Administrations in Washington and one from overseas.
As much as we would like to think Washington knows best, we have to be honest and admit we do
not necessarily always have all the answers.' The problem with Tutwiler, as it was with public diplomacy leaders in place at State, is that more often than not they rotated in and out or disappeared
altogether without cementing any lasting legacy. At six months, Tutwiler's tenure was the shortest.
The US military may wish for the Department of State to take the lead in public diplomacy, but
with such vacuum in leadership at the helm (Armistead 2010) DoD has stepped in to fill the void
with its own strategic communication, information operations, and psychological operations.

Conclusion

It has been almost a decade and a half since the events of 11 September 2001. The 9/11 Commission Report of 2004 called on what amounts to a total diplomacy in support of a total war that would include 'all elements of national power: diplomacy, intelligence, covert action, law enforcement, economic policy, foreign aid, public diplomacy, and homeland defense' (Kean and Hamilton 2004: Executive Summary).

With the drawdown of US and NATO forces in Iraq and Afghanistan, we are likely to see some shift away from the post-9/11 ideologically-driven and security-driven models of public diplomacy, although questions remain as to the matter of degree. Will the rise in Cold War-style rhetoric between the United States and Russia, and the rise of the Islamic State, in reality and in media consciousness, perpetuate this full-spectrum dominance in shaping perceptions and attitudes? Perhaps so. Most assuredly, the US model of public diplomacy, which has favoured the military-security paradigm tactical approach to 'winning hearts and minds', will remain the dominant model in funding and personnel, but not necessarily effectiveness.

The balance between government's drive for credibility through more openness and transparency, and non-state actors, many adversarial to state interests, to use whatever means necessary to win allegiance to their cause, puts democracy – and accountability – driven public diplomacy at a distinct disadvantage. As Gregory notes (2008: 2), 'Network societies challenge organizational hierarchies. Attention – not information – is today's scarce resource.' With or without public diplomacy, the balance of power of old, which favoured superpowers and big-power parity and stability, is neither equipped for nor fully invested in the challenges faced by the imbalance of power today.

Notes

1 The author was a United States Information Agency (USIA) official from 1992 to 1994, which was the US Government's official independent agency of foreign affairs (1953–99) devoted to public diplomacy. In 1999, USIA public diplomacy efforts were integrated into the Department of State, but many strategies and tactics of public diplomacy can be found throughout government agencies today. In the US, the Department of Defense uses affiliate names like strategic communication and information operations.
2 The author was involved with the establishment and expansion of two leading US postgraduate programmes in public diplomacy (University of Southern California; Syracuse University), as well as internationally (UiTM; Tsinghua University; Interdisciplinary Center-Herzilya).

References

Armistead, L. (2010) *Information Operations Matters*, Washington, DC: Potomac Books.
Barber, B. (1999) 'Group Will Battle Propaganda Abroad', *Washington Times*, 28 July.
Barstow, D. (2008) 'Behind TV Analysts, Pentagon's Hidden Hand', *The New York Times*, 20 April.
Bennett, W. L. (2003) 'Operation Perfect Storm: The Press and the Iraq War', *Political Communication Report, International Communication Association and American Political Science Association*, 13(3), Fall.
Bush, G. W. (2001) 'Address to a Joint Session of Congress', 20 September. Online. Available HTTP: <http://georgewbush-whitehouse.archives.gov/news/releases/2001/09/print/20010920-8.html> (accessed 13 November 2015).
Carroll, W. (1948) *Persuade or Perish*, Boston, MA: Houghton Mifflin.
Caslen, R. L. (2011) 'The Way the Army Fights Today', *Military Review*, March/April: 84–8.
Chapple-Sokol, S. (2013) 'Culinary Diplomacy: Breaking Bread to Win Hearts and Minds', *The Hague Journal of Diplomacy* 8(2): 161–83.
Cull, N. (2006) '"Public Diplomacy" before Gullion: The Evolution of a Phrase', *The CPD Blog*, 18 April. Online. Available HTTP: <http://uscpublicdiplomacy.org/blog/060418_public_diplomacy_before_gullion_the_evolution_of_a_phrase> (accessed 10 March 2015).

Dao, J. and Schmitt, E. (2002) 'A Nation Challenged: Hearts and Minds; Pentagon Readies Efforts to Sway Sentiment Abroad', *The New York Times*, February 19. Online. Available HTTP: <http://www.nytimes.com/2002/02/19/world/nation-challenged-hearts-minds-pentagon-readies-efforts-sway-sentiment-abroad.html?pagewanted=all> (accessed 13 November 2015).

Davis, R. T. (2009) *US Army and the Media in the 20th Century*, Fort Leavenworth, KS: Combat Studies Institute Press. US Army Combined Arms Center, Occasional Paper 31.

Economist (2001) 'Fighting Terrorism: The Propaganda War', *The Economist*, 4 October. Online. Available HTTP: <http://www.economist.com/node/806392> (accessed 10 August 2015).

Fitzpatrick, K., Fullerton, J., and Kendrick, A. (2013) 'Public Relations and Public Diplomacy: Conceptual and Practical Connections', *Public Relations Journal* 7(4): 1–21.

Gass, R. and J. Seiter (2009) 'Credibility and Public Diplomacy,' in N. Snow and P. M. Taylor (eds.) *Routledge Handbook of Public Diplomacy*, New York and London: Routledge, 154–65.

Gates, R. (2008) *Remarks of the Secretary of Defense Robert M. Gates*, US Global Leadership Campaign, Washington, DC: Office of the Assistant Secretary of Defense, 15 July. Online. Available HTTP: <http://www.defense.gov/Speeches/Speech.aspx?SpeechID=1262> (accessed 24 April 2015).

Golan, G., Yang, S. and Kinsey, D. (2015) *International Public Relations and Public Diplomacy: Communication and Engagement*, New York: Palgrave.

Green, F. (1988) *American Propaganda Abroad*, New York: Hippocrene Books.

Gregory, B. (2005) 'Public Diplomacy and Strategic Communication: Cultures, Firewalls, and Imported Norms', Paper presented at the American Political Science Association Conference on International Communication and Conflict. George Washington University and Georgetown University, Washington, DC.

Gregory, B. (2008) 'Public Diplomacy and National Security: Lessons from the US Experience', *Small Wars Journal*. Online. Available HTTP: <http://smallwarsjournal.com/jrnl/art/public-diplomacy-and-national-security>accessed 11 August 2015).

Gygax, J. and Snow, N. (2013) '9/11 and the Advent of Total Diplomacy: Strategic Communication as a Primary Weapon of War', *Journal of 9/11 Studies* 38(July). Online. Available HTTP: <http://www.journalof911studies.com/resources/2013GygaxSnowVol38Jul.pdf> (accessed 28 June 2014).

Hayden, C. (2007) 'Arguing Public Diplomacy: The Role of Argument Formations in US Foreign Policy Rhetoric, *The Hague Journal of Diplomacy* 2: 229–54. Online. Available HTTP: <https://www.academia.edu/2529463/_Arguing_Public_Diplomacy_The_Role_of_Argument_Formations_in_Foreign_Policy_Rhetoric_> (accessed 12 August 2015).

Heath, R. L. (2001) *Handbook of Public Relations*, Thousand Oaks, CA: Sage.

Holbrooke, R. (2001) 'Get the Message Out', *The Washington Post*, 28 October. Online. Available HTTP: <http://www.washingtonpost.com/wpdyn/content/article/2010/12/13/AR2010121305410.html> (accessed 11 August 2015).

Hughes, K. (2005) 'The Mission of Public Diplomacy, Nominee for Under Secretary for Public Diplomacy and Public Affairs. Testimony at confirmation hearing before the Senate Foreign Relations Committee', Washington, DC, 22 July. Online. Available HTTP: <http://2001–9.state.gov/r/us/2005/49967.htm> (accessed 12 August 2015).

Kean, T. and Hamilton, L. (2004) *The 9/11 Commission Report: Final Report of the National Commission on Terrorist Attacks upon the United States*, Washington, DC: Government Printing Office.

Kinzer, S. (2013) *The Brothers: John Foster Dulles, Allen Dulles, and Their Secret World War*, New York: Times Books/Henry Holt.

McHale, J. (2009) 'Public Diplomacy: A National Security Imperative. Under Secretary for Public Diplomacy and Public Affairs Address at the Center for a New American Security, Washington, DC'. Online. Available HTTP: <http://www.state.gov/r/remarks/2009/124640.htm> (accessed 23 January 2015).

McPherson, H. C. Jr (1980) 'Walter Lippmann's American Century', *Foreign Affairs* 59(1): 163–71.

Mullen, M. (2009) 'From the Chairman: Getting back to Basics', *Joint Forces Quarterly* 55: 1–4.

Nye, J. (2004) *Soft Power: The Means to Success in World Politics*, New York: Public Affairs.

Nye, J. (2009) 'Get Smart', *Foreign Affairs*, July/August. Online. Available HTTP: https://www.foreignaffairs.com/articles/2009-07-01/get-smart (accessed 11 August 2015).

Peterson, P. G., Bloomgarden, K. F., Grunwald, H. A., Morey, D. E., Telhami, S., Sieg, J., and Herbstman, S. (2003) *Finding America's Voice: A Strategy for Reinvigorating US Public Diplomacy – Report of an Independent Task Force Sponsored by the Council on Foreign Relations*, New York: Council on Foreign Relations Press.

Rockower, P. S. (2012) 'Recipes for Gastrodiplomacy', *Place Branding and Public Diplomacy* 8: 235–46.

Root, E. (1922) 'A Requisite for the Success of Popular Diplomacy', *Foreign Affairs* 1(1).

Root, E. (1937) 'A Requisite for the Success of Popular Diplomacy', *Foreign Affairs* 15(3).

Rumbaugh, R. and Leatherman, M. (2012) *The Pentagon as Pitchman: Perception and Reality of Public Diplomacy*, Washington, DC: Stimson. Online. Available HTTP: <http://www.stimson.org/images/uploads/research-pdfs/Pentagon_as_pitchman.pdf> (accessed 15 May 2015).

Saxon, W. (1998) 'Edmund Asbury Gullion, 85, Wide-Ranging Career Envoy', *The New York Times*, 31 March. Online. Available HTTP: <http://www.nytimes.com/1998/03/31/world/edmund-asbury-gullion-85-wide-ranging-career-envoy.html> (accessed 13 November 2015).

Schneider, C. (2005) 'Culture Communicates: US Diplomacy That Works', in J. Melissen (ed.) *The New Public Diplomacy: Soft Power in International Relations*, New York: Palgrave Macmillan, 147–68.

Snow, N. (2013) *Truth is the Best Propaganda: Edward R. Murrow's Speeches in the Kennedy Years*, McLean, VA: Miniver Press.

Snow, N. (2015a) 'Public Diplomacy and Public Relations: Will the Twain Ever Meet?', in G. Golan, S. Yang, and D. Kinsey (eds.) *International Public Relations and Public Diplomacy*, New York: Peter Lang, 73–90.

Snow, N. (2015b) 'Deconstructing Japan's Public Relations: Where Is the Public?', in J. L'Etang, D. McKie, N. Snow, and J. Xifra (eds.) *The Routledge Handbook of Critical Public Relations*, New York and London: Routledge, 321–334.

Snyder, A. (1987) *Warriors of Disinformation: American Propaganda, Soviet Lies, and the Winning of the Cold War*, New York: Arcade.

Snyder, A. (1995) *Warriors of Disinformation: American Propaganda, Soviet Lies, and the Winning of the Cold War*, New York: Arcade Publishing.

Sproule, J. (1997) *Propaganda and Democracy: The American Experience of Media and Mass Persuasion*, Cambridge: Cambridge University Press.

Steel, R. (1980) *Walter Lippmann and the American Century*, Boston, MA: Little, Brown.

Szondi, G. (2008) 'Public Diplomacy and Nation Branding: Conceptual Similarities and Differences', Discussion Paper in Diplomacy, Netherlands Institute of International Relations 'Clingendael'. Online. Available HTTP: <http://www.clingendael.nl/sites/default/files/20081022_pap_in_dip_nation_branding.pdf> (accessed 12 August 2015).

Taylor, P. M. (2003[1990]) *Munitions of the Mind: A History of Propaganda from the Ancient World to the Present Day*, Manchester: Manchester University Press.

Time (1950) 'Total Diplomacy', *Time*, 13 March, 55(11): 19.

Tutwiler, M. (2003) 'Margaret D. Tutwiler, Under Secretary for Public Diplomacy and Public Affairs. Testimony before the Senate Foreign Relations Committee', Washington, DC, 29 October.

Wike, R. (2012) 'Does Humanitarian Aid Improve America's Image?', Pew Research Center Global Attitudes and Trends, 6 March. Online. Available HTTP: <http://www.pewglobal.org/2012/03/06/does-humanitarian-aid-improve-americas-image/> (accessed 12 August 2015).

Wiseman, G. (2015) *Isolate or Engage: Adversarial States, US Foreign Policy, and Public Diplomacy*, Stanford, CA: Stanford University Press.

37
STATEBUILDING

Tobias Debiel and Patricia Rinck

Statebuilding became a central paradigm in the practice of international intervention in the first years of the twenty-first century (cf. Mallaby 2002; Rotberg 2002) for two main reasons located at the interface of security and development: first, countries torn by violent conflict and characterized by institutional dysfunctionalities became more numerous. Second, weak or failing statehood became a synonym for almost unpredictable security risks such as transnational terrorism, organized crime and drug trafficking, or the spread of contagious diseases after 9/11. Today, a quarter-century after 1989 and fifteen years after 9/11, the track record of the international community with building peaceful structures in war-torn countries, strengthening state capacities and implementing government and governance reforms is mixed at best. Against this background, critical Security Studies has gained influence – criticizing the social-engineering-based concept of 'liberal peace' and revealing the weaknesses of the 'peacebuilding-as-statebuilding' approach.

In the following, we reconstruct and reflect critically upon the statebuilding debate. We start by investigating how concepts of statehood and state failure became prevalent from the end of the 1990s onwards, and how they served as a stepping-stone for the development of statebuilding strategies. Second, we will illustrate how the latter can be understood as a social-engineering approach that aims to provide a shortcut to the Weberian state. A shortcoming of such an understanding is that it ahistorically assumes that a polity can be planned and administered from the outside, thereby ignoring important insights from the debate on state formation. The historical institutionalist critique is partly shared by post-liberal approaches that we look at in section three. Still, they are more far-reaching by transgressing the framework of the nation-state and taking an emancipatory stance. The fourth section, accordingly, analyses three main features of these perspectives that have turned the analytical focus to 'everyday peace' and resilience at the local level, aiming to investigate new forms of 'hybrid peace' at the international–local interface and to replace linear understandings of state and peacebuilding with complexity thinking. In our conclusion, we sketch out research perspectives that prioritize gaining a more in-depth empirical understanding of current statebuilding processes and of how political orders emerge after the end of violent conflict.

State failure and its reflection in policy discourses

The shift towards statebuilding gradually started at the beginning of the 1990s when the 'good governance paradigm' took into account that 'institutions matter' and that these are a prerequisite for market-based development, a counter movement to the neglect of the state in the 1980s. A few years later, a 'rehabilitation of the state' was heralded with the 1997 World Development Report. The report recognized that an 'effective state' is needed in order to serve the goal of development (World Bank 1997: iii–vi). Increasingly, issues of governance and state capabilities were viewed through a conflict prevention/post-conflict lens, given the high number of war-torn societies, or so-called post-conflict countries, which became a serious cause of concern in the field of development cooperation in the early 1990s. In order to cope with this particular challenge, the World Bank created the Task Force on the Work of the World Bank Group in Low Income Countries Under Stress (LICUS) in November 2001. The OECD/DAC developed a similar strategy to deal with 'difficult partners' or, as it was later termed, 'fragile states', who accordingly were seen to 'lack political will and/or capacity to provide the basic functions for poverty reduction, development, and to safeguard the security and human rights of their populations' (OECD/DAC 2007: 2).

In this debate, 'state failure' was generally defined as the inability of a state to provide security and public goods to its citizens, to collect taxes, and to formulate, implement, and enforce policies and laws. Central to such an understanding are conventional definitions of the 'state', which tend to use a Weberian concept of statehood. Thus, 'state failure' and 'state fragility' are usually defined as diverging – albeit to varying degrees – from an ideal (and idealized) type of the state (examples of such an approach are, with varying terminology, DFID 2005: 7; OECD/DAC 2007: 2; World Bank 1997: 20).

After the terrorist attacks on the World Trade Center and the Pentagon, the attention paid to 'state failure' issues further intensified. Western states placed the issue of failing and failed states at the top of their own agendas, in contrast to the earlier perception that saw them as a concern for humanitarian interventions and local/regional security. This trend led to a 'securitization' (Buzan et al. 1998) of the state failure discourse that had so far mainly been embedded in development thinking. Rather than concerns about how fragile states could achieve progress, for instance, with regard to the Millennium Development Goals (MDGs), security threats became the focus of attention. Strengthening state capacities was no longer seen primarily as a requirement for successful development cooperation, but rather as a tool to tackle supposed root causes of terrorism. This merging of security and development resulted in an increasing acceptance of military interventions into these 'failing states' which, in some cases, involved the temporary or even permanent suspension of de facto sovereignty.

Statebuilding: shortcut to the Weberian state?

For a long time, statebuilding was understood as a process that a country would naturally undergo, following the development of European states in history. In the 1950s and 60s, modernization theory assumed that post-colonial countries would follow a similar process after independence. The current debate, however, does not conceive of statebuilding as a 'natural' process that will simply run its course but assumes instead that external actors can actively 'build states'. As Ottaway argued, such social-engineering strategies at the development–security nexus more or less looked for a 'short-cut to the Weberian state' (Ottaway 2002: 1004). In the following, we first analyse how statebuilding elements have been integrated into the 'liberal peacebuilding' approach over the past two decades. Second, we deal with a different trajectory, namely 'counter-insurgency' strategies that have also taken up statebuilding measures, but at the same time have followed different logics and priorities.

Statebuilding and liberal peacebuilding: unfulfilled promises

When linked to multilateral goals of development and peace, statebuilding is understood as 'purposeful action to develop the capacity, institutions, and legitimacy of the state in relation to an effective political process for negotiating the mutual demands between state and societal groups' (OECD/DAC 2008: 14). This definition combines the criteria of institution building, legitimacy building, and state-society relations. In recent years, it has been an important goal to orientate the state towards 'resilience' (OECD/DAC 2008: 7–8), resilience being the 'capacity to positively or successfully adapt to external problems or threats' (Chandler 2012: 217).

Early on, the development-related policy discourse developed quite differentiated concepts within the emerging 'statebuilding paradigm'. Comparing strategic documents from several key institutions – the World Bank, the OECD/DAC, DFID and USAID – Debiel et al. (2007) identified several elements that were shared by the major multilateral and national development agencies: enhanced state capacities and economic, social policy, and democratic reform processes were pronounced as mid- to long-term goals in a manner that allowed statebuilding to be framed as part of a liberal peacebuilding perspective. At the same time, related strategies took the restricted capacities of 'fragile states' as well as legitimacy deficits into account and included 'quick impact' measures that promised to present visible successes to the population. Finally, although engagement with governments was the first choice, employing non-state actors as local partners also remained an option, especially in cases where countries were suffering from institutional breakdown and where governments showed no inclination to embark on development goals.

When the UN expanded its traditional peacemaking and peacekeeping activities and engaged in the huge peace missions of the 1990s, statebuilding became a top issue in post-conflict societies. The core goal of all these missions – whether in Angola, Bosnia, Cambodia, Nicaragua, or Timor-Leste – was to transform war-torn societies into peaceful market-based democracies by building institutions according to the Western role model of the liberal state in order to prevent future violence (Doyle and Sambanis 2006). A broad 'peacebuilding palette' (Smith 2004) was developed, which comprised institution building and other activities in the areas of security and the military, the socio-economic realm, and the political and diplomatic field, as well as justice and reconciliation. Statebuilding activities were included in the mandates of the peace missions, e.g. restoring the state's monopoly of force; strengthening political institutions such as the civil service, the military, the police, and the judiciary; and improving state capacity in service provision and financial management (Curtis 2013: 81–3).

Liberal peacebuilding and statebuilding are often portrayed as complementary, mutually dependent, and reinforcing by policy-makers and academics (Call with Wyeth 2008). Their relationship, however, is not necessarily unproblematic: policy-makers and practitioners usually face a trade-off between short-term stabilization and long-term transformation of post-conflict societies. For instance, international actors have tried to end many violent conflicts through power-sharing agreements – especially in sub-Saharan Africa – pursuing the idea that if former adversaries share political power, this will enable them to cooperatively decide on the country's future institutions, so that a strong state can be built (Jarstad 2013: 253). However, experience has shown that these agreements often do not only fail to achieve short-term stability but can also have negative consequences on longer-term peacebuilding goals (Mehler 2009; Roeder and Rothchild 2005). Even when some initial stability has been achieved, statebuilding activities may still endanger peacebuilding goals. For instance, military capacity building has often impeded political reform and even strengthened authoritarian regimes, for example in Uganda, Ethiopia, or Rwanda (Beswick 2014: 231). Hence, there is an inherent dilemma: while a strong, well-institutionalized state seems to be necessary for peaceful development, strengthening its coercive capacity also increases its capacity for oppression (Curtis 2013: 80).

Proponents of 'peacebuilding-as-statebuilding' (e.g. Collier et al. 2003; Doyle and Sambanis 2006; Paris 2004) acknowledge that external, top-down institution building may suffer from such a dilemma, as well as from a lack of local legitimacy and a poor consistency with other donor objectives. Still, they are convinced that such shortcomings can be ameliorated through a refined sequencing of different measures, better coordination among external actors, and negotiation with local elites (Curtis 2013: 84). The track record of such approaches, however, is very mixed. A look at the 'Fragile States Index' (Fund for Peace 2015) and other measures shows that many of the countries that have experienced violent conflict and received international assistance have remained unstable or weak, and that many contemporary conflicts (such as in Mali, South Sudan, or the Central African Republic) can be seen as the result of unresolved statebuilding processes.

Statebuilding and counterinsurgency: inconsistencies of the stabilization approach

Besides the context of liberal peacebuilding in war-torn societies, statebuilding has also become part of enforcement actions and counter-insurgency campaigns – such as the US-led military interventions in Afghanistan and Iraq, or the AU mission in Somalia. They differ from the liberal peacebuilding context in two ways: first, statebuilding takes place in the context of an ongoing armed conflict. Second, statebuilding is defined by the stabilization approach, which may consist of liberal elements, but primarily aims at creating a security arrangement that gets insurgency forces under control.

Counter-insurgency strategies have integrated elements of statebuilding and aim at 'localizing' the maintenance of order in a mid- and long-term perspective. Still, the combination of the two approaches is characterized by inherent tensions. As Astri Suhrke shows with regard to Afghanistan, the crucial unresolved question is how external actors can build peace or even a state while simultaneously fighting a war. The contradictions become particularly evident if the state's security sector is dysfunctional, due to the opposition of various local actors – including tribal authorities, large landowners, or religious leaders – who fear that the strengthening of state capacities may result in a loss of their authority (Suhrke 2013: 271, 281). Against this background, international interveners often decide to circumvent the central government. A case in point is the US' 'war against terror' in Afghanistan. The US relied on 'resilience' at the community level and supported armed local militias, co-opted potential spoilers, and tried to reconcile competing power brokers, thus building a 'hybrid model of governance' that integrated traditional institutions and governance mechanisms (Suhrke 2013: 271; Wardak and Hamidzada 2012: 82). Even though this resulted in a temporary improvement of local security, it turned out to be counterproductive later with regard to statebuilding issues such as the establishment of a monopoly of force and minimum criteria of 'good enough governance'.

The case of Somalia shows that external intervention, combining statebuilding and counter-insurgency elements, is limited even if regional actors such as the AU take the lead (Curtis 2013: 90). More than twenty-five years after state collapse, and despite various international efforts to stabilize the situation, there is still no state monopoly of force in Somalia (as would be required with statebuilding), with the exception of the quasi-independent Somaliland. At the same time, various local actors besides formal state actors provide different security functions (Hills 2014: 90). Though the countries differ in many aspects, a well-known phenomenon from Afghanistan can be observed here as well: Somalis superficially support statebuilding processes and donors' projects as these are perceived as opening up opportunities for patronage and assets. At a closer look, however, they often just mimic donors' models and carefully pay attention that these processes do not really result in statebuilding (Hills 2014: 94, 96, 103).

Statebuilding in the context of counter-insurgency operations is, contrary to 'peacebuilding-as-statebuilding', a very pragmatic approach, which primarily pays attention to security governance and emphasizes short-term outputs. It is based on a reductionist understanding of the state as reduced to the core institutions of the security sector. While it can better take account of the diversity of actors operating in the security area than the liberal model, it conceptually offers little more than the short-term stabilization of patchwork governance or the external brokering among local security actors. Therefore, it does not offer many clues of how statebuilding or state formation could be supported constructively from the outside.

Reminders from history: state formation as a coercive and violent process

The statebuilding strategies mentioned above mirror 'an attempt to develop such an entity quickly and without the long, conflictual, and often brutal evolution that historically underlies the formation of states' (Ottaway 2002: 1004). Experiences over the last two decades have indicated that such a goal is over-ambitious or even hubristic. In order to gain a more realistic understanding of how states can be established, a closer look at the analysis of state formation processes and what they can (and cannot) offer for today's challenges is useful.

In his well-known four-part framework, Tilly (1985) argued that the modern state was built following a monopolization of violence, through the centralization of power and solidification of the state as a political, controlling entity – here, the economy, resources, and taxation come into play. After external rivals have been eliminated (war-making), and internal rivals have been eliminated or controlled (state-making), state agents must ensure citizens' support by protecting and providing for them. A system of resource extraction is developed that finances the first three goals – in modern states, these resources are typically gained through taxation (Gibler and Miller 2014: 635; Kisangani and Pickering 2014: 188).

Historically, state formation has thus been a coercive and often violent process. A short assessment of empirical evidence shows that this historical pattern also holds for more recent conflicts/statebuilding processes outside of Europe, such as Sudan (1963–72), Rwanda (1963–4), Pakistan (1973–7), Mozambique (1979–92) or Timor-Leste (1999), to name but a few.

However, Tilly's model is tailored to a specific historical and regional setting and is therefore not sufficient for fully understanding today's varieties of state formation processes and the underlying political economies. First, while there is still a link between state formation and violence, Tilly's well-known claim that 'war makes states' (1985: 170) – based on experiences in sixteenth- and seventeenth-century Europe – does not seem to hold any more since the mid-twentieth century. Rather, many wars after 1945, and in particular the 'new wars' fought in the 1990s, have had the opposite effect by contributing to state failure rather than to state-making. One key difference is that since 1945, the newly emerging states of the global South have enjoyed a historically unprecedented level of protection (Jackson 1990). Thanks to the principles of self-determination and state sovereignty enshrined in international law, they were able to establish themselves as independent entities at the international level despite obvious deficits in their degree of state effectiveness. As a result, large-scale interstate wars have become uncommon and conquest has more or less disappeared from international politics. This, in turn, has mitigated the necessity to create internal coherence.[1] While European rulers in the sixteenth and seventeenth centuries were forced to seek internal support through alliances with their citizens in the face of external threats (Verkoren and Kamphuis 2013: 505), the biggest threat to the state is currently posed not by other state actors, but by home-grown, transnational insurgent groups whose success does not depend on balancing war-making, extraction, protection or state-making (Tilly 1985), but rather on linking their war economies up to the global market and financial system.

Second, statebuilding often does not result in a Weberian state. Verkoren and Kamphuis (2013) try to develop a more nuanced conceptual approach for today's realities. More specifically, they distinguish four models of state formation: the Western, developmental, rentier, and predatory paths, highlighting the significance of the underlying economic structure for a state's further development path. The developmental approach to state formation refers to the statebuilding approach chosen by the East Asian 'developmental states' such as Taiwan, South Korea, Singapore, and Malaysia, which achieved remarkable economic development through export-oriented growth, in a rather short time period, and in a peaceful manner. The rentier path to state formation follows a different logic, with the state deriving its income from rents (natural resources or development assistance) rather than taxes, and replacing input legitimacy (citizens' participation) by output legitimacy (provision of public goods). Finally, in predatory states, rents are simply exploited for the personal benefit of elites who, in the process, estrange themselves from the population. A predatory state is for instance illustrated by the case of pre-war Sierra Leone (Verkoren and Kamphuis 2013: 506–10).

Such a differentiated approach helps determine under which conditions the establishment of a Western-style democratic state may or may not be promising. Accordingly, Verkoren and Kamphuis argue that trying to turn a rentier state into a Western-style democracy will not work because the structure of the economy creates strong incentives for patronage-based rule, which is generally incompatible with democracy. Under these circumstances, the introduction of liberal institutions, as envisaged in the 'peacebuilding-as-statebuilding' approach, can even have negative consequences, in terms of destroying power balances among elites and fuelling violent conflict (Verkoren and Kamphuis 2013: 508–9). Within the context of a predatory state, the effects might even be worse.

Despite these limitations, there is a lot that we can learn from Tilly's framework. In all variants of statebuilding, the nature of the political settlement between contesting groups is key. It may result from a fight against internal and external rivals of the state, or it may represent a modality for political accommodation. The litmus test, according to Putzel and Di John, is concerned with determining whether the respective political settlement in a country properly reflects the contentions and bargains among various elites, between elites and non-elites, between different groups (e.g. genders, ethnic, linguistic, or religious), and between 'those who control the state and the wider society' (Putzel and Di John 2012: 1), and whether it is able to manage violence in a reliable manner.

The local turn, resilience, and hybridity as alternative perspectives

The historical perspective on state formation questions the short-term rationale of social engineering inherent in current statebuilding enterprises, but remains within the framework of the nation-state. Scepticism towards the liberal peacebuilding paradigm, in other words, is not concerned with the level of analysis. Rather, the aim has been to gain better-informed and empirically grounded insights of how state formation *really* works. On this basis, external actors might assist in more modest ways, e.g. by facilitating arrangements that are in line with historical path dependencies and which thereby promise to lead to a better accommodation of elite aspirations and the underlying societal interests.

Critical approaches in the field of security and peacebuilding studies share the assessment that external statebuilding, as we know it, reflects a rather technical, apolitical exercise by 'mainstream' politics and research (Chandler 2010; Goodhand and Sedra 2013: 242; Jabri 2013; Mac Ginty 2012). In contrast to historical institutionalist approaches, however, they move away from the level of the central state, as well as the issue of elite accommodation, and take a normative stance. Statebuilding, in this view, is seen to maintain 'conservative versions of peace' that neglect important issues of equality, class identity and the social contract, agency, and the international order, which are raised by more historical and structural, sociological, anthropological, and postcolonial perspectives respectively (Richmond 2013: 308). Accordingly, post-liberal research has shifted attention to the local context as well as to the 'hybrid' environment that results from external intervention and its interaction with local agency. Furthermore, post-liberal theories tend to move away from linear understandings of statebuilding and peacebuilding, and instead take up notions of complexity.

The crucial frame of reference is 'local peace' which is seen as the result of a complex process of an 'everyday and emancipatory type, in which authority, rights, redistribution, and legitimacy are slowly rethought' (Mac Ginty and Richmond 2013: 769, 771). Everyday peacemaking, in this view, functions without any kind of external intervention. At the same time, proponents of this school of thought concede that everyday peace can be a very limited form of conflict management, which tries to minimize the impact of conflict through tolerance and coexistence, rather than through more expansive forms of conflict transformation, aimed at addressing the underlying causes of the conflict (Mac Ginty 2014: 557, 559).

The 'local turn', secondly, is accompanied by more in-depth analysis of how local and international norms, institutions, and actors interact, and by considering whether, despite their shortcomings, liberal interventions might open up opportunities for a kind of 'hybrid peace' as a combination of both logics in mutual learning processes (Belloni 2012; Mac Ginty 2010). Such a 'hybrid peace', however, may have an emancipatory potential, but can – as Afghanistan shows – also result in a rather precarious situation (Goodhand and Sedra 2013: 243, 250).

Third, post-liberal research doubts that social engineering, based on linear and positivist understandings of causality, is possible. Instead, war-torn societies are understood as complex social systems that 'develop the ability to organize and maintain themselves not because of a centrally controlled hierarchy, such as a strategic framework or a strategic plan, but as a result of emergence' (de Coning 2013: 3–4). Accordingly, respective approaches do not place any significant degree of trust in the reform and transformation of formal institutions via governance strategies or in efforts that seek to strengthen the resilience of state capacities. Rather, 'resilience', as conceptualized by post-liberals, differs from related neoliberal understandings, as it does not primarily focus on the individual, its vulnerability, and its market-oriented coping mechanisms, but rather on communities.

From a statebuilding perspective, post-liberal approaches have highlighted severe shortcomings and traps of external strategies. At the same time, these approaches fall short of providing coherent and comprehensive conceptual alternatives (see Debiel and Rinck 2016). With their focus on local agency as well as on everyday practices, they tend to underestimate the relevance of institutional rules and structures – like the state security apparatus, justice system, parliament, parties, and authorities – and how they impact the causes of violence and can help to overcome these. While claiming to create space for negotiating local solutions, they do not pay close attention to the question of which rules are to apply in this space and whether the political constitution of regimes is significant or not. Not least, research in the wake of the local turn partly 'has proceeded on the assumption that international interveners and local communities either do or could interact in a manner that is unmediated by state intervention' (Hughes et al. 2015: 821).

A more promising starting point for analysing political order in war-torn societies might therefore be an analytical framework that Boege et al. developed. They interpret such societies as

> places in which diverse and competing institutions and logics of order and behaviour coexist, overlap, and intertwine: the logic of the 'formal' state, the logic of traditional 'informal' societal order, the logic of globalisation and international civil society with its abundance of highly diverse actors, such as non-governmental organisations (NGOs), multinational enterprises (MNEs), international organisations, development aid agencies, private military companies (PMCs), and so on'
>
> *(Boege 2011: 433)*

The resulting structures, which decide about the distribution of power and authority, are described as Hybrid Political Orders (HPO) in which the state has to share its sovereignty with a peculiar mix of 'local', private, transnational, and international actors and institutions (Boege et al. 2009; Carbonnier and Wennmann 2013). This notion of hybridity partly integrates the above-mentioned idea of a 'hybrid peace', combining and reconciling liberal peacebuilding concepts with local perceptions. At the same time, it is more differentiated with regard to the variety of domestic and trans-national/international actors that it recognizes, and refrains from attributing any kind of normative value to 'hybridity'.

Conclusion

This chapter has argued that mainstream understandings of statebuilding share a more or less teleological outlook, with the Weberian state as the 'natural' endpoint of postcolonial political development. They are rooted in concepts of 'state failure' that became prevalent in the development–security nexus of the late 1990s and early 2000s. Within the fragile states discourse, institutions and governance mechanisms have been analysed against the background of what is not there (or what is deviating from the Weberian ideal), thereby offering no guidance for understanding what actually is there outside formal structures (Goodhand and Sedra 2013: 242).

Statebuilding approaches became part of two distinct strategies: first of all, 'statebuilding-as-peacebuilding' tries to externally engineer institutional reforms, the introduction of market economies, and democratic political regimes. The liberal school is aware of tensions and dilemmas that, for instance, exist between short-term prerequisites, such as the quick provision of security, and long-term goals, such as the establishment of accountable state institutions as well as participatory and inclusive governance. Still, they maintain that sequenced and carefully calibrated strategies might result in a 'shortcut' to the Weberian state. Second, the integration of statebuilding approaches into counter-insurgency operations pursues more modest goals, explicitly puts a premium on security-related quick-impact measures, and draws, if considered necessary, on local governance mechanisms beyond formal state structures. At the same time, the inherent contradictions are even more evident than in the liberal approach, as it is extremely difficult to build up a legitimate state while continuing with military intervention and relying on institutions and actors that regard the state as a potential rival.

The mixed balance (liberal peacebuilding) or rather negative track record (counter-insurgency) of current statebuilding approaches has reminded mainstream approaches that state formation has always been a rather long and frequently violent process. Charles Tilly's seminal work on state-making can still serve as a frame of reference, as it brings political economy (extraction of resources) and the control of violent means (protection of territory and populations) back into our analysis. Still, we have argued that the rules of the international system after the Second World War have changed, and that new varieties of state formation (resulting, among others, in developmental and rentier states) have emerged. International actors, thus, are well advised to better understand how existing political orders work and how they might adapt, react, or even resist those measures that promote the Weberian or related models of the state.

Post-liberal critiques of statebuilding go beyond frameworks that focus on the national level and elite contestation and accommodation. By analysing how 'local peace' functions in everyday practices, they try to identify non-Western modes of managing conflict and governing post-conflict societies. Though being critical of liberal strategies, they still see opportunities resulting from the interaction of international and local norms, institutions, and actors, which in its sum has resulted in 'hybrid' structures that foster mutual learning processes. Empirically, however, such structures are rather precarious, as the case of Afghanistan has shown. Not least, post-liberals have advanced the idea that most war-torn societies are places with an unstable and unpredictable environment, in which the outcomes of one's interventions are not predictable but contingent (Dunn Cavelty et al. 2015: 4–5) and in which the resilience of communities might be the best leverage available for overcoming violence.

Despite their valuable contribution to the statebuilding discourse, we have argued that post-liberal approaches tend to be rather reductionist and, in particular, tend to fall short of recognizing that local politics can hardly be understood without addressing institutional rules and settings as well as the distribution of power and authority at the national level (see Debiel and Rinck 2016). By maintaining a liberal–local divide, they implicitly attribute 'otherness' to non-Western actors and institutions, and reproduce Eurocentric thinking, so to say, on a higher level (Sabaratnam 2013). Further research on statebuilding, thus, should not replace the confinements of the Weberian state framework by 'local reductionism', but would be better advised to integrate structural analysis of hybrid political orders that emerge at the interface of local, national, and international levels. From an epistemic and methodological perspective, linear thinking and respective methods and tools – such as sequencing models – do not allow us to properly grasp inherent complexities and emergent processes. Still, complexity does not mean the absence of causalities. Accordingly, statebuilding research is well advised to look for more elaborate, non-deterministic models that establish nuanced causal inferences regarding the legacies of statebuilding. Empirical research is still the key, and current methods, favouring conceptual analysis, large-*n* inferences, and single case studies, should increasingly be complemented by process tracing, counterfactual analysis, comparative studies, and the use of control cases (Tansey 2014: 174).

Note

1 There seems to be a positive link between external threats to the state and domestic peace, and state capacity. Applying standard models of state capacity and insurgency models of conflict on a sample of states from 1946 to 2007, Gibler and Miller find that external threats to a given territory increased state capacity by unifying the state and by increasing the government's power to repress potential regime dissidents (Gibler and Miller 2014: 634; cf. 644–5).

References

Belloni, R. (2012) 'Hybrid Peace Governance: Its Emergence and Significance', *Global Governance* 18: 21–38.
Beswick, D. (2014) 'The Risks of African Military Capacity Building: Lessons from Rwanda', *African Affairs* 113(451): 212–31.
Boege, V. (2011) 'Potential and Limits of Traditional Approaches in Peacebuilding', in B. Austin, M. Fischer, and H. Giessmann (eds.) *Advancing Conflict Transformation*, The Berghof Handbook II, Opladen; Framington Hills, MI: Barbara Budrich, 431–57.
Boege, V., Brown, A., Clements, K., and Nolan, A. (2009) 'Undressing the Emperor: A Reply to Our Discussants. Building Peace in the Absence of States: Challenging the Discourse on State Failure', in M. Fischer and B. Schmelzle (eds.) *Building Peace in the Absence of States: Challenging the Discourse on State Failure*, Berghof Handbook Dialogue Series 8, Opladen; Framington Hills, MI: Barbara Budrich, 87–93.
Buzan, B., Wæver, O., and de Wilde, J. (1998) *Security: A New Framework for Analysis*, Boulder, CO: Lynne Rienner.
Call, T. and Wyeth, V. (eds.) (2008) *Building State to Build Peace*, Boulder, CO: Lynne Rienner in collaboration with the International Peace Institute.
Carbonnier, G. and Wennmann, A. (2013) 'Natural Resource Governance and Hybrid Political Orders', in D. Chandler and T. Sisk (eds.) *The Routledge Handbook of International Statebuilding*, London: Routledge.
Chandler, D. (2010) *International Statebuilding: The Rise of post-Liberal Governance*, London: Routledge.
Chandler, D. (2012) 'Resilience and Human Security: The Post-Interventionist Paradigm', *Security Dialogue* 43(3): 213–29.

Collier, P., Elliott, L., Hegre, H., Hoeffler, A., Reynal-Querol, M., and Sambanis, N. (2003) *Breaking the Conflict Trap: Civil War and Development Policy, A World Bank Policy Research Report*, Washington, DC: World Bank.

Curtis, D. (2013) 'The Limits to Statebuilding for Peace in Africa', *South African Journal of International Affairs*, 20(1): 79–97.

Debiel, T., Lambach, D. and Reinhardt, D. (2007) *'Stay Engaged' statt 'Let Them Fail': Ein Literaturbericht über entwicklungspolitische Debatten in Zeiten fragiler Staatlichkeit*, Duisburg: Institut für Entwicklung und Frieden. INEF Report 90/2007.

Debiel, T. and Rinck, P. (2016) 'Rethinking the Local in Peacebuilding: Moving away from the Liberal / post-Liberal divide', in T. Debiel, T. Held, and U. Schneckener (eds.) *Peacebuilding in Crisis: Rethinking Paradigms and Practices of Transnational Cooperation*, London: Routledge, 240–256.

De Coning, C. (2013) 'Understanding Peacebuilding as Essentially Local', *Stability: International Journal of Security and Development* 2(1): 1–6. Online. Available HTTP: <dx.doi.org/10.5334/sta.as> (accessed 19 July 2015).

DFID (Department for International Development) (2005) *Why We Need to Work More Effectively in Fragile States*, London: Department for International Development.

Doyle, M. and Sambanis, N. (2006) *Making War and Building Peace: United Nations Peace Operations*, Princeton, NJ: Princeton University Press.

Dunn Cavelty, M., Kaufmann, M. and Søby Kristensen, K. (2015) 'Resilience and (In)Security: Practices, Subjects, Temporalities', *Security Dialogue* 46(1): 3–14.

Fund for Peace (2015) 'Fragile States Index 2015', *Foreign Policy*. Online. Available HTTP: <fsi.fundforpeace. org> (accessed 20 July 2015).

Gibler, D. and Miller, S. (2014) 'External Territorial Threat, State Capacity, and Civil War', *Journal of Peace Research* 51(5): 634–46.

Goodhand, J. and Sedra, M. (2013) 'Rethinking Liberal Peacebuilding, Statebuilding and Transition in Afghanistan: An Introduction', *Central Asian Survey* 32(3): 239–54.

Hills, A. (2014) 'Somalia Works: Police Development as State Building', *African Affairs* 113(450): 88–107.

Hughes, C., Öjendal, J., and Schierenbeck, I. (2015) 'The Struggle versus the Song – The Local Turn in Peacebuilding: An Introduction', *Third World Quarterly* 36(5): 817–24.

Jabri, V. (2013) 'Peacebuilding, the Local and the International: A Colonial or a Postcolonial Rationality?', *Peacebuilding* 1(1): 3–16.

Jackson, R. (1990) *Quasi-States: Sovereignty, International Relations and the Third World*, Cambridge: Cambridge University Press.

Jarstad, A. (2013) 'Sharing Power to Build States', in D. Chandler and T. Sisk (eds.) *The Routledge Handbook of International Statebuilding*, London: Routledge, 246–256.

Kisangani, E. and Pickering, J. (2014) 'Rebels, Rivals, and Post-Colonial State-Building: Identifying Bellicist Influences on State Extractive Capability', *International Studies Quarterly* 58: 187–98.

Mac Ginty, R. (2010) 'Hybrid Peace: The Interaction between Top-Down and Bottom-Up Peace', *Security Dialogue* 41(4): 391–412.

Mac Ginty, R. (2012) 'Routine Peace: Technocracy and Peacebuilding', *Cooperation and Conflict* 47(3): 287–308.

Mac Ginty, R. (2014) 'Everyday Peace: Bottom-Up and Local Agency in Conflict-Affected Societies', *Security Dialogue* 45(6): 548–64.

Mac Ginty, R. and Richmond, O. (2013) 'The Local Turn in Peace Building: A Critical Agenda For Peace', *Third World Quarterly* 34(5): 763–83.

Mallaby, S. (2002) 'The Reluctant Imperialist: Terrorism, Failed States, and the Case for American Empire', *Foreign Affairs* 81(2): 2–7.

Mehler, A. (2009) 'Peace and Power Sharing in Africa: A Not So Obvious Relationship', *African Affairs* 180(432): 453–73.

OECD/DAC (2007) *The Principles for Good International Engagement in Fragile States and Situations*, Paris: OECD/DAC.

OECD/DAC (2008) 'Concepts and Dilemmas of Statebuilding in Fragile Situations: From Fragility and Resilience', *OECD Journal on Development* 9(3): 61–148.

Ottaway, M. (2002) 'Rebuilding State Institutions in Collapsed States', *Development and Change* 33(5): 1001–23.

Paris, R. (2004) *At War's End: Building Peace after Civil Conflict*, Cambridge: Cambridge University Press.

Putzel, J. and Di John, J. (2012) *Meeting the Challenges of Crisis States, LSE Crisis States Research Centre Report*, London: London School of Economics and Political Science.

Richmond, O. (2013) 'The Legacy of State Formation Theory for Peacebuilding and Statebuilding', *International Peacekeeping* 20(3): 299–315.

Roeder, P. and Rothchild, D. (2005) (eds.) *Sustainable Peace: Power and Democracy after Civil Wars*, Ithaca, NY: Cornell University Press.

Rotberg, R. (2002) 'Failed States in a World of Terror', *Foreign Affairs* 81(4): 127–40.

Sabaratnam, M. (2013) 'Avatars of Eurocentrism in the Critique of the Liberal Peace', *Security Dialogue* 44(3): 259–78.

Smith, D. (2004) *Towards a Strategic Framework for Peacebuilding: Getting Their Act Together: Overview Report of the Joint Utstein Study of Peacebuilding*, Oslo: Royal Norwegian Ministry of Foreign Affairs. Evaluation Report 1/2004.

Suhrke, A. (2013) 'Statebuilding in Afghanistan: A Contradictory Engagement', *Central Asian Survey* 32(3): 271–86.

Tansey, O. (2014) 'Evaluating the Legacies of State-Building: Success, Failure, and the Role of Responsibility', *International Studies Quarterly* 58: 174–86.

Tilly, C. (1985) 'War-Making and State-Making as Organized Crime', in P. Evans, D. Rueschemeyer, and T. Skocpol (eds.) *Bringing the State back in*, Cambridge: Cambridge University Press, 169–91.

Verkoren, W. and Kamphuis, B. (2013) 'State Building in a Rentier State: How Development Policies Fail to Promote Democracy in Afghanistan', *Development and Change* 44(3): 501–26.

Wardak, A. and Hamidzada, H. (2012) 'The Search for Legitimate Rule, Justice and a Durable Peace: Hybrid Models of Governance in Afghanistan', *Journal of Peacebuilding and Development* 7(2): 79–88.

World Bank (1997) *The State in a Changing World: World Development Report 1997*, New York: Oxford University Press.

38

HUMANITARIAN INTERVENTION

Aidan Hehir

In the post-Cold War era the issue of humanitarian intervention has come to dominate the international political agenda in a way few could have predicted. With the advent of technological change – manifest most prominently in the emergence of 24-hour media and the Internet – the suffering of 'strangers' and overseas crises have permeated to the very centre of domestic political debate. Whilst public awareness of, and academic interest in, foreign humanitarian crises has increased, the international community's ability to respond to these crises remains limited. The desultory international response to the slaughter in Syria since 2011 is a sobering reminder of how, for all the talk of human rights, 'never again!', and international responsibilities, we have yet to solve the perennial problem posed by intra-state mass atrocities.

This chapter has four parts. It begins by assessing the definition of humanitarian intervention, showing that while the term is controversial, it usefully frames a particular debate. The second section looks at the controversy surrounding the threshold for intervention, before analysing the issue of authority in the third section. While in recent years there has been a degree of unanimity around what constitutes grounds for humanitarian intervention, the mechanisms by which action should be authorized remain hugely controversial and politicized. The fourth section examines the under-researched issue of reform: if, as the case of non-intervention in Syria suggests, we remain prey to a system which cannot ensure a consistent and timely response to intra-state humanitarian crises, should we think about systemic reform?

What is 'humanitarian intervention'?

There are literally hundreds of definitions of 'humanitarian intervention', and while there are differences between them, controversy stems not so much from profoundly different understandings but rather from normative assumptions (Hehir 2013: 15). The 'intervention' element is uncontentious and relatively easy to clarify. Normally, it refers to coercive action undertaken by a third party from outside the state, which differentiates it from three related practices: internal policing and/or the deployment of national militaries to quell domestic unrest; intervention undertaken with the consent of the host state, such as UN peacekeeping; and non-military intervention, such as the provision of humanitarian aid. Whether an intervention has to be legal is generally not considered a decisive factor. As discussed below, there is considerable debate about who has the authority to sanction and engage in intervention, but there have been cases where interventions have been deemed *illegal* but still described as a 'humanitarian intervention': NATO's military campaign against the Federal Republic of Yugoslavia in 1999 being a prime example (Independent International Commission on Kosovo (IICK) 2000: 4).

What creates more of a debate than 'intervention' is the word 'humanitarian' and its positive connotations. The difference between a 'military intervention' and a 'humanitarian intervention' relates not to the means, as both employ coercive force, but rather to the motives. Military interventions can be undertaken for a variety of reasons such as to acquire land, repel an attack, or as part of a counterterrorism operation. Humanitarian interventions, however, are generally deemed to necessitate the articulation of benevolent motives, namely to prevent or halt the suffering of others. How exactly this is to be determined, and to what extent such justifications must be articulated, is a controversial issue.

Only very few scholars have argued that a humanitarian intervention must exclusively be motivated by altruism (Miller 2000: 54). Most accept that an intervention can still be deemed humanitarian if there is some degree of national interest involved – how much is both a matter of dispute and methodologically difficult to determine. In any case, the majority of academics reject an either/or approach, suggesting that mixed motives are a fact of life and need not undermine the 'humanitarian' claim (Weiss 2007: 7). Provided there is some public declaration that force is being employed to prevent or halt oppression, then the intervention can potentially constitute a humanitarian intervention; 'potentially' because claiming an act is motivated by a desire to stop oppression does not foreclose debate about whether this was the 'real' motivation. For example, Russia claimed in 2008 that its invasion of Georgia was aimed at halting the 'genocide' being perpetrated by government forces against ethnic Russians, a claim that convinced few (Bellamy 2014: 147).

Furthermore, there are many examples of cases of intervention where determining the 'true' motivations is unclear, such as the 2003 invasion of Iraq, which inspired much acrimonious debate about the US-led coalition's intentions (Wheeler and Morris 2007). In response to this problem, some have suggested that the outcome rather than the expressed intentions of the intervener should determine whether an intervention counts as humanitarian. Nicholas Wheeler, for example, has argued that an intervention undertaken without any actual humanitarian motivation or justifications articulated by the intervening party can still count as a humanitarian intervention provided it has a positive humanitarian outcome (2002: 39).

For others, 'humanitarian intervention' is a misnomer precisely because military intervention always constitutes a politically motivated act and can never truly be 'humanitarian'. Many humanitarian aid agencies have criticized the term, arguing that only the impartial provision of aid is 'humanitarian' and this term should never be used in connection with the use of military force (Lu 2006: 44). In the developing world in particular, 'humanitarian intervention' has pejorative connotations since it is associated with colonial-era rhetoric of the 'white man's burden' and 'mission civilisatrice'.

Given these different viewpoints, it is highly unlikely that a consensus can emerge. However, this empirical contestation does not undermine the utility of the concept altogether; as in the cases of 'democracy', 'sovereign state', or 'good society', the absence of an agreed archetype does not render discussion about a concept irrelevant. Nevertheless, given the contestation surrounding the concept, it is perhaps better to think of 'humanitarian intervention' not as a precise descriptor but rather as a term that narrows the parameters of potential debate and creates a conceptual framework within which a set of interrelated issues can be discussed.

When is intervention warranted?

After the Second World War, the UN Charter established that all states were equal (Article 2.1) and entitled to exclusive authority over matters within their 'domestic jurisdiction' (Article 2.7). Decolonization led to an increase in the number of former colonial states in the UN. In general, these states championed sovereign inviolability, which ensured that the General Assembly routinely passed resolutions reaffirming sovereign inviolability.

Yet, while sovereign inviolability became increasingly codified and affirmed, a parallel trend in international law pointed towards consensus on the limits to domestic jurisdiction. Most obviously, the 1948 Genocide Convention affirmed that the international community did have a right to become involved to prevent or halt certain egregious intra-state atrocities. Throughout the Cold War, the General Assembly passed a number of resolutions which restricted the power of states (at least formally) by forbidding various practices, including torture (3452), racial discrimination (3379), and gender discrimination (3521). Yet, while these human rights abuses were outlawed, it was not clear what should be done if they were committed – and, most controversially, whether the commission of these crimes was ever grounds for external intervention. Regulating compliance with these international laws was, paradoxically, essentially seen as an internal matter (Henkin 1990: 250).

During the Cold War, East–West rivalry made it impossible to achieve consensus around an issue as controversial as thresholds for external intervention at the Security Council. Additionally, the 'spheres of influence' and nuclear stand-off made the potential costs of intervention excessively high. After the implosion of the Soviet Union, however, many hoped for a new era of cooperation at the UN, which could help to determine when the international community could intervene to protect human rights (Barnett 2010: 21–2; Berdal 2003: 9). Initially the optimism appeared to be well-founded: in 1991, for example, the Security Council passed Resolution 688, which described the oppression of the Kurds in Iraq as a threat to international peace and security. This was later used as the legal basis for 'Operation Provide Comfort', the imposition of no-fly zones over northern and later southern Iraq.

Yet, as the 1990s proceeded, cases of massive human rights violations were ignored while less grave situations were addressed. The pattern of sanctioned intervention appeared erratic and highly inconsistent (Chesterman 2002: 5). This was perhaps most apparent in 1994. That year the Security Council failed to respond while some 800,000 people were slaughtered in Rwanda; yet, via Resolution 940, the Council sanctioned a multi-national force to address the much less acute crisis in Haiti. As the following section suggests, this had more to do with geopolitics at the Security Council than confusion over the thresholds for intervention. The genocide in Rwanda and the desultory international response to the dissolution of Yugoslavia led to significant concern – particularly in the developing world – about the selective manner in which decisions to intervene were made. Calls for clearer guidelines on the thresholds for intervention followed.

The key concern, essentially, was that 'humanitarian intervention' constituted a threat to sovereign equality – and hence international order. Without clear guidelines on when intervention was warranted, the international system would regress to the subjective and malleable rules of colonial times when European states routinely justified their incursions into 'terra nullius' as benevolent and humanitarian (Ayoob 2002). Describing a situation as 'morally unconscionable' and determining that intervention was thus 'a moral imperative' (cf. Clinton 1999) necessarily constitutes a potential shift away from restrictive positive law to the more selective, and hence more easily abused, natural law (Bellamy 2004: 141).

This concern about thresholds for intervention led to a proliferation of lists of criteria outlining when intervention was warranted (Nardin 2003: 11–27; Wheeler 2002: 34). The majority of lists relied on the just war tradition and the 'just cause' criterion in particular. Yet, while these were generally sensible prescriptions, they were often vague. in its now-famous report *The Responsibility to Protect*, the International Commission on Intervention and State Sovereignty (ICISS) stated that:

> Military intervention for human protection purposes is warranted [when there is] large-scale loss of life actual or apprehended, with genocidal intent or not, which is the product either of deliberate state action or state neglect . . . or large-scale 'ethnic cleansing', actual or apprehended, whether carried out by killing, forced expulsion, acts of terror or rape.
>
> *(2001: xii)*

'Large scale' is obviously subjective, and many warned that this lack of specificity could facilitate precisely the politically motivated selectivity that had led to the establishment of the ICISS in the first place (Bellamy 2006: 148–9). To some extent, these fears were allayed when the 'Responsibility to Protect' (R2P) was formally recognized in the 2005 World Summit *Outcome Document*. Paragraphs 138 and 139 restricted R2P's application to genocide, ethnic cleansing, war crimes, and crimes against humanity. Yet, significant contestation surrounds the precise definition of these crimes, and again there is no mention of scale. Hence, the *Outcome Document* did not completely foreclose concerns about selectivity. Arguably, paragraph 139 even formally facilitates it by noting that the Security Council will assess each situation on 'a case-by-case basis'.

While some lamented that the *Outcome Document* did not outline specific criteria for military intervention (Evans 2008: 48), the fact that it clarified the types of crimes which constitute a basis for humanitarian intervention was deemed a major breakthrough. These 'four crimes' are now widely accepted as the only legitimate basis for humanitarian intervention. Concerns that politically and/or culturally specific human rights (such as the right to vote) or 'low-level' human rights abuses (such as denial of education or the right to drive a car) would be used as grounds for intervention, have largely been quieted (Bellamy 2014: 12).

Yet, while the 2005 World Summit *Outcome Document* outlined the grounds for humanitarian intervention, this has not addressed what Simon Chesterman described as 'inhumanitarian non-intervention' (2003: 54), namely those situations where the gravity of the crisis clearly passes the threshold for intervention yet no action is taken by the international community. This is most evident in regard to the crisis in Syria, which degenerated horrifically after it began in 2011, claiming, according to the UN, over 220,000 lives by January 2015 (Hadid 2015). While evidence from objective UN-appointed observers (as well as the majority of humanitarian organizations on the ground) unequivocally found that President Assad's forces were actively engaged in crimes against humanity and war crimes (BBC 2013), the international community failed to take robust action. While clarifying the grounds for intervention potentially removes the problem of spurious, unwarranted intervention, it does not in itself solve the more pressing question regarding the authorization of clearly warranted punitive measures.

Who sanctions interventions?

By far the most controversial question related to this debate is 'who is authorized to sanction a humanitarian intervention?' Under international law there are three possibilities: the first is that the Security Council can pass a Chapter VII resolution; the second is that the General Assembly can pass a resolution under the powers granted to it in the 1950 'Uniting for Peace' Resolution 377; the third is that regional organizations can act under Chapter VIII of the Charter. In reality, the

Security Council is the primary body. The 'Uniting for Peace' provision has rarely been invoked and a resolution authorized by the General Assembly sanctioning intervention against the wishes of one of the great powers or their allies would be highly unlikely to actually result in an intervention taking place (Krasno and Das 2008). Additionally, 'Uniting for Peace' cannot be invoked in situations under consideration by the Security Council. Likewise, while regional organizations have undertaken action which could be described as constituting a 'humanitarian intervention' – such as the Economic Community of West African States' interventions in Liberia in 1990 and Sierra Leone in 1997 – this is extremely rare, and in any event, the Charter states in Article 53.1 that such action must be approved by the Security Council.

The legality of unilateral intervention – action taken by a state or group of states without Security Council or General Assembly authorization – is controversial, but the majority view is that such action is illegal (ICISS 2001: 48–9). There have been occasions when it has been tacitly tolerated, however, such as when Tanzania intervened in Uganda in 1979 (Franck 2005: 219), though in more recent times the US-led invasion of Iraq in 2003 and Russia's intervention in Georgia in 2008 have generated renewed opposition to unilateral intervention.

Thus, Security Council authorization remains the most sound and practically viable legal basis for action. Under Article 42, the Security Council is empowered to 'take such action by air, sea, or land forces as may be necessary to maintain or restore international peace and security'. As stated earlier, the Cold War rendered this provision moribund, but since the dissolution of the Soviet Union, such action has been sanctioned on a number of occasions, most notably in 2011 when Resolution 1973 authorized the imposition of a 'no-fly zone' over Libya which eventually resulted in the overthrow of Gaddafi.

While some have argued that humanitarian crises are not actually 'a threat to international peace and security' and thus the Security Council is not actually empowered to launch a humanitarian intervention (IICK 2000: 196; White 2004), Council practice since 1991 has rendered this argument somewhat moot. That the Security Council can, and has, authorized coercive measures to relieve humanitarian crises within states is now firmly established (Chesterman 2011). This has not, however, ameliorated concerns regarding the inconsistent manner in which the Security Council has exercised this right.

According to Article 24.1 of the Charter, the Security Council is mandated to act on behalf of all UN member states; in practice, however, this has rarely been the case. The Security Council comprises 15 states but it is the permanent five members (P5) – China, France, Russia, the UK, and the US – who have the greatest influence, thanks to their veto power. While the formal use of the veto is relatively rare – 29 resolutions have been vetoed since the end of the Cold War – the threatened use of a veto also impacts on Security Council deliberation and action; draft resolutions that will definitely be vetoed are rarely put to the vote. Because the P5 can block any resolution put to the Security Council, and because P5 actions are strongly guided by national interests, achieving consensus around Chapter VII action has generally proved difficult. Also, a number of states have been shielded from external censure by virtue of having an ally amongst the P5. For example, in February 2011, the US blocked a resolution condemning Israeli settlements in Palestine, which was supported by the other 14 members of the Council. Russia and China have vetoed resolutions seeking to impose punitive sanctions against President Assad on four occasions since 2011.

This inconsistency has led many to question the legitimacy of the laws governing humanitarian intervention and specifically the Security Council's monopoly on the authorization of such action. NATO's intervention in Kosovo in 1999 highlighted this issue starkly: NATO acted without Security Council authorization to protect the Kosovo Albanians. While the action was thus technically illegal, it was deemed by many to have been necessary and laudable – 'illegal but legitimate' according to the Independent International Commission on Kosovo (IICK 2000: 4) – and thus it

highlighted the tension between the existing laws and a growing disposition in favour of humanitarian intervention. In the wake of Kosovo, many called for new laws on humanitarian intervention
or for a reliance on 'natural law' in cases where the legal route through the Security Council was
impossible (Nardin 2003: 23).

Yet, both alternatives to Security Council authorization – reform or reliance on natural law –
bring their own difficulties and potential drawbacks. In terms of reform, this has been discussed for
decades, and myriad proposals have been advanced (Buchanan and Keohane 2011; Hehir 2012: 228;
UN Commission for Global Governance 1995: 90; UN High-Level Panel on Threats, Challenges
and Change 2004: 57). The main stumbling block is that reform requires the Security Council's
consent which, unsurprisingly, has not been forthcoming; indeed one of the few issues the P5 have
consistently agreed upon is the need to maintain the organizational status quo and hence their
privileged position (Bourantonis 2007: 35). It has also been argued that the Security Council's
primary – albeit not exclusive – responsibility is to maintain international peace and security and to
ensure that there is no outbreak of hostilities between the great powers which could cause massive
loss of life (Jackson 2000: 291). The Security Council's monopoly on the authorization of the use
of force ensures that military action which is strongly opposed by one or more of the P5 cannot
be sanctioned; while this may occasionally mean that crises and human suffering go unaddressed, it
considerably reduces the possibility of a globally devastating conflict (Bosco 2009: 10).

The second alternative – maintaining the legal status quo and occasionally relying on 'natural
law' – has suffered greatly through its association with some of history's most controversial and
discredited 'humanitarian interventions'. The basic logic underpinning natural-law-based justifications is that there are laws which transcend positive law. These 'moral norms' constitute the
very fabric of our common humanity and though they are not always reflected in actual codified
law, they retain a position of primacy (Byers 2005).

The problem is, however, that the natural law argument is easily abused: the determination
that existing law is no longer legitimate necessarily constitutes subjective judgement, which
may actually mask more nefarious motives. Many fear that championing natural law constitutes
a regression to the pre-charter era when European states routinely justified their imperial conquests as benevolent, altruistic, moral acts (Evans 2005; Hehir 2012: 170). Without rules and clear
procedures on who may employ force, moral arguments might be spuriously invoked, leading to
oppression and the degradation of the very idea of humanitarian intervention. The 2003 invasion
of Iraq undoubtedly discredited both the idea of humanitarian intervention and the legitimacy
of unilateral action, as did the Russian invasion of Georgia in 2008.

The most prominent initiative in the contemporary era aimed at improving the manner in
which the international community responds to intra-state humanitarian crises is R2P. In its
original report ICISS affirmed the primacy of the Security Council, noting 'there is no better or
more appropriate body than the Security Council' and, cautioning against seeking alternatives,
suggested that the key task was 'to make the Security Council work better' (2011: xii). The focus
was, therefore, on changing the attitude of the P5 rather than their powers. With respect to the
veto, ICISS suggested that the P5 should abide by a 'code of conduct' whereby 'a permanent
member, in matters where its vital national interests were not claimed to be involved, would
otherwise not use its veto to obstruct the passage of what would otherwise be a majority resolution' (ICISS 2011: 51). The two paragraphs related to R2P in the 2005 World Summit *Outcome
Document* also reiterated the primacy of the Security Council, stating that external intervention was only permissible if sanctioned 'through the Security Council in accordance with the
Charter'. This has also been reiterated during subsequent key junctures in the evolution of R2P,
such as the 2009 General Assembly debate on the concept, and the six official reports published
by UN Secretary General Ban Ki-Moon since 2009.

Many have argued that R2P, despite having achieved significant international recognition, has ultimately failed to address the primary source of the inconsistent response to intra-state crises precisely because it has focused on moral advocacy rather than calling for substantive reform of the Security Council's powers (Reinhold 2010; Stahn 2007). The Security Council's response to the Arab Spring certainly suggested that the perennial problem of politicized selectivity remains: while the Security Council was quick to act against Gaddafi's oppression of pro-democracy protestors in Libya, the situation in Bahrain was essentially ignored (Hehir 2015; International Crisis Group 2011). Arguably more damaging to R2P's perceived efficacy has been the crisis in Syria. The Security Council has demonstrated a pronounced inability to act in a unified fashion due to the competing national interests of the P5. As Gareth Evans noted, 'the shame and horror of Syria' has led to 'a real sense of disappointment' (2014), and thus the search for a solution to the perennial problem of inconsistency and 'inhumanitarian non-intervention' goes on.

Duty or discretionary entitlement?

Many of the problems discussed above stem from a pivotal question that is rarely asked and remains under-researched: 'does anyone have a duty to prevent or halt mass atrocities; if not, should a body with just such a mandate be established?' States are bound under international law to protect their people from harm. This is reflected in the wording of paragraph 138 of the 2005 World Summit *Outcome Document*, which asserts 'Each individual State has the responsibility to protect its populations from genocide, war crimes, ethnic cleansing, and crimes against humanity'. Yet in recent years, the behaviour of various governments demonstrates that this injunction to protect is occasionally wilfully ignored. Historically, states have constituted the greatest threat to their citizens' livelihood: more people were killed by their own governments during the bloody twentieth century than by external forces (Lu 2006: 54). So, while states may legally have a duty to protect, this cannot be assured in practice.

The key issue, then, is: who assumes not just a right to protect but a *duty* to protect when the state fails to do so? This distinction between a 'right' and a 'duty' is of crucial importance: that individuals have rights under international law is incontrovertible; that there is a body charged with a *duty* to enforce these rights is, however, far from assured. There is no doubt that 'human rights' exist; this is reflected in both domestic and international legislation. Yet, positive international law may imbue individuals with certain rights and forbid states from engaging in certain acts but it does not by itself constitute a sufficiently comprehensive legal framework as it does not create a means by which these human rights can be enforced and protected.

As discussed earlier, the Security Council, and indeed the General Assembly and regional organizations, can act to enforce human rights, but they do not have a duty to do so.[1] This contrasts sharply with the nature of the (normative) domestic legal system: rights are enshrined in law but additionally a body – the police – are established with a duty to uphold these rights and a judiciary is mandated to try those who violate them. A police officer cannot – legally at least – choose when to enforce the law and is constitutionally bound to act whenever a citizen is imperilled. If a police officer fails to act then there are consequences. An individual citizen certainly has the right to come to the aid of a fellow citizen being attacked but this is a matter of personal choice; the intervening citizen has no obligation. The international response to intra-state crises is determined by the conscience – and interests – of citizen-like actors rather than the duties and obligations of a police-like entity. This has a number of grave consequences which help explain the record of humanitarian intervention.

First, in the absence of an obligation, decisions on whether or not to act will naturally be taken on the basis of factors extraneous to the suffering that is occurring. They are factors that relate in essence to the interests of potential interveners, including the relationship between the potential intervener and both the aggressor and the victim; the costs (military and economic) likely to be incurred by the intervener; the potential material interests that depend on the outcome of the case; and the particular political disposition of the intervener's government/citizenry/military at any given time. When all these factors are considered, it is no surprise that intervention rarely takes place and that 'inhumanitarian non-intervention' is the norm.

Second, the absence of a group constitutionally mandated to address intra-state crises potentially leads to unilateralism. Security Council inaction in response to certain atrocities has at times unsurprisingly led people to call for unilateral intervention (Lang 2014). While there may well be a strong moral basis for these calls, unilateral intervention cannot constitute a viable foundation upon which to construct a consistent means to respond to intra-state crises. Such action – even if morally warranted – by definition degrades international law and legitimizes extra-legal action which may not always be morally defensible.

Third, perpetrators of systematic human rights abuses can shield themselves from external censure if they have an alliance with one of the veto-wielding P5. In the contemporary era certain oppressive regimes have continued to focus on cultivating an alliance with a member of the P5 rather than change their illegal behaviour. In any system where legal censure is not guaranteed – because of the judiciary's ineffectiveness, its lack of coercive capacity, or its susceptibility to corruption and/or the influence of power – potential lawbreakers are naturally less wary of breaking the law and the preventative benefits of a non-political legal system are lost (Hurrell 2005: 16).

Thus, humanitarian intervention remains prey to the vagaries and anachronisms of the legal system designed by Stalin, Churchill, and Roosevelt over seventy years ago. Clearly, the P5 have an interest in maintaining the status quo and have worked conscientiously to do so, but there has also been an arguably surprising reluctance amongst some human rights advocates to lobby for reform. In particular, the global movement advocating R2P has, almost uniformly – Thomas Weiss being a notable exception (2009) – rejected the idea of legal reform and decried proposals aimed at improving the legal architecture as unrealistic and, even, potentially a threat to international peace and stability (Davies and Bellamy 2014; Evans 2008: 180). As the distribution of power shifts from the West to the emerging powers – notably Brazil, Russia, India, China, and South Africa – achieving agreement at the Security Council, and other international fora, is arguably likely to decrease, and thus the efficacy of initiatives – such as R2P – which depend on political consensus and diplomatic machinations is likely to diminish, to the detriment of universal human rights.

Conclusion

Despite the enormous contemporary upsurge in interest in the issue amongst the general public, academics, journalists, and policy-makers, humanitarian intervention remains a divisive, contested, and controversial subject. While this is lamentable – given the tragic nature of the core issue – it is arguably not surprising. Humanitarian intervention is a subject which incorporates a complex array of issues of profound importance, such as state sovereignty, human rights, state-society relations, universal morality, the international–domestic divide, and the legitimacy and efficacy of the use of force. The debate throws up myriad questions and conundrums, and this is one of the reasons it has remained such an alluring and unresolved focus of enquiry for a long time.

Unfortunately, it seems highly unlikely that the issue will lose its relevance any time soon; intra-state crises will continue to erupt and the calls for 'something' to be done will be reiterated. Any conceptions of 'human progress' must surely be tempered by the jarring juxtaposition of man-made egregious human suffering, and inaction on the part of those with the capacity to halt such wanton violence. One must hope that further research into this issue – on a variety of themes from prevention to human rights law and Security Council reform – will help to improve the international community's capacity to address mass atrocities and render such blights on humanity a thing of the past.

Note

1 In 2007 the International Court of Justice did note that states have an obligation to act to prevent and/ or stop genocide but noted that the nature of a state's obligation was determined by factors such as its capacity to act, geographic proximity, and political links with the parties involved (International Court of Justice 2007: 221). In this sense the court found that Serbia breached its obligations with respect to the violence perpetrated by Serbs in Bosnia, but a similar ruling would not, and could not, be made against neighbouring Slovenia or Croatia; the particularities of Serbia's relationship with the perpetrators of the crimes in Bosnia were the crucial determinant on the court's findings.

References

Ayoob, M. (2002) 'Humanitarian Intervention and State Sovereignty', *International Journal of Human Rights* 6(1): 81–102.

Barnett, M. (2010) *The International Humanitarian Order*, London: Routledge.

BBC (2013) 'UN Implicates Bashar al-Assad in Syria War Crimes', BBC Online, 2 December. Online. Available HTTP: <http://www.bbc.co.uk/news/world-middle-east-25189834> (accessed 7 November 2014).

Bellamy, A. (2004) 'Ethics and Intervention; The "Humanitarian Exception" and the Problem of Abuse in the Case of Iraq', *Journal of Peace Research* 41(2): 131–47.

Bellamy, A. (2006) 'Whither the Responsibility to Protect? Humanitarian Intervention and the 2005 World Summit', *Ethics and International Affairs* 20(2): 143–69.

Bellamy, A. (2014) *The Responsibility to Protect: A Defence*, Oxford: Oxford University Press.

Berdal, M. (2003) 'The UN Security Council: Ineffective but Indispensable', *Survival* 45(2): 7–30.

Bosco, D. (2009) *Five to Rule Them All*, Oxford: Oxford University Press

Bourantonis, D. (2007) *The History and Politics of Security Council Reform*, London: Routledge.

Buchanan, A. and Keohane, R. O. (2011) 'Precommitment Regimes for Intervention: Supplementing the Security Council', *Ethics and International Affairs* 25(1): 41–63.

Byers, M. (2005) 'Not yet Havoc: Geopolitical Change and the International Rules on Military Force' in D. Armstrong, T. Farrell, and B. Maiguashca (eds.) *Force and Legitimacy in World Politics*, Cambridge: Cambridge University Press, 51–70.

Chesterman, S. (2002) *Just War or Just Peace?*, Oxford: Oxford University Press.

Chesterman, S. (2003) 'Hard Cases Make Bad Law', in A. Lang (ed.) *Just Intervention*, Washington DC: Georgetown University Press, 46–61.

Chesterman, S. (2011) '"Leading from Behind": The Responsibility to Protect, the Obama Doctrine, and Humanitarian Intervention after Libya', *Ethics and International Affairs* 25(3): 279–85.

Clinton, W. (1999) 'A Moral Imperative', *Washington Post*, 16 April. Online. Available HTTP: <http://www.washingtonpost.com/wp-srv/inatl/longterm/balkans/stories/excerpts041699.htm> (accessed 7 November 2014).

Davies, S. and Bellamy, A. (2014) 'Don't Be Too Quick to Condemn the UN Security Council Power of Veto', *The Conversation*, 12 August. Online. Available HTTP: <http://theconversation.com/dont-be-too-quick-to-condemn-the-un-security-council-power-of-veto-29980> (accessed 25 August 2014).

Evans, G. (2008) *The Responsibility to Protect*, Washington, DC: Brookings Institution.

Evans, G. (2014) 'After Syria: The Future of the Responsibility to Protect', S. T. Lee Lecture, Institute for Advanced Study, Princeton, 12 March. Online. Available HTTP: <www.gevans.org/speeches/speech545.html> (accessed 2 June 2014).

Evans, M. (2005) 'Moral Theory and the Idea of a Just War', in M. Evans (ed.) *Just War Theory: A Reappraisal*, Edinburgh: Edinburgh University Press.

Franck, T. (2005) 'Interpretation and Change in the Law of Humanitarian Intervention', in J. L. Holzgrefe and R. O. Keohane (eds.) *Humanitarian Intervention: Ethical, Legal and Political Dilemmas*, Cambridge: Cambridge University Press.

Hadid, D. (2015) 'Syrian Rebels and Government Reach Truce in Besieged Area', *Huffington Post*, 15 January. Online. Available HTTP: <http://www.huffingtonpost.com/2015/01/15/syria-rebel-truce_n_6478226.html?ncid=txtlnkusaolp00000592> (accessed 8 August 2015).

Henkin, L. (1990) 'Compliance with International Law in an Inter-State System', *Academie de droit international, Recueil des cours 1989*, Dordrecht: Martinus Nijhoff.

Hehir, A. (2012) *The Responsibility to Protect: Rhetoric, Reality and the Future of Humanitarian Intervention*, Basingstoke: Palgrave.

Hehir, A. (2015) 'Bahrain: An R2P Blindspot?', *International Journal of Human Rights* 19(8): 1129–1147.

High Level Panel on Threats Challenges and Change (2004) *A More Secure World: Our Shared Responsibility*, 2 December. Online. Available HTTP: <http://www.un.org/secureworld/report.pdf> (accessed 11 November 2014).

Hurrell, A. (2005) 'Legitimacy and the Use of Force: Can the Circle be Squared?', in D. Armstrong, T. Farrell, and B. Maiguashca (eds.) *Force and Legitimacy in World Politics*, Cambridge: Cambridge University Press.

Independent International Commission on Kosovo (2000) *Kosovo Report*, Oxford: Oxford University Press.

International Commission on Intervention and State Sovereignty (2001) *The Responsibility to Protect*, Ottawa: International Development Research Centre. Online. Available HTTP: <http://responsibilitytoprotect.org/ICISS%20Report.pdf> (accessed 12 November 2015).

International Court of Justice (2007) 'Case Concerning Application of the Convention on the Prevention and Punishment of the Crime of Genocide (Bosnia and Herzegovina v. Serbia and Montenegro)', 26 February. Online. Available HTTP:< http://www.icj-cij.org/docket/files/91/13685.pdf> (accessed 11 November 2014).

International Crisis Group (2011) 'Popular Protests in the Middle East and North Africa: Bahrain's Rocky Road to Reform', Middle East/North Africa Report 111, 28 July. Online. Available HTTP: <http://www.crisisgroup.org/en/regions/middle-east-north-africa/iraq-iran-gulf/bahrain/111-popular-protest-in-north-africa-and-the-middle-east-viii-bahrains-rocky-road-to-reform.aspx> (accessed 12 November 2015).

Jackson, R. (2000) *The Global Covenant*, Oxford: Oxford University Press.

Krasno, J. and Das, M. (2008) 'The Uniting for Peace Resolution and Other Ways of Circumventing the Authority of the Security Council', in B. Cronin and I. Hurd (eds.) *The UN Security Council and the Politics of International Authority*, London: Routledge.

Lang, A. (2013) 'Syria: The Case for Punitive Intervention', 30 August. Online. Available HTTP: <http://www.carnegiecouncil.org/publications/articles_papers_reports/0169.html> (accessed 24 January 2014).

Lu, C. (2006) *Just and Unjust Interventions in World Politics*, Hampshire: Palgrave.

Miller, R. (2000) 'Humanitarian Intervention, Altruism, and the Limits of Casuistry', *Journal of Religious Ethics* 28(1): 3–35.

Nardin, T. (2003) 'The Moral Basis of Humanitarian Intervention', in A. Lang (ed.) *Just Intervention*, Washington, DC: Georgetown University Press.

Reinhold, T. (2010) 'The Responsibility to Protect: Much Ado about Nothing?', *Review of International Studies* 36: 55–78.

Stahn, C. (2007) 'Responsibility to Protect: Political Rhetoric or Emerging Legal Norm?', *American Journal of International Law* 101(1): 99–120.

UN Commission on Global Governance (1995) *Our Global Neighbourhood*, Oxford: Oxford University Press.

Weiss, T. (2002) *Saving Strangers*, Oxford: Oxford University Press.

Weiss, T. (2007) *Humanitarian Intervention*, London: Polity Press.

Weiss, T. (2009) *What's Wrong with the United Nations and How to Fix It*, Cambridge: Polity Press.

Weiss, T. and Morris, J. (2007) 'Justifying the Iraq War as a Humanitarian Intervention: The Cure is Worse than the Disease', in R. Thakur and W. P. S. Sidhu (eds.) *The Iraq Crisis and World Order*, New York: United Nations University Press.

White, N. D. (2004) 'The Will and Authority of the Security Council after Iraq', *Leiden Journal of International Law* 17(4): 645–72.

39

GLOBAL SECURITY GOVERNANCE

*Thomas J. Biersteker**

Although governance at the global level is certainly not new, the subject has become a central preoccupation in public policy and scholarly discourse over the past twenty-five years. Despite the growing interest, however, global governance remains a permissive concept. The frequency with which global governance is invoked in scholarly literature and policy practice far exceeds the number of times it is defined. As a result, the term is applied to a wide variety of different practices of order, regulation, systems of rule, and patterned regularity in the international arena. It is permissive in the sense that it gives one license to speak or write about many different things, from any pattern of order or deviation from anarchy (which also has multiple meanings) to normative preferences about how the world should be organized.

This chapter has four main parts. The first contains a survey of recent discussions of global governance followed by a synthetic definition that builds on them, with particular reference to the governance of security affairs. In the second part, it considers Inis Claude's classic three-fold typology for addressing the subject of power and international relations (Claude 1962), in which he distinguished analytically between different ways of governing security affairs: balance-of-power systems, collective security arrangements, and world government. In the third part, it will discuss how global governance is managed, from the international society of states (Bull 1977), to arguments about the importance of hegemony for order and governance (Gilpin 1975, 1981), international regimes (Keohane and Nye 1977), institutions (Keohane and Martin 1995; Martin 1992), international law (Abbott and Snidal 2000), global norms (Finnemore and Sikkink 1998; Katzenstein 1996; Keck and Sikkink 1998), private authority (Cutler et al. 1999; Hall and Biersteker 2002), or codes and routines (Sylvan 2013). In the fourth part, the chapter looks at the increased salience of different institutional actors, particularly non-state actors, involved in contemporary global governance.

Five core elements of global governance

Global governance first emerged in the early 1990s, with the pioneering introduction of the concept 'governance without government' by James Rosenau and E. O. Czempiel (Rosenau and Czempiel 1992). Rosenau defined global governance in very general terms as 'an order that lacks a centralized authority with the capacity to enforce decisions on a global scale' (Rosenau 1992: 7). His conception of global governance was that of a purposive order that is created for the management of global interdependence in the absence of a global state. The definition has relatively little to say about who makes decisions. It also has very little analysis of precisely how enforcement takes place or very much detail about the structures or mechanisms of governance. It is important, however, because it presciently identified an important emergent phenomenon and opened the way for subsequent theoretical reflection and analysis.

We do not lack detailed and more precise definitions of global governance today. In fact, we probably have too many. Still, the different conceptions and definitions of global governance (for some important ones see Weiss 2009 on the scope of issues and range of actors involved; Abbott and Snidal 2009, 2010 on regulatory issues; Held 2012 for a normative dimension; de Burca et al. 2013 for types of governance; Ruggie 2014 on guiding principles) offer a great many insights.

As diverse as they are, several key elements are common to all definitions: foremost is the centrality of the idea of rules, systems of rules, and/or rule-governed behaviour at the global level. These rules can be either formal or informal, and they can range from being formally legalized to being widely accepted norms involved in regulating behaviour. Institutions, whether of a formal organizational sort or as a more informal set of practices, are also common to all. As will be discussed more fully below, global governance arrangements increasingly involve a broad range of different actors, both public and private.

Altogether, there are five core elements for global governance. First, it requires some form of *patterned regularity* or recurring order at the global level (a necessary, but hardly sufficient condition). Second, following Rosenau, and with acknowledgement of Hedley Bull's important contribution to the study of order in international politics (Bull 1977), global governance must be *purposive* and/or oriented toward the achievement of some goal or goals. In this sense, and integrating it with the first element, global governance is order, plus intentionality, at the global level.

Third, governance connotes a *system of rule*, or rules. These rules can either be formal and embodied within formal institutions, or they can be informal and reside intersubjectively among a population or a set of key institutional actors. There can be different degrees of institutionalization associated with different forms of governance, and both formal and informal institutions may be necessary for governance (Stone 2011). It is not required, however, that these rules be universally recognized as legitimate, but only that they be widely shared, recognized, and practised on a global scale (on multiple continents) by relevant and important actors. Most actors tend to be norm-takers or norm-shapers, rather than norm-makers.

Fourth, the system of rule implied by global governance is *authoritative*, in the sense that there is a social relationship between the governed public or key institutional players and some governing authority. That is, there is a recognized set of 'rules of the game' that key players acknowledge and recognize as authoritative in a particular issue domain. Governance requires acceptance by a significant portion of some relevant population and therefore is 'as dependent on intersubjective meanings as on formally sanctioned constitutions and charters' (Rosenau 1992: 4). Governance requires the effective performance of some functions for its systemic persistence, which is why it is associated with the functions of government, rather than its formal institutional processes.

Even though much of the literature emphasizes the steering aspect of governance, global governance can also exist in the absence of an easily identifiable agent deliberately steering the direction of governance arrangements. Just as an engine can be said to be regulated and kept from overheating by a governor, so too can a governance arrangement be regulated independently of deliberate actions taken by someone steering the process (Börzel and Risse 2010). This is an important distinction, and it opens up space for exploring different bases of governance, including *self-regulation*. In this sense, a market, a set of market mechanisms, a network, or a widely used standardized code can also be said to govern, be allowed to govern, or be relied upon to govern in instances and some issue domains. The market can be constituted as authoritative by the public statements (speech acts) of leaders of important states and private institutions when they suggest that they are 'governed' by its behaviour. Alternatively, a network may be open to those who have a certain minimum level of technical expertise and through their actions reproduce its informal rules and norms.

Governance arrangements in global security affairs

In *Power and International Relations*, Inis Claude differentiated among three heuristic ways to manage power in international relations – balance-of-power systems, collective security arrangements, and world government (Claude 1962). He placed the three alternatives on a continuum, ranging from the least formally institutionalized arrangement (balance-of-power) on one end of the spectrum, to the most formally institutionalized (world government) on the other. Collective security arrangements were placed in the middle of the continuum. Each of the ideal types he sketched provides a basis for global governance of security affairs. They differ primarily according to their degrees of formal institutionalization.

In his analysis of the evolution of international society, Adam Watson developed a similar continuum to describe the spectrum of international systems, from absolute independence of individual states at one end of the spectrum to absolute empire at the other (Watson 1992: 13). Following in the tradition of Hedley Bull, Watson argued that order promotes peace, but it does so at the price of independence and constraints on freedom of action of states (due to its association with greater degrees of institutionalization). Independence, however, also has its price, in terms of economic and military insecurity and, as a result, states must form and rely upon alliances to provide for their security. Hegemony – where some power (or small group of powers) is able to 'lay down' the law – and suzerainty – where members of international society accept that hegemony as legitimate – are intermediate forms of global governance. Dominion and empire exist at the other end of Watson's continuum.

The principal basis for differentiation in both of these conceptions is the degree of institutionalization entailed in the governance arrangement. They are also differentiated by the principal mechanism of governance. Thus, both balance-of-power systems and state independence as arrangements for global security governance at one end of the continuum have relatively low levels of formal and informal institutionalization, and are essentially regulated by a form of market mechanism. They are governed or regulated principally through the separate actions of individual state actors pursuing their own security interests.

At the other end of the continuum – whether it is in the form of dominion, empire, or a world government – the systems of governance are essentially hierarchical, top-down, and highly institutionalized. They entail governance principally by governments (a single state in cases of dominion or empire, or a unitary government, in the case of a world state). In dominion, imperial authority determines the internal government of other communities, but they maintain their identity. Empire exists when the direct administration of others is carried out from a unitary imperial centre. Both require high levels of institutionalized authority. The same would obviously be true of world government.

In between these two extremes of complete state independence and world government are a large variety of informal institutions, complex combinations of formal and informal institutional arrangements, and a wide range of different social networks. Rather than being regulated principally by market mechanisms or hierarchical institutions, these systems of governance are regulated by networks composed of key institutional actors, who share a common concern with a particular issue domain, but not necessarily a common approach or method for addressing it.

Table 39.1 Framework for characterizing types of global security governance arrangements

Inis Claude	Balance-of-power systems	Collective security arrangements	World government
Adam Watson	Independent states	Hegemony Suzerainty	Dominion Empire
Degree of formal and informal institutionalization	Low	Medium	High
Principal mechanism of governance	Market	Network	Hierarchy

Their authority is sometimes contested, and different governance arrangements can often contradict one another, such as in regime complexes. Networks are ideally 'forms of organization characterized by voluntary, reciprocal, and horizontal patterns of communication and exchange' (Keck and Sikkink 1998: 8), but there are also aspects of hierarchy in many networks. The recent popularity of the idea of public–private partnerships in global governance constitutes one contemporary form of networked governance.

Hierarchical governance is probably the most efficient form, but it is relatively rare in the international system. Market governance is more widespread, but less guided, steered, or reliable. Networked governance is the most common form of contemporary global governance, but its effectiveness and reliability are also highly variable and uncertain. Table 39.1 summarizes this analytical framework for characterizing different global governance arrangements. Different periods in time may be associated with the general predominance of one or another of these forms of global security governance. However, in any given period, there is typically a complex blend of overlapping forms of global security governance, with different systems and elements of different systems coexisting in complex, and sometimes contradictory, ways (Biersteker 2014a).

Different bases of global governance

Much of the theoretical and policy debate about forms of global governance revolves around the different (and often complexly interrelated) underlying bases of governance. As mentioned above, there is variation in the principal governance mechanisms (market, network, hierarchy) as there is in degree of formal institutionalization (low, medium, high). The different bases for identifying and comprehending forms of contemporary global security governance are the society of states, hegemony, regimes, institutions, law, norms, private authority, and standardized codes. Global governance in most issue domains is provided by a complex combination of these different bases, rather than by any single one of them, but they illustrate well the complexity of the subject, as well as the range of institutional players involved. Table 39.2 compares and contrasts the different bases of global governance, which are discussed below.

Society of states

For Hedley Bull, the principal basis of global governance was found in the *society of states*. He terms this 'the anarchical society', because its core units are independent states coexisting in a systemic situation of anarchy (Bull 1977). The system of diplomatic rules and practices that regulates interstate interaction (reciprocal acceptance of practices of diplomatic recognition, diplomatic immunity, and the exchange of ambassadors) governs international society. Christian Reus-Smit

Table 39.2 Comparing different bases of global governance

What governs?	International society	Hegemony	Regimes and institutions	Law and norms	Private authority and codes
Who governs?	States (exclusively)	State(s)	States (primarily)	States and NGOs	Firms, NGOs, non-state armed groups
Principal governance mechanism	Network	Hierarchy	Hierarchy and market	Hierarchy and networks	Networks and hierarchy
Degree of formal institutionalization	Low	High	Medium	Medium	Low

develops Bull's concept of the international society of states (Reus-Smit 1997), arguing that contractual international law and multilateralism constitute deep structural elements underlying contemporary international society. While constitutional structures at the international level may have originated within the domestic cultures of dominant states (like the US after the Second World War), once embedded in the practices of other states, the values inherent within those constitutional structures condition the behaviour of all states and provide a basis for global governance.

Hegemony

State *hegemony* provides another basis for global governance. Both the hegemony of Great Britain in the nineteenth century and the hegemony of the US in the twentieth provided global leadership and underwrote the provision of collective goods, backed by their considerable political, economic, and military resources. State hegemony is a relatively hierarchical basis for global governance, maintained by structural power (Strange 1986), indicated by leadership, and occasionally operating with ideological hegemony, where direct coercion is rare and the leadership of the hegemon is widely accepted by other states (Cox 1987). Thus, hegemony has three meanings: capabilities, leadership, and ideological dominance. For Charles Kindleberger, writing about the governance of the global economy (Kindleberger 1973), and for Robert Gilpin, who extended Kindleberger's conception to the governance in the global security domain (Gilpin 1981), the essence of hegemony is political leadership of the hegemonic state and is indicated by its willingness to underwrite the costs of maintaining the governance of the economic, political, and/or military order.

International regimes and institutions

The concept of *international regimes* is best understood within the context of the debate about hegemonic decline and hegemonic stability. While Robert Gilpin worried about the consequences of US hegemonic decline and/or the potential temptation for the US to become a rogue hegemon, liberal institutionalists like Robert Keohane argued that international regimes could provide a basis for global governance even without a hegemon (Keohane 1984). Processes of path dependence ensured that once the institutions of global governance had been created by a hegemon, it would take a great deal to dismantle them. As long as the demand for regimes was sustained, they would continue. It is easier to maintain existing international regimes than to create new ones, but it was possible to imagine that new regimes could also be created to govern different issue domains, even after hegemony.

Regimes are defined as 'sets of implicit or explicit principles, norms, rules, and decision-making procedures around which actors' expectations converge in a given area of international relations' (Krasner 1983b: 2). International regimes are widely associated with the governance of the global economy, but the concept has been extended into the security domain, with consideration of the non-proliferation, arms control, peacebuilding, sanctions, and counterterrorism regimes. There has been a great deal of debate about the direct and indirect influence of international regimes, measured principally in terms of their effects on individual states (Haggard and Simmons 1987). Regimes constrain states by increasing the costs of defection from agreements enforced by regimes, and they therefore provide an institutionalized basis for global governance.

Closely related to the operation of international regimes are *institutions*, and when defined broadly (Keohane 1988; Young 1992), they are nearly identical. Robert Keohane defines institutions as 'related complexes of rules and norms, identifiable in space and time' (1988: 383). Institutions provide a system of authoritative rules at the global level and can provide a basis for governance by defining, constraining, and shaping actor expectations in different domains. Broad institutions such as multilateralism can provide solutions to a variety of different dilemmas of strategic interaction (Martin 1992: 766). One of the best indicators that institutions matter to states is that governments continue to invest in them (Keohane and Martin 1995: 40–1). Institutionalists do not restrict their claims to the international political economy and argue that institutions play a critical role in providing information in both economic and security relations (Keohane and Martin 1995: 43–4). Institutions reduce incentives for states to defect, lower transaction costs, link issues, and provide focal points for cooperation.

International law

Although it is widely viewed as a principal component of international regimes, *international law* (which constitutes a formalization of rules) can serve as a basis for global governance. International law codifies rules governing the behaviour of major actors, particularly of independent states. In their work on law in international governance, Kenneth Abbott and Duncan Snidal distinguish between what they term 'hard' and 'soft' law (Abbott and Snidal 2000). Hard law refers to legally binding obligations that are precise and restrict behaviour and sovereignty. EU law, which is backed by the European Court of Justice, is an example of hard law. Soft law refers to a weakening of hard law along one (or more) of three dimensions: obligation, precision, or delegation (Abbott and Snidal 2000: 422). If obligation, precision, and/or delegation are absent, as they often are in practice, there is still a form of legalization present. Abbott and Snidal make this distinction not only to illustrate the variety in degrees of legalization, but also to illustrate how widespread legalization has become globally. The UN Charter's injunction against state aggression, the international Convention on the Prevention and Punishment of the Crime of Genocide, the Non-Proliferation Treaty, and the activities of the International Criminal Court are all examples of soft international law that govern the security domain.

Norms

Global *norms* are another component of international regimes that can provide the ideational or normative underpinnings for governance. Adherence to norms is one of the best empirical indicators of the presence of global governance. Norms are standards of appropriate behaviour for actors with a given identity (Finnemore and Sikkink 1998: 891). Finnemore and Sikkink distinguish between different categories of norms: regulative, constitutive, and prescriptive. Regulative norms both order and constrain behaviour and are most closely associated with conceptions of global governance. Constitutive norms create new actors, interests, identities, or categories of actors. Prescriptive norms establish what 'ought' to be done.

Neta Crawford makes a distinction between norms as common practice and normative beliefs based on ethical prescriptions, but correctly notes that 'international relations theorists frequently use "norms" to denote both senses' (Crawford 2002: 40). If norms are internalized within major players, they become an authoritative base for a system of rules that operate at the global level. International norms are widespread and increasingly visible in the governance of the security domain – from justifications for the use of force and proportionality in war (derived from just war theory and practices) to proscriptions against the use of torture, norms against the first use of nuclear weapons, and in support of the idea of sovereign responsibility to protect. These norms are often contested, but they provide a basis for global governance (considered as an intersubjectively recognized, purposive order at the global level).

Private authority

Most of the different bases of global security governance considered up to this point (with the possible exception of global norms), are based on relations between states or evaluated predominantly in terms of their influence on state behaviour. Private, non-state actors can also provide a basis for governance, typically in association with states, but occasionally on their own (Daase and Friesendorf 2010). *Private authority* in the global political economy ranges from self-binding codes of conduct and standards setting schemes to coordinated lobbying efforts, independent rating and assessment agencies, and private regimes (Cutler et al. 1999).

Private authority has also emerged in the realm of global security governance (Avant 2005; Hall and Biersteker 2002). A great variety of non-state actors are engaged in global security governance, from advocacy networks like the International Campaign to Ban Landmines to public policy think tanks, private military companies, militia groups and warlords, transnational movements engaged in the commission of acts of terrorism, and, in some instances, even mafias and vigilante groups. They can be said to be authoritative because they establish standards, provide social welfare, enforce contracts, maintain security for certain populations, and offer an alternative basis for governance. Private authority in the security domain emerges when states delegate it, enable it, or passively allow it to develop. It can also emerge in spaces where the state has abdicated from its responsibilities, and in some instances, authority can be seized from the state.

Standardized codes

The creation or existence of a standardized *code* or mutually agreed–upon routine for regulating a particular domain can also provide a basis for governance (Sylvan 2013). Codes are often developed by private sector actors for self-regulating their behaviour to improve collective efficiencies and/or to reduce costs. Commonly accepted standards create a basis for the interoperability of complex systems, and the governance of the Internet provides a good illustration of the phenomenon. The standards developed by the Internet Engineering Task Force (IETF), an open network of technical specialists drawn almost entirely from the private sector, enables the 'network of networks' that constitutes the Internet to operate (Gahnberg 2014).

In a related way, the SWIFT code, developed originally by private financial institutions to improve the efficiency of their inter-bank transactions, not only governs international financial transfers, but has served as a basis for the financial surveillance being carried out in the name of global counterterrorism. Accessing the SWIFT database became a key priority of US Treasury

Department officials immediately following the attacks of 11 September 2001 in their effort to identify the networks behind the attacks by sifting through their financial transactions. This form of financial surveillance has been extended beyond countering the financing of terrorism to other security domains – countering proliferation, enforcing international sanctions, and prosecuting transnational crime.

The complexity of contemporary global security governance

During the past two decades, a great deal of innovative research has explored the role of non-state, private, and/or transnational actors engaged in contemporary global governance. Whether the phenomenon is described as the 'emergence of private authority' (Cutler et al. 1999; Hall and Biersteker 2002), the 'global public domain' (Ruggie 2004), the role of 'transnational advocacy groups' (Keck and Sikkink 1998), the emergence of 'trans-governmental networks' (Slaughter 2004), the growth of 'public–private partnerships' (Andonova 2010, 2014), the development of 'multi-stakeholder initiatives' (Jerbi 2012), 'transnational new governance' (Abbott and Snidal 2009), or the 'new power politics' (Avant and Westerwinter, forthcoming), there is a growing consensus that it is no longer possible to focus exclusively, or even predominantly, on states and their interactions in inter-governmental institutions to comprehend, understand, and analyse contemporary global governance. As de Burca, Keohane, and Sabel point out, we have moved well beyond the model of principal–agent relationships between states and hierarchical international organizations associated with the first generation international regimes, into a far more complex system of global governance (de Burca et al. 2013).

For example, Jonas Tallberg and his colleagues have documented empirically the growth in the formal access of non-state actors to the deliberations and activities of formal international organizations (Tallberg et. al. 2013). They have identified a secular increase in the formal access of non-state actors, beginning from 1970 in the case of United Nations organizations, and from the early 1990s in the case of all international organizations considered together. While there is significant variation in access by issue domain, there is evidence of greater formal access by non-state actors in global security organizations over time (particularly after 2000).

Securing formal access is significant, but as Cecilia Cannon has pointed out, the kinds of influence exercised by non-state actors, particularly in transnational advocacy campaigns, tend to vary over time (Cannon 2013). Cannon examines the influence of non-state actors in different phases of the policy process, differentiating initial issue definition from agenda setting, advocacy, public information, and standards creation. She finds that the influence of non-state actors appears to be greatest in earlier stages of transnational advocacy campaigns (in defining issues, in agenda setting, and advocacy), and that states re-emerge as more influential at the later stages of drafting common standards, monitoring, and of course, in legal codification. This pattern is clearly discernible in the recent negotiation over the convention to limit private military and security providers.

At times, the 'authority of expertise' exercised by some of these non-state actors enables them to play an active role in governance itself (Hall and Biersteker 2002: 14). The independent assessments of non-governmental human rights organizations are important for evaluating (and potentially challenging) existing inter-governmental governance arrangements routinely conducted largely by states. There are many other examples of non-state actors exercising authority in contemporary global governance, either jointly or alone, from the activities of ICANN in the governance of Internet domain names or the IETF in Internet governance to the independent evaluations of private bond rating agencies like Standard and Poors, who exercised their independent private authority in 2011 when they downgraded US public debt.

Non-governmental actors participate in contemporary global governance in a variety of different ways, sometimes through participations in 'transnational policy networks' (Biersteker 2014b). Transnational policy networks are broadly analogous to Pierre Bourdieu's concept of a specialized 'field' of expertise (Bourdieu 1990) with a structured social space with its own rules, roles, hierarchies, and range of legitimate views. They are constituted by a group of individuals who share a common expertise, a common technical language to communicate that expertise, broadly shared normative concerns, but not necessarily agreement on specific policy alternatives. Transnational policy networks might include individuals from non-governmental organizations associated with advocacy, but they are more technical in orientation and tend to avoid explicit engagement with advocacy. They are similar to trans-governmental networks and certainly include them (Slaughter 2004), but transcend them to include actors other than state officials – actors from the private sector, from international organizations, from international legal practice, and sometimes from academia. They are less formally institutionalized than most public–private partnerships and even most multi-stakeholder initiatives, and they are more focused on policy formation and the development and reform of policy instruments than on regulatory activities (that are the principal concerns of non-state market-driven regulatory systems and multi-stakeholder initiatives).

Transnational policy networks are not visible in the form of governance provided by 'the international society of states' and are largely absent in the governance arrangements provided by an individual state's hegemony or by many international regimes, but they are often major players in the production of new international norms and institutions in emerging domains of global security governance. Many governance initiatives at the global level begin with private standard-setting arrangements, but they are not able to sustain themselves because they lack public legitimacy. As a result, they turn increasingly to transnational advocacy networks to gain legitimacy, sometimes morphing into multi-stakeholder initiatives including states. Only at later stages do states or inter-governmental organizations try to come back into the process with greater formal regulation of activities, as seen recently in the cases of the 2013 convention on private military companies and in 2014 debates about Internet governance.

Conclusion

Global governance is a multifaceted concept: a lot of different definitions exist. With regard to the mechanisms of governance, there is again a range – from hierarchy in hegemonic systems to networks in governance by global norms and international society. Private authority, international law, regimes, and institutions as bases of governance tend to be governed by a combination of both hierarchy and network.

With regard to degree of formal institutionalization, there is again wide variation, both between different bases of governance and within them. International society and private authority operate with relatively low levels of formal institutionalization at the global level, while most forms of hegemony are associated with high degrees of formal institutionalization. Regimes, institutions, law, standardized codes, and norms tend to operate at an intermediate level of formal institutionalization, with a mix of formal and informal institutional arrangements.

The variety of different bases for identifying and comprehending forms of contemporary global security governance – the society of states, hegemony, regimes, institutions, law, norms, standardized codes, and private authority – illustrate well the complexity of the subject, as well as the range of institutional players and mechanisms involved. In spite of all of the disorder and complexity associated with global security issues, however, there is a great deal of purposive and authoritatively rule-governed order present in the contemporary international system. It is not always a very just or efficient system of governance, but it is governance nevertheless, and is central to any understanding of attempts to address contemporary security challenges.

Note

★ I would like to thank Myriam Dunn Cavelty, Victor Mauer, and Georg von Kalckreuth for their comments on a previously published version of this essay, and I would like to thank Thierry Balzacq and Myriam Dunn Cavelty for their patience and constructive comments on this version. I would also like to acknowledge and thank Dominika Ornatowska for her research assistance for this revised and updated version. A small portion of this essay was previously included in Robert I. Rotberg (ed.) (2015) *On Governance*, Waterloo: CIGI Press.

References

Abbott, K. and Snidal, D. (2000) 'Hard and Soft Law in International Governance', *International Organization* 54: 421–56.

Abbott, K. and Snidal, D. (2009) 'Strengthening International Regulation through Transnational New Governance: Overcoming the Orchestration Deficit', *Vanderbilt Journal of International Law* 42: 1–78.

Abbott, K. and Snidal, D. (2010) 'The Governance Triangle: Regulatory Standards Institutions and the Shadow of the State', in W. Mattli and N. Woods (eds.) *The Politics of Global Regulation*, Princeton, NJ: Princeton University Press, 44–88.

Andonova, L. (2010) 'Public–Private Partnerships for the Earth: Politics and Patterns of Hybrid Authority in the Multilateral System', *Global Environmental Politics* 10(2): 25–53.

Andonova, L. (2014) 'Boomerangs to Partnerships? Explaining State Participation in Transnational Partnerships for Sustainability', *Comparative Political Studies* 47(3): 481–515.

Avant, D. (2005) *The Market for Force: The Consequences of Privatizing Security*, Cambridge: Cambridge University Press.

Avant, D. and Westerwinter, O. (forthcoming) 'The New Power Politics: Networks and Transnational Security Governance'.

Biersteker, T. (2014a) 'Dialectical Reflections on Transformations of Global Security during the Long 20th Century', *Globalizations* 11(3): 711–31.

Biersteker, T. (2014b) 'Participating in Transnational Policy Networks: Targeted Sanctions', in M. E. Bertucci and A. F. Lowenthal (eds.) *Narrowing the Gap: Scholars, Policy-Makers and International Affairs*, Baltimore and London: Johns Hopkins University Press, 137–154.

Börzel, T. A. and Risse, T. (2010) 'Governance without a State: Can It Work?', *Regulation and Governance* 4(2): 113–34.

Bourdieu, P. (1990) *The Logic of Practice (Le sens pratique)*, Stanford, CA: Stanford University Press.

Bull, H. (1977) *The Anarchical Society: A Study of Order in World Politics*, New York: Columbia University Press.

Cannon, C. (2013) 'How Much Influence Do NGOs Really Wield? A Method for Isolating Influence in Processes of Normative Change', Unpublished paper presented at the PSIG Seminar on Governance, The Graduate Institute, Geneva.

Claude, I. (1962) *Power and International Relations*, New York: Random House.

Cox, R. (1987) *Production, Power, and World Order: Social Forces in the Making of History*, New York: Columbia University Press.

Crawford, N. (2002) *Argument and Change in World Politics: Ethics, Decolonization, and Humanitarian Intervention*, Cambridge: Cambridge University Press.

Cutler, C., Haufler, V., and Porter, T. (1999) *Private Authority and International Affairs*, Albany: SUNY Press.

Daase, C. and Friesendorf, C. (2010) *Rethinking Security Governance: The problem of unintended consequences*, London: Routledge.

de Burca, G., Keohane, R. O., and Sabel, C. (2013) 'New Modes of Pluralist Global Governance', *International Law and Politics* 45(3): 723–86.

Finnemore, M. and Sikkink, K. (1998) 'International Norm Dynamics and Political Change', *International Organization* 52: 887–917.

Gahnberg, C. (2014) 'Who Governs? Networks and Internet Standards: An Empirical Study of the IETF', MA Dissertation in International Relations / Political Science, The Graduate Institute, Geneva.

Gilpin, R. (1975) *US Power and the Multinational Corporation: The Political Economy of Foreign Direct Investment*, New York: Basic Books.

Gilpin, R. (1981) *War and Change in World Politics*, Cambridge and New York: Cambridge University Press.

Haggard, S. and Simmons, B. (1987) 'Theories of International Regimes', *International Organization* 41: 491–517.

Hall, R. and Biersteker, T. (2002) *The Emergence of Private Authority in Global Governance*, Cambridge and New York: Cambridge University Press.

Held, D. (2012) 'Toward the New Global Governance', *The Global Journal*, 6 March.

Jerbi, S. (2012) 'Assessing the Roles of Multi-Stakeholder Initiatives in Advancing the Business and Human Rights Agenda', *International Review of the Red Cross* 94(887): 1027–46.

Katzenstein, P. (1996) *The Culture of National Security: Norms and Identity in World Politics*, New York: Columbia University Press.

Keck, M. E. and Sikkink, K. (1998) *Activists beyond Borders: Advocacy Networks in International Politics*, Ithaca, NY: Cornell University Press.

Keohane, R. O. (1984) *After Hegemony: Cooperation and Discord in the World Political Economy*, Princeton, NJ: Princeton University Press.

Keohane, R. O. (1988) 'International Institutions: Two Approaches', *International Studies Quarterly* 32: 379–96.

Keohane, R. O. and Martin, L. (1995) 'The Promise of Institutionalist Theory', *International Security* 20: 39–51.

Keohane, R. O. and Nye, J. (1977) *Power and Interdependence: World Politics in Transition*, Boston, MA: Little, Brown.

Kindleberger, C. (1973) *The World in Depression, 1929–1939*, Berkeley: University of California Press.

Krasner, S. (1983), 'Structural Causes and Regime Consequences: Regimes as Intervening Variables', in S. Krasner (ed.) *International Regimes*, Ithaca, NY: Cornell University Press, 1–21.

Martin, L. (1992) 'Interests, Power and Multilateralism', *International Organization* 46: 765–92.

Reus-Smit, C. (1997) 'The Constitutional Structure of International Society and the Nature of Fundamental Institutions', *International Organization* 51: 555–89.

Rosenau, J. (1992) 'Governance, Order and Change in World Politics', in J. Rosenau and E.-O. Czempiel (eds.) *Governance without Government: Order and Change in World Politics*, Cambridge: Cambridge University Press, 1–29.

Rosenau, J. and Czempiel, E.-O. (eds.) (1992) *Governance without Government: Order and Change in World Politics*, Cambridge: Cambridge University Press.

Ruggie, J. G. (2004) 'Reconstituting the Global Public Domain – Issues, Actors, and Practices', *European Journal of International Relations* 10(4): 499–531.

Ruggie, J. G. (2014) 'Global Governance and "New Governance Theory": Lessons from Business and Human Rights', *Global Governance* 20(1): 5–17.

Slaughter, A.-M. (2004) *A New World Order*, Princeton, NJ: Princeton University Press.

Stone, R. W. (2011) Controlling Institutions: International Organizations and the Global Economy, Cambridge: Cambridge University Press.

Strange, S. (1986) *Casino Capitalism*, Oxford: Blackwell.

Strange, S. (1988) *States and Markets*, London: Pinter.

Sylvan, D. (2013) 'Global Internet Governance: Governance without Governors', in R. Radu, J.-M. Chenou, and R. Weber (eds.) *The Evolution of Global Internet Governance: Principles and Policies in the Making*, Basel: Schulthess, 23–36.

Tallberg, J., Sommerer, T., Squatrito, T., and Jönsson, C. (2013) *The Opening Up of International Organizations: Transnational Access in Global Governance*, Cambridge: Cambridge University Press.

Watson, A. (1992) *The Evolution of International Society: A Comparative Historical Analysis*, London and New York: Routledge.

Weiss, T. G. (2009) 'The UN's Role in Global Governance', *UN Intellectual History Project Briefing Note*, No. 15: 1–6.

Young, O. (1992) 'The Effectiveness of International Institutions: Hard Cases and Critical Variables', in J. Rosenau and E.-O. Czempiel (eds.) *Governance without Government: Order and Change in World Politics*, Cambridge: Cambridge University Press, 160–94.

40

RESILIENCE

David Chandler

This chapter seeks to introduce the paradigm of resilience and to contrast it to the liberal internationalist understandings of reactive international intervention to secure people threatened by conflict, deprivation, or disasters. Resilience is defined here as the capacity to positively or successfully cope with, adapt to, and recover from security crises, and is widely employed as a framework for addressing a broad range of interrelated security threats stemming from conflict, poverty, and environmental concerns. Resilience thus concerns the capacities of societies, communities, and individuals as the targets of security interventions rather than attempting to deal with security crises merely at the level of their manifestations – i.e. the provision of post-hoc aid or humanitarian relief or military intervention to remove war criminals or dictatorial regimes. Resilience seeks to address security questions at the deeper level of social causation in order to provide sustainable solutions enabling communities to understand, to cope with, and to successfully manage security threats.

This chapter has four parts. In the first, the resilient subject with its ascription of vulnerability is introduced. In the second, resilience is posited as a post-interventionist paradigm, where the agency for security lies with the resilient subject itself, which signifies a shift from a state-based to a society-based understanding of security practices. In the third, the chapter contrasts security interventions within the resilience paradigm with older modes of governance. In the fourth, the chapter illustrates the shift from liberal internationalist understandings of security to the post-intervention paradigm with a few examples.

The resilient subject

The resilient subject (at both individual and collective levels) is never passively conceived (as in the case of post-hoc or reactive paradigms of victims requiring saving interventions) but is an active agent, capable of achieving security goals through self-transformation. Resilience is a normative or ideal concept, and is a goal rather than a final state of being, and therefore can only be measured or calculated as a comparative or relative quality. Some individuals or communities may be understood to be more resilient than others, but none can be understood to be fully resilient. While we are aware that our fixed understandings, derived from the past, are a barrier to resilience we are also aware that our thought-processes and cultural and social values continue to bound or limit our openness to the need to adapt. We can only ever be somewhere along the continuum of resilience, and therefore ultimately are all in need of enabling to become more resilient. Resilience is thus conceived as a process, through which security problems and threats are dealt with through building capacities that enable threats to be managed rather than responded to after the event.

Subjects believed to lack the capacities for resilience are held to be vulnerable. The ascription of vulnerability suggests that the subject lacks the capacities for resilience. Polit and Beck, in a medical practice context, define vulnerability in terms of 'being incapable of giving informed consent' or 'at the high risk of unintended side-effects' (Polit and Beck 2004). This draws out the distinction between vulnerability as an internal attribute, in relation to the capacity to make reasoned choices, and vulnerability as a product of objective circumstances or susceptibilities (cf. Kottow 2002). In this sense vulnerabilities constitute our 'unfreedoms' or the restrictions, both material and ideological, which prevent us from being resilient (cf. Sen 1999). The interpellation as vulnerable can be applied to individuals – the 'at risk', the 'socially excluded', or the 'marginal' – as well as to communities – the 'poor', the 'indigenous', or the 'environmentally threatened' – as much as to states themselves – the 'failing', 'failed', 'fragile', 'low income under stress', or badly governed.

Post-intervention

Resilience provides a paradigm for international intervention aimed at securing societies and communities which can be seen as post-interventionist. This is because the securing agency is not the external actor but the community itself, seen to require intervention in order to secure itself. The conceptual framing of post-interventionism seeks to demarcate international security frameworks from those of humanitarian intervention, based on the reaction to abuses and the protection of victims; in a post-interventionist–resilience paradigm the emphasis is on prevention rather than intervention, empowerment rather than protection, and work upon the vulnerable rather than upon victims (cf. Chandler 2010a; Foucault 2008; Joerges 2010; Walker and Cooper 2011).

In articulating international security in terms of resilience and post-intervention, this chapter develops some of the themes in recent work, highlighting the links between discourses of resilience and the shift from a state-based to a society-based understanding of security practices (Brasset and Vaughan Williams 2011; Briggs 2010; Bulley 2011; Coaffee et al. 2009; Edwards 2009; Lenzos and Rose 2009; O'Malley 2010; UK Cabinet Office 2011). It seeks, in particular, to emphasize the shift to the agency of the objects of the interventionist discourse rather than that of the ostensible interveners. Discourses of resilience do not centrally focus upon protection as provided by external actors, nor the material attributes (military equipment, technology, welfare provisions, etc.) that can be provided through government as a way of protecting populations or responding after an event. Resilience concerns the inculcation of the agency of the other.[1] For this reason, discourses of resilience do not fit well with the liberal internationalist framings of security practices, which were dominant in the 1990s, as reactive post-hoc interventions.

The post-interventionist order is conceptually very different from that of the 1990s debates, which pitched human-centred against state-centred approaches. The post-interventionist world order no longer juxtaposes external intervention to sovereignty as if this were a zero-sum game, or articulates intervention in the language of a clash of rights or as a problem which needs a legal solution. The interventionist policy practices operating under the paradigm of resilience cannot be grasped in terms of the clash of liberal rights, in the formal spheres of law or politics. Using an entirely different register, resilience operates conceptually by reinterpreting external intervention as productive of capable and securing subjects.

In this paradigm, the external management of, or intervention in, post-conflict or post-colonial state policy-making is understood as a process of empowerment, of capacity- and capability-building. This shift is reflected well in discussions of intervention as bridging the 'sovereignty gap' (Ghani et al. 2005) and in Stephen Krasner's view of 'domestic sovereignty' being built up (or co-produced) by external actors on the basis of giving up 'Westphalian/Vattelian sovereignty' (Krasner 2004: 87–8; see further, Chandler 2010a). Despite the increased regulatory engagement, the discourse is one of prevention and the building of sovereignty, not of intervention and the denial of sovereignty. This policy emphasis on prevention, resilience, and empowerment is dominant in discourses of international regulation and intervention today.

The resilience paradigm as an articulation of an alternative or more progressive framework of security depends for its radical status upon the critique of liberal discourses of intervention posed in terms of sovereignty and rights. With the shift away from the liberal discourse of intervention privileged in the 1990s, resilience claims to offer an alternative to mainstream approaches – through emphasizing prevention, empowerment, and the agency of the post-conflict and post-colonial subject. There are three key distinctions: first, the discourse of resilience always operates preventively, never reactively or in the post-hoc manner of liberal international intervention. Second, the subject of international security practices is always the vulnerable subject in need of enabling agency to become resilient; never the passive victim, in need of external securing agency for protection. Third, the inculcation of resilience is a necessity, never an option, because the starting assumption is the lack of capacity of the subject to secure itself in the future unless its securing agency is empowered (see Table 40.1).

The framework of resilience is presented as a radical democratization of security, where the most dangerous threats are to the most vulnerable, who therefore need external intervention in order to enhance their capacities for security. This framework is that of intervention to protect through empowerment rather than through external sovereign intervention. The discourse of resilience inverts a traditional liberal understanding of sovereign securing power. The emphasis is no longer upon the intervening external sovereign or international actor as a securing agent; the

Table 40.1 The resilience paradigm

Liberal internationalism	Resilience
Liberal	Neoliberal / Post-liberal[1]
Intervention	Post-intervention
Rights / Law	Capabilities / Capacities
Post-crisis	Pre-crisis
Victims	Vulnerable
Coercive	Empowering
Consequences addressed	Causes addressed
Direct provision / responsibility	Indirect provision / responsibility
External agency	Internal agency
Top-down	Bottom-up
Sovereign power	Dispersal of power
Western responsibility	Western facilitation
State sovereignty undermined	State sovereignty strengthened
Endpoint exit / status quo ante	Ongoing process / open-ended

[1] *The distinction between the paradigm of resilience articulated here as central to understandings of human security and 1990s liberal internationalist discourses of intervention has parallels with that established by Foucault, in terms of neoliberal or biopolitical framings which he understood as 'inverting' and 'transforming' traditional liberal doctrines (2008:118) and is further explored in relation to the practices of post-liberal governance in Chandler (2010a).*

discourse of vulnerability, empowerment, and resilience insists that the emphasis must be upon a 'bottom-up' understanding of security. This is a far cry from the social contract framing of liberal modernity with the collective constitution of securing agency at the level of the state, tasking the sovereign with the post-hoc duty of intervention to correct any problematic outcomes of the free interplay of market forces or of democratic contestation.[2] Security discourses of resilience work in reverse. Rather than securing power being transferred to the sovereign, this securing power is decentralized or dispersed back into society (UNDP 1994: 33):

> An actor-oriented, agency-based resilience framework . . . reframes resilience from a systems-oriented to a people-centred perspective. It starts by considering social actors and their agency, arenas and respective agendas in the transformation of livelihoods in a resilient way. The framework proposes a normative context of entitlements, capabilities, freedoms and choices or, even more broadly, of justice, fairness and equity. An agency-based framework measures resilience in terms of how peoples' livelihood vulnerability can be reduced or, to put it more broadly, in terms of their human security. Mechanisms for *resilience-building*, from this perspective, are first and foremost about *empowering the most vulnerable* to pursue livelihood options that strengthen what they themselves consider to be their social sources of resilience.
>
> *(Bohle et al. 2009: 12, emphases added)*

In this dispersal of securing power, the task of the state (or external interveners) is to focus on empowering those held to be least able to secure themselves – least capable of securing themselves and adapting to potential security threats. In this way, no conceptual distinction is made between the empowering practices of the domestic state and of international interveners as both are constructed as pursuing the same tasks of dispersing the power or agency to secure, rather than as acting as securing actors per se.

In this framing, the understanding of failed and failing states as a security threat is precisely that they are vulnerable subjects in need of external policy interventions to build resilience capabilities. The existing regimes of liberal rules of law and democracy are often held to be problematic in the post-colonial world, precisely because of the lack of capacities at both individual and societal levels. For this reason, the problematic of the inculcation of resilience has been at the centre of academic security discourses. From Nobel prize-winning development theorists, such as Amartya Sen and Douglass North, to leading security theorists, such as Paul Collier, the problem of security has been seen to be that of the difficulty of facilitating better choice-making capabilities through intervention capable of empowering both individuals and societies (Collier and Hoeffle, 2004; Collier et al. 2006; North 1990; 2005; Sen 1999; see also Chandler 2010b).

Empowerment is therefore at the centre of the problematic of resilience. In the post-interventionist framework, the West no longer has the responsibility to secure, to democratize, or to develop the non-Western world. This is always the lesson learned from experiences of 1990s-style interventions and their corollary of the formalized external processes of international statebuilding, where responsibility is directly assumed by international actors. It is for these reasons that resilience approaches can easily mesh with the concerns of 'post-liberal' approaches to peace-building, where the emphasis is squarely placed upon 'the capacity of people to decide their own future' (Martin and Owen 2010: 223; see also Chandler 2010a; Richmond 2011). The regulatory mechanisms of empowerment, prevention, and capacity-building are premised upon the understanding that there can be no clash of rights between sovereignty and intervention: no inside and no outside. Responsibility once again stops at the boundaries of the sovereign state but this is a state understood as incapable of managing its autonomy without the help of external facilitators.

'Organic' versus 'political' understandings of intervention

Western policy-interveners increasingly claim that they are not thereby taking over decision-making processes and increasingly argue that they are also not setting external goals or even measuring progress using universal external yardsticks. Rather than the external provision of policy solutions or the use of 'conditionality' to guide states in specific directions, international actors are more likely to understand security interventions within the resilience paradigm in terms of enabling organic systems and existing knowledges, practices, and capacities. This model forwards more homeopathic forms of policy-intervention designed to enhance autonomous processes rather than undermine or socially engineer them (see, for example, Drabek and McEntire 2003; Kaufmann 2013 on emergent responses to disasters). Resilience approaches thereby problematize security interventions that seek to act merely at the level of the appearance of problems and crises, arguing that these approaches are often superficial, counterproductive, and unsustainable, failing to touch the real issues and relations at the societal level.

The shift from intervention at the level of surface appearances to addressing the underlying societal capacities has been predominantly discussed in relation to the need to take into account the 'law of unintended consequences'. Previous approaches which assumed that security problems were discrete and separable from social processes are thereby understood as too reductionist and mechanistic in their approach – failing to grasp the interrelations between different aspects of security. Resilience thereby takes a more 'holistic' and interconnected approach to security, which minimizes 'unintended consequences'. This heralds a profound shift in the understanding of the importance of social relations to international security intervention, and can be understood as a generalized extension of Ulrich Beck's view of 'risk society' with the determinate causal role of 'side effects' or of Bruno Latour's similar analysis of today's world as modernity 'plus all its externalities' (Beck 1992; Latour 2003). It seems that there is no way to consider intervention in terms of intended outcomes without considering the possibility that the unintended outcomes will outweigh these.

While, in 2002, the US State Department was focusing on extensive statebuilding operations to address the crucial question of state failure, in 2012, a decade later, the US Defense Strategic Guidance policy is illustrative of a different set of assumptions: that US forces would pursue their objectives through 'innovative, low-cost, and small-footprint approaches' rather than the conduct of 'large-scale, prolonged stability operations' (DSG 2012: 3, 6). In 2013, discussion over potential coercive intervention in Syria was dominated by fears that the unintended outcomes would outweigh the good intentions of external actors (Ackerman 2013). General Martin Dempsey, chairman of the US Joint Chiefs of Staff, warned that policy caution was necessary as: 'we must anticipate and be prepared for the unintended consequences of our action' (Ackerman 2013; see also Phillips 2013).

As Michael Mazaar argued in the influential US foreign policy journal *Foreign Affairs* in 2014, securing US goals of peace, democracy, and development in failing and conflict-ridden states could not, in fact, be done by instrumental cause-and-effect external policy-interventions: 'it is an organic, grass-roots process that must respect the unique social, cultural, economic, political, and religious contexts of each country ... and cannot be imposed' (Mazaar 2014). For Mazaar, policy would now follow a more 'resilient mindset, one that treats perturbations as inevitable rather than calamitous and resists the urge to overreact', understanding that policy-intervention must work with, rather than against, local institutions and 'proceed more organically and authentically' (Mazaar 2014). This shift is also reflected by high-level policy experts in the US State Department; according to Charles T. Call, senior adviser at the Bureau of Conflict and Stabilization Operations, current US approaches seek not to impose unrealistic external goals but instead to facilitate local transformative agency through engaging with local 'organic processes and plussing them up' (cited in Chandler 2014).

Security interventions, today, are increasingly understood to be problematic if they are based upon the grand narratives of liberal internationalism, which informed and drove the debate on international intervention in the 1990s, when issues of intervention and non-intervention in Africa and the Balkans were at the centre of international political contestation. International policy-intervention is not opposed per se or on principle, but on the basis of the universalist and hierarchical knowledge assumptions which informed policy-interventions and produced the hubristic and reductionist promises of transformative outcomes (see, for example, Mayall and Soares de Oliveira 2011; Mazaar 2014; Owen 2012; Stewart and Knaus 2012).

The focus therefore shifts away from international policies (supply-driven policy-making) and towards engaging with the internal capacities and capabilities that are already held to exist. In other words, there is a shift from the agency, knowledge, and practices of policy-interveners to that of the society, which is the object of policy concerns. As the 2013 updated UK Department for International Development, Growth and Resilience Operational Plan states: 'we will produce less "supply-driven" development of product, guidelines and policy papers, and foster peer-to-peer, horizontal learning and knowledge exchange, exploiting new technologies such as wiki/ huddles to promote the widest interaction between stakeholders' (DfID 2013: 8).

'Supply-driven' policies – which often assume universal solutions to security threats which are seen in isolation from their social, cultural, and political context – are understood to operate in an artificial or non-organic way, and to lack an authentic connection to the deeper societal relations which need to be accounted for. The imposition of external institutional and policy frameworks has become increasingly seen as artificial and thereby as having counterproductive or unintended outcomes. Resilience approaches seek to move away from the 'liberal peace' policy-interventions – seeking to export constitutional frameworks, to train and equip military and police forces, to impose external conditionalities on the running of state budgets, to export managerial frameworks for civil servants and political representatives or to impose regulations to ensure administrative transparency and codes of conduct – which were at the heart of international policy prescriptions in the 1990s and early 2000s (ActionAid 2006; Eurodad 2006; World Bank 2007).

It is argued that the 'supply-driven' approach of external experts exporting or developing liberal institutions does not grasp the complex processes generative of instability or insecurity. Instead, the 'top-down' model of liberal intervention is seen to create problematic 'hybrid' political systems and fragile states with little connection to their societies (Mac Ginty 2010; Millar 2014; Richmond and Mitchell 2012; Roberts 2008). The imposition of institutional frameworks, which have little connection to society, is understood as failing, not only in not addressing causal processes, but as making matters worse through undermining local capacities to manage the effects of problems, shifting problems elsewhere, and leaving states and societies even more fragile or vulnerable. This approach is alleged to fail to hear the 'message' of problematic manifestations or to enable societies' own organic and homeostatic processes to generate corrective mechanisms. Triggering external interventions is said to shortcut the ability of societies to reflect upon and take responsibility for their own affairs, and is increasingly seen as a counterproductive 'over-reaction' by external powers (see further, Desch 2008; Maor 2012). There is an increasingly prevalent view that, contrary to earlier assumptions, policy solutions can only be developed through practice by actors on the ground.

Examples of policy shifts

As noted above, conceptualization of security policy-interventions in terms of vulnerability, empowerment, and resilience evades the traditional disciplinary understanding of intervention as an exercise of external political power and authority. It does this through denying intervention as an act of external decision-making and policy-direction as understood in the political paradigm of liberal internationalist discourse. This can be illustrated through highlighting some examples of policy shifts in key areas of international security concern: conflict and the rule of law; development; and democracy and rights.

Conflict and the rule of law

Policy-interventions are increasingly shifting in relation to the understanding of conflict. As the UK government argues, in a 2011 combined DfID, Foreign and Commonwealth Office and Ministry of Defence document, conflict per se is not the problem. The problem which needs to be tackled is the state's or society's ability to manage conflict: 'in stable, resilient societies conflict is managed through numerous formal and informal institutions' (DfID et al. 2011: 5). Conflict management, as the UK government policy indicates, is increasingly understood as an organic set of societal processes and practices, which international policy-intervention can influence but cannot import solutions from outside or impose them. This understanding very much follows the approach long advocated by influential peace theorist, Jean Paul Lederach, who argued that: 'the greatest resource for sustaining peace in the long term is always rooted in the local people and their culture' (1997: 94). For Lederach, managing conflict meant moving away from universalist liberal internationalist forms of external intervention which see people as 'recipients' of policy, and instead seeing people as 'resources', integral to peace processes (1997: 95). One of the central shifts in understanding conflict as something that needs to be 'coped with' and 'managed' rather than something that can be 'solved' or 'prevented' is the view that state-level interventions are of limited use. Peace treaties can be signed by state parties, but unless peace is seen as an ongoing and transformative inclusive societal process these agreements will be merely superficial and non-sustainable (Lederach 1997: 135).

Just as peace and security are less understood as able to be secured through cause-and-effect forms of intervention, reliant on policy-interveners imposing solutions in mechanical and reductive ways, there has also been a shift in understanding the counterproductive effects of attempts to export the rule of law (Cesarine and Hite 2004; Chandler 2014b; Zimmermann 2007). The resilience approach is driven by a realization of the gap between the formal sphere of law and constitutionalism and the social 'reality' of informal power relations and informal rules. This perspective has also been endorsed by Douglass North, the policy guru of new institutionalist economics, who has highlighted the difficulties of understanding how exported institutions will interact with 'culturally derived norms of behavior' (1990: 140). The social reality of countries undergoing post-conflict 'transition' is thereby less capable of being understood merely by an analysis of laws and statutes. In fact, there increasingly appears to be an unbridgeable gap between the artificial constructions of legal and constitutional frameworks and the realities of everyday life, revealed in dealings between individual members of the public and state authorities.

Development

A key policy area where the shift to resilience approaches to security has had an impact has been in the sphere of developmental and environmental security threats. Coping with poverty and with disasters is clearly a very different problematic from seeking to use development policy to reduce or to end extreme poverty. However, discourses of disaster risk reduction have increasingly displaced those of sustainable forms of development because of the unintended side effects of undermining the organic coping mechanisms of communities and therefore increasing vulnerabilities and weakening resilience (see, for example, IRDR 2014; UNDP 2014). Claudia

Aradau has highlighted the importance of the UK Department for International Development (DfID) shift in priorities from poverty reduction strategies to developing community resilience, which assumes the existence of poverty as the basis of policy-making (Aradau 2014). As she states: 'resilience responses entail a change in how poverty, development and security more broadly are envisaged'; this is clearly highlighted in DfID's 2011 report outlining the UK government's humanitarian policy:

> Humanitarian assistance should be delivered in a way that does not undermine existing coping mechanisms and helps a community build its own resilience for the future. National governments in at-risk countries can ensure that disaster risk management policies and strategies are linked to community-level action.
>
> *(DfID 2011: 10, cited in Aradau 2014)*

As George Nicholson, Director of Transport and Disaster Risk Reduction for the Association of Caribbean States argues explicitly: 'improving a person's ability to respond to and cope with a disaster event must be placed on equal footing with the process to encourage economic development', highlighting the importance of resilience to disaster risk as an increasingly key security policy area (Nicholson 2014). Whereas development approaches put the emphasis on external policy assistance and expert knowledge, disaster risk reduction clearly counterposes an alternative framework of intervention, where it is local knowledge and local agency that count the most. Disaster risk reduction strategies stress the empowerment of the vulnerable and marginalized in order for them to cope and to manage the effects of the risks and contingencies that are concomitant with the maintenance of their precarious existence.

Democracy and rights

As emphasized above, the resilience approach does not seek to assert sovereign power or Western hierarchies of power and knowledge; in fact, resilience operates as a challenge to and reaction against universalist liberal internationalist framings, dominant until the last decade. These points are highlighted, for example, in Bruno Latour's critical engagement with modernist modes of understanding: arguing that Western societies have forgotten the lengthy processes which enabled them to build liberal institutions dependent on the establishment of a political culture, which has to be steadily maintained, renewed, and extended and cannot be exported or imposed (Latour 2013: 343).

This shift away from formal universalist understandings of democracy and human rights is increasingly evidenced in the shifting understanding of human rights-based approaches to empowerment. Understanding empowerment in instrumental cause-and-effect terms based upon the external provision of legal and political mechanisms for claims is increasingly seen to be ineffective. Rights-based NGOs now seek not to empower people to access formal institutional mechanisms but to enable them to empower themselves. The resilience approach places the emphasis on the agency and self-empowerment of local actors, not on the introduction of formal frameworks of law, supported by international human rights norms (Moe and Simojoki 2013: 404).

The approach of 'finding organic processes and plussing them up' (as articulated by the US State Department policy advisor, cited earlier) has been increasingly taken up as a generic approach to overcome the limits of liberal peace approaches. A study of Finnish development NGOs highlights that rather than instrumentally selecting groups or civil society elites, new forms of intervention deny any external role in this process (Kontinen 2014). A similar study notes the importance of being non-prescriptive and avoiding and 'unlearning' views of Western teachers as 'authorities' and students as passive recipients (Gillespie and Melching 2010: 481). Policy-intervention is articulated as the facilitation of local people's attempts to uncover traditional practices and in 'awakening' and 'engaging' their already existing capacities: 'by detecting their own inherent skills, they can more easily transfer them to personal and community problem solving' (Gillespie and Melching 2010: 490). These processes can perhaps be encouraged or assisted by external policy-interveners but they cannot be transplanted from one society to another, and even less can they be imposed by policy-actors.

Conclusion

The shift in understanding policy-intervention from reactive impositions of external policies to that of resilience – focusing on the problem society's own capacities and needs and internal and organic processes – has been paralleled by a growing scepticism of attempts to export or impose Western models. The approach of resilience therefore marks a fundamental departure from hierarchical universalist approaches of liberal internationalism, where international security actors were seen as securing, rescuing or saving the non-Western other. Rather than bringing specific resources, knowledge, or solutions, security threats and risks are understood in much more organic ways. Interventions of this sort require no specialist knowledge and, in fact, tend to problematize such knowledge claims, and instead could be understood to require more therapeutic capacities and sensitivities, more attuned to open and unscripted forms of engagement, mutual processes of learning, and unpredictable and spontaneous forms of knowledge exchange (see for example: Brigg and Muller 2009: 130; Duffield 2007: 233–4; Jabri 2007: 177).

Notes

1 As Miller and Rose astutely note, this 'ethical a priori of active citizens in an active society is perhaps the most fundamental, and most generalizable, characteristic of these new rationalities of government' (2008: 215; see also Dean, 2010: 196–7).
2 See, for example, Foucault's discussion of the liberal problematic of intervention, or 'liberal economy of power' (2008: 65).

References

Ackerman, S. (2013) 'US Military Intervention in Syria Would Create "Unintended Consequences"', *The Guardian*, 22 July. Online. Available HTTP: <http://www.theguardian.com/world/2013/jul/22/us-military-intervention-syria> (accessed 12 November 2015).

ActionAid (2006) *What Progress? A Shadow Review of World Bank Conditionality*, Johannesburg: ActionAid.

Aradau, C. (2014) 'The Promise of Security: Resilience, Surprise and Epistemic Politics', *Resilience: International Practices, Policies and Discourses* 2(2): 73–87.

Beck, U. (1992) *Risk Society: Towards a New Modernity*, London: Sage.

Bohle, H.-G., Etzold, B., and Keck, M. (2009) 'Resilience as Agency', *IHDP Update* 2: 8–13.

Brassett, J. and Vaughan-Williams, N. (2011) 'Performative Ecologies of Resilience and Trauma: A Critical Analysis of UK Civil Contingencies', Paper presented at the Open University, Centre for Citizenship, Identities and Governance workshop 'Resisting (In)Security, Securing Resistance', London, 12 July.

Brigg, M. and Muller, K. (2009) 'Conceptualising Culture in Conflict Resolution', *Journal of Intercultural Studies* 3(2): 121–40.

Briggs, R. (2010) 'Community Engagement for Counterterrorism: Lessons from the United Kingdom', *International Affairs* 86(4): 971–81.

Bulley, D. (2011) 'Producing and Governing Community (through) Resilience'. Paper presented at the 'Resilient Futures: The Politics of Preventive Security' workshop, Department of Politics and International Studies, University of Warwick, 27–8 June.

Cesarini, P. and Hite, K. (2004) 'Introducing the Concept of Authoritarian Legacies', in K. Hite and P. Cesarini (eds.) *Authoritarian Legacies and Democracy in Latin America and Southern Europe*, Notre Dame: University of Notre Dame Press, 1–24.

Chandler, D. (2010a) *International Statebuilding: The Rise of post-Liberal Governance*, London: Routledge.

Chandler, D. (2010b) 'Race, Culture and Civil Society: Peacebuilding Discourse and the Understanding of Difference', *Security Dialogue* 41(4): 369–90.

Chandler, D. (2015) 'Resilience and the "Everyday": Beyond the Paradox of "Liberal Peace"', *Review of International Studies* 41(1): 27–48.

Coaffee, J., Murakami Wood, D., and Rogers, P. (2009) *The Everyday Resilience of the City: How Cities Respond to Terrorism and Disaster*, Basingstoke: Palgrave MacMillan.

Collier, P. and Hoeffler, A. (2004) 'Greed and Grievance in Civil War', *Oxford Economic Papers* 56: 563–95.

Collier, P., Hoeffler, A., and Rohner, D. (2006) 'Beyond Greed and Grievance: Feasibility and Civil War', *Centre for the Study of African Economies Working Paper Series*, 2006–2010, 7 August.

Dean, M. (2010[1999]) *Governmentality: Power and Rule in Modern Society*, London: Sage.

Desch, M. C. (2008) 'America's Liberal Illiberalism: The Ideological Origins of Overreaction in US Foreign Policy', *International Security* 32(3): 7–43.

DfID (Department for International Development, Saving Lives, Preventing Suffering and Building Resilience) (2011) *The UK Government's Humanitarian Policy*, London: DfID.

DfID (Department for International Development, Saving Lives, Preventing Suffering and Building Resilience) et al. (2011) *Building Stability Overseas Strategy*, London: DfID, FCO, MoD.

DfID (Department for International Development, Saving Lives, Preventing Suffering and Building Resilience) (2013) *Operational Plan 2011–2015 DFID Growth and Resilience Department*, London: DfID.

Drabek, T. E. and McEntire, D. A. (2003) 'Emergent Phenomena and the Sociology of Disaster: Lessons, Trends and Opportunities from the Research Literature', *Disaster, Prevention and Management* 12(2): 97–112.

DSG (2012) Sustaining US Global Leadership: Priorities for 21st-Century Defense, Washington, DC: White House.

Duffield, M. (2007) *Development, Security and Unending War: Governing the World of Peoples*, Cambridge: Polity Press.

Edwards, C. (2009) *Resilient Nation*, London: Demos.

Eurodad (2006) *World Bank and IMF Conditionality: A Development Injustice*, Brussels: European Network on Debt and Development.

Foucault, M. (2008) *The Birth of Biopolitics: Lectures at the Collège de France 1978–1979*, Basingstoke: Palgrave.

Ghani, A., Lockhart, C., and Carnahan, M. (2005) 'Closing the Sovereignty Gap: An Approach to State-Building', *Overseas Development Institute Working Paper* 253(September).

Gillespie, D. and Melching, M. (2010) 'The Transformative Power of Democracy and Human Rights in Nonformal Education: The Case of Tostan', *Adult Education Quarterly* 60(5): 477–98.

IRDR (Integrated Research on Disaster Risk Programme) (2014) *Issue Brief: Disaster Risk Reduction and Sustainable Development*. Online. Available HTTP: <http://www.preventionweb.net/english/professional/publications/v.php?id=35831> (accessed 12 November 2015)).

Jabri, V. (2007) *War and the Transformation of Global Politics*, Basingstoke: Palgrave.

Joerges, C. (2010) 'Unity in Diversity as Europe's Vocation, and Conflicts Law as Europe's Constitutional Form', *LSE 'Europe in Question' Discussion Paper Series* 28(December).

Kaufmann, M. (2013) 'Emergent Self-Organisation in Emergencies: Resilience Rationales in Interconnected Societies', *Resilience: International Policies, Practices and Discourses* 1(1): 53–68.

Kontinen, T. (2014) 'Rights-Based Approach in Practice? Dilemmas of Empowerment in a Development NGO', Unpublished paper, presented for 'After Human Rights' workshop, University of Helsinki, 13–14 March.

Kottow, M. H. (2002) 'The Vulnerable and the Susceptible', *Bioethics* 17: 5–6, 460–71.

Krasner, S. (2004) 'Sharing Sovereignty: New Institutions for Collapsing and Failing States', *International Security* 29(2): 5–43.

Latour, B. (2003) 'Is Re-modernization Occurring – and If So, How to Prove It? A Commentary on Ulrich Beck', *Theory, Culture & Society* 20(2): 35–48.

Latour, B. (2013) *An Inquiry into Modes of Existence: An Anthropology of the Moderns*, Cambridge, MA: Harvard University Press.

Lederach, J. P. (1997) *Building Peace: Sustainable Reconciliation in Divided Societies*, Washington, DC: United States Institute of Peace.

Lentzos, F. and Rose, N. (2009) 'Governing Insecurity: Contingency Planning, Protection, Resilience', *Economy and Society* 38(2): 230–54.

Mac Ginty, R. (2010) 'Hybrid Peace: The Interaction between Top-Down and Bottom-Up Peace', *Security Dialogue* 41(4): 391–412.

Maor, M. (2012) 'Policy Overreaction', working paper, Hebrew University of Jerusalem. Online. Available HTTP: <http://portal.idc.ac.il/he/schools/government/research/documents/maor.pdf>.

Martin, M. and Taylor, O. (2010) 'The Second Generation of Human Security: Lessons from the UN and EU Experience', *International Affairs* 86(1): 212–24.

Mayall, J. and Soares de Oliviera, R. (eds.) (2011) *The New Protectorates: International Tutelage and the Making of Liberal States*, London: Hurst.

Mazarr, M. J. (2014) 'The Rise and Fall of the Failed-State Paradigm: Requiem for a Decade of Distraction', *Foreign Affairs*, January–February. Online. Available HTTP: <https://www.foreignaffairs.com/articles/2013-12-06/rise-and-fall-failed-state-paradigm> (accessed 6 June 2016).

Millar, G. (2014) 'Disaggregating Hybridity: Why Hybrid Institutions Do Not Produce Predictable Experiences of Peace', *Journal of Peace Research* 51(4): 501–14.

Miller, P. and Rose, N. (2008) *Governing the Present: Administering Economic, Social and Personal Life*, Cambridge: Polity Press.

Moe, L. W. and Simojoki, M. V. (2013) 'Custom, Contestation and Cooperation: Peace and Justice in Somaliland', *Conflict, Security & Development* 13(4): 393–416.

Nicholson, G. (2014) 'Inequality and its Impact on the Resilience of Societies', Association of Caribbean States, 22 July. Online. Available HTTP: <http://www.eturbonews.com/48253/inequality-and-its-impact-resilience-societies> (accessed 12 November 2015).

North, D. C. (1990) *Institutions, Institutional Change and Economic Performance*, Cambridge: Cambridge University Press.

North, D. C. (2005) *Understanding the Process of Economic Change*, Princeton, NJ: Princeton University Press.

O'Malley, P. (2010) 'Resilient Subjects: Uncertainty, Warfare and Liberalism', *Economy and Society* 29(4): 488–509.

Owen, D. (2012) *The Hubris Syndrome: Bush, Blair and the Intoxication of Power*, York: Methuen.

Phillips, D. L. (2013) 'Unintended Consequences of Striking Syria', *World Post*, 11 September. Online. Available HTTP: <http://www.huffingtonpost.com/david-l-phillips/unintended-consequneces-o_b_3902414.html> (accessed 12 November 2015).

Polit, D. F. and Beck, C. T. (2004) *Nursing Research: Principles and Methods*, Philadelphia, PA: Lippincott, Williams & Wilkins.

Richmond, O. P. (2011) *A post-Liberal Peace: The Infrapolitics of Peacebuilding*, London: Routledge.

Richmond, O. P. and Mitchell, A. (eds.) (2012) *Hybrid Forms of Peace: From Everyday Agency to post-Liberalism*, Basingstoke: Palgrave.

Roberts, D. (2008) 'Hybrid Polities and Indigenous Pluralities: Advanced Lessons in Statebuilding from Cambodia', *Journal of Intervention and Statebuilding* 2(1): 63–86.

Sen, A. (1999) *Development as Freedom*, Oxford: Oxford University Press.

Stewart, R. and Knaus, G. (2012) *Can Intervention Work?*, London: W. W. Norton.

UK Cabinet Office (2011) *UK Resilience*. Online. Available HTTP: <http://www.cabinetoffice.gov.uk/ukresilience> (accessed 12 November 2015).

UNDP (United Nations Development Programme) (1994) *Human Development Report 1994: New Dimensions of Human Security*, New York: UNDP.

UNDP (United Nations Development Programme) (2014) *Disaster Risk Reduction Makes Development Sustainable*. Online. Available HTTP: <http://www.undp.org/content/dam/undp/library/crisis%20prevention/UNDP_CPR_CTA_20140901.pdf> (accessed 12 November 2015).

Walker, J. and Cooper, M. (2011) 'Genealogies of Resilience: From Systems Ecology to the Political Economy of Crisis Adaptation', *Security Dialogue* 42(2): 143–60.

World Bank (2007) *Conditionality in Development Policy Lending*, Washington, DC: World Bank.

Zimmermann, A. (2007) 'The Rule of Law as a Culture of Legality: Legal and Extra-Legal Elements for the Realisation of the Rule of Law in Society', *ELaw – Murdoch University Electronic Journal of Law* 14(1): 10–31.

41

THE STUDY OF
CRISIS MANAGEMENT

Arjen Boin, Magnus Ekengren, and Mark Rhinard

We live in a world of crises. Media headlines and government agendas are dominated by a wide variety of threats, ranging from financial breakdowns to climate change, from urban terrorism to cyber-attacks. These crises are increasingly transboundary in nature: they reach across geographical, legal, cultural, and policy borders (Ansell et al. 2010; Beck 1992; Boin et al. 2013). This makes it hard for the traditional nation-state to deal with these crises.

Long-standing security paradigms no longer suffice to prepare for these modern threats (Jervis 1997). As traditional military threats take a backseat to 'new', transboundary threats, conventional conceptions of security are being rethought and refashioned. National and international security organizations have experienced a process of reforming, retooling, and recasting. Security governance and crisis management are increasingly becoming intertwined.

This chapter summarizes key findings of crisis management research and explores the relevance of these findings for the security community. Security scholars traditionally focused on existential threats to the nation-state. With strong foundations in International Relations (IR) theory, they studied issues of stability and peace. Since the early 1990s, they have begun to study threat agents other than aggressor nations and their militaristic behaviour. Security scholars now recognize a wide range of threats to stability and peace. These threats require more than a military response. To deal with them, national governments and international organizations must become adept at the principles of crisis management.

The interdisciplinary field of crisis management research concentrates on a society's efforts to prepare for, and deal with, urgent threats to its core values and life-sustaining systems. It comprises theoretical and empirical findings that help us understand how societies can protect themselves against a wide variety of hazards, be they man-made or natural in origin. An understanding of this research domain can be helpful to security scholars who seek to study the response capacity of nation-states in the face of new and unforeseen threats.

The overview of this research domain follows three steps. First, we briefly reflect on the crisis concept and present an overview of the various schools of thought on crisis development and crisis management. We then discuss the processes through which crises *emerge* and offer a framework for understanding the *response* to emerging threats. This chapter concludes by considering the complementary nature of crisis management research and Security Studies.

Studying crisis: schools of thought

There are many definitions of crisis, but most contain three elements: threat, urgency, and uncertainty. Using these elements, we define a crisis as 'a serious threat to the basic structures or the fundamental values and norms [of a society], which under time pressure and highly uncertain circumstances necessitates making vital decisions' (Rosenthal et al. 1989: 10; cf. Rosenthal 2001).

This definition of crisis covers a wide variety of adversity: natural disasters and environmental threats; financial meltdowns and surprise attacks; terrorist attacks and hostage takings; epidemics and exploding factories; infrastructural dramas and organizational decline. What these events have in common is that they create impossible conditions for those who seek to manage the response operation and to make urgent decisions – all while essential information about causes and consequences remains unavailable.

Crisis has been a key concept in sociology since Durkheim founded the discipline. In sociological terms, crisis marks the phase during which order-inducing institutions stop functioning – the threat of anomy lurks in the background. The empirical and theoretical findings of disaster research are particularly relevant. The thorough understanding of collective behaviour, disaster myths, and the pathologies of top-down coordination in times of adversity has proved particularly fruitful to understanding crisis dynamics (Barton 1969; Quarantelli 1988).

Another sub-field of sociology – organization theory – produced one of the most powerful theories informing crisis studies. In *Normal Accidents*, Charles Perrow ([1984]1999) applied two wholesale sociological concepts (complexity and coupling) to explain organizational breakdown. This and other similar work in organization theory helped raise a fundamental debate about the feasibility and desirability of entrusting dangerous technology to large-scale bureaucracies (Chiles 2001; JCCM 1994; Sagan 1993).

Scholars working within the field of IR have studied crises and crisis management from two different angles. The first angle uses a decision perspective to study international crises. This body of richly documented studies has taught us much about leadership behaviour in times of crisis (Ansell et al. 2010; Craig and George 1983; Hermann 1972; Janis et al. 1987) as well as dynamic interaction between parties (Brecher 1993). In explaining the escalation and outcomes of international conflicts, IR scholars study how pervasive perceptions, bureau-politics, and small-group dynamics affect the critical decisions made during a crisis (Allison 1971; George 1991; Jervis 1976; Lebow 1981).

A second group of IR scholars have looked at crises as part of a growing number of problems that threaten national security. Even before the end of the Cold War, scholars within the field of Security Studies began to criticize the monopoly held by military issues (Buzan 1983; Ullman 1983). They argued that attitudes on the nature of security differed dramatically across peoples and countries; in many areas, contingencies like severe weather or energy shortages stoked as much insecurity and posed as great a threat to the viability of societies as foreign armies.

When the prospects of a global nuclear conflagration faded after the Cold War, a litany of pre-existing problems stood out in sharper relief. Scholars turned their attention to what might be loosely called 'new security' challenges, ranging from civil or ethnic conflict, resource scarcity, environmental degradation, and uncontrolled migration to organized crime, international terrorism, and drug trafficking (Baldwin 1995; Rob 2007; Walt 1991). Scholars in this field studied how security policy elites struggle to design an effective policy response to such threats (Stares 1998; Bigo 2000), why such threats become subjectively 'securitized' (Buzan et al. 1998; Huysmans 1998), and how governments ready themselves for the prospect of crises and 'failed security' (Relyea 2003). This has led to a renewed interest in the crisis management capacities of international organizations such as the World Health Organization, NATO, and the European Union (Boin et al. 2013).

Social psychologists study how crisis managers make critical decisions under stress (Holsti 1979; Janis and Mann 1977). Their work shows that group decisions do not necessarily compensate for the shortcomings of the stressed individual's decision-making process ('t Hart 1994; 't Hart et al. 1997; Janis 1982). In addition, psychologists have done important work that helps us understand the relation between human error, technology, organizational culture, and the development of crises (Reason 1990). The natural decision-making perspective shows that well-trained operators make crisis decisions in a very particular way (Flin 1996; Klein 2001): they compare their situational assessment with mental slides of similar situations (they select the decision that comes with the slide that matches their assessment). It tells us that crisis decision-making differs quite dramatically from the incremental, semi-rationalistic way in which routine decisions tend to be made.

In yet another niche – tucked away in the field of communications studies – interesting work is being done on the relation between crisis actors, political stakeholders, (social) media, and civilians (Olsson 2014; Seeger et al. 2003). This body of research helps us understand why sound decisions may or may not help to manage a crisis, depending on the way they are communicated. It helps us understand how media 'frames' shape crisis reports, which, in turn, affect general perceptions of the crisis and the authorities managing it.

Our *tour d'horizon* would not be complete without mentioning the field of risk studies, itself an interdisciplinary social-scientific endeavor (Pidgeon et al. 2003). It studies why and how people act on negligible risks (avoiding flying) while they ignore others (smoking; driving without seatbelts). The hardcore stream in this field tries to calculate risks, which should help policy-makers make decisions on baffling issues such as genetically modified food, environmental pollution, or space travel. It helps us understand the difference between 'known unknowns' (those that happen with some sort of regularity) and 'unknown unknowns' (those that cannot be foreseen or even imagined). Risk management pertains to the former; crisis management is needed for the latter (cf. Taleb 2007).

These various schools have built an impressive body of theoretical and empirical research findings. In the following sections, we will explore how these findings enhance our understanding of the *causes* and *patterns* of crises. In addition, we will use these findings to construct a framework that helps us analyse governmental *responses* to different kinds of crises.

The emergence of crises

Crises can be viewed as the resultant of two types of processes (Turner 1978). One process pertains to the emergence of a threat agent. This threat could come from anywhere (ranging from earthquakes to human errors, from technological failure to suicide terrorism). The second process pertains to the inability of a social unit (an organization, town, or country) to minimize the consequences of an emerging threat.

These processes can interact in intriguing and devastating ways. Modern systems of technology, trade, communications, finance, and transport are complex and tightly coupled, which allows threat agents to escalate in unforeseen and often incomprehensible ways (Perrow 1999). The more complex a system becomes, the harder it is for anyone to understand it in its entirety. Tight coupling between a system's component parts and those of other systems allows for the rapid proliferation of interactions (and errors) throughout the system. Threat agents can thus remain unnoticed, while developing into full-blown crises.

Consider the financial crises that have rattled the global markets in recent years (Eichengreen 2014). Globalization and ICT have tightly connected most world markets and financial systems. As a result, a minor problem in a seemingly isolated market or with an ill-understood financial tool can trigger a financial meltdown in markets on the other side of the globe. Structural vulnerabilities in relatively weak economies may suddenly 'explode' on Wall Street and cause worldwide economic decline.

As complex systems cannot be easily understood, growing vulnerabilities go unrecognized. Ineffective attempts to deal with seemingly minor disturbances can, in effect, 'fuel' a lurking crisis. A minor 'trigger' can then initiate a destructive cycle of escalation, which may then rapidly spread across systems and countries. Crises may have their roots far away (in a geographical sense) but they can rapidly snowball through global networks, jumping from one system to another and gathering destructive potential along the way.

In hindsight, analysts and commentators often judge that policy-makers and political leaders 'should have seen it coming'. But research points to the near-inherent inability to recognize emerging threats in time. There are at least three reasons why many potential crises fail to gain recognition. First, threats to shared values or life-sustaining functions cannot always be recognized before their disastrous consequences materialize. As the crisis process begins to unfold, policy-makers often do not see anything out of the ordinary. Everything is still in place, even though hidden interactions eat away at the underlying pillars that uphold a system. It is only when the crisis is in full swing and becomes manifest that policy-makers can recognize it for what it is.

The second reason is found in the contested nature of crisis. A crisis rarely, if ever, 'speaks for itself'. More often than not people will differ in their perception and appreciation of a threat. Analysts agree, for instance, that citizens and politicians alike have become at once more fearful and less tolerant of major hazards to public health, safety, and prosperity. At the same time, citizens and politicians routinely and collectively ignore seemingly 'objective' threats such as global climate change, nuclear proliferation, energy shortages, and modern terrorism.

The definition of a situation is, as social scientists say, the outcome of a subjective process. In fact, we might say that crisis definitions are continuously subjected to the forces of politicization (Edelman 1977). Crises can have a discrediting effect on policies and institutions, as the perceived underperformance of government agencies undermines their legitimacy. This creates opportunities for opponents of the status quo to forward proposals for reform that in normal times would be politically unfeasible (Boin et al. 2008).

Even if consensus would exist that a serious threat is emerging, the status of this new problem is far from assured. Governments deal with urgent problems every day; as such, attention for one problem takes away attention from another (Jones and Baumgartner 2005). For a threat to be recognized as a crisis and placed on the urgent policy agenda, it must pass many cognitive, political, and institutional hurdles (Birkland 1997).

All this has clear implications for a society's ambitions and efforts to prevent crises. While societies can and should try to prevent crises that are to be expected (building levees to prevent flooding for instance), it would be an illusion to think that a society can be made 'crisis free'. New threat agents will develop in unforeseen ways and will not be recognized in time to nip a threat agent in the bud. Therefore, societies have to invest in crisis management capacities. We turn to this topic in the next section.

Crisis management: crucial challenges for leadership

One might argue that modern society is better equipped than ever to deal with routine failures: sophisticated hospitals, computers and telephones, fire trucks and universities, regulation and funds – these factors have helped to minimize the scope and number of crises that were once widespread (Wildavsky 1988). Others argue that the resilience of modern society – its capacity to bounce back and return to normalcy – has deteriorated: when a threat does materialize (an electrical power outage, for instance), the most modern systems suffer most. Citizens and organizations in modern Western cities are not used to coping with a sudden absence of amenities. It remains unclear what can be done to enhance a society's capacity to be resilient in the face of disaster (Comfort et al. 2010).

But we do have a fairly clear understanding of the types of challenges that typically present themselves to political leaders and their administrative support teams in times of crisis. Here we present a framework for understanding and analyzing what we consider the most critical challenges for strategic crisis management: sense-making, organizing a response, meaning-making, rendering accountability, and learning (Boin et al. 2005).

Making sense of a crisis

During a crisis, it is critically important that leaders understand what is going on: what happened? How many people died? What is the damage? Who did it? What might be next? These questions are often hard to answer in the thick of crisis. Crisis scholars have identified a variety of reasons that explain why crisis management officials fail to 'make sense' of available information that in hindsight appears painfully obvious.

One reason is the bewildering pace, ambiguity, and complexity of incoming information streams, which tend to overwhelm normal modes of situation assessment. Key information is often not readily available, whereas decision-makers drown in operational data and disinformation or rumours. Individual stress and small-group dynamics may further impair sense-making abilities.[1] Finally, the organizations in which crisis managers typically function tend to produce additional barriers to crisis recognition (Kam 1988; Turner 1978; Wilensky 1967).

Some researchers point to organizations that have developed a proactive culture of 'looking for problems' in their environment. These so-called high-reliability organizations have somehow developed a capacity for thorough yet fast-paced information processing under stressful conditions. The unresolved question is whether organizations can design these features into existing organizational cultures (Weick and Sutcliffe 2002).

Organizing a response: critical decision-making and coordination

Once a threat is recognized and understood, a response must be organized. This typically involves two different processes: making critical decisions and coordinating various partners in the response.

Critical decisions in times of crisis involve tough value trade-offs and major political risks (Janis 1989; Brecher 1993). Interestingly, many pivotal crisis decisions are *not* taken by individual leaders or by small informal groups of senior policy-makers. They emerge from local theatres and bureaucratic trenches ('t Hart et al. 1993). While the difference between strategic and operational issues is well recognized in normal times, crises tend to blur clear demarcations. This may result in strategic decisions made at the operational level and operational details rising to the strategic level (also known as micro-management).

The crisis response in modern society is best characterized in terms of a network comprising a wide variety of response organizations that may have never worked together before. An effective response therefore requires some form of interagency and intergovernmental coordination: only when response organizations work together is there a chance that effective implementation of critical decisions will happen.

Coordination is not a self-evident feature of crisis management operations (Boin and Bynander 2015). Most public organizations were originally designed to conduct routine business in accordance with such values as efficiency, fairness, and lawfulness. Getting public bureaucracies to adapt to crisis circumstances is a daunting – some say impossible – task. Agencies that have never cooperated before may find it difficult to align their actions. Sensitivities and conflicts that governed the daily relations between organizations that have worked together before do not simply disappear. Crisis managers must try to orchestrate cooperation, but the question of who is in charge typically arouses great passions.

A truly effective crisis response is to a large extent the result of a naturally evolving process.[2] It cannot be managed in a linear, step-by-step, and comprehensive fashion from a single crisis centre, however full of top decision-makers and equipped with state of the art information technology. There are simply too many hurdles that separate a leadership decision from its timely execution in the field ('t Hart et al. 1993).

Meaning-making

Once a crisis has materialized, political leaders are expected to reduce uncertainty and provide an authoritative account of what is going on, why it is happening, and what needs to be done. They must try to get others – citizens, opposition leaders, media representatives, fellow leaders – to accept their definition of the situation ('t Hart 1993). If they are successful in offering a 'winning' frame, their chances to effectively manage the crisis are enhanced. If they do not, their decisions, actions, and strategies will not be understood nor respected. If other actors in the crisis succeed in dominating the meaning-making process, the ability of incumbent leaders to decide and manoeuvre is severely constrained.

Two problems often recur. First, public leaders are not the only ones trying to frame the crisis. Their messages coincide and compete with those of other parties, who are likely to espouse various alternative definitions of the situation and advocate different courses of action. The proliferation of social media provides everyone with a platform to offer alternative frames. Censoring them is hardly a viable option in a democracy.

Second, authorities cannot always provide accurate information right away or in the right way. They struggle with mountains of raw data (reports, rumours, pictures) that are quickly amassed during a crisis. Turning data into a coherent picture of the situation is a major challenge by itself. Getting it out to the public in the form of accurate, clear, and actionable information requires a major communications effort. This effort is often hindered by the aroused state of the audience: people whose lives are deeply affected tend to be anxious, if not stressed. Moreover, they do not necessarily see the government as their ally. Pre-existing feelings of distrust towards a government do not evaporate in times of crisis.

Rendering accountability

Governments – at least democratic ones – cannot afford to stay in crisis mode forever. A sense of normalcy will have to return sooner or later. It is a critical leadership challenge to make this happen in a timely and expedient fashion. Crisis termination is twofold. It is about shifting back from emergency to routine mode. This requires some form of downsizing of crisis operations. At the strategic level, it is about rendering an account of what has happened and gaining acceptance for that account.

The burden of proof in accountability discussions lies with leaders: they must establish beyond doubt that they cannot be held responsible for the occurrence or escalation of a crisis. These accountability debates can easily degenerate into 'blame games' with a focus on identifying and punishing 'culprits' rather than discursive reflection about the full range of causes and consequences.

Crisis leaders can be competent and conscientious, but that alone says little about how their performance will be evaluated when the crisis is over. Crises have winners and losers, and it is all too easy to fall on the losing side. Policy-makers and agencies that failed to perform their duties prior to or during critical moments need not despair, however: if they 'manage' the political game of the crisis aftermath well, they may prevent losses to their reputation, autonomy, and resources. The political (and legal) dynamics of the accountability process determines which crisis actors end up where (Boin et al. 2008; Brändström and Kuipers 2003; Hood 2013).

Learning

Political and organizational *lesson-drawing* constitutes the final challenge discussed here. A crisis offers a reservoir of potential lessons for contingency planning and training for future crises. One would expect those involved in crises to study these lessons and feed them back into organizational practices, policies, and laws.

Lesson-drawing is one of the most underdeveloped aspects of crisis management (Lagadec 1997; Stern 1997). In addition to cognitive and institutional barriers to learning, lesson-drawing is constrained by the fact that *which* lessons are drawn influences how the crisis affects a society. Crises become part of collective memory, a source of historical analogies for future leaders (Khong 1992; Sturken 1997). The political depiction of crisis as a product of prevention- and foresight-failures would force people to rethink the assumptions on which pre-existing policies and rule systems rest. Other stakeholders in the game of crisis-induced lesson-drawing might seize upon the lessons to advocate measures and policy reforms that incumbent leaders reject. Leaders thus have a big stake in steering the lesson-drawing process in strategic directions. The crucial challenge is to ensure that feedback streams generated by a crisis are channelled to support pre-existing policy networks and public organizations.

The documentation of these constraints has done nothing to dispel the near-utopian belief in crisis *opportunities*, an assumption found not only in academic literature but also in popular wisdom (Boin and 't Hart 2003). A crisis is seen as a good time to clean up and start anew. Crises represent discontinuities that must be seized upon – a true test of leadership, the experts claim. President George W. Bush presents a good example: in the wake of the 9/11 attacks, the president introduced several reforms (the Patriot Act; the new Department for Homeland Security) that would prove revolutionary and redefine America's approach to security threats. Crisis research suggests, however, that crises generate just as many constraints as opportunities in their aftermath.

Conclusion: crisis and security reconsidered

Events in the past decades (notably since 11 September 2001) have prompted a wider understanding among policy-makers of the intersecting challenges of crisis management and security policy. Security institutions are being connected to national crisis management structures; international organizations are increasingly taking on crisis management tasks (Boin et al. 2013). These developments have prompted scholars to follow suit and pay attention to this intersection between crisis and security management. Several conceptual overlaps and opportunities for dialogue across scholarly disciplines are worth mentioning here.

First, crisis scholars remind us that even the wealthiest and most competent government imaginable can never guarantee that major disruptions will not occur. The rise of transboundary crises undermines any ambitions to prevent crises from happening all together. Crisis prevention remains a necessary and indeed vitally important strategy, but it pertains only to *known* threats – those which have happened before. It is impossible to prevent *unknown* threats, which are thus likely to cause crises. This requires a strategy of societal resilience and crisis preparation (Comfort et al. 2010; Wildavsky 1988).

This line of thinking is fairly new in the Security Studies community. It could usefully inform analyses of how governments address complex security threats (and how governments might avoid the 'failures of imagination' that can afflict their approaches to security policy-making). At a more practical level, crisis management scholars help to complement security policy scholars by identifying with greater precision the mix of policies, organizations, and tools (both military and civilian) needed to manage today's complex threats.

Second, crisis scholars, not unlike some security policy scholars, propose that the crisis concept is a label: a semantic construction people use to characterize situations or epochs that they somehow regard as extraordinary, volatile, and potentially far-reaching in their negative implications. The intensity or scope of a crisis is thus not solely determined by the nature of the threat, the level of uncertainty, or the time available to decision-makers. A crisis is to a considerable extent what people make of it. Policy-makers cannot focus solely on 'objective' threats. They will have to take into account the perceptions of citizens, which may not correlate with threats as suggested by 'experts'. Security Studies scholars working in a constructivist vein will see affinities between this approach and their own. The crowded security agenda following the end of the Cold War, and its increased complexity after 11 September 2001, means that public crisis management scholars and traditional security policy scholars interested in threat perceptions are studying the same empirical 'threat space'.

Scholars on both sides should be encouraged to borrow tools and concepts from one another to enrich their analysis. The erosion of the traditional distinction between domestic and international politics, between internal and external security, and between threats 'at home' versus those 'abroad' will likely facilitate closer interaction between the two disciplines. This will not come a minute too soon, as security policy and crisis management are becoming increasingly alike in a world of globalized threats and challenges.

Notes

1 Some categories of people are known for their ability to keep their cool and to stay clear-headed under pressure. They have developed a mode of information processing that enables competent performance under crisis conditions (Flin, 1996; Klein, 2001). Veteran military officers and journalists, as well as fire and police commanders, are known for this.
2 See, for instance, the improvised response in New York City to the 9/11 attacks on the twin towers (Kendra and Wachtendorf, 2003).

References

Allison, G. T. (1971) *Essence of Decision: Explaining the Cuban Missile Crisis*, Boston, MA: Little, Brown.
Ansell, C., Boin, A. and Keller, A. (2010) 'Managing Transboundary Crises: Identifying the Building Blocks of an Effective Response System', *Journal of Contingencies and Crisis Management* 18(4): 195–207.
Baldwin, D. A. (1995) 'Security Studies and the End of the Cold War', *World Politics* 48(1): 117–41.
Barton, A. H. (1969) *Communities in Disaster: A Sociological Analysis of Collective Stress Situations*, New York: Doubleday.
Beck, U. (1992) *Risk Society: Towards a New Modernity*, London: Sage.
Bigo, D. (2000) 'When Two Become One: Internal and External Securitizations in Europe', in M. Kelstrup and M. Williams (eds.) *International Relations Theory and the Politics of European Integration*, London: Routledge, 171–204.
Birkland, T. (1997) *After Disaster: Agenda-setting, Public Policy, and Focusing Events*, Washington, DC: Georgetown University Press.
Boin, R. A. and Bynander, F. (2015) 'Explaining Success and Failure in Crisis Coordination', *Geografiska Annaler: Series A, Physical Geography* 97(1): 123–35.
Boin, R. A., Ekengren, M., and Rhinard, M. (2013) *The European Union as Crisis Manager*, Cambridge: Cambridge University Press.

Boin, R. A. and 't Hart, P. (2003) 'Public Leadership in Times of Crisis: Mission Impossible?', *Public Administration Review* 63(6): 544–53.

Boin, R. A., 't Hart, P., Stern, E., and Sundelius, B. (2005) *The Politics of Crisis Management: Public Leadership under Pressure*, Cambridge: Cambridge University Press.

Boin, R. A., McConnell, A., and 't Hart, P. (eds.) (2008) *Governing after Crisis: The Politics of Investigation, Accountability and Learning*, Cambridge: Cambridge University Press.

Brändström A. and Kuipers, S. L. (2003) 'From "Normal Incidents" to Political Crises: Understanding the Selective Politicization of Policy Failures', *Government and Opposition* 38(3): 279–305.

Brecher, M. (1993) *Crises in World Politics: Theory and Reality*, Oxford: Pergamon Press.

Buzan, B. (1983) *People, States and Fear: The National Security Problem in International Relations*, Brighton: Wheatsheaf.

Buzan, B., Wæver, O., and de Wilde, J. (1998) *Security: A New Framework for Analysis*, Boulder, CO: Lynne Rienner.

Chiles, J. R. (2001) *Inviting Disaster: Lessons from the Edge of Technology*, New York: Harper Business.

Comfort, L. K., Boin, R. A., and Demchak, C. C. (eds.) (2010) *Designing Resilience: Preparing for Extreme Events*, Pittsburgh: University of Pittsburgh Press.

Craig, G. A. and George, A. L. (1983) *Force and Statecraft: Diplomatic Problems of Our Time*, Oxford: Oxford University Press.

Edelman, M. J. (1977) *Political Language: Words That Succeed and Policies That Fail*, New York: Academic Press.

Eichengreen, B. (2014) *Hall of Mirrors*, New York: Oxford University Press.

Flin, R. (1996) *Sitting in the Hot Seat: Leaders and Teams for Critical Incidents*, Chichester: Wiley.

George, A. L. (ed.) (1991) *Avoiding War: Problems of Crisis Management*, Boulder, CO: Westview Press.

't Hart, P. (1993) 'Symbols, Rituals and Power: The Lost Dimension in Crisis', *Journal of Contingencies and Crisis Management* 1(1): 36–50.

't Hart, P. (1994) *Groupthink in Government: A Study of Small Groups and Policy Failure*, Baltimore, MD: Johns Hopkins University Press.

't Hart, P., Rosenthal, U., and Kouzmin, A. (1993) 'Crisis Decision Making: The Centralization Thesis Revisited', *Administration and Society* 25(1): 12–45.

't Hart, P., Stern, E. K., and Sundelius, B. (eds.) (1997) *Beyond Groupthink: Political Group Dynamics and Foreign Policymaking*, Ann Arbor: University of Michigan Press.

Hermann, C. F. (ed.) (1972) *International Crises: Insights from Behavioral Research*, New York: The Free Press.

Holsti, O. R. (1979) 'Theories of Crisis Decision Making', in P. G. Lauren (ed.) *Diplomacy: New Approaches in History, Theory, and Policy*, New York: The Free Press, 99–136.

Hood, C. C. (2013) *The Blame Game: Spin, Bureaucracy and Self-Preservation in Government*, Princeton, NJ: Princeton University Press.

Huysmans, J. (1998) 'Security! What Do You Mean? From Concept to Thick Signifier', *European Journal of International Relations* 4(2): 226–55.

Janis, I. L. (1982) *Groupthink*, Boston, MA: Houghton Mifflin.

Janis, I. L. (1989) *Crucial Decisions: Leadership in Policymaking and Crisis Management*, New York: The Free Press.

Janis, I. L., Herek, G. M., and Huth, P. (1987) 'Decision Making During International Crises: Is Quality of Process Related to Outcome?', *Journal of Conflict Resolution* 31(2): 203–26.

Janis, I. L. and Mann, L. (1977) *Decision-Making: A Psychological Analysis of Conflict, Choice and Commitment*, New York: The Free Press.

Jervis, R. (1976) *Perception and Misperception in International Politics*, Princeton, NJ: Princeton University Press.

Jervis, R. (1997) *System Effects: Complexity in Political and Social Life*, Princeton, NJ: Princeton University Press.

Jones, B. and Baumgartner, F. (2005) *The Politics of Attention: How Government Prioritizes Problems*, Chicago: University of Chicago Press.

Kam, E. (1988) *Surprise Attack*, Cambridge, MA: Harvard University Press.

Kendra, J. M. and Wachtendorf, T. (2003) 'Elements of Resilience after the World Trade Center Disaster: Reconstituting New York City's Emergency Operations Center', *Disasters* 27(1): 37–53.

Khong, Y. F. (1992) *Analogies at War: Korea, Munich, Dien Bien Phu, and the Vietnam Decisions of 1965*, Princeton, NJ: Princeton University Press.

Klein, G. (2001[1999]) *Sources of Power: How People Make Decisions,* London: MIT Press.

La Porte, T., Perrow, C., Rochlin, G., and Sagan, S. (1994) 'Systems, Organizations and the Limits of Safety: A Symposium', *Journal of Contingencies and Crisis Management* 2(4): 205–40.

Lagadec, P. (1997) 'Learning Processes for Crisis Management in Complex Organizations', *Journal of Contingencies and Crisis Management* 5(1): 24–31.

Lebow, R. N. (1981) *Between Peace and War: The Nature of International Crisis*, Baltimore, MD: Johns Hopkins University Press.

Olsson, E.-K. (2014) 'Crisis Communication in Public Organisations: Dimensions of Crisis Communication Revisited', *Journal of Contingencies and Crisis Management*, 22(2): 113–25.

Perrow, C. (1999[1984]) *Normal Accidents: Living with High-Risk Technologies*, Princeton, NJ: Princeton University Press.

Pidgeon, N., Kasperson, R. E., and Slovic, P. (eds.) (2003) *The Social Amplification of Risk*, Cambridge: Cambridge University Press.

Quarantelli, E. L. (1988) 'Disaster Crisis Management: A Summary of Research Findings', *Journal of Management Studies* 25(4): 373–85.

Reason, J. (1990) *Human Error*, New York: Cambridge University Press.

Relyea, H. C. (2003) 'Organizing for Homeland Security', *Presidential Studies Quarterly* 33(3): 602–24.

Robb, J. (2007) *Brave New War: The Next Stage of Terrorism and the End of Globalization*, Hoboken, NJ: Wiley.

Rosenthal, U., Boin, R. A., and Comfort, L. K. (eds.) (2001) *Managing Crises: Threats, Dilemmas, Opportunities*, Springfield, IL: Charles C. Thomas.

Rosenthal, U., Charles, M. T., and 't Hart, P. (eds.) (1989) *Coping with Crisis: The Management of Disasters, Riots and Terrorism*, Springfield, IL: Charles C. Thomas.

Sagan, S. D. (1993) *The Limits of Safety: Organizations, Accidents and Nuclear Weapons*, Princeton, NJ: Princeton University Press.

Seeger, M. W., Sellnow, T. L. and Ulmer, R. R. (2003) *Communication and Organizational Crisis*, Westport, CT: Praeger.

Stares, P. B. (1998) *The New Security Agenda: A Global Survey*, New York: Japan Center for International Exchange.

Stern, E. K. (1997) 'Crisis and Learning: "A Conceptual Balance Sheet"', *Journal of Contingencies and Crisis Management* 5(2): 69–86.

Sturken, M. (1997) *Tangled Memories: The Vietnam War, the Aids Epidemic, and the Politics of Remembering*, Berkeley: University of California Press.

Taleb, N. N. (2007) *The Black Swan: The Impact of the Highly Improbable,* New York: Random House.

Turner, B. A. (1978) *Man-Made Disasters*, London: Wykeham.

Ullman, R. (1983) 'Redefining Security', *International Security* 8(1): 129–53.

Walt, S. (1991) 'The Renaissance of Security Studies', *International Studies Quarterly* 35(2): 211–39.

Weick, K. E. and Sutcliffe, K. M. (2002) *Managing the Unexpected: Assuring High Performance in an Age of Complexity*, San Francisco: Jossey-Bass.

Wildavsky, A. B. (1988) *Searching for Safety*, Berkeley: University of California Press.

Wilensky, H. (1967) *Organizational Intelligence: Knowledge and Policy in Government and Industry*, New York: Basic Books.

42

'KILLER ROBOTS' AND PREVENTIVE ARMS CONTROL

Myriam Dunn Cavelty, Sophie-Charlotte Fischer, and Thierry Balzacq

> When change is easy, the need for it cannot be foreseen; when the need for change is apparent, change has become expensive, difficult and time consuming.
>
> *(Collingridge 1980: 11)*

The Collingridge Dilemma (see above) indicates that policy-makers face a double-bind quandary in the regulation of emerging technologies: on the one hand, they are hesitant to endorse preventive measures in the absence of complete information about the characteristics and effects of the technology. On the other hand, once the technology is fully developed, controlling its further evolution comes at a high cost, mainly due to the level of investments made for its development and deployment, or the advantages the technology is bringing (cf. Williams and Edge 1996).

The dynamic described by Collingridge is also influencing the debate about the future regulation of 'Lethal Autonomous Weapons Systems' (LAWS), colloquially called 'killer robots'. In the not too far future, it could be technologically possible to build fully autonomous weapons that select and engage human targets in conflict without human intervention. However, since these weapons do not yet exist, designing them to minimize risks and optimize benefits is still possible – but so is banning them entirely. It is widely agreed upon among experts and policy-makers that the time to decide how to regulate their use is now, before the technology has become too 'hardened' – but there is no agreement on what kind of regulatory action should be taken, given different takes on the risks of these technologies, and different ethical and moral standpoints.

Three positions with regard to their regulation are discernible. Proponents of the first group lobby for a complete ban (or a prohibitory treaty) on killer robots. The second group of experts calls for an arms control regime of the 'regulatory' type, to restrict only specific features of autonomous weapons systems, or limit the context in which they are employed. The third camp advocates an adaptive 'norms' approach, defined by the 'gradual evolution of codes of conduct based on traditional legal and ethical principles governing weapons and warfare' (Anderson and Waxman 2013: 2), thus arguing that no special or additional international treaty is needed.

This chapter unpacks the assumptions about ethics, technology, and the future of warfare that inform these positions. It has three parts. In the first, we compare definitions of LAWS and give examples of technologies with differing degrees of autonomy. In the second, we look at the literature in Security Studies (broadly understood) with bearing on LAWS. In the third, we discuss the three regulatory options and the scholarly opinions that inform them in more detail. We conclude with thoughts on what the main issues are, going forward, and what type of further research is needed from a Social Science/Security Studies perspective.

The technology

Some define LAWS as weapons that 'once activated, can select and engage targets without further intervention by a human operator' (DoD 2012a: 13). Others include the learning capabilities of machines ('artificial intelligence'), and define an autonomous weapon as 'one that is programmed to learn or adapt its functioning in response to changing circumstances in the environment in which it is deployed' (Lawand 2013). However, there is no agreement on a standard definition of LAWS, which makes discussions about them across different groups of experts quite difficult (Anthony and Holland 2014: 424). It is particularly noteworthy that the words 'automatic', 'automated', and 'autonomous' are used in inconsistent, even confusing ways (Scharre and Horowitz 2015: 4–5). The add-on 'unmanned' is also often used to signify different degrees of autonomy, which further adds to the confusion.

Even though there is no agreed-upon definition, it is fairly common to distinguish between different types of weapons based on how much human supervision or involvement in their operation is needed. The 'decline' of human decision-making (Adams 2011) is indeed the single most important cause for the ethical and legal debates around the use of autonomous weapons in warfare, especially if coupled with the prospect of artificial intelligence. Making degrees of human control the defining feature, Human Rights Watch (2012) proposes a useful distinction between three types of robotic weapons:

- Human-in-the-loop weapons: robots that can select targets and deliver force only with a human command;
- Human-on-the-loop weapons: robots that can select targets and deliver force under the oversight of a human operator who can override the robots' actions;
- Human-out-of-the-loop weapons: robots that are capable of selecting targets and delivering force without any human input or interaction. Only this last type is considered fully autonomous.

Because it is likely that the continuous adaptation of existing weapons, rather than the design of radically new systems, is the pathway to fully autonomous (human-out-of-the-loop) weapons, it is noted that it makes sense to think of them as situated on an evolving spectrum of autonomy, rather than as fixed classes of items (or technologies).

At the moment of writing, there are many human-in-the-loop, a few human-on-the-loop, and no human-out-of-the-loop systems in use. Unmanned (automated) systems – they are either in-the-loop or on-the-loop – are currently being developed and deployed by several nations including the United States, Israel, South Korea, Britain, France, Germany, Denmark, Sweden, China, and India (Sparrow 2009b: 170). In particular, unmanned aircraft piloted from afar ('drones'), some of which are used for targeted killings, are a significant and well-known component of the US war-fighting arsenal. In Table 42.1, we list a few weapon systems for each category.

It is important to note that, depending on how the weapon systems are programmed and used, several of the on-the-loop systems can also be considered in-the-loop systems, and vice versa. Even though today's robotic weapons still have a human being in the decision-making loop and

Table 42.1 Examples of different robotic weapons technologies in use (see DoD 2013; DoD 2012b; USAF 2014; Scharre and Horowitz 2015)

Type	Current	Future/Planned
Human-in-the-loop	Uninhabited Air Vehicles (UAVs), e.g. Global Hawk Combat Aerial Vehicles (UCAVs), e.g. Predator and Reaper Unmanned Ground Systems Unmanned Maritime Systems	
Human-on-the-loop	Automatic weapons defense systems. e.g. US Navy's MK 15 Phalanx Close-In Weapons System, the US ship-based Aegis and the land-based Israeli Iron Dome Sentry robots, e.g. SGR-1s, Guardium) 2nd generation unmanned aircraft (like Navy X-47B, Taranis) Active protection systems for ground vehicles to automatically engage incoming rockets or missiles, e.g. The French Shark or Russian Arena systems	Scalable Swarms of Autonomous Robots and Mobile Sensors (SWARMS) Low-Cost Autonomous Attack System (LOCAAS)
Human-out-of-the-loop		Nano Swarms (no concrete plans known)

require human intervention before the weapons take any lethal action, several observers point out that the move towards increasing levels of autonomy is inevitable (Anderson and Waxman 2013: 2; Liu 2012; Schmitt and Thurnher 2013: 237). Robotic weapons with various degrees of autonomy will most likely be a key feature across battlefield environments, especially since the majority of contemporary robotics research is funded by the military (cf. Harris 2012; Sparrow 2009a).

The literature in Security Studies

The use of robotics in warfare is a relatively recent development – and the first major books about the topic appeared only in 2009 (cf. Arkin 2009; Krishnan 2009; Singer 2009). In Security Studies, there are two types of literature that address aspects of LAWS. Both are relatively small; the majority of writings on the topic currently exist in legal studies or are published by American think tanks. The first body of literature is of a military and strategic nature. It mainly discusses causes for and consequences of making weapons systems increasingly autonomous, often embedding the discussion in the larger context of the ongoing military-technical revolution (see Krepinevich 2002; also Marchant et al. 2011), which is characterized by the 'rise of computer-driven information systems coupled with the proliferation of mobile autonomous and semi-autonomous systems' (Adams 2011: 2). This type of literature is in the old tradition of accounts that look at how specific technology changes the nature of war and warfare.

The second type of literature focuses specifically on drone warfare and targeted killings, an actual and observable practice of warfare using in-the-loop weapons, and is in the tradition of critical Security Studies. Drone killing is seen as visible expression of profound transformations of some of the enduring material and ideational features of war as we once knew it. It mirrors many of the points raised in military strategic writings, but is less future-oriented, seeing that drone warfare is a reality already.

Military Strategic Studies

Debates over the legal and ethical dimensions of new weapons, and also emergent ones, have been a feature of military thinking for a long time (cf. Tripodi and Wolfendale 2011), with specialized journals like *Military Ethics*[1] building up a scholarly body of knowledge around them (see, for example, Johnson and Axinn 2013; Roff 2014; Sharkey 2010). The emergence of new technology tends to be accompanied by two types of debates: the one that praises its (strategic) advantages and the one that mainly focuses on its downsides and risks.

By those focusing on the advantages, robots, whether manned or unmanned, ground or aerial, are regarded as effective tools that enable states to reduce personnel costs, to access denied areas controlled by enemies, and to wage wars with minimal footprint. Robots either do things humans cannot do or take what human beings used to do to an unprecedented level of sophistication in terms of speed and precision. Thus, robots revolutionize both the instruments and methods of war, even calling for 'entirely new concepts of operation' (Scharre 2014: 10; also see Brimley et al. 2013). Furthermore, autonomy would enable armies to use robots as force multipliers: one commander is sufficient to lead and coordinate a broad-scale robot attack.

Most importantly, the use of automated robots in future warfare will be driven by a desire to minimize the risk for one's own soldiers, but also a belief that such systems and their precision-strike capabilities will reduce the risk of 'collateral damage' among civilians (Strategic Defence Intelligence 2015). Not least, humans are often depicted as a problem in the operation of modern systems, since they are prone to make mistakes or underperform more generally (Adams 2011: 7); giving some tasks solely to machines is then seen as a way to reduce risks. Some experts even claim that machines might be much better at complying with the law of war (Geiss 2015: 16; also Arkin 2007: 58) because they do not feel fear or other emotions. However, differences in opinion often come down to beliefs as to whether autonomous systems can be programmed to comply with the rules of international humanitarian law.

The more sceptical observers have multiple objections to the use of machines for killing. The first is a moral argument. US Colonel Lee Fetterman for example warns that 'the function that robots cannot perform for us – that is, the function we should not allow them to perform for us – is the decide function … We would be morally bereft if we abrogate our responsibility to make life-and-death decisions required on the battlefield' (cited in Davis 2007). This is related to questions of responsibility (and liability): who would be to blame if a machine committed a war crime? (see Asaro 2012; Human Rights Watch 2012; Sharkey 2012).

A second is also related to moral and ethical issues, but is more specific. An often-made argument in relation to new and 'better' weapons is that they have disrupted the prevailing norms of warfare by radically and illegitimately reducing combat risk to the party using them. There is therefore a fundamental dilemma in the trade-offs between substantial gains in the ability to make war less destructive and harmful, primarily through the benefits of greater automated weapon precision, and significant dangers that military force will be used more destructively and with less ethical virtue on the other (Anderson and Waxman 2013: 2). This is followed by claims that by removing human soldiers from risk and reducing harm to civilians through greater precision, the disincentive to resort to armed force is diminished (Asaro 2012) – a point raised previously, i.e. with respect to remotely-piloted UAVs, and high-altitude bombing before that.

Another objection is related to the loss of control that this technology could bring. As war begins 'to leave the realm of human senses' (Adams 2011: 1), moving away from what we can see and hear and away from human reaction times, there is fear in some military quarters that it will 'remove warfare almost entirely from human hands' (Adams 2011: 2). Believing in 'meaningful human control' becomes questionable as soon as the time to make a counter-decision gets reduced to nanoseconds – or if one considers unintended and unpredicted interactions between automated or autonomous systems, given the possibility for future artificial intelligence functions.

Critical Security Studies and drone warfare

The second body of literature is the contribution of critical approaches to security, which problematizes the ways in which the increasing use of drones brings together, and rearranges, strategies, practices, and technologies of war (Benjamin 2012; Grondin 2011). For critical scholars, the 'dronification of state violence' introduces three major turns in the way war is thought, waged, and experienced (Shaw and Akhter 2014): first, modern warfare was fought within tight geographical constraints; drone warfare erodes the importance of classical geography. Second, the modern way of war's objects and subjects were primarily sovereign states; in an attempt to develop a 'perfect war', drone warfare individualizes war, and hence makes 'life its target' (Anderson 2009; Shaw 2013: 540). Finally, drone warfare institutionalizes a permanent state of war, wherein pre-emption becomes the rule.

With advances in drone warfare, the material power of topography and the ability of states to project their power are disengaged. It is not the territory that is targeted; instead, drones' aims are spaces of circulation that are enacted by patterns of life. A drone does not only challenge distance, but it also takes killing from distance to an unprecedented level (Gregory 2011: 192). Distant areas, such as Pakistan, Somalia, Afghanistan or Yemen, are thus brought to the gaze of the pilot, who might be located thousands of miles away from the theatre of operations. In fact, by digitizing space, and bodies that transform it into matter of concern, drone deployment brings the faraway right into the intimacy of the pilot (Shaw 2013: 550). This intimacy is made possible through the creation of a 'scopic regime', that is, a regime of visibility that collapses 'here' and 'there' or makes 'there' available 'here' (Gregory 2011: 190), thanks to technological sensors that produce high-resolution images that surpass what conventional bomber pilots used to see.

The scopic regime brought about by drones leads to a new political geography. This new political geography is associated with two major transformations: first, it goes hand-in-hand with the compression of time, as drone warfare exerts a heavy pressure on the kill-chain. Killing occurs as the targeted body emerges on the screen. Second, the new political geography debases the classical distinction between 'inside' and 'outside', through which Hobbes' social contract operated. Without a clear centre, man-hunting now happens everywhere; it is no longer restricted to fields of interstate war, as evidenced by the Global War on Terror. It is thus the very idea of modern sovereignty that is called into question, as drones' primary targets are 'stateless' human bodies (Wilcox 2015: 129). In short, drone killing individualizes war. The 'predator empire', to use Shaw's words (2013), ignores a state's exclusive authority over a territory, and thrives in a seamless space wherein war has neither temporal nor geographical limits (Wilcox 2015: 128).

The targeting practices enabled by drones generate their own set of problems. On the one hand, the use of drones tends to privilege 'signature strikes' over 'personality strikes'. On the other hand, it disposes the kill-chain to rely on anticipatory and pre-emptive action. The two issues are interlinked. The difference between signature and personality strikes is that the latter concern persons whose identities are known and stored in a classified list of people to be killed, whereas the former deal with people's trajectories, that is, the traces that their lives enact. But this reliance on signatures is not immune to lethal mishaps; without a trial or a judicial hearing of suspects, the standard of evidence that would allow the kill-chain such a determination appears arbitrary. For Shaw (2013: 546), the focus on signatures (traces) explains the impressive increase in the number of people killed by drone strikes – from 9 (between 2004 and 2007) the numbers have soared to 300 (between 2008 and 2012). According to Braun (2007: 19), this kind of future-oriented biopolitics 'takes as its target potential rather than actual risks'. That is, pre-emption is asserted as the main rationale that shapes drone strikes globally.

Even though this particular literature does not focus much on the future of robotic warfare, many of the points raised are in line with those of the opponents of killer robots. For them, in-the-loop weapons that are in actual use today belie the dream that future war can be 'clean' (with little to no collateral damage); they already violate human dignity; the imperative of distinction and proportionality is made moot. Any further automation would only aggravate these issues.

Regulating killer robots: issues of arms control

Even though forecasts on the dangers that autonomous weapon systems will pose in the future remain largely speculative at present, in 2014 a group of states launched multilateral expert meetings on the implications of, and the necessity to preventively regulate, LAWS in the frame of the Convention on Certain Conventional Weapons (CCW). Since then, state delegates have convened twice a year with legal, technical, and policy experts, as well as representatives of NGOs, to discuss outstanding issues on LAWS and to chart the further course of the debate.

While the majority of states supports consultations on LAWS in a multilateral forum, the debate has suffered from a lack of common definitions, and from diverging conceptions about a suitable regulatory approach. Although far-reaching agreement exists that humans should always remain part of lethal decision-making processes, a major point of discussion remains how 'meaningful human control' in autonomous systems can be defined. Apart from outstanding definitional issues, governments support differing regulatory approaches ranging on a wide spectrum from a full-scale ban to a status-quo approach that deems existent international law as sufficient to cover LAWS (Campaign to Stop Killer Robots 2015).

The existing literature on the governance of these technologies mirrors the heated policy debate on the regulation of LAWS – and to some degree even informs it. While most scholars agree that LAWS might have the potential to violate international humanitarian law and therefore might require preventive regulation or at least continuous observation, their conclusions and recommendations on an adequate approach vary widely. Three prevalent streams can be identified in the current discourse, two of which are pro-treaty. One group postulates the creation of a binding multilateral treaty to preventively regulate the development and use of LAWS. However, within this camp, one side, backed by several NGOs, calls for a full-scale ban on LAWS in the form of a prohibitory treaty, while the other, less radical, side suggests a regulatory treaty that restricts only certain technological features, or the context in which the weapons may be used. The third group rejects the utility of a preventive approach and contends that norms governing the manufacture and use of LAWS can only evolve incrementally, along with the technology. In the following, we provide deeper insights into the main premises and potential shortcomings of the three approaches.

A prohibitory treaty: banning LAWS

The regulatory approach that has gained most public attention so far is an outright ban of LAWS. A cornerstone in the development of this proposal was the report 'Losing Humanity: The Case against Killer Robots' published jointly by Human Rights Watch and the Harvard Law School International Human Rights Clinic in 2012. According to the report, 'killer robots' would increase the risks for civilians in war and thereby violate basic principles of international humanitarian law. Therefore the development, production, sale, deployment, or use of fully autonomous weapons should be prohibited (Human Rights Watch 2012). The activist group 'Campaign to Stop Killer Robots', a growing coalition of currently fifty-five NGOs, took up the issue and urged governments to launch multilateral consultations on LAWS and to join the call for a ban. Over time, the proposal has gained increasing support from several prominent individuals and governments.

In 2015, a group of leading scientists in the fields of robotics and artificial intelligence announced their support for a prohibitory treaty of autonomous weapons without meaningful human control in an open letter released by the Future of Life Institute (Future of Life Institute 2015). Moreover, during the last sessions of the CCW on LAWS, Bolivia, Cuba, Ecuador, Egypt, Ghana, Pakistan, the State of Palestine, and the Holy See expressed their backing of a ban (Campaign to Stop Killer Robots 2015). However, other governments and especially those at the forefront of developing and already employing increasingly autonomous systems, like the US and China, remain reluctant to endorse such a far-reaching treaty (Foster and Haden-Pawlowski 2015).

A full-scale ban would outlaw LAWS as a weapons category and thereby declare them as illegal per se, independent of the targets they engage and the context in which they are used (Schmitt 2013). Proponents of a ban contend that fully autonomous weapon systems would not be able to adequately protect civilians in war. This claim is based on legal and ethical grounds. Legally, the argument goes, fully autonomous weapons systems could not adhere to fundamental principles of international humanitarian law, quoting in particular the principles of distinction and proportionality. A robot would never be capable of clearly distinguishing with its sensors between combatants and non-combatants, or of recognizing when a combatant surrendered (Sharkey 2012). From an ethical point of view, lethal decision-making should never be left to a machine alone and a significant degree of 'meaningful human control' needs to be maintained (Human Rights Watch 2012). Finally, only a ban would effectively stigmatize LAWS, thereby also forcing non-signatory states to comply with the newly created treaty obligations over time (Foster and Haden-Pawlowski 2015).

A prohibitory treaty could take different legal forms. Examples from the history of arms control have been repeatedly compared with a potential ban of LAWS. One option would be a sixth Additional Protocol to the CCW. Additional Protocols provide the opportunity to react to emerging conventional weapons of humanitarian concern that were not yet existent at the time when the Convention was created. The fourth Protocol on the prohibition of Blinding Laser weapons, the only successful pre-emptive ban of any weapon to date, could serve as a blueprint for a ban of LAWS. Another possibility would be an independent treaty modelled after the Ottawa Convention on Anti-Personal Landmines that was concluded in 1997 (Anderson and Waxman 2013). Considering that decisions in the frame of the CCW are taken by consensus and that several states currently reject a ban of LAWS, an independent treaty appears to be the more realistic option, although no consultation process independent of the CCW has been initiated yet.

A regulatory treaty: restricting levels of autonomy and the context of use

A less radical approach in comparison to a full-scale ban is a regulatory treaty that would restrict only specific features of autonomous weapons systems or limit the context in which they are employed. Although the proposal has received less public attention so far, several scholars advocate a regulatory treaty (Dickow and Mutschler 2015; Lewis 2015; Müller and Simpson 2014; Schmitt 2013). The Israeli delegation also proposed a regulatory approach at the CCW meeting in April 2015 (Campaign to Stop Killer Robots 2015).

Proponents of a regulatory treaty argue from a consequentialist point of view that autonomous weapons systems are not unlawful per se. Instead, the legality of the technology and its use should be carefully reviewed with regard to different settings and the potential consequences of its employment (Dickow and Mutschler 2015; Lewis 2015; Müller and Simpson 2014; Schmitt 2013).

Under certain conditions, robots might be able to act at least as ethically as soldiers, or even outperform them (Lucas 2014). They could minimize collateral damage and hence improve the protection of civilians, due to their ability to process large amounts of information quickly for the selection of targets, a higher precision in engaging them, and the absence of human emotions such as fear and stress (Arkin 2009). Moreover, as Schmitt (2013) argues, even if LAWS would never be able to fulfil the principle of distinction, it could still be legal to use them in uninhabited spaces and against non-human targets, thereby decreasing the risks for soldiers on the battlefield. Henceforth, considering that increasingly autonomous weapons systems could improve the protection of both combatants and civilians, it would be counter-intuitive to pre-emptively ban them.

Drafting a regulatory treaty would necessitate a nuanced review of the legality of different features of the evolving technology and the potential contexts of use. Article 36 of the first Additional Protocol to the Geneva Conventions of 1977 sets out the formal review procedure for 'new weapon, means or method of warfare', obliging states to 'determine whether a weapon's employment would, in some or all circumstances, be prohibited by international law'.[2] However, so far, only six of the two-dozen countries possessing armed drones have initiated a review procedure, and the results of even fewer countries are publicly available (Foster and Haden-Pawlowski 2015). For that reason, Lewis (2015) suggests a more concrete regulatory framework for LAWS with five distinct categories in which the legality of LAWS needs to be monitored, assessed, and possibly restricted. Among these categories are the characteristics of the weapons technology, the environment in which they are used, the opposing forces against which they are directed, and the degree of residual human control (Lewis 2015: 1322).

There are several examples of regulatory arms control treaties from which lessons for the regulation of LAWS could be drawn. Particularly relevant to the present challenge is the amended second Additional Protocol to the CCW, on 'Prohibitions or Restrictions on the Use of Mines, Booby-Traps and Other Devices'. The Protocol restricts inter alia several technical features of landmines, and the targets which they may engage.[3] In contrast to the Ottawa Convention, the additional Protocol was also endorsed by states that were not willing to entirely ban, but still to regulate certain features and applications of landmines. Based on the experience of regulating landmines and in light of the critical position of key states like the US and Israel towards a ban, Lewis (2015) argues that a regulatory treaty could be more effective in the case of LAWS.

Both options presented so far suffer from one major weakness: the treaty-making process would be based on a largely predictive analysis of the future technology, and thus would be influenced strongly by the Collingridge Dilemma. Logically, this analysis could only provide an incomplete assessment of the potential dangers of LAWS and their precursors. A prohibitory treaty based on such an analysis could then prematurely give away the potentially positive effects of increasingly autonomous systems in both the military and civilian realm. Critics even argue that a ban would run counter to its self-proclaimed objective, by prohibiting a technology that could potentially improve the protection of civilians in war. A regulatory treaty, on the other hand, could be rendered obsolete quickly, if the provisions were not specific enough and the technology developed further around them. A third regulatory approach, presented below, tries to circumvent the 'prediction problem' by postulating the gradual establishment of norms and best practices along with the incremental evolution of increasingly autonomous technologies.

The norms approach: developing norms and best practices incrementally

The approach proposed by the legal scholars Kenneth Anderson and Andrew Waxman (2013) stipulates the development of a set of legal and ethical norms and best practices for the design, manufacturing, and use of increasingly autonomous weapons systems. Like the proponents of a regulatory treaty, Anderson and Waxman reject the assumption that fully autonomous systems are illegal per se. They disagree however on the utility of a preventive and binding regulatory treaty. Instead, they contend that norms have to evolve as incrementally as the technology itself.

Anderson and Waxman's model stretches over two levels. First, norms and best practices have to be created and applied by a leading state on the national level. According to the scholars, norms in this context do not refer to customary law but imply 'widely held expectations about legally or ethically appropriate conduct' (Anderson and Waxman 2013: 22). The baseline for these norms should be the principles of distinction and proportionality as enshrined in international humanitarian law. In a second step, once these norms have been fleshed out and established nationally, they should be transferred to the international level and eventually be adopted also by other states. However, Waxman and Anderson leave open whether such rules should be binding or not. As a pioneering state in the development and use of autonomous systems, the United States should take a leading role in the evolution, promotion, and application of these norms. By applying the standards to its own weapons development and restraining it accordingly, it could set a formative example for other states contemplating the acquisition and employment of LAWS.

While the norms approach does not fall into the trap of predictive regulation, it can be criticized on other grounds. First, the technology might outpace the establishment of norms and best practices. As pointed out by Collingridge, once the technology is employed and potential benefits become visible, it will be difficult to create norms for its use retroactively. Moreover, it could be challenging for the United States to act as a 'norm entrepreneur' in the case of autonomous weapons systems, after having been reluctant so far to take any regulative measures regarding armed drones, despite increasing international pressure.

Conclusion

Autonomous weapons have not been developed yet to a point where lethal decision-making without any human intervention is possible. Only precursors of such technology exist, some of which provide a glimpse into the future development trajectory. The huge increase in interest in different aspects of this topic is mirrored by the amount of scholarly work that has started to appear in the last few years – most of it outside of Security Studies, however. In general, the policy debate is most strongly informed by legal scholars at the moment.

Across all the texts, one aspect that has received surprisingly little attention is the role of private technology companies. Although some technical experts were invited to the past meetings on LAWS at the UN, no observable dialogue on the issue has taken place with representatives of private technology firms. This is astonishing in view of the strong dual-use character of the software and hardware components used in increasingly autonomous systems.

While dual-use technologies are not new to the field of arms control, autonomous systems will create specific challenges in this regard. Progress in the field of autonomy is mainly driven by innovations in the civilian realm, ranging from self-driving cars to household robots. Many of the components used in these systems can often, with only slight modifications, be used for military applications. In contrast to state-driven research and development projects in the armaments sector, innovative products from private companies specializing in civilian technologies become available on the market more quickly, and will therefore also play an increasing role in autonomous technologies used in the military realm (Francois 2015). Including private technology companies that are at the forefront of developing future autonomous technologies in the process of finding a suitable regulatory framework for LAWS could make predictions about technological risks more reliable and hence a treaty regime more stable and legitimate.

Private technology firms will also inevitably be affected by any restrictions regarding the development and sale of certain autonomous technologies or specific features thereof. This inference has two implications that require further consideration: first, the potential effects of regulatory measures on civilian technology firms are certainly influential in shaping a country's preference for one or the other regulatory approach. South Korea, as an important technology exporting country, stressed for example that a regulatory regime must not affect the civilian development of autonomous technologies (Campaign to Stop Killer Robots 2015). Second, in the case of any regulatory approach, the narrowing gap between civilian and military autonomous technologies will give the private industry an important role to play in the verification of treaty commitments, as well as in avoiding the proliferation of those technologies to non-state actors.

Notes

1 http://www.tandfonline.com/loi/smil20#.VnF5KyurX54
2 https://www.icrc.org/ihl/WebART/470-750045?OpenDocument
3 https://www.icrc.org/ihl/0/e32aba4fd82027edc125641f002d20f6?OpenDocument

References

All links accessed on 21 December 2015

Adams, T. K. (2011) 'Future Warfare and the Decline of Human Decision-Making', *Parameters* 41(4): 1–15.
Anderson, K. (2009) 'Targeted Killing in US Counterterrorism Strategy and Law', Working Paper of the Series on Counterterrorism and American Statutory Law, Brookings Institution, The Georgetown University Law Center, and The Hoover Institution. Online. Available HTTP: <http://www.brookings.edu/~/media/research/files/papers/2009/5/11-counterterrorism-anderson/0511_counterterrorism_anderson.pdf>.
Anderson, K. and Waxman, M. (2013) 'Law and Ethics for Autonomous Weapon Systems: Why a Ban Won't Work and How the Laws of War Can', a National Security and Law Essay, Stanford University, The Hoover Institution. Online. Available HTTP: <http://www.hoover.org/sites/default/files/uploads/documents/Anderson-Waxman_LawAndEthics_r2_FINAL.pdf>.
Anthony, I. and Holland, C. (2014) 'The Governance of Autonomous Weapons', in SIPRI (ed.) *SIPRI Yearbook 2014: Armaments, Disarmament and International Security*, Oxford: Oxford University Press, 423–31.
Arkin, R. (2007) 'Governing Lethal Behavior: Embedding Ethics in a Hybrid Deliberative/Reactive Robot Architecture', Technical Report GIT-GVU-07-11, Georgia Institute of Technology. Online. Available HTTP: <http://www.cc.gatech.edu/ai/robot-lab/online-publications/formalizationv35.pdf>.
Arkin, R. (2009) *Governing Lethal Behavior in Autonomous Robots*, London: Chapman and Hall.
Asaro, P. (2012) 'On Banning Autonomous Weapon Systems: Human Rights, Automation and the Dehumanization of Lethal Decision-Making', *International Review of the Red Cross* 94(886) (Special Issue on New Technologies and Warfare): 687–709.
Benjamin, M. (2012) *Drone Warfare: Killing by Remote Control*, New York: OR Books.
Braun, B. (2007) 'Biopolitics and the Molecularization of Life', *Cultural Geographies* 14(1): 6–28.
Brimley, S., FitzGerald, B., and Sayler, K. (2013) 'Game Changers: Disruptive Technology and US Defense Strategy', Working Paper, Center for a New American Security. Online. Available HTTP: <http://www.cnas.org/files/documents/publications/CNAS_Gamechangers_BrimleyFitzGeraldSayler_0.pdf>.
Campaign to Stop Killer Robots (2015) 'Country Policy Positions, 25th March 2015'. Online. Available HTTP: <http://www.stopkillerrobots.org/wp-content/uploads/2015/03/KRC_CCWexperts_Countries_25Mar2015.pdf>.
Collingridge, D. (1980) *The Social Control of Technology*, New York: St. Martin's Press.
Davis, D. L. (2007) 'Who Decides: Man or Machine?', *Armed Forces Journal*, 1 November. Online. Available HTTP: <http://www.armedforcesjournal.com/who-decides-man-or-machine/>.
Dickow, M., Hansel, M., and Mutschler, M. M. (2015) 'Präventive Rüstungskontrolle. Möglichkeiten und Grenzen mit Blick auf die Digitalisierung und Automatisierung des Krieges', *Sicherheit und Frieden* 33(2): 67–73.

DoD (2012a) 'DoD Directive on Autonomy in Weapon Systems, 3000.09'. Online. Available HTTP: <http://www.dtic.mil/whs/directives/corres/pdf/300009p.pdf>.

DoD (2012b) 'Task Force Report: The Role of Autonomy in DoD Systems', Defense Science Board (DSB). Online. Available HTTP: <https://fas.org/irp/agency/dod/dsb/autonomy.pdf>.

DoD (2013) 'Unmanned Systems Integrated Roadmap. FY 2013-2038'. Online. Available HTTP: <http://archive.defense.gov/pubs/DOD-USRM-2013.pdf>.

Foster, M. and Haden-Pawlowski, V. (2015) 'Regulating Robocop: The Need for International Governance Innovation in Drone and LAWS Development and Use', *Sicherheit und Frieden* 33(2): 61–6.

Francois, C. (2015) 'Robots, War and Society', *Defense Dossier*, American Policy Council, 13(February): 11–15.

Future of Life Institute (2015) 'Autonomous Weapons: an Open Letter from AI & Robotics Researchers'. Online. Available HTTP: <http://futureoflife.org/AI/open_letter_autonomous_weapons>.

Geiss, R. (2015) 'The International-Law Dimension of Autonomous Weapons Systems', Study, Friedrich Ebert Stiftung. Online. Available HTTP: <http://library.fes.de/pdf-files/id/ipa/11673.pdf>.

Gregory, D. (2011) 'From a View to a Kill: Drones and Late Modern War', *Theory, Culture & Society* 28(7–8): 188–215.

Grondin, D. (2011) 'The Other Spaces of War: War beyond the Battlefield in the War on Terror', *Geopolitics* 16(2): 253–79.

Harris, S. (2012) 'Out of the Loop: The Human-Free Future of Unmanned Aerial Vehicles', An Emerging Threats Essay, Stanford University, The Hoover Institution. Online. Available HTTP: <http://media.hoover.org/sites/default/files/documents/EmergingThreats_Harris.pdf>.

Human Rights Watch (2012) 'Losing Humanity: The Case against Killer Robots'. Online. Available HTTP: <https://www.hrw.org/report/2012/11/19/losing-humanity/case-against-killer-robots>.

Johnson, A. M. and Axinn, S. (2013) 'The Morality of Autonomous Robots', *Journal of Military Ethics* 12(2): 129–41.

Krepinevich, A. F. (2002) 'The Military-Technical Revolution: A Preliminary Assessment', Working Paper, Center for Strategic and Budgetary Assessments. Online. Available HTTP: <http://www.csbaonline.org/wp-content/uploads/2011/03/2002.10.02-Military-Technical-Revolution.pdf>.

Krishnan, A. (2009) *Killer Robots: Legality and Ethicality of Autonomous Weapons*, Farnham and Burlington: Ashgate.

Lawand. K. (2013) 'Fully Autonomous Weapon Systems', Presentation at the ICRC Seminar on Fully Autonomous Weapon Systems, Mission permanente de France, Geneva, Switzerland. Online. Available HTTP: <https://www.icrc.org/eng/resources/documents/statement/2013/09-03-autonomous-weapons.htm>.

Lewis, J. (2015) 'The Case for Regulating Fully Autonomous Weapons Systems', *The Yale Law Journal* 124(4): 1309–25.

Liu, H. Y. (2012) 'Categorization and Legality of Autonomous and Remote Weapons Systems', *International Review of the Red Cross* 94(886): 627–52.

Lucas, G. R. Jr (2014) 'Automated Warfare', *Stanford Law and Policy Review* 25: 317–40.

Marchant, G. E., Allenby, B., Arkin, R., Barrett, E. T., Borenstein, J., Gaudet, L. M., Kittrie, O., Lin, P., Lucas, G. R., O'Meara, R., and Silberman, J. (2011) 'International Governance of Military Robots', *The Columbia Science and Technology Law Review* 12: 272–315.

Müller, V. C. and Simpson, T. W. (2014) 'Killer Robots: Regulate Don't Ban', *BSG Policy Memo*, November. Online. Available HTTP: <http://www.bsg.ox.ac.uk/sites/blavatnik/files/2014-Regulate-not-ban-PolicyMemo1.pdf>.

Roff, H. M. (2014) 'The Strategic Robot Problem: Lethal Autonomous Weapons in War', *Journal of Military Ethics* 13(3): 211–27.

Scharre, P. (2014) 'Robotics on the Battlefield Part I: Range, Persistence and Daring', Working Paper, Center for a New American Security. Online. Available HTTP: <http://www.cnas.org/sites/default/files/publications-pdf/CNAS_RoboticsOnTheBattlefield_Scharre.pdf>.

Scharre, P. and Horowitz, M. C. (2015) 'An Introduction to Autonomy in Weapon Systems', Working Paper, Center for a New American Security. Online. Available HTTP: <http://www.cnas.org/sites/default/files/publications-pdf/Ethical%20Autonomy%20Working%20Paper_021015_v02.pdf>.

Schmitt, M. N. (2013) 'Autonomous Weapon Systems and IHL: A Reply to the Critics', *Harvard National Security Journal Features*. Online. Available HTTP: <http://harvardnsj.org/wp-content/uploads/2013/02/Schmitt-Autonomous-Weapon-Systems-and-IHL-Final.pdf>.

Schmitt, M. N. and Thurnher, J. S. (2013) 'Out of the Loop: Autonomous Weapon Systems and the Law of Armed Conflict', *Harvard National Security Journal* 4: 231–81.

Sharkey, N. (2010) 'Saying "No!" to Lethal Autonomous Targeting', *Journal of Military Ethics* 9(4): 369–83.

Sharkey, N. (2012) 'The Evitability of Autonomous Robot Warfare', *International Review of the Red Cross*. Online. Available HTTP: <https://www.icrc.org/eng/assets/files/review/2012/irrc-886-sharkey.pdf>.

Shaw, I. (2013) 'Predator Empire: The Geopolitics of US Drone Warfare', *Geopolitics* 18(3): 536–59.

Shaw, I. and Akhter, M. (2014) 'The Dronification of State Violence', *Critical Asian Studies* 46(2): 211–34.

Singer, P. W. (2009) *Wired For War: The Robotics Revolution and Conflict in the 21st Century*, New York: Penguin.

Singer, P. W. (2011) 'Robots at War: The New Battlefield', in H. Strachan and S. Scheipers (eds.) *The Changing Character of War*, Oxford: Oxford University Press, 333–54.

Sparrow, R. (2009a) 'Predators or Plowshares? Arms Control of Robotic Weapons', *IEEE Technology and Society Magazine* (Spring 2009): 25–9.

Sparrow, R. (2009b) 'Building a Better WarBot: Ethical Issues in the Design of Unmanned Systems for Military Applications', *Science and Engineering Ethics* 15(2): 169–87.

Strategic Defence Intelligence (2015) 'Military Robotics – Emerging Trends and Future Outlook', Report, Sector Publishing Intelligence.

Tripodi, P. and Wolfendal, J. (eds.) (2011) *New Wars and New Soldiers: Military Ethics in the Contemporary World*, Farnham: Ashgate.

USAF (2014) 'RPA Vector: Vision and Enabling Concepts 2013–2038', Headquarters, United States Airforce. Online. Available HTTP: <http://www.defenseinnovationmarketplace.mil/resources/USAF-RPA_VectorVisionEnablingConcepts2013-2038_ForPublicRelease.pdf>.

Wilcox, L. (2015) 'Drone Warfare and the Making of Bodies Out of Place', *Critical Studies on Security* 3(1): 127–31.

Williams, R. and Edge, D. (1996) 'The Social Shaping of Technology', *Research Policy* 25: 865–99.

INDEX